D0084555

ILLUSTRISSIMAE
ST. ANDREAE APUD SCOTOS UNIVERSITATI
OB SUMMUM IN S.S. THEOLOGIA HONOREM SIBI OBLATUM
HUNC LIBRUM
GRATUS VENERABUNDUS
D. D. D.
RUDOLFUS BULTMANN

THEOLOGY

OF THE

NEW TESTAMENT

by

RUDOLF BULTMANN

Professor of New Testament,
University of Marburg

VOLUME I

TRANSLATED BY
KENDRICK GROBEL

CHARLES SCRIBNER'S SONS, NEW YORK

Contents

CONTENTS

PART II

CONTENTS

(N.B. Volume II will contain Part III, The Theology of John, and Part IV, The Development toward the Ancient Church.)

(N.B. The Indices to the entire work are included in Volume II.)

PART ONE

PRESUPPOSITIONS AND MOTIFS
OF
NEW TESTAMENT THEOLOGY

CHAPTER I

The Message of Jesus

1. *The message of Jesus* is a presupposition for the theology of the New Testament rather than a part of that theology itself. For New Testament theology consists in the unfolding of those ideas by means of which Christian faith makes sure of its own object, basis, and consequences. But Christian faith did not exist until there was a Christian kerygma; i.e., a kerygma proclaiming Jesus Christ—specifically Jesus Christ the Crucified and Risen One—to be God's eschatological act of salvation. He was first so proclaimed in the kerygma of the earliest Church, not in the message of the historical Jesus, even though that Church frequently introduced into its account of Jesus' message, motifs of its own proclamation. Thus, theological thinking—the theology of the New Testament—begins with the *kerygma* of the earliest Church and not before. But the fact that Jesus had appeared and the message which he had proclaimed were, of course, among its historical presuppositions; and for this reason Jesus' message cannot be omitted from the delineation of New Testament theology.

2. The synoptic gospels are the *source for Jesus' message.* Their use as history is governed by the so-called two source theory: i.e. Mark (which we know, however, only in a later redaction) is one source of Matthew and Luke; the other is a collection of Jesus' sayings (Q). Furthermore, throughout the synoptics three strands must be distinguished: old tradition, ideas produced in and by the Church, and editorial work of the evangelists. The critical analysis of these strands cannot be presented here; it is available in my book, *Die Geschichte der synoptischen Tradition,* 2nd ed. (1931). Throughout this book, passages from Mark are cited without the addition of "par." wherever the Matthew and Luke parallels offer no independ-

[3]

ent tradition; "par." is added to a passage from Matthew or Luke wherever a tradition taken from Q is involved. That is what "par." is intended to indicate.*

§ 1. The Eschatological Message

1. The dominant concept of Jesus' message is the *Reign of God.* Jesus proclaims its immediately impending irruption, now already making itself felt. Reign of God is an eschatological concept. It means the regime of God which will destroy the present course of the world, wipe out all the contra-divine, Satanic power under which the present world groans—and thereby, terminating all pain and sorrow, bring in salvation for the People of God which awaits the fulfilment of the prophets' promises. The coming of God's Reign is a miraculous event, which will be brought about by God alone without the help of men.

With such a message, Jesus stands *in the historical context of Jewish expectations about the end of the world and God's new future.* And it is clear that his thought is not determined by the *national* hope then still alive in certain circles of the Jewish people, in which the time of salvation to be brought in by God was thought of as the restitution of the idealized ancient kingdom of David. No saying of Jesus mentions the Messiah-king who is to crush the enemies of the People, nor the lordship of Israel over the earth, nor the gathering of the twelve tribes, nor the joy that will be in the bounteous peace-blessed Land. Rather, Jesus' message is connected with the hope of other circles which is primarily documented by the *apocalyptic* litera-ture, a hope which awaits salvation not from a miraculous change in historical (i.e. political and social) conditions, but from a cosmic catastrophe which will do away with all conditions of the present world as it is. The presupposition of this hope is the pessimistic-

* Quotations from the New Testament are given according to the Revised Standard Version (1946), with the kind permission of the copyright owner, Division of Christian Education, National Council of the Churches of Christ in the U.S.A., unless there is an indication to the contrary. "Blt." (= Bultmann's version) means that the author himself translated the passage into German, for which an English equivalent is here offered; "tr." (= translator's version) means that the author quoted only the Greek text, which the translator of this book felt compelled to translate anew in the sense implied by the author's context. Rarely King James or a modern private translation is quoted, and always by name.

dualistic view of the Satanic corruption of the total world-complex, which is expressed in the special doctrine of the *two aeons* into which the world's career is divided: The old aeon is approaching its end, and the new aeon will dawn with terror and tribulation. The old world with its periods has an end determined by God, and when the day He has determined is here, the judgment of the world will be held by Him or by His representative, the Son of Man, who will come on the clouds of heaven; the dead will arise, and men's deeds, good or bad, will receive their reward. But the salvation of the faithful will consist not in national prosperity and splendor, but in the glory of paradise. In the context of these expectations stands the message of Jesus. However, it is free from all the learned and fanciful speculation of the apocalyptic writers. Jesus does not look back as they did upon past periods, casting up calculations when the end is coming; he does not bid men to peer after signs in nature and the affairs of nations by which they might recognize the nearness of the end. And he completely refrains from painting in the details of the judgment, the resurrection, and the glory to come. Everything is swallowed up in the single thought that then God will rule; and only very few details of the apocalyptic picture of the future recur in his words.

The contrast between this aeon and that is barely mentioned. The passages which speak of the "sons of this age" (Lk. 16:8; 20:34f.) and of the reward in the age to come for having followed him (Mk. 10:30) are secondary. The expression "close of the age" (Mt. 13:49) may be genuine tradition, though it is secondary in the parable interpretations (Mt. 13:39f. and 24:3). "The present time," Καιρὸς οὗτος, meaning the remnant of time before the eschatological end, at Lk. 12:56 is probably original, but at Mk. 10:30, as the opposite of "the age to come," is secondary.

But it is evident that Jesus has this conviction: This age has run out. The summary of his preaching in the saying, "The time is fulfilled, and the Reign of God is at hand" (Mk. 1:15), is appropriate. Jesus is convinced that the world's present course is under the sway of Satan and his demons, whose time is now expired (Lk. 10:18). He expects the coming of the "Son of Man" as judge and savior (Mk. 8:38; Mt. 24:27 par. 37 par. 44 par.; [Mt. 10:23; 19:28];

Lk. 12:8f.; [Mt. 10:32f.]; Lk. 17:30).* He expects the resurrection
of the dead (Mk. 12:18–27) and the judgment (Lk. 11:31f. par.,
etc.). He shares the idea of a fiery Hell into which the damned are to
be cast (Mk. 9:43–48; Mt. 10:28). For the blessedness of the righteous he uses the simple term "Life" Ζωή (Mk. 9:43, 45, etc.). While
he can indeed speak of the heavenly banquet at which they will
recline at table with Abraham, Isaac, and Jacob (Mt. 8:11) and also
of his hope of drinking wine anew in the Reign of God (Mk. 14:25),
he nevertheless also says, "When they rise from the dead, they
neither marry nor are given in marriage, but are like angels in
heaven" (Mk. 12:25).

2. Thus Jesus does take over the apocalyptic picture of the future,
but he does so with significant reduction of detail. What is new
and really his own about it all is the certainty with which he says,
*"Now the time is come! God's Reign is breaking in! The end is
here!"* That is what the following words mean:

> "Blessed are the eyes which see what you see!
> For I tell you:
> Many prophets and kings desired to see what you see and did
>   not see it,
> And to hear what you hear, and did not hear it!"
>   (Lk. 10:23f. par.)

Now is no time to mourn and fast; this is a time of joy like that
of a wedding (Mk. 2:18f.). So he now cries his "Blessed are you!"
to the waiting, expectant ones:

> "Blessed are you poor, for yours is the Reign of God!
> Blessed are you that hunger now, for you shall be satisfied!
> Blessed are you that weep now, for you shall laugh!" (Lk. 6:20f
> Blt.)

Satan's reign is now collapsing, for "I saw Satan fall like lightning from heaven" (Lk. 10:18).

Signs of the time there are, indeed; but not such as those after
which apocalyptic fantasy peers. For "God's Reign comes not so
that it can be calculated; and none can say, 'Lo here or there!' For
lo, God's Reign is (all at once) in your midst!" (Lk. 17:21 Blt.).

* Formulations presumably due to the Church, or words edited by the evangelists are placed in brackets. Lk. 17:30 is perhaps original.

"And if you are told: lo here! lo there! do not go, do not follow them. For as the lightning flashes and lights up the sky from one side to the other, so will it be with the Son of Man in his day" (Lk. 17:23f. Blt.).

The people, it is true, are blind to the true signs of the time; they can well enough interpret the signs of the heavens (clouds and wind) and know when it is going to rain or be hot—why can they not discern the signs of the present? (Lk. 12:54–56). When the fig tree sprouts and gets green men know summer is near; so from the signs of the time they should know that the End is at hand (Mk. 13:28f.).

But what are the signs of the time? He himself! *His presence, his deeds, his message!*

> "The blind see, and the lame walk,
> Lepers are cleansed and the deaf hear,
> The dead arise and the poor have the message of salvation proclaimed to them" (Mt. 11:5 par. Blt.).

It can be asked whether these words only express the certainty that the prophetic predictions of salvation (Is. 35:5f.; 29:18f.; 61:1) will presently be fulfilled, or whether Jesus means that their fulfilment is already beginning in his own miracles. Probably the latter. For though he refuses the demand made of him to legitimate himself by a "sign from heaven" (Mk. 8:11f.), he nevertheless sees God's Reign already breaking in in the fact that by the divine power that fills him he is already beginning to drive out the demons, to whom he, like his contemporaries, attributes many diseases: "If I by the finger of God drive out demons, then God's Reign has come upon you!" (Lk. 11:20 par. Blt.). "No one can enter a strong man's house and plunder his goods, unless he first binds the strong man" (Mk. 3:27), hence, since he is robbing Satan of his plunder, it is apparent that Satan has been attacked by one stronger than himself.

All that does not mean that God's Reign is already here; but it does mean that it is dawning. Man cannot hasten the divinely determined course of events, either by strict observance of the commandments and by penance—as the Pharisees supposed—or by driving out the Romans by force of arms—as the Zealots fancied. For "with the Reign of God it is as if a man should scatter seed upon the ground and should sleep and rise night and day, and the seed should sprout and grow, he knows not how. The earth produces of itself, first the blade, then the ear, then the full grain in the ear. But when the grain is ripe, at once he sends the harvesters, because the harvest has come" (Mk. 4:26-29 Blt.).

From this *parable of the seed growing of itself*, in which "of itself" is the point, one must not draw the conclusion that God's Reign (or Kingdom) is an entity growing in history; rather it assumes that its coming is a miracle independent of every human act—as miraculous as the growth and ripening of seed, which proceeds without human help or comprehension. It is far from Jesus and the world he moved in to regard the growth of seed as a natural process of development. The meaning of the parable can be clarified by placing beside it a similar one, handed down to us in I Clem. 23, which is intended to picture how certainly the judgment of God will come: "O fools, compare yourselves with a tree, for instance a grapevine! First it casts off its old leaves, then young shoots arise, then leaves, then blossoms, then the tiny clusters, then the full bunch is there. You see how quickly fruit gets ripe. Verily, quickly and suddenly shall God's decree be accomplished. . . ."

Neither do the *parables of the mustard-seed and of the leaven* (Mk. 4:30-32 or Mt. 13:31f. par.) tell of a gradual development of the "Kingdom of God" in history. Their point is the contrast between the minuteness of its beginning and the magnitude of its completion; they do not intend to give instruction about the process which leads from beginning to completion. Both beginning and completion of God's Reign are miraculous, and miraculous is the happening which brings its fulfilment. Then Jesus' presence and activity are understood to be its beginning—that is, if these parables really have for their subject the beginning and completion of God's Reign. That is admittedly uncertain; the related parables in the Shepherd of Hermas (Mand. V 1, 5f.; XI 20f.) about the drop of wormwood which makes a whole jug of honey bitter, and about the hailstone which can cause great pain, have an entirely different meaning. The former intends to illustrate how practice in patience is brought to nought by an attack of wrath; the latter illustrates the power of the Holy Spirit. So it might be that the parables of the mustard-seed and of the leaven originally dealt with the individual and were intended to instruct him, either as a warning or as a consolation, how great a result may grow out of small beginnings.

The introductory formula, "The Kingdom is like" (ὁμοία

ἐστίν) or "is likened" (ὁμοιώθη) in these parables and in Matthew's so-called *Kingdom-of-Heaven parables* (Mt. 13:44, 45; 18:23; 20:1; 22:2; 25:1) does not mean that what is named in the parable is to be directly compared with the Reign of God, but does mean that the parable teaches a truth that in some way applies to the Reign of God—for example, that God's Reign requires sacrifice of men; for when it is said (Mt. 13:45), "The Reign of God is like a merchant," it is clear that the merchant is not a portrait of God's Reign, but that his conduct portrays the attitude required by it. Besides, the introductory formula, frequently at least, is due to the editing of the evangelist; it is missing in the Lucan parallel (14:16) to Mt. 22:2 as well as in all the parables peculiar to Luke. On the interpretation of the parables in general *cf.* Ad. Jülicher, *Die Gleichnisreden Jesus* I 2nd ed. (1899), II 2nd ed. (1910); R. Bultmann, *Gesch. d. synopt. Trad.*, 2nd ed. (1931), 179–222 (where further references are given).

3. All that man can do in the face of the Reign of God now breaking in is this: Keep ready or get ready for it. Now is the *time of decision,* and Jesus' call is the *call to decision.* The "Queen of the South" once came to hear the wisdom of Solomon; the Ninevites repented at the preaching of Jonah—"behold, something greater than Solomon is here! behold, something greater than Jonah is here!" (Lk. 11:31f. par.). "Blessed is he who takes no offense at me!" (Mt. 11:6 par.).

Basically, therefore, *he in his own person is the "sign of the time."* Yet the historical Jesus of the synoptics does not, like the Johannine Jesus, summon men to acknowledge or "believe in" his person. He does not proclaim himself as the Messiah, i.e. the king of the time of salvation, but he points ahead to the Son of Man as another than himself. *He in his own person signifies the demand for decision,* insofar as his cry, as God's last word before the End, calls men to decision. Now is the last hour; now it can be only: either—or! Now the question is whether a man really desires God and His Reign or the world and its goods; and the decision must be drastically made. "No one who puts his hand to the plow and looks back is fit for the Reign of God!" (Lk. 9:62 Blt.). "Follow me, and leave the dead to bury their own dead!" (Mt. 8:22 par.). "Whoever comes to me and does not hate his father and mother, wife and children, brothers and sisters, yes, and even himself, he cannot be my disciple" (Lk. 14:26

par. Blt.). "Whoever does not bear his own cross and follow me, he cannot be my disciple" (Lk. 14:27 par. Blt. or Mk. 8:34).

He himself renounced his relatives; "whoever does God's will, he is brother and sister and mother to me" (Mk. 3:35 Blt.). And evidently he also uprooted by his word a band of men out of their homes and occupations to accompany him in his wandering life as his "disciples"—i.e. his pupils (Mk. 1:16–20; 2:14). Still he did not found an order or a sect, far less a "Church," nor did he expect that everyone should or could forsake house and family.

The saying about the building of the "Church" (ἐκκλησία) Mt. 16:18 is, like the whole of Mt. 16:17–19, a later product of the Church; *cf. Gesch. d. synopt. Trad.*, 2nd ed., 147–150, 277f.; *Theol. Bl.* 20 (1941), 265–279. An excellent account of the discussion of this problem is given by O. Linton, *Das Problem der Urkirche in der neueren Forschung* (1932). For more recent literature, *cf.* R. N. Flew, *Jesus and his Church* (1938). J. B. Bernardin, "The Church in the N.T." [*Anglican Theol. Rev.* 21 (1939), 153–170]. F. C. Grant, "The Nature of the Church" (*ibid.* 190–204). B. S. Easton, "The Church in the N.T." [*ibid.* 22 (1940), 157–168]. F. J. Leenhardt, *Études sur l'Église dans le N.T.* (1940). Especially: N. A. Dahl, *Das Volk Gottes* (1941); W. G. Kümmel, *Kirchenbegriff und Geschichtsbewusstsein in der Urgemeinde und bei Jesus* (*Symb. Bibl. Upsal.* I) (1943); E. Fascher in the article, "Petrus" in Pauly-Wissowa-Kroll: *Realenzykl. der Klass. Altertumswiss.* XIX, 1353–1361.

But everyone is confronted with deciding what he will set his heart upon—on God or on worldly goods. "Do not lay up for yourselves treasures on earth. . . . For where your treasure is, there will your heart be also!" (Mt. 6:19–21 par.). "No one can serve two masters!" (Mt. 6:24 par.). How dangerous wealth is! "It is easier for a camel to go through the eye of a needle than for a rich man to enter the Reign of God!" (Mk. 10:25 Blt.). Most men cling to earthly goods and cares; and when the time for decision comes, they fail—as the parable of the banquet shows (Lk. 14:15–24 par.). A man must make up his mind what he wants, what degree of effort he is capable of, just as the means for building a tower or waging a war must first be estimated (Lk. 14:28–32). But for the Reign of God one must be ready for any sacrifice—like the farmer who finds a treasure and gives all he has to get possession of it, or like the merchant who sells everything in order to acquire the one precious pearl (Mt. 13:44–46).

"If your hand causes you to sin, cut it off! It is better for you to enter life maimed than with two hands to go to hell. . . . "

"If your eye causes you to sin, pluck it out! It is better for you to enter the Reign of God with one eye, than with two eyes to be thrown into hell" (Mk. 9:43, 47 Blt. or Mt. 5:29f.).

But this renunciation toward the world, this "unworldliness," is not to be thought of as asceticism, but as simple readiness for God's demand. For the positive thing that corresponds to this renunciation, the thing, that is, which constitutes readiness for God's Reign, is the fulfilment of God's will, as Jesus makes evident in combatting Jewish legalism.

§ 2. Jesus' Interpretation of the Demand of God

1. As interpretation of the will, the demand, of God, Jesus' message is a great *protest against Jewish legalism*—i.e. against a form of piety which regards the will of God as expressed in the written Law and in the Tradition which interprets it, a piety which endeavors to win God's favor by the toil of minutely fulfilling the Law's stipulations. Here there is no differentiation between religion and morality, nor are laws about worship and ethics separated from statutes of everyday law. This state of affairs is typified by the fact that the "scribes" are theologians, teachers, and lawyers all at the same time. What religion and morality require is prescribed by the Law, but civil and criminal law are also regarded as divine Law. The result is not merely that a mass of ordinances which have lost the meaning they once had under earlier conditions remain in force and so have to be twisted by artificial interpretation into relevance for today; not merely that regulations appropriate to the present have to be wrung out of the ancient Law by artificial deduction to meet new conditions of life. Nor is the result merely that a plethora of cultic and ritual laws are regarded as God's demand, or as ethical demand, and thus frequently overshadow the really ethical demands. The real result is that motivation to ethical conduct is vitiated. That is the result not only in the wide extent to which the idea of reward and punishment becomes the motivation, but also—and this is the characteristic thing for Judaism—that the obedience man owes to God and to His demand for good is understood as a purely formal

one; i.e. as an obedience which fulfills the letter of the law, obeying a law simply because it is commanded without asking the reason, the meaning, of its demand. And though many a scribe protests against the prevalence of reward and punishment as the motive for obedience, demanding instead an obedience from the heart which would fulfill the commandment not out of fear but out of love to God, nevertheless obedience cannot be radical, genuine obedience so long as man obeys only because it is commanded—so long, that is, as he would do something else if something else were commanded, or, rather, would not do the thing in question if it did not stand in the commandment. Radical obedience is only possible where a man understands the demand and affirms it from within himself. And only of such obedience is it meaningful to say that in fulfilling the ethical demand it fulfills God's demand, for God requires radical obedience. The error of Jewish legalism reveals itself finally in the following. A statute, unlike an ethical demand, can never embrace every specific situation of life; instead there inevitably remain many cases unprovided for, cases for which there is no command or prohibition; that leaves room not only for every desire and passion that may arise but also—and that again is characteristic of Judaism—for works of supererogation. In principle, when a man's duties are conceived of as the committing or omitting of specific acts under legal requirement, he can completely discharge them and have room left over for extra deeds of merit. So there developed in Judaism the notion of "good works" that go beyond the required fulfilment of the Law (such as almsgiving, various acts of charity, voluntary fasting, and the like), establishing literal merits and hence also capable of atoning for transgressions of the Law. This indicates that here the idea of obedience is not taken radically.

2. Seen against this background *Jesus' proclamation of the will of God appears as a great protest.* In it the protest of the great prophets of the Old Testament against the cultic worship of God in their time is renewed under altered circumstances. Whereas they had upheld justice and uprightness as God's demand in opposition to the cultic piety of the people, Jesus demanded radical obedience in opposition to that merely formal obedience which to a large extent regarded the fulfilment of the ritual prescriptions as the essential thing. He does not, as the prophets did, raise the demand for justice and right; for the preaching of these things, once decisive

for Israelitic national life, has lost its meaning now that there is scarcely any national life left. What Judaism has left as the product of the prophets' work is codified law, which now, however, no longer serves primarily to regulate national life but governs the relation of the individual to God. And that is just what Jesus protests against—that man's relation to God is regarded as a legal one. God requires radical obedience. He claims man whole—and wholly. Within this insight Jesus takes for granted that God requires of man the doing of the good and that ethical demands are the demands of God; to that extent religion and ethics constitute a unity for him, too. But excluded from the demands of God are all cultic and ritual regulations, so that along with ethics Jesus sets free the purely religious relation to God in which man stands only as one who asks and receives, hopes and trusts.

The antitheses (Mt. 5:21–48) *in the Sermon on the Mount* throw legalism and the will of God into sharp contrast: "You have heard that it was said to the men of old . . ., But I say to you . . .!" The meaning is this: God does not lay claim to man only so far as conduct can be determined by formulated laws (the only way open to legalism), leaving man's own will free from that point on. What God forbids is not simply the overt acts of murder, adultery, and perjury, with which law can deal, but their antecedents: anger and name-calling, evil desire and insincerity (Mt. 5:21f., 27f., 33–37). What counts before God is not simply the substantial, verifiable deed that is done, but how a man is disposed, what his intent is. As the laws concerning murder, adultery and perjury are thus radicalized, so others which were once meant to restrict arbitrary action but now are conceived as concessions defining an area of leeway for permissive acts, are from the point of view of God's intention altogether abolished: the provision for divorce, the law of retaliation, the limitation of the duty of love to one's neighbor alone (Mt. 5:31f., 38–41, 43–48). *God demands the whole will of man* and knows no abatement in His demand.

> Are grapes gathered from thorns,
>   or figs from thistles?
> Each tree is known by its own fruit;
>   a good tree cannot bear evil fruit.
>   (Mt. 7:16, 18 combined with Lk. 6:43f. Blt.)

[13]

> The eye is the lamp of the body.
> So, if your eye is sound,
> Your whole body will be full of light.
> But if your eye is not sound,
> Your whole body will be full of darkness.
> (Mt. 6:22f. par.)

Man, upon whose whole self God's demand is made, has no freedom toward God; he is accountable for his life as a whole—as the parable of the talents teaches (Mt. 25:14–30 par.). *He may not, must not, cannot raise any claim before God,* but is like the slave who only has his duty to do and can do no more (Lk. 17:7–10).

This parable is paralleled in the saying of a pre-Christian rabbi, Antigonus of Socho: "Be not like servants who serve their lord on condition of receiving reward; but rather be like servants who serve their lord under no condition of receiving reward" (Pirqe Aboth 1, 3). In demanding unconditional obedience Jesus and the rabbi agree. That the idea of obedience is taken radically by Jesus follows from the whole context of his ethical utterances.

Man must become like a child, who, knowing no such thing as appeal to any rights or merits of his own, is willing simply to be given a gift (Mk. 10:15). Those who proudly brag of their merits are an abomination to God (Lk. 16:15), and the virtue-proud Pharisee has to take a lower place than the guilt-conscious publican (Lk. 18:9–14). So Jesus rejects all this counting up of merit and reward: The worker who went to work in the last hour of the day is rewarded just as much as the one who had worked all day long (Mt. 20:1–15). And Jesus also refuses to regard the misfortune that befalls individuals as punishment for their special sins; no man is better than another (Lk. 13:1–5).

One must, of course, admit that for Jesus it is certain that God does reward faithful obedience; back of the demand stands the promise; and in view of his battle against the motive of retribution his position must be so described: He promises reward precisely to those who obey not for the sake of reward. Even so, his words are not without self-contradiction, since he does occasionally use the *idea of recompense* as motivation for a demand—either by referring to heavenly reward (Mt. 6:19f. par. Mk. 10:21 and elsewhere) or

[14]

by threatening with hell-fire (Mt. 10:28 par. Mk. 9:43, 47 and elsewhere). Still the contradiction can probably be resolved in this
way: The motive of reward is only a primitive expression for the idea
that in what a man does his own real being is at stake—that self
which he not already is, but is to become. To achieve that self is the
legitimate motive of his ethical dealing and of his true obedience, in
which he becomes aware of the paradoxical truth that in order to
arrive at himself he must surrender to the demand of God—or, in
other words, that in such surrender he wins himself. This paradoxical truth is taught in the following saying:

> "Whoever seeks to gain his life will lose it,
> But whoever loses his life will preserve it." (Lk. 17:33)

Both Mark and Q hand down this saying. At Mk. 8:35
"whoever loses it" has the addition: "for my sake and the gospel's." The parallels to this passage, Mt. 16:25 and Lk. 9:24,
read only "for my sake," and that is probably all they had found
in their Marcan text. To accord with it Mt. 10:39 also added
"for my sake" in the Q-parallel to Lk. 17:33. John also knew the
saying, and knew it without the addition, so that he corroborates the form of Lk. 17:33 as the original one when he says,
"He who loves his life loses it, and he who hates his life in this
world will keep it for eternal life" (12:25), though he, on his
part, has added "in this world" and "for eternal life."

3. From the standpoint of this radical attitude of Jesus toward
the will of God, what is to be said of *his position toward the Old
Testament?* Without contesting its authority he makes critical distinctions among the demands of the Old Testament. Yes, Moses did
permit divorce, but only "in consideration of your hard-heartedness."
By no means is that the actual intention of God; rather He intends
marriage to be inseparable (Mk. 10:2–9).

"Woe to you, scribes and Pharisees, hypocrites! For you tithe
mint and dill and cummin, and have neglected the weightiest in the
Law: justice and mercy and good faith; these things ought to be
done and the others not neglected. You blind guides, straining out
a gnat and swallowing a camel!" (Mt. 23:23f. Blt.). If the words
"These things ought to be done and the others not neglected" are
really an original component of this "woe" (they are missing in the
Luke-parallel 11:42 in Codex D), they indicate that a reformer's
polemic against the Old Testament legislation is far from Jesus'

intention. In any case these verses indicate a sovereign attitude assumed by Jesus toward the Old Testament, an attitude which critically distinguishes the important from the unimportant, the essential from the indifferent. This is in harmony with the rest of Jesus' words concerning the Old Testament.

God did indeed declare His will in the Old Testament. Whoever inquires about the will of God is referred to the ethical demands of the Old Testament—for instance, the rich man with his question: "What must I do to inherit eternal life?" or the "lawyer"-scribe with his query about the highest commandment (Mk. 10:17–19, 12:28–34). But the rich man straightway has to accept the accusation that his previous fulfilment of the commandments has been an illusion, since he is incapable of giving up everything—he cannot radically obey.

That Jesus did not polemically contest the authority of the Old Testament is proven by the course later taken by his Church; it clung faithfully to the Old Testament Law and thereby came into conflict with Paul. The Church formulated its standpoint—no matter whether against Paul or against other Hellenistic missionaries—in the words placed on Jesus' lips about the imperishability of even the tiniest letter in the Law and expressly declaring that Jesus did not come to abolish the Law, but to fulfill it (Mt. 5:17–19)—a saying that in view of other sayings of Jesus and of his actual practice cannot possibly be genuine; rather it is a product of the Church coming out of the later period of conflict over the Law. Yet clearly this conservative attitude of the Church would not have been possible if Jesus had called into question the validity of the Old Testament. Its authority stands just as fast for him as for the scribes, and he feels himself in opposition to them only in the way he understands and applies the Old Testament. Neither did he oppose *the pious practices of Judaism*—almsgiving, prayer, and fasting—though he did protest against their being put into the service of personal vanity and so becoming a lie (Mt. 6:1–4, 5–8, 16–18).

His answer to the question about fasting, Mk. 2:19, does not reject fasting on principle, but means that in the dawning of messianic joy the mourning custom of fasting (which in itself is not opposed) does not make sense. The original meaning of the sayings about the new patch on an old garment and new wine in old skins (Mk. 2:21f.) is no longer clearly discernible. It may have intended some such meaning as this, that in the messianic period the old mourning customs have become meaningless.

Polemic against the temple cult is completely absent from the words of Jesus. As a matter of fact it, too, had essentially lost its original meaning in his time; for Judaism was no longer a cultic religion, but had become a religion of observance. The temple cult was faithfully carried out, and at the great festivals really cultic piety probably revived. But in general the temple cult with its sacrifices was carried out as an act of obedience—for was it not commanded in the Law? The synagogue with its interpretation of the regulation of daily life by the Law had pushed the temple service into the background; for the people, the scribes had replaced the priests as the seat of authority. So Judaism, borne up by the synagogue and the scribes, survived the fall of the temple without disaster. In Mt. 5:23f. participation in the temple cult is taken for granted without misgiving. It may well be a genuine saying of Jesus, whereas Mt. 17:24–27 is a later legend, but one that proves, nevertheless, that the Christian Church paid the temple tax. In the same way accounts contained in Acts also show that the Church held gatherings within the temple area.

Actually the Old Testament legislation, so far as it consists of cultic and ritual prescriptions, has been lifted off its hinges by Jesus. As he rises above the Sabbath law, so he attacks *legalistic ritualism* which strives for an external correctness which can go hand in hand with an impure will. Thus he quotes the prophet (Is. 29:13):

"This people honors me with their lips
　But their heart is far from me.
　In vain do they worship me,
　Teaching as doctrines the precepts of men." (Mk. 7:6f.)
"Woe to you, scribes and Pharisees, hypocrites!
　For you cleanse the outside of the cup and of the plate,
　But inside you (*cf.* Lk. 11:39) are full of extortion and rapacity!" . . .
"Woe to you, scribes and Pharisees, hypocrites!
　For you are like whitewashed tombs, which outwardly appear beautiful,
　But within they are full of dead men's bones and all uncleanness.

[17]

So you also outwardly appear righteous to men,
But within you are full of hypocrisy and iniquity." (Mt. 23:25–
   28 par. Blt.)

How alms, prayer, and fasting can be misused to impress others
(Mt. 6:1–4, 5f., 16–18)! Unless fasting expresses real grief, it has no
meaning (Mk. 2:18f.). How God's command to honor one's parents
can be set aside by declaring a cultic command to be more important (Mk. 7:9–13)! The laws of cleanliness are meaningless, for
"there is nothing outside a man which by going into him can defile
him; but the things which come out of a man are what defile him"
(Mk. 7:15). "The sabbath was made for man, not man for the
sabbath" (Mk. 2:27). And though it is true that the same insight
flashes up now and then among the scribes, still Jesus is the first to
draw the consequence of it with his question:

"Is it lawful on the sabbath to do good or to do harm,
   To save a life or to kill?" (Mk. 3:4 Blt.)

that is, there is no third choice, no holy indolence. To do nothing
where an act of love is required would be to do evil. So Jesus is
"a friend of publicans and sinners" (Mt. 11:19 par., Mk. 2:15–17);
he cannot avoid being slandered as "glutton and drunkard" (Mt.
11:19), and he can actually use a Samaritan as a good example (Lk.
10:30–36).

4. What, positively, is the will of God? *The demand for love.*
"You shall love your neighbor as yourself!" as the second greatest
commandment belongs together with the first: "You shall love the
Lord your God with all your heart and with all your soul and with
all your mind and with all your strength" (Mk. 12:28–34). There
is no obedience to God which does not have to prove itself in the
concrete situation of meeting one's neighbor, as Luke (10:29–37),
probably unhistorically but with the right of correct understanding
of the subject-matter, makes clear by combining the illustrative narrative of the Good Samaritan with Jesus' discussion of the greatest
commandment.

The demand for love surpasses every legal demand; it knows no
boundary or limit; it holds even in regard to one's enemy (Mt. 5:43–
48). The question, "How often must I forgive my brother when he

sins against me? Is seven times enough?" is answered: "I tell you: not seven times, but seventy times seven" (Mt. 18:21f. par. Blt.).

The demand for love needs no formulated stipulations; the example of the merciful Samaritan shows that a man can know and must know what he has to do when he sees his neighbor in need of his help. The little words "as yourself" in the love-commandment pre-indicate both the boundlessness and the direction of loving conduct.

Jesus completely refrained from making the love-commandment concrete in specific prescriptions. That fact shows that his proclamation of the will of God is not an ethic of world-reform. Rather, it must be described as an eschatological ethic. For it does not envisage a future to be molded within this world by plans and sketches for the ordering of human life. It only directs man into the Now of his meeting with his neighbor. It is an ethic that, by demanding more than the law that regulates human society does and requiring of the individual the waiver of his own rights, makes the individual immediately responsible to God.

5. At this point it begins to be clear how *Jesus' eschatological message and his ethical message constitute a unity*—in other words, how the same Jesus can be both the prophet who proclaims the irruption of God's Reign and the rabbi who expounds God's Law.

There is such a unity, but it is a false unity if it is reached by conceiving God's Reign as the triumph of the Demand for Good either in the human mind or in historical human affairs. This misconception may say: God's Reign is a reigning of God in the mind which occurs when the divine Demand prevails there and takes shape in ethical character. Or it may say: It is a reigning of God in human affairs which occurs when the divine Demand prevails there and takes shape in an ethical social order. Both forms not only distort the concept Reign of God but also misunderstand the intent of God's demand—it aims neither at the formation of "character" nor at the molding of human society.

Neither is it feasible, recognizing the rivalry between the eschatological and the ethical message of Jesus, to deny one of the two to belong to the historical Jesus and pronounce it a later product of the Church. It cannot be maintained that Jesus was only a teacher of ethics who taught a "superior righteousness" and that it was the Church that first put into his mouth the eschatological message of

[19]

the irruption of God's Reign. For we can readily see that the origin of the Church lies in the certainty of that imminent End, but not that that certainty itself could have been a later community product. The tradition shows, on the contrary, that alarmed anxiety arose in the Church at the delay of the expected Reign of God. This alarm is expressed in words put into the mouth of Jesus (Lk. 12:35–38, Mk. 13:31, 33–37). But above all, the movement which Jesus evoked among the people and his crucifixion by the Roman procurator show that it was in the role of a messianic prophet that he appeared. On the other hand, it is just as impossible to regard only his eschatological message as historically genuine and his ethical preaching as a secondary product of the Church. For, aside from the fact that it would not be intelligible how the Church should have come to make a rabbi of him whom they regarded as Messiah, the scrupulous observance of the Law by the earliest Church indicates that the radical sayings about the Law and its observance cannot have originated in it.

The unity of the eschatological and the ethical message of Jesus may be so stated: Fulfilment of God's will is the condition for participation in the salvation of His Reign. Only "condition" in that statement must not be taken in the external sense of an arbitrarily set task, in place of which some other could have been set—a condition, that is, without inner relation to the gift for whose receipt it constitutes the presupposition—as it is taken to mean, for instance, when Jesus' interpretation of the divine demand is held to be no more than an "interim ethic" and its imperatives are therefore regarded as exceptional commands which only held for the last short interval until the end of the world. Rather, these imperatives are clearly meant radically as absolute demand with a validity independent of the temporal situation. Neither the demands of the Sermon on the Mount nor Jesus' attacks against legalistic morality are motivated by reference to the impending end of the world. But precisely Jesus' knowledge of the absolute validity of the divine demand is the basis of his radical verdict over "this evil and adulterous generation" ripe for divine judgment (Mt. 12:39 par., Mk. 8:38)—the same verdict, that is, that comes to expression in the eschatological proclamation. Then this is clear: The fulfilment of God's will is the condition for participation in the salvation of God's Reign in *this* sense, that it means nothing else but true readiness for it, genuine and earnest desire for it. The Reign of God, demanding of man decision for God against every earthly tie, is the salvation to come. Hence, only he is ready for this salvation who in the concrete moment decides for that demand of God which confronts him in the person of his neighbor. They who, conscious of their poverty, wait weeping and hungering for salvation, are identical with those who are merciful, pure of heart, and peace-makers (Mt. 5:3–9). Whoever has his will set upon God's Reign also wills to fulfill the commandment of love. It is not that he fulfills the commandment of love as an irksome requirement while his real will is directed at something else (viz. God's Reign), for the sake of which alone he obeys the commandment of God. Rather there is an inner connection: Both things, the eschatological proclamation and the ethical demand, direct man to the fact that he is thereby brought before God, that God stands before him; both direct him into his Now as the hour of decision for God.

6. Thus it happens that at the sight of the actual state of the leaders of the people and of the great mass of the people itself—at the sight of religion frozen into ritualism, at the sight of superficiality and love of self and the world—Jesus' message becomes *a cry of woe and repentance.*

"Woe to you, scribes and Pharisees! . . ."
(Mt. 23:1ff. par.; Mk. 12:38ff.)
"Woe to you that are rich, for you have received your consolation!
Woe to you that are full now, for you shall hunger!
Woe to you that laugh now, for you shall mourn and weep!"
(Lk. 6:24–26)

"The time is fulfilled, the Reign of God is at hand! Repent!" (Mk. 1:15)—this is the condensed summary of Jesus' cry. But this contemporary "generation" is "adulterous and sinful" (Mk. 8:38; Mt. 12:39). Men say "yes" to God's demand and then do not do what He requires (Mt. 21:28–31). They refuse to "repent," to turn about from their perverted way (Lk. 11:31f. par.), and so the judgment will break in upon sinners (Lk. 13:1–5), and all predictions of woe will come to pass (Mt. 23:34–36 par.), especially upon Jerusalem (Mt. 23:37–39 par.) and its temple: not a stone that will not be thrown down! (Mk. 13:2). Only in the despised—the publicans,

[21]

sinners, and harlots—is there readiness to repent; to them and not to the "righteous," Jesus considers himself sent (Mk. 2:17); these who first said "no" repent (Mt. 21:28–31), and God has more joy over one sinner who repents than over ninety-nine "righteous" (Lk. 15:1–10). They who await God's Reign aright, hungering and sorrowing, knowing how poor they are—to them pertains the promise of salvation (Lk. 6:20f. or Mt. 5:3–6).

§ 3. Jesus' Idea of God

1. Once one has understood the unity of the eschatological and the ethical preaching of Jesus, one also has the answer to the real meaning of the eschatological message, namely: the answer to the question, what *idea of God* is at work in it. For, in view of the fact that the proclamation of the irruption of God's Reign was not fulfilled—that is, that Jesus' expectation of the near end of the world turned out to be an illusion—the question arises whether his idea of God was not also illusory. This question is frequently avoided, it is true, by the escape-reasoning that Jesus saw the presence of God's Reign in his own person and in the followers who gathered about him. But such a view cannot be substantiated by a single saying of Jesus,* and it contradicts the meaning of "God's Reign." On the contrary, Jesus clearly expected the irruption of God's Reign as a miraculous, world-transforming event—as Judaism, and later also his own Church, did. Nowhere to be found in his words is there polemic against this view, so taken for granted by his time, or any correction of it.

But it is a fact that *prophetic consciousness* always expects the judgment of God, and likewise the time of salvation to be brought in by God, in the immediate future, as may be clearly seen in the great prophets of the Old Testament. And the reason this is so is that to the prophetic consciousness the sovereignty of God, the absoluteness of His will, is so overpowering that before it the world sinks away and seems to be at its end. The consciousness that man's relation toward God decides his fate and that the hour of decision is of limited duration clothes itself in the consciousness that the hour of decision is here for the world, too. The word which the prophet

---

* Not by Lk. 17:21 either. On the meaning of this saying, see p. 6 above.

is conscious of having to speak by God's commission takes the form of the final word by which God summons men to definitive decision.

So also with Jesus. He is certain that he is acquainted with the unswerving will of God, who sternly demands the good from man and, through the message by which He is preached, thrusts man into the alternative of salvation or condemnation. It is this certainty which gives Jesus the consciousness of standing at the end of time. His message grows neither out of weariness with the world and longing for the world beyond nor out of fanciful speculation, but out of knowing the world's futility and man's corruption in God's eyes and out of knowing the will of God. The essential thing about the eschatological message is the idea of God that operates in it and the idea of human existence that it contains—not the belief that the end of the world is just ahead.

2. God, in keeping with Old Testament tradition, is, for Jesus, *the Creator* who governs the world with His care, feeds the beasts and adorns the flowers, without whose will not a sparrow falls dead to earth, and who has counted every hair of our heads (Mt. 6:25–34 par., 10:29f. par.). All anxious care, all haste to get goods to insure life, is therefore senseless—yes, wicked. Man is at the mercy of the Creator's will; he can neither add a cubit to his height nor make a single hair of his head white or black (Mt. 6:27 par., 5:36). If he imagines himself self-insured by the wealth he has amassed and able now to take his ease, he has forgotten that he still can die this very night (Lk. 12:16–20). Trust in God and consciousness of dependence are both alike demanded of man.

In the above, Jesus' idea of God does not essentially differ from that of the Old Testament and of Judaism, though it is true that in the common piety of Judaism faith in God the Creator had weakened even while it was strictly preserved in its official theology and confession. God had retreated far off into the distance as the transcendent heavenly King, and His sway over the present could barely still be made out. For Jesus, God again became *a God at hand.* He is the power, here and now, who as Lord and Father enfolds every man—limiting and commanding him. This contrast finds expression in the respective forms of address used in prayer. Compare the ornate, emotional, often liturgically beautiful, but often over-loaded, forms of address in Jewish prayer with the stark simplicity of "Father"! The "Prayer of Eighteen Petitions," for instance, which the devout Jew is expected to say three times daily, begins, "Lord God of Abraham, God of Isaac, God of Jacob! God Most High, Creator of heaven and earth! Our Shield and the Shield of our fathers!" ° † The "Lord's Prayer" stands out above Jewish prayers not only in its simple address but in its direct simplicity throughout (Mt. 6:9–13, or Lk. 11:2–4). God is near; He hears and understands the requests which come thronging to Him, as a father understands the requests of his own child (Mt. 7:7–11 par.; *cf.* Lk. 11:5–8; 18:1–5).

But God has also come near as the "Demand-er" whose will need not wait to be found in the letter of the Law or its scribal exegesis. The remoteness interposed by Law and Tradition between God and man is closed up, and man's uncertain searching for what is forbidden and what allowed is over. A man learns what God wants of him immediately out of his own situation in the encounter with his neighbor. And so God also stands before every man as the Judge to whom he owes accounting. "I tell you, on the day of judgment men will render account for every careless word they utter" (Mt. 12:36). "Do not fear those who kill the body but cannot kill the soul! Rather fear him who can destroy both soul and body in hell!" (Mt. 10:28 par.).

But the demanding God of judgment is also the merciful *God of forgiveness*; and whoever turns back to Him in repentance can be certain of His forgiving kindness. The scribes shut the Kingdom of Heaven in men's faces with their legalism (Mt. 23:13 par.); Jesus' very call to repentance opens the way to it and they have no need of the long penitential prayers that are characteristic of Judaism. The publican who dares not raise his eyes to Heaven, but strikes his breast and says, "God be merciful to me, a sinner!" is accounted righteous (Lk. 18:9–14). The "prodigal son" says only, "Father, I have sinned against Heaven and before you; I am no longer worthy to be called your son"—and then fatherly kindness embraces him (Lk. 15:11–32). The proud and self-righteous are an abomination to God (Lk. 16:15; 18:9–14); but over the sinner who contritely repents, God rejoices (Lk. 15:1–10). But forgiveness has been truly received only when it makes the heart forgiving, as the parable of the wicked servant teaches (Mt. 18:23–35; *cf.* Lk. 7:47), and only

° Palestinian recension, Dalman's emendations, *Die Worte Jesu*, appendix.
† *Cf.* espec. IV Esdras 8:20ff.

he who is willing to forgive can honestly ask for God's forgiveness (Mt. 6:12, 14f.). God's forgiveness makes a man new; and whoever is willing to become new receives it.

3. Jesus no longer speaks, as the ancient prophets did, of the revelations of God in the history of the Nation and the nations. And when he refers to the coming judgment of God, unlike them he is no more thinking of catastrophes in the affairs of nations than he expects God's Reign to be fulfilled in the erection of a mighty and glorious Israelitic kingdom. Unlike the prophets' preaching, his preaching is directed not primarily to the people as a whole, but *to individuals*. The judgment is coming not on nations but on individuals who must give account of themselves before God; and it is individuals whom coming salvation will bless. Judgment and salvation are eschatological events in the strict sense; i.e. events in which the present world and all history cease to be.

Thus, *Jesus in his thought of God*—and of man in the light of this thought—"de-historized" God and man; that is, released the relation between God and man from its previous ties to history (history considered as the affairs of nations). While this was already more or less the case in Judaism (but not in the religion of the Old Testament prophets), Jesus' thought, in contrast to that of Judaism, also *radically "historized"* God in a different sense of "history." In Judaism God is de-historized by having become a distant God enthroned in heaven; His governance of the world is carried out by angels, and His relation to man is mediated by the book of the Law. And man in Judaism is de-historized by being marked off from the world by ritual and by finding his security within the ritually pure congregation. The Jewish congregation artificially accomplishes its de-secularization (*Entweltlichung*) by means of its legalism. For Jesus, however, man is de-secularized by God's direct pronouncement to him, which tears him out of all security of any kind and places him at the brink of the End. And God is "de-secularized" by understanding His dealing eschatologically: He lifts man out of his worldly ties and places him directly before His own eyes. Hence, the "de-historization" or "desecularization" both of God and of man is to be understood as a paradox (*dialektisch*): precisely that God, who stands aloof from the history of nations, meets each man in his own little history, his everyday life with its daily gift and demand; de-historized man (i.e. naked of his supposed security within his historical group) is guided into his concrete encounter with his neighbor, in which he finds his true history.

§ 4. The Question of the Messianic Consciousness of Jesus

1. The Church of Jesus' disciples understood his claim that men's destiny is determined by their attitude to him in such a way that they regarded Jesus himself as the Messiah they had been expecting, or else still awaited Jesus himself as the coming Son of Man. The common opinion is that this belief of the earliest Church rests upon the self-consciousness of Jesus; i.e. that he actually did consider himself to be the Messiah, or the Son of Man. But this opinion is burdened with serious difficulties. It does agree with the evangelists' point of view, but the question is whether they themselves have not superimposed upon the traditional material their own belief in the messiahship of Jesus. In discussing this question it is important to bear in mind that if the fact should be established that Jesus was conscious of being the Messiah, or the Son of Man, that would only establish a historical fact, not prove an article of faith. Rather, the acknowledgment of Jesus as the one in whom God's word decisively encounters man, whatever title be given him— "Messiah (Christ)," "Son of Man," "Lord"—is a pure act of faith independent of the answer to the historical question whether or not Jesus considered himself the Messiah. Only the historian can answer this question—as far as it can be answered at all—and faith, being personal decision, cannot be dependent upon a historian's labor.

Some advance the following reasoning as an argument from history: The Church's belief in the messiahship of Jesus * is comprehensible only if Jesus was conscious of being the Messiah and actually represents himself as such—at least to the "disciples." But is this argument valid? For it is just as possible that belief in the messiahship of Jesus arose with and out of belief in his resurrection. The scene of *Peter's Confession* (Mk. 8:27–30) is no counter-evidence— on the contrary! For it is an Easter-story projected backward into Jesus' life-time, just like the story of the Transfiguration (Mk. 9:2–8). The account of Jesus' baptism (Mk. 1:9–11) is legend, certain though it is that the legend started from the historical fact of Jesus' baptism by John. It is told in the interest not of biography but of

---

* Disregarding the distinction between Messiah and Son of Man; after all, both mean the eschatological bringer of salvation.

faith, and it reports Jesus' consecration as Messiah. It originated in the time when Jesus' life was already regarded as having been messianic, whereas the transfiguration story, originally a resurrection-account, dates his messiahship from the resurrection onward. The Temptation story (Mk. 1:12f. or Mt. 4:1–11 par.), which involves reflection about what kind of messiah Jesus was or what kind of messiah the Christian believes in, is legend. The story of Jesus' entry into Jerusalem has been colored by legend, and the passion-narrative is also to a considerable degree overspread with legend; for to the Church that venerated the Crucified as the Messiah it was soon perfectly certain that it was as Messiah that he had been crucified.

Moreover the synoptic tradition leaves no doubt about it that *Jesus' life and work* measured by traditional messianic ideas *was not messianic*. And Paul, like others, also did not understand it as messianic, as the Christ-hymn quoted by him at Phil. 2:6–11 indicates. It conceives Jesus' life as that of a mere man, without messianic glory. Likewise Acts 2:36 and Rom. 1:4, where Paul is evidently using a traditional formulation, show that in the earliest Church, Jesus' messiahship was dated from the resurrection. Actually, "Messiah" was the term for the eschatological ruler; the word means "the Anointed" and came to mean simply "king."* But it was not as a king, but as a prophet and a rabbi that Jesus appeared—and, one may add, as an exorcist. Nothing of the might and glory, which according to Jewish supposition would characterize the Messiah, was realized in Jesus' life—not in his exorcisms, for example, nor in his other mighty works. For though miracles were indeed a characteristic of the messianic period in Jewish belief, still the Messiah himself was not thought of as a miracle-worker. And even if it be said, in view of Jesus' words about the Son of Man, that Jesus thought of the Messiah not so much, or not at all, as the Davidic king, but rather as that other figure, the heavenly judge and salvation-bringer (viz. the apocalyptic Son of Man), that does not change the situation, for it was not as judge of the world and supernatural bringer of salvation that Jesus appeared.

* *Cf.* the substitution of the word "king" Βασιλεύς Mk. 15: 2, 9, 18, 26, 32; Jn. 1:49; Ps. Sol. 17:23, etc. See P. Volz, *Die Eschatologie der jüdischen Gemeinde im neutestamentl. Zeitalter* (1934), 173f.; W. Staerk, *Soter* I (1933), 48ff.

2. Well, then, it has often been asked, did Jesus *reinterpret the traditional Messiah-concept?* Did he "spiritualize" it by exercising his sovereign office through the effect of his word? Only the tradition could inform us as to that. But where in it is such a thing indicated? Where, in the words of Jesus, is there polemic against the conventional Messiah-concept? It is no more to be found than is any criticism of the Jewish conception of the Reign of God!

At the most, the question about the Son of David (Mk. 12:35-37) might be cited; it seems to contain a criticism of the conception of the Messiah as the Son of David: The Messiah is not a descendant of David since David himself called him his lord. In any case, that does not constitute a re-interpretation of the Messiah-concept of such sort that a prophet-and-teacher's life and activity are to be regarded as messianic, and there is no thought here of "spiritualization." What it does say is that when the Messiah is called Son of David, his rank and dignity are given too humble a name. What, then, is the implied but unexpressed Messiah-concept out of which the title "Son of David" is criticized? It could be the apocalyptic concept of the heavenly Son of Man, and it is not impossible that criticism of this sort might go back to Jesus or to the Church. In that case, however, it would be hard to understand how the view came to prevail in the Church that Jesus was a Son of David (*cf.* the lineages of Jesus—Mt. 1:1ff.; Lk. 3:23ff.; Rom. 1:3, and the unretouched report that Jesus was addressed as Son of David—Mk. 10:47; Mt. 9:27, etc.). Or is the title "Son of God" implied as the counter-concept? * If so, this could only be meant as Hellenistic Christianity meant it: as a term for supernatural origin; for in Jewish-Christian use, this term, like Messiah, is only a designation of the king (*cf.* W. Staerk, *Soter* I:89 and e.g. Mk. 14:61; Lk. 1:32, 4:41, etc.). But in that case the passage had its origin in the Hellenistic Church. But if the meaning of Mk. 12:35-37 is held to be that the Messiah is both Son of David and Son of Man (Schniewind's view), then this passage is all the more meaningless for deciding whether Jesus' life had messianic character.

3. Since alleged re-interpretation and spiritualization of the Messiah-concept to mean anything but the king of the time of salvation

* So understood by Barn. 12:10f.; see W. Wrede, *Vorträge und Studien* (1907), 171ff.

has now been ruled out, there remains only the frequently chosen escape of saying that Jesus was conscious of being the one *destined to be the future Messiah,* that his idea of the Messiah was "futuristic." Nothing could be cited in favor of this idea except those words of Jesus in which he speaks of the coming Son of Man (Mk. 8:38 or Lk. 12:8f. par.; Mt. 24:27, 37, 44 par.; Lk. 11:30). But it must be admitted that in them he speaks of the Son of Man in the third person without identifying himself with him. There is no question but that the evangelists—and likewise the Church which had handed down these sayings—make this identification; but can that be asserted of Jesus himself?

At any rate, the synoptic tradition contains no sayings in which Jesus says he will sometime (or soon) return. (Neither was the word παρουσία, which denotes the "coming" of the Son of Man, ever understood in the earliest period of Christianity as "return," but correctly as "arrival, advent." The apologete Justin in the second century was the first to speak of the "first" πρώτη and "second coming" δευτέρα παρουσία (Dial. 14:8, 40:4) and of the "coming back πάλιν παρουσία (Dial. 118:2). And how would Jesus have conceived *the relation of his return as Son of Man to his present historical activity?* He would have had to count upon being removed from the earth and raised to heaven before the final End, the irruption of God's Reign, in order to come from there on the clouds of heaven to perform his real office. But how would he have conceived his removal from the earth? As a miraculous translation? Among his sayings there is no trace of any such fantastic idea. As departure by natural death, then? Of that, too, his words say nothing. By a violent death, then? But if so, could he count on that as an absolute certainty— as the consciousness of being raised to the dignity of the coming Son of Man would presuppose? To be sure, *the predictions of the passion* (Mk. 8:31, 9:31, 10:33f.; *cf.* Mk. 10:45, 14:21, 41) foretell his execution as divinely foreordained. But can there be any doubt that they are all *vaticinia ex eventu?* Besides, they do not speak of his parousia! And the predictions of the parousia (Mk. 8:38, 13:26f., 14:62; Mt. 24:27, 37, 39, 44 par.) on their part, do not speak of the death and resurrection of the Son of Man. Clearly the predictions of the parousia originally had nothing to do with the predictions of death and resurrection; i.e. in the sayings that speak of the coming of the Son of Man there is no idea that this Son of Man is already here in person and must first be removed by death before he can return from heaven.

Observe in what unassimilated fashion the prediction of the parousia Mk. 8:38 follows upon the prediction of the passion and resurrection 8:31. In Mk. 9:1, 11–13 only the parousia is assumed (v 12b is an interpolation modeled after Mt. 17:12b), while the transfiguration 9:2–10, which the evangelist inserted between these originally connected verses, contains only the idea of resurrection. Later Mt. 17:12b connects the motif of the suffering Son of Man with the sayings that involve reflection about the parousia, and Lk. 17:23–25 likewise combines the passion-motif with prediction of the parousia (*cf.* Lk. 17:23–25 with Mt. 24:26–27)—an altogether secondary combination.

Furthermore, it is not to be doubted that the predictions of the parousia are older than those of the passion and resurrection; Q knows only the former and not yet the latter. The latter are probably later products of the Hellenistic Church, in which the title "Son of Man" was no longer understood in its original sense, while the predictions of the parousia are old and are probably original words of Jesus.

The synoptic Son-of-Man sayings fall into three groups, which speak of the Son of Man (1) as coming, (2) as suffering death and rising again, and (3) as now at work. This third group (Mk. 2:10, 28; Mt. 8:20 par., 11:19 par., 12:32 par.) owes its origin to a mere misunderstanding of the translation into Greek. In Aramaic, the son of man in these sayings was not a messianic title at all, but meant "man" or "I." So this group drops out of the present discussion. The second group contains the *vaticinia ex eventu* which are not yet present in Q; the first group alone contains very old tradition. The sayings belonging to it speak of the Son of Man in the third person. —The secondary material peculiar to Matthew or Luke does not need to be taken into account here; it is significant that for these later evangelists the original meaning of the title is lost and Son of Man has become so completely a self-designation of Jesus that Matthew can substitute either "I" for a traditional Son of Man (Mt. 10:32f. against Lk. 12:8f; *cf.* Mk. 8:38; *cf.* Mt. 16:21 with Mk. 9:31; Mt. 5:11 with Lk. 6:22), or, vice versa, Son of Man for an "I" (Mt. 16:13 against Mk. 8:27).

Now it is true that in the predictions of the passion the Jewish concept Messiah-Son-of-Man is re-interpreted—or better, singularly enriched—insofar as the idea of a suffering, dying, rising Messiah or Son of Man was unknown to Judaism. But this re-interpretation of the concept was done not by Jesus himself but by the Church *ex eventu*. Of course, the attempt is made to carry the idea of the suffering Son of Man back into Jesus' own outlook by assuming that Jesus regarded himself as Deutero-Isaiah's Servant of God who suffers and dies for the sinner, and fused together the two ideas Son of Man and Servant of God into the single figure of the suffering, dying, and rising Son of Man. At the very outset, the misgivings which must be raised as to the historicity of the predictions of the passion speak against this attempt. In addition, the tradition of Jesus' sayings reveals no trace of a consciousness on his part of being the Servant of God of Is. 53.*

The messianic interpretation of Is. 53 was discovered in the Christian Church, and even in it evidently not immediately. The passion story, whose telling is colored by proof of predictions, reveals the influence especially of Ps. 21 (22) and 68 (69), but not before Lk. 22:37 is there any influence from Is. 53; and in Mt. 8:17, even Is. 53:4, so easily applied to vicarious suffering, serves as a prediction not of the suffering, but of the healing Messiah. The earliest passages in which the Suffering Servant of God of Is. 53 clearly and certainly appears in the *interpretatio christiana* are: Acts 8:32f., I Pet. 2:22–25, Heb. 9:28; such interpretation may be older than Paul and perhaps is behind Rom. 4:25, probably a saying quoted by Paul. Whether Is. 53 is thought of in "according to the scriptures," I Cor. 15:3, cannot be said. It is significant that Paul himself nowhere adduces the figure of the Servant of God. The synoptic predictions of the passion obviously do not have Is. 53 in mind; otherwise why is it nowhere referred to? Only later do such specific references as I Clem. 16:3–14 and Barn. 5:2 come along. So far as it understood Is. 53 messianically, the synagogue applied precisely the suffering and death of the Servant not to the Messiah, but to the People (or to something else); *cf.* Str.-B. II 284; P. Seidelin, ZNW 35 (1936), 194–231.

---

* Hans Walter Wolff attempts to prove the opposite in his Halle dissertation: *Jesaja 53 im Urchristentum* (1942). The attempt is scarcely successful.

4. It was soon no longer conceivable that Jesus' life was unmessianic—at least in the circles of Hellenistic Christianity in which the synoptics took form. That Jesus Christ, the Son of God, should have legitimated himself as such even in his earthly activity seemed self-evident, and so the gospel account of his ministry was cast in the light of messianic faith. The contradiction between this point of view and the traditional material finds expression in the theory of the Messiah-secret, which gives the Gospel of Mark its peculiar character: Jesus functioned as the Messiah, but his messiah-ship was to remain hidden until the resurrection (Mk. 9:9). The demons, who recognize him, are commanded to be quiet; silence is also commanded after Peter's Confession (8:30), after the Transfiguration (9:9), and after some of the miracles. The motif of the disciples' incomprehension likewise serves the secrecy-theory: Though the disciples receive secret revelation, they fail to understand it. Of course, this secrecy-theory, whose existence and importance W. Wrede pointed out, was incapable of being consistently carried through; hence the Gospel of Mark has been rightly characterized by the paradoxical term, book of "secret epiphanies" (Dibelius).

The attempt to understand the Messiah-secret not as a theory of the evangelist but as historical fact (Schniewind), falls to pieces against the fact that its literary location is in the editorial sentences of the evangelist, not in the body of the traditional units. This understanding would further assume that Jesus had on the one hand spiritualized the conception of the Messiah's activity (for this was the case if his activity on earth was to be regarded as already secretly messianic) and on the other hand that Jesus regarded himself as the Son of Man whose secret would someday come out at his return. But against this assumption arise the already named difficulties of attributing to Jesus the supposition that he was himself the future Son of Man.

CHAPTER II

The Kerygma of the Earliest Church

Since Acts offers only an incomplete and legend-tinted picture of the earliest Church, an historical picture of it, so far as one is possible at all, can be won only by the route of reconstruction. The following serve as sources: 1. The tradition utilized by the author of Acts, so far as it can be ascertained by critical analysis; 2. data occurring in the Pauline letters; 3. the synoptic tradition; its collection, first of all, and its selection, too, of course, and, in part, its shaping all took place in the earliest Church, and hence the tendencies that were operative in the earliest Church cannot but appear in that tradition.

§ 5. The Problem of Relationship between the Message of the Earliest Church and the Message of Jesus

1. As the synoptic tradition shows, the earliest Church resumed the message of Jesus and through its preaching passed it on. So far as it did only that, Jesus was to it a teacher and prophet. But Jesus was more than that to the Church: He was also the Messiah; hence that Church also proclaimed him, himself—and that is the essential thing to see. He who formerly had been the *bearer* of the message was drawn into it and became its essential *content. The proclaimer became the proclaimed*—but the central question is: In what sense?

It is clear in the first place that when Jesus was proclaimed as Messiah it was *as the coming Messiah,* in other words *as Son of Man.* Not his *return* as Messiah, but his *coming* as Messiah was expected. That is, his then past activity on earth was not yet considered messianic by the earliest Church (see § 4, 3 and 4).

But that means that *in itself the proclamation of Jesus as Mes-*

[33]

siah or Son of Man keeps quite within the frame of Jewish eschata-logical expectation. Of course, if God has raised from the dead Jesus of Nazareth, the teacher and prophet crucified by the Romans, and made him Messiah, exalted him to be the Son of Man who is to come on the clouds of heaven to hold judgment and to bring in the salvation of God's Reign, then the indefinite mythical figure, Messiah, has become concrete and visible. The myth has been transferred to a concrete historical man, and the consequence will be that trust in it will have been immeasurably strengthened. But neither the picture of the future is thereby basically remolded as yet, nor is man's relation to God understood anew. For the latter is obviously not yet founded upon one's relation to the person of Jesus, but is merely externally mediated, if he is nothing more than the Judge and Salvation-bringer whom Judaism also expected. If he were only that, he would be merely the guarantor, so to speak, that the ancient dreams would shortly be fulfilled.

2. But a limit was set to these dreams by the fact that Jesus had been, and in the Church's preaching continued to be, *the proclaimer of the radical demand of God.* For grasping what kind of Messiah he was it could not be immaterial that the Messiah was *he* who, as prophet and teacher, had also expounded the will of God with inescapable clarity. And inasmuch as the proclamation of salvation can also be called "gospel," the bearing of that gospel upon the Law is well founded in the fact that the prophet and teacher is also the Messiah—a bearing which only gradually came to clear recognition. But Jesus' messiah-ship does not *rest* upon the fact that he was prophet and teacher. For, however much his preaching in its radicality is directed against Jewish legalism, still its content is nothing else than true Old Testament-Jewish faith in God radicalized in the direction of the great prophets' preaching. And though it surpasses the latter in its individualization of man's relation to God, because it places not the People but first of all the individual into the immediate presence of God, and because it views not the People's future but God's Reign as eschatological salvation, still even in that it is only the consummation of tendencies that underlie the preaching of the great prophets. The concepts of God, world, and man, of Law and grace, of repentance and forgiveness in the teaching of Jesus are not new in comparison with those of the Old Testament and Judaism, however radically they may be understood. And his criti-

cal interpretation of the Law, in spite of its radicality, likewise stands within the scribal discussion about it, just as his eschatological preaching does within Jewish apocalyptic. This is also the only way of understanding why the teaching of the historical Jesus plays no role, or practically none, in Paul and John, while, on the other hand, modern liberal Judaism can very well esteem Jesus as teacher.[*]

3. Neither does the messianic significance of Jesus rest in the eyes of the earliest Church upon regarding him as a great "personality" standing as impressive power behind his teaching. It was not as the one who was the living embodiment of the religion, the obedience, which he demanded nor as the one who filled those open to his influence with fascination and enthusiasm, kindling them to "imitation" of himself that he was esteemed. And so the earliest Church was also far from understanding his way to the cross as the deed of one who heroically sacrifices himself for his cause. Not the power of his "personality," however great it may factually have been, was what the Church beheld—nor was it *the mystery of his nature* as if the "numinous" had there taken form. True though it may be that as miracle-worker or exorcist he made an awesome, "numinous" impression—although the sentences that say or hint the like belong to the editorial work of the evangelists and are not old tradition—that plays no role in the kerygma of the Church. The Church proclaimed him as prophet and teacher and beyond that as the coming Son of Man, but not as the "divine man" θεῖος ἀνήρ of the Hellenistic world, who was a numinous figure. Not before the growth of legend on Hellenistic soil was the figure of Jesus assimilated to that of the "divine man." The Old Testament-Jewish world knew neither "heroes" in the Greek sense nor *homines religiosi* in the Hellenistic sense. And so it comes about that the personality of Jesus has no importance for the kerygma either of Paul or of John or for the New Testament in general. Indeed the tradition of the earliest Church did not even unconsciously preserve a picture of his personality. Every attempt to reconstruct one remains a play of subjective imagination.

4. It can be taken for granted that the earliest Church did not ponder over *the uniqueness of the place in history and the historical influence* of him whose "advent" as Son of Man would presently end all world history. Nor did their faith in him as Messiah rest upon

[*] *Cf.* Gösta Lindeskog, *Die Jesusfrage im neuzeitlichen Judentum,* 1938.

understanding the historical phenomenon of Jesus in the way the Old Testament and Judaism spoke of historical persons and events, calling them "mercies of God." His ministry was not understood as a decisive event for Israel's history like the call of Moses, the exodus from Egypt, the giving of the Law on Sinai, or God's raising up of kings and prophets.

It might appear that beginnings in this direction are present where, in keeping with the Jewish Messiah-theology, the Messiah Jesus and the "first redeemer" Moses are placed in parallel (Jn. 6:31f., 49f.; Acts 3:22), or where the situation of the Christian Church is compared with that of Israel in the desert (I Cor. 10:1-11; Heb. 3:7—4:11); also, for that matter, wherever the Messiah-Son-of-Man is regarded as the Son of David. But except for the last idea, these are theological reflections which scarcely go back to the earliest Church and are, at any rate, only later attested. But note, above all, that what is involved here is not a paralleling of historical persons and events, but an interpretation of Old Testament history as a foreshadowing of what would happen in the eschatological period.

These events and persons are important for their influence upon the history of the People; and they become meaningful—as acts of revelation or as mercies of God—to the individual through his membership in the People. Each thing that God did to the fathers, the People as a whole, He did to each individual, as it is expressly said in the Jewish Passover liturgy. But neither in the earliest Church nor anywhere in the New Testament is Jesus looked back upon as a deed of God by which—as by Abraham, Moses or David—He showed "mercy" upon the People. Of course not! For Jesus' importance as Messiah-Son-of-Man lies not at all in what he did in the past, but entirely in what is expected of him for the future. And once this expectation is fulfilled by the eschatological drama, that event will never become, like the crossing of the Red Sea, a past to which one could look back thankfully, drawing confidence from it, but it will be God's last deed of all, by which he puts history to an end.

5. Now it is clear that Jesus—that is to say, his coming, his cross, and his resurrection or exaltation—has for Paul, and still more radically for John, *the meaning of eschatological occurrence.* But how is it for the earliest Church, to which the meaning of messiah-ship is of course also eschatological, but to which the messiah-ship itself

is a thing still to come? If Jesus' significance to the earliest Church were exhausted in its expecting him as the coming Son of Man, it would still be only a Jewish sect and would not properly be called Christian Church. Nor would the additional fact that it proclaimed the Crucified as the Risen One, change matters. For so long, at least, as the resurrection means no more than proof of the exaltation of the Crucified to Son of Man, it is not yet understood as an event that breaks the frame of Jewish eschatology. And that the earliest Church was in danger of remaining a Jewish sect is shown by Paul's battle against its understanding of the situation created by Jesus' coming, dying, and rising. Nevertheless, however little the earliest Church explicitly developed an understanding of Jesus' person and fate as *the* eschatological occurrence in Paul's sense, it did implicitly understand him in this sense through the fact that it conceived of itself as the eschatological Congregation.

§ 6. The Earliest Church as the Eschatological Congregation

1. *That the earliest Church regarded itself as the Congregation of the end of days,* is attested both by Paul and the synoptic tradition. In the saying Mt. 16:18f. placed upon the lips of Jesus by the Church, Jesus' band of disciples is called the "Church" (Congregation) whose leader possesses the keys of the Kingdom of Heaven. This Congregation, therefore, is the vestibule, so to say, of God's Reign that is shortly to appear. Nor can it be overwhelmed by the powers of the underworld whose attack upon the Congregation of God is one of the predicted "woes" of the end of days. It is the "little flock" to whom God will give His Reign (Lk. 12:32). It is represented by "the Twelve," who, when God's Reign has appeared, will sit upon twelve thrones to rule the tribes of Israel (Mt. 19:28 or Lk. 22:29f.). The less likely it is that the twelve were called by Jesus himself, the more characteristic they are for the eschatological consciousness of the Church; for they are "the Twelve" not as apostles but as the eschatological regents.

2. Further testimony for eschatological consciousness is the fact that Jesus' disciples after the Easter experiences in Galilee soon betook themselves to *Jerusalem* as the focus of the coming Reign of God. Here the Congregation awaited the fulfilment of the promises. Further evidence is furnished especially by the designations of the

Church and its members that are attested by Paul. In understanding themselves as Congregation or Church the disciples appropriate to themselves the title of the Old Testament Congregation of God, the קְהַל־יְהֹוָה On the one hand, this title designates Israel as the People of God, and on the other hand, it had already become an eschatological term; for Judaism expected of the end of days that it would bring the gathering together of now scattered Israel and the revealing of the now hidden Congregation. By designating itself Congregation—more exactly, Congregation of God—the earliest Church declared that it itself was the fulfilment of the hopes of the apocalyptists. Its members accordingly bear the eschatological titles "the chosen" or "the elect" and "the saints."

On the discussion about what Aramaic word lies behind the word "Church" ἐκκλησία of the Greek New Testament, *cf.* the literature given at § 1, 3; in addition especially Leonh. Rost, *Die Vorstufen von Kirche und Synagoge im AT* (1938). K. L. Schmidt, especially, has concerned himself with the lexicographic problem [*Festgabe für Ad. Deissmann* (1927), 258–319]; he would like to establish not קְהָלָא (Heb. קָהָל,), "Congregation, Gathering," but כְּנִשְׁתָּא (Heb. כְּנֶסֶת) "Gathering, Synagogue," as the Aramaic word—hardly rightly. In content "Church (of God)" ἐκκλησία (τοῦ Θεοῦ) corresponds at any rate with (יהוה) קהל ל. For קהל, ἐκκλησία usually is found in the LXX (but significantly not where it would mean a heathen קהל!), and especially in Deut. (which was important because of the parallelism of the Christian Congregation with the Sinai-congregation) and in the Psalms which were so important for the self-consciousness of the Christian Congregation. In the LXX עֵדָה, "assembly of people" is never rendered ἐκκλησία; instead עדה in the great majority of cases, though not exclusively, is rendered συναγωγή, "Gathering, Synagogue," which occasionally also is the translation of קהל. In Ecclesiasticus, too, ἐκκλησία seems to stand only for קהל, never for עדה.

In the Psalms of Solomon, ἐκκλησία as a term for Israel (as the People of God) and συναγωγή as a term for individual congregations (hence in the plural, while ἐκκλησία occurs only in the singular) are clearly distinguished. Philo uses only ἐκκλησία for the Sinai-assembly and for the קהל־יהוה Deut. 23:1ff., and uses συναγωγή only for the synagogue-building. On the titles "saints" ἅγιοι and "elect" ἐκλεκτοί, see especially Kümmel, *Kirchenbegriff*, etc. (§ 1, 3), 16ff. It is not impossible that the members of the earliest Church called themselves "the poor," a term which even in the Psalms is already synonymous with "pious, religious." In the Psalms of Solomon the pious who constitute the true Israel are also called "the poor." According to Origen c. Cels. 2:1 (I 126, 19) and Epiphanius 30, 17, 2 (I 356, 2), the Jewish Christians were likewise called אֶבְיוֹנִים (the poor). This title would also characterize the earliest Church as "Israel of God," and to that extent would also be eschatological. But it is uncertain whether this title was already in use in the earliest Church; anyway that cannot (as K. Holl, H. Lietzmann, E. Lohmeyer and others think it can) be deduced from Gal. 2:10: "only they would have us remember the poor"; for Rom. 15:26 speaks of "the poor among the saints" πτωχοὶ τῶν ἁγίων indicating that the "poor" πτωχοί are only a part of the Congregation and hence that πτωχός here is used in the sociological sense and not as a religious term.

3. Without doubt, *baptism* is to be understood in this sense. It can be regarded as certain that from the very beginning it was practiced in the earliest Church as the rite of initiation, for Paul assumes that all Christians are baptized (Rom. 6:3, I Cor. 12:13). But the meaning of baptism can hardly have been different from that of John's baptism, which Jesus and his first "disciples" had themselves received. That is, baptism in conjunction with repentance was a bath of purification (closely connected with repentance) for the coming Reign of God—in other words, an initiation rite of the eschatological Congregation similar to the Jewish proselyte baptism, which was a purifying bath that (in conjunction with circumcision) made the baptized a member of the Congregation of Israel. A difference between these baptisms is admittedly present in the fact that Christian baptism made the baptized a member of the eschatological Congregation; but probably the greatest difference is that proselyte baptism was considered to free a man from ritual defilement, whereas Christian baptism, like that of John—corresponding to the fact that both presuppose confession of sin and repentance— evidently promised purity from sin. For the phrase "for the forgiveness of sins," a characteristic of John's baptism according to Mk. 1:4, was likely true of Christian baptism from the very beginning

(*cf*. Acts 2:38). Inasmuch as such purification was regarded as brought about by an immersion, baptism in the earliest Church (like John's baptism) already had sacramental character and hence completely deserves to be described as an eschatological sacrament which made one a member of the holy Congregation of the end of days. How early the additional view arose that baptism brings the baptized into sacramental relation with the person of Jesus as Son of Man, making him the property of the latter and putting him under the protection of his "Name," can no longer be made out. When Paul presupposes that baptism was done "into (or in) the name of Christ" εἰς τὸ ὄνομα τοῦ Χριστοῦ (I Cor. 1:13), that probably goes back to the usage of the Hellenistic-Christian congregations. But perhaps very early exorcistic effect (by means of naming "the name of Jesus Christ" ὄνομα Ἰησοῦ Χριστοῦ?) was already attributed to baptism. Since when the positive effect of endowment with the "Spirit" was also attributed to it, is uncertain. It probably arose as a Hellenistic-Christian conception.

The analogy which exists between early Christian baptism and the Jewish baptism of proselytes does not signify that the former originated out of the latter; for if that were the case, one would expect it to have been performed on Gentiles only. Certain testimony to the practice of proselyte baptism is not found before the end of the first century A.D. It may have been older, but that cannot be proved. At any rate, Christian baptism did not originate in it, but in the baptism of John. The best orientation concerning these questions is given by Jos. Thomas, *Le mouvement baptiste en Palestine et Syrie* (1935), 356–391.

4. Likewise, *the common meals* (the "breaking of bread") receive their character from the eschatological consciousness of the Congregation. According to the obviously retouched tradition in Acts 2:42–47 there prevailed at these meals ἀγαλλίασις, "gladness," which probably means the mood of eschatological joy.* And it is permissible to form an idea of these celebrations from the table-prayers of which Did. 9 and 10 offer a tradition even though we have no way of knowing whether or to what extent these prayers go back to the earliest Church.† Since these are Jewish table-prayers with Christian editing and they therefore derive from Jewish-Chris-

* See *Th. WB* I 19f.
† See M. Dibelius, *ZNW* 37 (1938) 32–41.

tian tradition, they may be taken as characteristic of the prayers προσευχαί mentioned at Acts 2:42. They show that an eschatological mood filled the Congregation at these meals. Besides thanks for the gifts given in Jesus (in the formulation of these, specifically Hellenistic phraseology occurs), their chief content is the petition for eschatological fulfilment: "Remember, Lord, thy Church, to deliver it from all evil and to make it perfect in thy love, and gather it together in its holiness from the four winds to thy kingdom which thou hast prepared for it! . . . Let [the Lord *] come, and let this world pass away!" (Did. 10:5f., Lake's tr.).

5. As Jesus scented the irruption of the end of days in the flight of the demons before the spirit that worked in him (Mk. 3:28f.; Mt. 12:28f.; *cf.* Lk. 11:20), and as for Paul, the Spirit πνεῦμα at work in the Church was the firstfruit ἀπαρχή (Rom. 8:23) or the guarantee ἀρραβών (II Cor. 1:22; 5:5) of the imminent fulfilment, so the earliest Church knew that it had been given *the Spirit,* that gift of the end of days which, according to the Jewish view, had departed from Israel with the last of the prophets, but whose impartation was promised for the end of days. Driven by this Spirit, prophets arise once more, as Acts 11:28; 21:9, 10ff. testify; and Paul as well as the Didache takes the presence of prophets in the Church for granted. In the power of this Spirit miracles occur (Mt. 10:8; Mk. 6:13; Acts 11:28; 21:10f.), as Paul also takes for granted (I Cor. 12:9, 28f.). In times of persecution the Spirit gives the right word in court (Mt. 10:19f. or Mk. 13:11). Whether the manifestations of the Spirit in ecstasy and speaking in tongues (I Cor. 14), which later played so great a role in Hellenistic congregations, had already appeared in the earliest Church, is uncertain. An account of one such event appears to underlie the legendary pentecost story (Acts 2:1–13), as the last verse betrays.†

6. There is no doubt that in the earliest Church *the proving of Old Testament predictions* was practiced, sometimes for edification, sometimes for missionary purposes, but especially for apologetic reasons. However, the Old Testament prophecies were regarded as

* This, following the Coptic text, is probably the correct reading and not ἡ χάρις, "grace."

† It is not hard to conjecture that the last sentence, 4:31, of the account worked into the fourth chapter of Acts by its author originally ran in the source: καὶ ἐπλήσθησαν ἅπαντες τοῦ ἁγίου πνεύματος καὶ ἐλάλουν γλώσσαις—"and they were all filled with the Holy Spirit and spoke with tongues"; *cf.* 10:45f.

predictions of the time of the End; hence, the Church's certainty that they had been and were still being fulfilled presupposes once more its eschatological consciousness. In I Cor. 10:11 the principle that proof of prophecy is to be sought in "us," the Church, is clearly formulated (*cf.* "for our sake" δι' ἡμᾶς, I Cor. 9:10 and Rom. 15:4). Which statements out of the ever-increasing body of predictions regarded as fulfilled go clear back to the earliest Church, naturally can no longer be ascertained. The tradition παράδοσις cited at I Cor. 15:3ff. with its "according to the scriptures" κατὰ τὰς γραφάς—a phrase not otherwise occurring in Paul—establishes the Christian use of such proofs before Paul's time; and the synoptic tradition shows us that Christians early began to understand Jesus' person and his work, especially the passion, in the light of realized prediction.

7. Belief in the immediately impending End also governs *the missionary activity* of the earliest Church; that is reflected by the "charge to the apostles" placed into the mouth of Jesus. They must hasten through the land to call Israel to repentance (Mt. 10, especially verses 7 and 9ff.); they will not have finished with all the towns of Israel before the Son of Man comes (Mt. 10:23).

8. Q, finally, the collection of Jesus' sayings that goes back to the earliest Church, testifies to the same belief. It is prefaced by the eschatological preaching of John the Baptist; the beatitudes, full of eschatological consciousness, follow; the close is constituted by sayings dealing with the parousia.

§ 7. Jesus' Meaning to the Faith of the Earliest Church

1. Thus, when regarded from the history-of-religions point of view, the earliest Church presents itself as an eschatological sect within Judaism, distinguished from other sects and trends not only by the fact that it awaits the crucified Jesus of Nazareth as the Son of Man, but especially by the fact that it is conscious of being already the called and chosen Congregation of the end of days. When the Church proclaims Jesus as Messiah-Son-of-Man, that does not mean that it has thereby added an item to Old Testament tradition and Jesus' message. Rather, the kerygma of Jesus as Messiah is the basic and primary thing which gives everything else—the ancient tradition and Jesus' message—its special character. All that

[42]

went before appears in a new light—new since the *Easter faith in Jesus' resurrection* and founded upon this faith. But if Jesus' person and work appear to them in the light of Easter faith, that means that his significance lay neither in the content of what he had taught nor in some modification of the Messiah idea. It does mean, though, that *Jesus' having come was itself the decisive event* through which God called His Congregation (Church). It means that Jesus' coming itself was already eschatological occurrence. Indeed, that is the real content of the Easter faith: God has made the prophet and teacher Jesus of Nazareth Messiah!

2. *To what extent the earliest Church itself already explicitly recognized* that the fact that Jesus had come was the decisive eschatological occurrence is another question. Statements like those of Paul that when the fulness of time was come, God sent his son (Gal. 4:4) or that by virtue of Jesus' death the "old" had passed away and (all) had become new (II Cor. 5:17) are still foreign to the earliest Church along with their consequences—that now the epoch of the Law is past and the Law is abolished. And that the earliest Church was distinctly conscious that the new age had dawned (Kümmel's opinion), is probably an exaggeration. As the synoptic tradition shows, the expectation of the imminent dramatic End, the parousia of Jesus as Son of Man, controlled the consciousness of the Church, and Jesus' advent and ministry was not yet clearly recognized as eschatological occurrence. Only implicitly in the Church's eschatological understanding of itself was this recognition present, and only beginnings toward its development are manifest—beginnings that lay under certain restraints.

That this recognition was implicitly present is shown in the first place by the fact that for the Church, as for Jesus himself, the content of his message was not the decisive thing. In his lifetime he had demanded decision for his person as the bearer of the Word; the Church has now made this decision. Jesus' call to decision implies a christology. That call does not justify speculation about him as a heavenly being. Nor does it support the Messiah-consciousness attributed to him. But it does imply a christology which will unfold the implications of the positive answer to his demand for the decision, the obedient response which acknowledges God's revelation in Jesus. Such christology became explicit in the earliest Church to the extent that they understood Jesus as the one whom God by the resurrection has made Messiah, and that they awaited him as the coming Son of Man. For it is apparent that in that very fact they understood his sending as God's decisive act. In expecting him as the Coming One they understood themselves as the Congregation of the end of days called by him. For them factually—no matter to what degree it may have been clearly conscious—the old had passed away and the world had become new.

In the synoptic tradition a series of sayings shows that Jesus' work was conceived as decisive happening, especially such as speak of him as *having come* or *having been sent*. They are scarcely (at least in the majority of cases) original words of Jesus, but mostly products of the Church. And so far as they had already arisen in the earliest (i.e. the Palestinian) Church (which cannot in every case be clearly made out), they testify that this Church in retrospect conceived the phenomenon of Jesus together with its meaning as a unity: It was a divine "sending" by which the Church was called, its destiny determined, its problems decided. He "came" not to call the righteous, but sinners (Mk. 2:17). He "was sent" to the lost sheep of the house of Israel (Mt. 15:24). He "came" to cast fire on the earth (Lk. 12:49). His "coming" means not peace, but a sword (Mt. 10:34–36 par.), i.e. it means the eschatological hour of decision and division. Whoever receives him, receives Him who "sent" him (Mk. 9:37 or Mt. 10:40); whoever rejects him, rejects Him who "sent" him (Lk. 10:16). Other related sayings will be discussed in another context.* That his sending meant doom for. Jerusalem is expressed by the saying Lk. 13:34f. par., probably in origin a Jewish prophecy concerning "Wisdom," perhaps once quoted by Jesus, but as we now have it, re-interpreted by the Church and put back into his mouth: It was he who had desired in vain to gather Jerusalem's "children" together, so that it now was forsaken.†

3. The decision which Jesus' disciples had once made to affirm and accept his sending by "following" him, had to be made anew and radically in consequence of his crucifixion. *The cross,* so to say, raised the question of decision once more. Little as it could throw into question the content of his message, all the more it could and did render questionable his legitimation, his claim to be God's mes-

---

* *Cf.* on the "I-sayings," *Gesch. d. synopt. Trad.,* 2nd edition, 161–176.
† *Cf. Gesch. d. synopt. Trad.,* 2nd edition, 120f.

senger bringing the last, decisive word. The Church had to surmount the scandal of the cross and did it in the Easter faith.

How this act of decision took place in detail, how the Easter faith arose in individual disciples, has been obscured in the tradition by legend and is not of basic importance. Mk. 14:28 and 16:7 indicate that after Jesus' arrest the disciples fled to Galilee and that there Peter was the first to behold the Risen One, as I Cor. 15:5 corroborates. A trace of this fact is also preserved in Lk. 24:34, and Lk. 22:31f. probably goes back to the same event (see *Gesch. d. synopt. Trad.*, 2nd edition, 387f.). This basic event is reflected in the narratives of Peter's confession [Mk. 8:27–29], the transfiguration [Mk. 9:2–8 (§ 4, 1)], and Peter's miraculous catch of fish [Lk. 5:1–11], as well as in the words about Peter, the Rock [Mt. 16:17–19 (§ 1, 3)]. The accounts of the empty grave, of which Paul still knows nothing, are legends. According to I Cor. 15:5–8, where Paul enumerates the appearances of the risen Lord as tradition offered them, the resurrection of Jesus meant simultaneously his exaltation; not until later was the resurrection interpreted as a temporary return to life on earth, and this idea then gave rise to the ascension story (Lk. 24:50–53, Acts 1:3–11). The appearances of the risen Lord probably were not confined to Galilee but also occurred at Jerusalem after the disciples had return there (Luke reports only such). How the appearances enumerated in I Cor. 15:5–8 are to be distributed between Galilee and Jerusalem cannot be known, and it is a mere supposition that the appearance to the five hundred brethren (I Cor. 15:6) is identical with the event of Pentecost. Concerning these matters see in recent literature: Lyder Brun, *Die Auferstehung Christi in der urchristl. Überlieferung* (1925); Selby Vernon McCasland, *The Resurrection of Jesus* (1932); Maurice Goguel, *La foi à la Résurrection de Jésus dans le Christianisme primitif* (1933); Kirsopp Lake in *The Beginnings of Christianity* V (1933), 7–16; Em. Hirsch, *Die Auferstehungsgeschichten und der christliche Glaube* (1940); W. Grundmann, ZNW 39 (1940), 110–121; Paul Althaus, *Die Wahrheit des kirchlichen Osterglaubens* 2 (1941).

The rise of the Easter faith made necessary *a way of understanding the cross* that would surmount, yes, transform, the scandal of the curse which in Jewish opinion had befallen the crucified Jesus (*cf.* Gal. 3:13); the cross had to make sense in the context of the salvation-process. How far such an understanding was worked out in the earliest Church cannot clearly be seen. Scripture proof explaining Jesus' suffering and death as divinely decreed in the manner of Lk. 24:26f. can be taken as characteristic of one stage of the earliest Church's reflection on the subject: " 'Was it not necessary that the Christ should suffer these things and enter into his glory?' And beginning with Moses and all the prophets, he interpreted to them in all the scriptures the things concerning himself." If that was their understanding, one would have to admit that as yet the stumbling-block of the cross had only been negatively removed so so long as it was only placed under the divine "must" (δεῖ), and that its positive meaning had not yet become clear. Yet even so in this surmounting of the σκάνδαλον (stumbling-block, scandal) it would have come to light that in the cross of Christ Jewish standards of judgment and human notions of the splendor of the Messiah are shattered. Thus, the acknowledgment of the Crucified as Messiah implicitly contains a new understanding of man-before-God.

But probably something more may be said. In the tradition that had come down to Paul, do not both "according to the scriptures" κατὰ τὰς γραφάς and "for our sins" ὑπὲρ τῶν ἁμαρτιῶν ἡμῶν go back to the earliest Church? Then Jesus' death would already have been conceived as an expiatory sacrifice in the earliest Church! In favor of this view speak two other passages from Paul; in them he is visibly leaning on traditional formulations, perhaps even quoting them —at least in part. One of these sentences is Rom. 3:24f., in which one only needs to set off the specifically Pauline expressions with parentheses as his additions: ". . . justified (by his grace as a gift) through the redemption which is in Christ Jesus, whom God put forward as an expiation by his blood (to be received by faith); this was to show God's righteousness, because in his divine forbearance he had passed over former sins" (Blt.). The designation of Christ as the ἱλαστήριον (expiation, mercy-seat) occurs only here in Paul; nor is it Paul's habit elsewhere (except Rom. 5:9 and, again following tradition, in reference to the Lord's Supper, I Cor. 10:16; 11:25, 27) to speak of "the blood" of Christ, but of "the cross." Finally the idea found here of the divine righteousness demanding expiation for former sins is otherwise foreign to him. Hence, what we are here dealing with is evidently a traditional statement, which perhaps can be traced back to the earliest Church. It is the same with Rom. 4:25—a sentence which in form (synthetic parallelism of members) makes the impression of a quotation. Perhaps this statement was formulated in reminiscence of Is. 53; if so, that would make it probable that in Is. 53, too, a prophecy of Jesus' passion had already been found by the earliest Church, though this discovery did not take place in its very earliest period (see § 4, 3).

The interpretation of Jesus' death as an expiatory sacrifice for sins was, in itself, not unnatural to Jewish thinking. For in it the idea of the expiating power of the suffering of the righteous, especially of the martyr, had been developed. *Cf.* Str.-B. II 275–282; W. Bousset, *Die Religion des Judent.*, 3rd edition, 198f.; G. F. Moore, *Judaism* I 547–549; E. Sjöberg, *Gott und die Sünder im paläst. Judentum* (1939), 174f., 222. However, to the Judaism of Jesus' time the idea of a messiah suffering for sinners is entirely foreign; *cf.* G. Dalman, *Der leidende und der sterbende Messias der Synagoge* (1888); W. Staerk, *Soter* I (1933), 78–84; Str.-B. I 273–299; G. F. Moore, l.c. 551f. A different opinion in Joach. Jeremias, *Jesus als Weltvollender* (1930).

4. Through the fact that the Church awaits the prophet and teacher as Son of Man and in the light of Easter faith understands Jesus' earthly ministry anew, *a power to determine the present is also attributed to the figure of Jesus.* The future ruler and bringer of salvation already exercises his royal sway in a certain manner now from heaven, into which he has been exalted. When his words are collected that is done not simply because of their didactic content, but because they are his, the coming king's, words. According to rabbinic ideas the Messiah, when he comes, will also act as a teacher of Torah*—the Church already possesses Jesus' exegesis of the Law and in his "But I say unto you!" hears him speak as Messiah. In his words they already have the wisdom and knowledge which according to the belief of the apocalyptic writers the Messiah will someday bestow.† Out of such conviction new "words of the Lord" arise whose purpose is to decide moot questions; such are: "Think not that I have come to abolish the Law and the prophets! I have come not to abolish them but to fulfill them . . ." (Mt. 5:17,

---

* *Cf.* P. Seidelin, ZNW 35 (1936), 194ff.; P. Volz, *Die Eschatologie der jüd. Gemeinde* (1934), 218.

† *Cf.* P. Volz, *l.c.*

cf. 18–19). "I was sent only to the lost sheep of the house of Israel" (Mt. 15:24). There also arise sayings that testify that whatever fate one now experiences is understood as sent from him and whatever one conceives to be his task as commanded by him: "Do not believe that I have come to bring peace to the earth—but rather the sword! . . ." (Mt. 10:34 par. Blt., *cf.* 35–36 par.; see above, 2). "Fear not little flock, for the Father has decided to give you the Reign" (Lk. 12:32 Blt.). It is he who sends the messengers who are to carry the cry of the approach of God's Reign through the land (Mk. 6:7ff. or Mt. 9:37ff. par.). In his name the prophets speak: "Lo, I send you out as sheep into the midst of wolves" (Mt. 10:16 par. Blt.). "Behold, I have given you authority to tread upon serpents and scorpions; . . . and nothing shall hurt you" (Lk. 10:19);—just as we also find in Revelation examples of Christian prophets speaking in the name of the exalted Christ (*cf.* Rev. 3:20; 16:15). The invitation "come unto me," promising rest to those "that labor and are heavy laden" (Mt. 11:28f.) probably comes from some old "Wisdom" book; perhaps the earliest Church already put this saying into the mouth of Jesus. Certainly out of the earliest Church come the words in which the risen Lord, with royal bearing, delegates to Peter the direction of the Congregation—which he even calls "my Congregation" (Mt. 16:17–19); likewise his promise to the twelve that they shall someday be the regents of the tribes of Israel (Mt. 19:28 or Lk. 22:28–30). It is easily understandable that rules of Church discipline, which become necessary in the course of time, are regarded as his orders (Mt. 18:15–18). Indeed the earliest Church seems to have transformed a saying already current among the Jews which spoke of the presence of God with two men occupied with interpreting the Torah, into the saying: "Where two or three are gathered in my name, there am I in the midst of them" (Mt. 18:20). And it is not impossible that the name of Jesus in reminiscence of his own banning of demons was used as an effective means for exorcisms and other miraculous deeds. If Mk. 9:38–40 (though it probably was lacking in Mark as it originally was) should have come out of the tradition of the earliest Church, it would be a witness to such practice; likewise Acts 3:6.

5. The *titles* the Church conferred upon Jesus to indicate his significance and dignity were borrowed from the tradition of Jewish messianic faith; in which motifs of diverse origin were admittedly

united. All these titles, though their original meanings may have been various, agree in being designations for the eschatological salvation-bringer. Naturally Jesus was given the ancient title *"Messiah,"* i.e. anointed king, as the synoptic tradition testifies and Paul, too, clearly implies. This is the only reason that the double name Jesus Christ could then arise, as it did, in Hellenistic Christianity.

However, the predominant title in the earliest Church, by the testimony of the synoptic tradition, was "Son of Man," which comes out of the apocalyptic hope and means a supra-mundane, pre-existent being who at the end of time will come down from heaven to hold judgment and bring salvation (§ 1, 1); whereas the Messiah-title, coming out of the national hope, designates the king (of David's line), who is thought of as a mere man, no matter how much his arrival and his deeds may be guided and determined by God's supranatural intervention.

The title *Son of David* also comes out of the national tradition and is synonymous with Messiah. This title seems not to have played any great role in the earliest Church, since its occurrence is relatively rare in the synoptic tradition (not found in Q at all). On the other hand, Paul must have found it in current use before him. For though the title is of no importance to him, he refers to it in Rom. 1:3, a sentence which is evidently due to a handed-down formula; he desires thereby to accredit himself to the unknown Roman Church as an apostle who advocates right doctrine. Released from its Pauline syntax and freed of Pauline additions, the formula may be regarded as having run as follows:

"(Jesus Christ) the Son of God,
    Come from the seed of David,
    Designated Son of God in power by his resurrection from the
    dead." (Blt.) °

Whether or not the mutually divergent lineages (Mt. 1:1–17 and Lk. 3:23–38), which were intended to demonstrate the Davidic descent of Jesus, go back to the earliest Church, or to what extent they may do so, cannot be said. If Mk. 12:35–37 originated in the earliest Church, then criticism against transferring this title to Jesus had

° II Tim. 2:8 is also to be regarded as going back to an old formula; *cf.* H. Windisch, *ZNW* 34 (1935), 213–216.

possibly arisen in it (§ 4, 2). At any rate the title promptly established itself.

The messianic king is also meant by the title *Son of God,* which Rom. 1:3 likewise attests as already traditional before Paul. Whether Son of God was already current as a messianic title in Judaism, is uncertain and debated; it has not been proved to have been so used. Still it must be regarded as perfectly possible, since Ps. 2, in which by the use of the ancient oriental formula of adoption, the king is called Son of God, was already interpreted messianically in Judaism as it was in the Christian Church. But it is clear that neither in Judaism nor in the Christian Church could this title have the mythological meaning it later had in Hellenistic Christianity; that is, it did not designate the Messiah as a supernatural being begotten by God, but was simply a royal title. Though the synoptic passages in which Jesus is called Son of God are mostly either secondary and of Hellenistic-Christian origin, or else were formulated by the respective evangelist, still the transfiguration with "this is my beloved son" (Mk. 9:7) goes back to early tradition. If it was originally an Easter story (§ 4, 1), then it may be regarded along with Rom. 1, 3 as proving that the earliest Church called Jesus Son of God (messianic) because that was what the resurrection made him. However, unlike the later Hellenistic Church it did not regard the earthly Jesus as a Son of God (mythological); and the legend of Jesus' birth from the virgin is unknown to it as also to Paul.

In the apocalypses, IV Ezra and II Baruch, occurs the messianic title *"Servant of God"* which means nothing else than Messiah or Son of God. It comes from the Old Testament, in which favored men of piety, found worthy of a special mission by God, such as Abraham, Moses, and the prophets, are so called, and also kings, and the title clings especially to David of whom it became traditional; in this last sense it also occurs at Lk. 1:69, Acts 4:25, Did. 9:2 (in the last case used both of David and of Jesus). Hence, it is easily understandable that the Messiah as Son of David also was given this title. In the more detailed description of the messianic Servant of God Deutero-Isaiah may occasionally have played a part —though not the Servant of God of Is. 53 suffering vicariously for sinners, for this servant was interpreted by Jewish exegesis as the people of Israel; and the apocalyptic writers' Servant of God is not a suffering figure, but the messianic ruler and judge. Still influence from Is. 42:1ff. or 49:1ff. is possible; for the dignity of being the "Light of the Gentiles" conferred upon the Servant of God in Is. 42:6; 49:6 is transferred to the Son of Man in I Enoch 48:4; i.e. it has become a messianic attribute. Early Christianity took over the title "Servant." Whether the earliest Church had already done so, we, of course, do not know, since it does not occur in the synoptic tradition; only Matthew introduced it (12:18ff.) in one of his reflective quotations (Is. 42:1ff.). It occurs later at Acts 3:13, 26; 4:27, 30, in the last two cases in a prayer of the Church, then in the table-prayers (Did. 9:2f.; 10:2f.) and in the prayer of the Roman congregation (I Clem. 59:2ff.); so it appears to have been early, at any rate, that it was taken into the liturgical vocabulary of the Church.*

The Pauline letters indicate that in the Hellenistic Church Jesus was called *"Lord"* Κύριος and was cultically worshiped. Since W. Bousset's book, *Kyrios Christos* (1913, 2nd edition, 1921), there has been debate whether this implies that the earliest Church had already entitled Jesus "Lord" and invoked him as such in prayer. Bousset, who vigorously denied it, is probably right. In any case, the earliest Church did not cultically worship Jesus, even if it should have called him Lord; the Kyrios-cult originated on Hellenistic soil.

Judaism, at any rate, never entitled the Messiah "Lord." At the very outset the un-modified expression "the Lord" is un-thinkable in Jewish usage. "Lord" used of God is always given some modifier; we read: "the Lord of heaven and earth,"* "our Lord" and similar expressions. Used of Jesus, therefore, at least *"our* Lord" or something similar would be required. The oldest stratum of the synoptic tradition does not speak of Jesus as Lord; in Q the title never appears, in Mark only in the legendary story 11:3, while Luke, and he alone, frequently uses an absolute ὁ Κύριος (the Lord) in narrative. The vocative "Lord" Κύριε, which also occurs in the old tradition, proves nothing, for it is only a translation of the Aramaic title of address used by a pupil ("disciple") to his teacher ("master"): "my (or our) lord"; and Lord Κύριε and Rabbi ῥαββί (= my great one) alternate in Mark and Matthew as titles of address to Jesus. The eschatological prayer "Maranatha!" μαρᾶν ἀθᾶ (מָרָנָא תָא   = "Our

---

* *Cf.* besides Bousset, *Kyrios Chr.*, 2nd edition, 56f., and W. Staerk, *Soter* I 24ff., 77ff.: Ad. v. Harnack, *Die Bezeichnung Jesu als "Knecht Gottes" und ihre Geschichte in der alten Kirche* [Sitzungsber. d. Preuss. Akad. d. Wiss., Phil.-hist. Kl. (1926), 28]; P. Seidelin, ZNW 35 (1936), 230f.

Lord, come!") found at I Cor. 16:22 certainly comes out of the earliest Church, but it likewise is no proof that the earliest Church invoked Jesus as Lord; for it can originally have meant God, even if it was later taken to refer to Jesus (cf. Rev. 22:20). And though the phrase "those who call on the name of our Lord Jesus Christ" (I Cor. 1:2; cf. Acts 9:14, 21; 22:16; II Tim. 2:22) became a current designation for Christians in the Hellenistic Church, that proves nothing for the earliest Church. On this point, besides Bousset's *Kyrios Christos*, cf.: P. Wernle, *Jesus und Paulus* NKZ (1915), 439–457, 513–545; W. Heitmüller, *Jesus und Paulus* ZThK 25 (1915), 156–179; W. Bousset, *Jesus der Herr* (1916); Werner Foerster, *Herr ist Jesus* (1924); E. Lohmeyer, *Kyrios Christos* (1928) (in which foreign literature is also tabulated); Wolf W. Graf Baudissin, *Kyrios als Gottesbezeichnung im Judentum und seine Stellung in der Religionsgeschichte* I–IV (1929); E. V. Dobschütz, Κύριος 'Ιησοῦς ZNW 30 (1931), 97–123.

In his book *Galiläa und Jerusalem* (1936), E. Lohmeyer developed the thesis, since carried out in other investigations and especially in his commentary on Mark, that there were really two "earliest Churches" on Palestinian soil, or at least two characteristically differing parties: the Galilean and that of Jerusalem. For the Galilean Church, or party, according to him, Jesus as Son of Man was characteristic; for Jerusalem, Jesus as Messiah—but the title "Lord" also comes from the Galilean Church. It is probably correct that there were various parties in the Palestinian Church—but scarcely from the very beginning; they probably developed only gradually. It is perhaps also right that Jesus' whole following in Galilee did not move from there to Jerusalem after the Easter experiences, and that a Galilean Church existed side by side with that at Jerusalem, though it scarcely had the importance that Lohmeyer attributes to it. Paul, at any rate, takes only the Jerusalem Church into account, where at first the twelve were at the head until James, the Lord's brother, won the leadership—all Galileans in origin and hence representatives of Galilean tradition. At any rate, it is evidently impossible to conceive the titles "Messiah" and "Son of Man" as expressions of two differing theological views about Jesus and hence as distinguishing marks of two differing Churches or parties. Both alike denote the eschatological salvation-bringer. The ancient title "Messiah," once expressing Israelitic national hope, was no longer confined to this narrower meaning but could just as well be transferred to the heavenly salvation-bringer awaited by the apocalyptists, as the salvation to be brought by the latter could, vice versa, take on nationalistic traits. In the parables of I Enoch, "Son of Man" and "Messiah" alternate as titles of the same figure; likewise in IV Ezra. In the latter the messianic title "Servant of God" also appears, and it is expressly given to the Son of Man (13:32, 37, 52), while in II Bar. 70:9 it is the Messiah who is designated Servant of God. Furthermore in II Baruch the Messiah is pictured in every respect as the supernatural salvation-bringer of apocalyptic expectation except that he does not bear the title "Son of Man." Neither does anything in the synoptic tradition indicate that the varying titles "Messiah" and "Son of Man" express varying conceptions of Jesus' person; moreover, Paul, who does not use the apocalyptic title "Son of Man," clearly does not use the term Christ (so far as that is a title for him, and not a personal name) in the sense of the nationalistic hope, but in that of apocalypticism.

§ 8. Beginnings toward Development of Ecclesiastical Forms

1. What consequences did the earliest Church draw from its eschatological consciousness for its practical everyday attitudes, particularly its conduct toward Judaism and its institutions and adherents? How far did it see the total reality of its life in the light of eschatological occurrence?

Naturally the eschatological Congregation does not regard itself as a new religion—i.e. a new historical phenomenon—*and does not draw a boundary between itself, as a new religion, and Judaism.* It remains loyal to the temple and the temple cult. According to Acts 2:46 it customarily gathers within the temple area; according to Mt. 5:23f. it did not give up the sacrificial practices of Judaism, as Jesus also had not polemized against the temple cult (§ 2, 3). And just as the legend (Mt. 17:24-27) testifies that the Christian Congregation paid the temple tax in spite of knowing its inner separation from the old Jewish congregation, so Mk. 13:9 or Mt. 10:17 testifies that it felt itself subject to synagogal jurisdiction. As the Congregation of the end of days it conceives of itself as that true Israel, which is the goal of Israel's salvation-history, and for which the promises of the Old Testament are now being fulfilled (§ 6, 6).

That is where the problem lies: how far is "true Israel" understood as a really eschatological thing and how far as only a selection out of the historical People? How far is "Israel"—the subject to whom salvation happens—understood as meaning an absolutely eschatological entity, as it is by Paul, and how far as just the empirical People of history? Will the earliest Church eliminate from the idea of the Chosen People whatever applies only to the historical People? In what sense will the Old Testament's consciousness of history be adopted?

2. The question becomes acute *over the validity of the Law.* Is the Old Testament Law binding upon the members of the eschatological Congregation? And is obedience to the Law, therefore, the condition for participation in eschatological salvation? At first, this question does not seem to have been clearly answered; in fact, it does not seem even to have been clearly asked at first. In practice, however, a relative liberty toward the cultic-ritual demands of the Law must have existed. For could men preserve Jesus' critical and polemic words against Jewish legalism without orienting themselves by them? Could a man pass on Jesus' words against counting up reward and against the pride of the legally correct and at the same time impose the condition of legal merit upon the sharing of salvation? It is freely granted that the antinomy uncovered by Paul— faith, or works of the Law—did not become explicit in the earliest Church. On the contrary, its attitude toward Hellenistic Christianity, especially toward Paul, indicates that it did not achieve freedom from the Law. Presumably a retrogression had taken place so that the old scruples and fidelity to the Law had gradually gained ground; such was completely the case later with Jewish-Christian sects. This is partly attributable to the personal influence of James, the Lord's brother, and is partly a reaction against the criticism of the Law and the temple-cult on the part of the Hellenistic Church. The conclusions drawn by the Hellenists were terrifying and thus originated the famous saying placed into Jesus' mouth, "Think not that I have come to abolish the law and the prophets; I have come not to abolish them but to fulfill them. For truly, I say to you, till heaven and earth pass away, not an iota, not a dot will pass from the law . . ." (Mt. 5:17f.). And if he who relaxes one of the least of the commandments is to be counted as least in God's Reign (Mt. 5:19), that is said with regard to the Hellenists, perhaps to Paul himself.

But this lack of certainty and clarity was probably heightened by the fact that another question mingled with the question of the Law as the way to salvation. For the Law was not merely the way to salvation, and its fulfilment had not merely the character of meritorious accomplishment. It was also the gift of God which gave the Chosen People its rank and dignity. The history of salvation was the history of the People of Israel, the eschatological Congregation was the true Israel. Hence, fulfilment of the Law was the condition for participation in salvation insofar as it was the condition for membership in the People of Israel. And it is now clear that the earliest Church clung to this condition. However much (at least in the beginning) it may (under the influence of Jesus' words) have had a critical attitude toward Jewish legalism, and however much it may have broken with the Jewish idea of merit, it clung to the Law as a characteristic of the Chosen People which it was conscious of embodying.

This is indicated, in the first place, by the fact that the *mission to the heathen* was not regarded as an obligation by the Jerusalem Church. Rather, the saying placed into Jesus' mouth, "Go nowhere among the Gentiles, and enter no town of the Samaritans, but go rather to the lost sheep of the house of Israel" (Mt. 10:5f.), shows that in the earliest Church there was at least a party which altogether rejected the mission to the Gentiles; the saying (Mt. 10:23) also assumes a message for Jews only. Perhaps there were various opinions on this subject; perhaps a development took place from one opinion to another. At any rate the legendary stories of the Centurion at Capernaum (Mt. 8:5–10 par.) and the Syrophoenician woman (Mk. 7:24–30), both variations on the same motif, inform us on the one hand that before long Gentiles, too, were received into the Congregation of salvation and on the other hand that that was only exceptionally and hesitantly done. And the tradition worked into Acts 10:1ff. about Cornelius the Centurion at Caesarea permits the same insight. But especially Galatians and the tradition on which Acts 15 is based indicate that it was required of Gentiles who wished to join the eschatological Congregation of salvation that they adopt the Law, especially circumcision. But that means: the condition for sharing in salvation is belonging to the Jewish People —the empirical People of history. This, then, is the point where the conflict breaks out, first within the Church in Jerusalem between the old followers of Jesus and the Hellenistic Jewish-Christians, then between the Jerusalem Church and Paul.

Hellenistic Jews who had returned to Jerusalem and had their

[55]

own synagogues there (Acts 6:9) as a matter of course took a more liberal stand toward the Law. It is understandable that when such men joined the Christian Congregation, criticism of the Law and the temple cult made itself heard from their midst; such is testified (Acts 6:11, 13f.) of Stephen, one of their number. The conflict that had broken out in the Jerusalem Church apparently lurks behind the choice of the "seven men" (Acts 6:1ff.). For those seven were not "deacons," but were, as their Greek names (6:5) show, representatives of the *Hellenistic party.* What is told of Stephen, and later of Philip, also indicates that their office was by no means serving table, but that they were proclaimers of the word. These Hellenistic Christians occasioned among the Jews an uproar that evidently was not directed against the old Jewish-Christian Congregation, but against the Hellenists. Stephen was stoned and his fellow-partisans were driven out, and thereby the problem was for the time being beaten down both for the Jews and for the Jewish-Christian Church. But it soon arose again—and partly in direct consequence of the missionary activity of those driven out (Acts 8:4ff.; 11:19ff.)—when Gentile-Christian congregations arose for which adoption of the Law and especially circumcision no longer held as the condition for admission to the Congregation and for participation in messianic salvation.

In the dispute with Paul and Barnabas at the *"apostolic council"* reported in Gal. 2:1–10,* the Jerusalem Church acknowledged the right of Gentile Christianity to exist free from the Law. But Gentile Christians were evidently not regarded as having fully equal rights, as appears from the fact that in Antioch, and presumably elsewhere, new conflicts broke out over the question of table-fellowship in mixed congregations (Gal. 2:11ff.). To settle the dispute, regulations were released in Jerusalem which demanded certain concessions from Gentile Christians. These constitute the so-called "apostolic decree" (Acts 21:25).†

In his monograph *Apostel und Jünger* (1921), Rol. Schütz attempted to prove that Torah-free Hellenistic Christianity was the earlier stage, i.e. that it consisted of the congregations which grew up in Galilee, Samaria and the Decapolis out of Jesus'

---

* A parallel account is found in Acts 15; but the source on which it rests told about another meeting and decision—*viz.*, the one which resulted in the so-called "apostolic decree."

† See the foregoing note.

preaching, and that the Torah-loyal Church in Jerusalem was a later formation. This view, based upon a questionable literary analysis of Acts, cannot be maintained. On the basis of an unsuccessful source-analysis, W. Grundmann unconvincingly discusses *"das Problem des hellenist. Christentums innerhalb der Jerusalemer Urgemeinde"* ZNW 38 (1939), 45–73. Concerning the various parties and the position of Peter, James, and Paul within the conflict, *cf.* H. Lietzmann, *Zwei Notizen zu Paulus,* Sitzungsber. d. Preuss. Ak. d. Wiss., Phil.-Hist. Kl. (1930), VIII; Em. Hirsch, *Paulus und Petrus,* ZNW 29 (1930), 63–76; Gerh. Kittel, *Die Stellung des Jakobus zu Judentum und Heidenchristentum,* ZNW 30 (1931), 145–157; W. Grundmann, *Die Apostel zwischen Jerusalem und Antiochia,* ZNW 39 (1940), 110–137.

3. The development of the Church concept in the earliest Church was of course also hindered in other ways by its ties to the Jewish congregation. The Church as eschatological Congregation had not yet found appropriate expression in a cult of its own, since it had not cut itself loose from the temple cult. Only beginnings in that direction are present in the fact that the Church met not only in the temple area, but also in private houses (Acts 2:46)—whether as a whole or in separate groups (*cf.* Acts 12:12), information is lacking. But with the increase of the Church, especially after the acceptance of Hellenistic members, they can probably only have been group meetings. It can be taken for granted that they here sought edification together by interpretation of Scripture and that they called to mind words of Jesus. Nor is it impossible that the earliest Church set up its own synagogue service, since a number of synagogues are known to have existed in Jerusalem for the various groups of Judaism; but about that we know nothing.

Baptism (§ 6, 3), of course, was also a point of departure for the development of cultic forms of their own, and even more so *the common meals* (§ 6, 4), but they were no more than points of departure. For though these meals can indeed be called celebrations of the Congregation, still they are not actual cultic celebrations, much less the sacrament of the "Lord's Supper" as celebrated in the Pauline or Hellenistic congregations, whose liturgy we know from Mark and Paul. Rather, they are the main meal of the day, for nourishment, made into a solemn occasion. When this meal is called "the breaking of bread" (Acts 2:42, 46), that implies that they outwardly resembled Jewish meals which began with the act of bread-breaking and the accompanying blessing. That bread-breaking and blessing belong together, the Christian accounts also show (Mk. 6:41, 14:22; Lk. 24:30; Did. 9:3, 14:1). Wine might, of course, be drunk at such a meal, too, when it was available, but it had no cultic significance; otherwise the meal could not have been called simply "the breaking of bread." The origin of these meal-celebrations lies without doubt in the table-fellowship which once had united Jesus and his "disciples." No special reference to Jesus' last meal is in them. That comes only in the "Lord's Supper" of the Hellenistic congregations.

On the differentiation of the two forms of the Meal, the Palestinian form of the earliest Church and the Hellenistic-Pauline form, *cf.* H. Lietzmann, *Messe und Herrenmahl* (1926); O. Cullmann, *La signification de la Sainte-Cène dans le Christianisme primitif* (1936). E. Lohmeyer has dealt extensively and instructively with the questions involving the Lord's Supper and with the discussion of them in recent literature in *ThR*, NF 9 (1937), 168–227, 273–312; 10 (1938), 81–99. He also distinguishes the two types but believes he has found both in the earliest Church and thinks he can attribute them to the respective parties that he thought he had distinguished in it (§7, 5): the "breaking of bread," he thinks, was the "Galilean" tradition, while the Lord's Supper was characteristic of the "Jerusalem" party; the latter, he maintains, was regarded as instituted in Jesus' last meal, and its center was the memorial of Jesus' death. He also developed this idea in *JBL* LVI (1937), 217–252.

4. *The direction of the Church* was at first in the hands of "the twelve." Yet this was not really an office of the Church. Borne along by the expectation of the approaching End, they at first naturally did not think of setting up any such thing. "The twelve," as the future princes of the twelve tribes of Israel (§ 7, 4), are not so much an institution as a symbol of the eschatological Congregation as the true Israel. Their practical work was evidently as proclaimers of the word both within the Congregation and outside, and on missionary journeys they seem to have left Jerusalem either temporarily or (like Peter) permanently. The dominant authority was at first

Peter, as is testified by Mt. 16:17–19, Lk. 22:31f. and by the role that Peter played both in the synoptic tradition as a whole and in Paul. Besides him, John, the son of Zebedee, and James, the Lord's brother, must soon have won a leading position; Paul speaks of those three as the "pillars" (Gal. 2:9, *cf.* 1:18f.). Then, when Peter had left Jerusalem and John (presumably about 44 A.D.) had been executed with his brother James, the Lord's brother James remained the recognized authority (Acts 12:17, 21:18).

The *"elders"* constitute a real office of the Congregation. In accordance with Jewish precedent elders were evidently chosen at a relatively early period—when, we do not know. They are first encountered in the source behind Acts 11:30; and in 21:18, another passage with a source behind it, they are named with James. It may be due to editing by the author that in Acts 15 (as in 16:4) "the apostles and elders" appear as leaders of the Congregation. Presumably James was chairman of the council of elders.

The question that really matters is: *What office can be appropriately instituted* for the direction of the eschatological Congregation? Undoubtedly it can only be one *founded upon the proclamation of the word*: It was clear to Paul that at the same time that God instituted "reconciliation" he thereby instituted "the ministry of reconciliation" διακονία τῆς καταλλαγῆς, "the message of reconciliation" λόγος τῆς καταλλαγῆς (II Cor. 5:18f.). This "service," this "message," was at first and above all the concern of "the twelve" in the earliest Church —not, of course, as the future twelve princes of the salvation time, but because they were proclaimers of the word and guardians of the tradition. For since the Congregation is not founded by the persons it includes, as if it were a club or an association, but is conscious of having been founded by God's deed, it, like the Old Testament-Jewish congregation, needs *tradition,* in which the history which founded it is preserved and made present. Secondarily this tradition is the passing on of Jesus' message, but primarily it is the passing on of the specifically Christian kerygma—and is the former only within the frame of the latter. The legendary story of the election to re-complete the number of the twelve quite correctly expresses the substance of the matter: "So one of the men who have accompanied us during all the time that the Lord Jesus went in and out among us, beginning from the baptism of John until the day when he was taken up from us—one of these men must become with us a witness to his resurrection" (Acts 1:21f.). And I Cor. 15:3–7 as well as 11:23 shows that a kerygma is developing in which the tradition about the occurrence of salvation was fixed. The significant question for the future is whether the traditional message will be conceived as the factor which constitutes the Church—and if so, how.

Tradition requires continuity, i.e. *succession,* which need not be one mediated by an institution or sacraments. In Paul, too (*cf.* I Cor. 12:28), and even as late as Eph. 4:11f., the succession is a free one; i.e. not institutionally regulated but left to the free sway of the Spirit. The apostle is called in the first place by having seen the Lord—i.e. the Risen One (I Cor. 9:1); then he is legitimated by his missionary labor ἔργον (I Cor. 9:1); and that also means he is accredited by "all patience, with signs and wonders and mighty works" (II Cor. 12:12. *Cf.* I Thess. 1:5, I Cor. 2:4f., Rom. 15:19, Heb. 2:4). The idea of apostolic succession as an institution, the custom of ordination by the laying on of hands, appears for the first time in the pastoral epistles. The restriction of the concept "apostle" to the "twelve," which is an incipient tendency in this direction, can scarcely have taken place in the earliest Church. It is true that the apostle-concept is determined by the idea of tradition and hence also by that of divine commission and legitimation. But it is not yet narrowed down to a closed number; for Paul calls all missionaries "apostles" (I Cor. 9:5; Rom. 16:7; II Cor. 11:5, 13; 12:11f.) and the same usage is still found in Acts 14:4, 14 and Did. 11:4–6.

Karl Holl in his article, "Der Kirchenbegriff des Paulus in seinem Verhältnis zur Urgemeinde," * asserts that in the earliest Church the apostolate was a legal institution and restricted to the twelve. The opposite view is convincingly maintained by Wilh. Mundle, ZNW 22 (1923), 20–42, and W. G. Kümmel, *Kirchenbegriff,* etc., 6f. *Cf.* also Ferd. *Kattenbusch, Die Vorzugstellung des Petrus und der Charakter der Urgemeinde in Jerusalem,* Festgabe für Karl Müller (1922), 322–351.

However, the idea of tradition and succession finds characteristic expression in the fact that *Jerusalem is regarded as the center of the whole Church*—and obviously is so regarded not merely in the con-

---

* "Sitzungsb. d. Preuss. Akad. d. Wiss., Phil.-hist. Kl." (1921), 920–947; reprinted in Holl's collected essays: *Gesammelte Aufsätze zur Kirchengeschichte.*

sciousness of the Jerusalem Church. Paul and the author of Acts also bear witness to that fact. Paul finds it very important that the Gentile Congregations, to whom this idea in itself was necessarily strange, shall preserve connection with Jerusalem. Under this point of view the decision of the "apostolic council" that the Gentile congregations shall raise funds for the poor in Jerusalem (Gal. 2:10) is of special significance. I Cor. 16:1–4, II Cor. 8–9, Rom. 15:25–28 show how much Paul was concerned with this collection, for the collection has not just the meaning of a simple act of charity, but that of an act of faith, inasmuch as it documents their connection with the history of salvation. It is neither "a pious work toward the circle of charismatics and ascetics at Jerusalem" (Er. Peterson *RGG*, 2nd ed., III 464) nor a church tax (K. Holl, *l.c.*). When in Acts the legal right of supervision over all Christian congregations is ascribed to the Jerusalem congregation, that is certainly legendary. Barnabas, who according to Acts 11:22 was dispatched from Jerusalem to the Antioch congregation, was in the source-account underlying 11:19–26 evidently not a Jerusalem inspector, but belonged himself (as a Hellenistic Jewish Christian, *cf.* Acts 4:36) to those Hellenistic exiles from Jerusalem who had founded the congregation in Antioch.

Against Holl's assertion that the Jerusalem Congregation claimed a legal right of supervision and direction over the younger congregations, see Kümmel, *l.c.*, 9, 25, 53f. (footnote 85).

5. As time went on and membership increased, *life within the congregation* naturally needed a *certain regulation* which could not be left to the council of elders to decide from case to case; but the sources barely permit us a glimpse of that. Mt. 16:19 and 18:18 testify that the authority "to bind and to loose," i.e. a disciplinary power, lay first in the hands of Peter, then in those of the Congregation—and that probably means, in the hands of the elders; and Mt. 18:15–17 gives rules for settling quarrels in the congregation. The passage on Jesus' authority to forgive sins, Mk. 2:5b–10, which is inserted into the old miracle-story, 2:1–12, is to be regarded as having originated in the earliest Church, which proved its right to forgive sins by referring it back to Jesus; the Church's legitimation to forgive sins is its power of miraculous healing.*

* See *Gesch. d. synopt. Trad.*, 2nd edition, 12f.

The right of apostle-missionaries to support by the congregations (I Cor. 9:1ff.), which is expressly referred to in a saying of the Lord (I Cor. 9:14; Mt. 10:10 par.) cannot be regarded as a regulation of church law; it corresponds to Jewish custom and is not limited to apostles, as Gal. 6:6 shows.

It is self-evident that in an eschatological congregation awaiting the near end of this world no special economic system was set up. What is often called the community of property in the earliest Church on the basis of Acts 2:45; 4:34ff. is in reality a practical sharing of property on the basis of love. To call this actual communism is out of the question, for it lacks both a social program and organized production.

As there are only tendencies and beginnings in the direction of institutional forms that would give the eschatological Congregation a shape appropriate to its own nature in the historical world, so also the danger is still avoided of regarding the Church as an institution of salvation which mediates salvation by virtue of its offices and sacraments. As the eschatological Congregation, it is the fulfilment of the promises, that is true, but it is also the Congregation that awaits the future.

The *questions* which arise for the future are: How will the eschatological-transcendent character of the Congregation assert itself against its ties with the Jewish people without tearing its ties with the history of salvation? How will the idea of tradition and succession take form? Will the Word remain the constitutive factor? And what institutions will be created to give order to tradition and the life of the Congregation? How in all of this will the relation of the Congregation to the person of Jesus be conceived?

The first answer will be given by Paul's viewpoints: freedom from the Law, the ministry or the message of reconciliation, the body of Christ, and being in Christ, ἐν Χριστῷ.

CHAPTER III

The Kerygma of the Hellenistic Church Aside from Paul

PRELIMINARY REMARKS

1. The historical presupposition for Paul's theology is not the kerygma of the oldest Church but that of the Hellenistic Church; it was the latter that mediated the former to Paul. His theology presupposes a certain development of primitive Christianity which it had undergone after the Christian message had crossed the boundaries of Palestinian Judaism, and congregations of Hellenistic Christians, both Jewish and Gentile, had arisen. Our next task must, therefore, be to sketch a picture of this pre-Pauline Hellenistic Christianity.

But *pre-Pauline Hellenistic Christianity was by no means a unity*. It soon branched out according to whether influences of the synagogue were operative or those of Gentile religions (especially those of the Gnostic stream). Therefore, it is not in every one of its forms that it is pertinent as a presupposition for Paul's theology, and, therefore, also, its significance is not exhausted in its being a pre-stage for Paul. Side by side with Paul it lived on and developed partly along paths of its own, partly under Pauline influence. Its various types unfold and some are represented in such important developments as the Johannine theology—without Pauline influence—or Ignatius of Antioch—under the influence of Paul.

As complete a picture as possible is here to be given of Christianity before and during the time of Paul. At the same time the post-Pauline period will be taken into account wherever it is a matter of indicating theological tendencies which may be recorded only in sources of later date (this could be purely accidental) or which perhaps did not even take effect until after Paul's time, but which were potentially present in the situation itself: the entrance of Christianity into the Hellenistic world and the problems arising therefrom. We must make visible *the whole field of conditions and possibilities* in which independent and significant theological phenomena arise and out of which the theological and ecclesiastical forms of the early Church gradually grow.

2. *For the delineation of Hellenistic Christianity before and contemporary with Paul* there are scarcely any direct witnesses available. The so-called catholic epistles all come from a later time. Hence, it is essentially by reconstruction that the picture must be derived. What means can this task employ? At its disposal stand (1) some few data in *Acts* which are contained in the (Antiochene?) source used in chapters 6–8 and in 11:19–30. Next (2) it must depend upon *inferences from the Pauline letters*. Primary material, of course, is offered by what Paul himself designates as tradition, like I Cor. 11:23ff. and 15:1ff., of which it must be asked in each case how far back such tradition may go. But beyond that, such propositions and terms may be claimed to be tradition as Paul treats as self-evident—generally accepted—matters which he does not introduce as new and neither proves nor defends; this refers to such things as honorific titles of Christ, eschatological propositions, his use of the Old Testament and his method of exegesis, statements about the sacraments, and the like. Finally (3) *inferences from other sources of later date* are both permissible and necessary, especially sources which represent a non-Pauline type of Hellenistic Christianity, such as Hebrews, Barnabas, I Clement, James, and the Kerygma Petri. Here, too, formula-like expressions, statements of a generally accepted character, are the material to be considered. Where these agree with corresponding expressions and statements in Paul, they bear witness not only to other primitive Christian types existing before and by the side of Paul but also to a general Christian kerygma in which all forms agree. Additional corroboration is lent at times by the agreement of such statements with motifs of the Hellenistic-Jewish missionary propaganda; for the Christian mission not only competed with it but also to a large extent inherited it. To this I Clement and the Shepherd of Hermas, and also the Epistle of James, bear witness.

§ 9. The Preaching of God and His Judgment, of Jesus Christ, the Judge and Savior, and the Demand for Faith

1. *Christian missionary preaching in the Gentile world* could not be simply the christological kerygma; rather, it had to begin with *the proclamation of the one God.* For it was not just a prevalent Jewish and Jewish-Christian opinion that the one true God was unknown to the Gentile world and that Gentile religion was polytheism and idolatry, but it was actually true that the Christian mission first reached those classes in which polytheism was still a living force.

The Jewish mission had anticipated the Christian in the preaching of monotheism. In the later literature of the Old Testament polemic against heathen religions is already beginning, with criticism of the worship of many gods and the manner of that worship, especially of their representation in tangible form. This is shown by the redaction of the second half of Isaiah, by the book of Daniel, and by the story of Bel and the Dragon appended to it in the LXX, also by the apocryphal Epistle of Jeremiah and especially by the Wisdom of Solomon. This last document shows at the same time that Hellenistic Judaism in its criticism of paganism took over both the criticism of naive polytheism and its cults that had developed within the Hellenistic enlightenment itself and also positive ideas of Hellenistic philosophic religiosity: God's rule over the world through Wisdom is conceived in analogy to the Stoic view of the administration διοίκησις of the world by the spirit. When IV Macc. places its story of martyrdom under the theme: "whether the Reason is supreme over the passions," εἰ αὐτοκράτωρ ἐστὶν τῶν παθῶν ὁ λογισμός (1:13), it is using a Stoic theme. Especially in Philo is the whole tradition of Greek philosophy pressed into the service of Jewish propaganda.

In this process the Old Testament-Jewish *concept of God* is frequently modified or obscured by the concept of God from the Greek philosophical tradition, a concept determined by the idea of the law and order of the cosmos. The "natural theology" of the Stoa is taken over with its proofs of the existence of God, and along with it its demonstration of God's providence πρόνοια in nature, and its proof of theodicy. God's demand is presented as rational moral law; the concept of virtue (ἀρετή), foreign to the Old Testament, and the notion of a system of virtues take root and along with them the idea of education and methods of education.

All these tendencies are taken along by Christian-Hellenistic missionary preaching, though at first only in individual motifs and with characteristically Christian modifications.

2. In its basic features *Hellenistic-Christian missionary preaching* and its language, which gave the faith of the Church its stamp, can be characterized as follows:

The pagan world is held to be sunk in ignorance ἄγνοια and error πλάνη.

Paul, who takes up (I Thess. 4:5) the Old Testament description of the Gentiles as "heathen who do not know God" (τὰ ἔθνη) τὰ μὴ εἰδότα τὸν Θεόν (Jer. 10:25, Ps. 78:6 LXX), says to the Galatian Gentile-Christians (Gal. 4:8f.): "Formerly when you did not know God (οὐκ εἰδότε Θεόν) you were in bondage to beings that by nature are no gods; but now that you have come to know God (γνόντες Θεόν) . . ." Acts 17:30 speaks of the pre-Christian period as the "times of ignorance" χρόνοι τῆς ἀγνοίας; and the Areopagus discourse takes the altar inscription "to an unknown god" ἀγνώστῳ Θεῷ (17:23) for its point of contact. Eph. 4:18 describes the Gentiles ἔθνη as "darkened in their understanding, alienated from the life of God because of the ignorance ἄγνοια that is in them"; and I Pt. 1:14 exhorts believers to conduct "not conformed to the passions of your former ignorance." The "Greeks" are described by Kerygma Petri 2 as "driven by ignorance and not knowing God" ἀγνοίᾳ φερόμενοι καὶ μὴ ἐπιστάμενοι τὸν Θεόν, and of their former sins it is said further on (3): "whatsoever sins one of you has done in ignorance not clearly knowing God" ὅσα ἐν ἀγνοίᾳ τις ὑμῶν ἐποίησεν μὴ εἰδὼς σαφῶς τὸν Θεόν. (Such utterances are not peculiar but typical and are handed down to later writers; for the apologetes, cf. Justin, Apol. I 12:11; Aristides 17:3, p. 27, 15 Geffcken; Athenagoras 28, p. 147, 10f. Geffcken; see also M. Dibelius on I Tim. 1:13 in Lietzmann's *Handbuch zum N.T.*) Similarly the "error" πλάνη of the Gentiles is spoken of in Rom. 1:27; II Pet. 2:18; II Clem. 1:7; Gentile Christians were once "led astray" πλανώμενοι Tit. 3:3 or "straying like sheep" ὡς πρόβατα πλανώμενοι I Pet. 2:25. Cf. Heb. 5:2—though perhaps the "ignorant and wayward" ἀγνοῦντες καὶ πλανώμενοι here named are not specifically the Gentiles but sinners of any kind.

Hence to accept the Christian faith is called "to know God" or "the truth."

"To know God" γινώσκειν (τὸν) Θεόν is used for conversion to the Christian faith by Paul (Gal. 4:9) and also, e.g., by I Clem. 59:3; II Clem. 17:1 (cf. 3:1) Herm. sim. IX 18, 1f. The compounds ἐπίγνωσις (full knowledge) and ἐπιγινώσκειν (fully know) are especially popular in this meaning; in such cases the object may be God (as in Herm. sim. IX 18, 1 and elsewhere), but more frequently is truth ἀλήθεια. To become a Christian means "to come to the knowledge of the truth" εἰς ἐπίγνωσιν ἀληθείας ἐλθεῖν (I Tim. 2:4) or "to receive the knowledge of the truth" λαβεῖν τὴν ἐπίγνωσιν τῆς ἀληθείας (Heb. 10:26) or to "know the truth" ἐπιγινώσκειν τὴν ἀλήθειαν. With this meaning ἐπιγινώσκειν or its noun also occurs at Col. 1:6; Tit. 1:1; II Pet. 1:3, 2:20f.; II Clem. 3:1; Kerygma Petri 3; Herm. sim. IX 18, 1. According to I Clem. 59:2, God called the Church "from ignorance to the full knowledge of the glory of His name" ἀπὸ ἀγνωσίας εἰς ἐπίγνωσιν δοξῆς ὀνόματος αὐτοῦ. That corresponds to the use of language in Hellenistic Judaism; cf. ThWB I 706, 22ff.

"Truth" ἀλήθεια in this context is right doctrine, right belief, in contrast to "ignorance" ἄγνοια and "error" πλάνη, so that Paul can characterize his apostolic activity as a "manifestation of the truth" φανέρωσις τῆς ἀληθείας (II Cor. 4:2) which is substantially synonymous with saying that God through him spreads "the fragrance of the knowledge of Him" ὀσμὴ τῆς γνώσεως αὐτοῦ (II Cor. 2:14). Christian faith is called "obedience to the truth" (I Pet. 1:22; cf. Gal. 5:7). The gospel itself can be called the "word of truth" λόγος τῆς ἀληθείας (II Cor. 6:7; Col. 1:5; Eph. 1:13 and often). This, too, corresponds to Hellenistic-Jewish language; cf. ThWB 244, 32ff.

I Thess. 1:9, where Paul reminds the Thessalonians "how you turned from idols to serve a living and true God," indicates that he began his missionary preaching with *the proclamation of the one God*; so does the reminder of having formerly worshiped "dumb idols" ἄφωνα εἴδωλα (I Cor. 12:2) or "beings that by nature are no gods" φύσει μὴ ὄντες θεοί (Gal. 4:8). I Cor. 8:4–6 shows how characteristic and rich in consequences monotheistic faith was for the whole congregation; the consciousness "that an idol has no real existence and that there is no God but one," leads the "strong" to a thoughtless attitude toward heathen cult-meals.

Such preaching of monotheism is of course not specifically characteristic of Paul. In it he is continuing the propaganda of Hellenistic Judaism, and from its writings some idea of primitive Christian missionary preaching, for which we have no direct sources, can be formed.

Cf. Ps. Aristeas 132ff.: "For he (our Law-giver) proved first of all that there is only one God and that his power is manifested throughout the universe." It goes on to say that God, as the Judge, views all that happens on earth, and no one is hidden from Him. (Then follows a polemic against polytheism and a defense of the Law.) Philo closes his commentary on the creation-story with this summary: "Five things Moses teaches through the creation-story: 1. that the Deity is and has been from eternity. . . . 2. that God is one. . . . 3. that the world came into being. . . . 4. that the world is one. . . . 5. that God also exercises forethought on the world's behalf." (*On the Creation* [*Opifex mundi*] 170–172 Whitaker tr.)

The other Christian missionaries contemporary with Paul and later speak in the same way. Examples of this are the discourses which the author of Acts has Paul deliver in Lystra and Athens (Acts 14:15–17; 17:23–30). Among the basic elements of Christianity is "belief in God" πίστις ἐπὶ Θεόν according to Heb. 6:1 (*cf.* I Pet. 1:21).

Correspondingly Herm. mand. 1 (where Jewish tradition has been re-worked): "First of all believe that God is one, who made all things and perfected them, and made all things to be out of that which was not and contains all things, and is himself uncontained. Believe then in him and fear him . . ." (Lake).

According to Kerygma Petri 3, Jesus sends out the apostles "to preach the gospel to men throughout the world that they should know that there is one God," and so the cry rings out (2): "Know ye then that there is one God who made the beginning of all things and hath power over the end." Further examples are II Clem. 1:4ff.; Aristides Apol. 15, 3 p. 23, 20ff. Geffcken; Ps. Clem. hom. 15, 11 p. 150, 10ff. Lagarde. Texts on the doctrine of God are compiled in Alfr. Seeberg, *Die Didache des Judentums*, 11–23.

Formula-like expressions, established locutions, are taken out of Old Testament-Jewish theology or out of the Hellenistic enlightenment-theology, enter new combinations, or, in some cases, arise for the first time. Philo's teaching "that God is one" (see above) occurs, as in Herm. mand. 1 and Kerygma Petri 2f. (see above), also at Jas. 2:19, Ign. Mag. 8:2 and similarly at Rom. 3:30; I Cor. 8:6; Eph. 4:6; I Tim. 2:5; I Clem. 46:6. *Cf.* also Er. Peterson, Εἶς Θεός (1926); H. Lietzmann, *ZNW* 21 (1922), 6f. A standing attribute of God is "only" μόνος, already current in the Old Testament and Judaism, but also found in Greek antiquity (see Bultmann, *Das Johannes-Ev.* 204, 2); *cf.* I Tim. 1:17, 6:15f. and the doxologies Rom. 16:27, Jude 25. Combining it with "true" ἀληθινός is especially popular: Joh. 17:3; I Clem. 43:6 and elsewhere (see Bultmann, *Joh.-Ev.* 378, 2 and H. Lietzmann *ZNW* 21 [1922], 6f.). The latter term, which likewise comes from the Old Testament tradition (אֱלֹהֵי אֱמֶת or אָמֵן 'א) also occurs alone, of course, or in other combinations; *cf.* I Jn. 5:20, Rev. 6:10, etc. (see ThWB I 250, 14ff.). In I Thess. 1:9 it is combined with "living," which is likewise an Old Testament-Jewish attribute for God (אֵל חַי) and one also used by Paul, II Cor. 3:3, Rom. 9:26 (quoted); *cf.* further [II Cor. 6:16] I Tim. 3:15; Acts 14:15; Heb. 3:12, 9:14, 10:31, 12:22; Ign. Philad. 1:2, II Clem. 20:1, Herm. vis. II 3, 2; III 7, 2; sim. VI 2, 2; heathen gods, by contrast, are dead νεκροί, II Clem. 3:1; *cf.* Sap. 15:17.

God is described as essentially the *Creator*, often in expressions of the Old Testament or Judaism. The prayer in Acts 4:24 says in broad liturgical style "Sovereign Lord, who didst make the heaven and the earth and the sea and everything in them"; likewise in the speech Acts 14:15 after which v. 17 further describes God's creating. Rev. 10:6 and 14:7 are similar; still more ornate is Herm. vis. I 3, 4. Briefer: Rev. 4:11, Did. 10:3 and Eph. 3:9 (3rd person) "thou didst create all things" or "God who gives life to all things" I Tim. 6:13. Or God may be described with a stronger expression: "who gives life to the dead and calls into existence the things that do not exist" Rom. 4:17 (*cf.* Herm. mand. 1, quoted above and Herm. sim. V 5, 2; VI 4). This creation out of nothing which is in accord with Hellenistic-Jewish tradition is emphasized also in Herm. vis. I 1, 6; mand. I 1; II Clem. I, 8.

    Cf. further the lengthy description of God's sway as creator in I Clem. 20, 59:3, 60:1. To the designation "creator," "father" is often joined: I Clem. 19:2, 62:2 and "father" of course also occurs alone or in other combinations: I Cor. 8:6; Eph. 3:14f., 4:6; Did. 1:5; I Clem. 23:1, 29:1; II Clem. 14:1; Ign. Rom. pr., combined with δημιουργός, "Creator," I Clem. 35:3 (the latter without "father" also found I Clem. 20:11, 26:1, 33:2, 59:2). "Almighty" παντοκράτωρ is added to "Father," Mart. Pol. 19:2 (as later in the Roman and the Jerusalem creeds) or also to "God" (I Clem. pr., 2:3, 32:4, 62:2; Pol. Phil. pr.) or to "Sovereign" (δεσπότης) (Did. 10:3); it occurs as an attribute of the "Will" of God, I Clem. 8:5, of His "Name," I Clem. 60:4; Herm. vis. III 3, 5 and it stands by itself or in apposition to "God" at Rev. 1:8, 4:8, 11:17, etc. (9 times). Participial characterizations are also common, such as: ὁ κτίσας (the maker, see above), ὁ ποιήσας (the maker, Did. 1:2; I Clem. 7:3, 14:3; Barn. 16:1), ὁ πλάσας (the molder, I Clem. 38:3; Barn. 19:2). Since the Creator of the world is also the Ruler of the world, God is often called "Sovereign" ὁ δεσπότης in such contexts (Acts 4:24; Rev. 6:10), "Sovereign of all" (I Clem. 8:2; 33:2, 52:1; joined with "Demiurge" δημιουργός I Clem. 20:11, 33:2). In addition, other terms occur, e.g. "Sovereign" δυνάστης (I Tim. 6:15) "king of ages" I Tim. 1:17, "King of kings and Lord of lords" (I Tim. 6:15), "who rules (κυριεύων) over all the world" Barn. 21:5. Concerning these and other terms for God as Creator, see W. Bousset, *Kyrios Chr.*, 2nd edition, 291f.; H. Lietzmann *ZNW* 21 (1922), 6f. On the equivalent Jewish terms for God: W. Bousset, *Die Religion des Judentums*, 2nd edition, 1926, 359f., 375ff.

In addition to these terms, certain Hellenistic (Stoic) formulations serve to describe God's creatorhood and rulership of the world. God is praised because "from him and through him and to him are all things" (Rom. 11:36); it is He "from whom are all things and through whom we exist" (I Cor. 8:6), "for whom and by whom all things exist" (Heb. 2:10), "who is above all and through all and in all" (Eph. 4:6. Here, however, the originally cosmological formulation is probably intended to be understood of the Church). Another formulation intended to express both God's immanence and transcendence at the same time is that of Herm. mand. I, 1 (see above): "(He) contains all things, and is himself alone uncontained" or, Kerygma Petri 2: "the . . . Uncontained, who contains all things"; this expression with variations also occurs in Hellenistic Judaism.

The Hellenistic parallels may be found in Lietzmann's commentary on Rom. 11:36 and Dibelius' on Col. 1:16f., both in the *Handbuch zum N.T.*, and in Ed. Norden's *Agnostos Theos* (1914), 240–250; see further Dibelius on Herm. mand. I, 1 in the supplement to the same *Handbuch*.

The Stoa's *"natural theology"* with its proofs of the existence of God—human intelligence divines the invisible creator from the visible world, the master-workman from his works—is taken over by Paul Rom. 1:19f. and to a still greater extent by the author of Acts in the Areopagus-address which he places in Paul's mouth, Acts 17:22ff.: The order of the allotted periods and boundaries of the earth proves God's governance of the world. Still more according to Stoic pattern is the description (I Clem. 20) of God's government (διοίκησις) of the universe manifested in the law and order of natural phenomena. In a proof of the resurrection of the dead, I Clem. 24:5, occurs the concept of divine "providence" (πρόνοια) in nature which is still absent from the New Testament because its thought is not concerned with nature, but with history, and because, consequently, it is governed by the concept of divine pre-determination (foreknow προγινώσκειν, pre-destine προορίζειν, etc.; *cf.* Rom. 8:29, etc.), rather than that of "providence." But as Hellenistic Judaism had taken over the concept of providence in nature, so Christianity also soon took it over, and we have no way of knowing whether it had already been taken over before or during Paul's time. The first witness after I Clement is Herm. vis. I 3, 4 where "providence" is coupled with Old Testament concepts descriptive of God's rule over nature. At any rate, Paul himself already took over the concept "nature" along with the phrases "according to" or "contrary to" nature (Rom. 1:26, 11:24); these phrases document the Stoic understanding of man as a being fitted into the totality of the cosmos.

That others besides Paul did this is shown by Jas. 3:7, Ign. Eph. 1:1, Tr. 1:1 (with the antithesis "by habit"—"by nature"), Barn. 10:7, II Pet. 1:4 actually uses the expression "that . . . you may become partakers of divine nature" (θείας κοινωνοὶ φύσεως). Other anthropological concepts from the tradition of popular philosophy, which were still foreign to the Old Testament, were also already taken over by Paul: "conscience" (Rom. 2:15, I Cor. 8:7, etc.), "what is proper" (Rom. 1:28 tr.), and ἀρετή in the sense of "virtue" (Phil. 4:8); they also have Christian attestation outside of Paul. ("Conscience" in the rest of the New Testament: Pastorals, Heb., I Pet., Acts; outside of New Testament: I Clem., Ign., Did. 4:14, Barn. 19:12. "Virtue": II Clem. 10:1, Herm. mand. I:2 VI 2, 3 and frequently. "The proper" or "the improper": I Clem. 3:4, 41:3; "properly" I Clem. 1:3; likewise "what is fitting": Did. 16:2, I Clem. 35:5, 45:1, 62:1, Barn. 17:1). The Hellenistic manner of describing the nature of God by the *via negationis* (the way of negation) is quickly appropriated by Christian language in its use of adjectives formed with the alpha-privative prefix. Such are: "*in*visible" (Rom. 1:20, Col. 1:15f., I Tim. I:17, Heb. 11:27, Ign. Mg. 3:2, Herm. vis. I 3, 4; III 3, 5, II Clem. 20:5 and "*in*corruptible" (ἄφθαρτος, Rom. 1:23, I Tim. 1:17). Ign. Pol. 3, 2 piles up the negatives: "time*less*, *in*visible, *im*palpable, *im*passive" (all α-privatives) and in Kerygma Petri 2 occurs this detailed description of God's nature: "the Unseen who sees all things, the Uncontained who contains all things, the Un-needy whom all things need and by whom they exist—incomprehensible, unending, incorruptible, unmade, who made all things by his word of power." Its "uncontained" occurs in Herm. mand. I:1, while un-needy takes up a characteristic Greek-Hellenistic motif which appears with variations in Acts 17:25, I Clem. 52:1, and later in the works of the apologetes. In all of this, of course, Hellenistic Judaism had already gone before.

Finally, let it be recalled that the Hellenistic idea of man's relatedness to God is already taken up in the Areopagus-discourse, Acts 17:28f., where it is expressed by nothing less than a quotation from the Stoic poet Aratus; also that "blessed" (μακάριος), a Greek attribute for the divine, already occurs in I Tim. 1:11 and 6:15.

3. According to Jewish opinion, there is a *causal connection between heathen polytheism and idolatry and the heathen world's degradation in sin and vice.* Paul took over this idea, too; in Rom. 1:24–32 the vices of the Gentiles appear as the consequence of—or as divine penalty for—the basic sin of idolatry. Thus, early Christian opinion takes for granted that heathen living is sinful living. Christians described that way of life in vice-catalogues such as Hellenistic Judaism had already taken over from the ethical parenesis of general Hellenism (Rom. 1:29–31, I Cor. 6:9f., Gal. 5:19–21, Col. 3:5, 8, Eph. 4:31, 5:3f., I Tim. 1:9f., I Clem. 35:5, Pol. Phil. 2:2, 4:3, etc.). Just as Paul (Rom. 6:17f., I Cor. 6:9–11) contrasts the former and the present states of Gentile Christians as their time of

sin and of righteousness, respectively, there soon develops a stereotyped scheme of primitive Christian preaching, in which this contrast of then and now is presented in variations (Col. 1:21f., 3:5ff.,
Eph. 2:1ff., 11ff., Tit. 3:3ff., I Pet. 1:14ff., 2:25, II Clem. 1:6ff.).

Hence, the call to believe in the one true God is simultaneously a
call *to repentance.* According to Heb. 6:1, "repentance from dead
works" in conjunction with "belief in God" (see above, 2) stands at
the threshold of Christianity—i.e. repentance from or turning back
from sinful deeds. Accordingly, the author of Acts lets Paul before
Agrippa say, "I declared . . . that they should repent and turn to
God . . ." (26:20). Rev. 9:20f. also shows that "conversion" to God
and repentance constitute a unity (*cf.* 16:9, 11). The specifically
Christian close of the Areopagus discourse begins, "The times of
ignorance God overlooked, but now he commands all men everywhere to repent" (Acts 17:30) and the Paul of Acts, looking back
upon his missionary labors, describes himself as "testifying . . . of
repentance to God" (20:21). In Paul's own writing, the idea of
"repentance" plays only a negligible role (Rom. 2:4, II Cor. 12:21;
II Cor. 7:9f. means the repentance of men who are already Christian) for which an explanation will be given later. But otherwise
"repentance" is represented as the basic requirement for conversion. In addition to the passages already named, Ign. Eph. 10:1 and
especially Kerygma Petri 3 illustrate this: "Whatsoever sins one of
you has done in ignorance, not clearly knowing God, when he has
come to know (God) and has repented, shall be forgiven him" (tr.).
Finally two other facts support this assertion. First, that the repentance which opens the way to salvation can be called a gift of
God, as at Acts 11:18, "Then to the Gentiles also God has granted
(ἔδωκεν) repentance unto life" (*cf.* 5:31), or I Clem. 7:4, where of
the blood of Christ it is said, "it brought the grace of repentance to
all the world" (*cf.* 8:5) or Barn. 16:9, where it is said of God, "giving
repentance to us" (*cf.* Pol. Phil. 11:4, Herm. sim. VIII 6, 1f.). Second, the fact that very early the possibility of a second repentance
was already being discussed. Whereas this is declared impossible
by Heb. 6:4–6, the author of Hermas feels himself called by a revelation to preach repentance to the Christian Congregation once more
for the last time (Herm. mand. IV 3).

But the call to repentance has its basis in the fact that *God the
Creator is also the Judge*; moreover His judgment takes place not in

the private fate of the sinner (or at least not only and not primarily there)—an idea which is both current in Judaism and not unknown to the Gentile world—but will soon be held over the entire world. Hence, Christian preaching of the one true God is at the same time *eschatological proclamation,* preaching of the impending *judgment of the world.* While Christian preaching thus agrees with Jewish apocalyptic (this motif had receded in Hellenistic Judaism), its peculiarity consists first in the fact that it proclaims the judgment of the world as close at hand and then in the fact that it binds the accomplishment of the judgment, or deliverance from its damning verdict, to the person of Jesus.

Acts 17:31 shows that the preaching of monotheism, the call to repentance, and the proclamation of the eschatological judgment form a unity; here the reason given for the call to repentance (see above) following upon the proclamation of the one God, is: "because he has fixed a day on which he will judge the world in righteousness by a man whom he has appointed." Likewise I Thess. 1:9f. attests the inter-relatedness of monotheistic and eschatological preaching: ". . . how you turned to God from idols, to serve a living and true God, and to wait for his Son from heaven, whom he raised from the dead, Jesus who delivers us from the wrath to come." According to Heb. 6:2, "the elementary doctrines" of Christianity include in addition to "repentance" and "belief in God" (also baptism and the laying on of hands), the doctrines of "resurrection of the dead" and "eternal judgment." Heb. 11:6 also characteristically says, "whoever would draw near to God must believe that he exists and that he rewards those who seek him." And in Herm. mand. I when "first of all believe that God is one" (see above, 2) is followed by: "Believe then in him, and fear him, and in your fear be continent," that also contains reference to God as Judge.

It is unnecessary to itemize *how the proclamation of the impending judgment* pervades all the writings of the New Testament. Only in the Gospel and Epistles of John is there a peculiar situation in regard to it; but though the idea of the judgment has found a peculiar new interpretation in them, that only proves how solidly the idea belonged to the structure of Christian thought. Understood in the traditional way, i.e., as the tremendous eschatological drama of the imminent world-judgment, it occurs both in Paul and in the deutero-Pauline literature, both in Acts and in Hebrews and James, and appears dressed in powerful pictures in Revelation; it is defended against doubt in II Pet. It is noteworthy and indicative of the extent to which Paul keeps within the frame of general Christian preaching, that he does not hesitate, in at least seeming contradiction to his doctrine of justification by faith alone, to speak of judgment according to one's works (I Cor. 3:13–15, 5:4, II Cor. 5:10, Rom. 2:5ff., 14:10–Rom. 2:16, however, is a gloss). So, also, the exhortation to be ready, the warning not to become negligent, runs through the whole New Testament. For "the appointed time has grown very short" (I Cor. 7:29); i.e. there is only a little time left until the End. "The night is far spent, the day is at hand" (Rom. 13:12 KJ; *cf.* Heb. 10:25, Jas. 5:8). "The end of all things is at hand" (I Pet. 4:7). "The moment is near" (Rev. 1:3, 22:10; *cf.* Ign. Eph. 11:1). Everything depends upon being kept "to the end" ἑώς τέλους (I Cor. 1:8), to be faithful "until the end" (μέχρι or ἄχρι τέλους —Heb. 3:6 ℵ D, etc., 3:14, 6:11, Rev. 2:26)—"for the whole time of your faith shall not profit you except ye be found perfect at the last time" (Did. 16:2).

The same terminology in all strata, even in details, shows that these are general-Christian ideas. God is called "the Judge" (Jas. 4:12, 5:9), "the Judge, God of all" (κρίτης Θεὸς πάντων Heb. 12:23), "the righteous Judge" (Herm. sim. VI, 3, 6). (On Christ as judge, see below.) His "judging" (κρινεῖν) is spoken of (Rom. 2:16, 3:6, Acts 17:31, Heb. 10:30, Barn. 4:12) or "being judged" (κρίνεσθαι) by Him (II Thess. 2:12, Jas. 2:12, 5:9, I Clem. 13:2, II Clem. 18:1); or the noun κρίσις (judgment) is used (II Thess. I:5, I Tim. 5:24, Heb. 9:27, 10:27, Jas. 2:13, 5:12, Jd. 6, II Pet. 2:4, 9; 3:7, Rev. 14:7, 18:10, Ig. Sm. 6:1, Pol. Phil. 7:1, Barn. 1:6); or the participle "coming" (μέλλουσα or ἐρχομένη) is added to the preceding (II Clem. 18:2, Herm. vis. III 9, 5); the eschatological judgment is called κρίμα (Pet. 4:17) or "κρίμα of God" (Rom. 2:2f.) or "coming" (μέλλον) or "eternal" κρίμα (Acts 24:25, Heb. 6:2). Κρίμα is also used as the eschatological verdict or condemnation (Gal. 5:10, Jas. 3:1, Jd. 2, II Pet. 2:3, Rev. 17:1, 18:20, I Clem. 21:1, Ign. Eph. 11:1); the same meaning is in "the judgments to come" (μέλλοντα κρίματα I Clem. 28:1).
Adapting the Old Testament phrase, "Day of Jahweh," various expressions speak of the "Day" of judgment: It is "the day of wrath when God's righteous judgment will be revealed"

(Rom. 2:2; "of wrath" also Rev. 6:17) or the "day of judgment" ἡμέρα κρίσεως (II Pet. 2:9, 3:7, Barn. 19:10, 21:6, II Clem. 16:3, 17:6) or "the day in which God will judge" ἡμέρα ἐν ᾗ κρινεῖ ὁ Θεός (Rom. 2:16), or, after Joel 3:4, simply "the day of God" (Acts 2:20, II Pet. 3:10, 12; or "the day of the Lord Jesus Christ," see below) or "the great day of God the Almighty" (Rev. 16:14) or "that day" ἐκείνη ἡ ἡμέρα (II Thess. :10, II Tim. 1:12, 18; 4:8), "the great day" ἡ μεγάλη ἡμέρα (Jd. 6; *cf.* Rev. 6:17, Barn. 6:4) and, altogether abbreviated, "the day" (I Cor. 3:13, I Thess. 5:4, Heb. 10:25, Barn. 7:9). Instead of "day," "*hour* of judgment" (Rev. 14:7), or "the hour to reap" (Rev. 14:7), or "the last hour" (I Jn. 2:18).

As the eschatological judgment can be called "day of wrath" ἡμέρα ὀργῆς, it can also be called simply "wrath" ὀργή (Rom. 5:9, *cf.* 12:19), or "coming (ἐρχομένη and μέλλουσα) wrath" (I Thess. 1:10, Ign. Eph. 11:1) or "the wrath of God" (Col. 3:6, Eph. 5:6, Rev. 19:15; *cf.* Rev. 11:18, 14:10, 16:19).

In the exhortations to be ready, the following figurative expressions occur again and again: "keep awake" (γρηγορεῖν), I Thess. 5:6, I Cor. 16:13, Col. 4:2, I Pet. 5:8, Acts 20:31, Rev. 3:2f., 16:15, Did. 16:1, Ign. Pol. 1:3; *cf.* Barn. 4:13; "arise (from sleep)" ἐγερθῆναι (Rom. 13:11) or ἐγείρειν intransitive (Eph. 5:14); "be sober" (νήφειν I Thess. 5:6, 8, I Pet. 1:13, 4:7, 5:8, Ign. Pol. 2:3, Pol. Phil. 7:2, II Clem. 13:1); also the figure of the "thief" κλέπτης which pictures the unexpected coming of "the Day" (I Thess. 5:2, 4, Rev. 3:3, 16:15, II Pet. 3:10). In addition many a traditional expression out of the Old Testament hope or Jewish apocalyptic occurs. It is noteworthy that among them the expression "Reign of God" is only seldom used. Paul has it only at Rom. 14:17, I Cor. 4:20, 6:9f., 15:50, Gal. 5:21 (I Thess. 2:12); of these I Cor. 6:9f., 15:20, Gal. 5:21 are certainly traditional, more or less crystallized statements which Paul either quotes or paraphrases—perhaps also Rom. 14:17, I Cor. 4:20. Add to these the following cases from deutero-Pauline literature: II Thess. 1:5, Col. 4:11, Eph. 5:5; from the rest of the New Testament: Acts 1:3, 8:12, 14:22, 19:8, 20:25, 28:23, 31 (Jas. 2:5). On the reign of Christ which Eph. 5:5 combines with that of God, see below. Beyond the New Testament, *cf.* Did. 9:4, 10:5 (in table-prayers); also (frequently in quotations): I Clem. 42:3, II Clem. (5:5, 6:9), 9:6, 11:7, 12:1ff., Barn. 21:1, Ign. Eph. 16:1, Phld. 3:3, Pol. Phil. 2:3, 5:3, Herm. sim. IX 12, 3 ff.; 13, 2; 15, 2f.; 16, 2ff.; 20, 2f.; 29, 2. In the Hellenistic sphere this concept is pushed into the background by that of "life (eternal)" ζωή (αἰώνιος), alongside of which "incorruption" ἀφθαρσία is used: Rom. 2:7, I Cor. 15:42, 50, 53f., Eph. 6:24, II Tim. 1:10, Ign. Eph. 17:1, Mg. 6:2, Phld. 9:2, Pol. 2:3, II Clem. 14:5, 20:5.

The preaching of *resurrection from the dead* is inseparable from that of God's judgment, for the dead, too, are to be brougnt to account for their former deeds. Closely connected with "eternal judgment" is "resurrection from the dead" among the elementary doctrines of Christian faith according to Heb. 6:2. To deny the resurrection is to deny the judgment (Pol. Phil. 7:1, II Clem. 9:1). The author of Acts distinctly feels the shocking novelty of such preaching to Gentile ears when he relates that Paul's preaching at Athens occasioned the misunderstanding: "He seems to be a preacher of foreign divinities"—and specifically: "because he preached Jesus and Anastasis" (Resurrection, mistaken for a proper name, Acts 17:18). He feels it again when he later has the audience interrupt Paul's speech where it comes to the resurrection theme: "hearing 'resurrection of the dead,' some mocked; but others said, 'We will hear you again about this'" (17:32). The same conclusion can be reached from Paul's own writings. He takes for granted that "the resurrection of the dead" belongs to the very core of Christian faith—if there is no such thing, then kerygma and faith are null and void (I Cor. 15:12–34). But this message is so incredible to his Corinthian audience that he has to prove its right to be heard. But in the Thessalonian Church, also, this portion of his preaching, which he surely cannot have skipped in his mission at Thessalonica, has died away without effect, so that he has to reassure that Church of the resurrection (I Thess. 4:13–18). I Clem. 24–26 is a detailed proof of the reality of the resurrection, and the resurrection is presupposed wherever the judgment is dealt with, whether expressly mentioned or not.

4. Inasmuch as He is the Creator, God is the Judge of the world. This inner connection, which also is emphasized in Judaism (IV Ez. 5:56–6:6, etc.) is occasionally made explicit, as at Kerygma Petri 2: "Know therefore that there is one God who made the beginning of all things and has power over the End."

Cf. also Kerygma Petri 3: the apostles are to preach "that there is one God," proclaiming at the same time "the things that are to come so that they who have heard and believed may be saved, and that they who do not believe though they have heard must bear witness thereto without the excuse of saying, 'We have not heard'" (tr.). The Creator is at the same time the Judge, I Clem. 20–23 declares; and to this theme of the divine governance of the world and its accompanying exhortation is joined the eschatological theme of the resurrection of the dead followed by its appropriate exhortation, 24–28.

Accordingly, Paul names God as the Judge of the world at I Thess. 3:13, Rom. 3:5, 14:10; *cf.* outside of Paul: I Pet. 1:17, Jas. 4:12, 5:4, Rev. 11:17f., 20:11ff., etc. (*cf.* the passages indicated on p. 75). But at this point the christological motif enters the kerygma: At God's side or in place of God *Jesus Christ appears as Judge of the world*; he represents God, so to say, as His plenipotentiary. Acts 17:31 phrases it: "He has fixed a day on which he will judge the world in righteousness by a man whom he has appointed." In general, no thought is taken to reconcile the ideas. In Paul, statements about God's judgeship stand unreconciled beside others about Christ as Judge of the world (I Thess. 2:19, I Cor. 4:5); Paul can speak both of the "judgment seat of God" (Rom. 14:10) and of Christ (II Cor. 5:10). Christ, too, is called "the righteous judge" (II Tim. 4:8); Christ will judge (Barn. 5:7, 15:5) and instead of "God's Reign" "Christ's Reign" is spoken of (Col. 1:13, II Tim. 4:1, 18, II Pet. 1:11, I Clem. 50:3, Barn. 4:13, 7:11, 8:5f.; implied by Paul I Cor. 15:24). Here, also, there is no reflection about reconciling the ideas; Eph. 5:5 presents a simple combination of the two: "in the kingdom of Christ and of God." Gradually the idea of Christ's office as Judge of the world comes to predominate. Rom. 14:9 already says: "For to this end Christ died and lived again, that he might be Lord both of the dead and of the living"; out of this a formula develops: Christ is he "who is to judge the living and the dead" (II Tim. 4:1, Barn. 7:2), "who is ready to judge the living and the dead" (I Pet. 4:5), "the one ordained by God to be judge of the living and the dead" (Acts 10:42), "the judge of the living and the dead" (Pol. Phil. 2:1, II Clem. 1:1)—down to the sentence in the Symbolum Romanum: "whence he comes to judge the living and the dead" (ὅθεν ἔρχεται κρῖναι ζῶντας καὶ νεκρούς).

Thus, *Christ* belongs in the eschatological kerygma—nevertheless not only as the Judge but in that very fact also as the Savior for those who belong to the Congregation of the faithful. According to I Thess. 1:9f., the preaching of this fact belongs intimately with the proclamation of the one God; the Thessalonians "turned to . . . the living and true God" "to serve" Him (see above 2) "and to wait for his son from heaven, whom he raised from the dead, Jesus who delivers us from the wrath to come." And when Paul says (Phil. 3:20), "But our citizenship is in heaven from which also we eagerly await a Savior (σωτήρ), our Lord Jesus Christ," that is all the more certainly an appeal to a common-Christian statement the more clearly we recognize how singular a phraseology this is to find in Paul, who does not otherwise use the title "Savior" for Christ. And Paul expressly appeals to the tradition when he describes the eschatological appearing of Christ to save the faithful (I Thess. 4:15–18). The expectation of the parousia or the manifestation (ἐπιφάνεια) of the Savior Christ Jesus was so taken for granted as an item of the Christian hope (Tit. 2:13) that "Savior" became a title for Christ used in a formula-like manner.

Of course, other influences are also at work in the use of the title "Savior." They are: first, the Old Testament tradition, in which God is called Savior (still so used in the New Testament: the pastoral epistles, Lk. 1:47, Jd. 25) and second, the Hellenistic usage in which both mystery and salvation deities and divinely worshiped rulers bear the title. See W. Bousset, *Kyrios Christos*, 2nd ed., 240–246, where the abundant literature on this subject is also cited, and M. Dibelius, Excursus on II Tim. 1:10 (Lietzmann's *Handbuch zum NT* 13, 2nd ed. (1931), 60–63). In a meaning clearly or probably eschatological the title occurs at Phil. 3:20, Tit. 2:13, Acts 5:31, 13:23. The hope of the parousia of Christ is attested by I Cor. 15:23, I Thess. 2:19, 3:13, 4:15, 5:23; then II Thess. 2:1, 8, Jas. 5:7f. (where, however, originally the parousia of God was meant), II Pet. 1:16, 3:4. In the same sense his "manifestation" (ἐπιφάνεια) is mentioned at II Thess. 2:8 (here tautologically combined: "the manifestation of his parousia"), I Tim. 6:14, II Tim. 4:1, 8, Tit. 2:13, II Clem. 12:1, 17:4; but the appearing of the historical Jesus is meant by the "manifestation of the Savior" at II Tim. 1:10 and by his parousia in Ign. Phld. 9:2. *Cf.* also the designation of Christ as "our hope," I Tim. 1:1, on which see Dibelius, *op. cit.*

Though the figure of Christ as the eschatological Judge and Savior corresponds to the Son of Man figure in Jewish apocalyptic and in the earliest Palestinian Church (§ 5, 1), nevertheless the *title* "Son of Man" drops out of Hellenistic Christianity, and—except in John, where it has a special meaning—is found in the rest of the New Testament only in Acts 7:56 (it is not as a title that Rev. 1:13 and 14:14 use it). Thus it comes about that Son of Man (Barn. 12:10, Ign. Eph. 20:2) can be contrasted with the title "Son of God" to indicate the mere humanity of Jesus. *The title "the Christ"* (ὁ Χριστός) also gradually is lost and "Christ" becomes a proper name; later, accordingly, in Latin-speaking Christendom, Χριστός is no longer translated, but simply transliterated Christus. As a title, "the Christ" was not understandable to the Hellenistic world and any such paraphrase as "the King" (ὁ βασιλεύς), which would have corresponded in content, was out of the question, in the first place because "King" had no soteriological meaning; and also because it would have exposed the Christian message to the misconception that it was a political program.

The favorite combination in which the proper name Christ is used is "Jesus Christ." "Christ" as a title is still relatively frequent in Acts (side by side with "Jesus Christ"), likewise in Rev., Jn., and I, II Jn.; also in Eph. (and Col.), where, however, it is often hard to decide whether "Christ" is really meant as a title. Only rarely does Paul use it as a title. Peculiar to him is "Christ Jesus," in addition to which he less frequently uses "Jesus Christ." But in either order, "Christ" is a proper name, as his frequent expression "our Lord Jesus Christ" shows. For Paul, "Lord" and not "Christ" is Jesus' title. The Pauline "Christ Jesus" persists in the literature dependent upon Paul along with the usual "Jesus Christ" down to the Symbolum Romanum, which exhibits it.

But in contrast to the Son of Man of the apocalypses and in agreement with the Son of Man of the earliest Church, the eschatological Judge and Savior Jesus Christ is none other than the crucified Jesus of Nazareth whom God raised from the dead and appointed to his eschatological role. Hence, the message of the *raising* or the *resurrection of Jesus* is a basic constituent of the Hellenistic kerygma, as the "tradition" of I Cor. 15:1ff. expressly attests, no matter whether any or all of its formulation goes back to the earliest Church or not. Accordingly, when Paul speaks (I Thess. 1:9f., see above) of the expectation of Christ as the coming Savior he expressly describes him as him "whom [God] raised from the dead." According to Acts 17:31 God gave proof that He had appointed Christ Judge of the world by raising him from the dead (*cf.* I Clem. 42:3, where it is said of the apostles: "being fully assured by the resurrection of our Lord Jesus Christ"). That God raised him from the dead is a statement that, obviously quite early, was a constituent of more or less crystallized creedal statements, for without doubt Paul is alluding to a creedal formula in Rom. 10:9.

"If you confess with your mouth that Jesus is Lord and believe in your heart that God raised him from the dead, you will be saved."

II Tim. 2:8 similarly exhorts: "Remember Jesus Christ risen from the dead, descended from David, as preached in my gospel." Likewise in Pol. Phil. 12:2 the object of faith is "our Lord Jesus Christ and his Father, who raised him from the dead." Christian faith is "faith in the working of God who raised him (Christ) from the dead" (Col. 2:12, Eph. 1:20), and "who raised him from the dead" becomes a formula-like attribute of God (Col. 2:12, Eph. 1:20, Gal. 1:1, I Pet. 1:21; *cf.* Rom. 8:11, I Cor. 6:14, II Cor. 4:14; also Ign. Tr. 9:2, Sm. 7:1, Pol. Phil. 1:2, 2:2f.).

An inner causal *connection between Jesus' resurrection and the general resurrection of the dead* becomes a subject for reflection only in a different thought context which is of fundamental importance in Paul and Ignatius (see § 15, 4c). In many cases, for instance in the speeches of Acts, there is no mention of such a connection, and Christ's resurrection is regarded only as his legitimation (17:31, see above). Nevertheless, we probably should everywhere assume the implied thought that our hope is founded on the resurrection of Christ, as formulated, for instance, in I Pet. 1:3, 21—that the risen Christ has the keys of Death and Hades (thus Rev. 1:18)—that he has destroyed death by his own death or by his resurrection (Heb. 2:14f., Barn. 5:6f.). According to I Clem. 24:1, God made "the beginning" of the resurrection of the dead by raising Christ; but the idea of I Cor. 15:20ff. is not present here. On occasion, even Paul can confine himself to a simple "as . . . so" without stopping to demonstrate the inner connection: *as* God raised Christ, *so* He will also raise us (see I Cor. 6:14, II Cor. 4:14).

According to the oldest view, Christ's resurrection coincides with his *exaltation* to heavenly glory (§ 7, 3); this remains the dominant view in Paul and others of his time. But whether the exaltation was thought to be identical with the resurrection or whether it was thought to be a little later than the latter (as, for example, in Lk. 24:36ff., Barn. 15:9, Ign. Sm. 3)—in either case the two belonged most intimately together. And just as belief in his resurrection crystallized in formula-like statements, so did the conviction of his exaltation. God "exalted" Jesus Christ (Phil. 2:9f, Acts. 2:33, 5:30f.; *cf.* Jn. 3:14, 12:32, 34) and so he "sits at the right hand of God" (Rom. 8:34, Col. 3:1, Eph. 1:20, I Pet. 3:22, Acts 2:33, 7:55f., Heb. 1:3, 13; 8:1, 10:12, 12:2; *cf.* I Clem. 36:5, Barn. 12:10, Pol. Phil. 2:1), and the Symbolum Romanum summarizing this conviction calls him "he who sitteth at the right hand of the Father" (καθήμενον ἐν δεξιᾷ τοῦ πατρός).

Two proofs of the resurrection of Jesus were current: testimony of eye-witnesses (I Cor. 15:5ff., Acts 1:22, 2:32, 3:15, 10:40ff.) and discovered agreements with the Old Testament—"according to the scriptures" (I Cor. 15:4, Lk. 24:27 and 44f.; Acts 2:30ff., 13:34ff.).

It is self-evident that the preaching which proclaimed the risen Lord had also to speak in some way *of the earthly Jesus and his death.* Rom. 1:3f. and II Tim. 2:8—both formula-like traditional statements (§ 7, 5)—indicate that the risen and exalted Lord was called *Son of David* in reminiscence of his preliminary humanity. To the Gentile world this term could be neither significant nor impressive; it is indeed still current in Ignatius (Ign. Eph. 18:2, 20:2, Tr. 9:1; Rom. 7:3; Smyr. 1:1), but otherwise it has dropped out of use. Barn. 12:10 even protests against Jesus' sonship to David (§ 7, 5). But to them it was all the more significant and impressive *that the risen Lord was he who had previously died on the cross.* Here, too, formula-like expressions promptly form, as the tradition of I Cor. 15:3f. again indicates, and also the description at Rom. 4:25:

"who was put to death for our trespasses
and raised for our justification."

—a statement that had evidently existed before Paul and had been handed down to him (§ 7, 3).

Especially in *Ignatius,* the inter-relation between Christ's passion (πάθος) and resurrection is often emphasized. Both together belong to the οἰκονομία, the divine dispensation of salvation, according to Ign. Eph. 20:1. Faith regards both of them together—Phld. intr., 8:2, Sm. 7:2, 12:2 (see also Pol. Phil. 9:2). These two data are supplemented, according to Mg. 11:1, by Christ's preceding birth or, according to Phld. 9:2, by his "parousia" (here = into earthly life).

The same thing is shown by the predictions put into Jesus' mouth in Mk. (and also in Mt. and Lk.) carrying back the Hellenistic kerygma into the preaching of Jesus. These "predictions" speak in schematic form of Jesus' death (or of his being "delivered up"—παραδοθῆναι—as in I Cor. 11:23) and of his resurrection "after three days" (Mk. 8:31, 9:31, 10:33f.). In them we have, so to speak, a pattern of the christological kerygma, and we can see in the somewhat fuller third form how the pattern could be worked out in preaching. From the likewise highly schematic sermons of Acts we can then form a somewhat more graphic notion of concrete preaching (Acts 2:14–36, 3:12–26, 5:30–32, 10:34–43, 13:16–41). In them the focal point is the kerygma of Christ's death and resurrection (and exaltation), which, supported by scripture proofs, furnishes the basis for the call to repentance. Reference is made to the eschatological role of Jesus—in 3:20f. as a promise, in 10:42 in the description of him as "the one ordained by God to be judge of the living and the dead."

In the sermons of Acts we also see how the pattern in particular instances could be expanded by taking up this or that detail from the tradition of Jesus' life for illustrative purposes. Acts 10:37f., 13:23–25 say that Jesus' ministry attached itself to that of John the Baptist. Reference is made to Jesus' miracles in 2:22, 10:38f. The expression "that the Lord Jesus on the night when he was betrayed . . ." (I Cor. 11:23) permits us to recognize that the telling of the passion story was clothed with some details, for does that expression not imply that the reader was oriented about the events of that night? The same thing is indicated by the mention of Pilate, Acts 3:13, 13:28, and is corroborated by the description of Christ Jesus in I Tim. 6:13: "who in his testimony before Pontius Pilate made the good confession . . ." Ignatius also mentions Pilate in connection with the passion (and resurrection) of Jesus (Tr. 9:1, Sm. 1:2,

Mg. 11:1) and this tradition flows on down to "crucified under Pontius Pilate and buried" (τὸν ἐπὶ Ποντίου Πιλάτου σταυρωθέντα καὶ ταφέντα) in the Symbolum Romanum.*

In the case of the Hellenistic mission and its churches, as in that of the earliest Church (§ 7, 3), it is hard to say to what extent there was theological reflection on the *death of Christ;* i.e. to what extent positive significance for salvation was ascribed to it. In the beginning Christian missionary preaching was built upon motifs and concepts from the Old Testament-Jewish tradition; yet very soon views and concepts out of Hellenistic syncretism, especially the mystery religions, also show their influence. These are to be treated later (§§ 13 and 15). First, we will proceed to sketch the conceptualization of Jesus' death which was determined by the Old Testament-Jewish tradition so far as it can be grasped.

The interpretation of Jesus' death as an *expiatory sacrifice for sins,* which we found attributable to the earliest Church (§ 7, 3), was without doubt also presented in the Hellenistic-Christian mission. It finds expression in the numerous statements and formulas which describe the death of Christ as having taken place "for you" (ὑπὲρ ὑμῶν; or "for us," "for many," or "for sins," etc.). Such sentences and formulas are scattered throughout the New Testament and the immediately succeeding literature (lacking only in Acts, James, Jude, II Peter, Didache, II Clement, and Hermas), a fact which indicates that we are here dealing with a by no means specifically Pauline, but a general-Christian idea—this ὑπὲρ ("for . . ."), as everyone knows, has its solid place in the liturgy of the Lord's Supper. To this train of ideas belong those statements which expressly speak of Jesus' death as a sacrifice, or of his blood poured out for us, or where Jesus' death is described as the means of forgiveness or deliverance from sin, or of sanctification or purification, and the like. From the same tradition come the interpretations of Jesus' death as a covenant-sacrifice or passover-sacrifice. In the latter, it is still clearer than in the other cases that Jesus' death is regarded as primarily significant not for the individual, but for the Congregation, the "People" of God—a view characteristic of the Old Testament-Jewish tradition which is here determinative.

* On the reconstruction of the christological kerygma, see M. Dibelius, *Die Formgeschichte des Evangeliums,* 2nd ed. (1933), 14–25.

For descriptions of Christ's death as *sacrifice* (θυσία, προσθορά, etc.), see Eph. 5:2, Heb. 7:27, 9:26, 28; 10:10, 12, Barn. 7:3 among others; as passover-sacrifice I Cor. 5:7; as covenant-sacrifice, the texts of the Lord's Supper and Heb. 13:10. Besides the words of the Lord's Supper and texts referring to them, the following passages deal with the *blood of Christ*: Rom. 3:25, 5:9, Col. 1:20, Eph. 1:7, 2:13, I Pet. 1:2, 19, Acts 20:28, Heb. 9:11ff., 10:19ff., 29; 13:12, 20, Rev. 1:5, 5:9, 7:14, 12:11, 19:13, I Jn. 1:7, 5:6–8, I Clem. 7:4, 12:7, 21:6, 49:6; specialized mention of "sprinkling" (ῥαντισμός) with Christ's blood: I Pet. 1:2, Heb. 9:13, 10:22, 12:24, Barn. 5:1, *cf.* 8:1–3. (The Ignatian passages are of a different character.) The idea of *expiation* is expressed in the terms ἱλαστήριον (Rom. 3:25), ἱλασμός (I Jn. 2:2, 4:10) and ἱλάσκεσθαι (Heb. 2:17). That Christ's death provides *forgiveness* of sin is said in these passages among others: Rom. 3:25f., Eph. 1:7, the Matthean saying accompanying the sacramental cup (Mt. 26:28) and Heb. 9:11ff., Barn. 5:1, 8:3. The idea of *release* or *deliverance* (ἀπολύτρωσις, λύτρωσις or phrases employing verbs) is found: Rom. 3:24, I Cor. 1:30, Col. 1:14, Eph. 1:7, Heb. 9:12, 15, I Clem. 12:7, Mk. 10:45, I Tim. 2:6, Rev. 1:5, Tit. 2:14, I Pet. 1:18f., Barn. 14:5f. Similar is the idea of ransom: I Cor. 6:20, 7:23, Gal. 3:13, 4:5, Rev. 5:9, 14:3f., II Pet. 2:1. From among the many statements about *justification*, Rom. 3:24f. and I Cor. 6:11 (*cf.* 1:30!) and Herm. vis. III 9, 1 belong in this context. More characteristic for the sacrificial outlook which dominates this cluster of ideas are the statements about *sanctification*, I Cor. 6:11 (*cf.* 1:30), Eph. 5:25f., Heb. 2:11, 9:13f., 10:10, 29; 13:12, I Clem. 59:3, Barn. 5:1, 8:1, Herm. vis. III 9, 1. Likewise those on purification: Heb. 1:3, 9:13f., 22; Tit. 2:14, Eph. 5:25f., I Jn. 1:7, 9, Herm. sim. V 6, 2. The idea of *reconciliation* seems to be peculiar to Paul (Rom. 5:10f., II Cor. 5:18ff.); Col. 1:20f. and Eph. 2:16 vary the expression, each in its own way. That it is the Congregation that is founded by Christ's sacrifice comes to the fore—aside from its interpretation as a covenant-sacrifice—explicitly in Tit. 2:14, I Pet. 2:9, I Clem. 64, where "God's own (= peculiar) people" is mentioned and in Heb. 2:17, 7:27, 13:12, Barn. 7:5, 14:6, where simply "the People" is used in breviloquence for the same idea; Eph. 5:25ff., Acts 20:28 use Congregation, Church in the same sense. With still other expressions the same idea occurs: Rev. 1:5f., 5:9f., (*cf.* I Pet. 2:9).

As more and more exact and stable formulas grow out of the kerygma and gradually crystallize into creeds, so there develops out of the kerygma *the literary form: Gospel.* Its oldest exemplification is for us the Gospel of Mark. The following probable stages in the development of "the gospel" can be named: 1. The germ-cell is the kerygma of the death and resurrection of Jesus, so that the gospels have been rightly called "passion-narratives with an extensive introduction." * 2. The brief kerygma of the passion and Easter required fuller visualization, as I Cor. 11:23–26 and 15:3–7 show, and also assignment of a place in the divine plan of salvation; to fill this need, both the account of the Baptist and the proofs of fulfilled prediction were taken in. 3. The Christian "sacraments" (on which see § 13) had to be accounted for in the life of Jesus, the cultically worshiped Lord. 4. A visualization of what Jesus had done was also indispensable, since his life, considered divine, served as proof of his authority, as Acts 2:22, 10:38f. show. Hence the collecting of miracle-stories and their incorporation into "the gospel" are readily understandable. 5. Probably the apophthegms (i.e. short stories whose point is a saying of Jesus and which in part also report miracles, like Mk. 3:1–6, 22–30, etc.) also stood in the service of this visualization. These draw others after them, and the apophthegms occasion the inclusion of still other sayings of the Lord. 6. The reason that sayings of the Lord, which at first were handed down separately from the christological kerygma, came more and more to be taken up into "the gospel" (in Mark still sparingly, whereas Matthew and Luke combine the kerygma and the tradition of Jesus' sayings into a unity) is that, while missionary preaching continued, preaching to Christian congregations took on ever-increasing importance and for these already believing congregations, Jesus in the role of "teacher" had become more important again. 7. Finally both the moral exhortation and the regulations of the Congregation had to be accounted for in the life and words of Jesus (*cf.,* for example, I Cor. 7:10, 9:14). Hence, current exhortations and congregational regulations currently in force were also taken into "the gospel." Example: Mt. 18:15ff.

* M. Kähler, *Der sogenannte historische Jesus und der geschichtliche biblische Christus,* 2nd ed. (1896), 80, 1. *Cf.* Ad. Schlatter, *Der Glaube im NT,* 4th ed. (1927), 477: "For each evangelist the gospel was the account of Jesus' way to the Cross": see also Jul. Schniewind, *Th. R., NF.,* 2nd ed. (1930), 179–188, and *cf. Gesch. d. synopt. Trad.,* 2nd ed., 395–400.

5. The substantive "evangel" (τὸ εὐαγγέλιον) soon appears in Hellenistic Christianity as the technical term for the Christian proclamation, and for the act of proclaiming the verb εὐαγγελίζεσθαι was used, usually in the middle voice, sometimes also in the passive and with either a personal or a non-personal object. However, the substantive can also be used for the act of proclaiming. The meaning of noun and verb is simply "message," "news" and "proclaim," "preach." The etymological meaning "*good* news" or "to proclaim *good* news" had already worn off in the LXX (and in Philo), even though it does occasionally reappear. If the intention is to emphasize that *good* news is meant, a complementary object such as ἀγαθά (good things) is added to the verb (e.g. III Kingdoms 1:42, Is. 52:7, and, quoting the latter, Rom. 10:15). Hence, this verb can be used even where it does not mean "good" news at all (Lk. 3:18, Acts 14:15, Rev. 10:7, 14:6). Certain objects of content that are added to the verb (or objective genitives to the noun) also indicate that only the meaning "proclaim" is implied (e.g. to proclaim "the word" or "the word of the Lord," Acts 8:4, 15:35); and note especially that "preach the gospel" εὐαγγελίζεσθαι τὸ εὐαγγέλιον is, in use, completely synonymous with "to herald . . ." κηρύσσειν, "to announce . . ." καταγγέλλειν, "to speak . . ." or "to testify to" the gospel and, correspondingly, "gospel" is synonymous with "the message," "kerygma" (κήρυγμα), and "the word," ὁ λόγος.

"Evangel" (or its verb) is strictly a technical term only when it is absolute—that is, used without any object of content to designate the Christian message, but simply implying its clearly defined content. This usage of Paul, which in his footsteps became widely current, has no analogy either in the Old Testament and Judaism or in Gentile Hellenism, and the wide-spread view that "evangel" is a sacral term of the emperor-cult cannot be maintained. This absolute use of the word seems to have developed in Hellenistic Christianity gradually, but relatively quickly. In many cases "evangel" is limited by an objective genitive (e.g. "of the Kingdom," Mt. 4:23, 9:35 or "of Christ," Rom. 15:19, I Cor. 9:12, etc.) or the verb is supplemented by an object of content (e.g. the "Reign of God," Lk. 4:43, "Jesus" or an equivalent expression, Acts 5:42, 8:35, Gal. 1:15, etc.; or "faith," Gal. 1:23, etc.).

Whether the absolute use is earlier than Paul cannot be said with certainty. Evidently it does not go back as far as the earliest Church; for the substantive εὐαγγέλιον, lacking entirely in Q, is found in Mark only in secondary formations (in Matthew partly following Mark, partly in phrases peculiar to Matthew). It is absent from Luke but occurs twice in Acts. Among these occurrences it is used technically, i.e. absolutely, in these cases: Mk. 1:15, 8:35, 10:29, 13:10, 14:9, Mt. 26:13, Acts 15:7. The verb, in the passive voice, is used once in Q (Mt. 11:5 = Lk. 7:22) quoting Is. 61:1, is lacking in Mark and Matthew, but frequent in Luke and Acts, though technical only in the following cases: Lk. 9:6 (20:1), Acts 8:25, 40; 14:7, 21; 16:10. In the New Testament, outside of the synoptics, Acts, and Paul, the noun occurs in the technical use only in the deutero-Pauline writings (II Thess., Col., Eph., Past.); the verb occurs technically I Pet. 1:12, 4:6, Heb. 4:2, 6. Not infrequently (especially in Paul) "of God" as a subjective genitive or genitive of the author is added. Not only from Luke but also from the following the noun is completely absent: Jn., I–III Jn., Heb., Jas., Jd., II Pet., Rev. (here the word occurs only in a different sense, 14:6). The verb is absent from Mark and Matthew and the following: Jn., I–III Jn., Past., Jas., Jd., II Pet., Rev. In the literature of the succeeding period neither noun nor verb is found in Hermas; the noun occurs absolutely in Did. 8:2, 11:3, 15:3f., I Clem. 47:2, II Clem. 8:5, Barn. 5:9, Ign. Phld. 5:1f., 8:2 (uncertain text), 9:2, Sm. 5:1, 7:2; the verb with complementary infinitive I Clem. 42:3, with object Barn. 8:3; absolute: I Clem. 42:1 (passive) middle voice: Barn. 14:9 (quotation of Is. 61:1), Pol. Phil. 6:3.

The technical use of κήρυγμα, *"the message,"* and κηρύσσειν, *"to herald,"* developed quite analogously. The verb, which can also take objects: "the Reign" (Lk. 9:2, Acts 20:25, 28:31) or "Christ" or equivalents (Acts 8:5, 9:20, I Cor. 1:23, II Cor. 4:5, etc.) is used absolutely in the technical sense: Mk. 3:14, Acts 10:42, Rom. 10:14f., I Cor. 9:27, I Clem. 42:4, Barn. 8:3, Herm. sim. IX 16, 5; 25, 2. In the spurious close of Romans (16:25) the noun has the objective genitive "of Jesus Christ"; similarly, with "of the Son of God" Herm. sim. IX 15, 4; it is used absolutely I Cor. 1:21, 2:4, 15:4, II Tim. 4:17, Tit. 1:3, Herm. sim. VIII 3, 2, IX 16, 5. "The word" (ὁ λόγος) goes through the same development. It is often qualified by an objective genitive, such as: "of the Reign" (Mt. 13:19), "of salvation" (Acts 13:26), "of grace" (Acts 20:32), "of the cross" (I Cor. 1:18), "of reconciliation" (II Cor. 5:19), "of truth" (Col. 1:5, Eph. 1:13, II Tim. 2:15); *cf.* Pol. Phil. 3:2; "truth" and "life," without the article, are probably qualitative genitives (Jas. 1:18 and Phil. 2:16). But "the word," absolute, also denotes the Christian message: I Thess. 1:6, Gal. 6:6, Phil. 1:14 (variant), Col. 4:3, I Pet. 2:8, 3:1, Acts 6:4, 8:4, 10:36, 11:19, 14:25, 16:6, 32; 17:11, Barn. 9:3, 14:5, 19:10, Pol. Phil. 7:2, Heϱm. vis. III 7, 3; usually, it is true, "of God" is added as a subjective genitive or genitive of the author.

Acceptance of the Message is called πίστις (*"faith"* and *"belief"*) or πιστεύειν (*"believing"* or *"having faith"*). "Faith" as the acceptance of the kerygma is described at length in Rom. 10:14–17. The object of faith is "the kerygma" (I Cor. 1:21, Herm. sim. VIII 3, 2, etc.), "the gospel" (Mk. 1:15, Acts 15:7, I Cor. 15:2, etc.), "the testimony" (II Thess. 1:10, I Jn. 5:10), "the word" (Acts 4:4, Eph. 1:13, Barn. 9:3, *cf.* 16:9), the ἀκοή (lit. "the hearing"—i.e. "what is heard," "the preaching," Rom. 10:16, Jn. 12:38). The importance of this act of believing acceptance of the message, the act which makes the believing one a member of the Congregation, had the result that the concept "faith" took on a meaning which it had not had either in the Old Testament or in other ancient religions. In Christianity, for the first time, "faith" became the prevailing term for man's relation to the divine; in Christianity, but not before it, "faith" came to be understood as the attitude which through and through governs the life of the religious man. The way for this semantic development was prepared by the missionary activity of Judaism and of Gentile religions that were spreading their propaganda in the Hellenistic world. For it is only in missionary activity that "faith" comes to be conceived as conversion to a new religion⁄ that is being preached, whereas in the Old Testament, as in all folk-religions of antiquity, the worship of a people's own divinity (or divinities) is taken for granted.

In accord with the specific content of the primitive-Christian message, "faith" or "believing" means in Hellenistic Christianity: 1. belief in the one God (I Thess. 1:8f., Heb. 6:1, 11:6, Herm. mand. I 1; see above, 2, p. 67f.); 2. belief in God's saving deed in Christ (I Cor. 15:11, Rom. 4:24). The content of such belief may be given in a subordinate clause (ὅτι-clause, Rom. 10:9, I Thess. 4:14, Jn. 20:31, etc.), or it may be intimated by abbreviated expressions like "believing in Christ Jesus" (Gal. 2:16), or "in the Lord" (Acts 14:23, Herm. mand. IV 3, 3), "in the name of the son of God" (I Jn.

5:13), or others. The development of just this abbreviated expression to "believe (or belief) in" (or "believe" alone, and "belief" plus an objective genitive), foreign both to Greek diction and to the Old Testament (LXX), is significant. It is likewise significant that soon "believe" and "belief" (= "faith") are used technically, without any qualifying phrase. "Pistis," with or without a qualifying phrase, besides meaning faith-belief, can mean the act of becoming a believer (*Gläubigwerden:* I Thess. 1:8, Acts 20:21, etc.), or the state of being a believer (*Gläubigsein:* I Cor. 2:5, Did. 16:2, Barn. 4:9, etc.), or the attitude of having faith (*Gläubigkeit:* Rom. 14:1, I Thess. 1:3, etc.). "To believe" likewise sometimes means to become a believer (Rom. 10:14, Acts 18:8, etc.) and sometimes, especially in the participle, to be a believer, so that "the believing" (οἱ πιστεύοντες or οἱ πιστεύσαντες) can be substituted for "Christians" (II Thess. 1:10, Herm. sim. IX 19, 1f., etc.). Finally, *pistis,* whose first meaning, of course, is "faith" (*fides qua creditur*), comes to mean also "belief" (*fides quae creditur*—that which is believed: Rom. 10:8, Acts 6:7); then πίστις means simply "Christianity" (I Tim. 4:1, 6)—and "after the common faith" (Tit. 1:4 KJ) means "Christian." Except for this last stage all these possibilities of usage had developed before Paul's time and continued to be worked out by his contemporaries. Only against this background of missionary terminology does Paul's distinctive understanding of faith stand out.

Nevertheless, even aside from Paul the concept of faith underwent an *expansion and enrichment* in earliest Christianity. That is readily explained in the first place by the fact that πιστεύειν (have faith) can mean "to trust" and that this meaning easily combines with that of the missionary terminology. As "faith" and "confidence" are combined in Eph. 3:12, I Clem. 26:1, 35:2, so "trust" πεποίθησις takes the place of "believe" (I Clem. 58:1, 60:1, Herm. sim. IX 18, 5), and I Cor. 2:9, Phil. 3:4ff. also show the affinity of the two verbs. In the second place, this kinship of meaning made it inevitable that an Old Testament-Jewish conception of man's relation to God should influence the Christian relation to God called *pistis.* The conception referred to is expressed by the verbs הֶאֱמִין (feel safe, trust, believe), בָּטַח (trust), חָסָה (find refuge in), קִוָּה (wait for, hope in)—i.e. an understanding of man's relation to God as one characterized both by trust and hope and by fidelity and obedience. The influence of this conception on the meaning of Christian "faith" was all the more inevitable because the regular LXX rendering of הֶאֱמִין is precisely πιστεύειν (have faith, trust); the other verbs, especially בָּטַח, are frequently rendered πεποιθέναι ("to trust").

Heb. 11 shows with special clarity the richness of nuance that the concept "faith" has under these influences. While in verse 3, and especially verse 6, the technical sense of missionary terminology emerges, in general the meaning "trust" and "hope" prevails (especially vss. 9f., 11, 13, 17), yet in such a way that in addition the meaning "obedience" and "fidelity" again and again asserts itself (vss. 5, 7, 8, 24ff., 30f., 33). Elsewhere, also, the meaning "trust" breaks through: (e.g. Rom. 4:17-20; I Clem. 26:1, 35:2, II Clem. 11:1), or that of "hope" (esp. in I Pet.; *cf.* 1:5-9, 21; elsewhere: I Clem. 12:7, Barn. 4:8), or that of "fidelity" (II Tim. 4:7, I Pet. 5:9, Rev. 2:13, 13:10) or that of "obedience," which is especially marked in Paul but also appears elsewhere—for instance, in the use of πείθεσθαι ("obey," "be persuaded" as synonymous with πιστεύειν (believe, trust) in Acts 17:4, 28:24, and in the designation of unbelief as ἀπειθεῖν ("disobeying" in Acts 14:2, 19:9, I Pet. 2:8, 3:1, Joh. 3:36, etc.).

Does "faith" (or "to believe") also indicate a personal relation to the person of Christ, or does it mean only a relation to God on the basis of God's deed in Christ? The expression "believe in him" (εἰς αὐτόν), at any rate, does not in itself assert a personal relation to Christ, since this expression is only an abbreviation for the fuller one "believe that . . ." followed by a clause (e.g. "that God raised him from the dead," Rom. 10:9). The LXX never describes man's relation to God as "believing in" (εἰς), and the expressions the LXX does use for this purpose occur almost nowhere in the New Testament to designate a relation to Christ. The LXX-phrases are: πιστεύειν with the dative and no preposition, and πιστεύειν ἐπί ("believe upon") with the dative. (The verb with dative alone is used of Jesus in the New Testament really only in John, with the meaning: believe him (his words); with ἐπί and the dative, I Tim. 1:16.) Rarely πιστεύειν ἐπί with the accusative, which elsewhere is also used of God, is used of Christ (Acts 9:42, 11:17, 16:31, 22:19); the use of πρὸς τὸν κύριον Ἰησοῦν, Phm. 5 ("faith toward the Lord Jesus"), is unique. So the answer that must be given to the initial question is that faith as a personal relation to the person of Christ is an idea that was at first foreign to the earliest Christian message; for such an idea to arise there must have been other factors at work.

From this survey of the message of the one God and His judgment and of Jesus Christ as Judge and Savior the *questions* that arise are: Will faith in the one God take on the character of an "enlightened" *Weltanschauung* or will God be understood as the Power who determines human existence and demands the whole will of man? Though the question seems to have been decided in the second of these two ways by the eschatological message, the question remains: To what extent will eschatological faith outgrow mythological imagination? Will it confine itself to simply waiting for a coming event, or will it understand the present in the light of an already happened eschatological occurrence? In what manner will eschatology be retained when the expectation of the imminent End pales and dies out? Further: Will the significance of Christ remain confined to the role of the future Judge and Savior? How will theological reflection understand his death and resurrection? Will theological propositions take on the character of theoretical speculation, and will "faith in him" thereby become mere belief in dogmas? How will the idea of "faith" develop and how will theological thinking be guided by it?

§ 10. Church Consciousness and the Christian's Relation to the World

1. The eschatological missionary preaching of Christians was a startling thing to at least a large part of Gentile hearers in the Greek-speaking world—especially the message of the resurrection of the dead. The account in Acts indicates this in 17:18, 32 when it lets the Athenian audience pay special attention and take offense when the theme of "resurrection" is touched (see above p. 77). Likewise I Thess. 4:13ff. and I Cor. 15 show the novelty and the offensiveness of such preaching. And yet, on the other hand, the proclaiming of an imminent eschatological drama, a cosmic revolution, was for many hearers nothing basically new or unheard of. Eschatological ideas of this sort had long since penetrated the Hellenistic world from the orient. It must be recognized, of course, that they had been largely divested of their originally mythological character either by

taking on the character of a theory of natural science, as in the Stoic teaching of the world-periods with a "conflagration" (ἐκπύρωσις) at the end of each, or by becoming a poetic figure for a turning-point in political history, as in the *Carmen saeculare* of Horace or in Vergil's *Eclogue* IV, which sings the birth of a coming savior of the world.

As the announcement of a cosmic turning-point the eschatological preaching of earliest Christianity could therefore count upon being rather generally understood. But so far as it was the earliest Christian view *that the imminent eschatological event was to be the closing act of a history of salvation,* the history of the Chosen People, "true Israel"—so far as it meant fulfilment of the promise for the benefit of the Chosen People—the presuppositions for understanding it were not present. How could the consciousness of the earliest Church of being the eschatological "Congregation" of the end of days, for whom the promises were now being fulfilled—how could the consciousness of being "true Israel" find a footing in Hellenistic congregations?

This is a decisive question, the question of the *Church concept.* Does the salvation proclaimed by the Christian message mean only the salvation of the individual, the release of the individual soul from the contamination of sin and from suffering and death? Or does it mean salvation for the fellowship of God's people into which the individual is incorporated? The fact that the earliest Church in its mission simply took the latter for granted essentially differentiates it from the propaganda of other oriental religions of redemption; and, viewed historically, therein lies a basic reason for Christianity's triumph over them. In Christianity, the individual believer stands within the Congregation, and the individual congregations are joined together into one Congregation—the Church. Nor is the primary motive of this joining together the practical need of organization. Rather, churchly organization arose primarily out of the consciousness that the total Church exists before local churches do. An indication of this is the terminology: "ecclesia" denotes at first not the individual church at all, but the "people of God," the fellowship of the chosen at the end of days. This was the usage not only in the earliest Church (§ 6) but also in Hellenistic Christianity. And though *in the latter* the individual Church before long is called "ecclesia," and "church" can then be used in the plural, the idea is, nevertheless, that the individual church is the manifestation of the one Church.

Paul is evidently following the common Hellenistic terminology when he uses "ecclesia" sometimes of the total Church, sometimes of the local congregation. Following Old Testament and earliest Christian usage he calls the total Church "Church of God": I Cor. 10:32, 11:22, 15:9, Gal. 1:13. "Church" by itself can also mean the total Church: I Cor. 12:28, Phil. 3:6. In Acts, the singular occurs only once where it certainly means the total Church: 9:31; perhaps also 20:28 ("the Lord's Church"); this use is frequent in Col. and Eph. and occurs also I Tim. 3:5, 16, in the Didache (in prayer to God: "thy Church," 9:4, 10:5; also 11:11), in Hermas ("thy = God's holy Church" vis. I 1, 6; 3, 4—also, sim. VIII 6, 4, IX 13, 1; 18 2f. ("of God"), and hypostatized to a mythical figure in vis. II 4, 1; III 3, 3 IV 1, 3; 2, 2; sim. IX 1, 1f.). It occurs, further, in Barn. 7:11, II Clem. 2:1, 14:1–4, and in Ignatius, who calls the Church sometimes "holy" (Tr.), sometimes "God's" (Tr. 2:3) or "Jesus Christ's" (Eph. 5:1) or "God's and Christ's" (Phld. pr., Sm. pr.) but also speaks of "the Church" without qualification, meaning the total Church (Eph. 17:1, Phld. 9:1); in his writings also occurs for the first time "the universal (catholic) Church" (ἡ καθολικὴ ἐκκλησία, Sm. 8:2).

That the local church is a manifestation of the total Church is probably meant in the expression occurring a number of times in the prefatory greetings: "To the Church (of God) so far as it is present at . . . (τῇ ἐκκλησία [τοῦ θεοῦ] τῇ οὔσῃ ἐν . . .), (I Cor. 1:2, II Cor. 1:1, Ign. Eph., Mg., Tr., Phld.), in place of which may also be said: "to the Church of God sojourning in . . . (τῇ παροικούσῃ, I Clem. pr., Pol. Phl. pr.).

The idea of the priority of the total Church over the local church is also indicated in the equating of the Church with the "body of Christ" which comprises all believers. Paul practically makes this equation in I Cor. 12; it is then explicitly made in Col. 1:18, 24, Eph. 1:22f., 5:23ff., II Clem. 2:1; but especially is this so in the speculations which early arose over the pre-existence of the Church—i.e. an existence which preceded its historical realization—Eph. 5:32, II Clem. 14, Herm. vis. II 4, 1 (cf. II, 1, 6; 3, 4).

This *Church-consciousness* likewise stands behind the effort of the Jerusalem Church to exercise a sort of oversight over the Gentile-Christian congregations of which we hear both from Paul and in Acts. It also stands behind Paul's own efforts to establish and strengthen the connection of Gentile-Christian congregations with Jerusalem. Seen from this point of view, the decree of the "apostolic council" (Gal. 2:10) that Gentile congregations should contribute funds for the poor of the Jerusalem Church is historically almost the most important decree of the council, for there was a greater danger that the unity of the congregations might be lost than that the Gentile congregations might accept an obligation to observe the Torah. That is the reason for Paul's eagerness about the collections of the Gentile Christians for Jerusalem (I Cor. 16:1–4, II Cor. 8–9, Rom. 15:26f., 31).

2. It is due not only to the efforts of Paul that a church consciousness did promptly form and develop in Hellenistic Christianity, but also to the fact that the Hellenistic congregations in part grew out of Hellenistic synagogues, and to the fact that—whether in each instance the latter was the case or not—that the *Old Testament had been transmitted to them as a holy book.* Though the influence of the Old Testament was not equally great in all congregations, yet by and large it was probably everywhere operative. The epistolary literature of the New Testament, with the exception of the Johannine epistles, shows that all the way through a certain familiarity with the Old Testament is assumed in the readers—a familiarity that, of course, may be of very uneven extent. The same thing is shown by the writings of the apostolic fathers, among which only the letters of Ignatius rarely refer to the Old Testament. Perhaps there soon existed anthologies, i.e. collections of Old Testament quotations on specific points of teaching, as the agreement among composites of quotations in various writings seems to prove. Individual writings, such as Hebrews and Barnabas, are almost entirely devoted to exegesis of the Old Testament.

While it makes a difference, of course, whether the Old Testament is read as a book of oracles serving to demonstrate the fulfilment of prophecy, or as a code of ethics and moral examples, or as the document of the history of salvation—still these various motives all work together toward creating in the Christian Congregation a consciousness *of solidarity with Israel and its history.* Abraham is the "father" of believers from the Gentile world, too (Rom. 4:1, 12, 9:7f., Gal. 3:7, 29, Jas. 2:21, I Clem. 31:2, Barn. 13:7; *cf.* Heb. 2:16.

6:13), and the Christian congregations dispersed in the world are the people "of the twelve tribes in the dispersion" (Jas. 1:1; *cf.* I Pet. 1:1, Did. 9:4, 10:5, I Clem. 59:2). They are the "Israel of God" (Gal. 6:16), the "chosen generation" and the "peculiar people" (I Pet. 2:9), "the portion of His choice" (I Clem. 29:1); they are "the true circumcision" (Phil. 3:3). So it is perfectly natural that the Old Testament witnesses of faith are their models (Heb. 11); they are to "fix their gaze" (ἀτενίσωμεν εἰς) upon the Old Testament men of faith (I Clem. 9:2); it is to them that Christians are to "cleave" (κολληθῶμεν, I Clem. 31:1, 46:4). Job is the model of patience and piety (Jas. 5:11, I Clem. 17:3), Lot and Rahab, the harlot, are examples of hospitality (I Clem. 11f.), Abraham and David are models of humility (I Clem. 17f.), etc. When in I Clem., 55 models of conduct from heathen history are ingenuously placed by the side of those from the Old Testament, it is evident to what an extent the Church has already made the history in the Old Testament its own history. No less the Old Testament furnishes them warning examples not to be followed: the disobedience and faithlessness of Israel in the desert (I Cor. 10:6ff., Heb. 3:7ff.), the jealousy of Cain, Esau, and others (I Clem. 4; *cf.* Heb. 12:16). This principle holds: "Whatever was written (in the Old Testament) in former days was written for our instruction, that by steadfastness and by the encouragement of the scriptures we might have hope" (Rom. 15:4; *cf.* I Cor. 10:11, Rom. 4:23f., I Cor. 9:9f., II Tim. 3:16).

Teaching and exhortation of this sort are an after-effect of the Synagogue's homiletic tradition, and two *conventional forms of preaching* soon appear in the earliest Church which were already present in Judaism: 1. Summaries of the history of God's People which point out the divine teleology of that history. Examples of this in the New Testament are the speech of Stephen, Acts 7:2–47, and that of Paul in Pisidian Antioch, Acts 13:17–25 (41). 2. Series of examples collected from history according to a particular catch-word. Of this nature is Heb. 11; shorter, Jd. 5–7; I Clem. contains many examples of this sort (4–6, 7–8, 9–10, 11–12, 51:3–5).

It must be recognized, however, that the *relation of the Church to Israel's history* is a peculiarly paradoxical one because the course of events from Jacob-Israel down to the present is not a continuous history but one broken by the eschatological occurrence in Christ. That is, the eschatological Congregation is not simply the historical successor and heir of the empirical Israel of history but the heir of the ideal Israel, so to say, the people of God which the historical Israel was indeed called to be, but which, in point of fact, it never actually was. For it was indeed the elect People of God; but its election always hovered above and ahead of it, so to say, as goal and promise. Israel's election determined its history in consequence of divine guidance in bane and blessing. Still the election never came to realization—or, when it did, only in exceptions like Abraham, the strong in faith (Rom. 4, Heb. 11:8ff., etc.), David in whom God was pleased (Acts 13:22) and in whom the Holy Spirit spoke (Acts 1:16, Rom. 4:6, etc.), the prophets and men of faith who now serve as models to the Church. But as a whole, on account of its disobedience and faithlessness and especially for its rejection of Jesus, Israel itself has been rejected. The Christian Church is the true People of God.

But this contrast with the historical Israel, this eschatological break in history, does not mean discontinuity in the history of salvation but precisely the opposite—continuity. The election of the People of God, which, so to say, had been awaiting its fulfilment, is now being realized in the Christian Congregation, which in contrast to "Israel after the flesh" (Ἰσραὴλ κατὰ σάρκα, I Cor. 10:18 KJ) is the "Israel of God" (Gal. 6:16), whose members are the true sons of Abraham (see above, and Rom. 9:7ff., Gal. 4:22ff.) with whom God has concluded the new covenant (II Cor. 3:6ff., Heb. 8:6ff., and see below). The rejection of the historical Israel had been foreseen from the beginning in the Old Testament, as scripture proof teaches, and the new covenant had been predicted. The worship of ancient Israel had been a foreshadowing anticipation of the occurrence of salvation in Christ (Heb. 7–10).

As this paradoxical relation of the Christian Congregation to the historical Israel is expressed in the concept of the new covenant, so also in its use of the *concept "the People"* (λαός). This word, seldom used in post-Homeric Greek literature, had become in the LXX the distinctive designation for Israel in contrast to "the nations" (τὰ ἔθνη)—so also Lk. 2:32, Acts 15:14, 26:17, 23. "The people" had meant Israel in the still undifferentiated double sense of the Hebrew people of history and the Chosen People of God. The Christian Congregation appropriates this designation to itself, retaining only the second meaning.

The peculiarities of the LXX usage recur in Christian usage: "the People" by itself in the technical sense (Heb. 2:17, 13:12, Herm. sim. V 6, 2f.); "the People of God" (or, depending upon the context, "my," "thy," "His" = God's: Heb. 4:9, 10:30, Rev. 18:14, I Clem. 59:4, Herm. sim. V 5, 3; or "his" = "of the Son of God," Herm. sim. IX 18, 4); "the holy People" (patterned after Deut. 7:6, etc.: Barn. 14:6; *cf.* ἔθνος ἅγιον, "holy nation," I Pet. 2:9); "a chosen People" λαος περιούσιος (patterned after Ex. 19:5, etc.: Tit. 2:14, I Clem. 6:4; *cf.* "a peculiar People" [KJ] or "a special People" RSV marg. [I Pet. 2:9]); "people of the inheritance," Barn. 14:4. Expressions like these recur: "they shall be to me for a people" (after Jer. 38:33, LXX = 31:32 Heb.) Heb. 8:10; *cf.* Rev. 21:3, Acts 18:10, "to take a people . . . for his name" (Acts 15:14), "to prepare himself a people" (Barn. 3:6, 5:7, 14:6). The prophecy of "not-my-people" which shall become "my people" (Hos. 1:10, 2:23 = 2:1, 25 Heb.) is applied to the Gentile Christians in Rom. 9:25, I Pet. 2:10; so is the promise of Ex. 19:5f. (I Pet. 2:9).

The idea of the *"new covenant,"* of which the death of Christ is held to be the instituting sacrifice, was evidently alive before Paul, as the liturgy of the Lord's Supper which had come down to him indicates (I Cor. 11:25). This idea, which testifies that the idea of eschatological occurrence is oriented around the Congregation as the People of God (§ 9, 4) is equally important to Paul (II Cor. 3:6ff., Gal. 4:24) and to the author of Hebrews (8:8, 9:15, 12:24) who in 8:10ff. quotes at length from Jer. 38:31ff. LXX (31:30ff. Heb. text) the promise of the new covenant made to the People of God.

The covenant idea plays a special role in *Barnabas*, with a peculiar modification, however, inasmuch as the author claims that Israel, in reality, never had a covenant with God, since by its folly of idolatry it had from the beginning trifled away the Covenant intended for it on Sinai (4:6-8, 14:1ff.). Therefore, he does not speak of a "new" covenant but of the one covenant (13-14), which, however, did not pertain to the "former people" (13:1) but to the "new People" (5:7, 7:5), the Christian Congregation.

[98]

3. Church-consciousness includes *a consciousness of separateness and delimitation from the world.* This is attested, first, by the fact that the attributes of the eschatological Congregation (§ 6, 2) are appropriated by Hellenistic Christianity, too. Believers are called "the chosen" (ἐκλεκτοί, Rom. 8:33, II Tim. 2:10, I Pet. 1:1, 2:4, etc.) or "the called" (κλητοί, Rom. 1:6, I Cor. 1:24, Jd. 1, Barn. 4:13, or κεκλημένοι, Heb. 9:15, I Clem. 65:2, Herm. sim. VIII 1, 1; IX 14, 5) or "the saints" (ἅγιοι, Rom. 8:27, I Cor. 6:2, Heb. 6:10, I Clem. 56:1, Barn. 19:10, etc.) or "the sanctified" (ἡγιασμένοι, I Cor. 1:2, Acts 20:32, 26:18, etc.) or combinations of these terms, such as "called saints" (Rom. 1:7, I Cor. 1:2) and others (Rev. 17:14, I Clem. pr., Jd. 1).

This separateness is first of all, of course, a self-exclusion from *non-Christian cults of every sort.* This is seldom mentioned in the texts because it was taken for granted. The clear-cut alternative is formulated in II Cor. 6:14–7:1. The polemic of I Cor. 10:1–22 * is directed against idolatry equated with participation in a heathen cult. Otherwise, idolatry (or the idolater) is only mentioned almost parenthetically among other vices as a practice that is out of the question for a Christian (I Cor. 5:10f., 6:9, Gal. 5:20, I Pet. 4:3, Rev. 21:8, 22:15, Did. 3:4, 5:1, Barn. 20:1); it simply belongs to "the time that is past" (I Pet. 4:3; *cf.* Barn. 16:7, II Clem. 17:1) and it is significant that in Christianity, as in Judaism before it, the concept is widened and transferred to other vices (Col. 3:5, Eph. 5:5). Of course, there were scrupulous souls who declared even the eating of food that had been offered to idols prohibited (Rev. 2:14, 20, Did. 6:3), and this prohibition is also the first provision of the so-called "apostolic decree" (Acts 15:20, 29; 21:25). But this provision did not go into general effect, and Paul, dealing with this matter in I Cor. 10:23–11:1, declares the eating of food offered to idols permitted so far as any principle is concerned.

* The contradiction between this passage and I Cor. 8:7ff. (where participation in heathen cult-meals is forbidden only out of consideration for "the weak") is probably to be explained by regarding I Cor. 10:1–22 as an excerpt from Paul's precanonical letter to Corinth (mentioned at I Cor. 5:9). Paul evidently had heard that members of the Congregation were taking part in heathen cult-meals and assumed that this participation was meant as worship of the heathen divinities. Those concerned replied that this assumption was false, and that they, having "knowledge," regarded idols as non-existent and hence could perfectly well take part in those meals. Thereupon Paul answers with 8:1–13, 10:23–11:1.

But every kind of sorcery (φαρμακεία, Gal. 5:20, Rev. 21:8, 22:15, Did. 2:2, 5:1, Barn. 20:1) or magic (μαγεία, Did. and Barn., *loc. cit.*) is forbidden as it had been in Judaism. Included under the ban of sorcery is the invoking of demons, which, according to Jewish and early Christian conceptions, the beings worshiped in idolatry really are (I Cor. 10:20f., Barn. 16:7, etc.).

4. But the separateness of the Church is above all its *delimitation from the world as the sphere of moral uncleanness and sin.* The Congregation is the holy temple of God, set apart from all that is worldly and sinful (I Cor. 3:16f., II Cor. 6:16, Eph. 2:21f., Ign. Eph. 9:1, Mg. 7:2); it is the "spiritual house" of God (I Pet. 2:5; *cf.* I Tim. 3:15, Heb. 3:6, 10:21, Herm. sim. IX 13, 9; 14, 1). The eschatological Congregation really no longer belongs to the perishing world. Its members have no home here; their πολίτευμα (citizenship) is in heaven (Phil. 3:20), their City is the one that is to come (Heb. 13:14). Here, in this world, they are away from home on a pilgrimage.

> Christians in this world are "away from home," ἐπὶ ξένης, as Herm. sim. I:1 sets forth at length. They are "strangers, temporary sojourners" (παρεπίδημοι, I Pet. 1:1, 2:11), "resident aliens," not full citizens (πάροικοι, I Pet. 1:17, 2:11, II Clem. 5:1; later, Diogn. 5:5, 6:8, who, in chapter 5, deals with this theme at length). Hence a local congregation can be described as "sojourning" (παροικοῦσα) in its particular place (I Clem. pr., Pol. Phil. pr.). The basic motif of the Epistle to the Hebrews can be called "the pilgrim-people of God" [thus E. Käsemann in his book with that title: *Das wandernde Gottesvolk* (1939)]; it is thematically handled in Heb. 3:7–4:13 by parallelizing the Christian Church with Israel on its wandering toward the promised land. This foreignness of the Church is parallelized with Israel's situation in another respect when the Church is described as being in the dispersion (Jas. 1:1, I Pet. 1:1).

The thing to do, then, is "to gird up one's loins" for the pilgrimage (I Pet. 1:13, Pol. Phil. 2:1). In such expressions *the paradox of the Christian situation* comes to expression which Paul characterizes as the situation between "no longer" and "not yet" (Phil. 3:12–14). But Paul has only reduced to a brief formula what everywhere is described in a great variety of terms as the Christian situation.

For, on the one hand, the eschatological church-consciousness feels itself separated from the world—i.e. from "this age," from its own past, and from its heathen environment. For Christians are sanctified and purified (§ 9, 4, p. 85) inasmuch as Christ accomplished "purification for sins" (Heb. 1:3). Through baptism, the purification has been carried out on one and all (Eph. 5:26); it is "the bath of regeneration and renewal" brought about "by the Holy Spirit" (Tit. 3:5). As the occurrence of salvation is for Paul a new act of creation by God (II Cor. 4:6) and the Christian is "a new creation" (II Cor. 5:17), so for Barnabas it means the fulfilment of the promise, "Lo, I make the last things as the first" (6:13), namely: a new creation. It means that God renewed us by the forgiveness of sins (6:11) and created us anew: "See, then, we have been molded (ἀναπεπλάσμεθα) anew" (6:14; *cf.* 16:8: "We became new, being created again from the beginning"). Or, as I Pet. 1:23 says, "You have been born anew."

However, when God is called he "who has begotten us again to a living hope" (I Pet. 1:3), that brings to the fore the paradox of which we have spoken: We are what we are in hope. For that is the other side of the Christian situation: though Christian existence can, on the one hand, be described by the indicatives—we are sanctified, we are purified—nevertheless, so long as it moves within this world, it stands under the imperative. Though, on the one hand, it is separated from its past and its environment, yet this separation must be newly made again and again. The *pure* and *sanctified* are exhorted: "Let us cleanse ourselves from every defilement of body and spirit and make holiness perfect in the fear of God" (II Cor. 7:1). Life must no longer be "conformed" (συσχηματίζειν) to the passions of one's earlier heathen period (I Pet. 1:14), one must "no longer live as the Gentiles do" (Eph. 4:17), but "be holy" and "conduct one's self in the fear of God throughout the time of one's pilgrimage" (I Pet. 1:15–17). What God wills is sanctification; thereto He called us (I Thess. 4:3–7). One must "keep one's self unstained from the world" (Jas. 1:27, II Pet. 3:14). Baptism must be kept "pure and undefiled" (II Clem. 6:9; *cf.* 7:6, 8:6). What has happened in principle must be brought to reality in practice: "Put to death therefore what is earthly in you . . . seeing that you have put off the old nature with its practices and have put on the new nature which is being renewed . . ." (Col. 3:5, 9f.), or "put off your old nature which belongs to your former manner of life . . . and be renewed in the spirit of your minds, and put on the new nature created after the likeness of God . . ." (Eph. 4:22–24). They who are new creations must be told: "create (reading ἀνακτίσασθε, not ἀνακτήσασθε) yourselves anew in faith" (Ign. Tr. 8:1). They who have been called out of darkness into light (I Pet. 2:9) must "cast off the works of darkness and put on the armor of light" (Rom. 13:12f., I Thess. 5:4ff.). "In the midst of a crooked and perverse generation" Christians must "shine," "blameless and innocent," "like the stars" (Phil. 2:15) and distinguish themselves from the Gentiles by their good conduct (I Pet. 2:12). They must go outside the "camp"—i.e. the world—to Christ (Heb. 13:13). We must "forsake our sojourning in this world, and do the will of him who called us, and not fear to go forth from this world" (II Clem. 5:1), and that means: "lead a holy and righteous life, ànd regard the things of this world as not our own (ἀλλότρια), and not desire them" (II Clem. 5:6; on the concept ἀλλότρια, "not our own, foreign" cf. Ign. Rom. pr., Herm. sim. I 3 and 11). The present world and the world to come are enemies, hence: "We must bid farewell to this world to consort with the one to come" (II Clem. 6:3–5).

It is not surprising that in the Hellenistic sphere, *asceticism* early became a means of delimitation from the world, for Hellenism knows many an ascetic movement. It does not mean asceticism proper, of course, when the eating of meat offered to idols is forbidden (Acts 15:20, 29; 21:25, I Cor. 8–10, Rev. 2:14, 20), or when fasting is recommended to strengthen prayer (Acts 13:3, 14:23, I Cor. 7:5 secondary koine-text, Did. 1:3), or to prepare for the reception of revelation (Acts 13:2, Herm. vis. II 2, 1; III 1, 2, etc.), or when regular fasting is prescribed on two days of the week (Did. 8:1). Did. 6:3, however, does combine the prohibition of food offered to idols with ascetic abstinence. *Food-asceticism* on principle (abstinence from meat and wine) is the standpoint of the "weak" (Rom. 14), whom Paul treats with consideration. It is not clear to what extent the demands for abstinence made by the false teachers condemned in Col. 2:16ff. were truly ascetic or whether they were simply harmless ritual commandments; the former seems to be the case with the false teachers combatted in I Tim. 4:3 (*cf.* Tit. 1:15), who also urged sexual asceticism. *Sexual asceticism* is even for Paul an ideal (I Cor. 7:7). It is evidently recommended in the merely suggestive words of Did. 6:2, and is probably meant in the enigmatic sentence Did. 11:11, *cf*. Eph. 5:32. At any rate, the ideal of chastity stands in high regard according to Rev. 14:1–5, I Clem. 38:2, 48:5, Ign. Pol. 5:2, and II Clem. 12 and 14:3 plead for it. A special form of sexual asceticism is already presupposed in I Cor. 7:25, 36f.—i.e. a "spiritual" marriage in which ascetic and virgin live together.* A vivid picture of this practice is furnished by Herm. sim. IX 11. The ascetic requirement of *renunciation of property* is not at first made, though distrust of wealth is great (I Tim. 6:6–10, Heb. 13:5, Jas. 5:1–6, and especially Herm.—e.g. vis. III 6, 5–7; 9:2–6; sim. II).

Such exhortations are naturally heightened again and again by *reference to the imminent end of this world* (e.g. Rom. 13:11f., I Thess. 5:1ff., I Pet. 1:5ff., 4:7, Heb. 10:25ff., Did. 16, Barn. 21:3, Ign. Eph. 11:1, Ign. Pol. 3:2, Herm. vis. II 3, 4). Paul expects to experience the parousia of Christ with the majority of his contemporaries (I Thess. 4:17; "we who are alive, who are left"; *cf.* I Cor. 15:51) and, of course, he was not alone in holding that view. In time, of course, the delay of the parousia becomes noticeable and references to it have to be strengthened by exhortations to be patient (Mk. 13:10, Jas. 5:7ff., Heb. 10:36ff.; indeed, even doubt of its coming must be combatted (II Pet. 3, I Clem. 23, II Clem. 11f.). The warning becomes necessary not to regard one's self as "already made righteous" (Barn. 4:10), "never to rest, as being called, and slumber in our sins" (Barn. 4:13). Nor do the exhortations "to watch" and "be sober" (§ 9, 3, p. 76) die out.

Since "forgetfulness of having been cleansed from former sins" (II Pet. 1:9) comes over many, the *exhortation to make Christian living a reality* takes on a sharper tone: "Cleanse your hands, you sinners, and purify your hearts, you men of double mind!" (Jas. 4:8). And while Heb. 6:4ff. warns: "it is impossible to restore again to repentance those who have once been enlightened" (I Jn. 1:7, 9), pointing to the blood of Christ which cleanses us, exhorts the believer to constant confession of sin. While I and II Clem. take for

---

* The woman in this relation was later technically known as παρθένος συνείσαχτος and *virgo subintroducta* or, rarely, *synisacta*. An abstract noun seems not to have developed as a name for the practice, but German scholars have created and use the barbarism: *Syneisaktentum*. If the need for a technical term with this meaning should ever be felt in English, "subintroduction" would be more apposite.

granted that repentance is the constant accompaniment of the Christian life, according to Hermas God is just once more offering a last renewed opportunity for repentance and hence offers the possibility of a second "renewal" (ἀνακαίνωσις or ἀνανέωσις, vis. III 8, 9; 13, 2; cf. vis. III 12, 3; sim. VIII 6, 3; 14, 3). Hence, now is heard anew the exhortation: "Therefore purify your heart from all the vanities of the world" (mand. IX 4, sim. V 3, 6; cf. vis. III 8, 11, mand. IX 7, XII 3, 4; 6, 5; sim. VII 2, VIII 11, 3).

Stereotyped forms of exhortation develop. As the gods of the Gentiles are "vain" (μάταιοι, Acts 14:15, imitating the LXX) and the Gentile way of life is "vain" (I Pet. 1:18) or "a walking in futility" (ἐν ματαιότητι, Eph. 4:17; cf. Rom. 1:21), as their understanding is "darkened by vain desires" (II Clem. 19:2), so "vain" with its derivatives becomes the specification for the worldly in general. I Clem. urges the giving up of "empty and vain cares" (7:2) or of "vain toil" (ματαιοπονία, 9:1); Pol. Phil. urges the renunciation of "the futility of the many" (7:2) or "empty vanity" (κενὴ ματαιολογία, 2:1). Barnabas cries: "Let us flee from all vanity" (4:10). Hermas speaks of "the vain desire(s) of this world" (mand. XI 8; XII 6, 5) and demands purification "from all the vanities of this world" (mand. IX 4, sim. V 3, 6).

As Gentile conduct is a walking *"in lusts"* (Rom. 1:24, Tit. 3:3, I Pet. 1:14), so ἐπιθυμίαι (lusts, passions, desires) become the earmark of the world. They are called "worldly" passions (Tit. 2:12, II Clem. 17:3) or "fleshly" (I Pet. 2:11; cf. Gal. 5:16, 24, Eph. 2:3) or "carnal and bodily" (Did. 1:4). I Jn. 2:16f. combines the two descriptions: "all that is in the world, the lust of the flesh . . . is of the world. And the world passes away and the lust of it." I Clem. 28 mentions "foul desires" (ε. μιαραί). Related to "passion" is "care" or "anxiety." As Paul warns against being "anxious about worldly affairs" (I Cor. 7:32–34), so I Clem. 7:2 warns against "empty and vain cares."

Cares entangle one in the "preoccupations of daily living" (Herm. vis. III 11, 3, vis. I 3, 1, mand. V 2, 2), or the "occupations of this world" (Herm. mand. X 1, 4; cf. vis. III 6, 5, sim. VIII 8, 1f.; IX 20, 1f.)—and these are what Hermas' exhortations are directed against; his book as a whole is a penitential sermon against the secularization of Christianity.

The Christian attitude toward the world is also described in *stereotyped phrases.* A much-used term for it is "abstaining" (ἀπέχεσθαι): "abstaining from immorality" (I Thess. 4:3), "from every form of evil" (I Thess. 5:22), "from the passions of the flesh" (I Pet. 2:11; *cf.* Did. 1:4), "from all unrighteousness" (Pol. Phil. 2:2), or, after a catalogue of vices, "from all these things" (Pol. Phil. 5:3), "from every evil desire" (Herm. vis. I 2, 4: *cf.* III 8, 4, mand. XI 8, XII 1, 3; 2, 2) "from the works of the devil" (mand. VII 3), and, referring to specific vices (mand. II 4, III 5, IV 1, 3 and 9, V 1, 7; 2, 8, IX 12).

As Paul urges the believer to "cast off (ἀποθέσθαι) the works of darkness" (Rom. 13:12), so Col. 3:8 says: "now cast off also all these" (a catalogue of vices follows); Eph. 4:22 (see above) is similar. *Cf.* also: Eph. 4:25, I Pet. 2:1, Jas. 1:21, Heb. 12:1, I Clem. 13:1, 57:2, II Clem. 1:6. A related idea (ἀποτάσσεσθαι, "bid farewell") is expressed in II Clem. 6:4f. and 16:2.

The positive correlative to "casting off" in Rom. 13:12 is "putting on" (the armor of light), a figurative expression which also occurs in I Thess. 5:8, Eph. 6:11, 14, and, as a pure metaphor, in Col. 3:12. Col. 3:8ff. speaks of "putting on" the new man in contrast to "putting off" (ἀπεκδύεσθαι), combining this expression with the metaphorical use of "put away" (ἀποθέσθαι), while Eph. 4:22–24 mixes the two expressions. This metaphorical "putting on" (already current in the Old Testament and Judaism) is an expression especially favored in Hermas—e.g. mand. I:2, "you shall cast away from yourself all wickedness, and shall put on every virtue of righteousness"; see further: vis. IV 1, 8, mand. II 3f., V 2, 8, IX 7 and 10; X 3, 1 and 4; XI 4, XII 1, 1; 2, 4; sim. VI 1, 2 and 4; 5, 3; VIII 9, 1, IX 29, 3; also Ign. Pol. 1:2.

Christians can be and are described as "fleeing from the corruption that is in the world because of passion" (II Pet. 1:4) or "fleeing from the defilements of the world" (II Pet. 2:20), and the exhortation to "flee" (φεύγειν) occurs again and again. That from which one is to flee may be "idolatry" (I Cor. 10:14) or "fornication" (I Cor. 6:18) or the vices of greed (I Tim. 6:11, *cf.* 6–10) or "youthful passions" (II Tim. 2:22), or a whole list of vices (I Clem. 30:1) or "ungodliness" (II Clem. 10:1). Equivalent to this expression are "put aside (ἀπολείπειν, I Clem. 7:2, 9:1, 28:1, Pol. Phil. 2:1, 7:1) and "forsake" (καταλείπειν, II Clem. 5:1, 10:1).

Two further *types of Christian preaching* (see above, p. 96) develop in which the novelty of Christian living is described in contrast to the worldly past according to the scheme:

"formerly . . . now": 1. Once salvation (God's plan of salvation) was hidden; now it has been revealed. This motif first appears in I Cor. 2:7ff., then Col. 1:26f., Eph. 3:4f., 9f.; its overtones are heard in II Tim. 1:9f., Tit. 1:2f.; I Pet. 1:20 uses it for exhortation, and it is woven into a doxology at Rom. 16:25f. (non-Pauline!). 2. Once we were heathen, sunk in darkness and vice —now we are illumined and cleansed by God. Paul sets the pattern for this motif, too: Rom. 6:17f., 7:5f., 11:30, Gal. 4:3ff., especially I Cor. 6:9ff. in connection with a catalogue of vices. Otherwise it occurs: Col. 3:5ff., Tit. 3:3ff.; *cf.* I Pet. 4:3f.; without the vice-catalogue: Eph. 2:1ff., 11ff., I Pet. 2:25. II Clem. 1:6ff. indicates that this scheme was expanded in actual preaching.

5. Church-consciousness and the consciousness of eschatological delimitation from the world can be termed a *dualistic view*—it is the eschatological dualism of Jewish tradition. Though this contains a cosmological motif in the expectation of the great final catastrophe of the world, still it is not speculatively interested in cosmology. Nevertheless, the question arises whether the purity of the eschatological motif will be maintained or whether cosmological speculations will take root. Since a negative attitude toward the world goes hand in hand with eschatological consciousness—the attitude of "abstention" or "flight," etc.—the further question arises whether eschatological delimitation from the world will be understood as an inner de-secularization arising out of what one already positively has, or whether it will be a purely negative attitude to the world taking rise from the expectation that he who now flees the world will have his renunciation richly compensated by future heavenly goods. The historical situation of the earliest Church being such as it was, the further possibility existed that the eschatological consciousness of delimitation from the world might mingle with or even be replaced by other motifs which were also grounds for a negative attitude toward the world. *Stoic ideas* could influence Christian thought. An easy point of contact could be the Stoics' battle against "desire" and their exhortation to "renounce" (ἀπέχεσθαι) and to "regard as foreign" (ἀλλότρια ἡγεῖσθαι) to one's self all that is not truly in one's power: i.e. everything external. Indeed the occurrence of this expression (Heb. 11:9, Herm. sim. I 1, II Clem. 5:6) in itself indicates Stoic influence, at least in terminol-

ogy. Furthermore * *the motifs of Gnostic dualism* could operate on Christian thinking even in conjunction with Stoic ideas, since for both Stoicism and Gnosticism the sphere of flesh and sensuality is degraded, although "the Spirit," which is the opposite of sensuality, is differently conceived by the two. Motifs of both kinds could become the foundation for a basically different asceticism from that of eschatological de-secularization (see above, 4).† Already in Paul the ascetic motif enters into a peculiar combination with the eschatological (espec. I Cor. 7); so also later in Hermas when, for example, he exhorts: "Guard this flesh of yours pure and undefiled" (Sim. V 7, 1). II Clem. 8:4, 6 also urges: "Keep the flesh pure and the seal (of baptism) undefiled," and presents queer, somewhat hazy ideas about the "self-control" (15:1) that is to be practiced in regard to the flesh (14:3–5). Especially Ignatius shows this influence; but with that we shall deal later (§ 15).

One is probably justified in saying that the *consciousness of the Gnostics* of constituting a community bound together in a mysterious unity and foreign to the world furnishes a certain analogy to Church-consciousness, a part of which is the consciousness of being delimited from the world. And actually the Fourth Gospel's consciousness of Church unity is influenced by Gnosticism, as we shall later show. The Epistle to the Hebrews also demonstrates how a churchly-eschatological and a Gnostic understanding of Christian existence can combine (§ 15). Nevertheless Gnosticism lacks the specific characteristics of Church-consciousness: a knowledge of its solidarity with the history of the People of God and a binding tie to the document of salvation, the Old Testament. In this detail, of course, the synagogue-congregations furnish an analogy; but otherwise the eschatological-churchly consciousness is something completely unprecedented in the Hellenistic world. That will change, of course, to the extent that the consciousness of being "the Israel of God," "the people of God" gives way to the notion of being a "third kind," τρίτον γένος, in contrast to Greeks (Gentiles) and Jews. The phrase occurs for the first time in Kerygma Petri 2: "For what the Greeks and the Jews have is antiquated, but it is we Christians

---

* *Cf.* M. Dibelius in the supplement to Lietzmann's *Handbuch* on Herm. sim. I 1. Sim. I, as a whole, is written in the style of the Cynic-Stoic diatribe.
  † See above, see below = these references always refer to something which precedes or follows *within the same section* (§).

who worship Him (*sc.* God) in a new way, a third kind, τρίτῳ γένει, (of worship)." But here it means the Christian manner of worship and is not a designation for Christianity itself,* as it later became. But the next question is: how will the problem of the Church's relation to Judaism be solved—a problem arising from its consciousness of being the true Israel—and how will the authority of the Old Testament be understood?

§ 11. The Church's Relation to Judaism and the Problem of the Old Testament

1. On the one hand *the relation to Judaism* means for Hellenistic Christianity the relation to the form of *Jewish Christianity* represented by the *earliest Church* in Palestine. For it, as we have seen (§ 8, 1), had not severed itself from Judaism and had not cut the bands between the eschatological Congregation and the Jewish People. It took for granted at first that the non-Jew who wanted to belong to the Congregation of salvation had to be circumcised and place himself under the Law—i.e. had to become a Jew (§ 8, 2). In contrast to this attitude there developed out of the mission of Hellenistic Jewish-Christians a Hellenistic Christianity of which circumcision was not required and which did not obligate itself to keep the Law. This Torah-free Gentile Christianity represented by Barnabas and Paul achieved recognition by the earliest Church at the apostolic council (§ 8, 2). The fact that in spite of the agreement Jewish-Christian Torah-enthusiasts, the so-called Judaizers, propagandized for the Law in Gentile-Christian congregations and even penetrated the Pauline mission field—as Galatians testifies and Philippians hints—need not be pursued further here, since, for the history of early Christianity and the formation of its theology, it remained an episode whose only importance is that it forced Paul into the theological discussion to which we owe the letter to the Galatians.

The problem of the Church's relation to Judaism obviously took a somewhat different turn in other Hellenistic churches in which the Christian congregation had grown out of the synagogue—in that at Rome, for instance, but presumably also in many another. Here *debate with Judaism itself* was necessary, as Paul's letter to the

* On which see Ad. v. Harnack, *Mission u. Ausbreitung*, 3rd ed., I 238–267.

Romans testifies. For it does not polemize against "Judaizers," nor is it occasioned like Galatians by the intervention of rival missionaries who want to compel Roman Christians to adopt circumcision. Rather, it develops in purely theoretical fashion the principle of Christian faith in antithesis to the principle of the Jewish Torah-religion. Such debate with Judaism did not need by any means to arise out of a practical situation of conflict, but was just as likely to arise as the necessary consequence of *reflection on the part of the Christian believer* upon the essence and the foundations of his faith. To such theological reflection especially Hebrews and the Epistle of Barnabas bear witness.

The problem arose from the simple fact that Hellenistic Christianity had taken over the Old Testament and acknowledged its authority but at the same time denied the validity of the Old Testament Law for Christians. How was this denial to be backed up? How was the Law, which after all was a basic portion of the authoritative book of revelation, to be interpreted?

2. The Torah-free attitude of Hellenistic Christianity is by no means simply a result of *Paul's* struggle against the "Judaizers," and much less was his defense of freedom from the Law either then or later the *only* one in force. Side by side with his solution of the problem, other *possibilities* not only existed but were realized in practice. A survey of these possibilities comes down far beyond the time of Paul and must do so. For it is clear that all these possibilities were present from the beginning in the historical situation; the scantiness of the sources makes it impossible to say where and how soon they were realized. And it is not only possible but probable that later attested ideas were being presented before and during Paul's time. The meaning and importance of Paul's teaching on the Law can be recognized and appreciated only after a survey of all the possibilities has been made. The most important types of possibility are the following:

a. *Radical Gnosticism.* Gnosticism is not a phenomenon that first appeared within the Christian Church. It cannot be described as a speculative Christian theology under the influence of Greek philosophical tradition. It is not properly regarded as the "acute Hellenization" of Christianity, as Harnack in his time supposed. It has its roots in a dualistic redemption-religion which invaded Hellenism from the orient. Seen as a whole, it is a phenomenon parallel or competitive to the Christian religion. Each of these movements, the Gnostic and the Christian, influenced the other in many ways, but of that we shall have to speak later on. At any rate, there was very soon a Christian Gnosticism which, in its radical form, completely rejected the Old Testament, thus constituting the most extreme of the possibilities to be surveyed; that is why it is here named first.

Here the God of the Old Testament, creator of the world and giver of the Law, is distinguished from the God of Christian faith, the God of redemption whose revealer is Christ. In this, too, many differentiations are possible, depending upon whether in a particular case the Old Testament God is considered a being subordinate to the highest God, following His intentions, though with limited power, wisdom, and mercy, or whether He is thought of as a being inimical to the highest God, self-impelled and disobedient, the very Satan himself. The Old Testament with its Law is, accordingly, either an antiquated proclamation by a subordinate god or it is a Satanic law. In either case, it is no longer valid for the Christian. The practical consequence that is then drawn from such a view can be a libertinistic ethic, but not inevitably; for such a view also contains the possibility of an ascetic ethic.

b. *The Epistle of Barnabas.* This not definitely dateable document, certainly written after 70 A.D. and before 140 and very likely after 100, deals thematically with the problem of the Old Testament and claims to teach the right understanding of it which has at last been made available to Christian faith or to Christian *"gnosis"* (knowledge). For the Jews—this is its author's thesis—completely misunderstood it: "an evil angel misinstructed (ἐσόφιζεν) them" (9:4; *cf.* 10:9). Israel never had a covenant with God; for when Moses came down from Sinai with the tables of the Law and saw the people fallen into the sin of idolatry he smashed the tables "and so their covenant was broken in order that the covenant of Jesus the Beloved should be sealed in our hearts in the hope of our faith in him" (4:6–8; *cf.* 13–14). How then is the Old Testament to be understood? Allegorically. By this method two things are to be found in the Old Testament. The first is ethical instruction; that is how the cultic and ritual commandments are to be interpreted. The law of circumcision means circumcision of the heart (ch. 9); the unclean beasts that are not to be eaten mean evil men with whom one is not to associate (ch. 10), and so on. And, second, the Old

Testament contains predictions of Christ and Christian salvation (ch. 5–8). Both in cultic laws and in narratives (e.g. the 318 servants of Abraham, 9:8) the author finds the cross of Christ foretold; he reads out of the ancient texts the proclamation of the gospel (8:3), the return of Christ (7:9), the future glory of the faithful (6:16ff.), and so forth.

The real problem of the Law as the way of salvation—i.e. the problem of legalism, the problem of good works as the condition for participation in salvation—escaped the author. "The ordinances of the Lord" (δικαιώματα κυρίου, 2:1, 10:11, 21:1) have taken the place of the laws of the Old Testament. These constitute "the new law of our Lord Jesus Christ" (2:6), described, however, as "being without the yoke of necessity"—but this description is applied only in one direction: This law requires no "man-made sacrifice."

c. *The Epistle to the Hebrews.* For it the Old Testament as a whole is prediction of Christ and his work. Christ himself speaks in the Old Testament (2:12f., *cf.* Ps. 22:23, Is. 8:17f.; 10:5–7, *cf.* Ps. 40:7–9). Christ was pre-depicted in Moses as the one "faithful in all God's house" (3:1–6), and in Melchizedek as the high priest (7:1–10). But the author's chief interest is in the interpretation of the Old Testament cult. He has in common with Barnabas the method of allegorical interpretation; but in contrast to him the author to the Hebrews is certain that the Old Testament laws once were in force in their literal sense, which only Christ has abolished. "A former commandment is set aside because of its weakness and uselessness" (7:18). But why was the always weak and useless Law of the Old Testament ever given at all, then? Because it contained "the shadow of the good things to come, not the essence of these things themselves" (10:1 tr.); it typifies and presages what will perfectly appear in Christ. For "the Law appoints men in their weakness as high priests, but the word of the (divine) oath, which came later than the Law, appoints a Son who has been made perfect forever" (7:28). Christ's sacrificial blood accomplishes what the blood of the Old Testament sacrifice could not (9:15–28).

Just why all this prefiguration of Christ's deed of salvation, which no one in the time before Christ could understand, should have been instituted at all, it would probably be fruitless to ask the author in his satisfaction over his interpretation.

Nor did he any more than Barnabas reflect over the real problem of legalism. He does not mention the ethical commandments of the Old Testament; but he repeatedly emphasizes that Christians much more than Jews, or Israel, must beware of all "transgression" and "disobedience," since an incomparably sterner judgment will befall erring Christians than erring Jews (2:2f., 10:28f., 12:25). It is significant of the author's own legalistic manner of thinking that he rejects the possibility of a second repentance (6:4ff.).

d. *I Clement.* This letter was written in 95 or 96 A.D. from the Roman Church to the Corinthian. The problem we are discussing does not seem to exist for its author; rather he quite naively claims the Old Testament as a Christian book. He assumes as a matter of course that the cultic and ritual laws of the Old Testament are no longer valid. On one occasion he offers a Hellenistic idea as the reason for this: "The Sovereign (= God) . . . is in need of nothing: he asks nothing of anyone, save that confession of sin be made to him" (52:1). Yet he also assumes that the cultic laws were once a valid ordinance of God. They serve him as an analogy to the regulations of the Christian Congregation (40, 41). He has no need of allegory. Only once does he use this art—when he interprets the red thread which Rahab the harlot hung on the house as a sign to the Israelites to mean the blood of Christ (12:7f.). Rather, the knowledge" (γνῶσις, 40:1, 41:4) that he possesses is the art of making the Old Testament useful for practice and edification. For Christians it is the book of ethical models. It furnishes the "patterns" and "models," to be imitated by Christians, of the "commandments and ordinances of the Lord" (or "which are given us by God," 2:8, 58:2, etc.).

And the author knew Romans and I Corinthians! But he does not sense the Pauline problem of legalism. Like Paul (Rom. 4:7), he quotes Ps. 32:1f., "blessed are those whose iniquities are forgiven," etc. (50:6f.), but Paul's query, "Is this blessing pronounced only upon the circumcised or also upon the uncircumcised," is far from occurring to him. He perceives no difference between the Old Testament and the gospel, and still less any contrast. To him "faith" is a virtue among others; for instance, hospitality: "because of faith and hospitality" Abraham was given a son in old age (10:7) and Rahab the harlot was saved (12:1).

e. *Ptolemy to Flora.* This is a letter written by Ptolemy (140–160 in Rome), a pupil of Valentinus, to a lady to instruct her in the right understanding of the Old Testament Law. According to him, it falls into three parts: 1. the legislation of God; 2, the legislation of Moses (to it is reckoned, for instance, the law of divorce, which really is not allowed according to God's commandment, but which Moses—as the author knows from Mt. 19:6ff.—permitted on account of man's hard-heartedness); 3. the decrees of the elders, who—as the author says, echoing Mt. 15:3ff.—by their "traditions" set aside the Law of God. Therefore, "that whole Law contained in the pentateuch of Moses was not legislated by One." But even "that one part, the Law of God Himself, is divided into three," viz.: 1. the pure and perfect moral law which Jesus did not abolish but fulfilled, the decalogue; 2. the law mixed with evil, such as that of retaliation, which Jesus did abolish; 3. the ceremonial law whose spiritual meaning Jesus revealed; it is to be understood allegorically and it requires not ritualistic but ethical conduct. Nevertheless, the god who gave this three-fold Law is not the highest God, but a being standing between Him and the devil; this middle-god is not to be called "perfect," though he is to be called "righteous."

In this moderate Gnosticism of Ptolemy there is a curious combination of historical criticism and critical analysis of the content. But the latter is not oriented to the gospel but to the ideal of a spiritual ethic, and the problem of the way to salvation, or the problem of legalism, is not raised here either.

f. *Justin Martyr*. In his Dialogue with Trypho the Jew, the apologete Justin (ca. 100–165 A.D.) deals with the problem of the Old Testament in a way that later became the typical view of the Church. He, too, divides the Old Testament Law into three parts, but distinguishes them only as to content, not according to both content and history as Ptolemy did: 1. The eternal moral law: "what is by nature good and godly and righteous" or "what is universally, naturally, and eternally good" (both, 45:3f.) or "that which is always and universally just" and is acknowledged as such "by every race of mankind" (93:1f.; *cf.* also 67:10). This moral law was not abolished by Christ, the "new law-giver" (14:3, 18:3; Christ himself is called "the new law and the new covenant" at 11:4), but he summed up its content in the double commandment of love to God and to one's neighbor (93). 2. The prediction of Christ ("but some injunctions . . . were mentioned in reference to the mystery of Christ," 44:2), which is to be derived by allegory. Thus, the Passover lamb, of course, means Christ, whose two "comings" are fore-told in the two goats of the Day of Atonement (40:1ff.); the twelve bells, which according to Justin were part of the high-priest's regalia, mean the twelve apostles (42:1); physical circumcision symbolizes the "true circumcision," "by which we are 'circumcised' (cut off) from error and wickedness," and which Christians have received in baptism (41:4, 43:2, 92:4). 3. The cultic and ceremonial law in its original and (for "Israel," or "the Jews") still valid sense. It was given the Jews by God, in part "for a sign," viz. to set apart this people from all others and protect it from idolatry (16:2, 19:6, 23:5), but in part—because the people were rebellious and disobe-dient—to discipline and exhort it day by day (18:2, "on account of your transgression and the hardness of your hearts"; *cf.* 22:11, 43:1; 20:1, "in order that in your eating and drinking you might have God before your eyes"; *cf.* 92:4). For Christians, of course, the law in this sense is abolished (see, e.g. 43:1).

It is apparent that Justin did not attack the problem of legalism, either. He, too, quotes (141:2) Ps. 32:2: "Blessed is he to whom the Lord shall not reckon sin," and goes on: "that is, having repented of the sins that he may receive remission (of his transgressions) from God"—an exegesis which does not rise above the Old Testa-ment-Jewish view.

3. If one keeps in mind this range of possibilities and adds to them what is incidentally said on this theme in early Christan liter-ature, this is the resulting picture:

a. *The Old Testament Law is regarded as abolished so far as it contains cultic-ritual demands.* It is not the sacrificial cult that pro-cures God's grace, nor is it the law of cleanliness that makes clean. The usual means of coming to terms with the cultic and ritual law is allegory, which in part interprets this law as a disguise of the moral law (Barnabas, Ptolemy, and, sometimes, Justin), in part as prediction of Christ (Barnabas, Justin). A special variety of this interpretation is also that of Hebrews, which understands the Old Testament cult as "the shadow of the good things to come." Yet even when the divine origin of the Law is not contested—as it was in Gnosticism—the opinion as to what meaning the Law had for the past, varies. Though according to Barnabas the Jews had never understood it, for Hebrews, as for I Clem. and Justin, it had once been in force in all seriousness.

But the question now is whether this abolition is understood as only the nullification of an old cult and ritual or as *the complete abolition of cult and ritual as the way to salvation.* This question was nowhere clearly put, it is true, but it is clear that everywhere—and especially in Hebrews—the idea is given up that God's grace must or can be won by humanly offered sacrifices; and that led by implication to the insight that the Church does not need persons of special quality (i.e. priests) to mediate between it and God. Christ's sacrifice made God's grace operative once and for all, and he is the high priest of the Congregation (Heb. 2:17, 3:1, 4:14, 5:1ff., 7:1ff., I Clem. 36:1, 61:3, 64, Ign. Phild. 9:1, Pol. Phil. 12:2). The Congregation itself is a "holy," a "royal priesthood" (I Pet. 2:5, 9, Rev. 1:6, 5:10); it offers God "spiritual sacrifices" (I Pet. 2:5), and one and all are urged to "present your bodies as a living sacrifice, holy and acceptable to God, which is your spiritual presentation of sacrifice" (Rom. 12:1 tr.). "To visit orphans and widows in their affliction and to keep oneself unstained from the world," according to Jas. 1:27, is "religion that is pure and undefiled before God and the Father." True sacrifice is the praise of God offered by the Congregation of those who bear His name, and, along with that, doing good and sharing what one has (Heb. 13:15f.; *cf.* Justin dial. 117:2). Hence the Congregation needs no cultic building, for it is itself the temple of God (§ 10, 4). The individual likewise can be described as the temple of God in which the Holy Ghost or God Himself dwells, and which he—by his ethical conduct—must keep clean (I Cor. 6:19, Barn. 4:11: "Let us become spiritual, let us become a perfect temple for God"; Ign. Eph. 15:3). For this conception it makes no substantial difference whether "the body" (I Cor. 6:19) or "the heart" (Barn. 6:15, 16:7–10) or even "the flesh" (II Clem. 9:3, Ign. Phld. 7:2) is specified as the "temple"; the meaning remains the same since all the figure intends to do is to emphasize the demand of spiritual worship of God and ethical purity.

These ideas are specifically Christian insofar as they are the positive counterpart of the rejection of sacrificial worship. Taken by themselves they are not specifically Christian. For the Old Testament already knows the concept of spiritual sacrifice and so does Judaism, which, especially after the temple cult had ceased with the destruction of Jerusalem, had further developed out of earlier origins the "theory of equivalence," according to which the former place of sacrifice is taken by other acts, especially prayer and charity. Spiritualization of cultic concepts is still more prevalent in Hellenism, both Gentile and Jewish. That man—especially his soul—is a temple of God, is said by the Stoics and in their footsteps by Philo; and the Hermetic writer (Corp. Herm. I: 31; XIII 18f., 21) also knows that to worship the deity with prayers of praise is to worship with "spiritual sacrifices" (λογικαὶ θυσίαι; cf. Rom. 12:1).

Still, will this position of non-cultic worship be consistently maintained? Will not the worship of Jesus Christ as "Lord" take on cultic character? Are not baptism and eucharist in the nature of the case congregational acts with cultic character? And will this character not expand and draw far-reaching consequences after it (§§ 12, 13)? Another possible point from which a cult could develop lies in the working out of an "order" of worship for the Christian Congregation. For the exhortation, "We ought to do all things in order," I Clem. 40–42, appeals to the Old Testament with its ordering of the cult which commands that "sacrifices and services be celebrated not in just any fashion or in a disorderly way but at fixed times and hours." Therefore, "let each one of us . . . be well pleasing to God in his own rank, with a good conscience, not transgressing the fixed norm of his cultic service (τῆς λειτουργίας αὐτοῦ), with all dignity (ἐν σεμνότητι)." Here the way for a specifically cultic order to develop is more definitely prepared than in the exhortation of Paul that in the meetings of the Congregation "all things should be done decently and in order" (I Cor. 14:40), for the concern of I Clem. is for the authority of the "bishops" (and "deacons"), the official leaders of Christian worship. Thus the question arises: Will the office of priest develop anew in the Christian Congregation?

b. *The Old Testament in its entire extent is generally regarded as a book of predictions,* which in Christ are partly already fulfilled, and partly proceeding toward fulfilment. The method of interpreting the Old Testament in this way—the use of allegory, that is—is everywhere the same. It is not specifically Christian, but was taken over from Judaism, especially from its Hellenistic branch, which in turn had taken it over from Greek Hellenism, where, especially among the Stoics, it had been developed as a method of interpreting the old mythology and the old poets, such as Homer. In the present context it does not matter whether the allegorical sense of a text was regarded as its only meaning or as a deeper meaning existing side by side with the literal one. In this context the distinction can also be ignored between allegory (the art of finding prediction or deeper truths of any sort in the wording of Scripture) and typology (the interpretation of persons, events, or institutions of the past as foreshadowing prototypes). But the decisive question is whether the meaning of the Old Testament to the Christian Congregation is exhausted in being a book of oracles. Insofar as it is understood in that way, it furnished the Church a means—an effective one in that day—of polemic and defense in the battle against and the competition for Jews and Gentiles, and hence is at the same time a means of strengthening its own security. But does that not shift the real basis for the power of the gospel message and for the Christian's own security by putting a faith in the letter in place of the genuine faith which seizes the word of God's grace addressed to one's conscience and self-understanding—seizes it on the basis of having been inwardly conquered by it and not on the basis of rational proofs?

Or will the proof of prophecy play an historically inevitable and dangerous but still subordinate role? And will the real significance of the Old Testament for the Christian Congregation, then, be that it keeps alive in the Church the consciousness of being the eschatological Congregation, the goal of a history guided by God? It is *the question of the Church-concept* (§ 10, 1) over again: Will the Church understand itself to be an organization constituted by the joining together of individuals on the basis of their common understanding of general truths and of common practical goals? Or will it understand itself as the "People of God" which is "called" by God's deed in Christ? For Gentile Christianity, the danger of regarding itself as a Jewish sect will not be great. But all the greater for it will be the danger of conceiving itself simply as a "new religion" in contradistinction to the heathen and to the Jews, a new religion resting upon progress in knowledge of God. This danger can be avoided by the continuing possession of the Old Testament, since it teaches an understanding of God according to which God deals with men in *history* and man becomes aware of God and of his own nature not by free-soaring thought but by historical encounter. For to the Old Testament God is not cosmic law, available to thought and investigation, but *the God who reveals himself in the course of history*. The possession of the Old Testament will, therefore, be a counterbalance against the ideas of "natural theology" (§ 9, 2) which soon came pushing in. The idea that God reveals Himself in what He *does* will be kept, thanks to the Old Testament, and in that idea the possibility of understanding the person of Jesus and his cross will be present. For it is also out of this idea that an understanding can and must be reached of what eschatological occurrence is, if this is to be anything more than merely mythological in character. Insofar as the idea of prediction and fulfilment—even though in primitive form—includes within itself the knowledge of a meaning and goal of history that transcends historical occurrence, it is one of the factors that preserves to the Church the consciousness of being a called-in-history, history-transcending, eschatological Congregation. But that means at the same time in the fact of possessing the Old Testament, the Church is also confronted with the theological problem of reason and revelation.

c. *So far as the Old Testament contains ethical commandments* or permits such to be read out of it by the help of allegory, *its authority remains uncontested and valid*—except in radical Gnosticism. Its validity in this direction can only be strengthened the more by the authoritative words of Jesus handed down within the Church, and these at the same time lend a unified direction and a clear meaning to the manifold ethical precepts of the Old Testament by causing them to be understood from the standpoint of the master-commandment of love (Rom. 13:8–10, Gal. 5:14, down to Justin dial. 93; see above in 2f.). Indeed, it was possible for the ethical commandments of the Old Testament and the sayings of Jesus to enter into combination with the demands of Greek (especially Stoic) ethics and the bourgeois morality of Hellenism. For there are heathens who "do by nature what the Law requires," because, as their conscience testifies, they bear "what the Law requires written on their hearts" (Rom. 2:14f.). Hence the Greek notion of "virtue" (ἀρετή) very early creeps into Christian parenesis (Phil. 4:8, II Pet. 1:5, II Clem. 10:1, Herm. mand. I:2; VI 2, 3; XII 3, 1; sim. VI 1, 4; VIII 10, 3; *cf.* also 9, 2). Just as Paul had already taken over Hellenistic catalogues of virtues and vices—in which, of course, he was not the pioneer, as Hellenistic Judaism shows—so the deutero-Pauline literature takes over the Hellenistic-Stoic scheme of the "Haustafeln" (tables of household duties), and in the pastorals the ideal of Christian living is often described in accord with the bourgeois ideal of uprightness current in the Greek world and is couched in the terms used in sepulchral and honorary inscriptions.

Nevertheless, the virtue-concept does not become the dominant idea in Christian parenesis; and that also means that it is not the concept of "the ideal" that determines Christian ethics. Rather, what remains determinative is the idea *that the demand of God is the good*—that man is responsible to God and must give an accounting for his deeds before the judgment seat of God. To substantiate this insight the Church does not, it is true, first appeal to the Old Testament, still it is constantly kept awake by the Old Testament so that the possession of the Old Testament is a counterbalance against natural morality, as it is against natural theology; ethics remains theonomous. The conversion of a heathen to Christianity does mean emancipation from "idolatry" and the fear in his life, but not from the claim of God upon him, which on the contrary is intensified to the uttermost.

But then the question arises: *How is the relation between God's demanding will and the grace of God* proclaimed by the gospel understood? The very fact that the Old Testament was taken over could not help becoming dangerous by promoting the conception that obedience to God's demand for good deeds is the condition for participation in salvation—i.e. that the good deed is to be understood as a meritorious work. Describing the divine demand as a "law of liberty" (Jas. 1:25, 2:12) as a "new law of the Lord" (Barn. 2:6) or as "the commandments and ordinances of the Lord" (I Clem. 2:8, 58:2, Barn. 2:1, 10:11, 21:1) has not basically changed anything in regard to Jewish legalism, if this "new law" or these "commandments and ordinances" have the character of a way to salvation. It is as a second Moses that Christ appears when he is called the "new law-giver" (Justin dial. 14:3, 18:3) or when he is himself called "the law and word" (Kerygma Petri 1), "law of God" (Herm. sim. VIII 3, 2) or "the new law and the new covenant" (Justin dial. 11:4). Indeed, the question is raised: Has not the situation of Christians become much more responsible and dangerous than that of the devout men of the Old Testament and Judaism? Does not a much more severe judgment await them because they have received the grace of God (Heb. 2:2f., 10:28f., 12:25)?

But what does grace mean then? In what does the salvation conferred in Christ consist? Only in the remission of sins committed

[119]

before baptism, with the result that after baptism the believer must depend upon his own works (Heb. 6:4–6)? The problem of sins committed after baptism becomes a burning one, and it is not fundamentally solved when Hermas considers himself authorized on the basis of a divine revelation to proclaim the possibility of a second repentance, which however is irrevocably the last. But Hebrews and Hermas remain isolated voices in this matter. For Paul and the earliest period in general, the problem does not arise because of the expectation of the near End; but when the problem has become visible the generally prevailing conception comes to be that the grace of God which became effective in Christ remains in effect, and hence that Christians in their transgressions can and must be *constantly called to repentance* (Rev., I–II Clem., Ign., Justin; *cf.* II Tim. 2:25, II Pet. 3:9, Did. 10:6, 15:3). Though in view of Christ Christian confidence in the forgiving grace of God is incomparably more certain than the Old Testament-Jewish trust in the effectiveness of repentance, still that does not yet mean a fundamental difference from the Old Testament and Judaism until the relation between God's demand—or the obedient doing of the good and the grace of God is defined anew. Does the forgiving grace of God only supplement the human deed? Or is there no such thing as human doing of the good until God's prevenient grace makes it possible? The problem can also be formulated as that of the *relation between a man's deed* which wins God's approval *and a man's faith* which seizes the proffered grace of God. Is the faith which accepts the gospel and leads to joining the Congregation understood as only the first act of Christian conduct, or as the attitude which permeates and rules the whole life of the Christian? Does it remain present only as knowledge of the object of faith, especially as knowledge that the one God exists, so that knowledge can be distinct from love (I Cor. 8:1ff., 13:2) or so that it can be said, "Even the demons believe . . . and shudder" (Jas. 2:14)? Or so that it can be asked, "What good does it do . . . if a man says he has belief but has not works? Can belief save him?" (Jas. 2:14 tr.)? Or so that it can be said of Abraham that he was not justified by belief alone, but only because "his belief was completed by his works" (Jas. 2:21f. tr.)? Or will a new obedience be founded upon the very gift of grace, so that grace and faith become the forces that determine all of life? The answer to this question is given in one direction by the Pauline doctrine of justification by faith alone, and in another by the rise of the ecclesiastical institution of penance. The basis of the problem Augustinianism versus Pelagianism is already present in the early days of Christianity.

§ 12. Lord and Son of God

1. That the Christian congregations into which the baptized had united themselves in the Hellenistic world met for services of worship needs no explanation—neither where they were congregations grown out of synagogue-congregations, nor where they were congregations mainly or entirely of Gentile origin. But to what extent are these meetings and the services held in them to be termed cultic in the strict sense? That depends upon the definition of cult. We venture a definition in three parts: 1. *Cult* means human action—especially sacrifice, but also other acts—which influences the deity, disposes Him graciously toward the congregation, and makes His power effective for it. 2. This action takes place at fixed, holy times, in a holy place, and according to holy rules or rites. 3. This action is performed by persons of special quality, priests, who mediate between the deity and the congregation; or, in case the congregation participates more than just passively, the action is led by such persons. If that is what cult means, then the *meetings and services of the Christian Congregation* obviously *cannot be termed originally cultic.* For in Christian worship of this period there is neither sacrifice nor priest, nor is it bound to holy places or times (§ 11, 3a). As in the synagogue services the "word" must at first have dominated the service of the mission congregations, both the preached word, which could be spoken by anyone who had the gift and felt himself called thereto, and the word of prayer and song whether uttered by individuals or by the whole congregation. In many congregations preaching probably consisted in the exegesis of words of scripture, and, at least in the congregations that had grown out of the synagogue, the reading of a passage from the Old Testament must have been a regular constituent of congregational worship, though it cannot be assumed to have been so in all congregations. For at first it was simply impossible for many congregations to get possession of an Old Testament—a whole one, especially. But probably early and everywhere apostolic writings and gospels along with

Jewish apocalypses that had undergone Christian revision either took the place of the Old Testament or supplemented it.

Public reading (in these cases probably from Old Testament scripture) is explicitly attested in I Tim. 4:13, II Clem. 19:1 and indirectly at Mk. 13:14 (= Mt. 24:15). Public reading of apostolic writings is mentioned in I Thess. 5:27, Col. 4:16, Rev. 1:3. According to Justin Apol. I 67, 3, "the memoirs of the apostles" (i.e. gospels) "or the writings of the prophets" are publicly read.

Although in the Hellenistic world Christian and Jewish worship services a peculiar phenomenon in being services of the "word," still it can *not* be said that *the cultic has been completely eliminated* from them; it is only *strongly reduced.* Sacrifice, it is true, is entirely missing, and in the apostolic and post-apostolic period the Lord's Supper is not yet by any means understood as a sacrifice; for the description of the eucharist as "sacrifice" (Did. 14) or of those administering it as "offering gifts" (I Clem. 44:4) is figuratively meant. Neither is there any priest in the Christian congregational meetings; nor, according to both Did. 7 and Justin Apol. 61, is baptism administered by specially qualified persons. But if the intent of cultic action is to bring about *the presence of the deity* for the celebrating congregation, then this intent is fulfilled in Christian services of worship, too, and the congregation's action or attitude in which God becomes present, must then also be termed cultic—though there may well be this distinction: that the act and attitude of worship in the Christian Congregation do not first summon the deity before He is there, but rest upon God's being already present. He is present in the *Spirit* by which the Congregation is conscious of being sustained and with which its speakers feel themselves filled (*cf.* I Cor. 14:25, and see § 14). But He is also present in the *word of scripture* in case such is read.

The exhortation (Did. 4:1) "to remember day and night him who speaks the word of God to thee and honor him as the Lord" is backed up by this characteristic reason: "for in the place out of which (his) Lord-ship is spoken, there the Lord is" (tr.). If this sentence belongs, as can hardly be doubted, to the Jewish "catechism" which was worked into Did. 2–6, it indicates that the synagogue service also had thoroughly cultic character. This is also attested by the fact that the removal of the Torah-roll from its shrine (the ark of the Torah) for the reading and its replacement after the reading were solemn liturgical acts. The *Numen praesens* (divine presence) is embodied in the Torah-roll.

Furthermore, the concept of cultic action must not be too narrowly restricted. It is not limited to sacrifice and ritual acts, but also includes the recitation of holy texts, *prayers* first of all, and the singing of *hymns*—in a word, what we are accustomed to call liturgy. Now, it is true, we are not able to say how soon in Gentile Christian Congregations prayers and songs—or rather, an arrangement of such into an order of worship—achieved fixed liturgical form; but it will be shown that it was at any rate quite early. Besides, the free prayer or song of the individual also achieves a special character within the framework of the congregational celebration—precisely a cultic character. And though the young Christian Church knows neither a holy place nor holy times, purely practical reasons demand the choice of definite places and regular times; and that these gradually acquire the quality of cultic "holiness" is illustrated by the history of Sunday.

Whether Paul already knows Sunday as the day for congregational worship is not made certain by I Cor. 16:2 (*cf.* Acts 20:7). At any rate, it soon became that; and when, as such, it is called Lord's (Day), κυριακὴ (ἡμέρα), (Rev. 1:10, Did. 14:1, Ign. Mg. 9:1) and when the seer, Rev. 1:10, receives his revelation on that day, that in itself shows that as a day it possesses a special quality, even if its choice as the "eighth day" (Barn. 15:9) should have been due originally only to contrast with Jewish custom (like the choice of the Christian fast-days, Did. 8:1). Its distinction among the days is given a justification as cultic acts are, out of the history of salvation: it is the day on which Jesus "rose from the dead and having appeared ascended into heaven" (Barn. 15:9, Ig. Mg. 9:1). In the course of time, then, the sabbath laws of the Old Testament are transferred to the Lord's Day, and it has completely become a "holy" day.

2. It is taken for granted that the deity whose presence is believed and experienced in the congregational gatherings of Christians, whose word is heard, and to whom prayers are offered, is the one true God to whom the heathen have been converted from their "idols." The same thing is attested by the prayers and doxologies at Rev. 4:8, 11; 7:12; 11:17f.; 15:3f.; 19:1f.; 7f., and by the long congre-

gational prayer in I Clem. 59–61. But as in Rev. 5:13, 7:10, the praise of God and the "Lamb" sounds forth, and as in Rev. 11:15, 12:10, "God and his Christ" are praised, so the closing formula of I Clem. 61:3 reads, "we praise thee through the high priest and guardian of our souls, Jesus Christ, through whom be glory to thee . . ." That means that Christ, too, has become a cultically worshiped figure present in the cult, and for the eschatological Congregation that is the really distinctive thing. For according to Phil. 2:10f., the saving occurrence accomplished in Christ has for its goal, "that at the name of Jesus every knee should bow, in heaven and on earth and under the earth and every tongue confess that Jesus Christ is Lord, to the glory of God the Father."

This is the distinctive feature of the eschatological Congregation in Hellenistic Christianity, for in it for the first time Jesus Christ figures not only as the eschatological savior but also as the cultically worshiped "Lord" (§ 7, 5). In place of the titles "Son of Man" and "Christ" (= messianic king), which are dying out, there appears in the Hellenistic congregations the *title "Kyrios," Lord.*

It is highly improbable that the title "Kyrios" as applied to Jesus is derived from the LXX, in which it is the usual translation for Yahweh. Rather, vice versa, the already accepted designation of Jesus as Kyrios made it possible for utterances of the LXX involving Kyrios to be transferred to him. But it is true that by this process the figure of Jesus as Kyrios increased in content and weight (*cf.,* for instance, the application of Is. 45:23 to Christ in Phil. 2:11; of Is. 40:13 in I Cor. 2:16; of Jer. 9:22f. in II Cor. 10:17; of Ex. 34:34 in II Cor. 3:16). Neither is the transfer of the Kyrios-title to Jesus to be understood as a counterpart to its use in the ruler-cults, or at least not primarily, although the adjective κυριακός (dominical) may have been taken over from it. Rather, the term Kyrios used of Christ is derived from the religious terminology of Hellenism, more specifically from that of oriental Hellenism, in which Kyrios was the Greek translation of typical terms in various languages which denoted the deity as "Lord." This usage was wide-spread in Egypt, Asia Minor, and especially in Syria, which in all probability is the land of origin of the term "the Lord" used absolutely. This origin of the Kyrios-title comes clearly into view in the antithesis of "one Lord Jesus Christ" to the "many lords" in I Cor. 8:5f.

Kyrios in this usage (as everywhere else except in the LXX) is an appellative and hence requires completion by a proper name (unless it is evident from the context) to indicate what deity is meant. In Christianity, therefore, "Jesus Christ" is added. Kyrios indicates the respective deity not primarily in his divine majesty and power, but in his "master" relation to the speaker (the corresponding term for the worshiper is "slave," δοῦλος). With this implication it characteristically appears in the frequent phrase "our Lord Jesus Christ" or "Christ Jesus my Lord," Phil. 3:8 (*cf.* Rom. 14:4, Eph. 6:9). The fact that Kyrios occurs so often in the New Testament without the added personal name is probably due not simply to the obviousness of the implied addition but also to the influence of the LXX at just that point. It comes from LXX-usage also that Christ is not only the lord of his worshipers (or of the Church) but is "Lord of all" (Rom. 10:12), Lord, indeed, of all the cosmic powers (Phil. 2:10f.), "the Lord of all the cosmos" (Barn. 5:5); likewise from the LXX comes such an expression as "the Lord of glory" (I Cor. 2:8).

That *Paul was not the first* to give Christ the title "Kyrios" but that it was *already current in the Hellenistic Church before him* is to be concluded both from the way in which he takes the use of the title for granted and from certain other observations. The Christ-hymn in Phil. 2:6–11 was not composed by Paul for this context, but is a quotation taken over by him, as E. Lohmeyer has shown. It is not to be doubted that in Rom. 10:9 Paul is referring to a common Christian confession when he writes: "If you confess with your lips that Jesus is Lord . . ." Just this, then, is the distinctively Christian confession: "Jesus (Christ) is Lord." As such, it is also cited at I Cor. 12:3 as the criterion for distinguishing between spirits. And when Paul (II Cor. 4:5) declares: "What we preach is not ourselves, but Christ Jesus as Lord," intending thereby to legitimate himself as a genuine apostle, it is clear that just this is held to be the Christian message: to proclaim Christ as the Kyrios. Also the formula derived from Joel 2:32 LXX, "those who call upon the name of the Lord (Jesus Christ)," a formula which clearly reveals the cultic character of the Kyrios-title, became a designation for Christians, but one which Paul had evidently found already in use (I Cor. 1:2, II Tim. 2:22, Acts 9:14, 21; 22:16). When Jas. 2:7 (again using an Old Testament-Jewish formula) speaks of the "good name" as "having been called over you," this "name" is probably none other than that of "the Lord (Jesus Christ)," as we read in Herm. sim. VIII 6, 4: "the name of the Lord which was called over you," or as Christians are called (sim. VIII 1, 1) "those who are called by the name of the Lord," or (sim. IX 14, 3) "those who call upon his name." These formulas indicate the cultic meaning of the Kyrios-title. The name of the Lord is evidently "called upon" the believer at baptism and at the same time his first "calling upon" the name also takes place (Acts 22:16), but the latter is constantly repeated in the celebrations of the congregation. And the wish expressed in the greetings of Paul's letters is evidently also a liturgical formula that had come down to Paul: "Grace to you and peace from God our Father and the Lord Jesus Christ." * Hence, it is conceivable how the Christian worship-service could have been called (Acts 13:2) "worshiping the Lord (Jesus Christ, understood)."

Nevertheless, *calling upon the Lord*" probably did not consist in liturgical prayers addressed directly to Christ. So far as we see, such prayers were preponderantly addressed to God alone; for it is hardly permissible to regard Jn. 14:14 as testimony to liturgical prayer by a congregation addressed to Jesus. For the period of the ancient Church only the apocryphal acts of the apostles attest liturgical prayers addressed to Christ. Rather, "calling upon the Lord" probably consisted in confessing him and in doxologies like II Tim. 4:18, I Clem. 20:12, 50:7, or like the ones offered to the "Lamb" in Rev. 5:9f. and 12, and also in single, formula-like invocations like the "Maranatha" interpreted as referring to Christ (§ 7, 5), which appears at Rev. 22:20 as "come, Lord Jesus." † Or at the close of the epistles, where "the grace of the Lord Jesus Christ" is wished for the readers (Gal. 6:18, Phil. 4:23, I Cor. 16:23, Rev. 22:21, I Clem. 65:2, etc.). Also in specific cases the Kyrios was probably invoked to intervene with his miraculous power.

A characteristic example for the last case is I Cor. 5:3-5, where Paul instructs the congregation to deliver to Satan the miscreant who is to be excluded. This is to happen, Paul says, "in the name of the Lord Jesus when you are assembled and my

---

* This was demonstrated by E. Lohmeyer ZNW 26 (1927), 162ff. by proving the divergence of this formula from the diction of Paul.

† In the table-prayer (Did. 10:6) the Coptic tradition attests the reading "let the Lord (in place of 'grace') come," which is perhaps the original text.

spirit is present with the power of our Lord Jesus Christ"; and it makes no difference whether "in the name of the Lord Jesus Christ" be connected with "when you are assembled" or with the following "deliver this man to Satan." In either case the invocation of the "name of the Lord" is to make his "power" effective in the congregation. The same point of view emerges in the legendary story of Acts 1:24. The Kyrios is implored to indicate by lot the right man to take the place among the twelve left vacant by Judas.

Related in content to the invocation of the *"name of Christ"* (I Cor. 5:3–5) is the use of the "name" for *exorcism* and miraculous deeds in general. Perhaps the earliest Church had already used the name of Jesus as a means of exorcism (§ 7, 4); at any rate this was done in Hellenistic Christianity, as the account of the Jewish exorcists who wanted to profit by the power of the "name of the Lord" (Acts 19:13–17) testify and also the editorial verse Lk. 10:17, according to which the seventy on returning to Jesus report to him, "the demons are subject to us in your name." In the same direction Mt. 7:22 also transforms the older tradition (Lk. 13:26f.): "Did we not in your name . . . cast out demons and do many mighty works in your name?" With this the outlook of the author of Acts is consistent (3:16, 4:7, 10; 16:18). But exorcistic formulas are ordinarily derived from liturgical material, and that this was true of the exorcistic use of the "name" of Christ is proved by Justin's account: "For every demon, when exorcized in the name of this very Son of God—who is the First-born of all creation, who was born of a virgin and became a man subject to suffering, who was crucified under Pontius Pilate . . . who died, who rose from the dead and ascended into heaven—is conquered and subjected" (Dial. 85:2; *cf.* 30:3, 49:8, 76:6, 121:3, 131:5). Here we see the statements of the liturgical confession of faith put into the service of exorcism. And when Justin declares (Dial. 30:3): "Thus it is apparent to all men that his Father has given him such power that even the demons are subjected by his name and by the dispensation of the suffering that he suffered," he, of course, does not mean that that had not been true before his, Justin's, time.

But *"calling upon the Lord"* has its place in liturgy, especially in the phrase "in his name" which accompanies prayers and doxologies addressed to God (Eph. 5:20; *cf.* also 3:21; Jn. 14:13, 15:16, 16:24,

26). Or prayers are offered to God "through him," for, as Paul says, clearly referring to liturgical usage, "that is why we utter the Amen through him, to the glory of God" (II Cor. 1:20). So it is *through him* that thanks is given to God (Rom. 1:8, 7:25, Col. 3:17) or praise (Did. 9:4, I Clem. 58:2, 61:3, 64, 65:2). And the formula which occurs in the letters of Ignatius, "I greet you in the name of Jesus Christ," probably also comes from liturgical usage (Ign. Rm. pr., 9:3, Sm. 12:2) and presumably likewise the "appeal through the name of our Lord Jesus Christ" (I Cor. 1:10, Rom. 15:30; *cf*. II Cor. 10:1). When the Kyrios-name is spoken every being must bow in homage to the glory of God (Phil. 2:10f.).

Outside of formal, liturgical worship, prayers evidently were said directly to Christ in the personal lives of individuals. Paul besought "the Lord" for his own person (II Cor. 12:8) and he prays to him for the weal of the Congregation (I Thess. 3:12; so also in the non-Pauline II Thess. 3:3, 5, 16, where the parallel passages in I Thess. 3:11, 5:23f. have 'God').

3. What is true of the name "Kyrios" is also true of the other name conferred on Christ: *He is the "Son of God."* Whereas according to Phil. 2:11 it is the Kyrios-name that crowns his work of salvation, according to Heb. 1:4 the "more excellent name" which God has conferred upon the exalted Christ and which lifts him above all angels is undoubtedly the name of "Son." Hence, Herm. sim. IX 14, 5 says, "the name of the Son of God is great and incomprehensible and supports the whole world." Both names occur in the exorcistic formulas (see above). They belong together inasmuch as Son of God denotes the divine nature of the Kyrios which is his as a cultically worshiped figure, and inasmuch as "Kyrios" correspondingly specifies the rank and function of him who by nature is Son of God.

The title "Kyrios" was first conferred upon Christ in the Hellenistic Church. But Hellenistic-Jewish Christians had brought along the *title "Son of God"* embedded in their missionary message; for the earliest Church had already called Jesus so (§7, 5). But one must recognize that the title, which originally denoted the messianic king, now takes on a new meaning which was self-evident to Gentile hearers. Now it comes to mean *the divinity of Christ, his divine nature*, by virtue of which he is differentiated from the human sphere; it makes the claim that Christ is of divine origin and is filled with divine "power."

That this meaning of the title was the one taken for granted in Hellenism is evident from a double fact. One part of it is that to the mind of Hellenistic Christians the salvation-event consists precisely in the paradoxical fact that a figure, divine by nature, appears as a man and suffers the fate of man (*cf.* the Christ-hymn quoted by Paul in Phil. 2:6–11), with the result that what had been a stumbling-block to the earliest Church—i.e. that Christ should be subject to, and subjected to, suffering (χριστὸς παθητός)—is no longer a stumbling-block to the Hellenistic Church, though it is a mystery (μυστήριον). The other part of the double fact is that the problem of how the humanity of the Son of God can be conceived becomes troublesome, and that the reality of Christ's humanity has to be defended (precisely for the sake of that paradox which the salvation-event is) against Gnostic heresy. While the term "Son of God" secondarily serves to differentiate Christ from the one true God and to indicate Christ's subordinate relation to God, it also serves—and this is the primary thing—to assert his divinity. So it is not surprising that II Clem. begins, "We must think of Jesus Christ as God"; for Heb. 1:1–14 had already taught Christ's elevation above the angels and described him as "the effulgence of the glory (of God) and the very stamp of His substance" (1:3 tr.).

In *describing Christ as "God"* the New Testament still exercises great restraint. Except for Jn. 1:1, where the pre-existent Logos is called God, and Jn. 20:28, where Thomas reverences the risen Christ with the exclamation, "My Lord and my God!" this assertion is made—at least by any probable exegesis—only in II Thess. 1:12, Tit. 2:13, II Pet. 1:1. Ignatius * on the contrary speaks of Christ as God as if it were a thing to be taken quite for granted (Tr. 7:1, Sm. 1:1, 10:1); usually he says "(Jesus Christ) our God" (Eph. pr., 15:3, 18:2, Rom. pr. twice, 3:3, Pol. 8:3). And that what concerns him is precisely that paradox is shown by such expressions as: "incarnate God" (ἐν σαρκὶ γενόμενος θεός, text of GL, Eph. 7:2, "God manifested himself as man" (Eph. 19:3), the mention of "God's blood" Eph. 1:1), of the "passion of my God" (Rom. 6:3) or of "the bread of God, that is, the flesh of Jesus Christ" (Rom. 7:3).

* The doxology in Rom. 9:5 is scarcely to be referred to Christ; in Jn. 1:18 and I Tim. 3:16 "God" is a secondary variant.

That the proclamation of "Christ, the Son of God," was so under-stood, is not to be wondered at; *the figure of a Son of God was familiar to Hellenistic ways of thinking,* familiar in several varia-tions. One among them was an inheritance from the Greek tradi-tion, which applied the mythological idea of being begotten by a god to men who seemed by their heroic deeds, mental accomplish-ments, or benefactions to humanity to transcend ordinary human proportions. The Hellenistic period knows a whole series of such "divine men" (θεῖοι ἄνδρες), who claimed to be sons of (a) god or were regarded as such, and some of whom were also cultically wor-shiped. In their case, there is no emphasis, or almost none, on the paradoxicality of the divine appearing in human form; moreover, this was no problem at all to Greek thinking in general, for which every man's soul is a divine entity. Hence, here the interest lies not in the (paradoxical) fact of the divine son's humanity but in the content of his life (βίος) marked by miracles and other divinely conferred phenomena. Another variation was the conception of divine sonship which was common in oriental Hellenism as an inher-itance from old oriental mythology: the idea of son-divinities, upon whom cultic worship was bestowed and who were regarded as saviors. About such divinities, worshiped in "mysteries," their myths related that they had suffered the human fate of death but had risen again from death. But according to the belief of their worshipers, the fate of these divinities establishes a salvation which is imparted to those who experience with the deity his death and resurrection in the rites of the mysteries. Akin to these divine figures, whose origin lies in ancient vegetation-gods, is the figure of the "Redeemer" in the Gnostic myth—whatever historical connections may underly this kin-ship—to the extent that in that figure the paradox that a divine being (a son-deity) should become man and suffer a human fate is most emphatically expressed.

The Gentile-Christian conception of Christ as Son of God varies according to which tradition influences it more. The synoptic gos-pels essentially represent the first type, inasmuch as they picture Jesus as the Son of God who reveals his divine power and authority through his miracles. This is a way of thinking which was also capable of being appropriated even by such Christian thought as was determined by Jewish tradition; this was done when it attrib-uted the "power" in the life of the "divine man" to the divine Spirit, by analogy with David and the prophets. This is the vein in which the Gospel of Mark tells its story. According to it, Jesus becomes the Son of God by the Spirit conferred upon him at the baptism. The same view clearly emerges in the "western" text (D it, etc.) of Lk. 3:22, according to which the heavenly voice says, "Thou art my son; to-day have I begotten thee." In keeping with this line of thinking Acts 2:22 calls Jesus "a man attested . . . by God with mighty works and wonders and signs which God did through him." But also the mythological conception of a divine son begotten by some deity—an idea which not merely Greek tradition knows, but which is also current in the Babylonian and especially the Egyptian king-legend—was evidently taken over by Jewish Hellenism in Egypt and transferred to the devout men of the Old Testament. Hence, it is no wonder that early in Hellenistic Christianity the legend springs up that Jesus was begotten by the Holy Spirit (Mt. 1:20) or by the "power of the Most High" (Lk. 1:35) and was born of a virgin. The fact that it was unknown to Paul, of course, does not prove that it may not have been current in circles other than Paul's even before his time. In the New Testament the virgin-birth concept does not occur outside of Mt. 1 and Lk. 1, and the understanding of Son of God which underlies it was surpassed by the *second type* of understanding, according to which Jesus Christ is the pre-existent Son of God become man. Paul (like John) takes this understanding for granted, and the pre-Pauline Christ-hymn (Phil. 2:6–11) proves that he was not the first to introduce it into Christian thinking. This view is also consonant with the recognition of the paradoxicality of the salvation-event; all emphasis lies upon the fact of the humanity and the human fate of the Son of God who became man. To this fact, the idea that Jesus proved himself to be God's Son in his earthly life by miracles is really contradictory, as Phil. 2:6–11 clearly shows. It is correspondingly foreign to Paul himself to conceive of Jesus' life as filled with the miraculous.

But in Hellenistic Christianity these two christologies joined together in a somewhat strained union. With the synoptic gospels is preserved their picture of the Son of God as the wonder-worker. In Ignatius "the virginity of Mary and her accouchement along with the death of the Lord" constitute the "three mysteries of a cry" (Ign. Eph. 19:1; *cf.* Sm. 1:1); although otherwise it is precisely Ignatius who emphasized the paradoxicality of the pre-existence christology (see above).

But still a *third type* of the son-of-God figure must be recognized. The son-divinity of Gnosticism often possesses not only soteriological but also cosmological significance; indeed, this was probably its primary meaning, and it was independently developed in mythologies and in religious-philosophical speculations like those of Philo, whose cosmic Logos is the "son" of God, and a similar development is found in the Hermetic writings. A parallel phenomenon is the cosmic figure of Wisdom which had already crept into the Wisdom-literature of the Old Testament and had become an object of speculation in Judaism, especially in Hellenistic Judaism. Very early this Logos and Wisdom speculation penetrated into Hellenistic Christianity. Already in I Cor. 8:6 Christ appears as he "through whom all things (are) and through whom we (exist)," a formula in which the cosmological and the soteriological roles of Christ are combined. Whether Paul was the first *to ascribe to Christ this cosmic role as mediator of creation,* cannot be said; the way he speaks of it as if it were a matter of course rather inclines one to conclude that he was not alone in doing so. The matter-of-fact way in which he terms Christ "the likeness of God" (II Cor. 4:4) makes the same impression; for this concept belongs in the context of the cosmological Son-of-God speculation and appears in that connection in Philo and in the Hermetic and Gnostic literature. After Paul, this cosmological significance of Christ is presented especially in Col. 1:15ff., where Christ is characterized as "the image of the invisible God, the first-born of all creation; for in him all things were created . . . and in him all things hold together (exist)." Ephesians, also, knows this speculation, but its author has turned it from cosmology to ecclesiology (1:20ff.), a change which Colossians had already begun to make. Besides Jn. 1:1ff., Hebrews attests that Christ as Son of God was regarded as a cosmic figure by others than Paul and his school; Heb. 1:3 describes Christ as "upholding the universe by his word of power" after having called him "the effulgence of the glory (of God) and the very stamp of his nature," which is only a paraphrase of the concept "image" (εἰκών). Similarly Hermas says (sim. IX 12, 2): "The Son of God is older than all his creation, so that he was the Father's counsellor of creation," behind which, of course, Prov. 8:27ff. hovers. But especially in sim. IX 14, 5, the cosmological role of the Son of God finds expression: "the name of the Son of God is great and incomprehensible and supports the whole world. If then the whole creation is supported by the Son of God . . ." The answer to the question here begun by Hermas draws an ecclesiological conclusion from this cosmological premise.

§ 13. The Sacraments

1. In the worship (the Kultus) of the congregation, the Lord Jesus Christ is present. An individual gets into the congregation through *baptism*; and that means that in this way he enters into relation with the Lord. In all probability it was as a rite of initiation into the eschatological Congregation that baptism had been practiced in the earliest Church (§ 6, 3), a sacramental bath which washes away the guilt of sin, and it was so that the missionaries had brought it to the Hellenistic Congregations. That baptism is the *indispensable condition for admission to the Congregation* and for participation in salvation is self-evident, and is at least indirectly expressed in Acts 4:12: "And there is salvation in no one else, for there is no other name under heaven given among men by which we must be saved" (supply: "than the name of Jesus Christ")—even if the author should not here be thinking of the "Name" spoken at baptism. According to Did. 9:5 and Justin Apol. 66:1, no unbaptized person may participate in the eucharist, and according to Herm. sim. IX 12, 4f. "no one shall enter the Reign of God unless he shall have received the name of the Son of God"—i.e. been baptized. In fact, according to sim. IX 16, even the righteous of the Old Testament can participate in salvation only after they have been baptized; for this purpose, apostles and teachers after death preached and baptized in the underworld.

As to the *rite of baptism*, it was normally consummated as a bath in which the one receiving baptism completely submerged, and if possible in flowing water as the allusions of Acts 8:36, Heb. 10:22, Barn. 11:11 permit us to gather, and as Did. 7:1–3 specifically says. According to the last passage, it suffices in case of need if water is three times poured on the head. The one baptizing names over the one being baptized the name of "the Lord Jesus Christ," later expanded to the name of the Father, the Son, and the Holy Spirit (first attested in Did. 7:1,

[133]

3, Justin Apol. 61: 3, 11, 13; also found in Mt. 28:19, but this is perhaps a case of later interpolation). That the "Name" was spoken over the person being baptized is implied by the formula "baptized in (into, εἰς) the name" (indirectly attested I Cor. 1:13, 15; directly in Acts 8:16, 19:5, Did. 9:5, Herm. sim. III 7, 3; "in," ἐν, in place of "into," εἰς: Acts 10:48; "to," ἐπί, Lk. 24:47—if "repentance" here implies baptism) and Acts 2:38 (*cf.*, besides these passages which speak only of "the name of the Lord," the passages cited above containing the trinitarian formula); it is corroborated by the formula "the name which has been spoken over you" (Jas. 2:7) or "over them" (Herm. sim. VIII 6, 4), and it is explicitly stated by Justin (Ap. 61:11). In keeping with this are also the expressions "receive the Name" (Herm. sim. IX, 12, 4 and 8; 13, 2 and 7) or "bear the Name" (Herm. sim. IX 14, 5; 15, 2). The one being baptized, on his part, speaks—either just before or just after the bath of baptism—the confession: "Jesus Christ is Lord," and belongs thereby to "those who call upon the name of the Lord" (§ 12, 2). If the "confession" of I Tim. 6:12 made "in the presence of many witnesses" is the baptismal confession, then it is surely to be thought of as preceding baptism. It would accord well with this if the act of baptism was preceded by the question and answer which O. Cullmann, *Urchristentum und Gottesdienst,* pp. 79–88, deduces out of Acts 8:36, 10:47, 11:17, Mt. 3:14, Gospel of the Ebionites in Epiphanius 30, 31—i.e. the question: "What is to prevent?" and the answer: "It is permitted" (or "nothing prevents"). In the scarcity of sources, it is impossible to say how early such ritual formulas developed. At any rate, according to Justin Apol. 61, 2, baptism is preceded by the commitment of the candidate that he "is able to live thus" (i.e. in accordance with the teachings he has received). Though in the earliest period baptism certainly often followed immediately upon the conversion which had taken place under the impression of missionary preaching (illustrated, for instance, by Acts 2:41, 8:12, 16:33, 18:8), later some instruction preceded baptism, as Heb. 6:2, Did. 7:1, Justin. Ap. 61:2, 65:1 presuppose. Since when a fast of one or two days mentioned by Did. 7:4, Justin Apol. 61:2 (here prayer is also mentioned) preceded baptism, we do not know. Neither do we know anything definite about the ritual act of laying on of hands, which, according to Heb. 6:2, Acts 19:5f. (*cf.* 8:17), belongs to baptism; but probably this was a regular component of it from the beginning, perhaps accompanying the speaking of the Name. It should be taken for granted that only adults were baptized (Joach. Jeremias, *Hat die älteste Christenheit die Kindertaufe geübt?* (1938), to the contrary notwithstanding). He who performed the baptism had no distinguishing quality, i.e. no priestly quality, see § 12, 1; only, according to Ign. Sm. 8:2, baptism is not to be permitted "without the bishop."

The meaning of baptism is determined by various factors which in part work together, in part independently. But in every case it is regarded as a *sacrament*—i.e. an act which by natural means puts supranatural powers into effect, usually by the use of spoken words which accompany the act and release those powers by the mere utterance of their prescribed wording. Indeed, the sacramental act may confine itself completely to the speaking of a word or a formula. The concept "sacrament" rests upon the assumption that under certain conditions supranatural powers can be bound to natural objects of the world and to spoken words as their vehicles and mediators. If the conditions are fulfilled (if, for instance, the prescribed formula is correctly spoken and the material is thereby "consecrated"—i.e. laden with supranatural power), and if the act is consummated according to the prescribed rite, then the supranatural powers go into effect, and the act, which apart from these conditions would be only a purely worldly, natural one like a bath or a meal, is itself a supranatural ceremony which works a miracle. Though in the primitive stage of the history of religions sacramental action can hardly be distinguished from magic, still in the course of history the difference becomes ever greater, depending upon what conditions must be fulfilled by those for whom the sacrament is to be effective and upon what supranatural powers are to be put into effect. The presupposed condition may be a specified state of the body, or it may be a state of spiritual preparedness. The powers may be such as only serve the enhancement of physical life, or such as promote the life of the spirit. In the latter case, it is true, the paradoxicality of the sacrament is increased: How can spiritual powers be bound to material elements as their vehicles? Finally, a sacrament can be etherealized into a symbol; then a psychological effect results instead of a miraculous one.

It is clear that in earliest Christianity the sacrament was by no means a symbol, but a miracle-working rite—most strikingly shown for the sacrament of the Eucharist in I Cor. 11:29ff. (see below), and for baptism in I Cor. 15:29. When people have themselves baptized for the dead, as they did in Corinth—i.e. when their intention is to have the supranatural powers that the sacrament bestows made effective for the dead—then no distinction is made between the sacrament and a magical act. It is of course self-evident that neither Paul nor other Jewish-Christian missionaries introduced this practice, and it is no less understandable that it was eliminated by the Church, though Gnostic sects still practiced it for a while. But it is significant that Paul mentions the custom without any criticism whatever; for the mode of thought behind it is precisely his own, too, as it was for earliest Christian thought in general (with the exception of John).

What is expected as the effect of baptism (corresponding to its origin; see above) is first: *Purification from one's sins*, and it is several times expressly said, from one's sins committed in the past (II Pet. 1:9, Herm. mand. IV 3, 1, Justin Ap. 61:10). Paul undoubtedly means purification by baptism when after describing the sinful heathen past of the readers he continues: "But you were washed, but you were made holy, but you were made righteous in the name of the Lord Jesus Christ and in the Spirit of our God" (I Cor. 6:11). All three verbs describe the sacramental bath of purification; and in this series "made righteous" is not meant in the specific sense of Paul's doctrine of justification, but, corresponding to "made holy," is meant in the general-Christian sense: cancellation of sin (§ 9, 4, p. 85). The related passages also show that Paul is here presenting the general-Christian view of baptism. In the deutero-Pauline literature such passages include: Eph. 5:26, where the purpose of Christ's work of salvation is "that he might make her (the Church) holy, having cleansed her by the washing of water with the word"; or I Pet. 3:21, where baptism is interpreted as "not a removal of dirt from the body," i.e. the bath of baptism is no external purification, but creates the possibility (by cleansing the believer of his sins) of "calling upon God with the consciousness of purity" (*cf.* Heb. 9:14, 10:2, 22). Similar passages occur in literature nearly or entirely independent of Paul. Since baptism takes place "for the forgiveness of sins" (Acts 2:38), Saul-Paul is commanded to "rise and be baptized and wash away your sins, calling upon his name" (Acts 22:16). According to Heb. 10:22 we, as Christians, have "our hearts sprinkled clean from an evil conscience and our bodies washed with pure water" in which "body" is separated from "heart" only for the sake of the rhetorical parallelism of members; for the washing is, of course, not limited to the "body," but applies just as much to the "heart." The "cleansing from one's old sins," II Pet. 1:9, is, of course, the cleansing received in baptism. According to Barn. 11:11 "we go down into the water full of sins and foulness, and we come up bearing the fruit of fear in our hearts and having hope on Jesus in the Spirit"; and according to 16:8f. we become a temple of God by "the remission of sins" (received in baptism). "When we went down into the water," Hermas says (mand. IV 3, 1), "we received remission of our former sins" (*cf.* Justin Ap. 61:10).

With the cleansing bath of baptism *the naming of "the name of the Lord"* is combined. Here a second factor joins the first, but it is hard to say when the combination took place (§ 6, 3). The calling of the Name is not what it became in the later Church, an *epiclesis,* a special prayer which summons the power of Christ into the water to give it the ability to purify and sanctify, but is a naming of the Name over the candidate, which imparts its power to him. Hence, at bottom, the naming of the Name is an independent sacrament competing with the bath of baptism. Still, since their effects more or less coincide, their combination is understandable enough. The meaning of this naming of the Name is first of all this: that by it the candidate is stamped as property of the Kyrios and placed under his protection. This is proved by the use of the term *"seal"* (σφραγίς), which Paul clearly presupposes, for baptism.

The statement made of God in II Cor. 1:22: "he has sealed (σφραγισάμενος) us and given us his Spirit in our hearts as a guarantee," undoubtedly alludes to baptism. Even if Paul does not necessarily· imply the actual use of the noun, "seal" (σφραγίς) for baptism, at any rate, behind the cognate verb used by him lies the idea that did lead to this terminology in later sources. The same is true of Eph. 1:13: "having believed in it (*sc.* the gospel), you were sealed (ἐσφραγίσθητε) with the promised Holy Spirit." But later on, in II Clem. 7:6, 8:6, Herm. sim. VIII 6, 3, IX 16, 3–7; 17, 4; 31, 1, the designation of baptism by the noun, "seal," is perfectly familiar; furthermore, in Hermas it is quite clear that baptism is called "seal" because it places the one baptized under the authority and protection of the Name; his phrase "receive the seal" (sim. VIII 6, 3, IX 16,

3; 17, 4) is equivalent to "receive the Name" (see above, p. 134). Perhaps Judaism already referred to circumcision as a "seal" before Paul did so (*cf.* Rom. 4:11, in which, however, "seal" could be a mere metaphor for "ratification"; likewise in Barn. 9:6); but that can be proved only for a later period. In the mystery-religions, too, "seal" was a technical term for the rite of initiation. But even though here Christian language may possibly have been influenced from that direction, the root meaning of the term has not died out. W. Heitmüller (*Neutest. Studien für G. Heinrici* [1914], 40–59) has demonstrated that just as in secular use so also in sacral use the word "seal" means the brand or trade-mark which indicates ownership and owner's rights, and that it is in this sense that the Name serves in baptism as a "seal."

The bath of baptism as a purification has a negative meaning (cancellation of past sins), but the naming of the Name has a double effect, both negative and positive. Negatively, it drives out evil spirits (widely regarded as the cause of sins) by its exorcistic power (see above, 2, p. 127). Positively, it puts the baptized under the protection of the Kyrios for the future, too, and secures him against demonic influences—and that means against sins, too, though also against other evils. In Col. 1:13f.—for this passage is probably alluding to baptism—this view is clearly expressed: "He has delivered us from the dominion of darkness and transferred us to the kingdom of his beloved Son, in whom we have redemption, the forgiveness of sins." Likewise in Barn. 16:7f.: once our heart was a "house of demons," but by virtue of the Name it has become a temple in which God dwells. The fast which soon came to be associated with baptism (see above) probably is connected with this view, for fasting is a means of driving out demons (e.g., Mk. 9:29 variant).

A positive effect of baptism important for the future is that *it bestows the Holy Spirit*. This also is a general-Christian view presupposed by Paul when he appeals to it as a thing to be taken for granted (I Cor. 12:13, II Cor. 1:22); also present in Eph. 1:13, 4:30 (see above). According to Tit. 3:5 baptism is a "bath of . . . renewal (brought about) by the Holy Spirit." In baptism the Holy Spirit is received (Acts 2:38; *cf.* 9:17f.), and it is in this that the Church sees the specific difference of its baptism from that of John (Acts 19:1–6; *cf.* Mk. 1:8). Water and Spirit, according to the traditional text of Jn. 3:5, bring about re-birth. Barn. 11:9–11 presupposes the same view, and Herm. sim. IX 13 expounds in broad allegory that a condition for salvation is to be clad by the twelve virgins with their garments; these virgins are building the tower of the Church, and Hermas interprets them as "holy spirits" and "powers of the Son of God."

The passages, Acts 8:14–17, 10:44–48, in which the receipt of the Spirit and baptism are not contemporaneous, are only an apparent exception. In reality, the intent of both passages is to teach precisely the inseparability of baptism and the receipt of the Spirit. A baptism which does not bestow the Spirit is no proper baptism and hence must be supplemented by the receiving of the Spirit (8:14–17). The bestowal of the Spirit by God means that baptism must be given to the one so favored (10:44–48).

The bestowal of the Spirit is a third factor in the meaning of baptism. This is also recognizable in the fact that it was attached to the special ritual act of laying on of hands—at least it is in Acts 8:17, 19:6, and presumably was from the beginning as soon as bestowal of the Spirit was associated with baptism at all. Since when that was the case we admittedly do not know. At any rate it was scarcely true in the earliest Church (§ 6, 3), because there, where Jewish tradition was dominant, the baptismal water-bath can scarcely have been conceived otherwise than negatively—i.e. as a purification. For Heb. 6:2, at any rate, the doctrine of baptism and of the laying on of hands belongs to the matter handed down by tradition. In its meaning the bestowal of the Spirit (by the laying on of hands) is more closely related to the naming of the Name than to purification by the water-bath; and perhaps it was from the beginning associated with the former rather than with the latter. It would be in line with this that, in Eph. 1:13, 4:30, the "sealing" is described as the work of the Spirit—i.e. in the mind of the author the naming of the Name (= the "sealing") and the impartation of the Spirit are identical. In fact, the driving out of demons and endowment with the Holy Spirit are correlates; exorcistic effect is likewise attributed to the laying on of hands, as it is to the Name. Of course, the cooperating factors are not differentiated in the general consciousness; hence, forgiveness of sin can also be connected with the naming of the Name and "forgiveness of sins" can be said to be received "through his name" (Acts 10:43), in which the Name is probably used *a parte potiori* (chief part for the whole) for the baptismal act as a whole.

But to the three interpretations of the sacrament of baptism—purification, sealing by the Name, and bestowal of the Spirit—still a fourth and very important one is added: *Baptism imparts participation in the death and resurrection of Christ.* This interpretation undoubtedly originated in the Hellenistic Church, which understood this traditional initiation-sacrament on analogy with the initiation-sacraments of the mystery religions. The meaning of the latter is to impart to the initiates a share in the fate of the cult-deity who has suffered death and reawakened to life—such as Attis, Adonis, or Osiris.

This interpretation, by which baptism was furnished with a hitherto missing reference to the salvation-occurrence, is clearly a secondary one, for the ceremony of baptism was in no wise adapted to serve as a reproduction or dramatization of what had happened at Jesus' death and resurrection. Jesus did not die by drowning; neither did the earliest Church consider baptism "a drowning of the old Adam," as Luther did. This interpretation could attach itself to baptism only because it was, after all, the Christian sacrament of initiation; and so it came to be explained as a Hellenistically understood initiation-sacrament. Such an interpretation is foreign to Old Testament-Jewish thinking, for it knows no cultic acts based on the fate of the Deity and intending to bring its effect into the present, but only such as have their basis in the history of the People. To understand Jesus' fate as the basis for a cult, and to understand the cult as the celebration which sacramentally brings the celebrant into such fellowship with the cult-divinity that the latter's fate avails for the former as if it were his own—that is a Hellenistic mystery-idea.

Correspondingly, the effect of baptism so understood is not considered to lie in purity from sins, the protection of the Kyrios, and the bestowal of the Spirit, but in conquest over death and the acquisition of life. In Rom. 6:2ff., it is true, Paul makes an effort to bring freedom from sin into relation with the latter by teaching the reader to understand the future resurrection guaranteed by baptism as an already present resurrection which realizes itself in ethical conduct. But the artificial turn of this understanding is obvious in v. 4: "We were buried therefore with him by baptism into death, so that as Christ was raised from the dead . . . we too"—not: "might be raised from the dead," as we would expect if the sentence were logical, but "might walk in newness of life." But the explanation added in v. 5 clearly indicates the understanding to which Paul is appealing: "For if we have been united with him in a death like his, we shall certainly be united with him in a resurrection like his." The same relation exists between vss. 6 and 8.

Thus Rom. 6:2ff. clearly implies that Paul was not the first to give baptism this mystery interpretation, but that it was already current before him in Hellenistic congregations, as his question (v. 3), "or do you not know . . ." might indicate by itself. It is implied by the additional fact that when he intends to explain the origin of the new ethical way of life in baptism he does not take as his point of departure the bestowal of the Spirit (one of its meanings), as one would expect from Rom. 8:11ff. or Gal. 5:25, e.g. Instead he simply makes use of the mystery-interpretation, which he feels free to presuppose in his readers. Actually, Paul's own particular interpretation of baptism is still another one, specifically, one determined by Gnostic thought, that the baptized is incorporated into the "body of Christ" (I Cor. 12:13, Gal. 3:27f.), which will be discussed later. It is also implied, finally, by I Cor. 15:29; for what else did this vicarious baptism for the dead, which Paul already found in use, intend but just this: to give even those who had died the benefit still of the life provided by Christ's resurrection?

The school of Paul follows his thought that the life mediated by baptism is already at work in the present. Col. 2:12ff. does so by saying that being "buried with him in baptism" is the basis of forgiveness of sin and emancipation from the spirit powers. From this, then, in 2:16ff. emancipation from cultic and ritual regulations is deduced: "If with Christ you died to the elemental spirits of the universe, why do you live as if you still belonged to the world?" (2:20). It is apparent how the various motifs here flow together. More closely connected with Rom. 6:2ff. is Col. 3:1ff.: "If then you have been raised with Christ, seek the things that are above . . . for you have died . . ." Similar is the use of the terminology of the baptismal mystery in Eph. 2:5f., where, however, the idea has considerably paled. For here, though being "made alive with Christ" and being "raised up with him" are spoken of, dying with Christ is no longer mentioned (rather the contrast is expressed as being "dead through our trespasses"). But the original mystery idea reappears (though without explicit mention of baptism) in II Tim. 2:11: "If we have died with him, we shall also live with him." Similar to this is the interpretation of the tower allegory in Herm. sim. IX 16, 1: "They had need . . . to come up through water that they might be made alive. For 'they could not' otherwise 'enter into the Kingdom of God' unless they put away the mortality of their (former) life." This is the more clearly a reference to a traditional interpretation of baptism as mystery thinking is otherwise foreign to Hermas. The wide circulation of the mystery idea is also implied by such brief allusions as the interpolation in Jn. 19:34b, 35: from the wound of the crucified flowed (blood and) water. For the meaning is evidently this: In Jesus' death lies the foundation of the sacrament (of the Lord's Supper and) of baptism. The same idea lies in the statement of Ignatius Eph. 18:2: ". . . who was born and baptized that by his passion he might purify the water."

It is in harmony with the mystery interpretation of baptism that its effect is also called *re-birth*, a usage which has parallels in the mysteries. Baptism, according to Tit. 3:5, is a "bath of re-birth." This is also the conception of the text of Jn. 3:3ff. as it has come down to us when it speaks of being "born (again) by water and the Spirit," i.e. by baptism. That is an echo of an apocryphal saying of Jesus which Justin quotes in Ap. 61:4: "Unless you are born again you cannot enter the Reign of God"; moreover, Justin quotes this saying to substantiate the conception of baptism as "re-birth" (61:3, 66:1). So, according to Justin Dial. 138:2, Christians are "(a race) regenerated by him (*sc.* Christ) through water, and faith, and wood." This terminology is also echoed when I Pet. 1:3 describes God as He "who has begotten us anew to a living hope through the resurrection of Jesus Christ from the dead." So Christians can be described (1:23) as "born anew, not of perishable seed . . ." in which fact here as in Paul lies their foundation for ethical living. This terminology is not found in Paul, but the same idea lies in II Cor. 5:17: "if any one is in Christ, he is a new creature"; for "being in Christ" comes about by "being baptized into Christ" (Gal. 3:27, Rom. 6:3; *cf.* I Cor. 12:13). Barn. 6:11 similarly says: "Since he has made us new by the remission of sins (i.e. by baptism) he made us another type, that we should have the soul of children (*cf.* I Pet. 2:2) as though he were molding us anew." Likewise 16:8: "When we received the remission of sins and put our hope on the Name, we became new, being created again from the beginning."

Calling baptism *"illumination"* or using "to illumine" for "to baptize" has this same meaning. The mystery term "illumination" specifically designating baptism first occurs in Justin Ap. 61:12 (the verb occurs at 61:12f.; 65:1; Dial. 39:2: "illumined through the Name of Christ"; 122:1ff.; 123:2). Justin interprets it as an "illuminating of the mind" (Ap. 61:12; *cf.* Dial. 39:2), whereas the term originally meant not the illuminating of the mind but transformation into a divine nature which is "Light" (= "Life"). As Heb. 6:4 shows, the term in this sense had already been taken over by Christianity at a much earlier time. "Those who have once been enlightened" can by the context here only mean the baptized, and that "to be enlightened" means "to be filled with divine powers" is shown by the additional description, "who have tasted . . . the powers of the age to come." The baptized are also called "the enlightened" in 10:32. Whether the figurative use of the expression in Eph. 1:18; 3:9; II Tim. 1:10 goes back to baptismal terminology may be left an open question.

Naturally, *the other interpretations of baptism were combined with the mystery interpretation.* When the effect of baptism, understood as purification from sins, is attributed to the "resurrection of Jesus Christ" in I Pet. 3:21—i.e. to the fate of the cult-divinity—two interpretations have flowed together. Or, once the relation of the baptismal bath to Jesus' death had been worked out, a mode of thought that moved within Jewish tradition and understood Christ's death as sacrifice (§ 9, 4) could easily combine the idea of a sprinkling with the blood of Christ with that of the purifying bath of baptism, as Heb. 10:22 does. Or, again, forgiveness of sin and renewal or rebirth are combined in Barn. 6:11; 16:18; Justin Ap. 66:1; and in Justin Dial. 39:2, the "illumination" is attributed to the Name and connected with the bestowal of the Spirit. Rebirth and bestowal of the Spirit are united in Tit. 3:5; Jn. 3:5; and, correspondingly, to the heavenly powers bestowed by the sacrament, according to Heb. 6:4f., belongs primarily the Spirit.

The decisive thing that had happened in the mystery interpretation of baptism is this: The Christian initiation sacrament of baptism had been given a relation to Jesus' death and resurrection—i.e. to the occurrence of salvation—which it did not originally have. What Ignatius expresses in enigmatic brevity by saying "that by his passion he might purify the water" Barnabas 11 developed more fully: "water" (= baptism) and "the cross" belong together. From Ps. 1:3–6 Barnabas draws the conclusion: "Mark how he (*sc.* God) described the water and the cross together. For he means this: Blessed are those who hoping on the cross descended into the water." It cannot be denied that this whole interpretation brought along with it the danger that Christian existence might be built up entirely upon Hellenistic sacramental magic instead of being understood as eschatological existence. But, on the other side, the possibility seized by Paul was also given: to interpret it as an existence determined by Christ's death and resurrection and hence to understand the sacrament as an actualization, here and now, of the occurrence of salvation.

2. Besides the initiation sacrament of baptism Hellenistic Christianity knows one other sacrament, *the Lord's Supper*; its celebration is regularly repeated by the congregation.

Paul calls this meal "the Lord's supper" (κυριακὸν δεῖπνον, I Cor. 11:20), but the term that became prevalent is "Eucharist" (εὐχαριστία, a giving of thanks). This term is found in Didache, Ignatius, and Justin, and means at first, as Didache clearly indicates, the prayers spoken at the celebration of the meal and then the whole sacramental celebration. In addition to the latter, Ignatius knows the name "Agape" (Sm. 8:2; Rom. 7:3? ἀγαπᾶν, Sm. 7:1 = "hold the Agape") which also occurs in Jd. 12. It is very doubtful whether "the breaking of bread" (Acts 2:42) or "to break bread" (Acts 2:46; 20:7, 11) was ever a technical designation of the Lord's Supper. So far as the latter was a meal, "breaking of bread" could be used of it, even though the phrase in itself did not denote the sacramental meal (thus I Cor. 10:16; Did. 14:1); in itself the phrase means simply a meal (e.g. Acts 27:35). It cannot be definitely said how frequently the Lord's Supper was celebrated or in what relation its celebration stood to worship by the word. According to Did. 14:1 the whole congregation celebrated the Eucharist "each (κατὰ) Lord's Day of the Lord"; but probably there were celebrations of the Supper

in smaller groups besides. Whether the meal on "the first day
of the week" in Acts 20:7 is the Lord's Supper, must remain in
doubt; Barn. 15:9 speaks of the celebration of the "eighth day,"
as the day of Jesus' resurrection, without mentioning the Eucharist. According to Justin Ap. 65, a Eucharist follows immediately after a baptism, and according to Ap. 67, the whole congregation celebrates the Eucharist (but it is no longer a real
meal; see below) just after worship by the word on "the day
called Sun's day." When Pliny in his letter to Trajan (ep. X
96, 7) reports of the worship and the meal-celebrations of the
Christians that they take place *stato die* (on a fixed day), he
undoubtedly means Sunday.

As long as the Eucharist was a real meal (see below), it
probably took place only in the evening, as the expression
"Supper" (δεῖπνον) itself suggests; whether it was at that time
connected with a service by the word, we do not know. So far
as congregations had come out of the synagogue or followed its
traditions, at least the services of worship by the word took
place in the morning, while the Eucharist was celebrated in the
evening (Pliny: *rursusque coeundi ad capiendum cibum,* "to
convene again to take food").* Probably varying customs were
in practice in different places and times; and there is as little
foundation for saying that worship by the word and the celebration of the Supper always and everywhere took place separately as for saying that the celebration of the Supper was
always and everywhere "the cause and purpose of all congre-
gating" (Cullmann). With certainty, only Justin Ap. 67 testifies
that in Sunday worship proclamation of the word and the Eucharist were combined; but here the Eucharist is no longer a
real meal but is only a liturgical ceremony.

In addition to this, we know that only baptized persons were
admitted to the Eucharist (Did. 9:5; Justin Ap. 66:1). According to Did. 14 a confession of sin precedes the celebration and
none may participate who has an unreconciled quarrel with his
brother. The celebration of the Supper was accompanied by
prayers (Did. 9f.; Justin Ap. 65:3; 67:2; Dial. 41:1).

The liturgical words which make the Lord's Supper a sacrament
have been handed down to us by Paul and Mark in essential agree-

---

* The morning celebrations, which according to Pliny take place *ante lucem*
(before daybreak), are probably not services of the word but baptisms; **see**
H. Lietzmann, *Geschichtl. Studien für Albert Hauck* (1916), 34–38.

ment with each other; Matthew and Luke are dependent upon Mark, Luke also upon Paul.

The text of I Cor. 11:23–25 in comparison with Mk. 14:22–24 has evidently been smoothed out. In Mark's saying over the cup the modifiers placed after "my blood"—"of the covenant" and "poured out"—collide with each other; but especially does "of the covenant" collide with "my" (literal Greek order: "This is the blood of me of the covenant . . ."), indicating that "of the covenant" is a secondary addition. The Pauline text has eliminated "poured out, etc." from the words said over the cup and has compensated for it by adding "for you" (τὸ ὑπὲρ ὑμῶν) to the words said over the bread; it avoids the collision of "blood of me" with "blood of the covenant" by the formulation: "This cup is the new covenant in my blood." The much-debated Lucan text (22:14–20) with its many textual variants is not to be regarded as having the value of independent tradition in any of its forms.

This liturgy contains *three motifs*: 1. the really sacramental interpretation of the act, which is expressed in the repeated phrase "this is," by which bread and wine are offered the partaker as flesh and blood of Jesus; 2. the words "of the covenant" which interpret Jesus' death as the sacrifice of the (new) covenant; 3. the words "poured out for many" (Mk. 14:24) or "for you" (I Cor. 11:24), which interpret his death as an expiatory sacrifice for sins, of which Matthew's addition "for the forgiveness of sins" (26:28) is a correct exegesis. There can scarcely be a doubt that the first interpretation is the original one, for the act is first and foremost a meal. Then, not only "of the covenant," which has already been shown on linguistic grounds to be an addition, but also "poured out for many" or "for you" is the result of secondary interpretation, and the original liturgical words are only:

"This is my body,
This is my blood."

And that is the wording in Justin Ap. 66:3, introduced by these words only: "This do in memory of me." The primary element of the text must be the words which interpret the act.

But what, then, is the *original meaning of the act*? When the

[146]

participants by partaking of bread and wine take into themselves the body and blood of Jesus, the basic idea is that of *sacramental communion*—communion of the partakers with the Kyrios. The question asked in this connection whether the sacrament bestows participation in the crucified physical body of Jesus or in the spiritual body of the exalted Christ is wrongly put. The "glory-body" of the exalted Christ is identical with the body put to death on the cross. That is just what the sacramental idea is: that the killed body of the cult-divinity is simultaneously the body filled with power and mighty in effect. This is also apparent in the warning at I Cor. 11:27: Whoever partakes unworthily of the sacramental body and the sacramental blood of the Kyrios makes himself guilty of the Lord's death. And when Rom. 7:4 says: "you have died to the law through the body of Christ," this "body" is the crucified body of Christ, which, as such (by virtue of the resurrection) is at the same time the glory-body, mighty in effect.

That sacramental communion is the real meaning of the Lord's Supper is also indicated by I Cor. 10:16: "The cup of blessing which we bless, is it not a participation (or communion) in the blood of Christ? The bread which we break, is it not a participation (or communion) in the body of Christ?" Paul's rhetorical questions indicate that he assumes this meaning to be the one self-evident to his readers. The following v. 17 confirms this by a peculiarly Pauline turn of thought: "Because it is *one* loaf, we who are many are *one* body, for we all partake of *one* loaf"; i.e. by sacramental communion the participants are united into one "body"—in which "body" is not a figurative term for unity, but means Christ's body. The unity of the celebrating congregation is explained by the unity of the bread only if the bread is the body of Christ (as v. 16, in fact, had said).

The same conception is expressed in Jn. 6:51b–58, a passage which is secondary within the Gospel of John. At the same time, this passage expresses what the effect of the sacrament for the participants is: Whoever eats the flesh ("flesh" as in Ignatius and Justin, instead of "body") and drinks the blood of Jesus thereby achieves Life. Ignatius, who in Phld. 4:1 defines the purpose of the cup as being "for union with his blood (*sc.* of Jesus Christ)," and for whom the Eucharist is "the flesh of our Savior" (Sm. 7:1), quite in this sense calls the eucharistic bread "the medicine of immortality, the antidote that we should not die, but live forever in Jesus Christ"

(Eph. 20:2). And in the same sense Justin Ap. 66:2 says that the elements of the Eucharist by the power of the prayer spoken become the flesh and blood of Christ and that by this nourishment "our flesh and blood are transformingly (κατὰ μεταβολήν) fed"—i.e. are transformed into a supranatural nature.

In Hellenistic Christianity the Lord's Supper, like baptism, is understood *as a sacrament in the sense of the mystery religions.* The idea of communion brought about by the sacramental meal is in itself not a specific idea of the mysteries, but is wide-spread in primitive and classic cults. But in the mysteries it plays a special role; in them it is communion with a once dead and risen deity, in whose fate the partaker receives a share through the sacramental meal, as we know from the mysteries of Attis and Mithra. Paul himself shows that the sacrament of the Lord's Supper stands in this context in the history of religions. He does so not only by calling the Lord's Supper "the table of the Lord," thereby using a Hellenistic term for cultic banquets (I Cor. 10:21; on which see Lietzmann in the *Handbuch zum NT*), but especially by the way he contrasts the cup and table of the Lord with heathen sacrificial meals: as these make the partakers "partners (or communicants) with demons," the Lord's Supper brings about "communion" (or partnership) with the Lord. And Justin declares the sacramental meal of the Mithra-initiates, in which bread and a cup of water are set before them with words of blessing, to be a demonic aping of the Eucharist (Ap. 66:4).

Like baptism, the Lord's Supper also is attributed, in keeping with the mode of thinking characteristic of the mystery religions, to the fate of the Kyrios as its founding cause—especially to Jesus' last meal with his disciples. That is the meaning of the prefatory words in I Cor. 11:23: "the Lord Jesus on the night when he was betrayed . . ." And it is in this direction that Mark cast his account of the last supper in the form of an etiological cult-narrative by working the eucharistic liturgy into an older traditional account which reported the last supper as a Passover meal. At bottom, it is the death of the Kyrios that is specified as the real foundation of the cultic meal when it is attributed to Jesus' last supper, for the body and blood of Jesus distributed by him at this meal are, of course (as precisely the secondary words of interpretation corroborate), in mysterious anticipation the body and blood of the crucified, sacrificed Christ. Paul clearly indicates that in the sentence added by him

(I Cor. 11:26): "For as often as you eat this bread and drink the cup, you proclaim the Lord's death."

That is, he conceives the eucharistic meal as a representational rite (δρώμενον) like the "acted rites" (δρώμενα) of the mysteries; the ceremony acts out the death of the Lord. And it is significant that Ignatius does not even mention the last supper of Jesus; for him the real institution of the Eucharist is the passion of Christ.

Quite understandably, the sacramental meal also received *other interpretations*. It was accompanied by various prayers, and in them "the proclamation of the Lord's death" which took place in the sacred act could be verbally expanded. It is not to be wondered at that such interpretations were then also adopted into the liturgy. The interpretations of Jesus' death as covenant sacrifice and as expiatory sacrifice were current, as we have seen (§ 9, 4, p. 84); and how easily such thoughts arose is indicated, e.g. by Jn. 6:51b ("for the life of the world") or Ign. Sm. 7:1 (Jesus' eucharistic "flesh" conceived as "having suffered for our sins") or by Justin Dial. 41:1. Though the additions "of the covenant" and "(poured out) for" are derived from the Jewish-Christian tradition, the sentences I Cor. 11:24f., which are without parallel in Mark, had their origin in the Gentile-Christian sphere—namely, the repeated instruction: "Do this in memory of me." They are apparently to be attributed to the fact that the Lord's Supper was conceived in analogy to Hellenistic memorial-ceremonies, for in the deeds of bequest for such ceremonies similar formulas occur (see Lietzmann on I Cor. 11:41f. in the *Handbuch zum NT*). According to Justin Dial. 41:4, also, the Eucharist is celebrated "in memory of the passion." "Out of these ideas grew the so-called Anamnesis,* in the most ancient liturgies."

In the course of development the *Eucharist came to be conceived of as a sacrifice*. It is called "sacrifice" in Did. 14:1, but there, it must be admitted, it is still meant figuratively—or rather the Eucharist is thereby designated as a cultic act which in the Christian congregation has taken the place of actual sacrifice. Ignatius, too, uses sacrificial terminology when, in urging unity upon the congregation gathered together under the bishop, he speaks of the "altar" or the "altar space" (θυσιαστήριον) within which the "bread of God" is dis-

---

* The "commemoration"-section of the eucharistic liturgy; (for examples see Lietzmann's commentary on I Cor. 11:26 and Lietzmann: *Messe und Herrenmahl*, pp. 50ff.).

tributed (Eph. 4:2), or when he speaks of the "one altar" which must be the only one in the congregation (Philad. 4). I Clem. prepares for this development of meaning in a different way when he places the Christian cultic officials in analogy with the priests of the Old Testament (I Clem. 40). Justin specifically calls the Eucharist a sacrifice (Dial. 41:3; 117:1), though he leaves us in doubt what he conceives the thing sacrificed to be. Only at a later stage of the development will that be made definite.

But another development, a presupposition for the last named one, takes place still earlier: *the divorce of the sacramental meal from an actual meal.* That the Lord's Supper was originally framed by a real meal for the satisfaction of the participants' hunger, or was itself the frame for such a meal, is attested by I Cor. 11; in a different way Didache also attests this combination (see below). But I Cor. also indicates that this arrangement led to irregularities; hence, Paul directs that hunger be satisfied by a meal at home before the sacramental celebration (11:21, 34). We do not know how soon in the various areas the real meal for hunger was eliminated from the cultic celebration; in Justin it has already been accomplished and the Eucharist has been combined with the service of the word (see above). But social meals continued to be held in the churches, and the title "Agape" stuck to them; they were occasions of sociability and charity.

The earliest witness to the sacrament of the Lord's Supper is Paul; but he created it no more than he did baptism; rather *he found it already present in Hellenistic Christianity.*

When, in I Cor. 11:23, he introduces the liturgical words with the sentence: "For I received from the Lord . . ." he is not appealing to a personal revelation from the Lord, though this is frequently assumed, but to a tradition that has been handed down to him, being ultimately derived from the' Lord. Our comparison of I Cor. 11:23–25 with Mk. 14:22–24 has shown that Paul's text represents an older one which has undergone editorial smoothing; and the analysis of the liturgical sentences showed that they imply a development in the course of which the various motifs combined. Another indication that Paul found the liturgical words already in existence is the fact that they speak of a "communion" with the (body and the) blood of the Lord. Can Paul, for whom "flesh and blood" are excluded from the Reign of God (I Cor. 15:50), have created this text? He also speaks in I Cor. 10:16 of sacramental communion as something self-evident for Christians; the "we" of these sentences is evidently the same as that of Rom. 6:2ff.

But did *Hellenistic Christianity* itself create the sacramental meal of communion—or is it, analogous to the mystery interpretation of baptism—the interpretation of a traditional custom, i.e. the fellowship meals derived from the earliest Church (§ 6, 4 and § 8, 3)? This question cannot be answered with certainty. It would be comprehensible if such meals, which were not really cultic ceremonies but were a bond and expression of fellowship in keeping with the tradition of Judaism and of the historical Jesus himself, should have been transformed into sacramental celebrations in Hellenistic Christianity. That may be regarded as the probable process. But in any case it must be borne in mind that the development in one place may have been different from that in another. The Didache apparently implies that at various places in Hellenistic Christianity, too, those fellowship meals continued to be held without developing into the sacramental Lord's Supper.

From Did. 9 and 10 we get a picture of a meal-celebration quite in keeping with Jewish tradition (§ 6, 4), in which there is no reference whatever to the death of Jesus and no mention of sacramental communion. It does appear to be true that the words of 10:6 are to be understood as a transition to the sacramental Eucharist, the liturgy of which does not need to be set down because it is familiar to all. But then it is clear that two celebrations of entirely different kind have been secondarily combined. Therefore, the celebration implied in Did. 9 and 10 existed at first by itself, and it must have been from it that the Lord's Supper took over the title "Eucharist" ("Thanksgiving"), which is a very strange term for the sacrament of the Lord's Supper.

3. Out of the facts set forth in §§ 12, 13 arise a number of questions for the future. First of all is the question already raised in § 11, 3a *whether a sacrificial cult and a priesthood will develop in the Christian Church.* At the same time the question arises *whether the cult will come to be considered one-sidedly as the means to salvation*, corresponding to Ignatius' conception of the Eucharist

as the "medicine of immortality" (see above p. 147)—that is to say, also corresponding to the conception of the Hellenistic mystery religions—or whether its meaning will remain that of being the self-representation of the eschatological Congregation, for which salvation is already present as anticipated future.

So far as salvation is held to be present in the cult, there is also the question how this presence is to be understood. Is the transcendent world present in the cult as a thing to be experienced and enjoyed, a reality of which one becomes aware by ecstasy and all sorts of "pneumatic" phenomena (§ 14)? That also means *how will the relationship between cult and eschatology be settled?* When Christ is worshiped as the present Lord, will the expectation of the coming Christ remain alive? Or will it fade out and thereby push the eschatological expectation clear into the background? Will the end of the world be postponed into an indefinite future, resulting in the reduction of Christian hope for the future to the hope for individual "immortality"? Or will the conception that the cult is the appropriate form for representing the eschatological transcendence of the Church win out? If so, will it do so through the idea that the congregation at worship is also a demonstration of God's judgment over the world, as Paul holds (I Cor. 14:21-25)? Will it win out by regarding the cult as that which calls the worshipers into question as earthly men and points them to that which they are not yet and yet, regarded from the view-point of the eschatological occurrence, already are, and which they must make manifest in their lives in order—as Paul puts it—to "shine as lights in the world" (Phil. 2:15)?

That also contains the question *in what relation will the cult and every-day life be placed to each other?* Is the cult—and with it "religion"—an interrupting and occasional thing within secular living? Is it to be understood as a guarantee of life after death and as having no relation to the present? Or is the whole person in his present every-day living determined by the cult? And if so, is his conduct negatively determined by regulations, either ritualistic or ascetic (§ 10, 4)? Or is one's conduct of life positively determined by the cult in this sense: that both the congregation and the individual are regarded as the temple of God and of His Spirit, a fact which each must confirm by ethical conduct so that one's whole life becomes service of God, or "cult," or "sacrifice" (§ 10, 4, p. 101f.; § 11, 3a, p. 115)? Similar questions will soon arise again.

§ 14. The Spirit

1. In baptism, the Spirit has been conferred upon all Christians (§ 13, 1, p. 138); it shows itself to be alive in them in the worship services of the congregation (§ 12, 1, p. 122). What is meant by "the Spirit"? How is Christian existence determined by it? Neither the conceptions of the Spirit (πνεῦμα) nor those of the individual's possession of the Spirit are entirely homogeneous.

> The variation in *terminology*, however, does not imply variation in content of meaning. The same thing is meant whether "Holy Spirit" (ἅγιον πνεῦμα, on the basis of the Old Testament-Jewish רוּחַ הַקֹּדֶשׁ, "Spirit of Holiness") is used, or simply "Spirit," or "Spirit of God." Since the gift of the Spirit was brought about by the salvation-occurrence accomplished in Christ, the Spirit can be regarded as God's and also as Christ's gift, hence one may also speak of the "Spirit of Christ" or "of the Lord."

So far as the *Spirit-concept* is concerned, the basic notion underlying it, is, to be sure, homogeneous. Right comprehension of it has often been hindered by the choice of "Spirit" to translate *pneuma*, inasmuch as "spirit" in modern languages, especially in German (*Geist*), can also mean "mind." *Pneuma* does not mean "spirit" in the Greek-Platonic and the idealistic sense; i.e. it does not mean mind in contrast to body (regarded as the vehicle of sensuous life), or in contrast to nature. "Mind" in this sense, the active subject in "mental" or "spiritual" life, is called in Greek νοῦς, or ψυχή ("soul"), or λόγος ("reason"). Rather, *pneuma* is the miraculous divine power that stands in absolute contrast to all that is human. This comes out in Paul when he denies that the Corinthians are "spiritual men" (πνευματικοί) and asks them in view of their conduct, "are you not (ordinary) men?" (I Cor. 3:1–4). Or again Ignatius expresses it (Eph. 5:1) when he describes his "fellowship" with the bishop of Ephesus as "not human, but spiritual." Generally, the sphere of the human is termed "flesh" (σάρξ) to indicate its contrast to *pneuma*—a usage which, though not peculiar to Paul, was especially developed by him and need not here be treated (see § 23). The manifestations of the Spirit are that in a man's conduct which is extraordinary, mysteriously or terrifyingly mighty, and seems inexplicable as coming from merely human capabilities and powers. This, then, constitutes the concept of *pneuma*: *it is the miraculous—insofar as that takes place in the sphere of human life—either in what men do or in what is done to them.* To the *pneuma* are attributed miracles and extraordinary psychic phenomena but also brilliant insights and deeds of heroism or of moral power—but such are regarded as "pneumatic" (spiritual) not because they are phenomena of the inner or ethical life but because they are miraculous.

Such phenomena are called "spiritual [gifts]" (πνευματικά, I Cor. 12:1, 14:1) or "gifts" (χαρίσματα, Rom. 12:6, I Cor. 12:4, 9, 28, 30f.; I Tim. 4:14; II Tim. 1:6; I Pet. 4:10; I Clem. 38:1; Ign. Sm. pr., 2:2). Specified as such gifts are: the "word of wisdom" and the "word of knowledge" (I Cor. 12:8); the two are probably joined together in the "gift of teaching" (Rom. 12:7; I Cor. 12:28f.; 14:26; *cf.* Acts 6:10). The "faith" in I Cor. 12:9 is certainly the faith that is capable of working miracles (*cf.* I Cor. 13:2). Not clearly distinguishable from this are the "gifts of healing" (I Cor. 12:9, 28, 30) and the "working of miracles" (I Cor. 12:10; *cf.* 12:28f.; Gal. 3:5; *cf.* Rom. 15:18f.; Heb. 2:4; Acts 6:8); in fact, as a rule the distinction between related gifts must not be too precisely made. The "gift of prophecy" is often mentioned (Rom. 12:6; I Cor. 12:10, 28f.; 13:2, 8f.; 14:5f.; I Thess. 5:20; Acts 19:6; *cf.* Rev. as a whole, espec. 22:9, for instance; also Ign. Philad. 7). How "revelation" (I Cor. 14:6, 26, 30) is related to this gift or to the "word of knowledge" can scarcely be said. Especially sought after by the Corinthian church is the gift, also highly regarded by Paul, of "tongues," ecstatic "speaking in tongues" (I Cor. 12:10, 28, 30; 14:18, 26; Acts 19:6; is it also meant by the Spirit that is not to be "quenched"? I Thess. 5:19), a gift which finds its complement in the "interpretation of tongues" (I Cor. 12:10, 30). Finally, Paul mentions the gift of "distinguishing between spirits" (I Cor. 12:10). This list of gifts, to the enumeration of which Paul restricts himself in I Cor. 12:7–10, evidently includes those generally recognized as such. Other gifts include prayers uttered "in the Spirit" (I Cor. 14:14f.; Eph. 6:18? Jd. 20; Mart. Pol. 7:2f.) and songs sung "in the Spirit" (psalms, hymns, spiritual songs; I Cor. 14:15, 26; Col. 3:16; Eph. 5:18f.), while it is a peculiarity of Paul that he reckons "services of help" and "powers of administration" (I Cor. 12:28), "service" (Rom. 12:7f.) and similar activities to the "gifts" of the Spirit. On the other hand, it is evidently a common Christian opinion that man is guided by the Spirit in important decisions (Acts 13:2, 4; 16:6f.; *cf.* Gal. 2:2); and when Paul regards the unmarried state as a special "gift" (I Cor. 7:7) that probably also corresponds to general Christian opinion.

There is also agreement that *the bestowal of the Spirit is an eschatological gift* and that its coming into effect in the Church is an eschatological event. The earliest Church had so understood the Spirit (§ 6, 5), and the Hellenistic Church likewise did. When Paul calls the Spirit "the first fruits" (Rom. 8:23) or the "guarantee" (II Cor. 1:22; 5:5) of future glory (in which Eph. 1:13f. follows his lead), he is only expressing the common Christian conviction. According to Heb. 6:4f., the baptized, who have become partakers of the Holy Spirit, have already "tasted . . . the powers of the age to come." That is perhaps also what is meant in Barn. 1:7, where it is said that God "has given us a foretaste of the things to come." At any rate, it is clear that for Barnabas, too, it is being filled with the Spirit (1:2f.) which makes the Congregation into the eschatological temple of God (16:5ff.). The outpouring of the Spirit at Pentecost is the fulfilment of Joel's prophecy for the end of days (Acts 2:16ff.). And for I Pet., it is self-evident (1:3ff.) that "sanctification by the Spirit" (1:2) makes the sanctified heirs-apparent of the eschatological salvation soon to appear.

Over against these agreements *the differences in conception relating to the Spirit* are relatively unimportant; nevertheless, one important matter is expressed in them, as will appear.

In *animistic thinking pneuma* is conceived as an independent agent, a personal power which like a demon can fall upon a man and take possession of him, enabling him or compelling him to perform manifestations of power. In *dynamistic thinking,* on the contrary, *pneuma* appears as an impersonal force which fills a man like a fluid, so to say. One or the other of these ways of thinking may be distinctly present in a given passage; but in general little emphasis is placed upon the distinction, and the two conceptions can intertwine in the same author.

The *animistic* conception is present, e.g. in Rom. 8:16; I Cor. 2:10-16; 14:14; likewise Acts 5:32; 10:19; 16:6f.; 20:23; Ign. Philad. 7:1f.; and also in John—though here it has faded to a figure of speech—14:26; 15:26; 16:8, 13-15. It is also apparent in the use of the plural for spirits that work in individual persons (I Cor. 14:12, 32; esp. in the Mandata of Hermas); or also from the fact that a spirit is mentioned which evokes a specific effect (as in the Old Testament also—thus, the "spirit of stupor" (Rom. 11:8 quoting Is. 29:10; also the "spirit of gentleness" I Cor. 4:21; *cf.* further: II Cor. 4:13; Gal. 6:1; Eph. 1:17; II Tim. 1:7; Rev. 19:10). Often, it is true, the original concrete idea no longer remains but has been sublimated to a mere form of speech (as in I Cor. 4:21; Gal. 6:1). The *dynamistic* conception is the usual one; and it is evidently present wherever the "giving" (διδόναι or δοθῆναι), the "gift," the "pouring out," or the "supplying" of the Spirit is mentioned (Rom. 5:5; II Cor. 1:22; 5:5; I Thess. 4:8; Acts 2:38; 10:45; Heb. 6:4—Tit. 3:6; Acts 2:17f.; 10:45; I Clem. 2:2; 46:6; Barn. 1:3—Gal. 3:5; Phil. 1:19). This conception is also clear cut in Rom. 8:11, or also where "Holy Spirit" is coordinated with definite terms like "wisdom," "faith," "joy" (Acts 6:3, 5; 11:24; 13:52), and especially where "Spirit" and "power" are united in a hendiadys (I Cor. 2:4; I Thess. 1:5; Lk. 1:17); but also where the "power of the (Holy) Spirit" is mentioned (Rom. 15:13, 19; Ign. Sm. 13:1; *cf.* also Herm. sim. IX 1, 2 "empowered by the Spirit"). It can almost be said that "Spirit" and "power" are synonymous; that is the case in Herm. sim. IX 13, 2 where the "holy spirits" are soon after called "the powers of the Son of God." It is also very significant that in Heb. 7:16 the contrast to "after the law of a carnal commandment" (KJ) is not formed by means of the concept "spiritual," as one would expect according to the usual antithesis of "flesh" and "spirit," but is formulated: "after the power of an endless life" (KJ). Since "power" and "glory" can be synonymous (*cf.* Rom. 6:4 with I Cor. 6:14), so "spirit" is also related to "glory," the life-giving power from heaven; the "spiritual body" (I Cor. 15:44) is the "body of glory" or "glorious body" of Phil. 3:21); the resurrection of "the spiritual body" is a raising up "in glory" and "in power" (I Cor. 15:43). The textual variants of I Pet. 4:14 ("spirit of glory" or "spirit of glory and of power") beautifully illustrate the kinship of the concepts "spirit," "glory," and "power." The synonymity of πνευματικόν ("spiritual gift") and χάρισμα ("gift"; lit. "token of grace") indicates that "grace" can also be synonymous with "spirit"—or that "grace" can be conceived as a spiritual "power." See I Cor. 15:10; II Cor. 12:9; this is very clear in Acts 6:8 where "full of grace and power" corresponds to "full . . . of the Holy Spirit" in 6:5. *Cf.* also Ign. Mg. 8:2 ("inspired, ἐμπνεόμενοι, by his grace"); Rm. pr., Pol. 1:2 (*cf.* Mart. Pol. 7:3).

Neither conception is foreign to the Old Testament. Nevertheless the animistic one must be regarded as characteristic for Old Testament thought. The same is true of another distinction which to a certain extent coincides with the animistic-dynamistic one. The Spirit can be conceived *as the power which seizes a man, or is given to him, for a specific situation or moment,* causing in him a temporary condition or eliciting specific deeds for that sole time. Or it can be conceived *as a power permanently allotted to him, resting in him, so to say,* which, of course, goes into effect on special occasions, but which also gives his whole mode of life a special character, imparting a supranatural quality to his nature. The former conception is that of the Old Testament and Judaism. The latter is apparently present there, too, in embryo, but it is characteristic of the Hellenistic world. Hellenism, in turn, also knows the former conception, especially the phenomenon of ecstasy, in which, for moments, divine power lifts a man out of the sphere of the earthly. Nevertheless, the typical "pneumatic" in Hellenism is the "divine man" (θεῖος ἀνήρ), who is of higher nature than ordinary mortals, filled with mysterious, divine power, which makes him capable of miraculous insights and deeds. The term for the power in him is not, it is true, as a rule *pneuma,* but *dynamis,* power ("grace" also occurs); but in substance it means the same thing as the *pneuma* of early Christianity (dynamistically understood).

2. The variety in regard to these points accounts for certain inconsistencies or contradictions in Hellenistic Christian conceptions of the Spirit. On the one hand, the general conviction is *that all Christians have received the Spirit in baptism* and have thereby been transformed into a new nature (§ 13, 1, p. 138). The Spirit thus possessed is ordinarily latent, so to say, but can manifest itself in miraculous deeds (Gal. 3:5); according to Paul, it is above all the power for ethical living. But this is an idea peculiar to him. Generally accepted, however, appears to be the view which is also self-evident to Paul—that possessing the Spirit, which is God's life-giving power, lends the assurance of triumph over death, *the certainty of the resurrection and of eternal life* (Rom. 8:10f.; *cf.* Gal. 6:8). The Spirit "gives life" (II Cor. 3:6); it is a "life-giving Spirit" (I Cor. 15:45; Jn. 6:63) or a "Spirit of life" (Rom. 8:2). The resurrection body is a "spiritual body" (I Cor. 15:44). Contrasted to the "service of death" stands the "service of the Spirit" (II Cor. 3:7f.).

"Sealing" by the Spirit guarantees future salvation (Eph. 1:13f.; 4:30), whose "first-fruits" or "pledge" is precisely the Spirit (see above; *cf.* also Heb. 6:4f.). Did. 10:3 gives thanks that God has bestowed upon the Church in the Eucharist "spiritual food and drink and eternal life." Whoever has received the Spirit in baptism is, according to Barn. 11:11, sure of eternal life; and II Clem. 14:5 even formulates the idea in such a way that the very flesh participates in "life" and "incorruption" when the Spirit has united with it. The angel of repentance in Hermas bases his promise of heavenly glory in fellowship with the Son of God upon these words: "for of his Spirit you have received" (Sim. IX 24, 4).

But elsewhere the fact of common possession of the Spirit is ignored—ignored in various respects. First, it is rather often mentioned *that there are people who are to be regarded as bearers of the Spirit* (πνευματικοί) *in a special sense,* or who so regard themselves. Paul (I Cor. 2:13–3:3) distinguishes between people in the Church who are Spirit-endowed (πνευματικοί) and those who are "unspiritual" (ψυχικοί; KJ: "natural") or "men of flesh" (σαρκικοί; KJ: "carnal")—contrary to the proposition that all the baptized have received the Spirit. He similarly distinguishes between the Spirit-endowed in the Church and those whom some trespass has overtaken and who therefore cannot be regarded as Spirit-endowed (Gal. 6:1). It means the same thing when he makes a distinction between "the mature" (τέλειοι, Phil. 3:15) and others; for according to I Cor. 2:6 (compared with 2:13ff.) "the mature" are identical with the "Spirit-endowed." Now this view that there are people specially marked as endowed with the Spirit, is evidently not peculiar to Paul —regardless of whether he ascribed this dignity to the same persons as others did, or not. It may be regarded as especially the view of gnosticizing Christians (§ 15); at any rate, it was wide-spread. For, since Paul can say, "If any one thinks that he is a prophet, or one Spirit-endowed" (I Cor. 14:37 tr.), he presupposes a usage of speech according to which the ecstatic speaker in tongues (in the context it can mean only him) is the "Spirit-endowed" *par excellence,* as if ignoring the fact that prophecy is also a gift of the Spirit.

One must ask whether in an inconsistency of this sort there does not appear a difference in the conception of what the Spirit is. When some in the Church as "Spirit-endowed" are distinguished from others, the Spirit is obviously not understood as the power that governs the Christian as Christian. How that can be understood must be shown further on. The conception *that one may possess the Spirit in varying quantity or intensity* is more easily reconciled with the idea that all Christians have the Spirit. When individuals are described as being "full of the Spirit and of wisdom" or "full of faith and the Holy Spirit" (Acts 6:3, 5; 11:24), that intends to affirm nothing more than that they are especially richly and powerfully endowed with the Spirit. Barn. 1:2f., for instance, shows how this conception is compatible with that of baptismal grace; the author rejoices that the readers have received (by baptism) "the implanted grace of the Spirit-gift" in such high degree (οὕτως) "that I truly see in you the Spirit of the Lord, whose fountain is rich, poured out upon you" (tr.).

Related to this conception is the view that there are not only *various gifts of the Spirit* ("apportionings of the Holy Spirit" Heb. 2:4; "distributions" KJ mg.), but that these also *vary in value*—a view which Paul assumes to be current in Corinth (I Cor. 12, 14), and which he also shares, himself, when he outlines a value-gradation among spiritual gifts, as it were (I Cor. 12:28), or exhorts: "earnestly desire the higher gifts" (12:31). That really contradicts the view that the Spirit has been bestowed upon all Christians at baptism. For it is the Spirit that accomplishes the decisive thing: It makes Christians new creatures. But in the conception under discussion the Spirit is spoken of as the miraculous power which grants the capacity for certain particularly excellent deeds or attitudes, and its operation is perceived in specific "gifts" so that Paul under certain circumstances has occasion to emphasize the unity of origin of the various gifts (I Cor. 12:4ff.).

But the Spirit not only shows differences in its particular gifts, *it also manifests its activity at particular moments.* It is at special times that a person is "filled with the Spirit" (Acts 4:8, 31; 13:9) or is "full of the Spirit" (Acts 7:55) or is "transported by the Spirit" (γίνεσθαι ἐν πνεύματι, Rev. 1:10; 4:2; *cf.* 17:3). In this, too, the possession of the Spirit by all Christians is ignored—and devout Jews can be spoken of in the same way (Lk. 1:41; of the Baptist, Lk. 1:15; of Jesus himself, Lk. 4:1). The same is true of the formula "speak (or "pray," or the like) in the Spirit" or "by the Spirit" (I Cor. 12:3; 14:2, 14ff.; Did. 11:7), which, of course, does not at all mean just speaking that is Christian, but rather a speaking in momentary seizure by the Spirit.

Finally, it is curious—and again not in harmony with the general view of baptism—that by the side of the ordinary view that the Spirit is the origin of all distinctly Christian phenomena, another view can find room: *that an effort or an appropriate attitude on man's part is needed to bring about the gift of the Spirit or of a particular spiritual gift*—or at least to increase or strengthen it. This is already implied in "earnestly desiring spiritual gifts" (I Cor. 12:31; 14:1) and in the exhortation: "strive to excel" (I Cor. 14:12) or "earnestly desire to prophesy" (I Cor. 14:39). So Barn. 4:11 directly urges: "Let us be spiritual" (somewhat different from the paradoxical exhortation at Gal. 5:25!), whereas II Tim. 1:6 more modestly urges the "rekindling" of "the gift of God" (in this case it is the specific gift of the teaching office that is meant). The means of achieving a particular gift of the Spirit is prayer, according to I Cor. 14:13. Fasting, according to Acts 13:2, is the preparation for revelation by the Spirit. This agrees with the traditional Jewish view. According to II Clem. 14:4, asceticism is the presupposition for the receipt of the Spirit. But according to I Clem. 2:2, it was on account of its model conduct that the Corinthian church had experienced a "full out-pouring of the Holy Spirit."

3. In the inconsistency—in fact, the contradictoriness—of these conceptions a significant fact in regard to the Spirit is reflected. Once it has been seen, this inconsistency can to a large extent be called appropriate to the nature of Spirit.

The view that all Christians receive the Spirit in baptism does not rest upon the idea that the individuals baptized have special "spiritual" or emotional experiences during the act of baptism, however much that may occasionally have been the case. Rather, it rests basically upon the fact *that the Spirit is given to the Church,* into which the individual is received by baptism. Hence, the Spirit bestowed upon the Church is often dwelt upon, or the gifts that are at work in the Church (I Cor. 1:4ff.; I Clem. 2:2; Barn. 1:2f.; Herm. mand. XI 14). Whoever imposes upon the Church deceives the Holy Spirit (Acts 5:3), and what the Church (through its leaders) decides and proclaims is thereby the Spirit's proclamation (Acts 13:2; 15:28). For the earliest Church there was no problem here at all, but for the Hellenistic Church there now arises the question how participation in the Spirit becomes a reality in all individuals. Do they possess the Spirit only in faith?—i.e. only in the conviction that in a manner at present hidden from view they are no longer of earthly nature but by the power of the Spirit dwelling within them will not perish with this world but in a changed form, a "spiritual body," will participate in the glory of the world that is soon to appear? Or, in case they die before the *parousia* of the Lord, that they will be awakened from the dead? Or do they already feel indications of possessing the Spirit? Is its life-giving power already at work in them?

The common Christian conviction is that the last of these is the case, and quite naturally *the workings of the Spirit are experienced above all in the service of worship*, in which the eschatological Congregation takes present form. It understands everything that is given it here as the gift of the Spirit, especially what transcends the limits of the ordinary—the word of instruction, which dispenses wisdom and knowledge, as well as prophecy, which uncovers the mystery of future events but which also reveals what lurks in the heart—prayers and songs and especially ecstatic speaking in tongues. However, it is clear that the criterion by which these utterances are judged to be gifts of the Spirit is not how Christian they may be, but how extraordinary their symptoms—the phenomena that accompany or precede them—may be. Doubtless the content of such enthusiastic utterances, except where they are completely unintelligible, is always assumed to be appropriate, but that is not what makes them "spiritual gifts." And we must think of the range between what was intelligible and significant in content and what was unintelligibly ecstatic or irrelevant in content as a wide one. Prayer may be anything from clear conscious speech to stammering in ecstatic tongues (I Cor. 14:14f.); it may be a wordless sigh (Rom. 8:26) or an ecstatic cry of "Abba" (Rom. 8:15; Gal. 4:6).

But the workings of the Spirit extend beyond these phenomena, which belong, primarily at least, to the cultic gathering. Its power manifests itself in all extraordinary achievements and modes of conduct. First of all, in *missionary activity* for which the Spirit gives instructions (Acts 13:2, 4; 16:6f.) and whose bearer, the *apostle* (I Cor. 12:28), is legitimated as a bearer of the Spirit by miracles (II Cor. 12:12; *cf.* Rom. 15:18f.; I Cor. 2:4; I Thess. 1:5; I Pet. 1:12; Heb. 2:4; I Clem. 42:3). *Prophecy and teaching* appear not only within the worship service as momentary gifts to one individual or another; they can also be the permanent possession of certain persons (for both prophets and teachers, see I Cor. 12:28; Eph. 4:11; Acts 13:1; Did. 11–13; for prophets, also Rev.—e.g. 22:9; Herm. mand. XI; for teachers, Jas. 3:1; Barn. 1:8; 4:9; Herm. vis. III 5, 1; mand. IV 3, 1; sim. IX 15, 4; 16, 5; 25, 2). But just as the gifts of prophecy and teaching can be given to any member of the congregation, so can the capacity for special acts, such as *healing and other miracles* (I Cor. 12:8ff., 28ff.). To these, Paul also reckons *gifts of "help" and "administration"* and various kinds of assistance, but that is peculiar to him. It is somewhat different when the officials of the congregation (by virtue of the laying on of hands) are later regarded as bearers of the Spirit. Also peculiar to Paul is the attribution of *ethical* conduct to the Spirit (Gal. 5:22-25; Rom. 8:4); outside of Paul and writings influenced by him ethical conduct is everywhere placed one-sidedly under the imperative. Very strange are the remarks of Herm. sim. IX 13 about the "virgins" who are building the tower of the Church (IX 2ff.); according to IX 15, 2f., they are "virtues," but in IX 13 they are interpreted as "holy spirits" or "as powers of the Son of God." Still, no serious attempt to found ethical conduct upon the Spirit is present here. Still less is that the case in the mandata (esp. mand. V) of Hermas; in them the idea of good powers dwelling in man as "spirits" is only precariously combined with the Christian conception of the Holy Spirit.

To sum up, *a double understanding of pneuma is discernible.* On the one hand, it is the power conferred in baptism which makes the Christian a Christian—a power which already in the present takes him out of this perishing world and "seals" him for the one to come. On the other hand, it is the power given now and again for the occasion to the Christian, enabling him to accomplish extraordinary things. If, now, it is taken seriously that the Spirit given in baptism truly determines Christian existence and is not just "believed in" in the sense that its possession guarantees resurrection or an eternal life, then—until a thinker like Paul takes hold of the problem—*inconsistent and contradictory statements will inevitably arise, because they are inherent in the matter itself.* For the statements which conceive the Spirit as a power given for the occasion and accomplishing extraordinary things are attempts to understand it as the power that determines Christian existence. In this contradiction it comes to light that the baptized Christian who, as such, belongs to the world to come, is, in his temporary present existence, not yet what he is to be and in the sight of God already is, but that his belonging to the world to come nevertheless determines his present existence. And in the contradiction that on the one hand the Spirit is the origin of a new attitude and capacity in the Christian, and on the other hand that his attitude qualifies him for ever-new endowment with the Spirit and that he must strive after spiritual gifts, an expression is provided for the insight that the might of the Spirit is not a magically (mechanically) working power, but is one that equally demands and presupposes a transformation of the will—although this paradoxical situation is clearly recognized only by Paul (Gal. 5:25).

Now the question arises, however, *how an understanding of existence founded and upheld by the eschatological divine power of the Spirit will develop.* It is the problem of delimitation from the world and of eschatological dualism (§ 10, 4 and 5). Insofar as the Christian's delimitation from and opposition to the world are believed to be founded and guaranteed by the gift of the Spirit and are so experienced, dangers arise for the Church. If the activity of the Spirit is seen in special deeds of power which are regarded as unambiguous signs of Spirit endowment, the existence of a Christian is in danger of being conceived as that of a Hellenistic "divine man" (θεῖος ἀνήρ), and the eschatological history of salvation comes to be regarded in the light of edifying legend—a danger which is already apparent in the New Testament, but which shows its full consequences in the apocryphal acts of the apostles. Simultaneously, the Spirit-endowed become arrogant, as the exhortations of I Cor. 12 already indicate. But if, instead, the real essence of Christian existence is held to lie in subjective emotional experiences and the activity of the Spirit accordingly to be the producing of emotional experiences, then an individualistic sort of Spirit-endowment will arise which may, of course, also express itself in deeds of power, but culminates in ecstasy. Then the Spirit will no longer be understood as the gift conferred upon the Church, nor will it any longer be the "first-fruits" or the "guarantee." Rather, eschatological de-secularization will be interpreted in terms of mysticism. I Cor. 12–14 and II Cor. especially indicate that these dangers existed. A sense of such a danger is shown also by the yet unsettled question which the Corinthian church evidently had asked Paul: By what criterion can divine and demonic ecstasy be distinguished from each other (I Cor. 12:2f.)? In other words, ecstasy is no unambiguous phenomenon in itself.

§ 15. Gnostic Motifs

PRELIMINARY REMARKS

In the Hellenistic world it was a historical necessity that the gospel should be translated into a terminology with which that world was familiar—this gospel of the one true God and of Jesus the Messiah-Son-of-Man with its eschatological message of imminent judgment and salvation, all of which had at first been embodied in the concepts of the Old Testament-Jewish tradition. How the Messiah-Son-of-Man, whose parousia was expected, became the cultically worshiped Kyrios has been shown in § 12. To express convincingly to Hellenistic ears his eschatological meaning and also the whole eschatological message and the eschatological dualism involved in it (§ 10, 5), Gnosticism and its myth offered a stock of terms that were intelligible to great numbers of people. Several times before now we have caught sight of Gnosticism (§ 10, 5; §11, 2a and e; § 12, 3; § 14, 2) and have had to call attention sometimes to its kinship with the Christian message, sometimes to its contrast with it. Here our task is to set forth connectedly the extent to which the understanding of the Christian message in Hellenistic Christianity was unfolded by means of Gnostic terminology.

Such a process does not, in the nature of the case, take place without some effect on the content of the ideas involved. As the development of the Kyrios-cult drew Hellenistic Christianity into *the syncretistic process*, the development, under Gnostic influence, of the doctrine of redemption did so still more. The extent to which that was the case varied greatly in different social levels and different localities; and side by side with positive influence from Gnosticism we also find rejection of it. But sometimes Christianity and Gnosticism combined. On the whole, one could be tempted to term Hellenistic Christianity a syncretistic structure. The only reason one may not do so is that it is not just a conglomerate of heterogeneous materials; in spite of all its syncretism in detail it retains from its origin an inherent drive toward an independent understanding, all its own, of God, world, and man. But the question is: Will this drive triumph and achieve clear form in a genuinely Christian theology? For the time being, all that is necessary here is to set forth the problematical situation and the issues arising therefrom.

1. For Christian missions, *the Gnostic movement* was a competitor of the most serious and dangerous sort because of the far-reaching relatedness between them. For the essence of Gnosticism does not lie in its syncretistic mythology but rather in a new understanding—new in the ancient world—of man and the world; its mythology is only the expression of this understanding. Whereas to ancient man the world had been home—in the Old Testament as God's creation, to classic Greece as the cosmos pervaded by the deity—the *utter difference of human existence from all worldly existence* was recognized for the first time in Gnosticism and Christianity, and thus the world became foreign soil to the human self (§ 10, 4); in fact, in Gnosticism, his prison. Gnostic thought is so radical that to it the impulses of one's own senses, instincts, and desires, by which man is bound to the world, appear alien and hostile—hostile to man's real self, which cannot achieve its own nature in this world at all, and to which this world is a prison in which his real self, related to and derived from the divine world of light, is shackled by the demonic powers of darkness.

To know of the heavenly origin of one's self (not of the "soul"—that would be misleading, for Greek-speaking Gnosticism distinguishes between the real self, the spark of light derived from the divine world and consisting of *pneuma* and the *psyche*, "soul," which, like the "body," is a garment imposed upon the real self by the demonic powers and holding it captive; this "soul" is the worldly vital urge, the urge that is found in the senses, instincts, and the will) to know of one's world-foreignness, the heavenly origin of one's self, and the way of redemption out of this world—*that is the definitive "knowledge," the Gnosis* ("knowledge") which gives the Gnostic movement its name. Salvation is bestowed upon the Gnostic ("knower") who has come to knowledge of himself, of his heavenly home, and of the way back to it, when the self separates at death from body and soul and soars, released, into the heavenly world of light.

This knowledge gives the Gnostic *his consciousness of superiority to the world.* The Gnostic—in whom the spark of heavenly light is alive—is the "spiritual man," the "pneumatic," who disdainfully looks down upon others who do not bear within them the spark of light but are mere "men of soul" (in the derogatory sense, as above), "men of flesh" or "men of matter." * Conscious of being already emancipated by his *Gnosis,* he demonstrates this freedom either by asceticism or libertinism, or even by a peculiar combination of both. By a meditative contemplation which culminates in ecstasy, he is able even now to enjoy the world of light which he is to enter after death, and he can demonstrate the power of the Spirit that dwells within him by miraculous deeds.

The history of the individual self stands in intimate relation *with that of the entire cosmos.* The individual self is only a spark or fragment of the light-treasure which is held prisoner by the demonic world-rulers in this world of darkness; and its redemption is only a detail of the redemption of all the sparks of light fettered here in prison but united with each other and with their origin by a "kinship of nature" (συγγένεια). Individualistic eschatology—i.e. the doctrine of the emancipation of the individual self at death and of its journey to heaven—stands within the context of a cosmic eschatology—i.e. the doctrine of the emancipation of all the sparks of light and their elevation into the light-world, after which this present world of mingled light and darkness will sink back into the primeval chaos of darkness, and the demonic rulers of the world will be judged.

The Gnostic myth depicts the cosmic drama by which the imprisonment of the sparks of light came about, a drama whose end is already beginning now and will be complete when they are released. The drama's beginning, the tragic event of primeval time, is variously told in the several variants of the myth. But the basic idea is constant: The demonic powers get into their clutches a person who originates in the light-world either because he is led astray by his own foolishness or because he is overcome in battle. The individual selves of the "pneumatics" are none other than the parts or splinters of that light-person. Hence, in their totality they constitute that person—who is frequently called Primal Man—and for whose total redemption they must be released and "gathered together." Inasmuch as the world structure made by the demonic powers will necessarily crash when the sparks of light are withdrawn from it, the

---

* The three-fold division of mankind found in churchly Gnosticism: *pneumatic, psychic, hylic* (or *sarkic*)—men of spirit, soul, matter (or flesh)—is secondary.

demons jealously guard their booty and attempt to stupefy the heavenly selves by the bustle and noise of this world, make them drunk and put them to sleep so as to make them forget their heavenly home.

Redemption comes from the heavenly world. Once more a light-person sent by the highest god, indeed the son and "image" of the most high, comes down from the light-world bringing *Gnosis*. He "wakes" the sparks of light who have sunk into sleep or drunkenness and "reminds" them of their heavenly home. He teaches them concerning their superiority to the world and concerning the attitude they are to adopt toward the world. He dispenses the sacraments by which they are to purify themselves and fan back to life their quenched light-power or at least strengthen its weakened state—by which, in other words, they are "reborn." He teaches them about the heavenly journey they will start at death and communicates to them the secret pass-words by virtue of which they can safely pass through the stations of this journey—past the demonic watchmen of the starry spheres. And going ahead he prepares the way for them, the way which he, the redeemer himself, must also take to be redeemed. For here on earth he does not appear in divine form, but appears disguised in the garment of earthly beings so as not to be recognized by the demons. In so appearing, he takes upon himself the toil and misery of earthly existence and has to endure contempt and persecution until he takes his leave and is elevated to the world of light.

What form the Gnostic religion took in its various groups and congregations, or how, in one place and another, doctrines developed and rites evolved, are secondary questions not to be dealt with here. We have little information—especially for the older period—about *Gnostic congregations*. At any rate the Gnostic movement did take a concrete form in various baptizing sects in the region of the Jordan; these also drew certain Jewish groups into their orbit. The movement evidently attached itself to local cults in the Near East, and in a syncretistic process melted together with them in the form of mystery-congregations; this happened, e.g. when the Gnostic Redeemer was identified with the Phrygian mystery-god, Attis. In this manner the movement also crept into Christian congregations, or the converse also happened—that Gnostic congregations adopted elements of Christianity. But the effect of Gnosticism extends beyond the circle of specifically religious groups: Its ideas were also at work in the speculations of Hellenistic religious philosophy down into neo-Platonism—likewise in the Jewish philosopher of religion, Philo of Alexandria.

2. Insofar as Christian preaching remained true to the tradition of the Old Testament and Judaism and of the earliest Church, *definitive contrasts between it and Gnosticism* are straightway apparent. In harmony with that tradition the Christian message did by and large hold to the idea that *the world is the creation of the one true God,* and hence that the creator-God and the redeemer-God are *one.* That immediately results in a contrast in *anthropology.* For in the genuinely Christian view, man is, body and soul, the creature of God, and no pre-existent spark of heavenly light—as if that were his real being—is to be distinguished from his psychosomatic existence. Hence, that division between those who bear the spark of light within, the "spiritual ones" (who, Gnostically speaking, are φύσει σωζόμενοι: "by nature saved") and the mere "men of soul" or "men of flesh" who lack the heavenly self, was not considered *a priori* to run through all mankind, though this Gnostic differentiation was taken over in another way (see below). Correspondingly, a contrast in *eschatology* persists almost consistently, insofar as the Christian proclamation does not know the idea of the heavenly journey of the self made possible by Gnosis and sacraments, but does teach the resurrection of the dead and the last judgment. However, the Gospel of John is peculiar in this respect, and in general it must be said that the Christian conception of the reception of the righteous into heaven and the idea of heavenly bliss were strongly influenced by Gnosticism. These differences entail a contrast in *christology,* since Gnosticism cannot acknowledge the real humanity of Jesus. Apparent humanity to a pre-existent heavenly being is only a disguise; and where Gnosticism adapts the Christian tradition to its own use, if it does not insist upon declaring Jesus' flesh and blood to be only seemingly a body, it has to make a distinction between the Redeemer and the historical person Jesus and assert some such thing as that the former was only transiently united with the latter (in the baptism) and left him before the passion.

The struggle against Gnosticism consists in part in mere warnings against "stupid, senseless controversies" (II Tim. 2:23; Tit. 3:9), "disputes about words" (I Tim. 6:4), "myths and genealogies" (I Tim. 1:4; 4:7; II Tim. 4:4; Tit. 1:14; 3:9), "the contradictions of

falsely named *Gnosis*" (I Tim. 6:20). In very pale fashion Gnostic
teachers are combatted in Herm. sim. VIII 6, 5; IX 19, 2f.; 22, 1ff.
But elsewhere there is spirited polemic and controversy against or
confutation of specifically Gnostic propositions. Christian congregations evidently first felt the contrast in *eschatology* and *christology*.
I Cor. 15, early as that is, is already a great polemic against the
gnosticizing party in Corinth which declares, "There is no resurrection of the dead." Paul, one must admit, misunderstands his opponents in attributing to them the view that with death everything is
over (I Cor. 15:19, 32). That, of course, was not their view, as the
custom of vicarious baptism (15:29) by itself suffices to show; they
were only contending against the realistic teaching of the resurrection as contained in the Jewish and primitive-Christian tradition.*
This view could also take the form of saying: "the resurrection has
already occurred"; i.e. the resurrection doctrine could be spiritualized (II Tim. 2:18; but *cf.* also Jn. 5:24f. and Eph. 5:14).

The detailed proof of the resurrection in I Clem. 23–26 is evidently not occasioned by Gnostic opposition, nor is the refutation of
doubt in the parousia, II Pet. 3:1–10, but by doubts of a general
nature. On the other hand, those who, according to Pol. Phil. 7:1,
deny the resurrection and the judgment are Gnostic teachers; and
II Clem. 9:1 also has such in view in the warning: "And let none of
you say that this flesh is not judged and does not rise again." The
warning emphasis upon the certainty of the parousia in II Clem.
10–12 is probably also motivated by Gnosticism. Later Justin Ap.
I 26, 4; Dial. 80, 4; Iren. I 23, 5; II 31, 2 bear witness to the same
motivation.

The true humanity of Christ is defended against the Gnostics in
I Jn. 2:22; 4:2, 15; 5:1, 5–8; II Jn. 7. I Jn. 5:6 seems to be specifically
directed against the Gnostic proposition that the Redeemer, though
united with Jesus at his baptism, separated from him before his passion. Similarly Ignatius does battle against the Gnostic christology,
which he encounters in the form of the claim that Christ had only a
seeming body (Eph. 7:2; 18–20; Mg. 11, Tr. 9f.; Sm. 1–3, 7); Polycarp does the same (Pol. Phil. 7:1).

---

   * It appears that in II Cor. 5:1–5, Paul, having been better informed in the
meantime, combats the Gnostic view that man's self at death will be released
from the body (and from the "soul") and will soar in the state of "nakedness"
into the heavenly world.

The contrast in the *doctrine of God and creation,* which constituted a main point for the later opponents of heresy, seems not to have come to the fore at first. The reason for this probably is that Gnosticism first crept into Christian congregations by the mediation of a syncretistic Judaism, a form of Gnosticism, that is, in which this contrast was not prominent. An additional reason may well have been that the Gnostic opinion of the world as it factually is did not greatly differ from the Christian; for both it is true that the world is ruled by Satan and "lieth" utterly "in wickedness" (I Jn. 5:19 KJ). I Jn. 1:5 probably contains polemic against Gnostic teachings which regarded the lower world of darkness as having originated by gradual emanations from the world of light, when it asserts, "God is light and in him is no darkness at all." Jd. 8–11 is unclear because of its merely allusive formulation; it appears to contain polemic against the Gnostic conception of the angel-world as a realm of enemy powers, which, however, are conquered by the Gnostic. It is probably gnosticizing Christians that are castigated in Rev. 2:2, 6, 14–16, 20–24 as "Nicolaitans" and as the (evidently identical) partisans of the prophetess "Jezebel." When these people claim for themselves knowledge of "the deep things of Satan" (Rev. 2:24), probably theogonic and cosmogonic speculations are meant. At any rate I Tim. 4:3–5; Tit. 1:14f. are aimed against Gnosticism's dualistic understanding of the world and the ascetic rules deduced therefrom.

3. Now it must be carefully noted that in all this Gnosticism is combatted not as if it were a foreign, heathen religion into which Christians are in danger of apostatizing. Rather, it is only dealt with so far as it is a *phenomenon within Christianity.* And it is also clear that the Gnostics here opposed by no means regard the Christian congregations as a mission field which they want to convert from Christianity to Gnosticism. Rather, they consider themselves Christians teaching a Christian wisdom—and that is the way they appear to the churches, too. Of course, the Gnostic apostles are regarded as interlopers by the representatives of the old tradition, and the author of Acts makes Paul predict (20:29): "I know that after my departure fierce wolves will come in among you . . ." But v. 30 lets Paul continue: "and from among your own selves will arise men speaking perverse things, to draw away the disciples after them." To Paul the apostles who have kindled a pneumatic-Gnostic movement in Corinth are interlopers, it is true—not, however, interlopers into the

Christian Churches as a whole, but into *his* Church, over which, since it is of his own founding, he alone has authority. It is perfectly clear that to the Church they have the standing of *Christian* apostles, though to Paul they are ministers of Satan "disguising themselves as apostles of Christ" (II Cor. 11:13). They proclaim Christ, though according to Paul "another Jesus than the one we preached" (11:4). In the churches of Ephesus, Pergamum, and Thyatira the false teachers opposed in Rev. 2 evidently dwell, or dwelt, as recognized teachers—recognized by a part of the churches, at least—as apostles and prophets.

Naturally Gnosticism, just like Christianity, is also spread by wandering teachers. It is against such false teachers coming into a church from without that II Jn. 10 and Did. 11:2 warn. But in I Jn. 2:19 it is said of the Gnostics: "They went out from us, but they were not of us; for if they had been of us, they would have continued with us." The case is no different with the false teachers at Colossae, and the polemic of the pastorals clearly shows that Gnosticism is an infra-ecclesiastical phenomenon. The Gnostics are such as have "fallen" from the faith (I Tim. 4:1; *cf.* 1:6; 6:21; II Tim. 2:18; 3:8); they are not heathens but "faction-makers" (αἱρετικοί, Tit. 3:10; *cf.* II Pet. 2:1). The letters of Ignatius and that of Polycarp reveal the same picture: False teaching is being imported into the churches by wandering teachers, and the churches are warned against receiving such teachers (Sm. 4:1; *cf.* Mg. 11). But they are Christian teachers and their doctrine has its advocates in many a church.

It is clear: Hellenistic Christianity is in the maelstrom of the syncretistic process; the genuinely Christian element is wrestling with other elements; "orthodoxy" does not exist at this early period but is still to develop.

At first, Gnosticism probably penetrated into the Christian congregations mostly through the medium of a Hellenistic Judaism that was itself in the grip of syncretism. The Gnostic Spirit-enthusiasts whom Paul opposes at Corinth are of Jewish origin (II Cor. 11:22). Whether the false teachings advanced in Colossae are also derived from a syncretistic Judaism, is not quite certain (*cf.* Col. 2:11, 14 and espec. 2:16). But in the case of the pastorals it is probably a Jewish-Christian Gnosticism that is involved (I Tim. 1:7; Tit. 1:10, 14). Ignatius polemizes against Ἰουδαϊσμός (Mg. 8–11; Phld. 6–9), "Judaism," but since its representatives are evidently identical with the opponents elsewhere inveighed against in his letters, it must be a Jewish-Christian Gnosticism that is meant by the term. Hence, it is doubly conceivable that Gnosticism could be regarded not as a heathen faith, but as a form of Christianity.

4. Now we must ask: In what manner did Gnosticism's thought, myth, and terminology influence Christian thinking and contribute to the development of Christian theological language?

a. It did so first of all by *further developing the concept of eschatological dualism* by carrying the latter beyond the dimensions of history-of-salvation thinking into those of cosmological thinking— or, better expressed, by further developing *cosmological thinking* in a more consistent manner. For even in Jewish eschatology, hopes for the future had already reached cosmic scope under the influence of Persian and Babylonian mythology, which were the sources of mythological thinking for Gnosticism also. It was from this influence that the differentiation between this age or world (עוֹלָם הַזֶּה, αἰὼν οὗτος) and the age or world to come (עוֹלָם הַבָּא, αἰὼν μέλλων) was derived—terms that were still unknown to the Old Testament. In this view, the forces that threaten Israel in the present are only superficially foreign nations or world empires; back of these are demonic powers or Satan himself. Accordingly, not revolutions on the plane of history (as is still the case in Deutero-Isaiah in spite of all its miraculous details) but a cosmic catastrophe will usher in the time of salvation, and the resurrection of the dead and the judgment of the world will bring the great change about. Here the judgment of the world is conceived as a "forensic" act—the act of a Judge in court—while the Old Testament (with the exception of Daniel and the late passage Is. 24–27, in which for the first time the ideas of cosmological eschatology occur) thinks of the judgment as taking place in the course of historical events. The figure of the Davidic king who was to appear in the time of salvation was more or less replaced by the figure of the Son of Man who was to come from heaven as the judge and salvation-bringer (§ 7, 5). The colors of the national political ideal had more or less faded in the popular conception of the time of salvation. The opinion that this world is the sinister stamping-ground of Satan—who in this role is still unknown to the Old Testament—and of his demonic hordes had spread abroad. And though the belief that the world had been created by

God was retained in accord with Old Testament tradition, that could be done only with a certain inconsistency. And if the difficulty was in a measure cleared up in apocalypticism by attributing to Adam's fall the consequence (still unknown to the Old Testament) of having brought upon Adamitic man and "this Aeon" the curse of sin, distress, and death, probably Gnostic ideas had already influenced this solution.

Under Gnostic influence such views could not help being further developed in Hellenistic Christianity. That is already quite apparent even in Paul; only it cannot be determined how much of this he may have brought along out of his Jewish past and how much Gnosticism may have influenced him at a later period.

It is Gnostic language when Satan is called "the god of this world" (αἰῶνος) (II Cor. 4:4), the "ruler of this world" (Jn. 12:31; 14:30; 16:11), "the prince of the power of the air" (Eph. 2:2), or "the ruler of this Aeon" (Ign. Eph. 19:1). Both in name and meaning "the rulers of this age" who brought "the Lord of glory" to the cross (I Cor. 2:6, 8) are figures of Gnostic mythology—viz. those demonic world-rulers who are also meant by the terms "angels," "principalities," "authorities," "powers" (Rom. 8:38f.; I Cor. 15:24, 26; Col. 1:16; 2:10, 15; Eph. 1:21; 3:10; 6:12; I Pet. 3:22) and are at least included in the "many gods and many lords" of I Cor. 8:4. As in Gnosticism, they are conceived to be in essence star-spirits; as such they are called "elemental spirits of the universe" (Gal. 4:3, 9; cf. Col. 2:8, 20) who govern the elapse and division of time (Gal. 4:10). Also Gnostic are the "world rulers of this present darkness" and the "spiritual hosts of wickedness in the heavenly places" (i.e. in the region of air, the lower sphere of the firmament, Eph. 6:12).

Aside from the terms for mythological figures, the *terminology* in which dualism is expressed shows extensive Gnostic influence. This is most apparent in John, whose language is governed by the antithesis "light—darkness." But the rest of the New Testament also knows this contrast (Rom. 13:12; I Thess. 5:4f.; II Cor. [6:14]; Col. 1:12f.; Eph. 5:8ff.; 6:12; I Pet. 2:9; cf. I Clem. 36:2; II Clem. 1:4; Barn. 14:5f.; 18:1; Ign. Rom. 6:2; Phld. 2:1). In this category also belongs the use of "truth" (and its opposite, "falsehood") to denote true (divine) reality in contrast to the seeming reality of the earthly. Here again this usage gives John its peculiar stamp—especially the related use of the adjective "true" (ἀληθινός), which occurs in this sense not only in John but also in Hebrews (8:2; 9:24). Hebrews expresses this same contrast in the antithesis "heavenly" (8:5; 9:23) as opposed to the earthly "shadow" (8:5; 10:1; *cf.* Col. 2:17) or to the "earthly" (9:1).

b. Gnostic mythology lies behind the allusion to the *fall of creation* in Rom. 8:20ff., which, because of its allusiveness, is difficult to explain in detail. According to it, creation "was subjected to futility" and has fallen into "bondage to decay," under which it groans in expectation of release. Rom. 5:12ff. interprets Adam's fall quite in keeping with Gnosticism, as bringing (sin and) death upon mankind; I Cor. 15:21, 44–49 goes even further when it derives Adamitic man's plight from his inborn quality of Adam, who, without any reference to his fall, is ψυχικός and χοϊκός—a man of mere "soul," not spirit (see § 14, 2) and "a man of dust." The contrast "psychic–pneumatic" ("man of soul"—"man of Spirit") to designate two basically different classes of men—a contrast which can be explained neither from Greek usage nor from the Old Testament but only from Gnostic anthropology—is an especially clear indication that Paul's anthropological concepts had already been formed under the influence of Gnosticism (I Cor. 2:14f.; 15:44–46; see further: Jas. 3:15; Jd. 19). It is likewise a piece of Gnostic thinking when Jn. 8:44 attributes enmity to Jesus to the descent of the unbelieving from the arch-liar, the devil. In fully Gnostic fashion those who are "of the devil" (Jn. 8:44; I Jn. 3:8)—or are "of the evil one" (I Jn. 3:12), "from below" (Jn. 8:23), "of this world" (Jn. 8:23 and elsewhere), or "of the earth" (Jn. 3:31)—are contrasted with those who are "from God" (Jn. 7:17; 8:47), "of the truth" (Jn. 18:37), "from above" (Jn. 8:23), or are "begotten of God" (I Jn. 2:29; 3:9; 4:7; 5:1).

Thus, Gnostic mythology serves to characterize *man's situation in the world* as a life which by its origin is destined for destruction, a life that is prone to be ruled by demonic powers. Paul even ventures in his polemic against Jewish legalism to contradict his basic view that the Torah comes from God (Rom. 7:12, 14) by appropriating the Gnostic proposition that on the contrary it was given by subordinate angel-powers (Gal. 3:19).

Correspondingly, the *terminology of parenesis* is to a large extent Gnostic when—in connection with the concepts "light" and "darkness"—it says that men have "fallen asleep" or are "drunk" and must be "awakened" or be "sober" (Rom. 13:11–13; I Thess. 5:4–6; I Cor.

15:34; 16:13; Col. 4:2; Eph. 5:14; II Tim. 2:26; 4:5; I Pet. 1:13; 5:8; Ign. Sm. 9:1; Pol. 1:3; 2:3; II Clem. 13:1—though, of course, γρηγορεῖν, "be awake" or "watch," is also already found in the Jewish-Christian tradition: Mk. 13:35; Rev. 3:2f.; Did. 16:1, etc.). The hymn (a fragment) in Eph. 5:14 is cast quite in Gnostic terms:

> "Awake, O sleeper,
> And rise from the dead,
> And Christ shall give you light."

c. But most of all the Gnostic stock of concepts served to clarify *the history of salvation.* According to these concepts the Redeemer appears as a cosmic figure, the pre-existent divine being, Son of the Father (§ 12, 3), who came down from heaven and assumed human form and who, after his activity on earth, was exalted to heavenly glory and wrested sovereignty over the spirit-powers to himself. It is in this conception of him that he is praised in the pre-Pauline Christ-hymn which is quoted in Phil. 2:6–11. This "mythos" is also briefly alluded to in II Cor. 8:9. The Gnostic idea that Christ's earthly garment of flesh was the disguise in consequence of which the world-rulers failed to recognize him—for if they had recognized him, they would not have brought about their own defeat by causing his crucifixion—lurks behind I Cor. 2:8. Further on, it will be indicated how the Gnostic Redeemer-myth of the incarnation of the pre-existent Son, and of his exaltation, by which he prepares the way for his own into the world of light, provides the terminology for the christology of John.

The descent and re-ascent of the Redeemer is the subject of Eph. 4:8–10. The expression, "descended into the lower parts of the earth," does not mean the descent into Hell, but corresponds to "he ascended" and means the pre-existent Son's journey to earth. And the idea that he conquered the inimical spirit-powers by his journey to heaven the author finds expressed in the words of the Psalter (68:19): "When he ascended on high he led a host of captives" (Eph. 4:8). That the exalted Lord won dominion over the realm of the cosmic powers, is also said in Col. 2:15: "He (God) disarmed the principalities and powers and made a public example of them, triumphing over them in him (Christ)." So, according to I Pet. 3:22, also, Christ's ascent to heaven is simultaneously the act of subjugating the demonic world-rulers; and 2:19f., whose original meaning * no more deals with the descent into Hell than does Eph. 4:9, follow the Gnostic myth, according to which the prison of the dead is not in the interior of the earth but in the region of the air, where the spirits of the stars, or of the firmament, keep them confined. This cosmic event is very briefly alluded to in Jn. 12:31: "Now is the judgment of this world, now shall the ruler of this world be cast out" (*cf.* 16:10f.). These words are spoken by Jesus as he prepares to go to his passion, which for John, however, means nothing less than his "exaltation" (12:32) or "glorification" (12:28).

Hence the whole cosmos—heavenly, earthly, and subterranean beings—must pay homage to the exalted "Lord" (Phil. 2:10f.). Thereby, God has appointed an end for the cosmic disorder which originated in the primeval fall and through him has "reconciled all things" (i.e. the universe) to Himself, as the hymn underlying Col. 1:20 says—a hymn which the author has rather strongly accommodated to the Christian tradition by his editing of it. The cosmic "peace" bestowed by the work of salvation is still more radically Christianized in Eph. 2:14ff., which interprets the "dividing wall of hostility," which according to the Gnostic myth divides the earthly from the heavenly world, as applying both to the enmity between Jew and Gentile (v. 14) and to the enmity between God and man (v. 16). Hebrews also follows the Gnostic Redeemer-myth: The pre-existent Son, who is here termed "the effulgence of the glory of God" and "the very stamp of his (God's) character" (1:3) in keeping with the Gnostic "image"-idea, abased himself (2:9) in becoming man and then was exalted above the angels; 1:5 applies to the enthronement of the exalted Redeemer. But here the figure is modified in the direction of Jewish-Christian eschatology by postponing the subjection of the total cosmos to him until the future parousia (1:6; 2:8). The myth is also contained in the lines of the hymn found at I Tim. 3:16:

---

* A Christ-hymn underlies I Pet. 3:18–22 (as in the case of Col. 1:15–20). As I Pet. 4:6 shows, the author of this epistle understood 3:19 as referring to the descent into Hell, a subject that is later treated in Ign. Mg. 9:3 and Herm. sim. IX 16, 5–7. On I Pet. 3:18–22 see R. Bultmann, *Coniectanea Neotestamentica* XI (1949), 1–14; on Col. 1:15–20 see E. Käsemann, *Bultmann-Festschrift* (1949), 133–148.

"Who was manifested in the flesh,
        Vindicated in the Spirit
     Seen by angels . . .
        Taken up in glory."

What is here hinted at is more extensively expressed in Ign. Eph. 19. Here we encounter again the motif that "the Prince of this world" is deceived. From him the "three mysteries of a cry" were kept hidden: the virginity of Mary, her giving birth, and the death of "the Lord." His death is followed by his glorious manifestation to the "Aeons" (by this Gnostic term the cosmic powers are here called; Lake translates misleadingly) as he triumphantly ascends on high—a drama whose goal and end is the destruction of "the old kingdom" (viz. that of the "Aeons" and of their Prince). Christ's passion and cross are conceived as a cosmic event by Ignatius, partly in Gnostic terms, partly in polemic against them.

d. For believers the cosmic triumph of Christ means *emancipation from the demonic world-rulers*, from sin, and especially from death; hence the declaration that "the resurrection has already occurred" (II Tim. 2:18; see p. 169 above) is comprehensible. In this connection the Gnostic idea is frequently utilized that the Redeemer by his ascent has prepared the way through the spheres of the spirit powers into the heavenly world. The exalted Redeemer will draw after himself his own (Jn. 12:32); he is, himself, the "way" (Jn. 14:6). The idea is expressed in Hebrews by the term "pioneer" (ἀρχηγός, 2:10; 12:2, *cf.* Acts 3:15; 5:31; II Clem. 20:5—same word in all five cases). Christ is the pioneer-guide to heaven; being, himself, "made perfect" by attaining heaven (τελειωθείς, 2:10, 5:9), he is also the "perfecter" (τελειωτής, 12:2) of his own. However, Hebrews re-interprets the Gnostic idea of the self's ascent to its heavenly "resting-place" (κατάπαυσις) into the idea that the People of God on earth is on pilgrimage to its heavenly home (3:7–4:11).

The Gnostic teaching of the "kinship" between the Redeemer and the redeemed by virtue of their mutual heavenly origin is so applied by Hebrews that the redeemed appear as brothers of the Redeemer (2:11f., 17), though they can also be called his children, since he has the priority. In the same sense, Paul calls the exalted Lord "the first-born among many brethren" (Rom. 8:29). Paul expresses Christ's meaning as Redeemer especially by paralleling him, as "the last Adam," with the (fallen) Primal Man Adam. As Adamitic man in his earthly-unspiritual (ψυχικός) nature, in his servitude to Death, is determined by Adam, so those who believe in Christ are determined by Christ, and that means by Spirit and Life. However, in so speaking, Paul does not draw the consistent Gnostic conclusion that "the resurrection has already occurred," but champions, instead, the old realistic resurrection-hope against the gnosticizing Corinthians; but in so doing, he gets into the difficulty of having to work out a paradoxical concept of Life—a life that is already present reality and yet is still future (Rom. 5; see §§ 18, 29). John, however, gives up the old realistic eschatology of the future parousia, resurrection, and last judgment.*

The Gnostic notion of the pre-existence of souls (or rather, thinking gnostically, the pre-existence of human selves) was, by and large, given up in the Christian congregations, and likewise the related idea of those who are "by nature saved," i.e. the idea that redemption has its foundation in a kinship between Redeemer and redeemed which antedates the decision of faith. But it recurs in John with a new interpretation when believers are held to be the ἴδιοι of the incarnate Logos ("his own," Jn. 1:11; supply: people, or relatives) whom he calls to himself and who hear and know his voice (Jn. 10) because they are "of the truth" (18:37b).

e. Hebrews takes *the Gnostic idea* that all "men of Spirit" who are delimited from the world *constitute a unity* (§ 10, 5) and combines it with the Old Testament-Jewish tradition of the People of God (besides 3:7–4:11, see 13:12–14). But Paul explains the inner unity of believers with each other and with the Redeemer by using the Gnostic term "body" (i.e. in the phrase "body of Christ," Rom. 12:4f.; I Cor. 12:12–27; also I Cor. 6:15–17) and in so doing very materially determines *the development of the Church-concept*.

Stimulated by Paul but also influenced, themselves, by Gnostic tradition, the authors of Colossians and Ephesians further developed this idea. Especially in Colossians the originally mythological or cosmological nature of the "body" concept of the Church is apparent. In Col. 1:15–20, the author builds upon a hymn which originally was in praise of the cosmic rank of Christ and understood the "body" whose "head" is Christ to be the cosmos, while the author interprets

---

* In the text that has come down to us churchly editing has "corrected" John by re-introducing the realistic eschatology; on this point, see Vol. II.

the "body" as the "Church" (by means of the addition in v. 18 and again in v. 24), thereby giving "the Church"—quite in keeping with Gnosticism—the character of a cosmic entity.

The same thing can be perceived in Ephesians. Here, however, in order to express Christ's relation to the Church, not only the "head" concept is used but also the Gnostic idea of the "divine marriage" (συζυγία): the Church is the bride, or the wife, of Christ (Eph. 5:25ff.; espec. 29–32).*

Though the idea this suggests—that the Church is pre-existent—is not expressed in this Ephesians passage—in fact, there may even be polemic against it in the emphatic words of v. 32: "but *I* mean . . ."—the author of II Clem. does draw this conclusion, speaking of "the first, the spiritual Church which was created before sun and moon" and "was made manifest at the end of days." The "body of Christ" (II Clem. 14:1f.) for him is the pre-existent Church.

In Hermas likewise (vis. II 4, 1) the Church, appearing in the guise of an old woman, is pre-existent: "she was created first of all things . . . and for her sake [or: through her] was the cosmos established." But the divine-marriage idea is not present here, and the "body" concept is only faintly echoed when the unity of the Church is described with the expression "one spirit and one body" (sim. IX 13, 5 and 7; cf. 17, 5; 18, 4). It is a Gnostic motif that is used when the virgins who are building the tower of the Church are called "holy spirits" and "powers of the Son of God" (sim. IX 13, 2); both the number of the virgins (seven in vis. III 8; nine in sim. IX 12ff.) and the description of the tower also betray the originally cosmological meaning of this presentation.† No very strong Gnostic influences affected the vague ecclesiological and christological arguments of Hermas.

The Gnostic myth also influenced the view of the Church found in Ignatius. The Church is the "body of Christ" (Sm. 1:2); he is its "head" (Tr. 11:2); Christians are "Christ's members" (Eph. 4:2; Tr. 11:2). Just as in the Gnostic myth the occurrence of salvation culminates in the gathering together of the sparks of light and their

---

* This conception is scarcely behind so early a passage as II Cor. 11:2, where the Corinthian church is regarded under the figure of the bride of Christ. It is more plausible at Rev. 19:7; 21:2, but there, too, it is doubtful.

† See Käsemann, *Leib und Leib Christi*, 85f.; Dibelius, *excursus on Hermas* vis. II 4, 1; III 2, 4; sim. V 6, 7 in the supplement to Lietzmann's *Handbuch*, IV, 451f., 459f., 572–575.

union into that figure of light, Primal Man, so for Ignatius the "unification" (ἕνωσις, or ἑνότης, "unity") of the Church is the goal that God had promised (Tr. 11:2; *cf.* Eph. 5:1; Pol. 8:3), and this "unification" is the constant refrain of his exhortation (Eph. 4:2; Mg. 7:2; Pol. 1:2); it is at the same time "unification" with Christ (Mg. 1:2; 13:2; Phld. 4:1). The concept of the divine marriage does not occur, for the statement that Christ "loved" the Church (Pol. 5:1) is probably a reminiscence of canonical Eph. 5:25, 29.

f. To come from polytheism to faith in the one true God was called "to come to knowledge of the truth" (§ 9, 2)—emancipating knowledge was a thing the Christian and the Gnostic had in common, and the Christian preacher could say in Gnostic terminology: "You will know the truth, and the truth will make you free" (Jn. 8:32). Paul in place of "faith" could speak of the "knowledge" which surpasses all that he once held to be gain ("the surpassing worth of *knowing* Christ Jesus," Phil. 3:8) and could set as his goal: to "be found in him" and to "*know* him and the power of his resurrection . . ." (Phil. 3:9f.). It is no wonder, then, that Christian and Gnostic zeal for "knowledge" united, and that in Corinth an eagerness after "knowledge" was unleashed (I Cor. 1:18). Nor is it any wonder that pride flourished over the fact that "we (all) have knowledge" (I Cor. 8:1ff.). Neither is it surprising that the Christian consciousness of delimitation from the world and of superiority over unbelievers should have taken on the Gnostic form of claiming to be "men of Spirit," because possessed of a higher nature, and hence of looking down upon mere "men of soul" (ψυχικοί) or "the weak" (ἀσθενεῖς). All this is the less to be wondered at because of the Christian awareness of possessing the Spirit through baptism (§ 13, 1).

This consciousness flaunted itself not only in the phenomena of enthusiasm and ecstasy (§ 14, 3) within the meeting of the congregation but also and especially in the genuinely Gnostic claim to have "*liberty*" and "*authority*," on the strength of which the "man of Spirit" disdained to be bound to the concrete ecclesiastical fellowship (I Cor. 8:1ff.) and also made light of being bound morally— "all things are lawful to me" (I Cor. 6:12ff.; *cf.* 10:23). In the struggle against false teachers, the accusation of immorality (Pastorals; Jd.; II Pet.; Herm. sim. V 7, 1ff.) and lovelessness (I Jn.) became so stereotyped that one cannot always be certain that it is a libertinism with a genuinely Gnostic basis that is meant. Yet precisely out of the conventionality of such accusations it follows that such libertinism had its representatives in Christian circles. How this consciousness of being a "knower" (i.e. a Gnostic) results in getting "puffed up" (I Cor. 4:6, 18f.; 5:2; 8:1) is shown by II Cor. 10–13: It causes men to "boast," to judge others arrogantly and to regard their own manifestations of "pneumatic" power as proof of their superiority to the Apostle, who only pursues his task "in weakness."

But Paul himself, obviously, also regards the Gnostic terminology as the appropriate form of expression for the Christian understanding of existence. He indicates this not merely by referring to the "knowledge" that is his foundation. Rather, being himself a *pneumatikos* (man of Spirit), he considers himself also to have at his disposal a "wisdom" which penetrates into the mysteries of the divine wisdom, "the deep things of God" (I Cor. 2:6ff. KJ). He feels himself exempted from others' judgment while he, as one who has the "mind (= Spirit) of Christ," has the right to judge others (I Cor. 2:15f.). He accepts not only the proposition that "we (all) have knowledge" (I Cor. 8:1) but also that "all things are lawful (to me)" (I Cor. 6:12; 10:23)—though with a specifically Christian correction, it is true (see below). He is just as proud of his "liberty" and "authority" as the Gnostics are—recognizing, however, the paradoxical character of this liberty (I Cor. 9:1–23). He declares himself to be "not in the least inferior to these superlative apostles" (II Cor. 11:5; *cf.* 10:3–5, 8; 13:3, 10)—pointing out, nevertheless, the paradoxicality of Christian "boasting" (II Cor. 11:16ff.; 12:1ff.). He belongs to the "mature" or "perfect" (τέλειοι, Phil. 3:15; *cf.* I Cor. 2:6)—but immediately assures the reader "Not that I have already obtained or am already perfect" (Phil. 3:12).

g. Undoubtedly, the Gnostic myth and its terminology offered the possibility of elucidating the eschatological occurrence as one inaugurated by the history of Jesus Christ and now at work in the present in process of consummation, and the possibility of comprehending the Church and the individual as placed in the grand context of a process of disaster and salvation. But the question now is whether this cosmic occurrence is to be understood as only a sublime process of nature which takes place by-passing, so to say, my conduct, my responsibility, my decisions—a process which has me at its mercy for better or for worse. *Will human history be conceived as natural process, or as genuine historical happening?* Is *Gnosis* only a speculative knowledge that exists alongside of all other knowledge and points of view, a knowledge the possession of which reassures me concerning my future after death? Or is it a genuine understanding of myself which dominates and determines my life in its every manifestation, especially in my conduct? Undoubtedly Gnosticism's intent is such an understanding of one's self; that is what comes to expression in the Gnostic consciousness of "liberty" and "authority." But the question is whether this liberty is to be conceived *as the liberty of responsibly existing man—man living, that is, in responsibility to and for his actual existence*—or whether it is to be conceived as man's withdrawal from his real existence. If it is to be conceived in the latter way, then, since such withdrawal is fundamentally impossible, man's "liberty" becomes a mere assertion or a meaningless theorem. In other words, the question is whether or not the paradoxical character of "liberty" is recognized. Or, asked in still another way, this is the question whether the state of being *pneumatikos* (a man of Spirit) is to be understood as if that were a quality of nature, or whether that state is kept in existence by an ever-repeated responsible decision because of the fact that the possibility of being *sarkikos* (a man determined by flesh), in accord with genuine existence in true history, continues to exist. Only in the latter case is liberty genuinely understood as liberty. Wherever this is not the case, the consequence will either be asceticism, which strives either to demonstrate or anxiously to preserve the "pneumatic" quality of liberty, or it will be libertinism, which either strives to demonstrate "liberty" or uses it as a pretext. Failure to recognize the reality of human existence in actual history involves a non-paradoxical misunderstanding of one's possession of the Spirit and of the liberty it brings, and this misunderstanding carries with it the surrender of the *idea of creation*. But retaining both the idea of the world as creation and the idea of de-secularization (Ent*welt*lichung—inward divorce from the world) through participation in the eschatological occurrence must establish such a dialectic (paradoxical) relation to the world as will be expressed in Paul's "as if . . . not" (I Cor. 7:29ff.). This Gnostic failure to recognize true human existence as fulfilling itself in one's actual history leads also to a non-historical interpretation of the "kinship" idea—

i.e. to a misconception of what *fellowship in the Church* is. Under this misconception, "knowledge" (γνῶσις) seeks its culmination in "de-historizing" ecstasy (i.e. an ecstasy which divorces its subject from his concrete existence) instead of finding it in the *Agape* which is its perfect realization—its genuine demonstration in the knower's actual history.

PART TWO

THE THEOLOGY OF PAUL

§ 16. The Historical Position of Paul

The historical position of Paul may be stated as follows: Standing within the frame of Hellenistic Christianity he raised the theological motifs that were at work in the proclamation of the Hellenistic Church to the clarity of theological thinking; he called to attention the problems latent in the Hellenistic proclamation and brought them to a decision; and thus—so far as our sources permit an opinion on the matter—became the founder of Christian theology.

Paul originated in Hellenistic Judaism; his home was Tarsus in Cilicia (Acts 9:11; 21:39; 22:3). There, without doubt, he received his first training in the rabbinic scriptural learning to which his letters bear witness. According to Acts 22:3 he is said also to have been a pupil of Gamaliel (the Elder) in Jerusalem; but the correctness of this information is debated and (in the light of Gal. 1:22) is at least doubtful. At any rate, in his home city he came into contact with Hellenistic culture and became acquainted with popular philosophy and the phenomena of religious syncretism. It remains uncertain, however, to what extent he had already appropriated in his pre-Christian period theological ideas of this syncretism (those of the mystery-religions and of Gnosticism) which come out in his Christian theology.

Not having been a personal disciple of Jesus, *he was won to the Christian faith by the kerygma of the Hellenistic Church.* The question thrust upon him by this kerygma was whether he was willing to regard the crucified Jesus of Nazareth, whom the kerygma asserted to have risen from the dead, as the expected Messiah. But for Paul, the fervent champion (ζηλωτής) of the traditions of the fathers (Gal. 1:14), straightway recognizing how basically the Torah was called into question by the Hellenistic mission, that meant whether he was willing to acknowledge in the cross of Christ God's judgment upon his self-understanding up to that time—i.e. God's condemnation of his Jewish striving after righteousness by fulfilling the works of the Law. After he had first indignantly rejected this question and become a persecutor of the Church, at his conversion he submitted to this judgment of God.

[187]

For just this is what his conversion meant: In it he surrendered his previous understanding of himself; i.e. he surrendered what had till then been the norm and meaning of his life, he sacrificed what had hitherto been his pride and joy (Phil. 3:4–7). His conversion was not the result of an inner moral collapse (which it is frequently assumed to have been on the basis of a misinterpretation of Rom. 7:7ff. as autobiographical confession). It was not rescue from the despair into which the cleavage between willing and doing had allegedly driven him. His was not a conversion of repentance; neither, of course, was it one of emancipating enlightenment. Rather, it was obedient submission to the judgment of God, made known in the cross of Christ, upon all human accomplishment and boasting. It is as such that his conversion is reflected in his theology.

His conversion brought him into the Hellenistic Church; it was in Hellenistic territory that he was soon working as a missionary in company with another Hellenistic missionary, Barnabas, who had sought him out and taken him to Antioch to collaborate with him (Acts 11:25f.). In company with him, Paul was the advocate of Hellenistic Christianity against the Palestinian Church at the "apostolic council" (§ 8, 2), and in company with him he undertook the so-called "first missionary journey" (Acts 13–14).

After his conversion he made no effort toward contact with Jesus' disciples or the Jerusalem Church for instruction concerning Jesus and his ministry. On the contrary, he vehemently protests his independence from them in Gal. 1–2. And, in fact, his letters barely show traces of the influence of Palestinian tradition concerning the history and preaching of Jesus. All that is important for him in the story of Jesus is the fact that Jesus was born a Jew and lived under the Law (Gal. 4:4) and that he had been crucified (Gal. 3:1; I Cor. 2:2; Phil. 2:5ff., etc.). When he refers to Christ as an example, he is thinking not of the historical but of the pre-existent Jesus (Phil. 2:5ff.; II Cor. 8:9; Rom. 15:3). He quotes "words of the Lord" only at I Cor. 7:10f. and 9:14, and in both cases they are regulations for church life. It is possible that echoes of words of the Lord are present in Paul's parenesis; e.g. Rom. 12:14 (Mt. 5:44); 13:9f. (Mk. 12:31); 16:19 (Mt. 10:16); I Cor. 13:2 (Mk. 11:23). The tradition of the Jerusalem Church is at least in substance behind the "word of the Lord" on the parousia and resurrection in I Thess. 4:15–17, though it is not certain whether Paul is here quoting a traditionally transmitted saying, or whether he is appealing to a revelation accorded to him by the exalted Lord. But of decisive importance in this connection is the fact that Paul's theology proper, with its theological, anthropological, and soteriological ideas, is not at all a recapitulation of Jesus' own preaching nor a further development of it, and it is especially significant that he never adduces any of the sayings of Jesus on the Torah in favor of his own teaching about the Torah. The concept, Reign of God, which was basic for the message preached by Jesus has lost its dominant position in Paul and occurs only at Rom. 14:17; I Cor. 4:20; 6:9f.; 15:50; Gal. 5:21 (*cf.* I Thess. 2:12); neither does Paul's description of the essence of salvation as "the righteousness of God" have a parallel in Jesus' preaching.

In relation to the preaching of Jesus, the theology of Paul is a new structure, and that indicates nothing else than that Paul has his place within Hellenistic Christianity. The so often and so passionately debated question, "Jesus and Paul," is at bottom the question: Jesus and Hellenistic Christianity.

But merely to recognize this historical fact does not in itself, of course, decide anything about the relation in content between Paul's theology and Jesus' message. This question, however, cannot be set forth and answered in advance, but must be developed and answered in the presentation of Paul's theology itself.

CHAPTER IV

Man Prior to the Revelation of Faith

1. As sources for Paul's theology only the undoubtedly genuine letters of Paul may serve: Rom., I–II Cor., Gal., Phil., I Thess., Phlm.

2. Paul did not theoretically and connectedly develop his thoughts concerning God and Christ, the world and man in an independent scientific treatise as a Greek philosopher or a modern theologian. He only developed them fragmentarily (except in Romans), always broaching them in his letters for a specific and actual occasion. Even in Romans, where he expresses them connectedly and with a degree of completeness, he does so in a letter and under the compulsion of a concrete situation. These facts must not be allowed to lead one to the false conclusion that Paul was not a real theologian, nor to the notion that to understand his individuality he must be regarded, instead, as a hero of piety. On the contrary! The way in which he reduces specific acute questions to a basic theological question, the way in which he reaches concrete decisions on the basis of fundamental theological considerations, shows that what he thinks and says grows out of his basic theological position—the position which is more or less completely set forth in Romans.

Nevertheless, this basic position is not a structure of theoretical thought. It does not take the phenomena which encounter man and man himself whom they encounter and build them into a system, a distantly perceived *kosmos* (system), as Greek science does. Rather, Paul's theological thinking only lifts the knowledge inherent in faith itself into the clarity of conscious knowing. A relation to God that is only feeling, only "piety," and not also a knowledge of God and man together is for Paul unthinkable. The act of faith is simultaneously an act of knowing, and, correspondingly, theological knowing cannot be separated from faith.

Therefore, Pauline theology is not a speculative system. It deals

[190]

with God not as He is in Himself but only with God as He is significant for man, for man's responsibility and man's salvation. Correspondingly, it does not deal with the world and man as they are in themselves, but constantly sees the world and man in their relation to God. Every assertion about God is simultaneously an assertion about man and vice versa. For this reason and in this sense Paul's theology is, at the same time, anthropology. But since God's relation to the world and man is not regarded by Paul as a cosmic process oscillating in eternally even rhythm, but is regarded as constituted by God's acting in history and by man's reaction to God's doing, therefore every assertion about God speaks of what He does with man and what He demands of him. And, the other way around, every assertion about man speaks of God's deed and demand—or about man as he is qualified by the divine deed and demand and by his attitude toward them. The christology of Paul likewise is governed by this point of view. In it, Paul does not speculatively discuss the metaphysical essence of Christ, or his relation to God, or his "natures," but speaks of him as the one through whom God is working for the salvation of the world and man. Thus, every assertion about Christ is also an assertion about man and vice versa; and Paul's christology is simultaneously soteriology.

Therefore, Paul's theology can best be treated as his doctrine of man: first, of man prior to the revelation of faith, and second, of man under faith, for in this way the anthropological and soteriological orientation of Paul's theology is brought out. Such a presentation presupposes, since theological understanding has its origin in faith, that man prior to the revelation of faith is so depicted by Paul as he is retrospectively seen from the standpoint of faith.

A. THE ANTHROPOLOGICAL CONCEPTS

PRELIMINARY REMARK

Paul, of course, did not draw up a scientific anthropology as if to describe man as a phenomenon in the realm of the objectively perceptible world. He sees man always in his relation to God. Still, it is in relation to God that he sees all that is or happens, and in this respect man has nothing to distinguish him from other beings. What, then, is the specifically human—that which gives man's relation to God its peculiar character? Precisely for the sake of understanding this relation, it is necessary that we clarify for ourselves the peculiarity of human existence, i.e. the formal structures of this existence.

§ 17. "Soma" (Body)

The most comprehensive term which Paul uses to characterize man's existence is *soma*, body; it is also the most complex and the understanding of it is fraught with difficulty. That *soma* belongs inseparably, constitutively, to human existence is most clearly evident from the fact that Paul cannot conceive even of a future human existence after death "when that which is perfect is come" as an existence without *soma*—in contrast to the view of those in Corinth who deny the resurrection (I Cor. 15, especially vv. 35ff.). However, the resurrection body will no longer be a body of flesh (I Cor. 15:50), not a "physical" (ψυχικόν) body or one of "dust" (I Cor. 15:44-49), but a "spiritual" (πνευματικόν) body, a "body of glory" (Phil. 3:21; *cf.* II Cor. 3:18). Hence, it was natural for interpreters to conceive *soma* to mean the body-form which could be stamped upon various materials—of fleshly or spiritual kind; and I Cor. 15:35ff. was a downright temptation so to conceive it. But it is a methodological error to choose this passage as the point of departure for the interpretation of *soma*; for in it Paul lets himself be misled into adopting his opponents' method of argumentation, and in so doing he uses the *soma*-concept in a way not characteristic of him elsewhere. In these verses only the underlying idea is genuinely Pauline: The only human existence that there is—even in the sphere of Spirit—is somatic existence; but the use of *soma* as "form," "shape" is un-Pauline. This is at once apparent when certain important statements are considered. When Paul warns, "Let not sin therefore reign in your mortal *soma*" (Rom. 6:12), or when he exhorts the Romans "to present your *somata* as a living sacrifice, holy and acceptable to God" (Rom. 12:1), it is clear that *soma* does not mean "body form" nor just "body," either, but that by "body" he means the whole person—undoubtedly in some specific respect which we have yet to define more exactly.

How little it is true that for Paul *soma* means "form," "shape," can be seen from the fact that he uses the words having the primary meaning of form and shape to designate the essence of a thing: the words *morphē* and *schema*. *Morphē* is the shape, the form, in which a person or thing appears, and in the LXX it is used synonymously with εἶδος (shape, form), ὁμοίωμα (likeness), ὅρασις (appearance), and ὄψις (appearance), not, however, in contrast to its essence, but precisely as the expression thereof. Hence, it is understandable that in Hellenistic usage *morphē* can be used to designate the divine nature (see Reitzenstein, *Hellenistische Mysterienreligionen,* 3rd ed., 357f.). It is used in the same way by Paul. Being "changed from glory to glory into the same image (with him)" which, according to II Cor. 3:18, takes place as a result of beholding the Lord, is an alteration not of one's form, but of one's nature. If the elect of God are to be "conformed to the image of his Son" (Rom. 8:29), that means that their nature will be, like his, a glory-nature. And Phil. 3:21 means the same thing: (Christ) "who will change our lowly body into conformity with his glory-body." The "form of God" in which the pre-existent Christ existed is not mere form but the divine mode of being just as much as the "form of a servant" is the mode of being of a servant (Phil. 2:6f.). The same is true of *schema.* He who "was found in human form" (Phil. 2:8) did not merely look like a man but really was a man "obedient unto death." The "change" (μετασχηματίζειν) of Phil. 3:21 (see above) denotes change of nature, and in Rom. 12:2 "conformed" (συσχηματίζεσθαι) and "transformed" (μεταμορφοῦσθαι) correspond in the same way. It is apparent that the perishing "form of this world" (I Cor. 7:31) means the world itself, not just its form. Only in II Cor. 11:13–15 is μετασχηματίζεσθαι (transform) used in its original sense of changing form; perhaps it is also so used in the obscure passage, I Cor. 4:6—i.e. instead of "applied" (RSV) perhaps "transformed this to apply . . ."

In defining the concept *soma,* the place to begin is the naive popular usage in which *soma* means *body*—as a rule, man's—which in a naive anthropological view can be placed in contrast with the "soul" or the "spirit" (I Thess. 5:23; I Cor. 5:3; 7:34). The body has its members, which comprise a unity within it (Rom. 12:4f.; I Cor. 12:12–26). Personal, physical presence is the "presence of the body" (II Cor. 10:10). Paul bears about on his body the "marks of Jesus" (Gal. 6:17)—evidently scars (resulting from mistreatment or accidents) which mark him physically—and he can describe his constant enduring of danger and sufferings as "carrying in the body the death of Jesus" (II Cor. 4:10). There are people who "deliver their bodies to be burned" (I Cor. 13:3); Paul "pommels and subdues his body" (I Cor. 9:27). In the *soma,* sexual life has its seat. Abraham beheld his body "dead"—i.e. no longer capable of procreation (Rom. 4:19). A wife does not rule over her body, nor a husband over his (I Cor. 7:4). Unnatural lust (homosexuality) is a "dishonoring of the body" (Rom. 1:24); unchastity in general is a sin which concerns the body (I Cor. 6:13–20, espec. v. 18).

But in a number of the above passages it is clear that the *soma* is not a something that outwardly clings to a man's real *self* (to his soul, for instance), but belongs to its very essence, so that we can say man does not *have* a *soma;* he *is* soma, for in not a few cases *soma* can be translated simply "I" (or whatever personal pronoun fits the context); thus, I Cor. 13:3; 9:27; 7:4 (see above), or Phil. 1:20 KJ ". . . Christ shall be magnified in my body (= me) whether by life, or by death." The same is thoroughly clear in the already mentioned exhortation, Rom. 12:1: "Present your bodies (= yourselves, or: your selves) as a living sacrifice, etc." Rom. 6:12f. is also instructive:

> "Let not sin therefore reign in your mortal *soma* . . .
> Do not yield *your members* to sin as tools of wickedness,
> But yield *yourselves* to God . . .
> And *your members* to God as tools of righteousness." (tr.)

Here "your members," which is a synonymous variation of "your body," stands parallel to "yourselves"; and in the following verses, both within v. 13 and in vv. 16 and 19, "yield yourselves" and "yield your members" are used synonymously. Likewise I Cor. 6:15, "Do you not know that your bodies are members of Christ?" and I Cor. 12:27, "Now you are the body of Christ and individually members of it," correspond to each other. In the former case, the subject of "being the members of Christ" is "your bodies"; in the latter case it is "you" without difference in meaning. In this usage, the word "members" denotes the individual faculties of human existence which are comprised in the *soma* as the whole, just as, correspondingly, the individual man, provided he is baptized, belongs to Christ's *soma* as a member.

The nuances of meaning in the word *soma* melt into one another in a strange fashion in I Cor. 6:13–20. "The body is not meant for immorality" (v. 13), evidently means that the body, insofar as it is the seat of sex-life, is not to be defiled by immorality. But when it goes on to say, ". . . but for the Lord, and the Lord for the body," this sexual implication of "body" can scarcely still be present. Moreover, when v. 14 says, "And God raised the Lord and will also raise us up," the word "us" has taken the place of the expected phrase "our bodies"; i.e. the equation "*soma* = self, person" hovers in the background. And when v. 15 begins, "Do you not know that your bodies are members of Christ," "your bodies" means "you" (*cf.* 12:27, see above). But when it continues, "Shall I therefore take the members of Christ and make them members of a prostitute?" the other meaning of *soma* as the physical body sounds through again. And when according to v. 16 he who joins himself to a prostitute becomes "one *soma*" with her, "soma" once more means physical body, even though the meaning tends toward the figurative in that it also means "unity," "one-ness." In v. 18 the meaning of *soma* is hard to determine; nevertheless, this much is clear: *Soma* here means that which is most intimately connected with man and amounts to the same thing as "self." In this formulation Paul is probably dependent upon the rabbinic idiom "to sin with the body," a term that can be used to denote unchastity. In v. 19, again, the meaning of *soma* fluctuates strangely, for when the *soma* is called the temple of the Spirit that dwells within the Christian, one is at first inclined to think of his physical body as the temple (*cf.* Rom. 8:11) in keeping with the basic tenor of the exhortation—that the Christian keep his body clean from immorality. But then it says, "*You* are not your own" instead of saying "your *bodies* are not your own property." Hence, the *soma* that is the Spirit's temple must be the Christian's whole person, not just his body. On the other hand, *soma* in the exhortation, "So glorify God in your *soma*" (v. 20), probably means "body"—i.e. within the whole context it means: do not yield your body to unchastity.

2. The result of all the foregoing is this: *Man, his person as a whole,* can be denoted by *soma.* It may also be significant that Paul never calls a corpse *soma*, though such a usage is found both in profane Greek and in the LXX. But what is the specific respect in which man is regarded when he is called *soma*? *Man is called soma in respect to his being able to make himself the object of his own action or to experience himself as the subject to whom something happens.* He can be called *soma*, that is, *as having a relationship to*

himself—as being able in a certain sense to distinguish himself from himself. Or, more exactly, he is so called as that self from whom he, as subject, distinguishes himself, the self with whom he can deal as the object of his own conduct, and also the self whom he can perceive as subjected to an occurrence that springs from a will other than his own. It is as such a self that man is called *soma*. Since it belongs to man's nature to have such a relationship to himself, a double possibility exists: to be at one with himself or at odds (estranged from himself). The possibility of having one's self in hand or of losing this control and being at the mercy of a power not one's own is inherent to human existence itself. But in the latter situation the outside power can be experienced as an enemy power which estranges man from himself or as the opposite, a friendly power that brings the man estranged from himself back to himself.

> The fact that *soma* can denote both the body and the whole man, the person, rests upon a point of view that is current both in the Old Testament (where the same holds true for בָּשָׂר, "flesh," "body," "self") and in Judaism. The reason for it is that for a person his body is not a thing like the objects of the external world, but is precisely *his* body, which is given to him, and he to it. He gets his primary experience of himself by experiencing his body, and he first encounters his thraldom to outside powers in his bodily dependence upon them. So the inward aspect of the self and the outward (its sensory given-ness) remain at first undiscriminated as phenomena.

That man is called *soma* in respect to his being able to control himself and be the object of his own action, is shown by the passages quoted above: he pommels or subdues *himself* (I Cor. 9:27); he can give *himself* to be burned (I Cor. 13:3); he can yield *himself* to the service of sin or of God (Rom. 6:12ff.; 12:1); he can expend *himself* for Christ (Phil. 1:20). Also, the statement that marriage-partners do not rule over themselves (I Cor. 7:4) ultimately belongs here, for the meaning is that though they can withhold themselves from each other, yet they are to place themselves mutually at the other's disposal; hence, it is up to them whether or not they make real the statement "he (she) does not rule . . ." The *soma* can be described as the actual tool of action; thus II Cor. 5:10 says, "that each may receive according to what he has done through the (= his) *soma*" (tr.). This has no other meaning than "according to his own deeds" —i.e. according to what he has done not with his body, but with himself, what he has made of himself.

Soma appears only once in Paul as the implied subject of an action: Rom. 8:13, where "deeds of the soma" are mentioned.* But these "deeds of the soma" recede strangely into the distance in reference to the acting human subject; these deeds are the object of his conduct ("if . . . you put to death the deeds of the soma"). So the expression is to be understood as arising from the fact that the soma-self (a self distinguished from the subject-self) has become so independent in Paul's thought that he can speak of its deeds. But that means nothing else than that the soma, so far as it brings forth deeds of its own, is under the sway of an outside power, which has seized from the self the power of control over itself; it simply means that in the "deeds of the soma" man no longer has himself in hand. The context shows that the outside power is "the flesh"; for the "deeds of the soma" correspond to "living according to the flesh." The same thing is indicated by the fact that Paul can speak of the "passions" of the "soma" (Rom. 6:12), for here, too, it is clear that what is meant by soma is that self which has fallen under the sway of "flesh"; precisely that self from which the real self distinguishes itself, or rather is urged to distinguish itself. The "passions of the soma" are nothing else than the "passions of the flesh" (Gal. 5:16f., 24; cf. Rom. 7:7ff.; 13:14). In the same sense, Paul can also speak of the "soma of sin" (Rom. 6:6)—i.e. the sinful self (the self that is under the sway of sin), while in Rom. 8:3 he speaks of the "flesh of sin" (= sinful flesh). In addition, soma receives adjectives and other qualifiers which express its captivation by an outside power, whether of destructive sort or of emancipating and beneficial sort. As subject to transitoriness and death, the soma is called psychikon (animate, but bound to lose its life, I Cor. 15:44), or "mortal" (Rom. 6:12; 8:11) or a "soma of humiliation" (Phil. 3:21); as the resurrection-body, it is a "spiritual body" (I Cor. 15:44), or a "glory-body" (Phil. 3:21).

The characterization of man as soma implies, then, that man is a being who has a relationship to himself, and that this relationship can be either an appropriate or a perverted one; that he can be at

---

* This lectio difficilior is to be preferred to the reading of DG et al.: πράξεις τῆς σαρκός (deeds of the flesh).

one with himself or at odds; that he can be under his own control or lose his grip on himself. In the latter case, a double possibility exists: that the power which comes to master him can make the estrangement within him determinative, and that would mean that it would destroy the man by entirely wresting him out of his own hands, or that this power gives him back to himself, that is, brings him to life. That man is *soma* means that he stands within such possibilities. The fact that he is *soma* is in itself neither good nor bad. But only because he is *soma* does the possibility exist for him to be good or evil—to have a relationship for or against God.

It can now be understood why Paul so zealously defends the resurrection of the *soma* against his Corinthian opponents—it must be understood from the basic meaning that the concept *soma* has as a characteristic of human existence. If man were no longer *soma*—if he no longer had a relationship to himself—he would no longer be man. Since Paul's capacity for abstract thinking is not a developed one, and he therefore does not distinguish terminologically between *soma* in the basic sense of that which characterizes human existence and *soma* as the phenomenon of the material body, he connects the idea of somatic existence in the eschatological consummation with a mythological teaching on the resurrection (I Cor. 15). In it *soma* must appear somehow or other as a thing of material substance, or as the "form" of such a thing. And since the substance of the resurrection-body cannot be "flesh and blood" (I Cor. 15:50), the unfortunate consequence is that *pneuma* must be conceived as a substance of which that *soma* consists. In distinction from this mythology the real intention of Paul must be made clear. It is that he asserts specific human existence, both before and beyond death, to be a somatic existence in the basic sense defined above.

It could be objected, to be sure, that in the resurrection-life the possibility seems to have dropped out that man could become estranged from himself, could get to be at odds with himself and fall victim to an inimical power that would tear him out of his own hands and destroy him. In fact, this has dropped out as a factual (ontic) possibility, for sin and death are destroyed at the consummation (I Cor. 15:26, 55f.). But that does not mean that the ontological structure of human existence will be destroyed, for if it were, no continuity at all would exist between a man before his death or resurrection and the resurrected individual. Actually, the statement that faith, hope, and love abide in the consummation (I Cor. 13:13) also testifies that Paul regards human nature as such (in its onto-logical structure) as unchanging, for in faith, hope, love man always also has a relationship to himself, since in them he makes up his mind about something, adopts a definite attitude. And the same conclusion results from the concept *soma pneumatikon* ("spiritual body"), rightly interpreted: "It does not in the end mean a body formed of an ethereal substance, but it does mean that the self is determined by the power of God which reconciles the cleft between self and self within a man and hence does presuppose a relationship of man to himself. But this cannot be cleared up until the concept *pneuma* (Spirit) is discussed.

3. Insofar as man is *soma* and thereby has a relationship to him-self, he can distinguish himself from himself, and he will do this all the more as he experiences outside powers trying to wrest him out out of his own control or even having done so. Then the temptation exists to let the perceived separation between himself and himself become a divorce—to misunderstand his relationship to himself as that between his self and a totally foreign being, a "not-I." In such misunderstanding the original naive meaning, *soma* = body, can come to the surface again so that the "double" to which the self is bound is regarded to be the material body. That is the understand-ing of the self that is found in (Gnostic) dualism, according to which man's self is imprisoned in the body, a prison foreign to its own nature, from which it yearns to be set free. To this view such a somatic existence as Paul expects to find at the consummation is, of course, unthinkable. And this dualism's attitude in practical life is mysticism and asceticism, that is, a turning aside from bodily (somatic) existence—a flight from the uncomfortable tension of a human existence in which a person unavoidably has a relationship to himself.

From the very fact that Paul conceives the resurrection-life as somatic, it is apparent that his understanding of the self was not shaped by this dualism. But, on the other hand, he sees so deep a cleft within man, so great a tension between self and self, and so keenly feels the plight of the man who loses his grip upon himself and falls victim to outside powers, that he comes close to Gnostic dualism. That is indicated by the fact that he occasionally uses *soma* synonymously with *sarx* ("flesh").

This does not refer to the use of *soma* or *sarx* to denote the physical body as in the following examples. II Cor. 4:10f. ". . . so that the life of Jesus may also be manifested in our bodies"; but in v. 11 the same statement ends ". . . in our mortal *flesh*"—synonymous parallelism of members. In Gal. 6:17, Paul bears on his "body" the marks of Jesus, but "body" can hardly mean anything else than "flesh" does in the phrase "ailment of the flesh" (Gal. 4:13 tr.), or the "thorn . . . in the flesh" (II Cor. 12:7). I Cor. 6:16 uses the two words synonymously, but only because Gen. 2:24 LXX "the two shall become one *flesh*" (tr.), is cited to prove that he who joins with a prostitute "becomes one *body* with her." In all such cases Paul is following the example of the LXX, in which בָּשָׂר is rendered sometimes *soma*, sometimes *sarx*, with no difference in meaning.

The passages named above (p. 197) which deal with the "passions" or the "deeds" of the *soma* (Rom. 6:12; 8:13) use *soma* in the sense of *sarx*—a sinful power at enmity with God. Here *soma* is to be understood as the self under the rule of *sarx*—and the "passions" and "deeds" that are meant are precisely those of *sarx* ("flesh"). The correspondence of the two clauses in Rom. 8:13— "if you live according to the flesh . . . if you put to death the deeds of the body"—shows that when the *soma* is under the sway of *sarx*, Paul can speak of the *soma* in just the same way as he does of *sarx* itself. The case of Rom. 7:14ff. is similar. Here the sin leading man to death is first attributed to the *sarx* (vv. 14, 18), but later the "law of sin" is spoken of as ruling in the "members"—i.e. in the *soma* (v. 23). Then when the question is asked, "Who will save me from this *soma* of death?" *soma* means the sin-ruled self, the self under the sway of sin—and that cry applies not to release from the *soma* absolutely, but release from this *soma* as it is ruled through and through by "flesh," and that really means release from "flesh" itself. According to Rom. 8:9, "flesh" is deposed, and when the next verse says "if Christ is in you, although your *soma* is dead because of sin," that means that the *flesh-ruled soma* (again equivalent to *flesh* itself) is eliminated (and it is eliminated "because of sin"—i.e. because sin has been condemned; *cf.* v. 3). Hence the estrangement between the self which is the bearer of man's real will (the "inmost self" of Rom. 7:22) and the self which slips away from this will and falls under the sway of flesh—exactly the cleft which Rom. 7:14ff. depicts—is regarded as so far-reaching that this second self seems almost a foreign one, not belonging to the same person. It is so completely ruled by flesh that the difference between *soma* and *sarx* is at the point of disappearing. And yet, the *soma* remains that self which is indissolubly bound to the willing self, as Rom. 7:14ff. also shows, and the basic difference between *soma* and *sarx* remains valid. For the Christian, the flesh is dead and deposed (Rom. 8:2ff.); it is excluded from participation in the Reign of God (I Cor. 15:50), while the *soma*—transformed, i.e. released from the dominion of flesh—is the vehicle of the resurrection-life. The *soma* is man himself, while *sarx* is a power that lays claim to him and determines him. That is why Paul can speak of a life κατὰ σάρκα (according to the flesh) but never of a life κατὰ σῶμα (according to the body).

Thus, Paul did not dualistically distinguish between man's self (his "soul") and his bodily *soma* as if the latter were an inappropriate shell, a prison, to the former; nor does his hope expect a release of the self from its bodily prison but expects instead the "bodily" resurrection—or rather the transformation of the *soma* from under the power of flesh into a spiritual *soma*, i.e. a Spirit-ruled *soma*. As the rescue from the "*soma* of death," for which Rom. 7:24 yearns, means release from the flesh (see above), so does the hope for the "redemption τοῦ σώματος" in Rom. 8:23 mean redemption from the *soma* as ruled by *sarx*, if it really means redemption *from* the *soma* (genitive of separation) and not just the *soma's* redemption (objective genitive).

The case of II Cor. 5:1ff. is different. Here Paul comes very close to Hellenistic-Gnostic dualism not merely in form of expression, by speaking of the *soma* under the figure of the "tent-dwelling" and "garment," but also in the thought itself. Here the *soma* appears as a shell for the self (the "inner nature," ἔσω ἄνθρωπος, of 4:16), moreover as an inappropriate shell, inasmuch as it is the earthly tent-dwelling in which the self at present still sighs with longing for a heavenly garment that would be appropriate to the self. Here, quite dualistically, to be "at home in the body" and its correlate to be "away from the Lord, our home" (tr.), confront their opposites: to be "away from (move out of?) our body-home and be at (move into our) home with the Lord" (vv. 6, 8, tr.). Furthermore, it is not the *soma* ruled by flesh (and sin)—ultimately sin itself, in other words—from which the self here desires to be freed, but the physical body distressed by care and suffering, the body mentioned at 4:10f. whose sufferings are described in 4:8f., the body that is an "earthen vessel" (4:7). So the Christian desires to be and will be redeemed from the *soma* in this sense. But that does not mean that this expectation contradicts the special sense of *soma* worked out above. It does not imply release from somatic existence altogether. Rather, the arguments of 5:1ff. contain indirect polemic against a Gnosticism which teaches that the naked self soars aloft free of any body. The Christian does not desire, like such Gnostics, to be "unclothed," but desires to be "further clothed" (ἐπενδύσασθαι, v. 4); he yearns for the heavenly garment, "for we will not be found naked when we have divested ourselves (of our present physical body)" (Blt., reading ἐκδυσάμενοι with D* etc. in v. 3).

In the same sense, as the physical body, *soma* is probably also to be understood in II Cor. 12:2–4, where Paul is speaking of a pneumatic experience of his, doubtless an ecstasy as mysticism uses the word. When he twice professes not to know whether this experience happened to him "in the body or out of the body," he is clearly reckoning with the possibility that the self can separate from the *soma* even in this present life, and this *soma* can only be the physical body. It would be meaningless here to think of the "*soma* of sin."

Though Paul shows himself to be influenced in II Cor. 5:1ff. and 12:2–4 by the Hellenistic-dualistic depreciation of the body conceived as physical corporeality, this influences goes still deeper in his treatment of the marriage question (I Cor. 7:1–7). For here, in keeping with ascetic tendencies of dualism, he evaluates marriage as a thing of less value than "not touching a woman" (v. 1); indeed, he regards it as an unavoidable evil ("on account of fornication," v. 2, tr.). It is to be noted, however, that he does not derive these ideas from the *soma*-concept, so that the latter remains quite in the background.

Nevertheless, it would be an error in method to proceed from such passages as these to interpret the *soma*-concept that is characteristic of Paul and determines his fundamental discussions. This characteristic concept, first meaning the physical body, comes to serve, as we have shown, to denote man's person in the respect that having a relationship to one's self belongs essentially to being man. More accurately, man is *soma* when he is objectivized in relation to

himself by becoming the object of his own thought, attitude, or conduct; he is *soma* in that he can separate from himself and come
under the domination of outside powers.

§ 18. *Psyche, Pneuma, and Zoe*

1. What does Paul call man, and how does he regard him, when
he is the *subject* of his own willing and doing, when he is his real
self who can distinguish himself from his *soma*-self? In Rom. 7:22
and II Cor. 4:16 as a formal designation for that self he uses the
term "the inner man" (ὁ ἔσω ἄνθρωπος), an expression that appears
to be derived from the anthropology of Hellenistic dualism. But it
has a purely formal meaning in Paul, as may be seen from the fact
that it means two things of different content in the two passages
cited. In Rom. 7:22, "the inner" is man's real self in contrast to the
self that has come under the sway of sin: "the *soma* of death" (7:24)
or "the *soma* of sin" (§ 17, 2, p. 200). In II Cor. 4:16 "the inner man
is still the real self, it is true, but in contrast to the physical body
(§ 17, 3, p. 201f.). Rom. 7:22 deals with unredeemed man under the
Law, II Cor. 4:16 with the Christian, in whom God's power is at
work (4:7), and in whom the Spirit dwells (5:5). The "inner man"
of Rom. 7:22 is identical in content with the *nous* ("mind"), which
belongs to man's essence (note how "inner man" is picked up, v. 23,
by the term "mind"), but "the inner man" of II Cor. 4:16 is the self
transformed by the Spirit (3:18). Thus the term "inner man" as
formal designation for the subject-self confirms our conception,
derived from the interpretation of *soma* (§ 17), of Paul's view of
human existence as the having a relationship to one's self. But
the investigation of other anthropological terms of Paul must teach
us how he more specifically understands that real self.

2. The term *psyche* (soul), so often used with *soma* to designate
man in his entirety, occurs relatively seldom in Paul—in connection
with *soma* in I Thess. 5:23, where *pneuma* is used in addition, so
that a trichotomous anthropology appears to be present. The investigation of Paul's use of *soma* has already shown that he does not
dualistically set body and soul in opposition to each other. Just as
Paul does not know the Greek-Hellenistic conception of the immortality of the soul (released from the body), neither does he use
psyche to designate the seat or the power of the mental life which

animates man's matter, as it had become the custom to do among the Greeks. Rather, *psyche* in Paul means primarily the Old Testament נֶפֶשׁ (rendered *psyche* in the LXX)—"vitality," or "life" itself. This corresponds, furthermore, with the older Greek usage. This is his use in Rom. 11:3 (quoting III Kingdoms 19:10), 16:4 ("risked their necks for my life"); II Cor. 1:23; Phil. 2:30; I Thess. 2:8. That is why lifeless instruments of music, which have no voice until the breath gives it to them, can be called "lifeless (ἄψυχα, 'soul'-less) things giving sound" (I Cor. 14:7). The use of "every soul" in the sense of "everyone" corresponds to Old Testament idiom (Rom. 2:9; 13:1). In this use it is already apparent that *psyche*, too, can take on the meaning "person," "self" (like נֶפֶשׁ). The *psyche* already mentioned in II Cor. 1:23, I Thess. 2:8 could be understood in this way and in any case must be so understood in II Cor. 12:15 ("I will most gladly spend and be spent for your souls" = for you).

It is very peculiar that Paul is influenced in addition by Gnostic usage, with the result that he uses *psyche* in a depreciatory sense. In I Cor. 15:45 he quotes Gen. 2:7: "The (first) man (Adam) became a living *psyche* (לְנֶפֶשׁ חַיָּה)" —quite in keeping with the Old Testament meaning, inasmuch as ψυχὴ ζῶσα (living "soul") denotes a living being, an animate person. But at the same, a foreign idea is smuggled into these words when "living soul" is qualified by the contrasting phrase "life-giving spirit." *Psyche* is now (as in Gnosticism) the merely natural, earthly vitality in contrast to the divinely given capacity for eternal life. And so the derived adjective *psychikos* can take on the meaning "second-rate," "limited," "transitory" (I Cor. 2:14; 15:44, 46; see § 15, 4b).

Nevertheless, where the contrast with *pneuma* is not involved, Paul uses *psyche* altogether in the sense current in the Old Testament-Jewish tradition; viz. to designate human life, or rather to denote man as a living being. But how his conception of this "life" is to be more adequately grasped is indicated by a number of passages. First, Phil. 1:27 ". . . that you stand firm in one spirit, with one mind (*psyche*) striving side by side for the faith of the gospel." The phrase "with one *psyche*" (like "in one spirit") means "in agreement"—i.e. having the same attitude or the same orientation of will; and there is no difference between *psyche* here and other expressions that mean the tendency of one's will, one's intention (*cf.* I Cor. 1:10, "united in the same mind—*nous*—and the same judgment"). **Words** compounded with the root *psych-* indicate the same thing: *Sympsychos* means "being in agreement" ("of one mind," Phil. 2:2 RSV); the *isopsychos* (Phil. 2:20) is the "like-minded." *Eupsychein,* "be of good cheer, hopeful, confident" (Phil. 2:19), offers a somewhat different nuance. It does not mean the willing of something, it is true, but it does also express the intention element of that vitality which is denoted by *psyche.* Hence, it is incorrect to understand *psyche* in Paul as meaning only the "principle of animal life" and as standing in close relation to "flesh" understood as the matter enlivened by that *psyche.* Rather *psyche* is that specifically human state of being alive which inheres in man as a striving, willing, purposing self. And even where *psyche* is depreciated in contrast to *pneuma,* it does not mean mere animal life but full human life—the natural life of earthly man, of course, in contrast to supranatural life. The man who is *psychikos* (I Cor. 2:14 "natural man" KJ; "unspiritual man" is RSV's interpretive rendering) is not a person who has only biological needs, but the person whose life is directed toward, and limited to, the earthly.

3. Just as in the Old Testament, נֶפֶשׁ (soul, life, self) and רוּחַ (spirit) are to a large extent synonymous, Paul, too, can use *pneuma* in a sense similar to that of *psyche.* This use, of course, must be carefully distinguished from his predominant use of *pneuma* for the Holy Spirit or the Spirit of God. In Rom. 8:16 the divine *pneuma* which Christians have received (v. 15) is expressly distinguished from "our *pneuma.*" Likewise, in I Cor. 2:10f., which is a case of conclusion by analogy—as only a man's "spirit" knows what is within him, so also the depths of God are available only to the divine "Spirit" (which has been bestowed upon Christians). When the unmarried woman or the maiden (I Cor. 7:34) is said to be anxious "how to be consecrated in body and spirit," "body and spirit" are evidently intended as a summary designation of the totality of a human being;* likewise, the wish (I Thess. 5:23) that "your spirit and soul and body may be kept sound and blameless" evidently means only that the readers may be kept sound, each in his entirety. So far as form is concerned, this is a trichotomous scheme of anthropology; but the formulation is to be explained as coming from litur-

---

* The totality of a person is designated in quite the same fashion by "flesh and spirit" in II Cor. 7:1; this verse, however, is non-Pauline like the whole of the inserted passage II Cor. 6:14–7:1.

gical-rhetorical (perhaps traditional) diction, so that nothing more is to be gathered from this passage than that Paul can also speak of a *pneuma* that is human.

In this use, *pneuma* can mean the person and take the place of a personal pronoun just as *soma* and *psyche* can. When I Cor. 16:18 says of the messengers from the Corinthian congregation, "they refreshed my *spirit* as well as yours," that means simply "me and you." That Titus' *pneuma* was set at rest (II Cor. 7:13) means only that he himself was set at rest. When Paul says in II Cor. 2:13, "I had no rest in my spirit" (KJ), he means that he found no inward rest (for there can be no thought of a distinction between his self and his "spirit"); but in the end the meaning is quite the same as that of II Cor. 7:5, "our flesh had no rest" (KJ). Both sentences mean, "I could not come to rest," and from them it is apparent how casual from case to case the choice can be of the anthropological term to designate the person. It is due to rhetorical pathos that in the closing wishes of some of the letters instead of the usual formula, "God . . . (or grace . . .) be with you all (or, with you)," we read the conclusion, "with your *spirit*," Gal. 6:18; Phil. 4:23; Phlm. 25. Probably Rom. 1:9 ("God . . . whom I serve with my *spirit*") should be included in this category; "with my spirit," in keeping with the pathos of the whole sentence, only emphasizes that Paul puts his whole person into the service of the gospel. Rom. 12:11 "fervent in *spirit*" (KJ), on the contrary, probably means "aglow with the Spirit" (RSV), since *pneuma* here seems to be the Holy Spirit conferred upon the Christian.

When Paul speaks of the *pneuma* of man he does not mean some higher principle within him or some special intellectual or spiritual faculty of his, but simply his self, and the only question is whether the self is regarded in some particular respect when it is called *pneuma*. In the first place, it apparently is regarded in the same way as when it is called *psyche*—viz. as the self that lives in a man's attitude, in the orientation of his will. Standing "in one *spirit*" (Phil. 1:27) is synonymous both with striving "with one mind" (*psyche* in the same verse; see above, 2) and with "in the same mind" and "the same judgment" of I Cor. 1:10. Phil. 2:1, also, scarcely means "participation in the Spirit" (RSV) or "unity bestowed by the Spirit," but simply unity of mind—i.e. unanimity of will. At any rate, this meaning of *pneuma* does occur in II Cor. 12:18 when Paul asks,

"Walked we not in the same spirit?" (KJ)—i.e. "Did we not (Titus and I) conduct ourselves in the same attitude (with the same intention)?" In distinction from *psyche, pneuma* seems also to mean the self regarded as conscious or aware. Thus Rom. 8:16: the divine Spirit "bears witness" to our spirit that we are God's children—i.e. makes us conscious of it, confers the knowledge of it upon us. And in the statement of I Cor. 2:11 that "man's *spirit* knows what is within him," *pneuma* approaches the modern idea of consciousness. It is apparent, therefore, that the meaning of *pneuma* departs from that of *psyche* and approaches that of *nous* ("mind"). Observe in this connection that in I Cor. 14:14 instead of the contrast between the divine *pneuma* and the human *pneuma* we find the contrast between the (divine) *pneuma* and the human *nous,* "mind," (for "my *pneuma*" here is not the human mind but the divine Spirit bestowed upon man)—exactly in a passage where it is essential to designate the conscious self.

Since the human self as a willing and knowing self can be called by the same term (*"pneuma"*) as the marvelous power of divine action (§ 14, 1), then the formal meaning of *pneuma* must possess this double possibility. As a matter of fact, a glance at what *pneuma* means as divine Spirit confirms what we have worked out for its meaning as human spirit. Paul does not conceive the divine Spirit as an explosively working power, so to say, but conceives it as guided by a definite tendency, a will, so that he can speak of its "endeavor" (φρόνημα, Rom. 8:6, 27) or even of its "desires" (ἐπιθυμεῖ, Gal. 5:17). It acts like a conscious subject certain of its goal (Rom. 8:26; I Cor. 2:10; II Cor. 3:6). Hence, to be "led by the (divine) Spirit" means to have one's will oriented in a particular direction (Rom. 8:14; Gal. 5:18). The same conclusion results from the fact that in I Cor. 2:16 Paul can let the expression νοῦς (κυρίου), which means "the planning (of the Lord)" (see below, § 19), take the place of *pneuma* (of God) because he wants to confirm his statement about the Spirit of God with the quotation from Is. 40:13.

It is from this point of view that certain passages are to be understood in which Paul, using an animistic terminology such as is frequently met in the Old Testament, speaks of a special *pneuma* which determines conduct in a specific case. It is clear that *pneuma* here means a special orientation of the will, although it cannot be said with certainty, whether *pneuma* in these passages is conceived as a specialization—a particle, so to say—of the divine Spirit, or whether it is simply a very pale locution approaching our own expression: "in the spirit of . . ."—i.e. "with the tendency of . . ." Thus Paul speaks of a "spirit of gentleness" (I Cor. 4:21; Gal. 6:1) or "of faith" (II Cor. 4:13). To this category, also, belongs the expression "the spirit of the world" in I Cor. 2:12. It must be left unanswered whether in this expression Paul is really imagining a concrete "power" inspired by the cosmos (a notion which, strictly speaking, is required by the contrast to "the Spirit which is from God"), or whether the formulation of the contrast is merely rhetorical, so that "spirit of the world" means *only* the worldly way of thinking and willing—a meaning which it would *include*, of course, in the other case, *too*.

I Cor. 5:3–5 presents difficulties. The contrast "absent in body—present in spirit" seems at first sight simply to contrast physical, personal absence (§ 17, 1) with presence in wish or will.* But v. 4 ("when you and my *pneuma* are gathered together") shows that for Paul it is not a matter of "mental" presence in his thoughts, but that his *pneuma* will be present as an active "power." Evidently a fluid transition takes place from one meaning of *pneuma* to another. Neither can the meaning of *pneuma* in v. 5 be determined with certainty: "for the destruction of the flesh, that his *pneuma* may be saved . . ." Is this *pneuma* the person, his real self, in contrast here to "the flesh" regarded as physical life (as in II Cor. 5:1ff., it is contrasted with the *soma*, § 17, 3)? Or is it the divine *pneuma* bestowed upon man in contrast to sinful flesh? Probably the former.

Rom. 8:10 and I Cor. 6:17 offer merely seeming difficulties which are due to their pointed, rhetorical formulation. Rom. 8:10: "(if Christ is in you), although your *bodies* are dead because of sin, your *spirits* are alive because of righteousness." This antithesis means that the flesh-ruled self is dead because sin is condemned (§ 17, 3); the new self ruled by the divine *pneuma* is alive because uprightness (of conduct; see "walk," v. 4) has now become reality. Still *pneuma* here does not mean simply the self, the person, but the divine *pneuma*, which has become the subject-self, so to say, of the Christian; the contrast

---

* In this sense Col. 2:5 says, "For though I am absent in the flesh, yet am I with you in the spirit" (KJ).

of *pneuma* to *soma* ("the *soma* of sin") requires this understanding. Hence, we have here a rhetorical paraphrase of the
simple thought: "If Christ dwells in you, then the life-giving
Spirit also dwells in you" (*cf.* v. 11). In I Cor. 6:16f. Paul supports his statement, "he becomes one body with her" with Gen.
2:24: "they shall become one flesh." In so doing, he gives "flesh"
the meaning of *soma* (§ 17, 3), but, of course, this *soma* is one
of "flesh." Then follows the contrasting statement, "But he who
is united to the Lord becomes one Spirit with him"; in compressed form this expresses the thought, "But he who joins himself to the Lord constitutes one body with him—a pneumatic
body."

4. In summary, this may be said: The various possibilities of
regarding man, or the self, come to light in the use of the anthropological terms *soma, psyche,* and *pneuma.* Man does not consist of
two parts, much less of three; nor are *psyche* and *pneuma* special
faculties or principles (within the *soma*) of a mental life higher than
his animal life. Rather, man is a living unity. He is a person who
can become an object to himself. He is a person having a relationship to himself (*soma*). He is a person who lives in his intentionality, his pursuit of some purpose, his willing and knowing (*psyche,
pneuma*). This state of living toward some goal, having some attitude, willing something and knowing something, belongs to man's
very nature and in itself is neither good nor bad. The goal toward
which one's life is oriented is left still undetermined in the mere
ontological structure of having some orientation or other; but this
structure (which for Paul is, of course, the gift of the life-giving
Creator) offers the possibility of choosing one's goal, of deciding for
good or evil, for or against God.

This analysis is also substantiated in the concept *zoe* (life),
wherever it is used as an anthropological term denoting the life that
is man's in the nature of the case when he has *psyche.* That man is
given natural *zoe* by God, that it is temporally limited and finds its
end in death, does not hit the meaning of the formal (ontological)
concept *zoe.* The supranatural life that is conferred upon the man
who is accounted righteous, or which stands in prospect for him, is
also *zoe* and has the same formal meaning as the concept *zoe* when
used to designate natural life. That is, what was said of the concept
soma (§ 17, 2) also applies here.

The way in which the verb "to live" (ζῆν) is used shows clearly that Paul does not understand life as a phenomenon of nature; but neither does he understand it in the Greek sense of "genuine" or "true" life—i.e. "mental" life. Rather, he understands it as the life a man leads in his concrete existence, the intentionality of human existence. His concept of life as lived by men is paradoxical in that *zoe* on the one hand means the life that a man lives as the subject of his own actions, his living self (i.e. his striving, willing self) and on the other hand, that this self-hood is not, like God, self-creative but is a thing entrusted to him—hence, that he factually lives only by constantly moving on, as it were, from himself, by projecting himself into a possibility that lies before him. He sees himself confronted with the future, facing the possibilities in which he can gain his self or lose it. This finds expression in the fact that he does not simply "live," but is always "leading his life" in some particular way. Living is always a "walking" (περιπατεῖν) and like the latter word is usually qualified by an adverb (to live "heathenishly" or "Jew-ishly," Gal. 2:14 tr.; *cf.* "to walk worthily . . ." I Thess. 2:12; "becomingly," Rom. 13:13; I Thess. 4:12) or by an adverbial phrase ("to live according to κατά—the flesh," Rom. 8:12; *cf.* "to walk . . . according to the flesh," Rom. 8:4; II Cor. 10:2; *cf.* "according to love," Rom. 14:15, tr.; "according to man," I Cor. 3:3 KJ mg.). Life is lived in some sphere and that sphere gives it its direction ("live in *it*"—by the context; in sin—Rom. 6:2; "in faith," Gal. 2:20; *cf.* "walking in craftiness," II Cor. 4:2; "by a spirit," II Cor. 12:18; Gal. 5:16). At the same time, man always lives "for" or "to" something (Rom. 14:7f.; II Cor. 5:15; Gal. 2:19), and just such statements show that a man's life can go astray in the illusion that he can live "for or to himself" instead of in dedication or self-surrender, renouncing the possibility of holding onto himself. In contradistinction to this aberration of "living for one's self," Paul admittedly does not set up a variety of possible ways of devoting one's self to a cause, but only the one basic possibility of living for God (Gal. 2:19) or for "the Lord" (Rom. 14:17f.) who for us died and rose again (II Cor. 5:15). But in these statements, which describe specifically Christian life, all that concerns us in this context is the bare ontological meaning they presuppose for "life" as a form of existence.

§ 19. Mind and Conscience

1. That being man means being a specific self that is the subject of its own willing and doing, is perhaps most clearly expressed by the term *nous* (usually translated "mind" or "understanding"). By it is meant not the mind or the intellect as a special faculty, but the knowing, understanding, and judging which belong to man as man and determine what attitude he adopts—except in the case that the human self is replaced by the divine Spirit in the state of ecstasy.

As the opposite of speaking in a "tongue," Paul speaks of speech "with the understanding" (τῷ νοΐ, I Cor. 14:14f., 19)—intelligent and intelligible speech. God's "peace" exceeds "all understanding," i.e. all that human "comprehension" (*nous*) understands—whether it be what man can think out or what he can receptively grasp (Phil. 4:7). The "unseen things" (KJ) of God, "his invisible nature" (RSV), have since the creation of the world been νοούμενα—i.e. perceived with the eye of νοῦς, "understanding thought" (Rom. 1:20).

Though in these passages the contemplative aspect inherent in the structure of *nous* is prominent, other passages show that *nous* is by no means just a contemplative attitude, but that it includes—like the Old Testament לֵב or לֵבָב ("heart," "mind") which it often represents in the LXX—the taking of a stand, a conscious or unconscious volition; it is an understanding intention, a "planning." In this sense, it is said of God's *nous*: "Who has recognized God's wondrous plan of salvation?" (Rom. 11:34 Blt., quoted from Is. 40:13, whose Hebrew text here has רוּחַ, Spirit). The same question occurs at I Cor. 2:16, where *nous* (16a and 16b) takes the place of the *pneuma* in the whole preceding discussion (vv. 10–15; *cf.* § 18, 3). Correspondingly, the ἀδόκιμος νοῦς to which God has given the heathen up (Rom. 1:28) is their "depraved inclination," their "miserable bent." Likewise, the exhortation to the Corinthian Church to be firm "in the same *mind* and the same judgment" (I Cor. 1:10; *cf.* § 18, 2 and 3) shows that *nous* is "what one has a mind to," the aim of one's will, the intent—i.e. *nous* is thinking that "has something in mind" or is making a plan for action. And when Rom. 12:2 exhorts: "Be transformed by the renewal of your *mind*," it is once more clear that what is meant is not a theoretical re-learning, but the renewal of the will. (Here as in Rom. 1:28 *nous* could almost

[211]

be translated: "character.") Rom. 14:5, "Let every one be fully convinced in his own *nous*," means "in his own judgment"—his judgment, that is, as to what is to be done and what not. Just as there is no willing and planning without knowing and understanding, so for Paul, knowing-and-understanding is everywhere of the sort that plans something, that contains an aim toward action.

The full meaning of *nous* is shown by Rom. 7:23: "But I see in my members another law at war with the law of my *nous*." The term *nous* takes up the term "inner man" (KJ) or "inmost self" (RSV) of v. 22 (§ 18, 1); the *nous*, therefore, is man's real self in distinction from his *soma*, the self which has become objectivized in relation to himself (§ 17, 2). And this self (the *nous*) is an understanding self that hears God's will speaking through the Law, agrees with it, and adopts it as its own. The *nous* is that self which is the subject of the "willing" in v. 15f. and 19–21, its aim is "the good" or "what is right," but its "doing" is frustrated by sin, which dwells "in the members." *

Admittedly there are grounds to wonder whether *nous* in Rom. 7:23 may not have lost its formal-ontological meaning, according to which it is an understanding volition that can turn toward either the good or the bad, while here it is presupposed that *nous*, as *nous*, turns toward the good. However, in Rom. 7:14ff. the ontological point of view (*nous* as a formal, neutral possibility capable of taking either direction) and the ontic point of view (*nous* already pointed in one specific direction) are peculiarly intertwined. It belongs to the nature of man (i.e. to his ontological structure) to desire "what is good," inasmuch as this good is nothing other than "life" itself. Since man can fail to achieve this thing that to him is "good," it also lies ahead of him as the requirement which he must fulfill if he is to achieve what he really desires. Factually, then, (ontically) the man who is under the Law—for that is *his* "ontic" situation—must actualize his human will for "good" by willing what the Law requires; for v. 10 says what the Law was given for: It was given "for life" (on which see § 27). Thus, behind the ontic meaning of v. 23 lies the ontological meaning. In the *nous* which affirms God's demand in the Law lurks the human *nous* whose innate inclination is toward

* In v. 25b, *nous* has the same meaning; but this sentence is very likely a gloss, which, in addition, has landed in the text at the wrong place; it belongs to v. 23.

"what is good," but as "depraved inclination" (Rom. 1:28), may factually be striving toward the bad, having in itself, as *nous,* the possibility of heeding or rejecting God's demand.

The very expression "being understood" (νοούμενα), they "are clearly seen" (Rom. 1:20 KJ), shows the same thing. For Paul so takes for granted that the understanding perception of God's nature includes knowledge of God's demand that he can describe the knowledge of God which is given (as possibility) to the heathen as "knowing God's demand (δικαίωμα)" (Rom. 1:32 Blt.); indeed, this is already implied by the fact that he can describe the sin of the heathen thus: "although they knew God, they did not honor him as God or give thanks to him" (v. 21). Knowledge of God is a lie if it is not acknowledgment of Him. Thus, it is clear that the *nous,* as such, is understanding will with the alternative of being for God or against Him. Man's volition is not an instinctive striving but is an understanding act of will which is always an "evaluating" act and therefore necessarily moves in the sphere of decisions between good and evil. It can go wrong in its judgment as to what is good or evil; it can become blind and be a "depraved intent." Hence, *nous* is not a higher principle in man any more than *psyche* or the human *pneuma* is, but is inherent to man as man and thereby has all the possibilities that human existence has.

2. The other derivatives of the root vo- indicate the same thing. The verb νοεῖν (understand) occurs in Paul only in the passage Rom. 1:20 already discussed; νόημα occurs more frequently. The *noemata* of Satan, II Cor. 2:11, are very clearly his "plots," his "designs" (RSV). When the *noemata* of the Jews are said to be hardened (II Cor. 3:14), the element of understanding thought is more prominent; but the very next verse "the veil is upon their *heart*" (KJ) indicates that the element of attitude or purpose is included, for that is just what is more clearly expressed by "heart" (§ 20, 1). Thus, both terms are combined into a hendiadys in Phil. 4:7: "The peace of God . . . will keep your *hearts* and your *minds.*" In II Cor. 4:4, the element of will is again more prominent when unbelief—which for Paul simultaneously means disobedience—is attributed to the fact that "the god of this world has blinded the *minds* of the unbelievers." This meaning is also clear in the description of the apostle's work, II Cor. 10:5: "taking captive every will (νόημα) to obey Christ" (tr.). Nor is it any different in 11:3: "I fear

. . . lest your *wills* (νοήματα) be led astray from single-hearted devotion to Christ" (tr.).

The terms διάνοια and διανοεῖσθαι (to consider, to purpose) do not occur in Paul; *metanoia* (repentance) occurs at Rom. 2:4 and II Cor. 7:9f., and *metanoein* (repent) at II Cor. 12:21. Its meaning here ("rue," "repent") clearly indicates that it is an act of the will that is meant.

A survey of the words on the root *phren-* can be added in confirmation of the above results. Φρένες in the sense of "understanding" appears only in I Cor. 14:20, where the context shows that what is meant is not just theoretical thinking but an intelligent (as opposed to childish) stand, or intelligent judgment. Φρονεῖν frequently occurs, and characteristic locutions indicate that it means one's "attitude" in which thinking and willing are one: τὸ αὐτό (or: τὸ ἕν) φρονεῖν, "have the same (or, one common) attitude" (RSV usually paraphrases: "live harmoniously" or "agree") Rom. 12:16; 15:5; II Cor. 13:11; Phil. 2:2; 4:2; "take a lofty attitude" (tr.), Rom. 11:20; 12:16; "adopting an earthly attitude," Phil. 3:19; "give way to the will of the flesh" (Blt.), Rom. 8:5. In the expression "be helpfully concerned for . . ." (Phil. 4:10 Blt.) the element of attitude is especially prominent. That φρόνημα means "intent" is clearly indicated by Rom. 8:6f., 27, where the *phronema* of the flesh and of the Spirit are mentioned. Φρόνιμος (wise, sensible) designates the one who has that intelligence or insight which has judgment as to right conduct (I Cor. 10:15; II Cor. 11:19); the "wise in their own conceits" (Rom. 11:25; 12:16) are the conceited ones who pride themselves on their own merits. The ἄφρων ("un-wise," "fool") is not just a dunce in thinking (I Cor. 15:35), but is a fool especially in attitude and conduct (II Cor. 11:16–19; 12:6, 11; "foolishness" in the same sense, 11:1, 17, 21); specifically the heathen are regarded categorically as "fools," Rom. 2:20. That σωφρονεῖν (have a sober or sane mind, Rom. 12:3; II Cor. 5:13) means an attitude of character, is self-evident.

3. According to Rom. 12:2, *nous* has for one of its functions δοκιμάζειν ("prove," "make a judgment"); when the judgment in question is a value-judgment, this word means "to consider worth" or "consider worthy." The element of will included in this meaning emerges clearly in Rom. 1:28: "since they did not *see fit* to acknowl-

dge God"—i.e. the heathen despised, rejected the acknowledgment
of God. Elsewhere, with persons as object, this verb means "find
worthy in the test" (I Cor. 16:3; II Cor. 8:22; said of God I Thess.
2:4; *cf.* also II Cor. 8:8: "to prove the genuineness of your love").
As the *nous* has the possibility of recognizing the demand for the
good, so the faculty of δοκιμάζειν ("proving," "approving") has the
ability to recognize τὰ διαφέροντα—i.e. "that which is essential"
(Rom. 2:18; Phil. 1:10 Blt.)—or "what is the good and acceptable
and perfect will of God" (Rom. 12:2, RSV mg.). In Rom. 14:22,
his verb obviously means deciding for what is required. Though
the verb also has the more specific meaning "test," this meaning, too,
is subordinate to the question concerning what is "good" (I Thess.
5:21: "test everything, hold fast what is good"); this is true in a
special way when the object to be tested is he who is to do the testing, himself ("himself" I Cor. 11:28; II Cor. 13:5; "his own work"
Gal. 6:4), in which it once more is apparent that the *nous* is the self
that makes itself the object of its own judging.

A special form of judging is κρίνειν, which in certain cases can
be almost synonymous with δοκιμάζειν (*cf.*, for instance, I Cor.
10:15: "judge for yourselves what I say" or 11:13 with I Thess.
5:21). It often means censorious judgment of others (Rom. 2:1f.;
14:3f., 10, 13; I Cor. 5:12; from the context also I Cor. 4:5, where it
is used absolutely; *cf.* also I Cor. 10:29. It is also used in this meaning, of course, of the decision of a judge I Cor. 6:2f. and often of
God's judging). Also, the self-condemnation that results from self-
examination belongs here (Rom. 14:22). In II Cor. 5:14 judgment
concerning a subject under discussion is meant: "making this judgment: that one died for all" (tr.; *cf.* I Cor. 10:15); discriminating
judgment is meant in Rom. 14:5 ("judges one day to be better than
another," etc., tr.). It means judgment concerning a course to be
chosen in Rom. 14:13 ("judge this rather, that no man put a stumbling-block . . . in his brother's way" KJ) and in I Cor. 2:2 ("I
reached the judgment not to know anything among you but Jesus
Christ," tr.)—also I Cor. 5:3f.; 11:13. Hence, κρίνειν can mean almost
"decide" (II Cor. 2:1, "I *made up my mind* not to make you another
painful visit," RSV; also, I Cor. 7:37) (RSV directly renders it
"decide" at Rom. 14:13; I Cor. 2:2, at least).

In part closely related to κρίνειν (and δοκιμάζειν) is λογίζεσθαι.
It likewise can denote judgment of a matter of fact ["we *hold* that

a man is justified by faith," Rom. 3:28 RSV; "*consider* yourselves dead to sin" (Rom. 6:11); "I *consider* that the sufferings . . . are not worth comparing" (Rom. 8:18); "who *considers* it unclean" (Rom. 14:14 tr.); "I do not *consider* . . ." (Phil. 3:13 RSV)]. Judgment about a person can also be meant: I Cor. 4:1 ("regard") II Cor. 10:2b; (a little differently, with a figurative use of a mercantile expression): II Cor. 12:6 (λ. εἰς ἐμέ = "give me credit"). In other passages one can waver in opinion whether this verb means judgment concerning a matter of fact or only means "think," "weigh," "ponder"; such cases are Rom. 2:3; II Cor. 10:2, 7 (RSV: "let him *remind himself* that as he is Christ's, so are we;"); 10:11 ("let such people understand," etc.); 11:5 ("I *think* that I am not in the least inferior . . ."). At any rate, in II Cor. 3:5 it means "consider" (not "think something up"); but in Phil. 4:8, on the contrary, it means merely "ponder," "think about," and in I Cor. 13:11 ("as a child") simply "think."

4. Other terms for "understanding" or "knowing" such as γινώσκειν and εἰδέναι have no specifically anthropological significance; i.e. they do designate acts that belong to man, but mean specific acts or states, from case to case, and neither characterize human existence as such nor contain the possibility of good or evil. Only the concept συνείδησις (conscience) belongs to the fundamental anthropological concepts. This word, which originally meant joint knowledge (συν-ειδησις) with another, had in Paul's time long since come to have the meaning of knowledge shared with one's self. Hellenistic Judaism had already appropriated the word in this sense, but any such term was still foreign to the Hebrew Old Testament (though not the phenomenon denoted by it; note, moreover, LXX Job 27:6: οὐ γὰρ σύνοιδα ἐμαυτῷ ἄτοπα πράξας, "for I am not conscious of having done wrong" = almost "my conscience does not accuse me of having done wrong"; LXX Eccles. 10:20 uses the noun, but in its original sense). It is in this sense that it is used by Paul, through whom, perhaps, it was first introduced into Christian language.

This term, too, denotes a relationship of a man to himself, though in a different way than *soma* does. While *soma* serves to distinguish the objectivized self from the real self and to characterize the *soma*-self as the object of one's own action or that of outside powers, συνείδησις ("conscience") is a man's knowledge ("consciousness") f his conduct as his own. Unlike *nous,* it is not a state of mind that includes an intent but one that, reflecting and judging, scrutinizes precisely this intent of one's own mind. Conscience judges; i.e. it s a knowledge about one's own conduct in respect to a requirement which exists in relation to that conduct. Hence, "conscience" is at one and the same time a knowledge of good and evil and of the corresponding conduct. This knowledge may point toward still unaccomplished conduct, a duty to be fulfilled, as well as critically judge already happened conduct. Both are involved in I Cor. 8:7–12; 10:25–30. For the idea is, on the one hand, that "conscience" forbids "the weak" to eat food that has been offered to idols, but on the other hand, Paul's thought evidently is that if "the weak" nevertheless eat it and thereby get their conscience "defiled" (8:7), they will have "a bad conscience." Rom. 2:15, also, probably refers first of all to the demanding, binding conscience, since "conscience" is to be regarded as a proof that the requirements of the Law are written in the hearts of the heathen. If, then, the added words apply not to social discussion (in which case one would translate: "while their discussions among themselves accuse or perhaps excuse," tr.) but to the conflict within a man, interpreting the term "conscience," as they probably do ("their conflicting thoughts accuse or perhaps excuse them," RSV), the consequence is that Paul is also thinking of the judging conscience which accuses the doer with an accusation which he (at times) resists.* If, according to Rom. 13:5, the citizen is to yield obedience to the government "for the sake of conscience," then it is the conscience that prescribes what is to be done. And when Paul as an apostle commends himself "to every man's conscience" (II Cor. 4:2), he means that the conscience of those who come to know him as an apostle forces them to an approving verdict as to his sincerity. Likewise, when he hopes not to be misunderstood by the Corinthians ("I hope to be revealed [for what I *am*] in your *consciences,*" II Cor. 5:11, tr.), if they let themselves be guided by their "conscience." That is, conscience demands in each case a specific attitude. Elsewhere, the word means the judging conscience that can either condemn or acquit. Thus, I Cor. 4:4: "for my conscience (συνοῖδα) has nothing against me" (tr.)—here the verdict is acquittal. Likewise, Rom. 9:1: Paul's "conscience"

---

* In any case v. 15 must not be combined with v. 16 into one sentence; v. 16 is a secondary gloss.

testifies that he is telling the truth. Also, II Cor. 1:12: his "conscience" testifies to him the sincerity of his way of life.

As Rom. 2:15 indicates, Paul considered conscience a universal human phenomenon—consistent with his view of human existence as we have thus far unfolded it. For if it is inherently human to have knowledge of one's self, and if the life a man has to lead lies ahead of him and can be won or lost (§ 18, 4), and if, therefore, the good that he seeks takes on the nature of requirement (see 1, above), then it is inherently human to have conscience. Paul takes it for granted that the heathen have a conscience. That he understands conscience as knowledge of the demand that is incumbent upon man, is to be concluded from the circumstance that this very fact of their having conscience testifies to him that the heathen know the demands of the Law, even though they do not have the Law; they are "written in their hearts," i.e. it is just by virtue of their "conscience" that they know them.

Insofar as the conscience's knowledge applies to *that which is demanded* of man, the decisive thing is that conscience knows that there *is* such a thing *at all*; for it is possible for it to err in regard to the *content* of that demand. That is true of the conscience of those in Corinth who suppose themselves to be obligated not to eat food offered to idols (I Cor. 8:7–12; 10:25–30); their conscience is called "weak," and they themselves, lacking correct "knowledge," are "weak." Nevertheless, the verdict of conscience which falls upon a man's conduct in view of what is demanded cannot err, but is valid. Those Corinthians, according to Paul, are really bound to the verdict of their conscience and may not be forced into conduct which their conscience condemns. Likewise, the certainty with which Paul appeals to the testimony of his conscience in defense of his conduct shows that its verdict is not subject to doubt (Rom. 9:1; II Cor. 1:12). But that rests upon the fact that the demand perceived by conscience has its foundation in a sphere transcendent to man; to acknowledge *that sphere* is in the end the decisive thing, though man may err in what he believes he hears as its demand. That is why Paul can motivate the duty of obedience to the government in a peculiarly double way (Rom. 13:5): The citizen owes the government obedience not only "for the sake of wrath," i.e. for fear of its power to punish (*cf.* v. 4; "*God's*" in v. 5 RSV is an interpretative addition!), but also "for the sake of conscience," i.e. for fear of the transcendent source of authority that stands behind conscience—or Paul, of course, God. And just as here "conscience," which was originally man's knowledge, is conceived as independent of him and used by metonomy for that authority of which the knowledge in "conscience" knows, so in Rom. 9:1; II Cor. 1:12 the conscience is accorded separate existence ("personified") as an authority beyond man—which indicates that the essential thing about "conscience" is just this obligation to its transcendent source of authority. Conscience, so to say, steps in as an independent witness with the man whose binding obligation she is.

Here again we see that Paul understands a man's self as the specific self which becomes his by his assuming responsibility, irrespective of the judgments of men, for the particular life turned over to him from outside himself. Precisely in "conscience," which a man has by virtue of a power which transcends it, his self constitutes itself as his specific self. The verdict of conscience is absolutely valid, inasmuch as in it obedience to the transcendent power takes place, hence, precisely in "conscience" man has his "freedom" (I Cor. 10:29). No other person has the right to force his judgment upon me: "for why is my freedom decided by any other conscience [than my own]?" (tr.)

This sentence is not to be taken as the objection of an opponent (Lietzmann). V. 27 (and 25, too,) had said, one need not ask for conscience' sake whether meat served at a meal has been offered to idols (i.e. there is no obligation to refuse such meat under any and all circumstances). If, however, the heathen host points out (with good or evil intent) that the meal served is sacrificial meat (v. 28), it is to be declined—declined not only for the informer's sake, but also for conscience' sake. V. 29 then comments on the motive for declining—not because one's own conscience demands it, but for the sake of the other's (i.e. the "weak" one's) conscience, lest he be caused to act contrary to his conscience. If "I" (Paul) supposed that I had to decline for the sake of *my* conscience, I would have submitted to another's judgment and surrendered my freedom; in principle, I am free to eat anything that I can eat with thanksgiving (i.e. with a "good conscience"; v. 30); but I do not surrender my freedom either, if I decline out of consideration for another's conscience.

The situation is the same when what is involved is not judgment concerning a duty still to be fulfilled but judgment of conduct already carried out. He whose conscience acquits him is no longer subject to any human authority—or rather such judgment is indifferent to him (I Cor. 4:3f.).

Since Paul takes for granted that the transcendent authority, whose demand and verdict conscience knows, is known by Christians as God, he can substitute "faith" for "conscience," insofar as faith (on whose complete structure see § 32) is obedience to God's demand. It is through this insight that the fact is to be understood that Paul argues on the basis of "faith" in the analogous question of Rom. 14 quite as he does on the basis of "conscience" in I Cor. 8 and 10. "One man has the faith (πιστεύει) that he may eat anything" (Rom. 14:2, tr.) means exactly that the verdict of one man's conscience permits him to eat anything. And the concluding statement, "and whatever does not proceed from faith is sin" (v. 23b, tr.), corresponds to the assertion that it would be a "stumbling-block" (i.e. seduction to sin) to cause "the weak" to act against his conscience (I Cor. 8:9) and that "the weak" would thereby fall into "ruin" (I Cor. 8:11; *cf.* Rom. 14:15). Thus, the verdict of "conscience" coincides for the Christian (as a man of "faith") with the verdict of "faith"; and the verdict of faith, like that of conscience, has validity even if it is mistaken as to what is required of it. He who is "weak in faith" (Rom. 14:1f.) corresponds to the weak in conscience (I Cor. 8:7, 9, 12). And when the term *nous* (mind, judgment) takes the place of the term "faith" ("Let every one be fully convinced in his own *judgment*," Rom. 14:5, tr.; see 1, above), that is only possible because the term "faith" includes just that element of conscious judgment which is present in the term "conscience." Vice versa, the analogy between "conscience" and "faith" confirms our conclusion that conscience means the self's knowledge of itself (the conduct that is demanded of it, or its conduct subject to the Judge's verdict) in responsibility to the transcendent power (of God).

§ 20. Heart

1. Just as in the LXX לֵב (heart) is rendered either by καρδία (heart) or by νοῦς (mind), Paul uses "heart" to a large extent synonymously with *nous*; viz. to designate the self as a willing, plan-

ing, intending self. In II Cor. 3:14f., "minds" and "heart" are parallel in content (RSV renders both: "minds"), and in Phil. 4:7, the two terms constitute a hendiadys (§ 19, 2). Just as the *nous* (or the οήματα, "minds," "wills") can be detestable, hardened, blinded, or corrupted (Rom. 1:28; II Cor. 3:14; 4:4; 11:3), so can "the heart" (Rom. 1:21; 2:5; 16:18); and as the *nous* must be renewed (Rom. 12:2), so must "the heart" be illumined (II Cor. 4:6). Since the "heart" is called "impenitent" (Rom. 2:5), it is apparent that penitence (μετάνοια, change of mind) is a matter of the "heart."

Like *nous*, "heart" is a man's self, and in most cases where it is used it performs the service of a personal pronoun. For the "heart" is the subject that desires (Rom. 10:1), lusts (Rom. 1:24), purposes (I Cor. 4:5), decides (I Cor. 7:37; II Cor. 9:7), grieves (Rom. 9:2), suffers (II Cor. 2:4), and loves (II Cor. 7:3; 8:16; Phil. 1:7). Clearly the "heart" is not a higher principle in man, any more than *nous* is, but just the intending, purposing self—which decides within itself or is moved from without—which can turn to either the good or the bad. As it can be "darkened," and "hardened" (Rom. 1:21; 2:5), it can also be the victim of deception (Rom. 16:18) or have evil desires (Rom. 1:24). God "who searches hearts" (Rom. 8:27) or "tests" them (I Thess. 2:4, after Jer. 11:20), will bring to light the purposes of men's hearts and judge them (I Cor. 4:5).

Moreover, the heart doubts as well as believes (Rom. 10:6–10). As refusal of faith is hardening of the *heart* (II Cor. 3:14f.), so faith arises when God causes light to dawn in the *heart* (II Cor. 4:6). It is God who can "establish" hearts (make them firm, I Thess. 3:13); he confers the gift of the Spirit upon our hearts (II Cor. 1:22; Gal. 4:6); his love has been poured into the hearts of believers by the Spirit (Rom. 5:5). Everywhere "heart" stands for the self (*cf.*, for example, II Cor. 1:22 with 5:5). The statement that "the demands of the Law are written in the heart of the heathen" (Rom. 2:15) simply means that in their "conscience" they know these demands (§ 19, 3).*

Paul can use (τὰ) σπλάγχνα ("bowels," KJ) almost synonymously with "heart," except that "bowels" is confined to a much narrower territory, viz. to denote the self as moved by love,

---

* The expression "from the heart"—i.e. with dedication of one's whole person—occurs in a secondary gloss: Rom. 6:17; *cf.* Mk. 12:30, 33 parrs.; I Tim. 1:5; II Tim. 2:22; I Pet. 1:22.

II Cor. 6:12 (RSV: "affections"; here the word is parallel with "heart"); 7:15 and Phlm. 12 (RSV here renders it "heart"!). By metonymy, σπλάγχνα stands for "love" itself in Phil. 1:8; 2:1. In Phlm. 7 and 20 ("refresh the heart") it substitutes for a personal pronoun in the very phrase in which *pneuma* does the same (at I Cor. 16:18; II Cor. 7:13).

The difference between *nous* (mind) and *kardia* (heart) lies in the fact that the element of knowing which is contained in "mind" and can be prominently present is not emphasized in "heart," in which the dominant element is striving and will and also the state of being moved by feelings (pain and love). Another nuance of difference exists in this: the term "heart" can express the idea that the self's intent and will may be a hidden thing; "heart" is the "interior" in contrast to the "exterior," the real self in contrast to what a man appears to be. As in I Thess. 2:17, the external separation of the apostle from the congregation is contrasted as being a separation "on the surface" (ἐν προσώπῳ) with a separation "in the heart," so in II Cor. 5:12 a "boasting about the exterior" (ἐν προσώπῳ, i.e. on the basis of externally visible, impressive merits) is contrasted with a "boasting about the interior" (ἐν καρδίᾳ, i.e. on the basis of invisible qualities). Similarly, in Rom. 2:28f. "external, physical circumcision" and "inward (καρδίας) circumcision" confront each other in contrast. The "purposes of hearts" (I Cor. 4:5) are hidden until God brings them to light; the "secrets of the heart" are disclosed by the prophet-inspiring Spirit (I Cor. 14:25).

II Cor. 3:2 is complicated and not entirely clear (that is why the text-tradition is also uncertain): The Corinthian Church is Paul's letter of recommendation—a letter that can be universally seen and read, since anyone can perceive that Church ("known . . . by all men"); and yet Paul also calls this a letter "written in your hearts" (read "your" following ‭א‬ pc., not "our") because he wants to contrast it with a literal document of recommendation; to that extent, therefore, it is an invisible letter, a letter not written with ink, as v. 3 proceeds to say, but with the divine Spirit. But now another thought is woven in: The recommendation with which God has equipped Paul is not written on "tablets of stone" but on "hearts of flesh" (read: ἐν καρδίαις σαρκίναις!); now it is contrasted with the Law of Moses, and with a formulation determined by reminiscences of the Old

[222]

Testament. That is, the description of "hearts" as "fleshly" which means "living hearts" (in contrast to the "tablets of stone") is derived from Ezek. 11:19; 36:26. At any rate, "heart" is clearly regarded to be that inward sphere which is the seat of life.

The exterior and the interior, separately named, can also be combined to designate the totality of man. Thus, "mouth" and "heart" stand in parallelism of members in Rom. 10:9f.; II Cor. 6:11 (for which "we" is introduced in v. 12), quite as "eye," "ear," and "heart," combined in the apocryphal quotation, I Cor. 2:9, describe man's possibilities of perception.

2. The strivings of the "heart" can actualize themselves in conscious volition. The words that designate this possibility are primarily θέλειν (to will) and θέλημα (will).

Θέλειν means "to will" in various nuances, and its meaning is frequently incapable of being very precisely defined. A willing, which is definite decision, is meant in these places (disregarding the passages where it is said of God): Rom. 9:16; I Cor. 4:21 ("what do you wish?" = decide!); 10:27; Gal. 4:9; Phlm. 14; it is expressly distinguished from execution (ποιῆσαι, "do" or ἐνεργεῖν, "work"): II Cor. 8:10f.; Phil. 2:13. Elsewhere, it means "desire," "long for": II Cor. 5:4; 11:12; 12:20; Gal. 4:17 or a wishing which may be ardent: Rom. 16:19; I Cor. 7:32; 10:20; Gal. 4:20; I Thess. 2:18, or may be less ardent, "like": "I should like . . .": I Cor. 7:7; 14:5; Gal. 3:2 or "I prefer," I Cor. 14:19; finally, it can be used quite unemphatically as in phrases like "I *would* not have you ignorant," KJ: Rom. 1:13; I Cor. 10:1, etc.

Θέλημα is used mostly of God's will, his deliberative decree (in such phrases as "by the will of God," Rom. 15:32; Gal. 1:4, etc.) or his demanding will (Rom. 2:18, etc.). It is also used of the decision or the intention of man (I Cor. 7:37; 16:12).

It is important to note that human "will" can aim at the "good" (Rom. 7:15–21) as well as at the bad or perverse (Gal. 1:7; 4:9, 21; 6:12), but especially that "will" need not penetrate into the field of consciousness at all, but may designate the hidden tendency of the self. The rhetorical question (Rom. 13:3): "*Would* you have no fear of him who is in authority?" presupposes that everyone "wills" to live without fear of the public authorities without necessarily being conscious of this will. When Paul characterizes his opponents in

Gal. 6:12 as "those who want to make a good showing in the flesh," he is not naming their conscious intention but their secret motive hidden even from themselves; likewise, when he says of them (6:13): "they desire to have you circumcised that they may glory in your flesh." The willing of the "good" in Rom. 7:15–21 is the self's innermost tendency which is covered up and hidden by the conscious desires which bring forth deeds. And if the consequence of the battle between Flesh and Spirit over man, according to Gal. 5:17, is that man does not do what he "wills" to do, then this passage also does not have in mind what man in the specific case actually does will but what he wills *at heart,* an intention which can be perverted in his concrete will (through the influence of Flesh). The case of Gal. 4:21 is somewhat different. "You who *desire* to be under law" does not, it is true, pertain to the Galatians' conscious will, but neither does it mean the real desire of their "heart"; rather, it means the "unintentional" consequence of their purpose to combine obedience to the Law (or at least certain of its regulations) with faith; for they do not perceive the exclusive antinomy between "life under Law" and "life under grace." Gal. 1:7 is a related case; here Paul's opponents are called they who "want to pervert the gospel of Christ." The perverting of the gospel into its opposite is, of course, not the intention of these people, but is the hidden meaning of their willing —hidden even from themselves.

A few times Paul uses βούλεσθαι (decide, purpose) for human intention (II Cor. 1:15, 17) or wish (Phil. 1:12; Phlm. 13). The "strivings (βουλαί) of hearts" (I Cor. 4:5) are purposes that need not be actualized in conscious will. God's βούλημα (will) is mentioned in Rom. 9:19.

The expression "desires of their hearts" (Rom. 1:24) indicates that "desire" is an activity of "the heart." Admittedly, Paul frequently uses the verb or the noun (ἐπιθυμεῖν, ἐπιθυμία) not as an anthropological term denoting desire in general, but in a qualified sense, in which "desire" (used absolutely) is in itself evil. This is the case in the formula, "Desire not!" (Rom. 7:7 tr., 13:9; also I Cor. 10:6b, though here it is easy to supply the object "evil" from 6a). "Desire," as such, is also evil in Rom. 1:24; 7:7f.; I Thess. 4:5, and in Rom. 13:14; Gal. 5:16, 24 is attributed to the flesh (as in Rom. 6:12 to the flesh-dominated "body"). Nevertheless, the very fact

[224]

that Spirit as well as Flesh can have "desires" (Gal. 5:17) by itself indicates that the original meaning of "desire" is simply the direction in which one yearns. This is its meaning in Phil. 1:23: "My desire is to depart and be with Christ," and in I Thess. 2:17: "we endeavored . . . with great desire to see you face to face." In both cases "desire" has the meaning of "longing," and in itself therefore is nothing evil.

Θυμός in classic Greek frequently meaning, among other things, "desire," "appetite" and any "passion," occurs in Paul only in the qualified meaning, "wrath" (Rom. 2:8; II Cor. 12:20; Gal. 5:20); but the derivatives προθυμία ("readiness," "zeal for the good," II Cor. 8:11f., 19; 9:2) and πρόθυμος ("eager," Rom. 1:15) occur in the old, neutral sense.

Other verbs that denote striving and purpose with various nuances are the following:

Σκοπεῖν (II Cor. 4:18) means "focus upon . . ." i.e. upon an object as the goal worth striving for, just as σκοπός is the "goal" which guides the "onward pressing" of Phil. 3:14. Selfish striving is meant by τὰ ἑαυτοῦ σκοπεῖν, Phil. 2:4—looking to one's own interests. When σκοπεῖν is used in the sense of "wary attention to . . ." or of "bewaring of . . ." (Rom. 16:17; Gal. 6:1; Phil. 3:17), it still has the basic meaning of a conduct-guiding "viewing" in one's own interest. Ζητεῖν (to seek), too, means striving as such—after either good or evil. Its object may be "incorruption" (Rom. 2:7) or "wisdom" (I Cor. 1:22). Paul and Peter are "endeavoring to be justified in Christ" (Gal. 2:17). Paul exhorts: "strive to excel in building up the church" (I Cor. 14:12); he describes his relation to the Corinthians: "I seek not what is yours, but you" (II Cor. 12:14). Foolish "seeking" would "seek glory from men" (I Thess. 2:6) or seek "the favor of men" (Gal. 1:10); the Jews "seek to establish their own (righteousness)" (Rom. 10:3). "Seeking one's own" (τὰ ἑαυτοῦ ζητεῖν, I Cor. 10:24, 33; 13:5; Phil. 2:21) is selfish purpose; its opposite is "seeking (the advantage) of the many" (I Cor. 10:33 tr.). Intense purpose is called ζηλοῦν (be zealous after), whose object likewise can be good or evil. Paul is "zealous" (or "jealous"—ultimately both are the same word) for the Church with "a divine zeal" (or "jealousy"), II Cor. 11:2, while the preachers of the Law in Galatia are "zealously after" ("make much of," RSV) the Galatians in order that the latter in turn may "make much of" them. The apostle urges that "spiritual gifts" be "zealously sought after" (I Cor. 12:31; 14:1, 39). Like "desire," ζηλοῦν can also be used absolutely; when it is, it is used with a qualified (pejorative) meaning (I Cor. 13:4: "Love is not jealous"), and ζῆλος, "jealousy" (likewise, used absolutely), is, correspondingly, a vice characteristic of heathen nature (Rom. 13:13; I Cor. 3:3; II Cor. 12:20; Gal. 5:20). But the fact that ζῆλος, "zeal," can be directed toward either right or wrong ends indicates that its basic meaning is that of a non-qualified striving. Paul concedes to the Jews that they have "a zeal for God" and he himself is "zealous with a divine zeal" (II Cor. 11:2, see above), and he praises the "zeal" of the Corinthians for the collection (II Cor. 9:2). There is such a thing as "zeal" for another's welfare (II Cor. 7:7: "for me"; cf. v. 11); but there is also reprehensible "zeal" (Phil. 3:6: "as to zeal a persecutor of the church"). The same is true of ζηλωτής (one who is zealous, I Cor. 14:12; Gal. 1:14). Διώκειν (to pursue) in the figurative sense means, much like ζηλοῦν, eager striving, but it is not used absolutely in a qualified (pejorative) sense, but in itself is neutral, receiving any qualification only from its object—as it happens (accidentally), always a good qualification (Rom. 9:30f.: "righteousness" or "the Law of righteousness"; 12:13: "hospitality"; 14:19: "what makes for peace"; I Cor. 14:1: "love"; I Thess. 5:15: "the good"; figurative Phil. 3:12, 14). Μεριμνᾶν (be anxious about), finally, denotes solicitous care of a thing or a person. That it can operate in opposite directions, is indicated by I Cor. 7:32–34, where "worldly affairs" and "the affairs of the Lord" are named as its objects. It means "solicitude," "care for another's welfare" in I Cor. 12:25 ("for one another") and Phil. 2:20 ("anxious for your welfare"), and the noun is used in the same sense in II Cor. 11:28. Still, Paul can also use μεριμνᾶν, like "desire," absolutely in the qualified sense of something wrong in itself (Phil. 4:6), and hence he can write, I Cor. 7:32: "I want you to be free from all anxieties (ἀμερίμνους)."

So far as the "heart" is the self which is stirred by feelings and emotions, it may express itself in χαίρειν (rejoicing), λυπεῖσθαι (sorrowing), or κλαίειν (weeping). All these verbs describe human conduct simply as such, not as either good or bad, as particularly Rom. 12:15 and I Cor. 7:30 show in the case of joy and sorrow. I Cor. 13:6 shows that joy can relate to either good or bad. Analogously, II Cor. 7:9–11 distinguishes between "godly grief" and "worldly grief." Specifically, Christian joy is joy "in" (Rom. 14:17) or "of" (I Thess. 1:6) "the Holy Spirit."

B. FLESH, SIN, AND WORLD

§ 21. Creation and Man

1. As the investigation of the term *soma* showed (§ 17, 2), man, according to Paul, is a being who has a relationship to himself, is placed at his own disposal, and is responsible for his own existence. But this existence of his, as the investigation of the terms *psyche, pneuma, zoe, nous,* and *kardia* showed (§§ 18–20), is never to be found in the present as a fulfilled reality, but always lies ahead of him. In other words, his existence is always an intention and a quest, and in it he may find himself or lose his grip upon himself, gain his self or fail to do so. This brings in the possibility that man can be good or bad; for just because he must first find his life (that which is "good"—meaning the existence that at heart he wants), this existence comes to have for him the character of the "good"—in the sense of that which is required of him (§ 19, 1).

If, up to this point, the ontological structure of human existence, as Paul sees it, has been clarified, this, nevertheless, only affords the presuppositions for his ontic statements about man in which his real interest lies. It has already become apparent that several anthropological terms which have a primarily unqualified ontological meaning are at times used by Paul in a qualified ontic sense. *Soma,* since it is factually dominated by "flesh," can be used synonymously with "flesh"; i.e. ontically regarded, the *soma* is a "*soma* of sin" (§ 17, 2, 3). *Vice versa, nous* can mean the affirmation, though a fruitless one, of the demand for the good (§ 19, 1), while "desire," in the other direction again, can have the qualified sense of *evil* desire (§ 20, 2); so can ζηλοῦν ("be zealous," but also "be jealous") and μεριμνᾶν ("be solicitous," but also "be anxious," § 20, 2).

These phenomena indicate that Paul is of this opinion: *Man has always already missed the existence that at heart he seeks,* his intent is basically perverse, evil. Indeed, the view that all men are sinners, which he develops at length in Rom. 1:18–3:20, is a basic one for his doctrine of salvation; through Adam, sin and death came into the world as dominant powers (Rom. 5:12ff.); "the scripture consigned all men to sin" (Gal. 3:22, tr.).

[227]

In order to understand this view it is necessary to clarify what the meaning of evil is according to Paul. And since in his cogitations the presupposition is taken for granted that evil is in any case "sin"—rebellion against God, guilt toward God—his idea of God, so far as it is pertinent to this context, must first be presented.

2. Paul constantly sees man as placed before God. The ontological possibility of being good or evil is simultaneously the ontic possibility of having a relationship to God; and God, for Paul, is not the mythological designation for an ontological state of affairs but the personal God, man's Creator who demands obedience of him. The ontological possibility of being good or evil is ontically the choice of either acknowledging the Creator and obeying Him, or of refusing Him obedience. The demand for good which is made upon man is God's demand, which, as such, is a "life-giving demand" (Rom. 7:10, tr.); and disobedience is, therefore, sin.

In accordance with the Old Testament tradition Paul speaks of God as the Creator. It is God who once commanded light to shine forth out of darkness (II Cor. 4:6 from Gen. 1:3), and created man (I Cor. 11:8–12; *cf.* 15:45, 47). The earth with its contents is His, as I Cor. 10:26 in allusion to Ps. 24:1 says. God's creatorship is not, for Paul, a cosmological theory which professes to explain the origin of the world and its existence as it is. Rather, it is a proposition that concerns man's existence. It concerns him, for instance, in the fact that the earth as God's creation is at man's disposal for his needs, as the Old Testament creation-story (Gen. 1:26) had already said; hence, there is nothing on the earth that is unclean or untouchable (I Cor. 10:25f., 30; Rom. 14:14, 20).

"All things are yours" (I Cor. 3:21f.), is not relevant here, because it applies specifically to Christians and has a different meaning. Neither can it be said (see W. Gudbrod, *Die Paulinische Anthropologie*) that the goal of God's work of creation is stated in I Cor. 15:28: "that God may be all in all" (KJ); for the drama described in I Cor. 15:20–28 does not come from the tradition of the creation-story, but from Gnostic cosmology and eschatology. What I Cor. 15:28 deals with is the end of the battle against the Powers that are at enmity with God.

But knowledge of God as Creator contains primarily knowledge of man—man, that is, in his creatureliness and in his situation of

[228]

being one to whom God has laid claim. Yes, Paul does use familiar ideas of Stoic "natural theology" in Rom. 1:19f., but not in order to prove the sheer existence of God and His world-dominating providence so that he may thereby enlighten man and free him from "ignorance of God" and from fear. Rather, he uses them in order to accuse, specifically to expose, the guilt of the heathen: With evil will they refused to pay heed to the possibility of knowing God that was given to them. To know God means in itself to acknowledge God, obey His demand (δικαίωμα, 1:32), bow before Him in grateful adoration (1:21; *cf.* I Cor. 10:31).

That God's existence is not an objectively perceptible, mere existing like that of a thing, is indicated by I Cor. 8:4–6. If God were being spoken of as only a cosmic Thing, the statement, "there is no God but one," would not be right at all; for in this sense of "is," other "gods" and "lords" "are." The "uniqueness" of God is His εἶναι ἡμῖν, His being "*for us.*" That is, His being (existence) is understood aright only when it is understood as significant-for-man being; hence, it is not understood aright unless at the same time man's being is also understood as springing from God ("from whom are all things") and thereby oriented toward Him ("and toward whom we exist," I Cor. 8:6).

Here, as also in Rom. 11:36, "for from him and through him and to him are all things," Paul is using a formula of Stoic pantheism. But in this Romans passage it is especially clear how far Paul is from orienting his concept of God to the cosmos in the Greek sense. For, as the closing sentence of chapters 9–11, the formula has lost its original cosmological meaning and serves the purpose of expressing Paul's theology of history: The history of nations is salvation-history, and its origin, its guidance, and its goal are all in God.

3. For Paul, the word *cosmos,* accordingly, has in the great majority of cases a meaning different from that of the Greek conception of the world (§ 26). As the created world, here and now existing, Paul calls it "creation," with reference to its Creator (Rom. 1:25). When the world is so regarded, man is excepted from it, even though as "mortal man" (Rom. 1:23) he belongs to it. But as a being endowed by God with special dignity and responsibility (*cf.* I Cor. 11:3, 7, "he is the image and glory of God"), man stands between God and the creation and must decide between the two.

The "creation" is characterized by creaturely transitoriness (φθαρτόν, Rom. 1:23; 8:20f.). In obscure words, which evidently go back to a myth, Paul hints that it was not always so, but that the creation was involuntarily subjected to "futility," "bondage to decay" —subjected, moreover, by "him who subjected it"—but that some day it, like "the children of God," will be set free from the curse of transitoriness (Rom. 8:20f.). Since it is unclear whom Paul means by the "subjector" (God? Satan? Adam?), we cannot understand this in detail; all that is clear is that the "creation" has a history which it shares with men—a fact which once again indicates how completely the cosmological point of view recedes for Paul behind that of his theology of history.

When Rom. 8:20f. speaks of the "creation" subject to transitoriness and longing for freedom, what is meant is evidently the earth and its creatures subordinate to man, not the *cosmic powers* which are enumerated in 8:38f. Although this enumeration strings together heterogeneous elements when it combines "death" and "life" (the former of which, it is true, could conceivably be a cosmic power in keeping with I Cor. 15:26) and "things present" and "things to come" with the cosmic powers, still in the case of "angels," "principalities" and "powers" at least, and probably also in the case of "height" and "depth," it does name cosmic powers which belong to the world created by God. This would be the case even if the additional remark, "nor any other created thing," did not directly say so. While this sentence testifies on the one hand that the activity of such powers is restricted by the will of God, nevertheless it presupposes, on the other hand, that there is an area of the creation in which rebellious powers, at enmity with God and man, hold sway.

Thus, the creation has a peculiarly ambiguous character: On the one hand, it is the earth placed by God at man's disposal for his use and benefit (I Cor. 10:26, see above, 2); on the other, it is the field of activity for evil, demonic powers. The historical observation, correct as far as it goes, that Old Testament tradition and Gnostic tradition have flowed together here, does not sufficiently explain the facts. Paul is able to appropriate the cosmological mythology of Gnosticism because it enables him to express the fact that the perishable "creation" becomes a destructive power whenever man decides in favor of it instead of for God (Rom. 1:25, see above); i.e. when he bases his life upon it rather than upon God. Hence, it owes to man himself such independence as it has toward God; how this is so, must be clarified later by investigation of the term "flesh" (sarx). But this much is already clear: Paul's conception of the creation, as well as of the Creator, depends upon what it means for man's existence; under this point of view the creation is ambivalent.

4. As God and the creation are regarded as being within the horizon of a theological view of history—i.e. in regard to their significance for man and his history—correspondingly *man's being* is understood in its relatedness to the Creator and the creation.

Only rarely does Paul use the word "man" (*anthropos*) to designate the species man as one of the creatures of this world in distinction from other living beings, such as beasts (I Cor. 15:39) or angels (I Cor. 4:9; 13:1).

> We here leave out of account the passages where *anthropos* is used unemphatically for "some one," "any one" or "one" (Rom. 7:1; I Cor. 4:1; II Cor. 12:2f.; Gal. 6:1, 7) or where πᾶς ἄνθρωπος with no definite antithesis means "everyone" (Gal. 5:3) or where its plural means simply "all" (Rom. 12:17f.; I Cor. 7:7; 15:19; II Cor. 3:2; Phil. 4:5; I Thess. 2:15).

In most passages, *anthropos* means man in his creaturely humanity, and that means also man in his relation to God. It is in his creatureliness that man is regarded when Paul rhetorically says that the "foolishness of God" is wiser than men and the "weakness of God" stronger than men (I Cor. 1:25), or when he asks, "O man, who are you to answer back to God?" (Rom. 9:20 tr.). Before God, every human complaint must become dumb: "Let God be true though every man be false" (Rom. 3:4). God's authorization puts Paul's legitimation beyond doubt as "an apostle not from men nor through man, but through Jesus Christ and God the Father" (Gal. 1:1; *cf.* 1:11f.). It is to God and not to man that one must look to find the right norm for apostolic activity (I Thess. 2:4, 6; Gal. 1:10), and the apostle's word is God's word, not man's (I Thess. 2:13); whoever disdains it, despises not men but God (I Thess. 4:8).

Before God, all human distinctions vanish; before him Jew and Greek stand alike as "man" (Rom. 3:28f.). Human greatness and human evaluations are nil before God. It would be madness for one chosen by God as a slave of Christ to make himself a slave of men by orienting himself according to human evaluations (I Cor. 7:23). It would be madness to boast of men (I Cor. 3:21). Praise from

God alone, not from men, has any importance (Rom. 2:29). Wherever jealousy and strife still find room, there things are still going in human fashion (I Cor. 3:3). The paradoxicality of the salvation-occurrence finds expression in the Christ-hymn which had been taken over by Paul (Phil. 2:6f.): he who had been in the form of God (= of divine nature) appeared on earth as a man, in human form; in so doing he "emptied himself"—therefore, there is nothing divine about man or in him! This understanding of man is the background of the formula, "I speak in a human way" (Rom. 3:5; I Cor. 3:3; 9:8; Gal. 3:15; *cf.* Rom. 6:19), which designates the form of a statement about things divine as really inappropriate to its content; the apostle must so speak only "on account of the weakness of the flesh" (RSV paraphrases interpretively: "because of your natural limitations," Rom. 6:19).

§ 22. The Term "Flesh" (Sarx)

Evil, our investigation of Paul's anthropological terms has shown (§§17–20), is perverse intent, a perverse pursuit, specifically a pursuit which misses what is good—i.e. misses "life," what man at heart is after—and it is evil, because the good it misses is also that which is required of a man. But to miss what is required is also sin, rebellion against God, who as Creator is the origin of life and whose commandment is a "commandment unto life" (§ 21). Hence, the alternative to lay hold of one's true existence or to miss it is synonymous with the alternative to acknowledge God as the Creator or to deny Him. And denial of God means failure to acknowledge one's own creatureliness. And since all pursuit, even the perverted sort, is, in intention, pursuit of life, this means seeking life where it is not —in the created world. For to deny God as Creator is to turn away from Him to the creation (§ 21). But the creation stands at man's disposal; hence, to seek life in it means to have the presumption to seek life in the disposable, i.e. to presume to have life at one's own disposal. Hence, the ultimate sin reveals itself to be the false assumption of receiving life not as the gift of the Creator but procuring it by one's own power, of living from one's self rather than from God.

Paul developed this train of thought neither so abstractly nor so compactly as this; but it underlies his discussions of sin, as is apparent in his statements about creation and man (§ 21), and as investigation of the term "flesh" will above all make clear.

2. *Sarx* means, first of all, "flesh" as man's material corporeality. In contrast to χρέας ("meat," animal flesh intended for food, Rom. 14:21; I Cor. 8:13), it is the animate flesh of man, active in its sensual manifestations and perceptible to the senses. *Sarx*, therefore, (in spite of I Cor. 15:39; see § 17, 1) does not mean simply "matter" (ὕλη) in contrast to "form"; while, though it does primarily mean a material, it means a material only as it is formed and animated in the human body. That is the only reason that *sarx* can occasionally be used synonymously with *soma* (§ 17, 3). Bodily sickness is "infirmity of the flesh" (Gal. 4:13 KJ); physical suffering is denoted by the figure of "the thorn in the flesh" (II Cor. 12:7). Circumcision, an operation on the body, is "circumcision which is outward, in the flesh" (Rom. 2:28 KJ). The outward cares of living are "trouble in the flesh" (I Cor. 7:28 KJ). Flesh is mortal (II Cor. 4:11), and death, as the end of physical life, is "destruction of the flesh"(I Cor. 5:5).

Inasmuch as man in his earthly existence is bound to fleshly corporeality, *sarx*, using Old Testament terminology, can mean man in general in the phrase "all flesh" (πᾶσα σάρξ = כָּל בָּשָׂר = everyone, Rom. 3:20; I Cor. 1:29; Gal. 2:16; *cf.* "every soul," § 18). In fact, like *psyche* and *pneuma* (§ 18, 2 and 3), *sarx* can even be used to designate the person himself (II Cor. 7:5 KJ: "our flesh had no rest" = "I found no rest"). In this usage the humanity of the person can be emphasized by adding "blood" to "flesh" in Jewish fashion (בָּשָׂר וָדָם) as in Gal. 1:16: "I did not confer with flesh and blood." While in this passage "flesh and blood" means a person in his humanness, in I Cor. 15:50 it means humanity as such, human nature: "flesh and blood cannot inherit the kingdom of God." *Sarx* by itself can also have this meaning, as Rom. 6:19 shows: "I speak after the manner of men because of the infirmity of your flesh" (= because of your limitations of human nature), which is synonymous in content with "I speak in a human way" (Rom. 3:5; I Cor. 9:8; § 21, 4, p. 232). "To remain in the flesh" means "to remain alive"— alive in the sphere of earthly life—in contrast to the wish "to depart and be with Christ" (Phil. 1:23f.).

Further examples indicate that *sarx* can denote not only the

[233]

concrete body of flesh but also "fleshliness," carnality, meaning the nature of the earthly-human in its specific humanness—i.e. in its weakness and transitoriness, which also means in opposition to God and His Spirit (*cf.* espec. Gal. 1:16; I Cor. 15:50). Not Abraham's "children of the flesh" (Rom. 9:7f. KJ), i.e. his natural, earthly offspring, are to be regarded as the "children of God," the true "seed of Abraham." The meaning of *sarx* undergoes an extension, however, in the fact that it means not only human nature as it is perceived at work in and on man himself but that the sphere of the human is expanded to include the environment with which man has to do. Thus, *sarx* can mean *the whole sphere of that which is earthly or "natural."* According to Rom. 2:28f. it may be termed the sphere of the "outward":

> "For the true Jew is not he who is outwardly a Jew
>   but he who is a Jew deep within;
>   nor is true circumcision the outward flesh-circumcision
>   but a spiritual, not a literal, heart-circumcision" (tr.).

"Flesh" here means, first of all, simply the physiological flesh on which circumcision is performed, and flesh in this sense by the juxtaposition of "outward" is brought into the wider sphere of "the outward." But the antithesis, especially by using "spirit" as a contrasting term, makes it clear that the sphere of "the outward" is precisely the sphere of "flesh." It will later be explained (§ 23, 1) that this is also the sphere of "the letter" or "the literal." "The seen" or "the visible" is synonymous with "the outward" (which, itself, should literally be translated "the visible"). The men of faith who surrender their "outward man" (II Cor. 4:16 KJ) to destruction—and that means their "body," their "mortal flesh" (II Cor. 4:10f.)—fix their gaze not on "the things that are seen," but on the "things that are unseen" (II Cor. 4:18); and when it is said, "for the things that are seen are transient," that is a direct characterization of the sphere of the "flesh." Those who by faith are no longer "in the flesh" (Rom. 8:9) live in a hope which hopes for that which is not visible (Rom. 8:24f.). While in Rom. 2:28f. the antithetical term to "the outward" is "the heart" (as the "hidden" sphere within a man), the contrast in II Cor. 5:12 to "priding one's self on a man's heart" is "priding one's self on appearance" (ἐν προσώπῳ)—i.e. on his externally visible

merits; but that means glorying "after the flesh" (II Cor. 11:18 KJ);
"boasting of worldly things" (RSV). Hence all that is "outward"
and "visible," all that has its nature in external "appearance" belongs
to the sphere of "flesh." In this sense, "flesh" becomes synonymous
with the term "world" (κόσμος), insofar as *cosmos* denotes the
world of created things which is the stage and the life-condition for
"natural" life, the world which is at man's disposal, giving him the
possibility to live from it and to be anxious about it (for further discussion of "world," see § 26). The "wisdom of this world" at I Cor.
1:20; 3:19 is the wisdom of those who are "wise . . . after the flesh"
(I Cor. 1:26 KJ). Life in worldly affairs with all its hustle and
bustle, its weal and woe, is "using the world" (I Cor. 7:31 KJ; "mixing in the world," Moffatt) and the care of husband or wife for the
other is being "anxious about worldly affairs" in contrast to being
"anxious about the affairs of the Lord" (I Cor. 7:32–34). "Worldly
grief" is contrasted with "godly grief" (II Cor. 7:9f.). To Paul, the
"world" is crucified in the cross of Christ (Gal. 6:14); this is synonymous in substance with the other statement (Gal. 5:24): "And those
who belong to Christ Jesus have crucified the *flesh* with its passions
and desires."

This is also the way to understand the phrase "in the flesh"
(except where it means "on the body," as in Rom. 2:28), a phrase
which can be explained neither from the Old Testament nor from
Greek usage. This formula shows that according to Paul a man's
nature is not determined by what he may be as to substance (in the
way the Old Testament says man is flesh) nor by what qualities he
may have (as Greek thinking would put it), but that his nature is
determined by the sphere within which he moves, the sphere which
marks out the horizon or the possibilities of what he does and experiences. The meaning of "in the flesh" becomes clear in the fact that
it corresponds antithetically to the formula "in the Spirit," in which
Spirit means the miraculous, life-giving power of God (§ 14, 1); its
territory is the "hidden interior" (τὸ κρυπτόν), the "unseen," the
"heart."

"In the flesh"—i.e. in the sphere of the obvious, or the earthly-
human, or the natural—takes place man's "living" (Gal. 2:20; Phil.
1:22), or "walking" (II Cor. 10:3)—also Christian man's in this aeon.
Or, differently said, "to live" or "to walk in the flesh" means nothing
else than simply "to lead one's life as a man," an idea which in itself

does not involve any ethical or theological judgment but simply takes note of a fact; not a norm but a field or a sphere is indicated by "in the flesh." Only it must be borne in mind that with this phrase there hovers in the air the opposite possibility that there is also another dimension in which life can move. Thus, Paul may speak of Onesimus as a brother "both in the flesh and in the Lord" (Phlm. 16 KJ)—i.e. both as a person and as a Christian. And insofar as the believer, having his true existence by faith, is already beyond the sphere of the merely human and belongs to the sphere of the Spirit, his "existence in the flesh" can be proleptically denied, and Paul can say: "when we *were* in the flesh . . ." (Rom. 7:5 KJ) and: "ye are not in the flesh but in the Spirit" (Rom. 8:9 KJ).

Whatever pertains to natural human life and is necessary for it can be called "fleshly" in contrast to "spiritual." Accordingly, Paul motivates his exhortation to Gentile Christians to contribute to the collection for the Jerusalem Church: "for if the Gentiles have come to share in their spiritual blessings, they ought also to be of service to them in material blessings" (σαρκικοῖς, lit.: "fleshly things"—Rom. 15:27 RSV). In the same way, he defends his apostle's right to support by the Churches: "If we have sown spiritual good among you, is it too much if we reap your material (σαρκικά) benefits?" (I Cor. 9:11).

While "flesh" in itself only means the human sphere as that of the earthly-natural and of the weak and transitory, nevertheless the use made of the formula "in the flesh" in Rom. 7:5; 8:8f. indicates that life "in the flesh" is a spurious life; in fact, everywhere the formula expresses an explicit or implicit antithesis to a life "in the Spirit" (Rom. 8:9), "in Christ" (Phlm. 16), "in faith" (Gal. 2:20), or the like. The sentence Rom. 8:8, "those who are in the flesh cannot please God," especially indicates that the sphere of "the flesh" can also be regarded as the sphere of sinning. So regarded, it is not merely the earthly-transitory contrast to the transcendent-eternal God but opposes God as His enemy. In this sense, Rom. 8:7 says: "The attitude of flesh is enmity to God" (tr.). How "flesh" comes to have this meaning comes into view when we examine the use of the phrase "according to the flesh."

3. The formula κατὰ σάρκα ("after the flesh" KJ) is used in a double sense, characterizing primarily a person, or a human relation-

ship, in regard to facts present within natural life and verifiable by everyone. However, it is true of this formula, as of "in the flesh," that a contrast between it and another possible point of view hovers behind it or is expressed. Abraham is "our forefather according to the flesh" (Rom. 4:1)—i.e. the natural progenitor of the Jews. The Jews are Paul's "kinsmen according to the flesh" (Rom. 9:3; or, abbreviated: "my flesh," 11:14)—in contrast, of course, to his "brothers in Christ." The Israelitic people of the Old Testament is "Israel after the flesh" (I Cor. 10:18 KJ) in contrast to the "Israel of God" (Gal. 6:16). Ishmael, Abraham's son born without God's promise, is called "he who was born according to the flesh" (Gal. 4:29; cf. v. 23: "But the son of the slave was born according to the flesh, the son of the free woman through promise"); i.e. he is Abraham's son only in the sense of natural human progeny in contrast to Isaac who was miraculously begotten "through the promise." Christ, too, can be described according to what he humanly is. "According to the flesh" he is a descendant of David and is from the people of Israel (Rom. 1:3; 9:5) in contradistinction to what he is "according to the Spirit of holiness": "Son of God" (Rom. 1:4). That in all these cases nothing more is meant than the sphere of the "natural" —that which is given and present in earthly fact—becomes clear in the insight that "we who are Jews by nature" (Gal. 2:15 KJ) would mean just the same thing if it read: "we who are Jews according to the flesh," or that instead of "uncircumcision which is by nature" (Rom. 2:27 KJ) Paul could just as well have said "uncircumcision according to the flesh."

"According to the flesh" in this sense serves as a rule (Gal. 4:23, 29 are exceptions) to modify substantives (including proper names). As a modifier of verbs the phrase has an altogether different meaning: It stamps *an existence or an attitude* not as natural-human, but *as sinful.* In this meaning we read of "purposing according to the flesh" (II Cor. 1:17 KJ), "knowing" (II Cor. 5:16), "walking" (II Cor. 10:2; Rom. 8:4), "warring" (II Cor. 10:3), even "being" after the flesh (Rom. 8:5)—and the last is given what amounts to a definition: "for they who exist according to the flesh are they who have the attitude of the flesh" (tr.). The antitheses here implied or expressed are: "according to the Spirit" (Rom. 8:4f.), "according to the Lord" (II Cor. 11:17 tr.), "according to love" (Rom. 14:15 tr.), and the like.

Σαρκικός ("fleshly," see above) can also have the meaning of κατὰ σάρκα (I Cor. 3:3; II Cor. 1:12; 10:4), and one might say that κατὰ σάρκα fills the place of an adverb σαρκικῶς (which occurs in Ignatius, but not in the New Testament). Paul uses σάρκινος also in this same sense (Rom. 7:14; I Cor. 3:1), though it properly means "consisting of flesh (as matter)" (so used in II Cor. 3:3).

Now it is of decisive importance to comprehend that in such usage the word "flesh" does not, as might be assumed, have another meaning than it has in those other cases where it designates the sphere of the humanly natural and transitory. That is to say, we do not have here, as it might seem, a mythological concept, as if "flesh" were conceived as a demonic being. Neither do we have a physiological concept, as if "flesh" here meant sensuality. Rather, the sinful has its origin in "flesh" in this respect: That that conduct or attitude that directs itself according to "flesh," taking "flesh" for its norm, is sinful—as the cited sentence, Rom. 8:5, clearly says: "existence in the flesh" realizes itself in "setting the mind on the things of the flesh" (RSV), i.e. in the pursuit of the merely human, the earthly-transitory.

A comparison of Rom. 9:5 with I Cor. 1:26 makes clear the difference between the two uses of "according to the flesh." When Christ is here qualified as "according to the flesh," that means Christ regarded as an empirical phenomenon within the world—in that respect he was of the Jewish race. But when the "wise" are called "wise after the flesh," the addition does not mean "so far as they are empirical phenomena within the world," but "(wise) so far as a wisdom according to the norms of 'flesh' is concerned"; "the wise" is equivalent to a verb in the above discussion. What corresponds in the former case to the recognition of a "Christ according to the flesh" is the manner in which such a Christ is perceived; this manner itself is also "according to the flesh"—i.e. Christ as a phenomenon in the world is perceived in the worldly manner of seeing.

The old debate over II Cor. 5:16 can be decided in a similar way: "Wherefore henceforth know we no man after the flesh: yea, though we have known Christ after the flesh, yet now henceforth know we him no more" (KJ). The question is, does "after the flesh" in these two clauses modify the objects ("no man" and "Christ") or the verbs? The latter is the more probable, it seems to me. But this decision means nothing for the sense of the total context, for a "Christ regarded in the manner of the flesh" is just what a "Christ after the flesh" is.

§ 23. Flesh and Sin

1. Man, and hence the Christian, too, lives his natural life "in flesh" (§ 22, 2). But the crucial question is whether "in flesh" only denotes the stage and the possibilities for a man's life or the determinative norm for it—whether a man's life "*in* flesh" is also life "*according* to the flesh" (§ 22, 3)—or, again, whether the sphere of the natural-earthly, which is also that of the transitory and perishable, is the world out of which a man thinks he derives his life and by means of which he thinks he maintains it. This self-delusion is not merely an error, but sin, because it is a turning away from the Creator, the giver of life, and a turning toward the creation—and to do that is to trust in one's self as being able to procure life by the use of the earthly and through one's own strength and accomplishment. It is in this sense, then, that "fixing the mind on the things of flesh" is to be at war against God (Rom. 8:7).

The sinful self-delusion that one lives out of the created world can manifest itself both in unthinking recklessness (this especially among the Gentiles) and in considered busy-ness (this especially among Jews)—both in the ignoring or transgressing of ethical demands and in excessive zeal to fulfill them. For the sphere of "flesh" is by no means just the life of instinct or sensual passions, but is just as much that of the moral and religious efforts of man.

The "passions and desires" of the flesh, which, according to Gal. 5:24, the man of faith has crucified, are the "vices" of sensuality and self-seeking which are enumerated in 5:19–21 as the "works of the flesh." When 5:13 warns against misusing Christian freedom as an "opportunity for the flesh," the antithesis in vv. 14, 15 shows that what is meant is natural human self-seeking, to which Christian freedom is not to give free rein. The same thing, in all likelihood, is meant by the "sinful passions" which were at work in us when we were "in the flesh" (Rom. 7:5), and probably also by the "deeds of the body" in which living "according to the flesh" (Rom. 8:13) consists. The accusation that the Corinthians are still "of the flesh" (σαρκικοί) is evidenced by the fact that "jealousy and strife" prevail in the congregation (I Cor. 3:3). The complaint made against Paul of "fleshly wisdom" (KJ, II Cor. 1:12) or of "walking according to the flesh" (II Cor. 10:2) consisted in accusations of unreliability and insincerity and of arrogance and the will to dominate, as his debate with his opponents shows.

Elsewhere, it is not always clear what specific attitude Paul had in mind when he spoke of fleshly attitude or conduct. It may be an "anxiety for things of the world," but this need not be immoral conduct; rather it may consist of normal human affairs whenever a man devotes himself to them without the reservation of "as if . . . not" (I Cor. 7:29ff.). To the category of conduct "according to the flesh" belongs above all zealous fulfillment of the Torah; it does so because a man supposes he can thereby achieve righteousness before God by his own strength. The Galatian Christians who want to adopt the Torah and be circumcised are indignantly asked: "Having begun with the Spirit, are you now ending with the flesh?"—ending, that is, not in sensual passions but in observance of the Torah (Gal. 3:3). In fact, not only zeal for the Law but also pride in all the pious Israelite's merits and titles of honor belongs to the attitude of flesh—or, the Torah and the merits and dignities of Israel fall within the concept "flesh" as belonging to the sphere of the visibly occurring and the historically demonstrable (Phil. 3:3-7). This passage makes it especially clear that the attitude which orients itself by "flesh," living out of "flesh," is the self-reliant attitude of the man who puts his trust in his own strength and in that which is controllable by him. For the renunciation of this attitude means, according to Phil. 3:9, renunciation of one's own righteousness; and according to Rom. 10:3, the basic sin of the Jews is that they want—even though motivated by "zeal for God"—to establish "their own righteousness." Thereby it also becomes clearer why "the letter" (i.e. the Law of Moses) constitutes the antithesis to Spirit and belongs to the sphere of "flesh" (Rom. 2:29; 7:6; II Cor. 3:6). It does so to the extent that it serves man as a means for that effort to win "righteousness" and "life" by his own strength through "works"—that is, through what he accomplishes (see § 27). The Torah is "letter" as the code of formulated and defined rules which can be discharged by performing definite acts corresponding to them.

Arrogance, which in the Jewish world takes the form of zeal for fulfilling the Torah and of pride over one's accomplishments in doing so and over Israel's titles to honor, appears in the Hellenistic world *as a striving after wisdom and as pride in knowledge and pneumatic endowment*. The "wise after the flesh" (I Cor. 1:26) are the wise who trust in themselves, who are not willing to smash their wisdom before God and let it become foolishness. The opponents against whom Paul writes in II Cor. 10–13, who boast "after the flesh" (11:18) and, as the allusion 10:4 implies, conduct their campaign with "fleshly weapons," are the people who boastfully compare themselves with others and commend themselves (10:12–18), and who give themselves airs with their "visions" and "revelations" (12:1). When they demand of Paul a "certification" (δοκιμή 13:3), they thereby betray their position that a tangible accomplishment capable of being presented for inspection is to them the proof of possessing the Spirit.

Whether, then, it is a matter of giving one's self up to worldly enticements and pleasures, either in frivolity or swept along by the storm of passion, or whether it is the zealous bustle of moral and religious activity that is involved—life in all of these cases is apostasy from God—a turning away from Him to the creation and to one's own strength, and is, therefore, enmity toward God (Rom. 8:6) and disobedience to the will of God (Rom. 8:7; 10:3; II Cor. 10:5). All human wisdom, power, and greatness must come to naught in the presence of God (I Cor. 1:26–31).

2. This judgment about flesh and sin finds characteristic expression, further, in the verbs Paul uses to describe this specifically human attitude. This purpose is served by the verb *"desire"* when used in Paul's negatively qualified sense (§ 20, 2). The divine commandment says: "You shall not desire," but it thereby only arouses sinful desire (Rom. 7:7f.). And it has its seat in "flesh," so that Paul can go so far as to make "flesh" (or the fleshly *soma*, § 17, 2) the subject which "desires" or has "desire" (Gal. 5:16f., 24; Rom. 6:12; *cf.* Rom. 13:14). The evil "desires of hearts" are the desires of such as have turned to the worship of creation (Rom. 1:24), and the vices to which they have given themselves up (1:26ff.) are none other than the "works of the flesh" of Gal. 5:19f. Clearly a life "after the flesh" is a life of "desire"—a life of self-reliant pursuit of one's own ends.

This self-reliant attitude of man likewise lurks in his μεριμνᾶν (*"care,"* § 20, 2). In it, through his will to dispose over the world, he factually falls victim to the world. Natural human "care," except as it may mean worrying dread of the future, is the pro-vision, foresight (behind which, of course, that dread always lies), which self-reliantly strives to forestall the future. The intention of such "care" is to insure one's self for the future, or also, to keep what now is for the future. This attitude is care "about worldly affairs" (I Cor. 7:32ff.), which rests upon the illusion that a man can insure his life by that which is worldly, controllable. As antithesis to this sort of "care" stands "care about the Lord's affairs"—and to have the latter, is to be "care-free" (I Cor. 7:32) or to be "care-ful for nothing" (Phil. 4:6 KJ). (In both these cases, "care" has the qualified sense of worldly care.)

The attitude of sinful self-reliance finds its extreme expression in man's *"boasting"* (καυχᾶσθαι). It is characteristic both of the Jew, who boasts of God and the Torah (Rom. 2:17, 23), and of the Greek, who boasts of his wisdom (I Cor. 1:19-31). It is also a natural tendency of man in general to compare himself with others in order to have his "boast" thereby (Gal. 6:4). How characteristic "boasting" is for the Jew, Rom. 3:27 shows. After Paul has stated his thesis of righteousness by faith alone without works, he clarifies the meaning of this thesis by the rhetorical question, "then what becomes of our boasting?—It is excluded," and then refers to Abraham, who, having believed God, had no "boast." In "boasting" is revealed a misconstruing of the human situation, a forgetting of the fact implied by the question, "What do you have that you have not been given? And if it has been given you, why do you boast as if it had not been given you?" (I Cor. 4:7 tr.). And God insists upon this: All standards of human greatness must be shattered "so that no human being may boast before God" (I Cor. 1:29 tr.). There is only one valid boast: "Let him who boasts, boast of the Lord" (I Cor. 1:31; II Cor. 10:17). Therefore, the Christian must be warned also against haughtily looking down on others (Gal. 6:4; Rom. 11:17f.). And when Paul does once boast, he does it in the "fool's" role (II Cor. 11-12) which he has adopted; and yet in so doing he turns his "boasting after the flesh" into a paradoxical "boasting," by boasting of his "weakness" (II Cor. 11:30; 12:9; *cf.* Rom. 5:2). Thus he confesses, "Far be it from me to boast except in the cross of our Lord Jesus Christ, by which the world has been crucified to me, and I to the world" (Gal. 6:14; *cf.* Rom. 5:11).

[242]

Very closely related to "boasting after the flesh"—in fact even synonymous with it—is *"putting one's confidence in the flesh."* In Phil. 3:3 it constitutes the antithesis to "boasting in Christ Jesus." *

While the latter means the surrender of all worldly accomplishments and titles of honor as mere "loss" and even "refuse" (Phil. 3:4–8) and also means the renunciation of a righteousness of one's own (3:9), "confidence in the flesh" is the supposed security which a man achieves out of that which is worldly and apparent, that which he can control and deal with. It is the rebellious pride which in the Jew expresses itself in his "boasting in the Torah" (Rom. 2:23) and misleads him to be "confident of being a guide to the blind, etc." (Rom. 2:19). "Putting confidence in the flesh" is nothing else than man's confidence in himself, and this is just what must come to naught before God; as there should be a "boasting" only "in the Lord," so there should be a "reliance" (= confidence, πεποιϑέναι) upon God alone. When God caused Paul to despair of his life he learned by experience "that we should not rely upon ourselves but upon God who raises the dead" (II Cor. 1:9 tr.).

3. The hidden side of "boasting" and "putting confidence in the flesh" is the *fear* which the man who is concerned for himself has, a fear which arises both from zeal in the works of the Law and from zeal in wisdom. This fear may remain hidden from the man himself, even though it unmistakably manifests itself in "care" (μεριμνᾶν). That the worldly man is full of fear (φόβος) is indicated by Paul's reminder to the believers, "for you did not receive the spirit of slavery to fall back into fear" (Rom. 8:15). The period before faith, that is, was under the sway of fear. This sentence also shows that it was a period of *"slavery."* And that holds true not only insofar as both Judaism and paganism are under slavery to the "elemental spirits of the universe," which for the Jews are represented by the Torah, for the Gentiles by "beings that by nature are no gods" (Gal. 4:1–10), but it especially holds true insofar as "life after the flesh" leads into slavery to "flesh" and "sin." Both he who "desires" and he who is "anxious with care," both he who "boasts" and he who "relies upon" something, in reality makes himself dependent upon that

---

* The affinity between "boasting" and "confidence" is also attested by a comparison of II Cor. 1:12 with 3:4; the same conclusion is to be drawn from the interchange between "confidence," or "be confident," and "boast" in II Cor. 10:2, 7f.

which he supposes he can control. Hence, the warning to the Galatians who want to achieve their own righteousness by observing the Torah, or who want to get to the goal "by flesh" (Gal. 3:3; see above, 1): "For freedom Christ has set us free; stand fast, therefore, and do not submit again to a yoke of slavery" (Gal. 5:1). The wisdom-proud Corinthians must be reminded: "all things are yours" (I Cor. 3:21f.); i.e. they must be warned against delivering themselves into dependence upon human authorities—that would be dependence upon "flesh and blood." And whoever has the notion that he has to shape his life according to the norms of human evaluations must hear the warning: "You were bought with a price; do not become slaves of men" (I Cor. 7:23). And when those who, by a misunderstanding of Christian freedom, regard unrestricted sexual intercourse as permitted are warned: "You are not your own; you were bought with a price" (I Cor. 6:20), that brings to light the whole paradox that he who apparently belongs to himself and has himself at his own disposal is a slave. Man is "bought free" from his previous slavery; but even so, he nevertheless does not belong to himself; for there is for man no absolute belonging-to-one's-self, but belonging to God or "the Lord" is man's freedom—namely, freedom from "flesh" and "sin" (Rom. 6:15ff.; 7:5f.). Indeed, one might say, he who lives "after the flesh" makes "flesh" his god; for Rom. 16:18 (KJ) gives a warning against those who "serve not our Lord Christ but their own belly," and Phil. 3:19 polemizes against those "whose god is their belly" (KJ).

The fact that *"flesh,"* and through it also *"sin," can become powers* to which man falls slave finds especially clear expression in the circumstance that Paul can speak of both as personal beings as if they were demonic rulers—but in such a way that we do not have the right actually to ascribe to him a mythological concept of "flesh" and "sin." Man is in danger of becoming a "debtor" to the "flesh" (Rom. 8:12) or of opening the door to it, so to say, or of offering it his hand (Gal. 5:13, tr.: "do not [offer] your freedom to the flesh as a base of operations"). Paul can even attribute "desire" to the "flesh" itself (Gal. 5:17: "for the desires of the flesh are against the Spirit"). Or he can speak of the "intent" (φρόνημα) of the flesh" (Rom. 8:6f. tr.), or of its "passions" and "desires" (Gal. 5:24) and its "works" (Gal. 5:19) or "deeds" (Rom. 8:13; § 17, 3). Moreover, he can personify the world in the same way when he speaks of its "wisdom" and its "knowing" (I Cor. 1:20f.). "Sin" particularly appears in this way as if it were a personal being. It "came into the world" (Rom. 5:12) and "achieved dominion" (Rom. 5:21 Blt.). Man is enslaved to it (Rom. 6:6, 17ff.), sold under it (Rom. 7:14); or man places himself at its disposal (Rom. 6:13) and it pays him wages (Rom. 6:23). Sin is also thought of as if it were a personal being when it is said to have been dead but to have revived (Rom. 7:8f.), or to have used the Torah to rouse desire in man and to have deceived and killed him (Rom. 7:8, 11, 13), or to "dwell" and act in man (Rom. 7:17, 20).

Little as all this constitutes realistic mythology—it is not that, but figurative, rhetorical language—it is, nevertheless, clear that this language stamps *flesh and sin as powers to which man has fallen victim* and against which he is powerless. The personification of these powers expresses the fact that man has lost to them the capacity to be the subject of his own actions. The strongest expression of this is found in Rom. 7:14, "I am carnal (= flesh-ly), sold under sin," and Rom. 7:18, "for I know that nothing good dwells within me, that is, in my flesh." While it may be that "that is" possibly has a limiting meaning here ("so far as I am flesh") and that the true, willing self is thereby dissociating itself from this self that is fallen victim to flesh, it is, nevertheless, significant that "I" and "my flesh" can be equated. Under the viewpoint of "doing," they are identical; but if they can be opposed to each other in regard to "willing," then it is apparent that the subject-self, the true self of a man, is inwardly split. That self which in Rom. 7:17, 20 distinguishes itself from the "sin which dwells within me," is flatly labeled in v. 14 as "carnal" and "sold under sin"—just as the first person is used throughout vv. 14–24 both in regard to willing and to doing. Therefore "I" and "I," self and self, are at war with each other; i.e. to be innerly divided, or not to be at one with one's self, is the essence of human existence under sin.

This inner dividedness means that man himself destroys his true self. In his self-reliant will to be himself, a will that comes to light in "desire" at the encounter with the "commandment," he loses his self, and "sin" becomes the active subject within him (Rom. 7:9). Thereby the self—the "I"—dies; selfhood, of course, belongs to the nature of man, and it is just the "commandment," given "for life," that ought to bring his selfhood to reality. Man fails to achieve it by attempting self-reliantly to realize it in "desire." In this false will toward selfhood man's destination to be a self—his will toward "life" —is pervertedly preserved; that is just the reason why it is possible to describe human existence as the struggle between "self" and "self" within a man. In the fact that man is a self—that he is a being to whom what matters and should matter is his "life," his self—lies the possibility of sin. In the fact that God's commandment is meant to give man "life" lies the possibility of misunderstanding: Man, called to selfhood, tries to live out of his own strength and thus loses his self—his "life"—and rushes into death. This is the domination of sin: All man's doing is directed against his true intention—viz. to achieve life.

§ 24. Sin and Death

1. Since all man's pursuit ultimately aims at life, even though in each case it seeks some specific end, it follows that a false, aberrant pursuit walks the way that leads to death.

For Paul, in the train of Old Testament-Jewish tradition, it is axiomatic that sin draws death after it. The "sting" of death is sin, whose power lies in the Torah (I Cor. 15:56); i.e. the transgressing of the Torah, which is occasioned by sin, draws death after it. *Death is the punishment for the sin a man has committed;* sinners are "worthy of death" (Rom. 1:32 KJ), they have "earned" death. So Paul can also say that sin pays her slave his "wage" with death (Rom. 6:16, 23), or that the sinner by his death pays his debt, atones for his sin (Rom. 6:7). In such statements, death, we must recognize, is first thought of as the death which is natural dying, as Rom. 5:12ff. shows, according to which death as the punishment for sin was brought into the world by Adam's sin. Nevertheless, they also presuppose that this death will be confirmed—made final, so to say— by the verdict condemning them to "destruction" which God will pronounce over sinners on the judgment day (Rom. 2:6-11).

2. Still Paul's thoughts on flesh and sin lead beyond this traditional juristic conception of death as punishment. If as we have concluded sin is man's false pursuit of life, and if this consists in leading one's life "after the flesh,"—i.e. living out of the created, the earthly-natural and transitory—*then sin leads with inner necessity into death:* "If you live according to the flesh you will die" (Rom. 8:13).

He who derives life out of the transitory must, himself, perish with the perishing of the transitory. "He who sows to his own flesh will from the flesh reap corruption" (Gal. 6:8). "Anxiety for the affairs of the world" clings to "the world," whose σχῆμα ("substance," not just "form") "passes away" (I Cor. 7:31); he who so lives clutches at emptiness, so to say, and all he gets himself is death. "Worldly grief" brings death to him who has it (II Cor. 7:10). Why? Because in it he clings to that which is doomed to death.

Thus, death grows out of flesh-ly life like a fruit—organically, as it were: "While we were living in the flesh, our sinful passions, aroused by the law, were at work in our members to bear fruit for death" (Rom. 7:5). Death is the "end" of the "fruit" of sinful life (Rom. 6:21 KJ). The *soma* of flesh in which sin "dwells" is thereby a "*soma*" of death" (Rom. 7:24; § 17, 3). When II Cor. 3:6 says: "for the written code kills, but the Spirit gives life," there is no reflection in this context over the question whether the individual under the reign of Law brings death upon himself by transgressing the Law or by his zeal for it. But the sentence is spoken not in regard to Jewish transgressions of the Law, but in polemic against the Jewish esteem for the Torah as an eternal Law diffused with glory. In opposition to this esteem Paul says that the ministry of Moses is a "ministry of death" and its "splendor" or "glory" a fading one. The Torah, therefore, belongs to the sphere of "flesh" (§ 23, 1, p. 240) in contrast to the "new covenant," which is a "covenant of the Spirit." Hence, serving the Torah leads with inner necessity to death.

The perversion of human striving that pursues life and yet only garners death is described at length in Rom. 7:7-25, a passage in which Paul so depicts the situation of man under the Torah as it has become clear to a backward look from the standpoint of Christian faith. V. 10 says that the commandment was given to man "for life"; and man, whose longing is to have life, completely agrees with this intention (v. 16: "I agree . . ."; v. 22: "I delight in . . ."). But the commandment nonetheless leads factually into death; it does so by arousing "desire" in man (vv. 7–11).

It may be that in these verses Paul does not reflect over the question whether "desire" tempts man to transgress the Law or whether it misleads him to a false zeal for fulfilling it. Yet the latter must at least be included; for if 7:7–25 describes the situation of being under the Law in a way that holds true for every one who is under it, then the attitude (described in Phil. 3:4–6) of being "blameless" "as to righteousness under the Law" must be contained in it. In this case, then, the "desire" aroused by the Law is the "unenlightened zeal for God" of Rom. 10:2 (tr.).

Sin's "deceit" (Rom. 7:11) consists in deluding man to think that if he follows his "desire" he will gain life, whereas he only acquires death. Victimized by this deceit, man does not know what he is doing: "for what I am bringing about I do not know (v. 15a tr.); i.e. he does not know that by what he is doing he is only reaping death.

These words cannot mean: "I don't know how it happens that my good resolutions always get broken," in the sense of Ovid's line, *video meliora proboque, deteriora sequor* (I see the better and approve; the lower I follow, *Metamorphoses* 7, 21). For nothing is said about good resolutions that come to nothing in actual conduct. What the encounter with the commandment arouses is not good will, but "desire"! Rather, the point of the passage in its context is that what man brings about is an "evil," whereas according to his intention (which is the guiding factor in "desire"), it was to be a "good." Since κατεργάζεσθαι in v. 13 does not mean "do," but "bring about" or "reap," it is natural to take it to mean the same in v. 15 (and then also in v. 17 and v. 20 in spite of 2:9f.) and to supply there the object named in v. 13–"death" (*cf.* also II Cor. 7:10: "worldly grief brings about —κατεργάζεται—death"); then "the good thing" which is the object of the same verb in v. 18 is "life." Then the "doing" (πράσσειν, vv. 16, 19, or ποιεῖν, vv. 19, 20, 21) of evil and good must be correspondingly interpreted as meaning the bringing about of the evil thing (= death) and of the good thing (= life), which might be a conceivable locution in pointed speech. But even if the simple verbs (πράσσειν and ποιεῖν) are understood literally (linguistically the more natural assumption) as the "doing" of evil or of good (in which case κατεργάζεσθαι would also have to be so understood, at least in vv. 17, 18, and 20), the basic meaning still remains the same: In pursuing his "desire" man thinks he is doing something good (i.e. life-bringing) and actually is doing something evil (i.e. life-destroying). In either case, the gruesome contradiction which characterizes human striving is being described: It wants to gain life and only achieves death.

Fundamentally, then, death is already a present reality, for man "sold under sin" (v. 14) has lost himself, is no longer at one with himself (§ 23, 3). This is clearly expressed in the formulation of vv. 9–11: ". . . but when the commandment came, sin revived and I died . . . for sin . . . deceived me and . . . killed me" (see § 27).

3. The juristic conception of death as the punishment for sin and the conception of death as a fruit organically growing out of sin are not harmonized with each other. Nor does either conception agree with the view set forth in I Cor. 15:45–49 that Adamitic man was created "earthy," and being earthy is flesh and blood (v. 50), and therefore "perishable" (v. 53f.). The disagreement between this view and the two preceding is obscured only by the fact that Paul here avoids the term "fleshly" (σαρκικός) and uses ψυχικός ("animate"—but non-spiritual) instead—which, however, amounts to the same thing (*cf.* I Cor. 2:14 with 3:1, 3; § 18, 2).

§ 25. The Universality of Sin

1. *The power of sin* operates not only in the fact that it completely dominates the man who has become its victim, but also in the fact that it forces all men without exception into slavery: "for all have sinned" (Rom. 3:23; *cf.* 3:9, 19), "scripture has encompassed all men under the power of sin" [Gal. 3:22 tr.—πάντα, "all," is probably a generalizing neuter referring to persons; (see Blass-Debrunner, § 138, 1)].

What reason is given for this proposition? Rom. 8:3 seems to give a reason by saying that "what the law could not do" (i.e. the Law's incapacity to bring man life) has its cause in the "flesh." Though that is understandable, still the question, Does not "flesh" first achieve its power when man lives "according to the flesh"? remains. And is there a necessity that natural human "life in the flesh" must without exception become "life in the flesh" in the negatively qualified sense—i.e. must it become "life according to the flesh"?

That is evidently Paul's opinion. In man—because his substance is flesh—sin slumbers from the beginning. Must it necessarily awaken? Yes, because man encounters the Torah with its commandment: "you shall not desire" (Rom. 7:7ff.).

Although, judging from the whole train of thought in this epistle, Paul is thinking only of the Jewish Law, the same holds true for the Gentiles, too, among whom the place of the Law of Moses is taken by the demands of conscience (Rom. 2:14f.). And it is quite possible that in Rom. 7:7–11 Paul has Adam in mind, the prototype of mankind, who, of course, also lived without the Law of Moses.

If, now, the demand of the "commandment" is this "you shall not desire," its intent is to snatch man out of his self-reliant pursuit of life, his will to rule over himself. When it is further said that by this very demand, sin is awakened, that rests upon a conviction that man fundamentally strives in the wrong direction. The life that the Torah offers him (v. 10: "for life") he wants to attain himself, by his own power.

2. Can reasons be given for this conviction, or is it simply derived from experience? Unless the guilt-character of sin were to be denied, it obviously could only have its origin in experience. For its guilt-character would be sacrificed if the universality of sin were attributed to some quality necessarily inhering in man—for instance, thinking Gnostically, to a sensuality having its basis in the matter of which man consists, or, Gnostic again, to a fateful event which occurred in the hoary past, because of which the curse of sin weighs upon all men. Paul's statements on this subject are not consistent with each other.

When Paul prefaces the thesis of righteousness by faith without works with *a demonstration of the universality of sin* in Rom. 1:18–3:20, he does not have recourse to a cause lying behind the factual sinning of men nor does he speak of a curse existing since primeval times, but only sets forth the fact that all men—both Gentiles and Jews—are factually sinners. To be sure, God did give them up to sin (1:24ff.), but only as a punishment for the proto-sin of apostasy from the Creator—and this, of course, does not take away the guilt-character from sinning, but only means that apostasy, the sin of sins, necessarily draws the vices after it. If sin is here a curse, it is "the curse of the evil deed" which, "begetting, must bear evil" (Schiller, "Piccolomini" 5, 1). That sin of sins is not elicited by matter nor by a primeval fate, but is real guilt. Neither, obviously, is this proto-sin meant as the sin of mankind's first parents at the beginning of time, but as the proto-sin of apostasy which repeats

[250]

itself in every Now in the face of that possibility of knowing God which is open to every Now. Consistent with this is Rom. 2:1ff., where Paul refuses to get involved in argument with those who set themselves up as judges over notorious sinners, but simply tells them to their faces that they likewise are sinners.

But the case is quite different in Rom. 5:12–19; here *the sin of all men is attributed to Adam's sin*; i.e. the idea of "original sin" (*Erbsünde:* "inherited sin") is enunciated: "for as by one man's (Adam's) disobedience the many were made sinners . . ." (v. 19). Here, in describing the curse that lies upon Adamitic mankind, Paul is unquestionably under the influence of the Gnostic myth (§ 15, 4b).

However, he avoids slipping off into Gnostic thinking by not letting Adam's sin be caused by something lying behind it, either by the matter of which Adam consists, or by Satan, or—following a rabbinic teaching—to "the evil tendency." Instead he holds to the idea that sin came into the world by sinning; and to this extent Rom. 5:12ff. is compatible with 7:7ff.—i.e. Adam's "transgression" (v. 14) or "disobedience" (v. 19) is the violation of the divine "commandment," which woke the sin slumbering within him.

I Cor. 15:44ff., however, is not applicable here. According to it Adam was ψυχικός and χοϊκός (non-spiritual and earthy) and hence had no possibility whatever of perceiving God's will (§ 24, 3) because the "unspiritual man" has no perception of the Spirit (I Cor. 2:14) whereas God's commandment is "spiritual" (Rom. 7:14). According to the Corinthian passage, further, Adam was doomed to death by his origin in "dust"; and, consequently—if it is to hold true that death is punishment for sin (§ 24, 1)—he must have been sinful by nature. Otherwise, one would have to say—if it could be justified—that death as the natural end of physical life pertained to Adam even before he sinned, but did not get its true death-character (as "destruction") until he sinned. But Paul makes no such distinction.

Nevertheless, it cannot be denied that in Rom. 5:12ff. the sin of humanity after Adam is attributed to Adam's sin and that it therefore appears as the consequence of a curse for which mankind is not itself responsible. At the most, men sinning under the curse of Adam's sin could be regarded as guilty only in a legal sense, inasmuch as law deals only with the guilty deed; but then we would have no right to speak of guilt in the ethical sense.

Now it must be noted that the real theme of Rom. 5:12ff. is not the origin of sin but the origin of death; more accurately, even the origin of death is the theme only as the negative aspect of the positive theme, the origin of life, for the meaning of the passage in its context is this: The certainty of the Christian hope set forth in 5:1–11 has its foundation in the fact that Christ has obtained life for the mankind instituted by him, and obtained it with the same certainty with which Adam brought death upon Adamitic mankind (so also in I Cor. 15:21f.). Then, since death is held to be the punishment or the consequence of sin, *Adam's* sin had to be brought in, too. For the context, it would have been sufficient to mention only Adam's sin; there was no need to speak of the sin of the rest of men, for whether they were sinners or not, through Adam they had simply been doomed to death—an idea that was expressed not only in Judaism but also by Paul himself (v. 14). However, Paul gets into obscurity here because he also wants to have the death of men after Adam regarded as the punishment or consequence of their own sin: "and so death spread to all men—because all men sinned" (v. 12)! Verse 13 is completely unintelligible: "sin indeed was in the world before the law was given, but sin is not counted where there is no law." What sort of sin was it if it did not originate as contradiction of the Law? And how can it have brought death after it if it was not "counted"? These questions cannot be answered. Suffice it to say that because Paul regards death as the punishment or consequence of sin, he cannot content himself with speaking of the inherited death brought about by Adam but is prompted to go on to the proposition of inherited sin (v. 19).

If one takes one's bearings from what is said of Christ, the antitype of Adam, then it becomes clear that the effect of Christ's "obedience" is by no means regarded as one that takes place with inevitable necessity. Not all men since Christ, it is clear, receive life, as all since Adam became the victims of death, but only those who have faith (= "those who receive," v. 17). Through Christ, that is, there was brought about no more than the *possibility* of life, which, however, in men of faith becomes certain reality. That suggests, then, that one should assume by analogy that through Adam there was brought about for Adamitic mankind the *possibility* of sin and death—a possibility that does not become reality until individuals become guilty by their own responsible action. Whether that may be regarded as Paul's real thought must, to be sure, remain a question; at any rate the universal fallenness of Adamitic mankind to sin and death is beyond all question to Paul.

It might seem that Abraham is an exception and hence a source of difficulties. He need not be, for the special position that he occupies (also David? *Cf.* Rom. 4:6; possibly the prophets, too?) is his not as one who is sinless, but as one who has faith—and that a faith in "him who rightwises the ungodly" [*] (Rom. 4:5 tr.).

In Rom. 5:13f. it is perhaps possible to discover a differentiation between sin for which man is responsible and sin for which he is not responsible and from that insight to make this inference: At the base of the idea of inherited sin lies the experience that every man is born into a humanity that is and always has been guided by a false striving. The so-derived understanding of existence applies as a matter of course to every man; and every man brings himself explicitly under it by his concrete "transgression," thereby becoming jointly responsible for it. Since human life is a life with others, mutual trust is destroyed by a *single* lie, and mistrust—and thereby sin—is established; by a *single* deed of violence defensive violence is called forth and law as organized violence is made to serve the interests of individuals, etc.—ideas at least hinted at by I Cor. 5:6: "do you not know that a little leaven ferments the whole lump of dough?" So everyone exists in a world in which each looks out for himself, each insists upon his rights, each fights for his existence, and life becomes a struggle of all against all even when the battle is involuntarily fought. So sin is always already here, and the divine command always encounters man as a "thou shalt" or "thou shalt not" which he must transform into an "I will" or "I will not" by first conquering himself. The fact that the good always demands a sacrifice testifies that in his living man has a tacit understanding of himself that is basically sinful. Paul, it is true, never expounds this train of thought, but our right to develop it for the understanding of his statements is suggested by his conception of "world."

[*] The translator has ventured to revive and to use here and especially in § 28 an obsolete Middle English verb "rightwise(n)"—the true English counterpart of the adjective "righteous" (Anglo-Saxon: rihtwís) and the noun "righteousness" (Anglo-Saxon: rihtwísnes). The only alternative seems to be to use consistently the Latin cognates just, justify, and justification—but they are alive in English with other very misleading meanings.

§ 26. The Term "World" (Cosmos)

1. In Greek antiquity, the conception "universe" was expressed by the word "*kosmos*." They conceived it as a totality bound together by rationally comprehensible relationships of law into a unified structure containing heaven and earth and all living beings, including gods and men. This conception is foreign to the Old Testament; it contains no term corresponding to the Greek "kosmos." It does occasionally speak of the "all" (הַכֹּל) and, much oftener, of "heaven and earth"—but always in such a way that God himself is not included in it, but is always distinguished from it as the Creator. In this restricted sense, Hellenistic Judaism took over and used the term "kosmos," and it is in this sense that the New Testament, inclusive of Paul, uses it.

From the phrase "since the creation of the world" (Rom. 1:20) it is apparent that for Paul "kosmos" can mean "the creation"; and, in keeping with Old Testament thought, he can place "in heaven . . . on earth" (I Cor. 8:5) in parallelism with "in the 'kosmos'" (v. 4). Probably Gal. 4:3 ("the elemental spirits of the 'kosmos'") and Phil. 2:15 ("as lights in the 'kosmos'") are to be reckoned to the few passages in which "kosmos" denotes the (total) world of creation.

Since statements about the "kosmos" as a rule have a bearing on men, it is quite understandable that "kosmos" occasionally means "world" in the restricted sense of the stage on which human life is played—that is, the "earth." That is the case when Abraham is called "the inheritor of the earth" (Rom. 4:13 tr.), and probably also in the reference to the many "sorts of languages" that there are "in the *kosmos*" (I Cor. 14:10 tr.).

However, "kosmos" does not always mean "earth" as the mere stage for man's life and living but often denotes the *quintessence of earthly conditions of life and earthly possibilities.* It embraces all the vicissitudes included between the pairs of polar terms "life . . . death," "things present . . . things future" (I Cor. 3:22). Accordingly, human life in its worldly aspects, in its hustle and bustle, in its weal and woe, is a "dealing with the world" (I Cor. 7:31)—and as the antithesis to the "affairs of the world," "the affairs of the Lord" hover in the background (7:32–34; see § 22).

As "kosmos" is *not a cosmological term here, but an historical one*, so it also is in the numerous passages where it is used in the sense of *"the world of men," "mankind"*—a usage, moreover, which Hellenistic Judaism also knows. Such a passage as Rom. 1:8 shows the transition to it: "your faith is proclaimed in all the world," which is evidently synonymous in substance with 16:19: "for your obedience is known to all." When Paul declares he has behaved with sincerity "in the 'kosmos'," he is not thinking of "kosmos" as the cosmic stage, but as the sphere of human relationships, as his added remark, "especially toward you," itself indicates (II Cor. 1:12). I Cor. 4:9 in naming angels in addition to men ("we have become a spectacle to the 'kosmos,' to angels and to men") also shows that when "kosmos" is used it can mean not the stage, but the persons existing upon it.

When it is said that God will judge "the world" (Rom. 3:6), or that before God every mouth must be stopped and all "the world" stand guilty (3:19; *cf.* v. 20 "all flesh"), "world" denotes men in their entirety. God's chastening is said to have the purpose, in Christians, that they may not fall under the verdict of condemnation "along with the world" (I Cor. 11:32); that means, with the rest of mankind. When it is said that by a man sin came into the "world" (Rom. 5:12f.), once again "world" does not mean the stage, but mankind; likewise, in the statement that God reconciled "the world" to Himself, for the comment follows: "not counting their (= the world's!) trespasses against them" (II Cor. 5:19). The "reconciliation of the world" (Rom. 11:15) is to be understood in the same sense. "Riches for the world" and "riches for the Gentiles" stand in parallelism (Rom. 11:12); similarly "refuse of the world" and "offscouring of all (men)" (I Cor. 4:13). The "wisdom of the world" (I Cor. 1:20) is human wisdom in contrast to God's; "the foolish of the world" (μωρὰ the generalizing neuter for the masculine!) with what follows (I Cor. 1:27) denotes the despised and outcast among men (v. 28).

2. Most important of all, however, is the fact that the term "kosmos" often contains a definite *theological judgment*. In many of the already cited passages, "kosmos" constitutes the implicit or explicit antithesis to the sphere of God or "the Lord," whether "kosmos" denotes the totality of human possibilities and conditions of life (I Cor. 3:22, 7:31ff.), or whether it implies persons in their attitudes and judgments (I Cor. 1:20, 27f.) or in their sinfulness and enmity toward God (Rom. 3:6, 19; 11:15; II Cor. 5:19). But

this is especially true where Paul says *"this world."* The human wisdom which shuts itself off from divine wisdom is "the wisdom of this world" (I Cor. 3:19). Sinners are described as "the immoral of this world" (I Cor. 5:10). The present is characterized by the sentence: the *schema* (essence) of this world is passing away" (I Cor. 7:31b). But "kosmos" alone, which can interchange with "this 'kosmos,'" has the same meaning (I Cor. 1:20f., 27f.; 2:12; 7:31a, 33f.; also II Cor. 7:10; Gal. 6:14).° "This world" can also interchange with "this age" (αἰών). The "wisdom of this age" (I Cor. 2:6, 8; 3:18) is the "wisdom of the world" or "of this world"; the wise who exemplify the wisdom of this world are the wise men, the scholars, the investigators "of this age" (I Cor. 1:20). "The *schema* of this world" (I Cor. 7:31) is "the present evil age" of Gal. 1:4.

Now this means that "kosmos"—used in the above sense—is much more a time-concept than a space-concept; † or, more exactly, it is an *eschatological concept.* It denotes the world of men and the sphere of human activity as being, on the one hand, a temporary thing hastening toward its end (I Cor. 7:31), and on the other hand, the sphere of anti-godly power under whose sway the individual who is surrounded by it has fallen. It is the sphere of "the rulers of this age" (I Cor. 2:6, 8) and "of the god of this age" (II Cor. 4:4).

This power, however—and this is the distinctive thing about Paul's view—does not come over man, either the individual or the race, as a sheer curse of fate, but grows up out of himself. The "kosmos," as the sphere of earthly life's conditions, achieves power over the man whose caring is directed toward "the affairs of the world" (I Cor. 7:32–34), as "flesh" does over him who lives "after the flesh" (§ 22). As a matter of fact, let us recall that the terms "flesh" and "kosmos" can be synonymous (§ 22, 2). Then the eerie fact is that *the "kosmos," the world of men, constituted by that which the individual does and upon which he bestows his care, itself gains the upper hand over the individual.* The "kosmos"

° In some of these passages various textual witnesses understandably (and correctly so far as the meaning is concerned) supply the demonstrative pronoun.

† This corresponds to the fact that in later Judaism the terms "kosmos" and עוֹלָם (originally a time-concept, "age," but gradually shading over into the meaning "world"), mutually influenced each other. I Cor. 5:10 indicates how the time-concept and the space-concept can interpenetrate each other: It is not at all "the immoral of this world" (with whom you are not to associate)— "since then you would need to go out of the world."

comes to constitute an independent super-self over all individual selves. In Paul's usage this clearly emerges in the fact that what is actually practiced or felt by individuals is attributed to the "kosmos" as the active or sentient self. It is the "world" that through its wisdom did not come to know God (I Cor. 1:21); and as the "world" has its "wisdom" (I Cor. 1:21; 3:19), it also has its "grief" (II Cor. 7:10). Indeed, Paul can even express the fact that the world masters those who constitute it by speaking of the "spirit of the world" (I Cor. 2:12)—no matter whether that is only a rhetorical phrase as an antithesis to "the Spirit which is from God," or whether "the spirit of the world" is conceived as an actual mythical reality. In modern terms, "the spirit of the world" is the atmosphere to whose compelling influence every man contributes but to which he is also always subject.

This sense of "kosmos" is also apparent wherever it is said that even though Christians are still in "the world" (considered as the stage and sphere of earthly life) because they are still "in the flesh" (§ 22, 2) and cannot flee out of the world (I Cor. 5:10), they are, nevertheless, already beyond "the world"—"the world" this time regarded as the anti-divine power that controls men. With all its menacing and tempting possibilities, it lies, so to say, beneath their feet; they have mastered it (I Cor. 3:21f.: "for all things are yours . . . whether . . . the world, etc."). They have received not "the spirit of the world" but "the Spirit which is from God" (I Cor. 2:12). To them "the world" is crucified on the cross of Christ and they to it (Gal. 6:14). For them the "elemental spirits of the 'kosmos'" to which they were once enslaved, have been unmasked as "the weak and beggarly elemental spirits" (Gal. 4:9). Therefore, they will someday be judges over the world (I Cor. 6:2f.). All this is true because, in point of fact, they have become new persons (II Cor. 5:17).

3. This eschatological-historical meaning of "kosmos" and along with it the understanding of man's situation as an enslavement to powers for whose dominion he nevertheless is himself responsible, comes out, finally, in the interpretation of Paul's *mythological statements* about these powers.

The "kosmos," although on the one hand, it is God's creation, is, on the other hand, *the domain of demonic powers:* the "angels," "principalities" and "powers" (Rom. 8:38; I Cor. 15:24; see § 21, 3), "the rulers of this age" (I Cor. 2:6, 8), "the elemental spirits of the 'kosmos'" (Gal. 4:3, 9; see §15, 4a). These are "the enemies of God," the last of whom is "death" (I Cor. 15:26). The head of these anti-divine powers is Satan (Rom. 16:20; I Cor. 5:5; 7:5; II Cor. 2:11; 11:14; I Thess. 2:18), the "god of this age" (II Cor. 4:4).

Like the character of the "kosmos," *the character of the spirit powers has a peculiar ambiguity,* for it is clear, in the first place, that Paul does not think in the dualistic manner of Gnosticism, recognizing side by side with the divine world of light an equally eternal, competing, devilish world of darkness (§15). Instead, he considers the spirit powers also to belong to God's creation (Rom. 8:39); God can make use even of an angel of Satan (II Cor. 12:7). It is clear, in the second place, that the "existence" of these powers has significance only for those who let it be an existence "for us"—in which sense, in reality, only God exists (I Cor. 8:5; see §21, 3). Hence, ultimately it is from men that they derive their power, and for the Christian they are already "dethroned" (I Cor. 2:6 Moffatt). In reality, they can no longer harm him. To be sure, the Christian, too, still lives "in the world," "in the flesh," and the ultimately unmythological meaning of the "powers" is also manifested in the fact that their "dethronement" is conceived unmythologically. A Christian's existence is not magically transformed but even after he becomes a Christian his life continues to be an historical existence as long as he is "in the flesh." His existence is ever threatened by danger; and if he, too, must still suffer under the enmity of those "powers," what is expressed in such statements is nothing else than the state of constant threat that menaces his existence. The "powers" come upon the Christian in the vicissitudes of his particular lot— i.e. in his "tribulations" and "distresses," etc. (Rom. 8:35; *cf.* I Thess. 2:18: "Satan hindered us")—which, however, can no longer basically harm him (Rom. 8:31–39). They also come upon him in his temptations; Satan is the "tempter" (I Thess. 3:5) against whom one must be on guard (I Cor. 7:5; II Cor. 2:11).

Hence, the mythological notions of the spirit powers and Satan do not serve the purpose of cosmological speculation nor a need to explain terrifying or gruesome phenomena or to relieve men of responsibility and guilt. When Paul speaks of the event by which death came into the world he takes recourse not to the devil, as Wis. 2:24 does, but to Adam's sin (Rom. 5:12ff.; §25, 3). Though

Death does appear in the mythological role of the "last enemy," I Cor. 15:26, yet in 15:56 it is "sin" that is the "sting of death." It is out of man's deeds that death grows as their fruit (§ 24, 2). Paul may indeed speak in naive mythology of the battle of the spirit powers against Christ or of his battle against them (I Cor. 2:6–8; 15:24–26). In reality, he is thereby only expressing a certain understanding of existence: The spirit powers represent the reality into which man is placed as one full of conflicts and struggle, a reality which threatens and tempts. Thus, through these mythological conceptions the insight is indirectly expressed that man does not have his life in his hand as if he were his own lord but that he is constantly confronted with the decision of choosing his lord. Beyond this, they also contain the conviction that natural man has always already decided against God, his true Lord, and has let the threatening and tempting world become lord over him.

§ 27. The Law

1. The true will of man—the "inward man" (§ 18, 1)—insofar as it is νοῦς, (understanding intent, § 19, 1) strives toward life as that which to him is "good"; and since he can miss this "good," it straightway takes on for him the character of the "good," in the sense of that which is demanded (§§ 19, 1; 21, 1). *God's demand* encounters man concretely in the νόμος, *the Law of the Old Testament,* the purpose of which is no other than to lead man to life (Rom. 7:10; *cf.* Rom. 10:5; Gal. 3:12b).

By νόμος (whether with the article or without) Paul understands the Old Testament Law or the whole Old Testament conceived as law, except in a few passages where νόμος has the general meaning of norm or of compulsion, constraint, as in Rom. 7:2f., 22–8:1. Here there is a play on the term νόμος (the "law of God" is contrasted with the "law in my members"; the "law of my mind" with the "law of sin and death"; and the latter, finally, with the "law of the Spirit of life"). Other such passages are Rom. 3:27 (νόμος, "principle of faith") and Gal. 6:2 ("the law of Christ"). Elsewhere, Paul's νόμος means the Old Testament Law or the whole Old Testament. Pentateuch passages from Moses' time are regarded as νόμος as much as the actual Law of Moses is: Rom. 4:13–16 (Gen. 17:10f.; 18:18; 22:17f.); 7:7ff. (Gen. 2:17); I Cor. 14:34 (Gen. 3:16). In Rom. 3:10–19, passages from Psalms and the prophets are put together and regarded as νόμος. In I Cor. 14:21, Is. 28:11f. figures as νόμος. Nor is any distinction made between the cultic or ritual commandments (Gal. 4:10; 5:3) and the ethical requirements (Rom. 7:7ff.); both are called νόμος. In place of νόμος, Paul may also say ἐντολή, "commandment" (Rom. 7:8ff.), whereas in strict usage the Law contains a multitude of "commandments" (*cf.* Rom. 13:9; I Cor. 7:19).

The Old Testament Law is conceived in the meaning it has for the Old Testament and Judaism. That is, it is not conceived as the principle of an ideal of man, individual or social, which is unfolded in specific requirements. In other words, it is not the rational moral law inherent in man's intellect and giving rise to discussion of such problems as education and the itemized content of "the good." Rather, the Law is *the totality of the historically given legal demands,* cultic and ritual as well as ethical; and the human attitude demanded by it is not that of Goethe's "ever-striving endeavor" (Faust II, Act V)—orientation to an ideal—but is obedience, obedience again and again in the concrete case.

To be sure, except when Paul has specific occasion to speak of the ritual law as in Galatians, in his statements about the Law he is thinking essentially of its *ethical* demands, in particular of the decalogue, as Rom. 2:1–3:20 proves (*cf.* especially 2:21f.); likewise, Rom. 13:8–10; Gal. 5:14 (*cf.* 5:23). This is also indicated by his assertion that for the heathen the demands of the Law are attested in their conscience (Rom. 2:14f.); for what their conscience hears is certainly not the cultic-ritual regulations of the Old Testament. Again, the δικαίωμα τοῦ Θεοῦ, "God's decree" (Rom. 1:32), or the δικαίωμα τοῦ νόμου, Rom. 2:26 ("precepts of the law"); 8:4 ("just requirement of the law") can also only mean the ethical demand.

Nevertheless, Paul, unlike the prophets and Jesus, did not define the nature of obedience under the demand of God by contrasting the ethical demand of the cultic-ritual demands and by criticizing the latter from the standpoint of the former. In his battle against false obedience to the Law he never appeals to a saying of Jesus (§ 16, p. 189). He did not ask how it is that fulfilment of cultic-ritual commandments can be regarded as obedience offered to God at all—a question which it seems superfluous to ask in the case of the ethical demands. The reason why no difference between them is apparent to Paul is that, thinking Jewishly, he does not evaluate the cultic-ritual commandments in regard to their content, but considers them only in regard to the fact that they, like the ethical commandments, are *demands*. Nevertheless, it is apparent from the matter-of-fact way in which he names the ethical demands of the decalogue (Rom. 13:8–10; Gal. 5:14) as the abiding content of the Law obligatory even for the Christian, that the identity of meaning in the cultic-ritual and the ethical demands exists only for the man who has not yet come to faith, and that in faith itself an unconsciously-working principle of criticism is provided.

Under God's demand stand the Gentiles as do the Jews, except that for the former this demand has not taken shape in the Law of the Old Testament. But Paul explicitly says that when the Gentiles, who do not have the "Law," do "by nature" (φύσει) the demands of the Law—so Gentile fulfilment of the Law does occur, no matter how rare or how frequent it may be—they testify that the "work of the Law," i.e. the deed demanded by the Law, is written in their hearts. Conscience also, which they have, too, testifies the same thing (Rom. 2:14f., § 19, 4).* Of course, Paul does not mean "practical reason," (Kant) which unfolds a rational moral law out of itself, when he speaks of conscience in the Gentiles; rather, he means that the Gentiles can hear the command of God which confronts them in the specific case. It takes concrete form for them, for instance, in the state, whose regime is ordered by God and serves Him, and is therefore to be obeyed for conscience' sake (Rom. 13:1–5). It also takes concrete form in convention—in all that is regarded as "true, honorable, just, pure, lovely, and gracious," all that is in repute as a "virtue" or "worthy of praise" (Phil. 4:8).

2. *Naturally, the Law had been given by God in order to be fulfilled.* According to Rom. 2:20, it is "the embodiment of knowledge and truth," and the "inward man" (man's "inmost self" RSV) approves of it (Rom. 7:14ff.). From the fact that the Law, being unable to lead to "righteousness" and leading, rather, only to death, is radically abolished for the man of faith (Rom. 1:18–7:6; Gal. 3:1–5:12) it is not to be inferred that it does not contain *God's obligatory demand.* Paul himself counters such misunderstanding (Rom. 7:7) with the question, "What then shall we say? That the

---

* Rom. 2:26 ("if the uncircumcision keeps the precepts of the Law") probably refers not to the heathen but to Gentile Christians.

law is sin?" (τί οὖν ἐροῦμεν; ὁ νόμος ἁμαρτία); and shortly after (v. 12) avers: "So the law is holy and the commandment is holy and just and good" and characterizes the Law as "spiritual" (v. 14). The "legislation" (νομοθεσία) accorded to Israel is one of Israel's titles of honor of which Paul is proud (Rom. 9:4). As the Law was given "for life" (with life-giving intent), the keeping of it would bestow life (Rom. 10:5; Gal. 3:12). The doers of the Law will be "right-wised" * (Rom. 2:13), and "eternal life" and all salvation will be accorded him who is faithful in "well-doing" (Rom. 2:7) or "who does good" (Rom. 2:10)—i.e. in the context, to him who fulfills the Law.

The presupposition for understanding the proposition that not works lead to "righteousness," but only faith, is the acknowledgment that the Law's demand is just, *that God is the Judge who demands good deeds of man* (Rom. 1:18–3:20). The preaching of faith does not introduce a new concept of God as if God were not the Judge who requires good works but were only the Merciful. No, we may speak of God's "grace" only when we also speak of His "wrath." That is how it happens that Paul, in words that sound open to misunderstanding, can refer the Christian, who achieves "righteousness" not by works of the Law but by faith, to the judgment in which recompense is made according to works (I Cor. 1:8; 3:12–15; 4:4f.; I Thess. 3:13; 5:23, etc.; especially II Cor. 5:10: "For we must all appear before the judgment seat of Christ, so that each one may receive good or evil, according to what he has done in the body"). Though the Christian in a certain sense is no longer "under Law" (Gal. 5:18; Rom. 6:14), that does not mean that the demands of the Law are no longer valid for him; for the *agape* demanded of him is nothing else than the fulfilment of the Law (Rom. 13:8–10; Gal. 5:14). Having received the possibility of proving "what is the good and acceptable and perfect will of God" by the "renewing" of his "mind" (Rom. 12:2), he is able to know by himself what the Jew can know as one "instructed in the law": "know the will (of God) and approve what is excellent" (Rom. 2:18). The will of God revealed to the Christian is identical with the demand of the Law.

The reason why man's situation under the Law is so desperate is not that the Law as an inferior revelation mediates a limited or even false knowledge of God. What makes his situation so desperate is

* See footnote p. 253.

he simple fact that prior to faith *there is no true fulfilment of the Law.* "For all who rely on works of the law are under a curse; for it s written, 'Cursed be every one who does not abide by all things written in the book of the law, and do them'" (Gal. 3:10). The arguments of Rom. 1:18–2:29 are summarized in 3:9: "I have already charged that all men, both Jews and Greeks, are under the power of sin." Then, after he has substantiated that by a composite of quotations, vv. 10–18, he concludes, "for no human being will be justified in his sight (God's) by works of the Law" (v. 20)—the primary meaning of which is that no man *can* procure his own "rightwising" by works of the Law. He cannot because he cannot exhibit "the works of the Law" in their entirety. That is why the "ministration of the Law" is a "ministration of death" or "of condemnation" (II Cor. 3:7, 9); that is why "the written code kills" (II Cor. 3:6); that is why the Law is "the law of sin and death" (Rom. 8:2). The reason why man under the Law does not achieve "rightwising" and life is that he is a transgressor of the Law, that he is guilty before God.

But Paul goes much further still; he says not only that man *can* not achieve salvation by works of the Law, but also that he is not even *intended* to do so. Paul thinks in this manner in consequence of his concept of God, according to which whatever factually is or happens, is or happens according to divine plan. In its context, Rom. 3:20—"no human being will be justified . . . by works of the law"—means, "no one can be justified on the basis of works of the Law," but that this impossibility was also *intended* is indicated by Gal. 2:16, where the same sentence means in this context: "no one *is to be* justified on the basis of works of the Law." A Jew would contradict Paul's assertion that a man can be justified only on the basis of absolutely perfect keeping of the Law ("who . . . abides by all things . . ." Gal. 3:10), still more would he contradict the proposition that *justification by works of the Law and justification by divine grace appropriated in man's faith exclude each other.* But that is the decisive thesis of Paul: "for Christ is the end of the law, that every one who has faith may be justified" (Rom. 10:4); i.e. "Christ means the end of the Law; he leads to righteousness everyone who has faith." Paul reminds the Galatians, who are by no means giving up their faith in Christ or rejecting the grace of God but only wish to combine with it the taking over of circumcision,

"You are severed from Christ, you who would be justified by the law; you have fallen away from grace" (Gal. 5:4). The way of works of the Law and the way of grace and faith are mutually exclusive opposites (Gal. 2:15–21; Rom. 4:4f., 14–16; 6:14; 11:5f.).

But why is this the case? Because *man's effort to achieve his salvation by keeping the Law* only leads him into sin, indeed this effort itself in the end *is already sin.* It is the insight which Paul has achieved into the nature of sin that determines his teaching on the Law. This embraces two insights. One is the insight that sin is man's self-powered striving to undergird his own existence in forgetfulness of his creaturely existence, to procure his salvation by his own strength (§ 23, 1), that striving which finds its extreme expression in "boasting" and "trusting in the 'flesh'" (§ 23, 2). The other is the insight that man is always already a sinner, that, fallen into the power of sin (§ 23, 3), he is always already involved in a falsely oriented understanding of his existence (§§ 25, 26). The reason, then, that man shall not, must not, be "rightwised" by works of the Law is that he must not be allowed to imagine that he is able to procure his salvation by his own strength; for he can find his salvation only when he understands himself in his dependence upon God the Creator.

Simultaneously, this answers the question that arises in Rom. 7:7 after it has been established in 3:21–7:6 that "righteousness" is bestowed only upon the faith which appropriates the grace of God and not upon the works of the Law. This is the question: *What meaning does the Law still have?* The two questions belong together and each of the answers given interprets the other.

The answer given in Rom. 7:7ff. expands what had already been briefly said in 3:20: "through the law comes knowledge of sin." For this sentence (coming after vv. 10–19) does not, of course, mean that *through the Law* man is led to knowledge of what sin is, but does mean that by it he is *led into sinning.* What is meant is practical "knowledge," the "knowing how" to sin, just as "knowing sin" in Rom. 7:7 or II Cor. 5:21 is the practice of sin (*cf.* II Cor. 5:11 where "knowing the fear of the Lord" is not a theoretical knowledge about the fear of the Lord but means "being experienced in fearing the Lord"). This is just the idea that Rom. 7:7–11 develops:

"I would never have come to know sin except through the Law; for I would never have come to know desire, were it not that the

Law says, 'You shall not desire.' But sin took advantage of the commandment and thereby brought about in me every sort of desire. For without the Law sin was dead, but I was once alive without the Law. But when the commandment came, sin came to life and I went to death. And the result was that the commandment which was intended to lead men to life led me straight to death. For sin took advantage of the commandment and deceived me and with its help killed me" (Blt.).

Thus, the Law brings to light that man is sinful, whether it be that his sinful desire leads him to transgression of the Law or that that desire disguises itself in zeal for keeping the Law. But what appears in Rom. 7:7ff. as a wile of sin is actually God's intention: "Law came in (*sc.* between Adam and Christ) to increase the trespass"; and the continuation shows what meaning that has: "but where sin increased, grace abounded all the more" (Rom. 5:20). Thus, the Law leads into sin the man who has forsaken his creaturely relation to God and wants to procure life for and by himself; it does this in order thereby to bring him back again to the right relation to God. This it does by confronting him with the grace of God which is to be appropriated in faith.

Gal. 3:19 says the same thing: "Why then the law? It was added for the sake of transgressions (i.e. in order to evoke transgressions), till the offspring should come to whom the promise had been made (i.e. until Christ, in whom God's grace becomes effective)." It is just by evoking sin that the Law must bring about the fulfilment of the divine promises: "Is the Law then contrary to the promises (of God)? By no means! For only if the Law had been given as one that could make alive would righteousness actually have its origin in the Law. But instead the scripture shut up all things under sin in order that the promise might be bestowed on the basis of faith in Jesus Christ upon those who have faith. Before faith came, however, we were confined under the Law, kept under restraint in prospect of the faith that was to be revealed. Hence, the Law became our discipliner until Christ, in order that we might be rightwised on the basis of faith. But since faith has come we are no longer under the discipliner" (Gal. 3:21–25 Blt.).

Rom. 4:13–16, finally, has the same meaning: "The promise given to Abraham or his descendants that he should be the heir of the world was not founded upon the Law, but upon the righteousness of faith. For if the right to the inheritance were founded upon the Law, faith would be done for (primarily faith in the promises is meant, but this is regarded as identical with Christian faith) and the promise would be void; for the Law only yields wrath. But where there is no Law, there is no transgression (and hence no wrath, either. What was the Law for, then? Why, it was intended to yield wrath; its purpose was to cause transgression!). 'On the basis of faith' holds true for just this reason: In order that 'on the principle of grace' may hold true, making the promise sure for every descendant . . ." (Blt.).

Though the purpose of the Law is, or was, that of being a *paidagogos to Christ,* it is not conceived in either the Greek sense or the modern sense as an educator who is to train man up to a higher level of mental (and especially of ethical) life. Is faith opening up to divine grace the product of education? Of course not. It does not even become possible except upon the basis of God's grace working in Christ. The "educating" done by the Law leads, on the contrary, into sin, and "educates" indirectly toward faith, it is true, because by it the sinner can understand the alternative—*either* works of the Law *or* faith—when grace confronts him. But the Law does this not by leading man into subjective despair, but by bringing him into an objectively desperate situation which he does not recognize as such until the message of grace hits its mark in him. Gal. 3:21–25 does not have the development of the individual in mind but the history of mankind, and Rom. 7:14–24 is not a confession of Paul describing his erstwhile inner division under the Law, but is that picture of the objective situation of man-under-the-Law which became visible to him only after he had attained the viewpoint of faith. The cry, "Wretched man that I am! Who will deliver me from this body of death" (v. 24) was not uttered by Saul-Paul struggling and groaning in time past under the Law—how *that* Paul regarded himself, Phil. 3:4–6 says. Not *that* Paul utters this cry, but Paul the Christian, who puts it into the mouth of the Jew and thereby exposes the situation of the Jew which is not visible to himself.

Nor does Paul elsewhere argue against the way of the Law with the argument that this way leads to subjective despair, and he never praises faith as the escape from an inner division caused by conscience, or as a release from an unbearable burden. His accusation against Jews and Judaizers is that the way of the Law is wrong not because in consequence of transgressions it does does not lead to the goal, but because its *direction* is wrong, for it is the way that is supposed to lead to "one's own righteousness" (Rom. 10:3, *cf.* Phil. 3:9). It is not merely evil deeds already committed that make a man reprehensible in God's sight, but man's intention of becoming righteous before God by keeping the Law and thereby having his "boast" is already sin.

To lead man into sin, therefore, is *the purpose of the Law in the history of salvation,* not only by arousing his desires to transgression but also by offering him the uttermost possibility of living as a sinner by perverting his resistance to the commandment into a striving after a "righteousness of his own" through keeping the commandment—a highly plausible perversion, for in the knowledge that transgression is sin (a knowledge that is directly given with the possession of the Law or is awakened by conscience; § 19, 4) and in the fear of transgressing, lies the foundation of a false supposition that Law-observance—which, as a conquering of desire, takes on the appearance of a good work—can procure "righteousness." That fear and this supposition show how deep in sin man lies ("in order that sin . . . through the commandment might become sinful beyond measure," Rom. 7:13); and bound up with this in the very nature of the case is man's ignorance of the situation he is in: It is hidden from him that his life is steering not toward life but toward death ("for what I am bringing about, I do not know," Rom. 7:15; see § 24, 2).

Then *the ultimate purpose of the Law is to lead man to death* and thereby to let God appear as God, for the Law gives sin its power; while sin is the "sting" of death (I Cor. 15:56); sin kills man by means of the commandment by dangling before him the deceptive promise of procuring him life (Rom. 7:11). So it can also be said, "The letter (i.e. the Law itself) kills" (II Cor. 3:6). The fruits of the "sinful passions" aroused by the Law ripen for death (Rom. 7:5; see § 24, 2). But by this process the Law leads man to God as the Creator who bestows life and from whom alone life can be given to man—this man who on the way to "his own righteousness," the way of "boasting," has blundered into death. It is as this God that he appears in the "grace" of the salvation-occurrence, and it is this God toward whom faith is directed. Abraham (Rom. 4:2), who has no "boast" (i.e. nothing to boast about), believes in "God who gives life to the dead and calls into existence the things that do not exist"

(Rom. 4:17). And for Paul, the upshot of the "affliction" he has experienced is that he has pronounced the sentence of death upon himself, "in order that we might not trust in ourselves but in God who raises the dead;" just that is also the upshot of the "educating" done by the Law (II Cor. 1:9).

3. At the end, then, it becomes apparent that even *the demand of God embodied in the Law* is grace only. It was already grace that God gave the Law "for life" (Rom. 7:10). And though this life-giving purpose was defeated by man's sinful desire, that still was not able to wipe out God's grace, for it is still God's grace that the Law factually led "to death," because by this route man is led to God, the "God who gives life to the dead." The Law is not "against the promises of God" (Gal. 3:21); the unity of the divine will is clear: It wills now nothing else than it always has, and God's law, the "spiritual law" (Rom. 7:14), remains in effect as the "law of Christ" (Gal. 6:2) and in *agape* (see above, p. 262) is kept by those who have faith. Now for the first time its real intention comes to fulfilment: God has removed the powerlessness of the Law ("what the law weakened by the flesh could not do") "in order that the just requirement of the law might be fulfilled in us, who walk not according to the flesh but according to the Spirit" (Rom. 8:3f.).

The difference between the Law as the eternal will of God and the Law that is abolished is expressed to a certain degree in Paul's terminology, in which frequently the Law as abolished by Christ figures as the *Law of Moses*. Thus, Christ and Moses are contrasted in Rom. 10:46f.; likewise, in II Cor. 3:7–18 in the comparison between the ministry of the old and the new covenant (*cf.* also I Cor. 10:2). The Law that intervened (Rom. 5:20) is identified by v. 14 as the Law of Moses. Especially significant is the fact that in the polemic of Gal. 3:19f., Paul can take up the Gnostic myth of the giving of the Law by angels in order to prove that the Law of Moses is not attributable to God Himself. Paul can do that only because he views the Law as a matter of course in the role in which the Jew lets it encounter him.

As the unity of the divine will is clear, so is the *unity of man's existence* clear as he moves from the situation under the Law to the situation under grace. No break takes place; no magical or mysterious transformation of man in regard to his substance, the basis of

[268]

his nature, takes place. Rather, his new existence stands in historical continuity with the old—not, indeed, in a continuity of development as understood within the Greek-idealistic picture of man. Compared with that kind of continuity we really do have to do here with a break: A new understanding of one's self takes the place of the old—it does so, nevertheless, in such a manner that historical continuity is preserved; indeed, it thereby becomes one's own true history, for the transition from the old existence to the new does not take place as a mental development from sin to faith; rather, faith is decision in regard to the grace which encounters a man in the proclaimed word. However much Paul's view of the history of salvation is oriented toward mankind, and not the individual (see above, p. 266), it still is true that the situation of mankind is also that of the individual. He, the sinner who is in death, is confronted by the gospel when it reaches him with the decision whether or not he is willing to understand himself anew and to receive his life from the hand of God. The possibility of understanding is given him in the very fact that he is a sinner, that he is in death. This rescue of man from death does not take as its point of departure some higher spiritual principle or faculty in him that is not under the power of sin, if there were such; what it rescues is not—as the Gnostic myth maintains—a fully inconceivable and only negatively describable self, the pre-existent spark of light, but precisely the sinner, the innerly divided and self-misunderstanding human self. Salvation is naught else than the realization of that destined goal of "life" and selfhood which are God's will for man and man's own real intention, but which were perverted under sin (§ 23, 3).

CHAPTER V

Man under Faith

A. THE RIGHTEOUSNESS OF GOD

§ 28. The Concept of Righteousness

1. Since Paul regards *man's existence* prior to *faith* in the transparency it has gained to the eye of faith, therefore *man's existence under faith* has already been indirectly pre-sketched in the presentation of pre-faith existence. If pre-faith man is man fallen into the power of death, man under faith is man who receives life. If man's death has its cause in the fact that man in his striving to live out of his own resources loses his self (§ 23, 3), life arises out of surrendering one's self to God, thereby gaining one's self.

This is just what is expressed in Paul's manner of interpreting the *"righteousness,"* or the *"being rightwised"* [*] (KJ "justification"), which is the presupposition for receiving life. In the thesis that salvation, the receipt of life, is dependent upon and conditioned by a man's righteousness, Paul is only repeating at the outset what Jewish tradition takes for granted. But the way he understands the possibility and the actualization of righteousness or rightwising—even speaking of it as the very substance of salvation—indicates the basic contrast between him and Judaism and reveals his new grasp of man's existence before God.

Strictly speaking, *righteousness is the condition for receiving salvation or "life."* As Abraham's (faith-)righteousness was the presupposition for his receiving the promise (Rom. 4:13), so now he who is righteous (by faith) *will* receive life (Rom. 1:17; Gal. 3:11). It is to those who are rightwised ("justified therefore . . .") that salvation will be imparted (Rom. 5:1ff.). As sin led to death, so righteousness leads to life (Rom. 5:17, 21; 8:10). The goal ahead of

[*] See footnote p. 253.

[270]

him who has righteousness is the gain of life (Phil. 3:9f.); God's rightwising act is followed by His glorifying act (Rom. 8:30).

But since this connection between righteousness and salvation is so tight and inevitable, *righteousness itself can become the essence of salvation.* "Striving after righteousness," the concern of the Jews (Rom. 9:30f.; Gal. 2:16), is the same thing as "striving after salvation," for in the former, one has the latter. Though in Rom. 5:9, salvation ("being saved") lies in the future awaiting the "right-wised," yet in Rom. 10:10, "righteousness" and "salvation" are used in synonymous parallelism. As Christ's death brought it about that we are "alive," it is also said, meaning the same thing, that we in him are "the righteousness (of God)"—i.e. that we have the standing of righteous men (II Cor. 5:15, 21). The "ministry of righteousness" (whose opposite is the "ministry of condemnation," i.e. of condemnation to death) is identical with the "ministry of the Spirit" (whose opposite is the "ministry of death"—II Cor. 3:7–9). Further, "righteousness" can be joined with other terms that also denote the state of salvation (I Cor. 1:30: "righteousness and consecration and redemption"; *cf.* 6:11). That which was brought to light by the occurrence of salvation in Christ, and which is the content of "the gospel," is the new possibility of a "righteousness" which shall be a "righteousness of God" (Rom. 1:16f.; 3:21); just for that reason the office of apostle can be called the "ministry of righteousness" (II Cor. 3:9). But it is possible to speak so of "righteousness" not only because of the tight connection that exists between "righteousness" (as condition) and "life" (as result), but especially because *not merely salvation (the result) is the gift of God but even the condition for it is already the gift of God Himself.* For what, we must now ask, is meant by "righteousness" and especially by "righteousness of God"?

2. The word *dikaiosyne* (righteousness) is (like its Hebrew analogue, צְדָקָה) ambiguous. We must here disregard a number of meanings which the word can have in both Biblical and secular usage, for instance, the very important meaning of "distributive justice" dealt out by a judge, which occurs in Paul (Rom. 9:28), according to many manuscripts at any rate, in his quotation from Is. 10:22. Aside from such meanings, *dikaiosyne* (and likewise *dikaios*, "righteous") is used in both an ethical sense (then meaning "uprightness") and a forensic sense. When it denotes the condition

for (or the essence of) salvation, *dikaiosyne is a forensic term.* It does not mean the ethical quality of a person. It does not mean any quality at all, but a relationship. That is, *dikaiosyne* is not something a person has as his own; rather it is something he has in the verdict of the "forum" (= law-court—the sense of "forum" from which "forensic" as here used is derived) to which he is accountable. He has it in the opinion adjudicated to him by another. A man has "righteousness," or is "righteous," when he is acknowledged to be such, and that means, in case such acknowledgment of him is in dispute: when he is "rightwised," "pronounced righteous" (*cf.* the parallelism between "righteous before God" and δικαιωθήσονται— be pronounced righteous"—in Rom. 2:13). Specifically, the "righteous" one is that one in a legal action (κρίνεσθαι; note the parallelism between "be justified" and "prevail"—win out—in Rom. 3:4), who wins his case or is acquitted. Normally, therefore, he is the "innocent" one—but he is "righteous" not to the extent that he may *be* innocent, but to the extent that he is *acknowledged* innocent. "Righteousness" then is the "favorable standing" that a person has in the eyes of others; it is that "right" which a man seeks to establish by process of law as "his rights." In this sense Michael Kohlhaas (in Kleist's story of the same name) is the type of the man who "demands righteousness"—viz. that he be acknowledged to be in the right.

This is in accord with Old Testament-Jewish usage. In exhorting men to trust Jahweh, the Psalmist says (Ps. 37:6):

"He brings forth thy righteousness (צְדָקָה,
LXX: δικαιοσύνη) as the light,
And thy judgment (מִשְׁפָּט, κρίμα) as the noonday."

Or he implores (Ps. 17:2, 15):

"Let my right (מִשְׁפָּט, κρίμα) come forth from thy presence . . . May I behold thy face in righteousness (צֶדֶק, δικαιοσύνη).

In this sense it may also be said of God that He is "declared righteous," in other words that He is acknowledged to be in the right. Thus, we read in the passage quoted at Rom. 3:4 (Ps. 51:4):

"Against thee, thee only, have I sinned and done this evil in thy sight

[272]

That thou mightest be justified (pronounced right, תִּצְדַּק, δικαιωθῇς) when thou speakest

And be clear (תִּזְכֶּה, νικήσῃς) when thou judgest."

This use is also frequent in the Psalms of Solomon (2:16: "I will justify thee [acknowledge thy righteousness] O God; 3:5; 4:9; 8:7, 27ff.); likewise, Lk. 7:29 ("and all the people and the tax-collectors 'justified' God"); *cf.* Lk. 7:35 and its parallel, Mt. 11:19).

The more Jewish piety came to be determined by eschatology—i.e. the more the pious expected God's rightwising verdict to come from His eschatological judgment—the more *the forensic term "righteousness" became an eschatological term*. By those who "hunger and thirst after righteousness," Mt. 5:6 obviously does not mean those who "ever striving, endeavor" to attain ethical perfection, but those who long to have God pronounce the verdict "righteous" as His decision over them in the judgment. What the pious Jew endeavors to do, however, is to fulfill the conditions which are the presupposition for this verdict of God; these conditions are, of course, keeping the commandments of the Law and doing good works. Hence, Paul can call the righteousness sought by the Jews "righteousness from the Law" (Phil. 3:9), while his thesis is that "righteousness" (as "God's righteousness") has been revealed "apart from the Law" (Rom. 3:21).

But before we proceed further to clarify the contrast between the Pauline and the Jewish conception, it must be clearly recognized that *there is complete agreement between them as to the formal meaning of* DIKAIOSYNE: *It is a forensic-eschatological term.* The forensic meaning of "righteous" and "be rightwised" is already a clear implication of Rom. 2:13 (see above) as it also is of the expressions modeled after Gen. 15:6 that speak of "being reckoned (λογίζεσθαι) as righteousness" (Rom. 4:3, 5, 22; Gal. 3:6; *cf.* "to reckon righteousness to . . ." Rom. 4:6), in which "reckon" has the same forensic meaning as the Hebrew חָשַׁב (Lev. 7:18; II Sam. 19:19 [19:20 in Heb.]; Ps. 32:2), for which the LXX uses precisely the same Greek verb (or its compound, διαλογίζειν). The eschatological meaning of *dikaiosyne* is clear as day in the passages that speak of a future verdict of righteousness to come in the eschatological judgment; such are Rom. 2:13 again and also Gal. 5:5 ("we wait for the hope of righteousness").

[273]

The future tenses in Rom. 3:20 ("no human being will be justified") and 3:30 ("he [God] will justify") are perhaps not genuine futures, but gnomic (or logical) futures. Rom. 5:19, "many will be made righteous," is evidently said as if uttered in Jesus' time (the dividing point of the ages); hence it is already true in the present in which Paul is speaking (*cf.* vv. 17, 21). On the other hand, neither is the present used in the present-tense statements of Gal. 2:16; 3:11; 5:4 a genuine present, but the timeless present of didactic statement and may therefore apply in spite of the tense to the decision of God in the coming judgment.

§ 29. Righteousness as a Present Reality

1. The first difference from Jewish usage is that Paul asserts of this forensic-eschatological righteousness that *it is already imputed to a man in the present* (on the presupposition that he "has faith"). After Rom. 3:21–4:25 has dealt with faith as the presupposition for being "rightwised," Rom. 5:1 begins: "Rightwised therefore by faith we have peace with God." [*] And in keeping with this v. 9 says: "Since therefore we are now rightwised . . . how much more shall we be saved . . ." For the present that exists since Christ the purpose expressed in v. 21: "that . . . grace might reign through righteousness to eternal life," is being fulfilled. Rom. 8:10 also applies to the present: "if Christ is in you, although your bodies are dead because of sin, your spirits are alive because of righteousness" (which is scarcely to be understood with Lietzmann as meaning: "because of the sin you have committed" and "because of the righteousness you will practice," but rather: "because sin is condemned [*cf.* v. 3]" and "because righteousness has been established," as Barth interprets). Though one may understand "those whom he called he also rightwised" (Rom. 8:30) as proleptic (like the following "he also glorified"), Paul, nevertheless, says to the Corinthians "you *were* rightwised" (I Cor. 6:11) and says of the Gentiles "who did not pursue righteousness," "they *have attained* righteousness" (Rom. 9:30). And Rom. 1:17 is to be understood in this same way when it says that in the preaching of the gospel the righteousness of God "is revealed." For this does not mean that the preached gospel expounds some teaching about righteousness, but that through it right-

[*] The variant reading ἔχωμεν (let us have) is not to be entertained.

eousness becomes a possibility (which in faith becomes reality) for the hearer of the gospel.

"Revealed" has the same meaning in Rom. 1:18: "the wrath of God is revealed from heaven"; i.e. God's wrathful judgment (see § 31, 1) appears, takes place—likewise in the present. The same meaning is also found in Gal. 3:23: "Now before faith came, we were confined under the law, kept under restraint until faith should be revealed"; this expected "revealing" has now become a thing of the present ("now that faith has come," v. 25); this does not mean that now a hitherto unknown teaching about faith is being expounded, but that it has now become a possibility and, in those who have faith, a reality—faith has made its appearance, for this is just what *"be revealed"* (ἀποκαλύπτεσθαι) or its noun "revelation" (ἀποκάλυψις), and also "be manifested" (φανεροῦσθαι, Rom. 3:21), mean when used as eschatological terms—appear on the scene, become possibility, or become operative. The awaited "revelation of the Lord Jesus Christ" (I Cor. 1:7 KJ mg.) is not some communication that he will impart, but his appearing in person at his parousia, just as the "revelation" of God's righteous judgment (Rom. 2:5) is the effective execution of it. And when I Cor. 3:13 says of the Day: "it will be revealed with fire," that means that the judgment day will fierily appear. "To appear on the scene" is also the meaning in Rom. 8:18f.: "I consider that the sufferings of this present time are not worth comparing with the glory *that will make its appearance in us.* For the creation waits with eager longing for the revealing (= the appearing) of the sons of God." The same usage occurs in II Thess. 1:7; 2:3, 6, 8; I Pet. 1:5, 7, 13; 4:13; 5:1; Lk. 17:30. Of course, both the verb and the noun can also mean the disclosing of something hitherto hidden, the divulging of a secret (I Cor. 14:6, 26, 30; II Cor. 12:1, 7; Gal. 1:12; 2:2; Phil. 3:15, and elsewhere).

This "appearing on the scene" or "becoming effective," since either is an event occurring to or for men, does, of course, *enable man to understand or perceive the event.* While that is true, it is not the perceiving of the event but the event itself that is denoted by "being revealed." The "revealing" of God's wrath (Rom. 1:18) takes place even though those concerned are not even aware of it themselves. In I Cor. 3:13 the clause "the Day will disclose it" does make a distinction between this informing function of revelation and revelation as actual occurrence (viz.

the occurrence of the judgment day meant in: "it will be 're-vealed' with fire"), but this disclosure will take place not through any proclamation but in the event itself. (*Cf.* R. Bult-mann, "Der Begriff der Offenbarung im NT" [1929] in *Glauben und Verstehen* [1933], pp. 153–187; the article: "Offenbarung" in *RGG*, 2nd ed.)

2. At this point it is of basic importance to comprehend that by his thesis that *righteousness is a present reality* Paul, nevertheless, does not rob it of its *forensic-eschatological meaning*. The paradoxi-cality of his assertion is this: God already pronounces His eschato-logical verdict (over the man of faith) in the present; the eschato-logical event is already present reality, or, rather, is beginning in the present. Therefore, the righteousness which God adjudicates to man (the man of faith) is not "sinlessness" in the sense of ethical perfection, but is "sinlessness" in the sense that God does not "count" man's sin against him (II Cor. 5:19).

That disposes of many questions that arise only from the fact that "righteousness" is not understood in its forensic-eschatological sense but is misunderstood as ethical perfection. When God right-wises the sinner, "makes him righteous" (Rom. 4:5), that man is not merely "regarded as if" he were righteous, but really is righteous—i.e. absolved from his sin by God's verdict. What consequences this has for his ethical conduct will be considered later (§ 38). That it must have such consequences is clear from the outset, for the "right-wised," being men who have been transplanted into eschatological existence, are also "saints" who can have no further contact with sin. Christ is "our righteousness and our consecration" (I Cor. 1:30); and side by side with "you were rightwised" stands "you were con-secrated" (I Cor. 6:11). But that is not expressed by the term "righteousness" itself, and the relation between "righteousness" and "consecration" ("sanctification" KJ) is for the present unclear. Be-fore it can be clarified the meaning of "rightwising" must first be clearly determined. Its meaning becomes apparent from such a sen-tence as Rom. 5:19:

> "For as by one man's disobedience
>   many were made sinners,
> so by one man's obedience
>   many will be made righteous."

Just as certainly as Adamitic men were not "merely regarded as if they were sinners," but really were sinners, so are the members of the humanity founded by Christ really righteous. II Cor. 5:21 indicates the same thing:

> "For our sake he made him to be sin who knew no sin,
>   so that in him we might become the righteousness of God."

It would be an error to regard the main clause as meaning that God treated the (ethically) sinless Christ "as if" he were a sinner (which in itself would not be untrue). Rather, this clause intends to express the paradoxical fact that God made the (ethically) sinless Christ to be a sinner (in the forensic sense)—viz. by letting him die on the cross as one accursed (*cf.* Gal. 3:13). Correspondingly, the purpose clause says that we (through him) are to become righteous (in the forensic sense). Thus, the old debate over whether he who is rightwised is really righteous or is only regarded "as if" he were righteous, rests upon a misunderstanding. So does the question: How is it possible for him to be a truly righteous man? So does the temptation to supply an "as if." So, finally, does the problem how Paul can, nevertheless, proceed to place these truly righteous, and hence "sinless," men under the ethical imperative. These perplexities all rest upon the misunderstanding that "righteousness" denotes the ethical quality of a man, whereas in truth it means his relation to God.

If one takes Paul's statements as they stand, without a supplied "as if," and yet fails to recognize the forensic-eschatological meaning of "righteousness," two wrong tracks are easy to take: 1. the idealistic and 2. the Gnostic misunderstanding. According to 1. "rightwising" means that one takes into his consciousness a new principle, the principle of obedience to the idea of the good. When one has done this, a "qualitative fulfilment of the Law" has taken the place of a "merely quantitative" fulfilment; man is righteous since his will affirms the ethical law in its totality (F. C. Baur). Righteousness, then, denotes the "ideal" character of the man whose living tends toward the good; "striving toward not sinning" (Epictetus, Diss. IV 12, 19) is the characteristic of the man who is "progressing" ($\pi\varrho o\varkappa\acute{o}\pi\tau\omega\nu$), to use Stoic terminology; by approaching in endless progress toward the ideal of ethical uprightness he can be regarded, *sub specie* of the idea, as righteous. He stands under the imperative," become what thou art" (viz. what thou, *sub specie* of the

[277]

idea, art). 2. The other misunderstanding is one related to Hellenistic Gnosticism, in which "righteousness" is considered a divine "power" (δύναμις) which flows into the initiate along with other divine powers in the mystery of re-birth and drives out the demonic powers which have hitherto reigned in him (Corp. Herm. 13:9 [Mead]: "We are made righteous, son, by the departure of Unrighteousness"). This is the sense R. Reitzenstein (*Hellenistische Mysterienreligionen,* 3rd ed., 257–261) professed to find in Rom. 6:7; 8:30; I Cor. 6:11. Even if it should turn out that Paul was influenced in these passages by the terminology of the mysteries, his conception of "righteousness" and "rightwising" would still not be explainable as a whole from the mystery terminology.

3. The *present reality* of righteousness rests upon its having been "revealed" by the occurring of salvation in Christ (Rom. 3:21–26; II Cor. 5:21; *cf.* I Cor. 1:30). This saving occurrence, however, is the *eschatological event* by which God ended the old course of the world and introduced the new aeon. For "when the time had fully come, God sent forth his son" (Gal. 4:4); so now "the old has passed away" and "the new has come" and whoever is "in Christ" is a "new creature" (II Cor. 5:17). The New Covenant (II Cor. 3:6ff.) predicted for the eschatological period by Jeremiah has taken the place of the Old Covenant, and the "acceptable time" prophesied by Isaiah has arrived (II Cor. 6:2).

The forensic-eschatological sense of "righteousness" is also corroborated, finally, by its parallelism with the term "*adoption to sonship*" (υἱοθεσία), which is also both a legal term (though not derived from the trial-court) and an eschatological term. Just as the salvation-occurrence can be described as having taken place "for our justification" (rightwising), Rom. 3:25f.; 4:25; 5:18; II Cor. 5:21), its purpose can also be given by the expression, "that we might receive adoption as sons" (Gal. 4:5). "Adoption" has the same peculiar double nature as "righteousness" has. On the one hand, it is a thing of the future, a longed-for goal (Rom. 8:23: "we wait for adoption as sons"); on the other hand, it is a present thing, as is attested by the fact that in the Spirit—that eschatological gift—we cry "Abba!" (Rom. 8:15f.; Gal. 4:6f.).

4. The contrast between Paul and Judaism, then, is not that each has a different conception of righteousness as a forensic-eschatolog-

ican entity. Rather, the immediate contrast is that what for the Jews is a *matter of hope* is for Paul a *present reality*—or, better, is also a present reality. But how can it be both? That can only be cleared up in the course of our further investigation of Paul's thinking. For the present, the problem itself must be pointed more sharply. It emerges clearly in the arrangement of Romans. After the section 1:18–3:20 has demonstrated that before the revealing of "God's righteousness" both Gentiles and Jews stood under the "wrath of God," the thesis of righteousness now established by the occurrence of salvation in Christ is presented in 3:21–31 and the Scripture proof of it is offered in 4:1–25. For the Jew, with whom Paul is debating in all these arguments, the assertion of the present reality of eschatological righteousness could only appear absurd; for where, he could ask, are the blessings that were to be given along with righteousness? Where is "life"? Are not death and sin still present realities?

Paul replies in chapters 5–8. In chapter 5 he endeavors to demonstrate that eschatological life, though a matter of hope, is, nevertheless, in a certain manner already a present reality. Further, he shows in 6:1–7:6 that even sin has lost its domination for the rightwised. Then, after a digression (7:7–25) has discussed the significance of the Law in the history of salvation, chapter 8 is the conclusion; it deals once more with freedom from sin (8:1–11) and from death (8:12–39), pointing out again the peculiar double character of salvation: future and yet already present.

§ 30. Righteousness as God's Righteousness

1. The contrast between Paul and Judaism consists not merely in his assertion of the present reality of righteousness, but also in a much more decisive thesis—the one which concerns the condition to which God's acquitting decision is tied. The Jew takes it for granted that this condition is keeping the Law, the accomplishing of "works" prescribed by the Law. In direct contrast to this view Paul's thesis runs—to consider its negative aspect first: "*without works of the Law.*" After the demonstration, Rom. 1:18–3:20, that Gentiles and Jews are fallen under sin has ended with "No human being will be justified ("rightwised") in his (God's) sight by works of the Law," the next verse enters like a new theme stating the thesis: "But now

the righteousness of God has been manifested apart from law," and after a short discussion v. 28 sums it up: "For we hold that a man is justified (rightwised) by faith apart from works of law" (in which by the context "by faith" certainly means "*sola fide*"—"by faith alone"). For this thesis, chapter 4 offers the Scripture proof: Even Abraham did not achieve his righteousness by his works. In the arguments about the fate of the Jewish people (chapters 9–11) this thought recurs at 9:31f.; 10:4–6; 11:6, particularly in the pithy sentence 10:4: "For Christ is the end of the law, that every one who has faith may be justified (rightwised)." The same assertion is defended in Galatians against the Judaizers who want to combine Christian faith with the acceptance of the Law (Gal. 2:16; 3:11, 21; 5:1); 2:21 in particular formulates the idea in utmost pointed form: "for if justification (rightwising) were through the law, then Christ died to no purpose." In his other letters, where Paul is not contending with Judaism and Judaizing Christians, such sentences are quite naturally missing except for one example in Philippians (3:9: "not having a righteousness of my own, based on law").

The negative aspect of Paul's thesis does not stand alone; a positive statement takes its place beside it: "*by, or from, faith.*" Right in the thematic sentences at Rom. 1:16f. where the "gospel" is described as "a power for salvation," the reason given for this description is: "For in it the righteousness of God is revealed through faith for faith," in support of which Hab. 2:4 is cited as Scripture proof. Accordingly, the negative sentence quoted above, Rom. 3:21, receives its positive complement in v. 22: "the righteousness of God through faith in Jesus Christ for all who believe." Similarly, in v. 28 (see above) "by faith" and "apart from works of the law" are brought together, and the catch-word "faith" appears in vv. 25 and 30. So Abraham in chapter 4 is the Scripture proof both for "apart from works of Law" and for "by faith" on the strength of Gen. 15:6. The new discussion beginning at 5:1 starts with "Therefore, since we are justified (rightwised) by faith . . ." and the catchword "faith" recurs again in 9:30–32, 10:4–6 (here "righteousness based on law" and "righteousness based on faith," both personified, are contrasted each with the other) and 10:10. Once again Galatians contains the same declarations (2:16; 3:6, 8, 11, 24; 5:5) and the same passage in Philippians (3:9) contrasts "righteousness based on law" with "righteousness from God that depends on faith."

[280]

2. What does this antithesis of Paul's to the Jewish view signify? Its full significance will emerge in our investigation of the structure of the concept "faith" (§§ 35ff.). But for the time being one thing is clear about it: *"faith" is the absolute contrary of "boasting."* The announcement of the thesis "by faith, apart from the Law," Rom. 3:21–26, is followed by a question addressed to Paul's Jewish opponent: "Then what becomes of boasting? It is excluded. On what principle? On the principle of works? No, but on the principle of faith" (Rom. 3:27). "Boasting (in the Law)" is the fundamental attitude of the Jew, the essence of his sin (Rom. 2:17, 23 and see § 23, 2), and the radical giving up of boasting is faith's attitude. Thus, Paul can say of Abraham, who was rightwised not by his works but by his faith, that he has no "boast" (4:2). Righteousness, then, cannot be won by human effort, nor does any human accomplishment establish a claim to it; it is sheer gift.

This may also be expressed by naming *"grace"* (with or without the specification *"God's"*) as the basis of rightwising. "Righteousness through faith" (Rom. 3:22) has an equivalent in v. 24: "justified (rightwised) by his grace as a gift," in which "as a gift" further emphasizes the gift-character of righteousness already stated in the term "grace." "Grace" and "gift" also appear in combination in Rom. 5:15, 17: ". . . how much more have the grace of God and the free gift in the grace . . . abounded." " . . . how much more will those who receive the abundance of grace and the free gift of righteousness reign . . ." (*cf.* v. 21 and the synonymous term χάρισμα in v. 15f. and 6:23).

Therefore, *"grace,"* like "faith" *can be placed in direct antithesis to "works of the Law."* "You are not under law but under grace" (Rom. 6:19), Paul reminds the rightwised. He speaks still more pointedly in Gal. 5:4: "You are severed from Christ, you who would be justified (rightwised) by the law; you have fallen away from grace." Paul declares of himself on the contrary, "I do not nullify the grace of God; for if justification (rightwising) were through the law, then Christ died to no purpose" (Gal. 2:21). While a remnant of the Jewish people has come to have faith, it did so "chosen by grace. But if it is by grace, it is no longer on the basis of works; otherwise, grace would no longer be grace" (Rom. 11:5f.). In the same way, "faith" and "grace" in conjunction are contrasted with the Law in the compressed and somewhat tortuous train of thought,

Rom. 4:14-16: verse 13 had established through scriptural proof that Abraham and his posterity had received the promise thanks not to the Law but thanks to his "faith-righteousness." Verse 14 then continues: "If it is the adherents of the law who are to be the heirs, faith is null and the promise is void." The promise, Paul assumes, makes sense only for "faith" (= those who have faith); under the Law this promise cannot come to fulfilment, "for the law brings wrath" (v. 15a). Then the thought turns from the negative to the positive significance of the Law. For when v. 15b goes on to say: "but where there is no law there is no transgression," this evidently means the Law is also intended to bring about transgression, for it is by doing just that that the Law confirms that the promise was given to faith: "the reason why it (righteousness) depends upon faith is: that it (righteousness) may depend upon grace" (v. 16, see § 27, 2, p. 265).

The paradox in "grace" is that it is precisely *the transgressor, the sinner,* to whom it applies, just as God in Rom. 4:5 is He "who justifies (rightwises) the ungodly." Rom. 3:23f. also says it: "all have sinned . . . they are justified (rightwised) by his grace as a gift," and so, especially, does Rom. 5:20: "Law came in to increase the trespass; but where sin increased, grace abounded all the more." Gal. 3:22, without explicitly mentioning "grace," says in substance the same thing: "the scripture consigned all men to sin that what was promised to faith in Jesus Christ might be given to those who believe" (tr.). Rom. 11:32 similarly: "For God consigned all men to disobedience, that he may have mercy upon all."

The term ἔλεος (mercy) used in Rom. 11:32 (here in verb-form) in place of the term "grace," means substantially the same thing, but more strongly emphasizes the eschatological character of God's act (when He rightwises). "Ἔλεος (or rather חֶסֶד, which the LXX as a rule renders ἔλεος) had taken on this eschatological emphasis in salvation-history (see *ThWB*, II 477, 4ff.; 478, 15ff.; 480, 8ff.). Paul speaks of God's "mercy" (except in the benediction, Gal. 6:16) only in his reflections on the history of salvation in Rom. 9-11, specifically 9:15-18 (after Ex. 33:19); 9:23; 11:30-32 and 15:8f. (We are naturally not concerned here with the passages that deal with his personal experience of God's "grace" and "mercy"—I Cor. 15:10; II Cor. 12:9 and I Cor. 7:25; II Cor. 4:1, respectively). Only rarely does he speak of God's "kindness" (χρηστότης, Rom. 2:4a, 11:22; or χρηστόν, Rom. 2:4b). In the Psalms of Solomon the reverse is true: "grace" does not occur, but (God's) "mercy" and "kindness" are frequently met. In the deutero-Pauline literature, "mercy" again becomes more frequent; here, too, "kindness" appears only a few times (Eph. 2:7; Tit. 3:4).

One readily understands, then, that just as "righteousness by faith" can designate the content of the gospel (see above, 1.), in the same way the content and significance of the message and the character of Christian existence can be denoted by the simple term "grace." Paul urges the Corinthians "not to accept the *grace* of God in vain" (II Cor. 6:1). To "nullify the grace of God" (Gal. 2:21) or to "fall away from grace" (Gal. 5:4; see § 32, 1) would mean to forsake the saving way of faith—the Christian faith itself.

It may serve to consolidate what has been said up to this point in § 30 if we pause to refute such a misinterpretation as that advocated by W. Mundle (*Der Glaubensbegriff des Paulus,* (1932), 99ff.). Mundle denies that the rejection of "works" as the condition for rightwising is to be understood to mean rejection of absolutely every accomplishment that can get or earn something for the doer. He maintains that when Paul rejects works, only the works demanded by the Mosaic Law are meant. And if faith, which appropriates God's grace, is an act of obedience, then "there is always a certain measure of activity on man's own part assumed in it." Against this interpretation must be said 1. Mundle does not ask himself *why* it is, according to Paul, that "works" do not rightwise. If the reason they do not is that man must not have any boast before God (Rom. 3:27; 4:2), then the "works *of the Law,*" on which Paul naturally concentrates in this discussion with the Jew, represent works in general, any and all works as works-of-merit. 2. Paul explicitly emphasizes the contrariety of "working" and a "gift" (or "act of grace") and contrasts "grace" (or "gift") and "due (wage)" (Rom. 4:4f.); he therefore understands "work" in the fundamental sense—to earn claim to a reward. 3. Although according to Paul, the man of faith also is required—but from an entirely new point of view—to keep the Law (Rom. 13:8–10; Gal. 5:14), it is clear that the works of the Law not as to their content but as to the manner of their fulfilment are meant. 4. Mundle overlooks the parallelism between Paul's polemic against "one's own righteousness based on law" and his polemic against the "Greeks" (§ 23, 2). This parallelism shows that the former was aimed not against the accomplishment of specific acts—viz. those required by the Mosaic Law—but against the attitude of that man who wants to pass muster before God on his own strength. If Mundle protests that faith's act of obedience "involves a certain measure of activity on man's own part," it must be said that faith, as decision, is even preeminently the deed of man; but Mundle overlooks the distinction between "deed" and "work," with which the analysis of the term "faith" will deal (§ 35).

"Righteousness," then, has its origin in God's grace—i.e. in His act of grace accomplished in Christ. "Grace" can mean simply to be graciously disposed toward another. The extent to which "grace" surpasses this meaning and means a deed or event—eschatological in either case—will soon be discussed in greater detail (§ 32). But it is already apparent at this point that God in His grace acts as the absolutely free God who has not been brought into debt by any human claim and who acts, therefore, as "the gracious One" in a radical sense. To the extent that a man wishes by his own accomplishment to have a boast before God, he brings divine grace to naught for himself. The receipt of grace presupposes on the contrary that man be utterly brought to naught; it is just the sinner to whose lot it falls. This meaning of grace is clearly corroborated by the passages in which Paul speaks of the grace of God at work in his own person, I Cor. 15:9f.: he, "the least of the apostles," the erstwhile persecutor of God's Church, says of himself: "by the grace of God I am what I am, and his grace toward me was not in vain. On the contrary, I worked harder than any of them, though it was not I but the grace of God which is with me" that worked. Recall, further, II Cor. 12:9, where Paul reports a word that the Lord had imparted to him: "My grace is sufficient for you, for power is made perfect in weakness" (omitting "my" before "power" with Nestle).

God's grace, therefore, is not His kindliness and goodness which cause Him to take man's weakness into account and, in view of his endeavor toward the good, to excuse an occasional mistake, or even many, to forgive small sins, or even great ones. On the contrary, that endeavor is exactly what the grace of God repudiates—for in it is just where man's sin of sins lurks, his arrogance, his fooling himself that he can live on his own. And however much this man may be struggling, fighting with himself, pleadingly looking for divine help and redemption, even so the grace of God comes to him, not as approval of his striving and a prop for his failing strength, but as the decisive question: Will you surrender, utterly surrender, to God's dealing—will you know yourself to be a sinner before God?

3. The reason why "righteousness" is called "*God's righteousness*" is just this: Its one and only foundation is God's grace—it is God-given, God-adjudicated righteousness (Rom. 1:17; 3:21f., 26; 10:3). The meaning of this phrase (i.e. the classification of the genitive as a genitive of the author) is unequivocally determined by Rom. 10:3: "For, being ignorant of the righteousness *that comes from God,* and seeking to establish *their own,* they (the Jews) did not submit to *God's* righteousness," and Phil. 3:9: "not having a righteousness *of my own,* based on law, but that which is through faith in Christ, the righteousness *from God* that depends on faith." As "their own" or "my own" means the righteousness which man exerts himself to achieve by fulfilling the "works of the Law," so "God's righteousness" means the righteousness from God which is conferred upon him as a gift by God's free grace alone.

In the New Testament, outside of Paul, the expression "righteousness of God" occurs at Jas. 1:20 and II Pet. 1:1. In the former of the two it means "what is right in God's eyes." This is the meaning the rabbis gave to the "righteousness of Jahweh" at Deut. 33:21 (though some interpreted it as an act of beneficence such as Yahweh does). Here, then, the term is used in the ethical sense, not in the forensic one. In the other passage, the word is used in an indeterminate and formula-like fashion in the salutation-formula: "To those who have obtained a faith of equal standing with ours in the righteousness of our God and Savior Jesus Christ." Here *dikaiosyne* appears to be the "distributive justice" which apportions to each his due, and the genitives apparently are subjective genitives.

§ 31. Reconciliation

Another term can be substituted for the term "righteousness" (or the cognate verb) as the designation of the new situation which God Himself has opened up to man: "reconciliation" (or the cognate verb—καταλλαγή and καταλλαγῆναι). Examination of Paul's statements on "righteousness" and of those on "reconciliation" results in mutual corroboration. Since "we have peace with God" (Rom. 5:1) means the same as if Paul had said "we are reconciled," and is a result of "being rightwised," then strictly speaking "reconciliation" is a consequence of "righteousness." But in point of fact "we have peace" only unfolds the meaning of "righteousness": "as rightwised men we have peace with God." So in Rom. 5:9, "we are rightwised" from v. 1 is picked up again and in vv. 10f. is paraphrased in the words, "For if while we were enemies we were *reconciled* to God . . ." and "much more, now that we are *reconciled* . . ." Just as "rightwising" is effected through Christ (Rom. 3:24), Christ is he "through whom we have now received our *reconciliation*" (5:11). The winning of the heathen world to the gospel can be equally well described as "the reconciliation of the world" (11:15) or by saying: "the Gentiles . . . have attained . . . righteousness" (9:30). The gospel, through which the "righteousness of God" is revealed (Rom. 1:16f.) is also called "the message of reconciliation" (II Cor. 5:19), and the office of its proclaimer is called both "ministry of righteousness" (II Cor. 3:9 Blt.) and "ministry of reconciliation" (II Cor. 5:18). The man of faith "receives" reconciliation (Rom. 5:11) as he "receives" righteousness (5:17).

The use of the word "reconciliation" makes clear that a complete reversal of the relation between God and men has taken place. Hitherto, men had been "enemies" of God (Rom. 5:10), which can have either active meaning—"hostile" (Rom. 8:7), or passive—"hated" (Rom. 5:10; 11:28); the connection between the two meanings is indicated by Rom. 8:7f.: the latter is the consequence of the former. The reversal of this relation takes place, as II Cor. 5:19 indicates, by God's not counting men's sins against them; and this takes place—quite as being "rightwised" does—not because of any human deed or attitude, but on God's own initiative: "all this has its origin in God who through Christ reconciled us to himself" (II Cor. 5:18). We were reconciled with God "while we were (still) enemies" (Rom. 5:10; *cf.* v. 6)! That is, the "reconciliation" precedes any effort—indeed any knowledge—on man's part, and "reconciliation" does not mean a subjective process within man but an objective factual situation brought about by God. All man can do is to "receive" the reconciliation (Rom. 5:11); therefore, at the same time God set up reconciliation He also set up the "ministry" or the "message" of reconciliation, and men are invited henceforth on their side **to** accomplish the subjective alteration in themselves: "be reconciled to God" (II Cor. 5:20). The "word of reconciliation," then, is not the conciliatory and reconciling word but the proclamation of the already accomplished reconciliation, and "be reconciled" is the invitation to faith. God's "reconciling" is His restoration of peace by no longer letting His "wrath" (§ 32, 1) prevail. One might almost say that in using the term "reconciliation" Paul's intention to show man's radical dependence upon the grace of God is still more clearly expressed than when he uses the term "righteousness of God," for while the latter means that *without* our doing anything we arrive at "peace" with God (Rom. 5:1), the former means that *before* any effort of man God made an end of enmity (Rom. 5:10). But in substance, of course, there is no difference: both "without us" and "before us" intend to declare the absolute priority of God.

The old question, "How is God to be reconciled?" is wrongly put. Naturally all pagan notions that men must do something to reconcile (propitiate) God, are far from Paul's thought. It never occurs to him at all that *God* needed to be reconciled; it is *men* who receive the reconciliation which God has conferred —not by removing their subjective resentment toward Him but by removing the objective state of enmity which, in consequence of sins, existed between Him and men.

It is noteworthy that Paul hardly ever speaks of the "forgiveness of sins," which plays so large a role in the earliest Christian preaching (§ 13, 1) and soon reappears in deutero-Pauline literature (Col. 1:14; Eph. 1:7), though he does describe God the reconciler as "not counting their trespasses." Only in the quotation from Ps. 32:1 do we encounter: "Blessed are they whose iniquities are forgiven" (Rom. 4:7); and only in Rom. 3:25 does he speak of God's "passing over former sins," a phrase probably based on a traditional formula (§ 7, 3). His avoidance of the term "forgiveness of sins" (which is connected with his avoidance of the term "repentance," § 35, 1) is evidently due to the fact that "forgiveness of sin" is insofar ambiguous as it seems to declare only release from the guilt contracted by "former sins," whereas the important thing for Paul is release from *sinning*, release from the power of sin (§ 38).

B. GRACE

§ 32. Grace as Event

1. God's "grace" is not a quality, not His timeless kindliness (§ 30, 2), and what the gospel brings is not enlightenment as to God's hitherto misunderstood nature as if till now He had been wrongly conceived as wrathful and ought henceforth to be regarded as gracious. On the contrary! Now, as then, "*God's wrath*" pours out "against all ungodliness and wickedness of men" (Rom. 1:18). Paul warns the unrepentant: "you are storing up wrath for yourself on the day of wrath when God's righteous judgment will be revealed" (Rom. 2:5; *cf.* 2:8). "To inflict wrath" belongs inherently to God's "faithfulness," "truthfulness," and judicial "justice" (Rom. 3:3–6). God continues to be the Judge, and Christian faith in the grace of God does not consist in the conviction that God's wrath does not exist or that there is no threateningly impending judgment (II Cor. 5:10), but in the conviction of being rescued from God's wrath: "Since, therefore, we are now justified (rightwised) by his blood, much more shall we be saved by him from the wrath of God" (Rom. 5:9; I Thess. 1:10; 5:9).

That misunderstanding, however, is based upon the false notion that *God's wrath* is a quality, an emotion, wrathfulness—a notion against which the ancient Church, under the influence of Stoic thinking, thought it had to defend God. In reality "wrath of God" means an occurrence, viz. *the judgment of God.* God is He who "inflicts wrath" (Rom. 3:5); when the "wrath of God" is said to be "revealed" (Rom. 1:18), that does not refer to a didactic communication about it but to its becoming effective (§ 29, 1). When the "wrath of God" is described (Rom. 1:18–32), it is shown to be identical with that which factually already takes place in the heathen world: abandonment to the "lusts of their hearts" (v. 24), to "dishonorable passions" (v. 26), to a "base mind" (i.e. corrupted intent, v. 28). The "day of wrath" is "the day when God's righteous judgment will be revealed," the future judgment day (Rom. 2:5). "Wrath" as the verdict of condemnation has its counterpart in the gift of "eternal life" (Rom. 2:7f.) or of "salvation" (I Thess. 5:9). The "wrath" of Rom. 5:9 and I Thess. 1:10 is likewise the punishment (soon) to take place. Though for the most part the future judgment is meant (*cf.* in addition Rom. 9:22), Rom. 1:18–32 means the judgment that is constantly taking place; so does Rom. 13:4f. where governmental authority is called "the servant of God to execute wrath (= punishment) on the wrong-doer" and the Christian is exhorted to practice civil obedience not only "on account of wrath (i.e. punishment)." "Wrath" without temporal limitation means divine punishment: Rom. 4:15, "for the law brings wrath"; Rom. 12:19 probably has the same meaning: "leave it to the wrath (of God)" (rather than KJ: "give place unto wrath").

The above observations yield two insights for the understanding of "*grace*": 1. God's grace is not His hitherto unknown or misconceived graciousness, but is His now occurring act of grace. 2. This act of grace does not, as it might seem, take the place of God's previous judgeship, but is His gracious dealing precisely as the Judge. God's "wrath" continues to be at work and will soon take effect decisively and definitively on the "day of wrath" (Rom. 2:5) as certainly as God is the Judge who is to be feared (Rom. 11:20; II Cor. 5:10f.; Phil. 2:12; see § 35, 4). The "grace of God" is the grace of the judge who "rightwises" the guilty (§ 30, 2).

2. The grace of God, as His judicial act of grace, can be still more precisely defined: It is not a mode of dealing which God has decided henceforth to adopt, but is *a single deed* which takes effect for everyone who recognizes it as such and acknowledges it (in faith)—"grace" is *God's eschatological deed.*

When Rom. 3:24 says of "rightwised" men, "they are rightwised by his (God's) grace as a gift," the word δωρεάν (gratis, without price, in the manner of a gift) emphasizes the gift-character of grace; grace itself is the act of grace which is described in the following words: "the redemption which is in Christ Jesus, whom God put forward as an expiation by his blood, to be received by faith." That is, God's deed of grace consists in the fact that He gave Christ up to die—to die as a propitiatory sacrifice for the sins of men. The *deed of God* "who gave him (his Son) up for us all" (Rom. 8:32) has its analogue in the "obedience" of the Son "who gave himself for me" (Gal. 2:20) and was "obedient unto death" (Phil. 2:8). Therefore, just this *occurrence of Christ's obedience* (which Paul contrasts with Adam's "disobedience" or calls Christ's "act of righteousness" in contrast to Adam's "trespass," Rom. 5:15–21) can also be regarded as the "deed of grace." As the occurrence of Adam's fall brought death over mankind, so the occurrence of Christ's obedience brought life, and the latter occurrence constitutes "grace," which instead of the usual word (χάρις) can also be called χάρισμα (gift of grace) because it is for the benefit of men (Rom. 5:15f.). The divine deed of grace is, as such, a *gift* of grace—the gift which is the event that takes place in Christ's obedience. Therefore Paul can equate "the grace of God" and "the free gift in the grace of that one man Jesus Christ" (Rom. 5:15) or speak of "the abundance of grace and the free gift of righteousness . . . through the one man Jesus Christ" (Rom. 5:17).

In one passage the thing emphasized may be that "grace" is the deed of God or Christ, in another that it is the occurrence which is bestowed upon men as a gift, in a third both emphases may meet, but in every case the same deed, the identical occurrence is meant. In II Cor. 6:1 when Paul urges the reader "not to accept the grace of God in vain," what he means by "grace" is that deed of God (*cf.* 5:21) which is at the same time the deed of Christ (5:14f.: "he died for all"); but simultaneously "grace" here means the gift which man must "accept" as in Paul's expression (I Cor. 2:12) for God's saving deed: "the gifts bestowed on us by God." In II Cor. 8:9 he reminds his readers of the event of salvation as the deed of Christ: "For you know the grace (i.e. gracious *deed*) of our Lord Jesus Christ, that though he was rich, yet for your sake he became poor" (in which, of course, he has in mind all that is said in Phil. 2:6–8). And "God's (deed of) grace" which he declares he does not "nullify" (Gal. 2:21) consists of just that deed of Christ described in the preceding verse: "who loved me and gave himself for me."

Because this deed or occurrence is the decisive eschatological event in which the time of salvation, "the acceptable time" (II Cor. 6:1), has dawned, therefore grace may be spoken of as a personified power which works against the power of sin and takes over its lost command: "but where sin increased, grace abounded all the more, so that, as sin (had) reigned in death, grace also might reign through righteousness to eternal life through Jesus Christ our Lord" (Rom. 5:20f.). The meaning of "grace" approaches actual identity with that of "spirit" (see § 38, 2f. and *cf.* above § 14, 1). That is the reason that *the new situation* into which men of faith—they who have received the Spirit (Gal. 4:6, etc.)—are put can also be called "grace"; here "grace" means the territory of the divine deed's sway. The Christian is called "to grace" (Gal. 1:6) and "stands" in it

(Rom. 5:2); he must beware not to "fall out of grace" (Gal. 5:4). Thus, Paul can address the Philippians as "partakers with me of grace" (Phil. 1:7; i.e. my fellow-participants in grace—unless "grace" is here used in a narrower sense, meaning the shared grace of suffering bestowed upon both Paul and the Philippians. (*Cf.* v. 29.)

Even where "grace" does not mean the eschatological occurrence, it still mean's God's gracious deed or dealing which man experiences as a gift. Combined with "peace" (= salvation!) in the greetings at the beginning or end of the epistles, "grace" is that which God does and confers for salvation.

The apostle's office committed to Paul as a gift—but also as a commission to be fulfilled—can be called a "grace," i.e. a gift: Rom. 1:5; 12:3; 15:15; I Cor. 3:10 (see RSV!); Gal. 2:9. Gal. 2:8 ("for he who worked through Peter . . . worked through me also") shows how much the "grace" of the following verse denotes God's working through Paul; Rom. 15:18 ("For I will not venture to speak of anything except what Christ has wrought through me") is the same kind of commentary to Rom. 15:15. The exercise of the Christian obligation to love is likewise a "gift" of God, a "grace": II Cor. 8:1, 4, 6f., 19; and so, in the end, is every manifestation of Christian living: I Cor. 1:4; II Cor. 9:8 and 8:7. Special gifts given to individuals are called *charismata*: Rom. 12:6; I Cor. 7:7. *Charis* is contained in both the word and the idea; that this *charis* means the mighty working of God is abundantly attested by the synonymity of *charismata* (gifts of grace) and *pneumatika* (spiritual gifts; see § 14, 1) and by the remark which refers to the latter: "it is the same God who inspires (lit. effects) them all in every one" (I Cor. 12:6).

The following passages, especially, indicate that God's "grace" is a power that determines the life of the individual: I Cor. 15:10 ("by the grace of God I am what I am"), II Cor. 1:12; 12:9 ("My grace is sufficient for you"). I Cor. 15:10 and II Cor. 12:9 particularly show that "grace" and "power" (§ 14, 1) can be synonymous.

3. In the same way as Paul speaks of "grace" and with the same meaning, he can speak of (God's or Christ's) *agape* (love); therefore, a consideration of his statements about *agape* confirms our treatment of "grace." It may be that in *agape* the sentiment (of love) is emphasized more than in the case of "grace"; but Paul

speaks of *agape* as it reveals itself in a deed, *agape at work, in action.* When he says in Rom. 5:8, "God shows his love for us in that while we were yet sinners Christ died for us," *agape* certainly has, as part of its meaning, the sentiment of love, but Paul speaks of it only as God "shows" it—by letting Christ die for us. V. 5 must be interpreted similarly: ". . . because God's love (subjective genitive!) has been poured into our hearts through the Holy Spirit which has been given us": through the Holy Spirit, God's deed of love, which v. 6f. describes as being the deed of Christ, attains certainty and effectiveness for us. The question of Rom. 8:35: "Who shall separate us from the love of Christ?" refers in its word "love" to the salvation-occurrence named in the preceding verse—the death and resurrection of Christ. Christ is "he who loved us," and his "love" consisted in giving himself up to death (Rom. 8:35; Gal. 2:20). And the identity of God's deed with Christ's deed is expressed in Paul's assurance that nothing will be able to separate us from "God's love (i.e. deed of love) in Christ Jesus our Lord"—in other words, from the salvation which God brought about through Christ (Rom. 8:39). When II Cor. 5:14 says that we are "controlled" by the love of Christ (subjective genitive!), this love is paraphrased in the next clause as Christ's "dying for all." Here *agape*, like *charis*, is also represented as a personified power.

Like "grace," "love" also appears occasionally in formula-like expressions, sometimes taking the place of "grace" (II Cor. 13:11: "the God of love and peace will be with you"), sometimes combined with it (II Cor. 13:14: "the grace of the Lord Jesus Christ, and the love of God . . . be with you all"). In such cases, *agape* like *charis* means all that God has done or bestowed for salvation. The activity of the Holy Spirit for salvation is termed "love" when Paul makes an appeal (Rom. 15:30) "by our Lord Jesus Christ and by the love of the Spirit."

§ 33. Christ's Death and Resurrection as Salvation-occurrence

1. The deed of divine grace consists in the fact that God gave Christ up to die on the cross (§ 32, 2); Christ is preached as "the crucified" (I Cor. 1:23; 2:2; Gal. 3:1). Therefore, the gospel can be called the "word of the cross" (I Cor. 1:18), a "stumbling-block" (Gal. 5:11) to natural man, or a "stumbling-block and folly" (I Cor.

1:23). The enemies of the gospel are "enemies of the cross of Christ" (Phil. 3:18; *cf.* I Cor. 1:17; Gal. 6:12). But the death and the resurrection of Christ are bound together in the unity of one salvation-occurrence: "he who died" is also "he who was raised up" (Rom. 8:34; II Cor. 5:15; 13:4), and it may also happen that Paul refers to the resurrection alone without mentioning the cross (I Thess. 1:10; I Cor. 6:14; II Cor. 4:14; Rom. 1:4; 8:11; 10:9) and terms God accordingly "he who raised him from the dead" (see references in § 9, 4, p. 80f.)

The salvation-occurrence, then, includes the death and the resurrection of Jesus. Such was the tradition that Paul had received (I Cor. 15:1–4), and such was the tradition that he passed on. He is quoting or paraphrasing statements of tradition which were obviously more or less definitely formulated when he speaks of Jesus' death (Rom. 3:24f.; § 7, 3, p. 46) or his resurrection (Rom. 1:4; 10:9; § 7, 3, p. 49; § 9, 4, p. 80), or of both together (Rom. 4:25; I Cor. 15:3f.; § 7, 3, p. 46; § 9, 4, p. 82; § 7, 3, p. 44) also, of course, when he speaks of baptism (Rom. 6:2–5, § 13, 1, p. 140f.) or of the Lord's Supper (I Cor. 11:23–26), the celebration of which "proclaims" Christ's death (§ 13, 2, p. 148). Strictly speaking, the incarnation is also a part of that one salvation-process; for he who gave himself up to die is no other than the pre-existent Son of God (Phil. 2:6ff.; II Cor. 8:9; Rom. 15:3; § 12, 3, p. 128f., p. 131). Yet the incarnation is never accorded a meaning independent from the crucifixion; rather it and his death are bound together in Christ's total deed (active and passive) in which his "obedience" took place (Phil. 2:8; Rom. 5:19). It plays a separate role only in the hint (I Cor. 2:8; § 15, 4c) that the demonic cosmic powers were deceived by the redeemer's human disguise. However, this motif does not belong to the actual proclamation, the "word of the cross," but belongs in the area of a "wisdom" intended for the "perfect" (I Cor. 2:6 KJ).

Jesus' death-and-resurrection, then, is for Paul the decisive thing about the person of Jesus and his life experience, indeed, in the last analysis it is the sole thing of importance for him—implicitly included are the incarnation and the earthly life of Jesus as bare facts. That is, Paul is interested only in the *fact* that Jesus became man and lived on earth. *How* he was born or lived interests him only to the extent of knowing that Jesus was a definite, concrete man, a Jew, "being born in the likeness of man and being found in human form" (Phil. 2:7), "born of woman, born under the law" (Gal. 4:4). But beyond that, Jesus' manner of life, his ministry, his personality, his character play no role at all; neither does Jesus' message (§ 16). To Paul, Jesus is not the teacher and prophet. It is true that as the exalted Lord he is also the law-giver of the Church (I Cor. 7:10f., *cf.* v. 25, 9:14) and Paul accompanies his exhortations with appeals to the authority of "the Lord" (I Thess. 4:1f.; Rom. 15:30; I Cor. 1:10). But Paul is not thinking of the historical Jesus here. Nor is he when he refers to Christ's example (Phil. 2:5ff.; II Cor. 8:9; Rom. 15:3); for in these cases he means the pre-existent Christ, and his appeal to the "meekness and gentleness of Christ" (II Cor. 10:1) is precisely an appeal to him who "emptied himself," "humbled himself," "became poor," "did not please himself."

It is self-evident that neither for Paul nor for the earliest Jerusalem Church (§ 5, 3) did Jesus and his passion and death appear in a heroic light like the heroes of the hero-cults. Likewise, every sort of pietistic-edifying absorption in a contemplation of the passion is unknown to him; and when he says he has "publicly portrayed" Christ as crucified "before the eyes" of the Galatians (Gal. 3:1), he means nothing else than the preaching of the "word of the cross" as the fact of salvation. By human norms, the cross cannot be recognized as the fact of salvation, but remains a "stumbling-block" and "folly." Any "evaluation" of the historical person Jesus according to human categories would be a *kata sarka* (flesh-wise) regarding of Christ and hence would mean seeing him as a "*kata sarka* Christ" (§ 22, 3).

2. It is clear that the salvation-occurrence, viz. Christ's death and resurrection, is the deed of the prevenient grace of God; and that the various expressions which describe this deed intend to express its unprecedented nature and its might which so radically transformed the human situation. It is an occurrence purely by God's initiative; for man, pure gift; by accepting it he is released from his perverse striving to achieve life or self-hood by his own efforts—in which he does the very opposite—only to be given it as a gift in the "righteousness of God."

The question now is *how can this occurrence be recognized and experienced by man as the deed of grace?* For only then can it take effect as a compelling and transforming power, when it can be

understood as directed at man, reaching him, happening to him—
i.e. when the challenge to accept it as salvation-occurrence thrusts
him into genuine decision. So far as it is an event that God causes
to occur to the pre-existent son of God, it seems to take place in a
mythical sphere outside the realm of human experience.

Let it be granted that there is a difference between this and the
salvation-occurrences related by the myth of the mystery-religions
and by Gnosticism: Here the subject is an historical person, Jesus,
and his death on the cross only a few years earlier is at the center
of the salvation-occurrence. Still, how is one to recognize that this
death has such vast significance? Is it so important because a pre-
existent divine being died it? If so, then does not faith in the saving
significance of this death presuppose a previous faith that Jesus is
the incarnate son of God? And if faith in salvation by Jesus is only
made complete by faith in the resurrection, does that not also demand a previous faith? For the resurrection, of course, simply cannot be a visible fact in the realm of human history. When Paul is
pushed to do so by Gnosticizing objections to belief in any resurrection whatever, he does, I grant, think he can guarantee the resurrection of Christ as an objective fact by listing the witnesses who
had seen him risen (I Cor. 15:5–8, § 15, 2).* But is such a proof
convincing?

3a. In order to describe the significance of the salvation-occurrence, Paul uses a series of terms originating in a number of different
thought-complexes. One group is composed of the statements which
understand Jesus' death in terms of Jewish sacrificial practice—and
that also means in terms of the juristic thinking that dominated it—
regarding his death as a propitiatory sacrifice by which forgiveness
of sins is brought about; which is to say: by which the guilt contracted by sins is canceled. Jesus' death is the "*hilasterion* in his
blood," the means of reconciliation efficacious through his blood, by
which God, to prove that He is a righteous judge, made possible the
"passing over of previously committed sins" (Rom. 3:25f. tr.). The
same thought occurs tersely formulated in Rom. 5:9: "justified
(rightwised) now by his blood." The liturgy of the Lord's Supper

---

* It has been denied, I know, (by K. Barth) that the listing of the witnesses
has this meaning; the contention is that it only intends to guarantee the identity
of Paul's message with that of the earliest Jerusalem Church. Undoubtedly that
is one of its purposes (v. 11); nevertheless, its primary purpose is the one indicated above.

in I Cor. 11:24f. (§ 9, 4, p. 84) is likewise governed by the conception of Jesus' death as a propitiatory sacrifice merged with a conception of it as a covenant sacrifice. The propitiatory idea is also behind the passages in which Jesus is described as he who died "for our sins" (I Cor. 15:3; II Cor. 5:14) or simply died "for us" (Rom. 5:6, 8; 14:15; I Thess. 5:10; *cf.* I Cor. 1:13), or he who was "given up" or "gave himself up" for us (Rom. 4:25; 8:32; Gal. 1:4; 2:20).

In all these cases, Paul is following a tradition which probably originated in the earliest Church (§ 7, 3) and, at any rate, was widespread in Hellenistic Christianity (§ 9, 4); Paul is in part quoting or paraphrasing the crystallized formulations of this tradition (see above under 1). At any rate, the above passages do not contain Paul's characteristic view. Neither does the only once-suggested thought (I Cor. 5:7) that Jesus' death is a passover-sacrifice, in Jewish eyes a sin-removing sacrifice. The same is true of the covenant-sacrifice idea that we find woven into the eucharistic liturgy (I Cor. 11:25).

(b) Closely related to the idea of propitiatory sacrifice is that of *vicarious sacrifice*, which likewise has its origin in the field of cultic-juristic thinking (§ 7, 3). The same phrase (ὑπὲρ ἡμῶν) that is translated "for us" can also express this idea, meaning now: "instead of us," "in place of us." Thus: Gal. 3:13, "becoming a curse in our stead" (tr. *cf.* Goodspeed); II Cor. 5:21: "he made him who was unacquainted with sin to be sin in our stead" (tr. §29, 2). The idea is probably also present in Rom. 8:3: "having sent his own son (clad) in (our) self-same, sin-ruled flesh and (sent him) to take sin's place, God (in condemning Christ to die) condemned (our) sin (= Christ) in the flesh (he shared with us)" (tr.). The ideas of vicarious and propitiatory sacrifice merge in II Cor. 5:14f. V. 14b, "therefore all have died," interprets the phrase in 14a εἷς ὑπὲρ πάντων ἀπέθανεν (which could mean either "one died *for the sake of all*" or "one died *taking the place of all*") as having the vicarious meaning: "one died in the place of all, therefore all have (vicariously) died." But in v. 15 the ὑπέρ in "he died ὑπέρ all" means "for the sake of"—contains, in other words, the propitiatory idea. But still another conception of Christ's death plays a part here—the conception, soon to be treated (see "e" below), that it was a cosmic event, for within the conception of vicarious representation "all have died" can only mean "all *are regarded as dead*," but by analogy with

Rom. 6:3, 5 this certainly also means in the mind of Paul: "all *are* dead."

(c) The vicarious death of Christ, according to Gal. 3:13, is the means by which men are "*redeemed*" (ransomed)—redeemed, that is, from the "curse of the Law"—and that evidently means from the punishment imposed upon sin (which is here equated with transgression of the Law). This view agrees with the statements containing the propitiatory sacrifice idea in this: the sacrifice cancels guilt or the punishment for guilt. Nevertheless, that is not the full extent of the thought, for it is scarcely permissible to isolate Gal. 3:13 from 4:4f. What the latter passage names as the means to "redemption is not Jesus' death, it is true; yet it does name his humanity and his subjection to the Law—and in these his death is involved. But here, according to the context, the resulting freedom (here = "adoption as sons") is not considered to be freedom from the punishment contracted by transgressing the Law, but freedom from the Law itself. Into this same context one must probably bring, finally, Gal. 1:4; here the purpose attributed to Christ's death is: "to deliver us from the present evil age." The "present age" is subject to the Law and because of that is subject to the power of sin and death. Hence the freedom bought by Christ's death is not only freedom from punishment but freedom from those "powers" (sin and death) and thereby is freedom not only from the guilt of sin but above all from sin as a power—i.e. freedom from the compulsion to sin. This interpretation is confirmed by the statement in I Cor. 6:20 and 7:23: "you were bought with a price," which in the context of 6:12–20 means: to freedom from sin; and in the context of 7:17–24: to freedom from men—i.e. from the standards and evaluations which prevail in this sin-dominated age.

For Paul, that takes care of the question to whom the τιμή (price or payment) earned by Christ's death was paid: It was paid to those powers who lay claim to man who has fallen into their grasp, primarily the Law. The expression is figurative, and the mythological idea of a bargain with the Devil is far from Paul's thought.

The essential thing, then, is that here the categories of cultic-juristic thinking are broken through: *Christ's death* is not merely a sacrifice which cancels the guilt of sin (i.e. the punishment contracted by sinning), but is also *the means of release from the powers of this age: Law, Sin, and Death.*

(d) The question then arises how Christ's death can have such an effect. It finds an answer in the statements in which *Paul describes Christ's death in analogy with the death of a divinity of the mystery religions.* This view, too, which had attached itself to the initiation-sacrament of baptism and which lay behind the sacrament of the Lord's Supper (§ 13, 1 and 2, p. 140–142; 147f.), had already come down to Paul out of tradition. But he gave it a new, more comprehensive meaning. The original meaning is, as we have seen, that participation in the fate of the mystery-divinity through baptism and sacramental communion grants the *mystes* (initiate) participation in both the dying and the reviving of the divinity; such participation, that is, by leading the *mystes* into death delivers him from death. One could have a good statement of this general conception by altering the words of Rom. 6:10—and applying them both to the god and to his initiate—to read: "The death he died he died *to death* once for all." Only Paul says ". . . he died to sin . . ."! That applies primarily to Christ, but for that very reason (v. 11) it also applies to those who are baptized "into his death" (v. 3). To Paul, release from death is simultaneously—no, primarily—release from the power of sin. What is true of baptism is, of course, also true of the Lord's Supper, even though Paul—following the traditional liturgy—does not expressly say so, but only points out that the rite "proclaims" Christ's death—i.e. both proclaims it and grants the participants a share in Christ's death (I Cor. 11:26).

(e) But Paul expands the mystery idea. He does so by simultaneously interpreting Christ's death *in the categories of the Gnostic myth,* regarding his death as unified with his incarnation and resurrection or exaltation. In so doing he is again following a tradition that is to be inferred as having existed in Hellenistic Christianity before him, inasmuch as he cites the Christ-hymn (Phil. 2:6–11) in which that tradition had taken form (§ 15, 4c and d). The Gnostic myth, in itself, contains only the notion of the Redeemer's coming and going as his humiliation and exaltation, not necessarily implying that his departure from the earth is caused by a violent death. It is plausible to assume that that mystery-conception (d, above) readily combined with the Gnostic myth in certain Gnostic groups organized as mystery-cults. In one such group, for example, the mystery-god Attis had coalesced with the Gnostic Redeemer-figure. At any rate, such a combination is present in Paul.

Now, for the Gnostic view it is an essential presupposition that men (or, rather, the Gnostics among men) together with the Redeemer constitute a unity. This unity is conceived in terms of substance: they and he belong to *one soma* (body). Just as the Redeemer himself is a cosmic figure and not really an individual person, so is his *soma* a cosmic entity (§ 15, 1 and 4d, p. 166, 178). What happens to the Redeemer, or happened while he tarried in human form on earth, happens to his whole *soma*—i.e. not to him alone but to all who belong to that *soma*. So if he suffered death, the same is true of them (II Cor. 5:14). If he was raised from the dead, the same is true of them (I Cor. 15:20–22). And just as his return to the heavenly home as the "redeemed Redeemer" means his release from the sinister powers that rule this world below, likewise they who are bound up with him into one body share in this release or "redemption."

It is in this light that Paul sees baptism. According to I Cor. 12:13 it unites the baptized with Christ into one *soma*. By baptism into his death we who have faith are "grown together" with him (Rom. 6:5). That is why the believer's whole life is stamped by Christ's death, but also by his resurrection. As Jesus' dying continues to occur in the apostle's body, so Jesus' life also lives in it (II Cor. 4:7–12; *cf.* 1:5). But this is by no means true for the apostle only, but for all believers, as Phil. 3:10f. shows. Here Paul only takes himself as one example among the many when he describes the goal of faith to be "that I may know him and the power of his resurrection and may share his sufferings, becoming like him in his death, that if possible I may attain the resurrection from the dead."

Christ's death and resurrection, accordingly, are cosmic occurrences, not incidents that took place once upon a time in the past. By them the old aeon along with its powers has been basically stripped of power. Its powers are already "destroyed" (κατεργού-μενοι, I Cor. 2:6), even though the life of the believer is not yet visible in the present but is hidden under the mask of death (II Cor. 4:7–12). For the present is only a short interval: "the time is short" (I Cor. 7:29 KJ; perhaps more literally: "the allotted time has shrunk together," tr.) . . . "for the form of this world (= this world itself) is passing away" (I Cor. 7:31). Therefore, Paul can also triumphantly say: "the old has passed away, behold the new has come" (II Cor. 5:17). As the first Adam ushered in the old mankind, so Christ, the "last Adam," ushered in the new. As the old, Adamitic mankind received its stamp from the transitory, earthly first parent who had brought sin and death into the world, so the new received its stamp from Christ, who, through his obedience (in becoming man and dying) and his resurrection, brought life and freedom from the annihilating powers (Rom. 5:12–19; I Cor. 15:21f., 44–49).

4. Clearly Paul found none of these thought-complexes and none of their terminologies adequate to express his understanding of the salvation-occurrence. Why did he not confine himself to presenting the significance of Jesus' death in the categories of Jewish cultic and juristic thinking? Because in them the meaning of the resurrection had no chance to come into its rightful place. Why did he, rather, also resort to the categories of the mysteries and the Gnostic myth? He obviously did so because through them the salvation-occurrence could be interpreted as happening actually to and for and in man. But in regard to all his formulations must not the question be raised whether the hearer of such a message must not have a preliminary conviction that Jesus Christ is by nature the pre-existent Son of God, that he became man and rose from the dead, if he is to believe in the saving significance of these events—especially in the saving significance of the sole objectively tangible fact: his death? What justification is there for demanding such a preliminary faith to serve as the necessary basis for actual salvation-faith?

If, simply copying, one reproduces the statements of Paul, it becomes evident, therefore, that, in reality, *two acts of faith or belief and consequently also two concepts of faith-belief* must be distinguished. The first is belief (in the narrower popular use of the English word): willingness to consider true (= believe) the facts reported of the pre-existent Son of God—incarnation, crucifixion, resurrection from the dead—and to see in them a demonstration of the grace of God. The second is a faith which is self-surrender to the grace of God and which signifies the utter reversal of a man's previous understanding of himself—specifically, the radical surrender of his human "boasting."

A homogeneous concept of faith-belief and a single decisive act of faith-belief would be detectable only if the decision-question whether a man is willing to give up his old understanding of himself and henceforth understand himself only from the grace of God and the question whether he will acknowledge Jesus Christ as the Son of God and Lord should turn out to be one and the same question. That is just what they evidently are in the real intention of Paul.

5. At any rate, one thing is clear: Paul can speak of Christ as "the Son of God who loved me and gave himself up for me" only as the Paul who has waived his own righteousness and given up his self (his ἐγώ) to die (Gal. 2:19f.; Phil. 3:4–11). He knows of that Christ only by knowing himself anew in the same act of recognition. From the outset, Paul, the "zealot" for the "traditions of the fathers" (Gal. 1:14), understood the proclamation of Christ the Son of God and Lord when it reached him as the demand that he give up his former sort of "zeal for God" (Rom. 10:2; § 16). It was as such a demand that he passed on the proclamation of Christ, not as "wisdom-discourse" (σοφία λόγου, I Cor. 1:17)—instruction like that of the mysteries concerning mythical events and metaphysical entities—but as the "word of the cross," which to natural man is a "scandal" and "folly": "so that no human being might boast in the presence of God" (I Cor. 1:18–31) and as the "word of reconciliation" (II Cor. 5:18–6:2 KJ), face to face with which there can be no "boasting over externals" (II Cor. 5:12, tr.).

It accords with the above that in Romans, where Paul is connectedly presenting the main ideas of his message to a hitherto unknown congregation in order to legitimate himself as a genuine apostle, he—unlike the Hermetic tractates with their initial cosmological teachings—does not first present the salvation-occurrence, the credibility of which would first have to be acknowledged. Instead he begins by exposing the plight of mankind, so that then the proclamation of God's salvation-deed becomes a decision-question. In keeping with this is the train of thought in Rom. 7:7–8:11: after man-under-the-Law has been made to see his situation under it as that of the "miserable wretch" groaning for deliverance from the "body of death," he can then see the salvation-occurrence as salvation-bringing.

But if it is true that the proclamation of the salvation-occurrence is not a preparatory instruction which precedes the actual demand for faith, but is, in itself, the call for faith or the challenge to give up one's previous self-understanding or the cry, "Be reconciled to God!"

—if that is so, then that means that *the salvation-occurrence is nowhere present except in the proclaiming, accosting, demanding, and promising word of preaching*. A merely "reminiscent" historical account referring to what happened in the past cannot make the salvation-occurrence visible. It means that the salvation-occurrence continues to take place in the proclamation of the word. The salvation-occurrence is eschatological occurrence just in this fact, that it does not become a fact of the past but constantly takes place anew in the present. It is present not in the after-effect of a significant fact of world-history but in the proclamation of the word, which, unlike world events, does not get absorbed into the evolution of the human mind. Paul expresses this by saying that at the same time that God instituted reconciliation He also instituted the "ministry of reconciliation" which is the "message (lit. "word," KJ) of reconciliation" (II Cor. 5:18f.). Consequently, in the proclamation Christ himself, indeed God Himself, encounters the hearer, and the "Now" in which the preachèd word sounds forth is the "Now" of the eschatological occurrence itself (II Cor. 6:2).

Here, then, the question asked above (2, p. 294) finds its answer: *How can the salvation-occurrence* be understood *as an occurrence directed at man, reaching him, and happening to him?* It takes place in the word, which accosts the hearer and compels him to decide for or against it. Moreover, this answer transposes the salvation-occurrence, which in the Gnostic myth remained in the dimension of cosmic-natural occurrence, into the dimension of genuine occurrence in man's actual life. The union of believers into one *soma* with Christ now has its basis not in their sharing the same supernatural substance, but in the fact that in the word of proclamation Christ's death-and-resurrection becomes a possibility of existence in regard to which a decision must be made, and in the fact that faith seizes this possibility and appropriates it as the power that determines the existence of the man of faith.

The transformation which the Gnostic categories have to undergo comes to light in Rom. 5:12–19. Since in mankind after Adam there was no choice but to be like Adam fallen under the power of sin and death, the logical consequence would be that after Christ, the second Adam, there is also no choice but to be like him under the power of "obedience" and "life." In point of fact, however, after Christ the necessity to decide between the

[302]

two possibilities exists—and the reservation "those who receive" (v. 17) in the Christ-aeon has and can have no correlative limitation in the Adam-aeon (for the participle λαμβάνοντες implies a condition: if, or so far as, they receive). Likewise, in consistent logic the meaning of I Cor. 15:22, "For as in Adam all die, so also in Christ shall all be made alive," would have to be: all men will be made alive by (in) Christ. But in point of fact the meaning is: All receive the possibility of being made alive; but only for them "that are Christ's" (v. 23 KJ) will the possibility be realized.

6a. Also answered, then, is the question *by what sign the cross of Christ is recognizable as salvation-event.* Not by preparatory instruction concerning the Crucified. He cannot first be recognized in his divine quality in order that one may then advance to faith in the significance of the cross—for that would rob the "word of the cross" of its scandal-and-folly character. It gets that character by the fact that a crucified one is proclaimed as Lord; and only in the fact that this proclamation occurs is the cross recognizable as salvation-event. But that means such recognition takes place only as acknowledgment. This is the decision-question which the "word of the cross" thrusts upon the hearer: whether he will acknowledge that God has made a crucified one Lord; whether he will thereby acknowledge the demand to take up the cross by the surrender of his previous understanding of himself, making the cross the determining power of his life, letting himself be crucified with Christ (I Cor. 1:18–31; Gal. 6:14; *cf.* 5:24). The fact that this acknowledgment does take place demonstrates that Christ's death is a "cosmic" event; i.e. that it may no longer be considered as just the historical event of Jesus' crucifixion on Golgotha. For God made this event the eschatological occurrence, so that, lifted out of all temporal limitation, it continues to take place in any present moment, both in the proclaiming word and in the sacraments (§ 34, 3). The apostle bears about in his body the dying of Jesus and is stamped with the "*stigmata* of Jesus" (II Cor. 4:10f.; Gal. 6:17); the sufferings of Christ overflow abundantly upon him (II. Cor. 1:5).* But it is not only in the proclamation that the cross thus becomes present; it also

* A disciple of Paul so formulated this thought as to let the apostle say (Col. 1:24) he is completing through his own sufferings for the Church what is still lacking in the sufferings of Christ.

does so in all those who let it become the determining power of their lives, those who are united with Christ into one *soma*.

(b) To the extent that the statements about *Christ's pre-existence and incarnation* are of mythological nature, they neither have the character of direct challenge nor are they expressions of the faith that is surrender of "boasting." Yet in context within the proclamation they express a decisive fact: The origin and significance of Jesus' person and his fate are not within earthly occurrence, but God was acting in them and this action of His took place "when the fulness of time was come" (Gal. 4:4). That is, that it is the eschatological deed of God—a deed, furthermore, for the salvation of men, for whose sake He delivered Christ up (Rom. 8:32). The fact of Christ's pre-existence, so understood, does not make faith in the Crucified easier (as if the assertion of the cross's salvation-significance would be credible, once it were recognized that it was precisely the pre-existent Son of God who died on the cross) but itself becomes a "scandalous" and "foolish" matter of faith at one with the "word of the cross."

As to the assertion that *Christ's incarnation is also his own deed of obedience and love* (Phil. 2:8; Gal. 2:20; Rom. 8:35, 39), it must first be admitted that the "obedience" and "love" of the pre-existent Son are not visible data and cannot be experienced as directly aimed at the man who is challenged to believe. However, they are indirectly experienced in the fact that Christ is present in the "ministry" of the proclaimer. As he by his incarnation became a "servant to the circumcised" (Rom. 15:8), so the proclaimers are "servants of a new covenant" (II Cor. 3:6), "servants of God" (II Cor. 6:4) or "of Christ" (II Cor. 11:23; *cf.* I Cor. 3:5), "slaves" or "servants" of Christ (Rom. 1:1; Gal. 1:10; Phil. 1:1; I Cor. 4:1) and thereby are "servants" (δοῦλοι) of men" (II Cor. 4:5; I Cor. 9:19), in whom he who "took the form of a servant (δοῦλος)" (Phil. 2:7) is actively present. What is true of the pre-existent Son—he "did not please himself" but took all reproach upon himself (Rom. 15:3)—is also true of the apostle: "I please all in all things" (I Cor. 10:33), and he, too, travels his way through reproach and shame (I Cor. 4:9–13; II Cor. 6:8f.). As Christ gave himself up to die in order to obtain life for men, so death is at work in the apostle in order that life may be at work in the hearers of his preaching (II Cor. 4:12); the "love of Christ" (Rom. 8:35) dominates the apostle (II Cor. 5:14—subjective genitive!). Hence he can exhort men not only to imitate Christ (Phil. 2:5; Rom. 15:3; II Cor. 8:9) but, as the representative of Christ to his hearers (II Cor. 5:20), he can even urge them: "be imitators of me" (I Cor. 4:16; *cf.* Gal. 4:12; Phil. 3:17; 4:9) and may add as motivation for such exhortation: "as I am of Christ" (I Cor. 11:1; *cf.* I Thess. 1:6).

Therefore, the incarnation of the pre-existent Son also has "cosmic" dimension—i.e. in reality, *historic dimension* (a locus in the actual living of men, which is true "history"). The incarnation is present and active in the Christian proclamation. Differently formulated: There exists a divinely authorized proclamation of the prevenient grace and love of God; this is the fact that finds mythological expression in what is said of the pre-existence of Christ. What the hearer affirms when he believes the pre-existence of Christ is that what has encountered him is the word of God.

Even the role of mediator in the creation of the world is attributed to the pre-existent Christ ("through whom are all things," I Cor. 8:6 = through whom the universe exists; see § 12, 3, p. 132). But the next phrase ("and we through him"—supply: are what we are: men under grace) intimately binds this role with his role as mediator of salvation. This intimate connection by itself indicates that the cosmological and soteriological roles are to be understood in unity with each other. That is, what is said of the pre-existent Christ as the mediator of creation expresses the faith that creation and redemption constitute a unity: The love of God which encounters the hearer in the word of proclamation originated before all time.

(c) Nothing preceding the faith which acknowledges the risen Christ can give insight into the reality of *Christ's resurrection*. The resurrection cannot—in spite of I Cor. 15:3-8—be demonstrated or made plausible as an objectively ascertainable fact on the basis of which one could believe. But insofar as it or the risen Christ is present in the proclaiming word, it can be believed—and only so can it be believed. Belief in the resurrection and the faith that Christ himself, yes God Himself, speaks in the proclaimed word (II Cor. 5:20) are identical. For in the proclamation Christ is not in the same way present as a great historical person is present in his work and its historical after-effects. For what is here involved is not an influence that takes effect in the history of the human mind; what does take place is that a historical person and his fate are raised to the rank of the eschatological event. The word which makes this proclamation is itself a part of this event; and this word, in contrast to all other historical tradition, accosts the hearer as personal challenge. If he heeds it as the word spoken to him, adjudicating to him death and thereby life, then he believes in the risen Christ.

Any counter-questioning as to the proclamation's right to its claim means that it is already rejected. Such questioning must be transformed into the question which the questioner has to ask himself—whether he is willing to acknowledge the Lord-ship of Christ which is putting this decision-question to his self-understanding. The meaning of Jesus' resurrection is not that he is translated into the beyond, but that he is exalted to the status of Lord (Phil. 2:11), which status he has until he gives it back to the Father (I Cor. 15:24). That is, he has it now—the now that is made Now by the now-sounding proclamation. At his command, the proclamation is being made (Rom. 10:17). The apostles are his "ministers," "slaves," and "servants" (see above). In them he is speaking (II Cor. 5:20; 13:3) and through them he is working (Rom. 15:18). When the apostle comes, it is "with the fulness of Christ's blessing" (Rom. 15:29) that he comes. It is as the risen Christ that Christ is present in the apostle; for in bearing about in his body the dying of Jesus, Paul is manifesting in his body the life of Jesus (II Cor. 4:10f.); through the apostle, Christ is demonstrating his power to the hearers: "For as he was crucified out of weakness but lives out of the power of God, so we, too, are weak through him but we shall live out of the power of God toward you" (II Cor. 13:4 Blt.)—i.e. the risen Christ himself encounters the hearer in the apostle.

§ 34. The Word, the Church, the Sacraments

1. The salvation-occurrence is the *eschatological occurrence* which puts to end the old aeon. Though Paul still expects the end of the old world to come as a cosmic drama that will unfold with the imminent parousia of Christ (I Thess. 4:16; I Cor. 15:23, 51f., etc.), that can only be the completion and confirmation of the eschatological occurrence that has now already begun. For with the sending of Christ "when the fulness of time was come" (Gal. 4:4) it decisively began, so that it can already be said now: "the old has passed away, behold, the new has come" (II Cor. 5:17). Eschato-

ogical "righteousness" and "adoption" are already present realities (§ 29); the Spirit, that "first-fruit" (Rom. 8:23) or "guarantee" of the coming consummation (II Co. 1:22; 5:5), has already been given to the Church (Gal. 4:6; Rom. 8:15). Though Paul describes the present actuality of the new Life in Gnostic terminology (§ 33, 3a), he nevertheless has lifted the present eschatological occurrence out of the dimension of cosmic occurrence into that of historic (§ 33, 5) by regarding it as taking place in the preaching of the word which proclaims Jesus as the crucified and risen Lord. In this proclamation the judgment already is taking place, for it spreads abroad death for refusal of faith and life for faith (II Cor. 2:15f.). Paul has historized the Jewish apocalyptic speculation of an intermediate messianic reign preceding the new aeon by conceiving the time of the Messiah's reign as the time between Christ's resurrection and parousia—i.e. as the Now in which the proclamation is sounding forth (I Cor. 15:23–28).

In the "word," then, the salvation-occurrence is present (§ 33, 5). For the proclaimed word is neither an enlightening *Weltanschauung* flowing out in general truths, nor a merely historical account which, like a reporter's story, reminds a public of important but by-gone facts. Rather, it is *kerygma*—herald's service—in the literal sense—authorized, plenipotent proclamation, edict from a sovereign. Its promulgation requires authorized messengers, "heralds," "apostles" (= sent men) (Rom. 10:13–17). So it is, by nature, personal address which accosts each individual, throwing the person himself into question by rendering his self-understanding problematic, and demanding a decision of him.

If the salvation-occurrence is present in the proclamation, then the latter belongs to the former as a part of it; as "ministry" or "word" of "reconciliation" (II Cor. 5:18f.; § 33, 5) it was instituted at the same time. In it, therefore, the eschatological occurrence is taking place; the eschatological "acceptable time," the "day of salvation" foretold by Is. 49:8, is present reality in the Now in which the word encounters the hearer (II Cor. 6:2; § 33, 5).

Then the proclaimer, *the apostle,* who represents Christ and God to his hearers (II Cor. 5:20; § 33, 6a and b), whose word is God's word (I Thess. 2:13), belongs to the eschatological occurrence. He spreads abroad the "fragrance of the knowledge of him (God)" (II Cor. 2:14); and if, through his preaching, God causes the "light of the knowledge of the glory of God in the face of Christ" to flare up, then He who once said, "Let light shine out of darkness," is thereby now accomplishing His new creation (II Cor. 4:6). Therefore the apostle must lay claim to the obedience of his congregations (II Cor. 2:9; 7:15; Phil. 2:12; Phlm. 21) exposing himself to being misunderstood as a tyrant over the believers (II Cor. 1:24), whereas, being himself a believer, he is under the same Lord as they, and, proclaiming him, makes himself the "slave" of the men to whom he preaches (II Cor. 4:5; I Cor. 9:19-23). Nevertheless, in the function of apostle he must demand that the congregation's "obedience to Christ" prove itself in obedience to him (II Cor. 10:5f.).

2. The preachèd word calls and gathers men into the *ecclesia,* the *Church,* the *Congregation* of those who are "called" and "saints" (§ 10, 3). It is the eschatological Congregation, and hence its existing belongs to the eschatological salvation-occurrence. As it was called into existence by the proclaimed word, its existence in turn is the foundation of preaching. Only in the *ecclesia* is there authorized preaching; the "ministry of reconciliation" is the "ministry of a new covenant" (II Cor. 3:6ff.)—i.e. apostolic preaching stands from the outset within the frame of the salvation-history of the People of God. The apostles, to whose missionary work the separate congregations owe their origin, are, nevertheless, themselves within the Congregation (I Cor. 12:28). If Paul could not be assured that his work has the approval of the Jerusalem Church—the original Congregation—he would have to believe he "had run in vain" (Gal. 2:2).

The fact that *ecclesia* sometimes means the total Church, sometimes the local congregation (§ 10, 1), reflects the peculiar double character of the eschatological Congregation. On the one hand, it is no phenomenon of the world but belongs to the new aeon; on the other hand, this eschatological Congregation, which as such is invisible, takes visible form in the individual congregations within the world. The *ecclesia* is just as ambiguous a phenomenon as the cross of Christ: visible as a worldly fact, invisible—yet to the eye of faith also visible—as a thing of the world to come.

The eschatological Congregation takes its purest form from time to time in the cultic gathering in which Christ is confessed as Lord (I Cor. 12:3; Phil. 2:11). In their "assembling as a congregation" (I Cor. 11:18) he is present and demonstrates his presence by the working of the Spirit in the various "spiritual gifts" (I Cor. 14).

Indeed, God himself, who "inspires them all (the gifts) in every one" (I Cor. 12:6), is present; and the outsider present as a guest when struck by the prophetic word has to confess: "truly God is among you" (I Cor. 14:25 tr.).

The eschatological holiness which takes form in the cultic gathering determines the structure of the Congregation and its life in general. Since the Congregation is withdrawn from the world, this world's distinctions have lost their meaning. Hence:

> "There is neither Jew nor Greek,
> there is neither slave nor free,
> there is neither male nor female;
> for you are all one in Christ Jesus."
> (Gal. 3:28; *cf.* I Cor. 12:13)

The indifference of worldly distinctions also emerges in the admonition: "let each one remain in the state in which the call of God encountered him" (I Cor. 7:17–24 Blt.)—i.e. the negation of worldly differentiations does not mean a sociological program within this world; rather, it is an eschatological occurrence which takes place only within the eschatological Congregation.

From the surrounding world, the "outsiders" (I Cor. 5:12f.; I Thess. 4:12), the "unrighteous" (I Cor. 6:1), the Congregation is *set apart* as the temple of God (I Cor. 3:16f.), the Congregation of the "saints." Believers are to be "children of God without blemish in the midst of a crooked and perverse generation" and are to "shine as lights in the world" (Phil. 2:15). The Christian, it is taken for granted, does not take part in heathen worship (I Cor. 10:1–22; § 10, 3). Neither is he to go to law in the heathen courts (I Cor. 6:1–8), though he is expected conscientiously to fulfill his duties toward governmental authority (Rom. 13:1–7). It is not as if all intercourse with "unbelievers" were to be cut off, however (I Cor. 5:9f.; 10:27). Still, it is not only in its cultic gathering that the eschatological Congregation makes its appearance. From it as a center there develops a secular faith-determined community of living in which there is mutual obligation and mutual service: "assistances" and "administrations," the functions of "presiding" (προΐστασθαι), "laboring" (κοπιᾶν), and "ministering" (διακονεῖν) in various forms (I Cor. 12:28; 16:15f.; Rom. 12:7f.; I Thess. 5:12). As official representatives of a Congregation *episkopoi* and **diakonoi** ("administrators" and "assistants" rather than "bishops" and "deacons") appear for the first time in Phil. 1:1. I Cor. 6:1ff. also prepares the way for the development of a Christian court of arbitration.

Paul may designate the eschatological character of the Church in keeping with the general Christian view in terms of the Old Testament history of salvation. He does so when he connects it with the "new covenant" (II Cor. 3:6ff.; I Cor. 11:25) or calls it "the Israel of God" (Gal. 6:16), or speaks of Abraham as the father of those who have faith (§ 10, 2). Such designations characterize the Church as the end and goal of the history of salvation; in the Church all promises find their fulfilment (Rom. 15:4; I Cor. 10:11; *cf.* 9:10). But Paul may also express the supramundane, eschatological character of the Church in Gnostic terminology. He is doing so when he calls it the *"body of Christ"* (I Cor. 12:27) or "one body in Christ" (Rom. 12:5; § 15, 4e). These terms express both the unity of the Church and the foundation of this unity in an origin transcendent to the will and deed of individuals and hence express its transcendental nature. The *ecclesia* is not a club in which like-minded individuals have banded together, though seen from without it may seem so; it is not a conglomeration of the Spirit-endowed, each of whom has and enjoys his private relationship to Christ. It is just this misconception, which has emerged in Corinth, that Paul combats in I Cor. 12:12–30. In doing so, he secondarily designates the Church as an organism (*soma*), using this metaphor from the classic Greek tradition, which in the latter means an organically developed and compact community. But he uses that association only secondarily (v. 14–26). Primarily he is describing the Church as the "body of Christ." His guiding thought is not that the several members of the body, being various, constitute the whole and therefore, in their variety, are equally important for the body. His main thought is, rather, that the members are equal because they belong to Christ, and therefore their differences are unimportant (v. 12f.). It is not the members that constitute the body but Christ (Rom. 12:5 implies the same). Christ is there, not through and in the members, but before they are there and above them. Thus, the body of Christ is, to speak Gnostically, a cosmic thing; however, Paul's Gnostic terminology serves to express the comprehensive historic complex, instituted by the salvation-occurrence, into which the individual is

[310]

placed (§ 33, 5). But it is quite natural that cosmological speculations about the *ecclesia* soon arise in connection with the term "body of Christ" (§ 10, 1; § 15, 4e).

3. The individual is taken into the "body of Christ" by the *sacrament of baptism*; "for by one Spirit we were all baptized into one body" (I Cor. 12:13). Or it may be said instead, simply: "into Christ" (Gal. 3:27; II Cor. 1:21) with the result that now Christian existence can be called existence "*in Christ*": "for you are all one in Christ Jesus" (Gal. 3:28). To belong to the Christian Church is to be "in Christ" or "in the Lord" (Rom. 16:7, 11; I Cor. 1:30), and Christian congregations may also be called congregations "in Christ" (Gal. 1:22; I Thess. 2:14). "In Christ," far from being a formula for mystic union, is primarily an *ecclesiological* formula. It means the state of having been articulated into the "body of Christ" by baptism, although baptism need not be directly implied in every instance (such as Rom. 8:1; II Cor. 5:17; Gal. 2:17). It must also be noted that from this basic meaning the formula took on an extension of meaning: It often expresses in a quite general way the state of being determined by Christ whereby it supplies the lack of the not yet coined adjective "Christian" or a corresponding adverb. Since the Church, into which baptism incorporates the member, is the *eschatological* Congregation, the formula "in Christ" has not only ecclesiological but at the same time eschatological meaning: "if anyone is in Christ, he is a new creation" (II Cor. 5:17). Similarly, the fact that "in Christ" can interchange with "in the Spirit" also indicates the eschatological meaning of "in Christ" (Rom. 8:9; 14:17). But since the Spirit is conferred by baptism (I Cor. 12:13; II Cor. 1:22; § 13, 1, p. 138), "in the Spirit" can also be regarded vice versa as an ecclesiological formula, though it, like the other, also underwent an extension of meaning.

But what is the relation between incorporation into the Church by the sacrament of *baptism* and the dynamic process in which the salvation-occurrence continues itself through the proclaimed *word* (§ 33, 5 and 6)? If baptism grants participation in the death and resurrection of Jesus, does it do so in another way than the word proclaimed and heard in faith? Paul found baptism already conceived before his time as a sacrament of the mystery religions and strove so to interpret it as purification from sin as to see in it the founding of a new ethical life (§ 13, 1, p. 140). To be sure, it is scarcely permissible to say that he completely freed himself of the mystery-conception of sacrament as having a magical effect; for he leaves vicarious baptism, which rests upon such a conception, at least uncontested (I Cor. 15:29) and also shows himself influenced by it in his view of the Lord's Supper (see below). Nevertheless, he by no means unconditionally attributes magic influence to baptism, as if receiving it guaranteed salvation. As the desert-generation of Israel, which once had received prototypes of the Christian sacraments, was not thereby preserved from destruction, so baptized Christians must be warned: "Therefore let any one who thinks that he stands take heed lest he fall" (I Cor. 10:1–12). When Paul emphatically says, "For Christ did not send me to baptize but to preach the gospel" (I Cor. 1:17), baptism obviously plays a subordinate role to the word. The baptizer does not have the character of priest as in the mysteries, and the act of baptizing does not, as was often the case in them, establish some mysterious relationship between the baptizer and the baptized.

Nevertheless, baptism is an objective occurrence which happens to the baptized, not simply a symbol for a subjective process within him. Whatever inward experiences the one being baptized may have, Paul does not reflect about them. As an event occurring objectively to the baptized, baptism certifies to him participation in the salvation-occurrence, the death and resurrection of Jesus. It, then, makes the salvation-occurrence present for him just as the proclaiming word also does, only this time with special reference to him, the one being baptized, as valid for him. But the appropriation on his part is the same as the appropriation of the salvation-occurrence when it comes through the preachèd word. For if, as can scarcely be doubted, Rom. 10:9 is a reference to the confession made at baptism—"if you confess with your lips that Jesus is Lord and believe in your heart that God raised him from the dead"—then baptism on the part of him who is being baptized is an act of faith confessing itself. And as acceptance of the word in faith is the acknowledgment of the Lord who is speaking in it, so baptism also brings a man under the domination of the Lord. To be "in Christ" is also to be "of Christ"—i.e. to belong to Christ as one's Lord (*cf.* Gal. 3:29 with 3:27f.; 5:24; II Cor. 10:7; Rom. 8:9; 14:8). As the acceptance of the "word of the cross" means willingness to let one's self-understanding and one's conduct be determined by the cross (§ 33, 6a), so baptism means crucifixion with Christ (Rom. 6:6). Consequently, the indicative (of Rom. 6:6 and 8, for example, which imply you already share Jesus' death and resurrection) now furnishes real justification for Paul's imperative: "yield yourselves to God as men who have been brought from death to life" (Rom. 6:13). Or, as another example, Gal. 3:27 says: "For as many of you as were baptized into Christ have put on Christ," which Paul can also say in the imperative: "Put on the Lord Jesus Christ" (Rom. 13:14).

Similarly, in Paul's conception of the *Lord's Supper* mystery-ideas unite with his own view of the salvation-occurrence. Paul took over from the Hellenistic Church (§ 13, 2) both the celebration of the Lord's Supper and a conception of it as a sacrament which effects communion with the crucified and risen Christ by means of bread and wine, eaten and drunk. Two facts indicate how little Paul consciously disavows the idea that the Supper has a magical effect. One is that he regards its effect as analogous to that of heathen cult-meals (I Cor. 10:20f.; p. 148). The other is his opinion that partaking in an unworthy manner results in damage to the partaker's body or even in his death (I Cor. 11:29f.). But when Paul formulates his thought of "communion" by saying that the participants become one "body" (the "body" of Christ, I Cor. 10:16f.), it is beyond doubt that his view of the "body of Christ" also determines his view of the Lord's Supper. And when he calls the process by which the Lord's Supper makes Christ's death a present reality a "proclaiming" (I Cor. 11:26)—using the same word that he otherwise uses for preaching (Rom. 1:8; I Cor. 2:1; 9:14; Phil. 1:17f.)—that indicates that the sacrament of the Lord's Supper like that of baptism is also coordinate with the word-proclamation and ultimately only a special mode of it. The particular effect of this sacrament, like that of baptism, is its special application of the salvation-occurrence just to those who here and now are celebrating it. Besides this, it has the additional effect of instituting fellowship among the celebrants (I Cor. 10:16f.), an effect not explicitly emphasized in the case of word-proclamation and baptism. Obviously, then, the efficacy of the sacrament—in spite of the influence of mystery ideas—does not really rest upon the elements, the bread and wine partaken, but rests upon the doing of this act as an act of "proclamation." In any case, the Lord's Supper is for Paul not a "medicine of immortality" (§ 13, 2, p. 147), the taking of which guarantees immortal life; his warning against supposed security (I Cor. 10:1–12) holds for the Lord's Supper just as for baptism. In the Lord's Supper, too—as the name κυριακὸν δεῖπνον itself implies—the lordship of the Lord is set up over believers and acknowledged by them.

C. FAITH

§ 35. The Structure of Faith

The attitude of man in which he receives the gift of "God's righteousness" and in which the divine deed of salvation accomplishes itself with him is *faith*. We inevitably caught sight of it in our earlier discussion of "God's righteousness" (§ 30), and its nature was indirectly clarified by our investigation of "grace" (§§ 32–34). Our present task is to set forth faith in its full structure and meaning.

At the outset, it may be simply said that "faith" is the condition for the receipt of "righteousness," taking the place of "works," which in the Jewish view constitute that condition. It may also be simply said at the outset that such "faith" is the acceptance of the Christian message (§ 9, 5)—following a usage that developed in the missionary enterprise of Hellenistic Christianity. An understanding of such acceptance, or a concept of "faith," was developed by several others besides Paul (p. 99), but by him it was given a characteristic and decisive stamp.

1. *Paul understands faith primarily as obedience;* he understands the act of faith as an act of obedience. This is shown by the parallelism of two passages in Romans: "because your faith is proclaimed in all the world" (1:8) and "for your obedience is known to all" (16:19). Thus, he can combine the two in the expression ὑπακοὴ πίστεως ("the obedience which faith is," Rom. 1:5) to designate that which it is the purpose of his apostleship to bring about.

Cf. further, I Thess. 1:8: "your faith in God has gone forth everywhere" and Rom. 15:18: "For I will not venture to speak of anything except what Christ has wrought through me to win obedience from the Gentiles." Further, he says of Jews who have not come to faith, Rom. 10:3: "they did not submit to (= obey) God's righteousness," and 10:16: "they have not all heeded (= obeyed) the gospel." Correspondingly, the Jews' refusal of faith is denoted by "disobey" and "disobedience" in

Rom. 11:30–32; *cf.* Rom. 15:31; Gal. 5:7. II Cor. 9:13 describes faith as "obedience in acknowledging the Gospel of Christ." Paul considers it his task, according to II Cor. 10:5f., to "take every thought captive to obey Christ," and warns the unruly Corinthians that he will "punish every disobedience when your *obedience* is complete" (for obedience rendered to the apostle is identical with obedience to Christ, § 34, 1). But he substitutes the word "faith" where we might expect to read "obedience" when he expresses the hope that he will become greater through them when their *faith* is increased (see II Cor. 10:15 KJ).

For Paul the acceptance of the message in faith takes the form of an act of obedience because of the fact that the message which demands acknowledgment of the crucified Jesus as Lord demands of man the surrender of his previous understanding of himself, the reversal of the direction his will has previously had (§ 33, 6a). "Faith's obedience" is the genuine obedience which God's Law had indeed demanded, but which had been refused by the Jews by their misuse of it to establish "their own righteousness," using it as a means for "boasting" (§ 23, 1 and 2). Faith's attitude is the radical opposite of the attitude of "boasting" (§ 30, 2); nor can faith take credit for itself—that would be "boasting." Accordingly, he warns even the man of faith, who is no longer under the Law, with a warning that corresponds to his opinion about Jewish boasting: "What have you that you have not been given? And if you have been given it, why do you boast as if you had not been given it" (I Cor. 4:7 tr.)? He exhorts the Gentile Christians who have been grafted into the cultivated olive tree as shoots from the wild olive: "Do not boast over the branches. If you do boast . . . it is not you that support the root, but the root that supports you" (Rom. 11:18). For the purpose of God's salvation-deed is: "that no flesh may boast before God" (I Cor. 1:29 tr.), and there is only one boast left: "Let him who boasts, boast of the Lord" (I Cor. 1:31; II Cor. 10:17). Accordingly, Paul thus describes the faith of Abraham: "he grew strong in his faith as he gave glory to God" (Rom. 4:20).

As true obedience, "faith" is freed from the suspicion of being an accomplishment, a "work" (§ 30, 2, p. 283). As an accomplishment it would not be obedience, since in an accomplishment the will does not surrender but asserts itself; in it, a merely formal renunciation takes place in that the will lets the content of its accomplishment be dictated by an authority lying outside of itself, but precisely in so doing thinks it has a right to be proud of its accomplishment. "Faith"—the radical renunciation of accomplishment, the obedient submission to the God-determined way of salvation, the taking over of the cross of Christ (§ 33, 6a)—is the free deed of obedience in which the new self constitutes itself in place of the old. As this sort of decision, it is a deed in the true sense: In a true deed the doer himself is inseparable from it, while in a "work" he stands side by side with what he does.

As free deed of decision, the obedience of faith is also insured against another misconception. "Faith" is not an "experience," not the "truly religious in religion," not a state of soul, not a διάθεσις (propensity, disposition) or an ἀρετή (virtue, excellence). It is not —as if it were the perfected state of the soul—salvation itself. Rather —as genuine obedience—it is the condition for receiving salvation.

The frequently made comparison with *Philo's* concept of "faith" is instructive (see Bousset, *Kyrios Christos,* 2nd ed., 145–149; *cf.* H. Windisch, *Die Frömmigkeit Philos* (1909); Schlatter, *op. cit.,* 66–86). Philo understands "faith" as a "propensity" (διάθεσις) of the soul, the soul's perfect state, an excellence (ἀρετή). In his thought, therefore, "faith" stands at the end "as the goal of life's movement toward God" (Schlatter), while for Paul it stands at the beginning furnishing the basis for the new life.

W. Michaelis (following Deissmann) attempts to escape the misconception of faith as an accomplishment which would be the condition for rightwising by altogether eliminating its condition-character and declaring that "righteousness by faith" (Rom. 1:17; 10:6) is only an antithetic formula to "righteousness from the Law." In reality, according to him, faith is the experience of being rightwised, fellowship with Christ. But he has overlooked, first, that "faith" equals "obedience" and, second, has ignored such expressions as "reckoned as righteousness" (Rom. 4:3, 5ff.; Gal. 3:6) and "believe unto righteousness" (Rom. 10:10 KJ), which clearly show that faith is not righteousness but the condition for it. The condition-character of "faith" is the clear implication of the passages that speak of rightwising or righteousness ἐκ ("from," "on the basis of") "faith": Rom. 3:30; 5:1; 9:30; 10:6 (*cf.* also 1:17; 3:26; 9:32), especially Gal. 2:16: "we have believed in Christ Jesus in order to be justified (rightwised) by (ἐκ) faith in Christ," and also Gal. 3:7f., 11f., 24; 5:5. The same is true of the synonymous formulas using διὰ πίστεως ("through faith," Rom. 3:22, 30; Gal. 2:16; 3:14; Phil. 3:9), ἐπὶ τῇ πίστει ("that depends on faith," Phil. 3:9), or the simple dative (Rom. 3:28). Paul's position seems incomprehensible or contradictory only to those who can conceive the fulfilling of a condition only as an accomplishment, whereas for Paul "faith" is precisely the waiver of any accomplishment whatever and thereby is radical obedience.

Neither is it adequate to understand faith as trust, founded on repentance, in God's gracious forgiveness which brings the sinner back to the way of the Law which in his transgressions he had forsaken (Schlatter). The very rarity of the terms "forgiveness of sins" and "repentance" in Paul (§ 31) and the similar rarity of ἐπιστρέφειν ("turn to"—only at I Thess. 1:9 and II Cor. 3:16 in Paul; § 9, 3) indicate that the movement of will contained in "faith" is not primarily remorse and repentance. Of course, they are included in it; but it is primarily the obedience which waives righteousness of one's own. Phil. 3:7–9 is not the self-condemnation of Paul's previous life as one soiled by trespasses, not condemnation of that which even in existence under the Law and by one so existing could be and, as IV Ezra shows, was condemned. Rather, it describes his sacrifice of all that had been his pride and "gain" in existence under the Law. It is evident that "faith" has the character of obedience and is an act of decision.

2. "Faith" is further insured against such misconceptions by the fact that *it is simultaneously "confession."* "Faith" is "faith in . . ." That is, it always has reference to its object, God's saving deed in Christ.

Hence, "confess" and "believe" correspond to each other:
> "If you confess with your lips that Jesus is Lord and
> believe in your heart that God raised him from the
> dead, you will be saved." (Rom. 10:9)

The object of belief or faith is expressed by a ὅτι-clause, as here, in I Thess. 4:14; Rom. 6:8. Equivalent locutions are "believe in" or "faith in" (εἰς in both cases with "Christ Jesus" as object) Gal. 2:16; Rom. 10:14; Phil. 1:29; πρός (faith toward) Phlm. 5; ἐν (in) Gal. 3:26; ἐπί ("on, in" quoted from Is. 28:16) Rom. 9:33; 10:11. An abbreviating substitute is the

[317]

objective genitive (§ 9, 5) with "Jesus Christ" as object: Gal. 2:16; 3:22; Rom. 3:22, 26; Phil. 3:9; or other objects: Son of God (Gal. 2:20), the gospel (Phil. 1:27).

Faith, therefore, is not "piety" or trust-in-God in general. Rather, it has "dogmatic" character insofar as it is acceptance of a word: "the word of faith" (Rom. 10:8) or "the heard word" (ἀκοή, KJ: "the hearing") of faith (Gal. 3:2, 5). Hence, faith can also be called "faith of the gospel"—i.e. faith in the gospel (Phil. 1:27).

"Faith," which arises from "what is heard" (Rom. 10:17), consequently contains a *knowing*. That is why Paul can, at times, speak as if knowledge were the basis of faith. For instance, Rom. 6:8f.: since we *know* that death no longer has power over the risen Christ, we *believe* that if we have died with him we shall also live with him (*cf.* II Cor. 4:13f.). But since this knowledge can be appropriated only in obedient, comprehending faith, and hence contains an understanding of one's self, knowledge may also appear as arising out of faith. It is so in Rom. 5:3 where the knowledge "that suffering produces endurance" is just the knowledge of those who are "rightwised by faith." So also in II Cor. 1:7; 5:6. Thus, "we know" or "you know" sometimes makes an appeal to a "dogma"—i.e. a statement in the *kerygma* (I Thess. 5:2; Rom. 6:3; II Cor. 5:1; 8:9)—and sometimes to truths which "faith"-ful reflection must draw as consequences (Rom. 8:28; 13:11; 14:14; I Cor. 3:16; 6:2f., 9; 15:58). Ultimately "faith" and "knowledge" are identical as a new understanding of one's self, if Paul can give as the purpose of his apostleship both "to bring about the obedience of faith" (Rom. 1:5) and "to give the light of the knowledge of the glory of God in the face of Christ" (II Cor. 4:6; *cf.* 2:14: "God ... who ... through us spreads the fragrance of the knowledge of him"). The same conclusion is to be drawn from his saying that he has given up "confidence in the flesh" for the sake of "the surpassing worth of knowing Christ Jesus" and his then proceeding to develop the purpose of "righteousness from God that depends on faith" as this: "that I may know him and the power of his resurrection and may share his sufferings . . ." (Phil. 3:4–10). An additional clarification of the character of "knowledge" lies in the fact that human "knowing" has its basis in a "being known by God" (Gal. 4:9; I Cor. 13:12).

"Faith," that is, also has, on the other hand, "undogmatic" character insofar as the word of proclamation is no mere report about historical incidents: It is no teaching about external matters which could simply be regarded as true without any transformation of the hearer's own existence. For the word is *kerygma,* personal address, demand, and promise; it is the very act of divine grace (§ 34, 1). Hence its acceptance—faith—is obedience, acknowledgment, confession. That is the reason why "grace" as well as "faith" can likewise be named as the opposite of "works" to designate the basis for rightwising (§ 30, 2); for "faith" is what it is only with reference to the "grace" which is actively present in the word.

In his "confession" of faith, the believer turns away from himself, confessing that all he is and has, he is and has through that which God has done. Faith does not appeal to whatever it itself may be as act or attitude but to God's prevenient deed of grace which preceded faith (§ 31). That is why Paul (and the New Testament in general) never describes faith as a state of soul nor its genesis as a psychological process. Though Gal. 3:23–26 sketches the preparation and the "coming" of "faith," what is sketched is not the individual's development but the history of salvation. The attention of the believer does not turn reflectively inward upon himself, but is turned toward the object of his faith. "Faith," then, as "obedience," is also "confession."

3. This same thing, that the believer is turned away from himself, is also expressed by the fact that *"faith" is also "hope."* "Faith" is no self-contained condition of man's soul, but points toward the future: "he who by faith is righteous shall live" (Gal. 3:11; Rom. 1:17). "For if we have died with Christ, we believe that we shall also live with him" (Rom. 6:8; *cf.* I Thess. 4:14). "For with the heart man believeth unto righteousness and with the mouth confession is made unto salvation" (Rom. 10:10 KJ).

The "righteousness" which is the goal of "faith" is no quality which adheres to man, but is his relation to God (§ 28, 2). If it has become a present possibility (§ 29, 1), this "present-ness" is not a temporal and therefore a temporary state. Rather, its "present-ness" is that of the eschatological Now. That is, it is always both here and ahead of the already rightwised believer as future to him. That is why we can be said to be both "rightwised by faith" (Rom. 5:1) and "waiting for the hope of righteousness" "through the Spirit, by faith" (Gal. 5:5). That is why "righteousness" and "salvation" correspond to each other in Rom. 10:9f. Though men of faith may already be called the "saved" (I Cor. 1:18; II Cor. 2:15), still: "in this hope we were saved. Now hope that is seen is not hope. For who hopes for what he sees? But if we hope for what we do not see, we wait for it with patience" (Rom. 8:24f.).

This "hope" is the freedom for the future and the openness toward it which the man of faith has because he has turned over his anxiety about himself and his future to God in obedience. For the sin of unbelief is just this: The unbeliever insists upon living out of his own resources and so is anxious about his own future in the illusion of being able to dispose over it. Though the man without faith naturally has his hopes, too—just as those "who have no hope" (I Thess. 4:13), of course, also live with certain hopes—still they are no real hopes. The man who is concerned for himself factually lives in fear (§ 23, 2), shutting himself up against the future, which is not at his disposal. The man of faith is relieved of this fear because in faith he has let anxiety about himself go. He hopes where humanly there is nothing to hope, following the example of Abraham, who "hoping against hope believed" (Rom. 4:18 tr.). He lives, that is, in the true hope "which does not disappoint" (Rom. 5:5). It manifests itself in the patient waiting (Rom. 8:25; see above) or "patience," of which "rejoicing in our sufferings" (Rom. 5:3) is characteristic. Believers "rejoice in hope," are "patient in tribulation" (Rom. 12:12). "Hope," like "love" (see § 39, 3) is bound up with "faith" in a unity (I Cor. 13:13); the "work of faith," the "labor of love" and the "steadfastness of hope"—all three together belong to the totality of Christian existence (I Thess. 1:3; *cf.* 5:8). When Paul prays for the perfecting of Christian existence, he prays: "May the God of hope fill you with all joy and peace in believing so that . . . you may abound in hope" (Rom. 15:13).

4. Such "hope," nevertheless, has a peculiar correlative in *"fear"* (φόβος), which is an indispensable constitutive element in "faith," inasmuch as it guarantees the centering of the believer's attention upon God's "grace." How it does so is illustrated by Paul's description of his conduct on arriving at Corinth (I Cor. 2:1–5). He came to Corinth "in weakness and in much fear and trembling"—so far, that is, as he looked to himself. But since he waived any eloquence or wisdom of his own and determined to know one thing only, "Jesus Christ and him crucified," he was effective with a "demonstration of

Spirit and power" having as its purpose and result: "that your faith might not rest in the wisdom of men but in the power of God."

That this is the appropriate attitude of the man of faith is also declared in the warning directed to the Gentile Christians who want to boast of their faith, comparing themselves with unbelieving Jews (Rom. 11:20-22): "They were broken off because of their unbelief, but you stand fast (only) through faith. (So) do not become proud, but stand in awe (i.e. do not be haughty—toward them—but rather fear—for yourself) . . ." Faith would be cheated of its purpose if the believer were to consider himself insured by it. God's "kindness," in which faith takes comfort, is only valid "provided you continue in his kindness." The man of faith, who in view of God's "grace" is freed from fear, must not forget that the grace that emancipates him is the "grace" of a Judge. When the man of faith looks to himself, his faith must ever contain "fear" as the knowledge of his own insignificance and his constant dependence upon God's "grace." Thinking of the "judgment seat of Christ" before which we must all be arraigned (II Cor. 5:10), Paul says: "knowing the fear of the Lord . . ." (v. 11). This sentence runs parallel with "since we have such a hope" (3:12), demonstrating the unity of "hope" and "fear." This sentence also shows, however, that "fear" has not only the negative purpose of destroying false security and directing the believer's attention away from himself toward God's "grace" which alone supports him (as in Rom. 11:20), but also the positive purpose of making man conscious of his responsibility, which he can assume now that he is no longer under Law but under "grace" (Rom. 6:14). Just because he has been set free (§§ 38, 39), what he does—previously a thing of no account—now really matters, and he can be exhorted (Phil. 2:13f.): "work out your own salvation with fear and trembling; for God is at work in you, both to will and to work for his good pleasure."

As long as the believer lives "in the flesh," his is a constantly threatened existence exposed to temptations (§ 26, 3). Therefore, he is not to look down in a false security of faith upon one overtaken in some trespass, but is to look to himself, lest he, too, fall into temptation (Gal. 6:1). Satan lies in wait (II Cor. 2:11) to tempt believers (I Thess. 3:5; I Cor. 7:5). Hence the exhortation that a man is to "test" himself (πειράζειν) or "examine" himself (δοκιμάζειν) as to whether he truly stands fast in faith (II Cor. 13:5; I Cor. 11:28;

Gal. 6:4). Hence the warning: "let anyone who thinks that he stands take heed lest he fall" (I Cor. 10:12), and the exhortation: "stand firm in your faith" (I Cor. 16:13; *cf.* Gal. 5:1; Phil. 1:27; 4:1) and "be immovable" (I Cor. 15:58). Hence, also, Paul's petition in his prayers for the believers that God may establish or strengthen or sustain them (I Thess. 3:13; 5:23; *cf.* I Cor. 1:8; II Cor. 1:21).

Though "hope" and "fear" equally belong to the structure of "faith," that does not mean that Christian existence is a wavering between hope and fear; rather, hope and fear belong together as correlatives: Just because faith is "hope," it is also "fear" and vice versa. This fact makes clear the obedience aspect of faith: the man of faith utterly surrenders to God's care and power, waiving all care or power of his own and all security that might be at his own disposal. Paul is describing this aspect of faith in Phil. 3:12–14:

> "Not that I have already obtained this or am already perfect;
> but I press on to make it my own,
> because Christ Jesus has made me his own.
> Brethren, I do not consider that I have made it my own;
> but one thing I do, forgetting what lies behind
> and straining forward to what lies ahead,
> I press on toward the goal for the prize of the upward call . . ."

Existence in faith, then, is a movement between "no longer" and "not yet." "No longer": The decision of faith has done away with the past; nevertheless, as true decision, the decision must be maintained—that is, made again and again anew. As that which is overcome, the past is always with us, and faith must remember the past as that which constantly threatens. Paul's "forgetting" does not mean putting the past out of mind, but does mean constantly holding it down, not letting one's self be caught by it again. "Not yet": giving up that which is past, i.e. surrendering a possession which had given a supposed security, precludes taking a new possession in exchange for it. Viewed from man's side no one can say, "I have made it my own"; and yet in view of the fact that "Jesus Christ has made me his own," it can be said, "Nevertheless the hoped-for has already occurred."

5. To the extent that faith is "hope" which has its foundation in "grace" and hence "does not disappoint" (Rom. 5:5), faith is naturally also *confidence*; thus, "since we have such a hope" (II Cor.

[322]

3:12) corresponds to "such is the confidence that we have" (3:4). In fact, precisely as obedience, faith in the end is confidence, trust; for in the radical sense confidence in or trust in God is nothing else than complete surrender of one's own care and strength to God: In other words, the obedience of faith. In this sense, faith is trust in God—but not just trust-in-God in general; rather, that trust which, by accepting the cross, lays its foundation upon God's deed of salvation. Paul makes this unmistakably clear by never using πιστεύειν in the simple sense of "trust" and hence never construing it with the dative, which it takes in the Septuagint and often has in the rest of the New Testament (§ 9, 5), except in the Old Testament quotations about the "trust" of Abraham, Gal. 3:6; Rom. 4:3. Instead, Paul distinguishes between the trust-aspect and the obedience-aspect of faith by using for the former πεποιθέναι or πεποίθησις.

For the man of faith, "trusting in one's self" (II Cor. 1:9) or "in the flesh" (Phil. 3:3f.) has ceased and given place to "trusting in God who raises the dead" (II Cor. 1:9). Similarly, natural man's "boasting" (§ 23, 2), almost synonymous with "trusting," has been replaced by "boasting of the Lord" (see above: 1) and even by "boasting of sufferings" (Rom. 5:3), which is nothing else than "trusting in God who raises the dead." In such "trust" fear is overcome; out of it grows that "boldness" which has no fear of being "put to shame" (Phil. 1:20). Or it is synonymous with the "boldness" which is founded on "hope" (II Cor. 3:12, *cf.* 3:4). It is the opposite of ἐγκακεῖν ("losing heart" or "being cowardly," II Cor. 4:1, 16; *cf.* "fearlessly" in relation to "made confident" in Phil. 1:14).

Only in II Cor. 1:9 (and by implication Phil. 3:3f.) does πεποιθέναι ("trust") denote the trusting surrender to God that is contained in "faith" and characterizes Christian existence in general. More frequently, Paul speaks of that trust in God arising from faith that gives him his apostolic consciousness and supports him in his ministry as an apostle (II Cor. 3:4; 10:2). He trusts in God's guidance and assistance for himself and the Church (Phil. 1:6, 25; 2:24). The trust which he places in a Congregation (Gal. 5:10; II Cor. 1:15; 2:3; *cf.* 8:22) or a friend (Phlm. 21) is probably also to be understood as flowing out of his "faith," especially since he characterizes it as a confidence "in the Lord" (Gal. 5:10, though B omits ἐν κυρίῳ).

Paul does not speak of trust in God in the traditional Old

Testament sense (found especially in Psalms), since his message has for its theme not the lot of individuals but eschatological salvation. For the contrary, see I Pet. 5:7, for example.

§ 36. Life in Faith

1. "Faith" as man's relation to God also determines man's relation to himself; for human existence, as we have seen (§ 17), is an existence in which man has a relationship to himself. "Faith" is the acceptance of the *kerygma* not as mere cognizance of it and agreement with it but as that genuine obedience to it which includes a new understanding of one's self. Therefore, it cannot be an act that takes place once and then becomes a thing of the past. Neither is it a quality of man that mysteriously and imperishably clings to him like, for instance, the "incorruption" imparted in the mysteries. Still less is "faith" an "experience," mystical or otherwise, to which one might look back contentedly and which could either occasionally repeat itself, interrupting the course of everyday life, or else maintain itself as one's "life-feeling." Rather, *it determines one's living in its manifold historical reality,* and there is no moment in which the man of faith is released from the obedience of constantly living out of the "grace" of God. Therefore, "whatever does not proceed from faith is sin" (Rom. 14:23). The Christian must "continue in (God's) kindness" (Rom. 11:22), and "the life I now live in the flesh I live by faith in the Son of God" (Gal. 2:20). Hence, there are no special practices designated for the man of faith—"for in Christ Jesus neither circumcision nor uncircumcision is of any avail (and that also means: no specifically religious practices), but faith working through love" (Gal. 5:6). Accordingly, *"faith" both as to degree and to kind realizes itself in concrete living: in the individual acts of the man of faith.* As to degree: A weakness in faith (Rom. 14:1) exists, so do "lacks of faith" (I Thess. 3:10); there is also "progress" (Phil. 1:25) and "increase" (II Cor. 10:15) in faith. A believer may be overtaken in some "trespass" (Gal. 6:1) and the exhortation that one should "correct" or "restore to a proper condition" (καταρτίζειν and καταρτίζεσθαι) occurs again and again (Gal. 6:1; I Cor. 1:10; II Cor. 13:11); so does the prayer that God may establish, strengthen, sustain, or the like (II Cor. 13:9; Rom. 15:13; I Thess. 3:13; 5:23; *cf.* § 35, 4). The fact that the "weakness in faith" of

Rom. 14:1f. fully corresponds to the "weak conscience" of I Cor. 8:7–12 clearly indicates that "faith" realizes itself in knowledge of what one has to do or not to do in the specific instance (*cf.* § 19, 4). The Christian henceforth is to consider himself only as one who has faith; that is just the reason why "whatever does not proceed from faith is sin." The life of the believer, therefore, will be a continual movement in which that basic movement between "no longer" and "not yet" (§ 35, 4) takes concrete form, heeding the exhortation: "Let those of us who are mature be thus minded (i.e. "strain forward to what lies ahead"); and if in anything you are otherwise minded, God will reveal that also to you. Only let us hold true to what we have attained" (Phil. 3:15).

"Faith," however, is also individualized as to kind, viz. according to the "measure of faith" which God has assigned to each one (Rom. 12:3). This "measure of faith" is equivalent to one's share of the "gifts" which God or the Spirit bestows (§ 14, 1). For as "faith" is individualized in various concrete ways of acting, so divine "grace" is also individualized in various concrete "gifts of grace": "having gifts that differ according to the grace given to us" (Rom. 12:6). As Paul was given the "grace" of apostleship to the Gentiles (Rom. 1:5; 12:3; 15:15; I Cor. 3:10; Gal. 2:9) and the "gift" of celibacy, so others were given other things: "each has his own special gift from God, one of one kind and one of another" (I Cor. 7:7). Paul's lists of such "gifts" in Rom. 12:6ff.; I Cor. 12:4ff., 28ff. show that he considers as "gifts" not only striking phenomena that were generally so considered, such as ecstatic glossolalia, the gift of prophecy and the working of miracles, but also includes all demonstrations of brotherly love (§ 14, 1 and 3). Moreover, the modifiers "in liberality," "with cheerfulness," and "genuine" (unfeigned) attached to the gifts of contributing, acts of mercy, and love, and designating in each case the norm of the respective activity, are equivalent to the phrase "in proportion to our faith" which is appended to prophecy (Rom. 12:6, 8f.). We see, then, that by virtue of all such gifts Christian existence in faith takes concrete shape in individually varied forms. As "faith" founded upon "grace" is at work in "love" (Gal. 5:6), love's activity itself can be called "grace" (II Cor. 8:1, 4, 6f., 19): "God is able to make every grace (= activity of love) abound in you, so that you may always have enough of everything and may provide in abundance for every good work" (II Cor. 9:8 tr.).

2. One eminent "gift" is *knowledge,* γνῶσις, and it already came to light in our analysis of the structure of "faith" that it contains a knowledge both capable of further development and requiring such (§ 35). The outward contradiction between I Cor. 8:1, "we know that all of us possess knowledge," and 8:7, "however, not all possess this knowledge," indicates that there are differences within that knowledge. The "weakness in faith" (Rom. 14:1) is a lack in knowledge (see 1, above), just as "not all possess this knowledge" is said in reference to the "weak." He who is "strong" is to be considerate of such "weak" ones and is not to judge them; for each one is responsible only to the Lord (Rom. 14:4, 22). When it is said: "let each one be fully convinced in his own mind" (v. 5), it is clear that each one is independent in his "faith" and is to achieve his own knowledge. So it is explicitly said: "Have the faith that you have by yourself before God . . ." (v. 22f., tr.).

This does not mean, however, that each is to insist upon his own standpoint. Just as Paul leaves no doubt but that he approves the knowledge of the "strong" (Rom. 14; I Cor. 8), he wishes for the Philippians: "that your love (here denoting the Christian attitude as a whole) may abound more and more with knowledge and all discernment so that you may approve what is excellent" (Phil. 1:9f.). Likewise Rom. 12:2: "be transformed by the renewal of your mind that you may prove what is the will of God . . ." In the meetings of the congregation the "word of wisdom" and the "word of knowledge" play an important role (I Cor. 12:8) and Paul is glad when he can boast that a congregation is rich in "understanding" (λόγος) and "knowledge" (I Cor. 1:5; II Cor. 8:7; Rom. 15:14), and he is proud that, though he is "unskilled in speech," he is not so in "knowledge" (II Cor. 11:6).

Such "knowledge" or "wisdom" develops the knowing that is contained in "faith" into ever clearer and more comprehensive knowledge. Paul stimulates his readers in this direction with his queries, "Are you ignorant?" "do you not know?" and the like (§ 35, 2). In Rom. 6:3, for example, he refers the Romans to a knowledge which he obviously presupposes them to have: "Do you not know that all of us who have been baptized into Christ Jesus were baptized into his death?" and then in v. 11 makes them aware of the consequence: "so you must consider yourselves dead to sin and alive to God . . ."

[326]

Knowledge as a special aspect of "faith" is a gift of the Spirit (see 1); this, nevertheless, does not mean that it is not to be conceived as a task or that it is not to be developed, as Phil. 1:9f. and Rom. 12:2 (see above) clearly show. Though here and probably in the majority of cases the knowledge meant is knowledge of the will of God—i.e. one's grasp of ethical duties—elsewhere it is knowledge of the mysteries of the history of salvation or of the eschatological occurrence (Rom. 11:25; I Cor. 2:7; 15:51). For by the power of the Spirit knowledge can soar aloft to a "wisdom" which lies beyond the paradoxical, foolish-seeming "wisdom" of the proclaimed cross; this higher "wisdom," however, is reserved for "mature" Christians (I Cor. 2:6). There is a Spirit-given "searching of the depths of God" (2:10). However great the danger is that *gnosis* may separate out of "faith" as speculation—a danger which has undoubtedly become reality in the Gnostics of Corinth—in Paul it retains its basic character of an existential knowledge in which faith unfolds itself. For Paul defines its purpose to be: "that we may understand the gifts bestowed on us by God" (2:12). To understand God's gift means to understand one's self as the receiver of it; hence, this highest "wisdom" and "knowledge" must simultaneously be the clearest understanding of one's self.

The restriction of this "wisdom" to those who have ethical maturity (I Cor. 3:1-3) likewise indicates that in Paul, knowledge has not been cut loose from its inner mooring to "faith" to become a free-floating speculation (or a neutrally investigating science). I Cor. 8, above all, indicates that Christian *gnosis* is the understanding of one's self under divine "grace." For "knowledge" is not genuine if it leads to getting "puffed up" and hence damages the "love" (ἀγάπη) in which "faith" ought to be working. So here, too, it becomes clear that "knowledge" in all its forms and degrees besides being an understanding of its object is simultaneously an existential understanding of one's self in "faith" (§ 35, 2). So far as this self-understanding unfolds as object-knowledge—i.e. as ever more penetrating knowledge of divine grace—it remains only partial knowledge, which will not be succeeded by clear comprehension without riddles until the consummation "when that which is perfect is come" (I Cor. 13:10-12); for now "we walk only by faith, not by sight" (II Cor. 5:7).

3. In this way the formula "*in Christ*" takes on a meaning beyond or in addition to its ecclesiological and eschatological meaning (§ 34,

3): It denotes not, to be sure, an individual mystical relationship to Christ, but the fact that the individual actual life of the believer, living not out of himself but out of the divine deed of salvation, is determined by Christ. It makes no difference whether Paul speaks of the believer's being in Christ or of Christ's being in the believer (Rom. 8:10; II Cor. 13:5; Gal. 2:20; *cf.* 4:19). Either one means nothing else than that conditioning of concrete life which Paul also calls the "law of Christ" (Gal. 6:2). Furthermore, as there is a "standing fast in faith" (§ 35, 4), there is also a "standing fast in the Lord" (I Thess. 3:8; Phil. 4:1). As there are degrees of "faith" (see 1 above), so there are degrees of existence in Christ, such as "babes in Christ" (I Cor. 3:1), "approved in Christ" (Rom. 16:10), or "wise in Christ" (I Cor. 4:10).

The believer's existence as a member of the "body" of Christ (§ 34, 2), eschatological existence, in other words, while he lives "in the flesh" realizes itself in his "walk," his conduct, which is no longer a "walking according to the flesh" (Rom. 8:4; II Cor. 10:2; § 38). For to have died with Christ—as the believer has—means "that our old self was crucified with him so that the sinful body might be destroyed, and we might no longer be enslaved to sin" (Rom. 6:6). Or "those who belong to Christ Jesus have crucified the flesh with its passions and desires" (Gal. 5:24). Thus, Paul confesses of himself: "far be it from me to glory (boast) except in the cross of our Lord Jesus Christ, by which the world has been crucified to me, and I to the world" (Gal. 6:14). Correspondingly, he describes "gaining Christ and being found in him" as the state of being completely determined by the salvation-occurrence; for that is the force of the words: "that I may know him and the power of his resurrection, and may share his sufferings, becoming like him in his death" (Phil. 3:10). His meaning is the same when he says, "I have been crucified with Christ; it is no longer I who live, but Christ who lives in me" (Gal. 2:19f.). Christ's sufferings overflow upon the apostle (II Cor. 1:5); in his body he carries about the dying of Jesus (II Cor. 4:10). But what is true of the apostle only exemplifies what is true of all Christian existence: "we suffer with him (Christ) in order that we may also be glorified with him" (Rom. 8:17).

How this basic determination of one's life by the deed of salvation (or by faith) extends even to details is indicated by the manifold use of the formula "in Christ" or "in the Lord." These phrases fill the place of an adjective or adverb which the linguistic process had not yet developed: "Christian" or "as a Christian," "in a Christian manner." They are used to characterize all sorts of conduct and attitudes: speech (II Cor. 2:17; 12:19) and exhortation (Phil. 2:1), boldness (Phlm. 8) and greetings (Rom. 16:22; I Cor. 16:19), concord (Phil. 4:2), brotherly love (Rom. 16:8; I Cor. 16:24), and friendly reception (Rom. 16:2), as well as effort and concern for the congregation (I Thess. 5:12; Rom. 16:12). Not only what the believer does but also what happens to him has taken on the new stamp denoted by the phrase "in Christ": "in Christ" Paul's imprisonment has become known (Phil. 1:13); for the believer to die is to "fall asleep in Christ" (I Cor. 15:18), and the Church's dead are "the dead in Christ" (I Thess. 4:16). For "whether we live or whether we die, we are the Lord's" (Rom. 14:7–9).

§ 37. Faith as Eschatological Occurrence

Faith as response to the proclaimed word (which is called ἀκοὴ πίστεως, "preaching of faith"), like that word itself, is part of the salvation-occurrence, the eschatological occurrence. As new *possibility* faith is the newly opened way of salvation. It is in this sense that the "principle of faith" can be contrasted with the "principle of works" (Rom. 3:27). Faith can also be said to "come" and "to be revealed" (Gal. 3:23, 25).

This, of course, does not take from the concrete "faith" of the individual that decision-character which belongs to its very nature as "obedience" (§ 35, 1). Nevertheless the concrete realization of the possibility of faith in the individual's decision of faith is itself eschatological occurrence. Since the believer experiences the possibility of the faith-decision as grace, it is only as a gift of grace that he can understand his decision—his own decision! And because he knows that it is God who accomplishes his willing and doing—his concrete, historical existing in "faith"—he is conscious not of being relieved of responsibility for it but on the contrary of being made responsible for it (Phil. 2:13f.; § 35, 4).

Thus, Paul can say that faith in Christ is "granted" as a gift (Phil. 1:29). In fact, he can speak of it in downright predestinarian terms (Rom. 8:29; 9:6–29). If such statements about God's "foreknowing" and "predestining" or His "electing" and "hardening" be taken liter-

[329]

ally, an insoluble contradiction results, for a faith brought about by God outside of man's decision would obviously not be genuine obedience. Faith is God-wrought to the extent that prevenient grace first made the human decision possible, with the result that he who has made the decision can only understand it as God's gift; but that does not take its decision-character away from it. Only so does the imperative, "be reconciled to God" (II Cor. 5:20; § 31) make sense. The predestinarian statements express the fact that the decision of faith does not, like other decisions, go back to this-worldly motives of any sort whatever—that, on the contrary, such motives lose all power of motivation in the presence of the encountered proclamation.

The eschatological nature of faith is testified, lastly, by the fact that Paul does not describe faith as inspired, attributable to the "Spirit." * Just the opposite: The Spirit is the gift which faith receives (Gal. 3:2, 5, 14) and in which the grace of God appropriated by faith becomes effective in concrete living (§ 38, 3). Therefore, Paul calls the "love" ($\dot{\alpha}\gamma\dot{\alpha}\pi\eta$) in which "faith" is operating the "fruit of the Spirit," just as he regards the Christian "virtues" as a whole to be such fruit (Gal. 5:22). A comparison between the parallel sentences Gal. 5:6 and 6:15: in Christ neither circumcision nor uncircumcision has any meaning, but (in the first case) "faith working through love" or (in the other case) "a new creation," reveals that the existing of a Christian in the faith that operates in love is eschatological occurrence: a being created anew.

D. FREEDOM

§ 38. Freedom from Sin and Walking in the Spirit

1. Faith's obedient submission to God's "grace," the acceptance of the cross of Christ, is the surrender of man's old understanding of himself, in which he lives "unto himself," tries to achieve life by his own strength, and by that very fact falls victim to the powers of sin

---

* In II Cor. 4:13 "Since we have the same spirit of faith . . . (so we speak)," "spirit of faith" does not mean the Spirit which bestows faith, but the spirit that is typical of faith. Ultimately "spirit of faith" here means "kind or sort of faith." When I Cor. 12:3 gives the cry, "Lord Jesus" as the criterion for possession by the Spirit, this does not intend to attribute the confession of faith to the Spirit, but to state the means by which spiritual and demonic ecstasy are to be distinguished.

and death and loses himself (§§ 23, 24). Therefore, "faith"—as "obedience of faith"—is also released from these powers. The new self-understanding which is bestowed with "faith" is that of *freedom,* in which the believer gains life and thereby his own self.

This freedom arises from the very fact that *the believer,* as one "ransomed," *no longer "belongs to himself"* (I Cor. 6:19). He no longer bears the care for himself, for his own life, but lets this care go, yielding himself entirely to the grace of God; he recognizes himself to be the property of God (or of the Lord) and lives for Him:

> "None of us lives to himself
>   and none of us dies to himself.
> If we live, we live to the Lord,
>   And if we die, we die to the Lord;
> So then, whether we live or whether we die,
>   We are the Lord's."
>   (Rom. 14:7f.; *cf.* 7:4; Gal. 2:19f.; II Cor. 5:14f.)

The mightiest expression of freedom is I Cor. 3:21–23:

> "For all things are yours . . .
> whether the world or life or death
> or the present or the future,
> all are yours."

But the concluding clauses are "and you are Christ's; and Christ is God's."

The life of him who is released from the power of death is no phenomenon of nature, either, but is the life of the striving, willing self which is always after something and is always faced with its various possibilities, but it is constantly faced with those two basic possibilities: to live "according to the flesh" or to live "according to the Spirit"—to and for one's self or to and for God or the Lord (§ 18, 4). This alternative also presents itself to the man of faith (Gal. 6:7f.; Rom. 8:12f.), and *the freedom to which he is set free* is not a "freedom (to be offered) as a base of operations to the flesh" (Gal. 5:13 tr.)—i.e. not a release from all binding norms, from the law of God, but rather a new servitude (Rom. 7:6), the service of the "living God" (I Thess. 1:9) or of Christ (Rom. 14:18; 16:18), an enslavement not to "sin" any longer, but to "righteousness" (Rom. 6:16–18). A paradoxical servitude! For the "slave of Christ" is, at the same time, "a freedman of Christ" (I Cor. 7:22). It will presently appear that this servitude is also a "serving of one another" (Gal. 5:13) and can demand that one make himself "a slave to all" (I Cor. 9:19). At any rate, the "obedience of faith" proves itself genuine when the believer places himself at God's disposal to obey Him (Rom. 6:16), and his members as "instruments of righteousness" (Rom. 6:12ff.); for "God condemned sin in the flesh, in order that the just requirement of the Law might be fulfilled" in the "walking according to the Spirit" which our "walking" has become (Rom. 8:3f.).

Neither is this freedom a mysterious emancipation from sin and death considered as powers of nature. It is not a decisionless capacity henceforth to do the good only—which would itself be a capacity of nature and hence also a supranatural compulsion. "Sinlessness" is not a magical guarantee against the *possibility* of sin—the believer, too, must beware of the "tempter" (I Thess. 3:5; I Cor. 7:5; II Cor. 2:11; §26, 3)—but release from the *compulsion* of sin. Freedom from sin consists in the possibility, once flung away, of realizing the commandment's intent to bestow life (§27). That which to man is good—"life"—both before and after his emancipation is also that which is required of him (§19, 1; §21, 1; §27, 1). Therefore, freedom from death means possessing genuine future, whereas man under the power of death, as he formerly was, had no future (§24, 2).

Therefore, the *imperative*, "walk according to the Spirit," not only does not contradict the *indicative* of justification (the believer is rightwised) but results from it: "Cleanse out the old leaven that you may be fresh dough, as you really are unleavened" (I Cor. 5:7f.). In a certain sense, then, "Become what thou art!" is valid—but not in the sense of idealism, according to which the "idea" of the perfect man is more and more closely realized in endless progress. In this idealistic sense the transcendence of "perfection" is conceived as the "idea's" transcendence, and man's relation to it is regarded (Stoically expressed) as a "progressing" or a "tending" toward it. Rather, "sinlessness"—i.e. freedom from the power of sin—is already realized in the "righteousness of God" (§29, 2); its transcendence is that of the divine verdict, and man's relation to it is that of "obedience of faith." The way the believer becomes what he already is consists therefore in the constant appropriation of grace by faith, which also means, in the concrete, "obedience," which is henceforth possible in his "walking": "for sin will have no dominion over you, since you are not under law but under grace" (Rom. 6:14). Likewise, the indicatives "you were washed, you were consecrated" (I Cor. 6:11) are the motivation for the preceding exhortation. In Rom. 6, Paul develops this idea on a broad scale. He is opposing a purely sacramental understanding of baptism as the means by which one achieves assurance of a future life. He does so by showing that the life conferred by baptism must prove itself in the present by its freedom from the power of sin (§ 13, 1; p. 140; § 34, 3): "so you also must consider yourselves dead to sin and alive to God in Jesus Christ" (v. 11). Likewise, the imperative "walk by the Spirit" (Gal. 5:16ff.) concludes with the paradoxical statement, "If we live by the Spirit, let us also walk by the Spirit" (v. 25)—a sentence open to misunderstanding so far as it seems to imply that there could be a "living by the Spirit" without a "walking by the Spirit." But the purpose of this formulation is to avoid the opposite misunderstanding that there must first be a "walking by the Spirit" which would then establish this "living by the Spirit." The meaning is clear: the faith-bestowed possibility of "living by the Spirit" must be explicitly laid hold of by "walking by the Spirit." The indicative is the foundation for the imperative.

2. The believer has been given (in baptism) the *gift of the Spirit.* What that means is just this: He has been given freedom—freedom from the power of sin and death.

Paul, as a matter of course, shares the general Christian view that the Spirit is conferred by baptism (I Cor. 6:11; 12:13; II Cor. 1:22; § 13, 1, p. 139) and also the conception of the Spirit as a miraculous, divine power (Rom. 15:19; I Cor. 2:4, etc.; § 14, 1). In speaking of the Spirit, he uses animistic and dynamistic terminology promiscuously (p. 155), a fact which in itself indicates that he is unconcerned with any speculative interest in the idea of Spirit. Corresponding to a mode of thinking that is undeveloped in the direction of abstraction, locutions occur in which the Spirit is conceived as a non-worldly *material* or as borne by such. At least Paul can speak of the Spirit as a something that can take residence in a man (Rom. 8:9, 11; I Cor. 6:19), and therefore is bound to a locality. But such a locution is scarcely to be taken strictly, since it can also be used in reference to the congregation (I Cor. 3:16), in which case a conception strictly corresponding to the literal wording is inconceivable. Nevertheless, Paul's term "spiritual body" (I Cor. 15:44, 46) strongly suggests that Paul conceived of the Spirit as a material, just as the term "glory" (§ 14, 1; p. 156), closely related to that of Spirit, undoubtedly denotes a (heavenly) substance in I Cor. 15:40f. Moreover, though II Cor. 3:7 naively speaks of the externally visible brightness of "glory," still Paul's contrasting of the glory of the old and the new "covenant" (3:7ff.) indicates by itself that he does not stick to this conception; for the "greater splendor" of the "new covenant" is not visible at all, but is a power which demonstrates itself in its effect—and that is that it produces freedom. When Paul says of those who along with the Spirit of the Lord have received freedom: "we are being transformed from glory into glory . . ." (v. 18), it is clear that this present glory is no shining material. It is nothing other than the power by means of which the "inward self" (§ 18, 1) is renewed day by day (4:16); recall that "glory" and "power" can be synonymous (§ 14, 1; p. 156).

We may accordingly say that the sporadically occurring notion of the Spirit *as a material* is not one that is really determinative for Paul's concept of the Spirit. That is sufficiently indicated by Paul's characterization of the Law as "spiritual" (Rom. 7:14), where the notion of materiality is out of the question, but also by such constructions as "spiritual gift" (Rom. 1:11) and "to share in spiritual blessings" (Rom. 15:27; *cf.* I Cor. 9:11) or the contrast of "letter" to "Spirit" (Rom. 2:29; 7:6; II Cor. 3:6), or the description of mature Christians as being "spiritual" (I Cor. 2:13, 15; 3:1; Gal. 6:1). Then the true meaning of Paul's Spirit-concept must be reached in some other way.

The Spirit is the opposite of "flesh" (Gal. 5:16; 6:8; Rom. 8:4ff., etc.). As "flesh" is the quintessence of the worldly, visible, controllable, and transitory sphere which becomes the controlling power over the man who lives "according to the flesh" (§ 22), so "Spirit" is the quintessence of the non-worldly, invisible, uncontrollable, eternal sphere (p. 234) which becomes the controlling power for and in him who orients his life "according to the Spirit." And as the power of "flesh" is manifested in the fact that it binds man to the transitory, to that which in reality is always already past, binds him to death, so the power of the Spirit is manifested in the fact that it gives the believer freedom, opens up the future, the eternal, life.

For freedom is nothing else than being open for the genuine future, letting one's self be determined by the future. So Spirit may be called the power of futurity.

The expression of this conception is the fact that the Spirit is the eschatological gift: the "first-fruit" (Rom. 8:23), or the "guarantee" (II Cor. 1:22; 5:5). For such statements declare that the believer's life is determined by that future which is his origin and his strength as well as his norm—just as "glory" is ultimately the power that flows out of the opened future and determines the present (II Cor. 3:18). Therefore, the Spirit is also called "the Spirit of adoption to sonship" (Rom. 8:15; *cf.* Gal. 4:6; § 29, 3); by its receipt in baptism we are "rightwised" (I Cor. 6:11) and incorporated into the "body of Christ" (I Cor. 12:13; *cf.* Gal. 3:27f.). As the eschatological existence can be called a "being in Christ" (§ 34, 3), so it can also be called a "being in the Spirit" (Rom. 8:9), and the locutions "to have the spirit of Christ" or "Christ in you" (v. 9f.) can take its place with no difference in meaning. What Paul has done "in the power of the Spirit" Christ has wrought through him (Rom. 15:18), and "being minded according to Christ Jesus" (Rom. 15:5) corresponds antithetically to "being minded according to the flesh." The believer has freedom "in Christ" (Gal. 2:4); Christ has freed us for freedom (Gal. 5:1). On the other hand, commenting on "to the Lord" from Ex. 34:34, Paul can say, "now the Lord is the Spirit" and add "and where the Spirit of the Lord is, there is freedom" (II Cor. 3:17). As to the last phrase of v. 18, καθάπερ ἀπὸ κυρίου πνεύματος, it is hard to decide whether it means "from the Lord of the Spirit" or "from the Lord who is the Spirit"—not to mention other possibilities.

"To be in the Spirit" no more denotes the state of ecstasy than "to be in Christ" is a formula of mysticism. Though Paul is familiar with ecstatic experience as a rare exception (II Cor. 12:1–4; v. 2: "fourteen years ago"), the Spirit, nevertheless, does not mean to him the capacity for mystical experiences. Rather, everything indicates that by the term "Spirit" he means the eschatological existence into which the believer is placed by having appropriated the salvation deed that occurred in Christ. To have received the Spirit means to be standing in grace (Rom. 5:2); when II Cor. 1:12 contrasts behavior "in fleshly wisdom" with behavior in "the grace of God," the latter phrase is synonymous with "according to the Spirit." Hence, Paul can say to describe rhetorically the whole of the salvation-occurrence: "the grace of the Lord Jesus Christ and the love of God and the fellowship of the Holy Spirit" (II Cor. 13:13). Again, the fact that the future has been opened up by the Spirit on the basis of the divine deed of salvation is expressed in the reason given for the certainty of Christian hope: "because God's love (§ 32, 3) has been poured into our hearts through the Holy Spirit which has been given to us" (Rom. 5:5).

3. There is a peculiar double meaning about the term "Spirit," because it can denote both the miraculous power that is bestowed upon the man of faith and is the source of his new life, and also the norm of his earthly "walk." This is the same paradox as in that utterance of Gal. 5:25: "If we live by the Spirit, let us also walk by the Spirit"—in which the first "Spirit" means the power, the second the norm, for it stands in place of a κατὰ πνεῦμα ("according to the Spirit," as in 5:16). The primary idea is that of the miraculous power of God; then, since it has the effect of emancipating from the power of sin and death (Rom. 8:2)—i.e. it grants freedom of action and opens up the possibility of "reaping eternal life" (Gal. 6:8)—it is also the norm for "walking." The newly opened possibility of laying hold of "life" by its very nature contains the ethical imperative (see 1, above). Freedom and demand constitute a unity: Freedom is the reason for the demand, and the demand actualizes the freedom. Only when this unity is understood, is Paul's thought of the Spirit understood aright—and that means: when the Spirit is conceived of not as a mysterious power working with magical compulsion but as the new possibility of genuine, human life which opens up to him who has surrendered his old understanding of himself, letting himself be crucified with Christ, in order to experience the "power of his resurrection" (Phil. 3:10). For it is clear that to be "led by the Spirit" (Rom. 8:14; Gal. 5:18) does not mean to be dragged along willy-nilly (*cf.* I Cor. 12:2) but directly presupposes decision in the alternative: "flesh" or "Spirit" (Rom. 8:12-14; Gal. 5:16-18). That unity of power and demand is likewise hidden in those seemingly mythological expressions, "the mind of the Spirit" (Rom. 8:6, 27) and the "desires of the Spirit" (Gal. 5:17; § 18, 3), for these expressions mean that the Spirit founds a new will, whose origin is not within man but within the salvation-deed of God—a will that has definite direction, free from the "flesh" and in battle against it, guided by the demand of God. Therein lies the solution of the con-

tradition that the Spirit is, on the one hand, the gift conferred upon all Christians at baptism and that, on the other hand, it shows its operation in special deeds (§ 14, 3). For, on the one hand, along with faith the possibility of eschatological existence is given to all, and, on the other hand, this possibility must actualize itself in the concrete deed from case to case.

In the view that the "Spirit" is miraculous power, Paul, it must first be said, simply shares without reflection popular notions, according to which "miraculous" events—i.e. strange phenomena that fall outside the frame of normal life—are regarded as spirit-wrought: glossolalia, prophecy, miracles of healing, etc. (§ 14, 1). Indirectly, however, he is already contesting the allegedly obvious meaning of such phenomena when he only so far recognizes them to be caused by the Spirit of God as they produce unity in the congregation— having themselves unity of origin in "the same Spirit" (I Cor. 12:4-6)—and serve for the "edification" of the congregation (I Cor. 12 and 14). The really characteristic feature of his conception of the Spirit, however, is the fact that he reckons the ministrations of love within the congregation among the Spirit's workings, an idea evidently foreign to the popular view (§ 14, 1 and 3; § 36, 1), and the further fact that he attributes ethical conduct to the Spirit (Rom. 8:4-9). The Spirit is at war with the "flesh" (Gal. 5:17), and the "virtues" (Gal. 5:22; *cf.* Rom. 14:17) are the "fruit" of the Spirit. This is no spiritualizing, ethicizing re-interpretation of the "Spirit" concept. It means that free, ethical obedience can have its origin only in miracle—quite in keeping with the view that from the fetters of flesh and sin man must be freed to obedience by the deed of God.

In respect to its meaning freedom from death and the source and power of the life to come, "Spirit" will come up for further discussion. So far as it produces freedom from sin and is the source and power as well as the norm of present conduct, those statements are characteristic in which *conduct* is described by such locutions as: "serve . . . in the newness (καινότητι) of the Spirit" (Rom. 7:6), "walk by the Spirit" (Gal. 5:16) or "be guided" (στοιχεῖν) (Gal. 5:25) by it, or "walk according to the Spirit" (Rom. 8:4), "be in the Spirit" (Rom. 8:5), "set the mind on the things of the Spirit" (Rom. 8:5); likewise the expression "Spirit of gentleness" (I Cor. 4:21; Gal. 6:1—semitizing for: the gentle Spirit) and "the love of the Spirit" (Rom. 15:30). Since λογικός ("reasonable," KJ Rom. 12:1f.), following Hellenistic usage, has for Paul the meaning "spiritual," the λογικὴ λατρεία ("spiritual worship" RSV) which has its foundation in the renewal of the νοῦς—i.e. of one's "character" (§ 19, 1)—and results in "proving what is the good and acceptable and perfect will of God," is only another expression for the same thing. Also characteristic, lastly, is the fact that the Spirit is received by the "heart" (Gal. 4:6; II Cor. 1:22; Rom. 5:5; *cf.* 8:27), i.e. is taken up into the will of man (§ 20); and also the fact that Paul describes his "conscience" as speaking "in the Holy Spirit" (Rom. 9:1).

Other descriptions of the Christian "walk," though not explicitly using the word "spirit," express substantially the same thing: the power and the obligation given when one is brought into eschatological existence—the Christian must walk "becomingly as in the day" (Rom. 13:13), "worthily of God who calls you into his own kingdom and glory" (I Thess. 2:12), "according to love" (Rom. 14:15). Where such conduct has its origin is betrayed by the characterization of the opposite kind as a "walking according to man," which is coordinate with being "of the flesh" (I Cor. 3:3).

The Spirit is the "Holy Spirit," πνεῦμα ἅγιον, and the use of the holiness-concept is likewise significant for the unity of the indicative and the imperative—i.e. of power and obligation. Believers are ἅγιοι, ἡγιασμένοι ("holy," "made holy"—though English translations through the influence of the Vulgate conventionally render the first "saints" and the second "sanctified" or "consecrated"—§ 10, 3), which means in the first place those who have been taken out of the world and transplanted into the eschatological existence by Christ's salvation-deed (I Cor. 1:2: as those "made holy in Christ Jesus") which in baptism was carried over to them (I Cor. 6:11: "but you were washed, you were made holy," etc.). Christ is to us "righteousness and consecration and redemption" (abstract expression for the concrete: "he who makes us righteous and holy and redeemed" I Cor. 1:30). But from this very fact arises our obligation to the active "holiness" which God demands of us (I Thess. 4:3; Rom. 6:19, 22); whoever disregards this demand disregards God who gave us His Holy Spirit (I Thess. 4:8). Our body is the Holy Spirit's temple, which must be kept clean (I Cor. 6:19). The congregation also is the holy temple of God, and God will destroy the destroyer of this temple (I Cor. 3:16f.). Similar are

Paul's wishes that God, or the Lord, may establish believers' hearts "unblamable in holiness" and utterly sanctify them (I Thess. 3:13; 5:23). The bestowal of holiness through baptism can be called "putting on Christ"; but in addition to the indicative, "you have put on Christ" (Gal. 3:27), we also find the imperative: "put on the Lord Jesus Christ" (Rom. 13:14).

4. It may seem strange that in the list of virtues at Gal. 5:22f. "joy" appears as a fruit of the Spirit second only to "love." But "joy" actually is one of the qualities of the eschatological existence founded by the Spirit, for the nature of the Reign of God is "right-ousness and joy and peace in the Holy Spirit" (Rom. 14:17). The combination of "joy" and "peace" occurring here and elsewhere (Gal. 5:22; Rom. 15:13) permits us to recognize "joy," too, as an eschatological phenomenon, for "peace" here means "salvation" in the eschatological sense, as Rom. 2:10; 8:6 (joined with "life"!) indicate, or the wish at Phil. 4:7, or the formula "the God of peace" (Rom. 15:33; 16:20; Phil. 4:9; I Thess. 5:23).*

The believer's existence, being eschatological, is an existence in joy. Paul hopes that he may yet work for the congregation in Philippi "for your progress and joy in the faith" (Phil. 1:25); to the Corinthian congregation he wants to be only a "fellow-worker for your joy" (II Cor. 1:24); his wish for the Romans is: "May the God of hope fill you with all joy and peace in believing" (Rom. 15:13). When God is called "the God of hope" in this wish, it is clear that the joy of the present is based upon the reference of Christian existence to the future; "rejoicing in hope" is one of the characteristics of believers (Rom. 12:12). Indeed, this joy, which is not a joy over anything within this world, is itself the Christian's relatedness to the future, insofar as it is consciously realized. And he *should* be conscious of it: hence, Paul's exhortations to be joyful (I Thess. 5:16; II Cor. 13:11 [English tradition here renders it "farewell"; but do ancient letters confirm this as a *closing* formula?] Phil. 3:1; 4:4). This is a joy that wells up in the midst of worldly tribulation (II Cor. 6:10) as a "joy inspired by the Holy Spirit" (I Thess. 1:6). Such eschatological joy actualizes itself furthermore in the fel-

---

* Of course, εἰρήνη can retain its root-meaning, "peace." This specific meaning is demanded by the context in II Cor. 13:11; it also occurs at Rom. 5:1; I Cor. 14:33. The succession of Rom. 14:19 upon 14:17 indicates how closely related these two meanings are.

lowship and mutual helpfulness of those whom it binds together
It is right and proper that the apostle or the congregation should
cause the other joy or rejoice in the other (II Cor. 1:15?; 2:3; Rom.
15:32; 16:19; Phil. 2:2, 17f.; 4:1, 10; I Thess. 2:19; 3:9) or give each
other reciprocal joy (II Cor. 8:2) or rejoice with each other (Rom
12:15).

§ 39. Freedom from the Law and the Christian's Attitude toward Men

1. The "power of sin" is "the Law" (I Cor. 15:56; § 27, 2)—or
rather, for believers: it was. For to them Christ is the "end of the
law" (Rom. 10:4); "in him" or "through him" we have freedom from
the Law (Gal. 2:4). For freedom he set us free (Gal. 5:1); to it we
were "called" (Gal. 5:13). The Christian Church is the Congregation of the free, while Judaism is under bondage to the Law, as the
Sarah-Hagar allegory (Gal. 4:21–31) sets forth. The old period of
the "custodian's" restraint lies in the past; the man who once held
the position of a slave under the Law has been set free, to be no
longer a ward; now he has the rights of a son (Gal. 3:23–4:7). The
"old covenant" and the "ministration of death" and "of condemnation" which "faded away" have been replaced by the "new covenant" and the "ministration of the Spirit" and "of righteousness"
which is "permanent" (II Cor. 3:6–11).

Since "flesh" has been condemned by the salvation-occurrence,
sin has been condemned with it, for God "condemned sin in the
flesh" (Rom. 8:3). For it is in the "flesh" that sin had its origin
(§ 22, 3; § 23) and it was awakened in the flesh by the Law (§ 27,
2). Since the power of sin is destroyed for those who share in the
salvation-deed of the cross (Gal. 5:24), for them the Law, and hence
also sin, have both lost their power: "for sin will have no dominion
over you, since you are not under law but under grace" (Rom. 6:14).
"When we were living in the flesh, there worked in our members the
sinful passions aroused by the law, so that we bore fruit for death.
But now we are free of the law, dead to that by which we were
fettered, so that we serve in the new Spirit and not in the old letter"
(Rom. 7:5f.). As those who are "led by the Spirit" (Gal. 5:18),
believers are no longer under the Law, and so far as they produce
the fruit of the Spirit Paul says: "against such people there is no

law" (Gal. 5:23). That is the reason for Paul's struggle against the Judaizers in Galatia and for his exhortation to those freed by Christ: "stand fast, therefore, and do not submit again to a yoke of slavery" (Gal. 5:1).

It is clear that Christ is the end of the Law so far as it claimed to be the way to salvation or was understood by man as the means of establishing "his own righteousness" (§ 23, 1; § 27, 2), for *so far as it contains God's demand* (§ 27, 2), *it retains its validity*. Of course, it is self-evident that so far as the νόμος of God is represented to Paul's mind by the Old Testament Torah with all its cultic and ritual rules (§ 27, 1), it cannot be valid in its whole extent. Paul's struggle in Galatia against the Law as the way to salvation is simultaneously a struggle against the ritual and cultic rules, particularly against circumcision and the Jewish festivals (Gal. 4:10). Where Paul calls the Law "holy" and "spiritual" (Rom. 7:12, 14) he is thinking only of the ethical commandments summarized in the formula, "you shall not desire" (v. 7)—likewise where he calls "love" the fulfilment of the Law (Gal. 5:14; Rom. 13:9f.; *cf.* § 27, 1). Then, however, freedom from the Law also actualizes itself in the freedom to differentiate between the valid and the non-valid, according to its content, within the Law as it has been handed down. Paul did not work out this problem in detail, but the obligation to practice such criticism is contained in the capacity of "proving what is the good and acceptable and perfect will of God" (Rom. 12:2) or of "approving what is excellent" (i.e. "distinguishing what is important"—Phil. 1:10).

2. Freedom from the Law, therefore, has a dialectic or paradoxical character: freedom from its demand and obligation to it nonetheless—depending upon the sense in which the demand is understood. This freedom can find expression in the formula, "All things are lawful for me" (I Cor. 6:12; 10:23), which was evidently a slogan of the Gnosticizing Christians in Corinth (§ 15, 4f.). Paul approves of it, but when he adds: "but not all things are wholesome (tr.) . . . but I will not be enslaved by anything," the ambiguity of the formula becomes apparent: It is to be rejected so far as it asserts that man is released from all obligations and that his subjective caprice is given free rein. If this were true, then this principle would have the consequence hinted at in the words, "but I will not be enslaved by anything," viz.: that man would fall into

subjection to whatever exercises motivating power upon his personal choice. "All things are lawful for me" in its true sense has for its presupposition inner freedom from the world, a freedom in which all claims from within the world have lost their motivating power and all worldly things and situations have sunk down into indifference. This freedom, however, arises precisely out of the believer's binding obligation to the Lord or to God: "for you are not your own" (I Cor. 6:19; § 38, 1). The sense, then, in which the reservation "not all things are wholesome" limits the principle that "all things are lawful for me" is not that within the field of "all things" there is this or that which is "not wholesome," for "nothing is unclean in itself" (Rom. 14:14) and "all things are clean" (14:20). It does assert, however, that the whole field of "all things" becomes "an unwholesome thing" as soon as I lose my freedom to anything whatever in which that field encounters me. The indifference of everything worldly disappears in the concrete situation of personal responsibility.

But this situation receives its stamp not alone from the demands that apply to the individual by himself, such as that of chastity (I Cor. 6:12ff.), but especially from the obligations that arise from human fellowship. In this respect "all things are lawful for me" is restricted by the limitation (I Cor. 10:23b): "but not all things build up"—some things do not contribute to building up fellowship. This limitation is also given in positive form: "let no one seek his own good, but the good of his neighbor" (I Cor. 10:24). Neither does that mean a quantitative diminution of "all things"; it does mean that this basic freedom may at any moment take on the form of *renunciation*—seemingly a renunciation of freedom itself, but in reality it is a paradoxical exercise of that very freedom, such as is expressed in Paul's declaration, "for though I am free from all men, I have made myself a slave to all" (I Cor. 9:19). Out of Christian "freedom" flows *"authorization"* (ἐξουσία), which is expressed in "all things are lawful for me" (which could just as well be translated: "for me all things are authorized"). This authorization is the Christian's independence from all worldly claims, among which are the ritual and cultic rules of the Torah. It is the authorization, or the right, to find for one's self, by that independent "proving," what the "good" is—and hence, is also independence from the judgment of any other person's conscience (I Cor. 10:29b; *cf.* Rom. 14:5). In his respect, of course, there can be no waiving of "authorization"; for in this respect it is "freedom" itself. But so far as "authorization" is regarded as a personal right to inconsiderate exercise of "freedom," Paul distinguishes between it and "freedom": the latter manifests itself, in case consideration for one's brother demands it, precisely in waiving "authorization" as a personal right. As a personal right it would no longer be Christian freedom but a legal claim, which higher purposes naturally may demand that one give up, as Paul makes clear by his own waiver of the apostle's right to support by the churches (I Cor. 9:1–23). Exercise of freedom in this sense is just what is being demanded when Paul urges: "take care lest this liberty (authorization) of yours somehow become a stumbling-block to the weak" (I Cor. 8:9; *cf.* Rom. 14:13). He is perfectly willing to give up what in principle is completely permissible to him, if enjoyment of it would be a cause of offense to his brother (I Cor. 8:13; *cf.* Rom. 14:21). However, it is clear, as the letter to the Galatians shows, that this consideration must be dropped in the situation of witness-bearing to one's faith—whenever, that is, it would expose itself to being misunderstood as the surrender of "freedom." Only as the exercise of freedom for a brother's sake does consideration have validity, but as that it is demanded of the Christian.

Consideration for one's brother does not mean dependence upon his judgment (I Cor. 10:29b; Rom. 14:5). On the contrary, Christian freedom is *freedom from all human conventions and norms of value.* The social distinctions of freedom and slavery as well as those of sex and race have lost their significance "in Christ" (Gal. 3:28; I Cor. 12:13) and "do not become slaves of men" (I Cor. 7:23) applies to all desires for emancipation, for they stem from human evaluations. The Christian, then, is free from all men, and yet there is a proper subjection of himself as "slave to all" (I Cor. 9:19) and the imperative, "be servants of one another" (Gal. 5:13) still stands. Here again, however, this is no surrender of freedom, but precisely the exercise of it.

3. "Be servants of one another" does not stand alone but has the modifier "through love," which gives it its character. For the believer has the freedom that is his as a "slave" of the "Lord" (§ 38, 1), and he who is "not under the law himself" has become a slave "to those under the law" and "to those outside the law" as "one outside the law" because he is within "the law of Christ" (I Cor. 9:20f.). And

the "law of Christ" (Gal. 6:2) is *the demand that one love.* Th
"bearing" of "one another's burdens" which Paul terms the fulfillin
of this "law," is nothing else than a manifestation of being "servant
of one another through love." It is love (ἀγάπη) which builds u
the congregation and hence requires the waiving of one's "authoriza
tion" or "right" (I Cor. 8:1; Rom. 14:15). It is love that requires th
Christian not to "seek his own good, but the good of his neighbor
(I Cor. 10:24; 13:5). Love is the fulfilment of the Law. whose de
mands are summed up in "You shall love your neighbor as yourself
(Rom. 13:8–10; Gal. 5:14).

Such fulfilling of the law, however, is no "work" in the sense c
meritorious accomplishment, but is a deed done in freedom. T
perform this deed of love believers are "God-taught" (θεοδίδακτοι
I Thess. 4:9). Love, then, is an eschatological phenomenon; in it th
faith which transplants men into eschatological existence is at worl
(Gal. 5:6). Love, as sheer existence for one's neighbor, is possible
only to him who is free from himself—i.e. to him who has died witl
Christ, to live no longer for himself but for him who for his sake die
and was raised (II Cor. 5:15) and hence is obedient to the "law o
Christ," the love commandment. Placing the parallel statements o
I Cor. 7:19; Gal. 5:6; and 6:15 side by side makes clear the natur
of "love": for the man of faith the characteristics "circumcision" an
"uncircumcision," which once determined a man's classification, have
sunk into insignificance; all that now matters is "keeping the com
mandments of God" (I Cor. 7:19)—or, in the second case, "faitl
working through love"—or, in the third case, "a new creation." Tha
is, God's demand is for love; it becomes real as the manifestation o
faith in living, and it is just in this that eschatological existence
becomes reality; this existence, moreover—the "new creation"—is to
be found only "in Christ" (II Cor. 5:17). Love is also designated a
an eschatological phenomenon by the fact that it is the primary frui
of the Spirit (Gal. 5:22). Though Paul lists other fruits after it
I Cor. 13 shows that love really cannot be regarded as just one of the
Spirit's gifts by the side of others. This chapter calls it the "stil
more excellent way," the way that exceeds all other "gifts" and with
out which all the others are nothing. Though all the Spirit's othe
gifts will disappear when "that which is perfect" comes, yet love
like faith and hope, will abide—and not only abide, but will be the
greatest of the three. It can be called nothing less because in it the

[344]

ossibility opened up by "faith" and "hope" becomes reality in concrete existence.

A special phase of *agape* is "*humility*" (ταπεινοφροσύνη). Phil. 2:3, representing Christ as the example of it, is an exhortation to it. It is described as "each counting the other better than himself," a parallel formulation to Rom. 12:10: "in honor preferring one another" (KJ). This "humility" does not mean a "disposition" of soul nor man's relation to God, as II Cor. 7:6, for instance, does, but means man's relation to men. Humility pays heed to their claim and does not insist upon pushing through one's own claims: "looking not to one's own interests, but each one looking to the interests of others" (Phil. 2:4; *cf.* I Cor. 10:24; 13:5). Humility, therefore, is a form of love. Its special character is indicated by the fact that it is placed in contrast with ἐριθεία (self-seeking, egoism) and κενοδοξία (conceit, egotism). Its opposite is "haughtiness," which looks down upon others and "boasts"—the attitude against which Gal. 6:3 warns: "For if anyone thinks he is something, when he is nothing, he deceives himself. But let each one test his own work, and then his reason to boast will be in himself alone and not in his neighbor." All such comparing of one's self with others and all judging of one's neighbor (II Cor. 10:12–18; Rom. 14:4, 10, 12f., 22) has ceased in "love."

§ 40. Freedom from Death

1. Freedom from the Law and sin is also freedom from death, for death is the "wage" and the "fruit" of sin (Rom. 6:23; 7:5; etc.; § 24). The believer, having died with Christ, also shares in his resurrection. Paul expresses this in language that stems from the mystery religions and Gnosticism (§ 33, 3d, e) in order to say: By faith in the word in which the risen Christ himself speaks to him, man lets the resurrection of Christ, like his cross, become the power that henceforth determines his life (§ 33, 6c). He now no longer lives—so Paul can paradoxically say—but in him Christ lives (Gal. 2:19).

However, Paul differs from the view prevalent in the mysteries and Gnosticism in not understanding the "life" thus mediated by Christ as a power, like those of nature, infused into man, a power of immortality which has become the property of the soul (or of the innermost self), and by means of which, after the death of th body, the soul soars into the sphere of divine blessedness, th heavenly world of light. Instead, he holds fast to the traditiona Jewish-Christian teaching of *the resurrection of the dead*, and in s doing he also retains the apocalyptic expectation of the last judg ment and of the cosmic drama which will end the old world an introduce the new world of salvation, "that which is perfect" (I Cor 13:10). He expects the "day" (or the "coming"—*parousia*) of th "Lord" (I Cor. 1:8; 5:5; 15:23; II Cor. 1:14; Phil. 1:6, 10; 2:16 I Thess. 2:19; 3:13; 4:15; 5:2, 23) which will also be the end of hi reign, which began with the resurrection, and the dawn of th period of salvation, in which God will be all in all (I Cor. 15 24–27).

The form of imagery in which Paul expresses the view that "life" has a future beyond the death of the body is that of the Jewish-Christian tradition (§ 9, 3; p. 77): *the resurrection of the dead.* Paul presents this teaching, strange to Hellenistic ears, in I Thess. 4:13–17 and defends it at length in I Cor. 15. The details in his picture of the cosmic drama have no theological importance. But it is important that Paul, in contrast to Jewish apocalypticism and Gnostic mythology, refrains from depicting the condition of the resurrection life, for a complex of future conditions could only be painted on analogy with earthly life, as an ideal picture of earthly life, and that would directly contradict the character of the future as that which is "not seen" (II Cor. 4:18). So Paul goes no further than to speak generally of the "glory" that is to be revealed (Rom. 8:18; II Cor. 4:17) or of "being with Christ," which will then begin (I Thess. 4:17; 5:10; Phil. 1:23; II Cor. 5:7f.). "Walking by sight" (II Cor. 5:7) will then take the place of "walking by faith." What we now behold is only a mirrored image full of riddles; then we shall see "face to face." "Now I know in part; then I shall understand fully, even as I have been fully understood" (I Cor. 13:12). Indeed, Paul actually gets into contradiction with the resurrection doctrine when he hopes in Phil. 1:23 that his "being with Christ" will begin immediately after his death. (As to II Cor. 5:1ff., where many interpreters find the same view expressed, see § 17, 3). This contradiction betrays how little difference it makes what images are used to express the fact that "life" has a future beyond life in the "flesh."

As resurrection-life beyond bodily death, "life," then, is a future thing yet to come. In Rom. 5:1–11, Paul has to defend his thesis that eschatological righteousness is already present, against the objection that the other signs of eschatological salvation are not yet to be seen. Hence, he also has to point out that "life" is already bestowed upon the rightwised (§ 29, 4). When he does this, he first does it by speaking of "life" as a thing of the future which determines the present as only a "hope of the glory of God"—but such a hope, be it noted, as "does not disappoint," for its foundation is the spirit-given knowledge of God's "love."

This present time in which we "live" and "walk in the flesh" (§ 22, 3) is, of course, no "glory"-present yet, but one of "tribulations" and "sufferings"; the resurrection life with its "eternal weight of glory" is yet to come (II Cor. 4:17; Rom. 8:18). Even believers still groan in "bondage to decay" (Rom. 8:21), in the earthly body (II Cor. 5:1ff.) and long for their heavenly one, "the spiritual body" or "the glory-body" (I Cor. 15:44; Phil. 3:21). "In hope we were saved" (Rom. 8:24; § 35, 3), and we now lead our lives only "by faith", not yet "by sight" (II Cor. 5:7; *cf.* I Cor. 13:12); being far from the Lord, we long to be united with him (II Cor. 5:6, 8; Phil. 1:21, 23). The cosmic drama which will bring "redemption of the body" (Rom. 8:23) has, nevertheless, already begun with the resurrection of Christ, and the consummation lies near ahead (I Thess. 4:15; I Cor. 15:51; *cf.* Rom. 13:11f.). Christ is the "first fruit of them that sleep" and those who believe in him will follow him, but "each in his own order," and not until the coming of Christ at the end of the world will death be destroyed as the "last enemy" (I Cor. 15:20–27).

Nevertheless, it is to be noted that Paul's recourse to the Gnostic proto-man idea (Rom. 5:12–21; § 15, 4d), in order to prove that "life" is bestowed upon the rightwised, shows that the futurity of "life" and "glory" is not conceived simply according to the scheme of Jewish eschatology as a mere contrast between Now and Then. As Adam brought death upon Adamitic mankind, so Christ brought life for the new mankind; in him it is already present even though it will not actualize itself for the believer until the future (v. 17, 21). Life is already here; for Christ's resurrection is conceived not just as the first case of rising from the dead, but as the origin of the resurrection life of all believers, which necessarily proceeds from it and hence can be regarded as already present in its origin. Also in I Cor. 15:12–16 the logic of the argument is not that the possibility of any resurrection is proved by *one* case of resurrection such as demonstrably occurred with Christ; rather, the resurrection of all believers is comprised in that of Christ, which is the origin of theirs, as v. 21f. clearly shows. A disciple of Paul discovered a fitting formulation for this idea: "for you have died, and your life is hid with Christ in God . . ." (Col. 3:3f.). Paul himself formulates it more paradoxically when he says: "it is no longer I who live, but Christ who lives in me" (Gal. 2:20).

2. Thus, in a certain sense, *"life" is a present thing after all*—present to hoping faith, though not as an "experience" in the life of the soul. For in baptism, too, which also brings participation in Christ's death and resurrection, the important thing is not what takes place in the soul. What it really is, is the bestowal of the salvation-occurrence and the appropriation of it by the faith of him who in it confesses his faith (§ 34, 3); accordingly, Rom. 6:8 characterizes the "life" mediated by that sacrament as a life to come: "but if we have died with Christ, we believe that we shall also live with him." Nevertheless, "life" already actualizes itself in the present, for he who is baptized has received the gift of the Spirit as the "firstfruit" or "guarantee" of future salvation (Rom. 8:23; II Cor. 1:22; 5:5). Thanks to this gift his hope will not disappoint him (Rom. 5:5), thanks to this gift—and here Paul approaches the manner of thinking found in the mysteries and Gnosticism—our future resurrection is certain (Rom. 8:11). The Spirit proves itself the ruling power of the present, however, in the fact that the latter is determined by the future. The Spirit is both the norm and the source and power of the Christian's new "walk" (§ 38, 2–3). "Life" is a present reality in the Christian's openness for the future and in his being determined by it. For the person one used to be is crucified with Christ; his *"soma* of sin" (his sin-ruled self) is destroyed, the "world" for him no longer exists (Rom. 6:6; 7:4–6; Gal. 5:24; 6:14); he is a "new creation," for "the old has passed away, behold, the new has come" (II Cor. 5:17). Hence, the exhortation: "consider yourselves dead to sin and alive to God in Christ Jesus . . . yield yourselves to God as men who have been brought from death to life" (Rom. 6:11, 13). Like "life," so is "glory" a thing of the present, so that Paul can say of God in bold anticipation: "and those whom he justified (right-

vised) he also glorified" (Rom. 8:30). Hence, the believer's life can be described not only as a daily renewal of our inner nature (II Cor. 4:16) but also as a transformation "from glory to glory" (II Cor. 3:18; § 38, 2).

Not alone in "walking" by the power and according to the norm of the Spirit does that future "life" make itself known as present— it also does so powerfully in *triumph over suffering*. Paul is as little concerned with theodicy as the rest of the New Testament is. Suffering in its implications for the present condition of this world does not need to be justified or defended, because this world is the old aeon hastening toward its end and under the dominion of death; therefore one of its essential qualities is suffering, in which death, ever future, is, nevertheless, always at work in the present, for it is the power behind transitoriness. So the real problem for early Christian thinking is not suffering but death. But for the believer this problem is solved by Christ's victory over death, which the believer, having died with Christ, shares. Therein he has won a new understanding of suffering, by which he becomes master over it—but since it flows out of his new understanding of himself it does not, of course, lay bare to him the cosmic meaning of suffering in general, but in the suffering that strikes his own person he finds a question addressed to himself and a new possibility of his life. The dominion of death which makes itself known in suffering (II Cor. 4:12), the transitoriness of everything earthly—"for the things that are seen are transient" (II Cor. 4:18)—all this warns him not to let himself get bound to the world by desire and care—"for the *schema* of this world (= this world itself) is passing away" (I Cor. 7:31)—and compels him to focus his gaze on the "things that are unseen, eternal" (II Cor. 4:18).

Suffering, which makes man aware of his weakness and insignificance, becomes a compulsion, indeed a help, to the believer, who, in the "obedience of faith" (§ 35, 1), has basically renounced his own strength to make real this renunciation and his radical surrender to "grace" in concrete living. In the face of threatening death, Paul learns to pronounce the death-verdict over himself, "in order that we should not rely upon ourselves but on God who raises the dead" (II Cor. 1:9 tr.). The treasure of grace bestowed upon him he carries in an earthen vessel, "in order that the transcendent power may be from God and not from us" (II Cor. 4:7); and lest he should

get haughty, he was struck with a bodily ailment (II Cor. 12:7)
Though at first he struggled against it, he was permitted to hear
the voice of the Lord saying: "My grace is sufficient for you; for
power comes in weakness to perfection" (II Cor. 12:8 Blt.). So he
wants to boast of his very weaknesses in order that the power of
Christ may come over him; so, for Christ's sake, he accepts whatever
sort of sufferings may strike him, "for when I am weak, then I am
strong" (II Cor. 12:9f.). This strength Paul illustrates in the following antitheses:

> "When reviled, we bless;
>   when persecuted, we endure;
>   when slandered, we try to conciliate." (I Cor. 4:12f.)
> ". . . as impostors, and yet true;
>   as unknown, and yet well known;
>   as dying, and behold we live;
>   as punished, and yet not killed;
>   as sorrowful, yet always rejoicing;
>   as poor, yet making many rich;
>   as having nothing, and yet possessing everything."
> (II Cor. 6:9f.)

In such acceptance of sufferings, the believer, as one "who is
made like him (Christ) in his death," concretely experiences the
"fellowship of his sufferings" (Phil. 3:10). The traces of past sufferings which he bears on his body are to him the "marks of Jesus"
(Gal. 6:17). To stand with such an understanding in the storm of
sufferings means nothing else than to bear about in one's own body
the dying of Jesus in order that the life of Jesus may be manifested
in one's own body (II Cor. 4:10f.). As Christ was "crucified in
weakness," so it is true of Paul: "we are weak in him." As Christ
"lives by the power of God," so the apostle: "we live with him by
the power of God"—and so live "for you" (II Cor. 13:4); for "fellowship" with Christ is also "fellowship" with all who belong to his
soma (I Cor. 12:25f.)—which means, thinking gnostically, all who
are related to Christ by having a common origin with him. To Paul,
though, it is a relationship of concretely living for each other, in
which what happens to one cannot but be full of consequence to the
other. Through the "fellowship of suffering," the sufferer is released

from the loneliness of his suffering. The sufferings of Christ overflow abundantly upon Paul, in order that he, comforted by Christ, may also comfort others (II Cor. 1:5-7). If death is at work in him, it is in order that life may be at work in others (II Cor. 4:12-13).

It is clear that the "fellowship of suffering" does not mean simply the historical relationship of follower and master which leads the follower of Jesus into suffering. It means the bond with Christ which takes place in faith, conceived in the cosmological terminology of Gnosticism (§ 33, 3e), but factually accomplished by the decision of faith. Nor is this "fellowship" artificially induced by an *imitatio Christi*—furthermore, it is by no means restricted to those sufferings into which one is led by following Christ, whether one's specific following be that of the apostolic office or simply that of confessing faith. Rather, it comprises all the sufferings which strike man, such as the physical affliction of Paul (II Cor. 12:7). Paul's dictum "for power comes in weakness to perfection" (II Cor. 12:9) is spoken as a basic principle and holds true for any "weakness." Moreover, it is mistaken to speak of this as "passion-mysticism." For this "fellowship" or "sharing" does not take place in absorbed meditation on the passion or in the soulful appropriation of Christ's suffering in mystical experience (the "marks of Jesus" are visible on Paul's body—his battle-scars as a soldier of Christ!). It does take place in the understanding of suffering learned beneath the cross. In that understanding, sufferings are overcome and become things to boast of. The believer's sufferings have become transparent to him as the process in which that "crucifixion" takes place by which the "world" sinks into insignificance for him.

Given freedom from death, *freedom from the world and its powers* (§ 26) are also given. The man of faith is freed from the care of one who relies upon himself, has the world (supposedly) at his disposal, and yet is its victim (§ 23, 3). He knows only one care, "how he may please the Lord" (I Cor. 7:32) and only one ambition: "to please the Lord" (II Cor. 5:9). Free from the world's care which binds one to perishing things, free from "worldly grief" which produces death (II Cor. 7:10), he faces the world free, as one who rejoices with those who rejoice and weeps with those who weep (Rom. 12:15), one who participates in the tumult of the world but does so with an inner aloofness—"as if (he did it) not":

"let those who have wives be as if they had not,
and those who mourn as if they mourned not,
and those who rejoice as if they rejoiced not,
and those who buy as if they possessed not,
and those who have to do with the world as if they
had nothing to do with it."
(I Cor. 7:29–31 tr.)

—in other words, as a free man. So Paul can boast: "for I have learned in whatever state I am to be content. I know both how to be abased and how to abound; to any and all circumstances I am initiate: to be full and to hunger, to have abundance and to be in want. I can endure anything in him who is my inward power" (Phil. 4:11–13 tr.).

Since neither life nor death can separate us from the love of God in Christ (Rom. 8:38), since in life as in death we belong to Christ (Rom. 14:7–9), then life and death as we know them as men "in the flesh" have lost their charm and terror, respectively (*cf.* II Cor. 5:9). He who belongs to Christ, and through him to God, has become master of everything:

"For all things are yours . . .
whether the world or life or death,
or things present or things future,
all are yours;
but you are Christ's, and Christ is God's."
(I Cor. 3:21–23)

In God, freedom, righteousness, and life have their cause, and it is in them that the glory of God as ultimate meaning and ultimate goal comes to its own. To the glory of God, Christ is confessed as Lord (Phil. 2:11). To the glory of God, prayers of praise and thanksgiving are to sound forth in the congregation (Rom. 15:6; II Cor. 1:20; 9:12–15). Our eating and drinking and our every undertaking it to be done to His glory (I Cor. 10:31) as well as the work of the apostle (II Cor. 4:15). To His glory, Christ accomplished his work (Rom. 15:7) and to Him he will resign his reign "in order that God may be all in all" (I Cor. 15:28 KJ).

Table of Abbreviations

Anglican Theol. Rev. = Anglican Theological Review

Ap, *see* Justin Ap.

AT (in German titles) = Altes Testament (Old Testament)

B = codex Vaticanus of the Bible

Barn. = Epistle of Barnabas (in Apostolic Fathers)

Blass-Debrunner = *Grammatik des neutestamentlichen Griechisch* by Friedrich Blass, revised by Albert Debrunner, 5th ed. (1921)

Blt. after a Biblical reference = Bultmann, signifying that the German text offered Bultmann's rendering of the Greek text into German, of which the wording here offered is a faithful English equivalent

c. Cels., *see* Origen

I Clem. = First Epistle of Clement (in Apostolic Fathers)

II Clem. = Second Epistle of Clement (in Apostolic Fathers)

Corp. Herm. = Corpus Hermeticum (edition by W. Scott, 1924)

D = Codex Bezae of the New Testament

D* = the original hand of the above MS

Dial., *see* Justin

Did. = Didache (in Apostolic Fathers)

Diogn. = The Epistle to Diognetus (in Apostolic Fathers)

ed. = edition

Epictetus, Diss. = Epictetus' "Dissertationes"

Ev. Theol. = *Evangelische Theologie*

IV Ez. = IV Ezra or IV Esdras (Latin numeration) = II Esdras (KJ numeration)

Expos. Times = *Expository Times*

f = and the following verse

ff = and the following verses

G = codex Boernerianus of Paul's epistles

Gesch. d. synopt. Trad., 2nd ed. = Rudolf Bultmann, *Geschichte der synoptischen Tradition*, 2nd ed. (1931)

Harnack, *Mission u. Ausbreitung* = Adolf von Harnack, *Die Mission und Ausbreitung des Christentums in den drei ersten Jahrhunderten*, 3rd ed. (1915) (English translation by James Moffatt, 1908: *The Mission and Expansion of Christianity in the First Three Centuries*—translates the second German edition)

[353]

Herm. mand. = Shepherd of Hermas (in Apostolic Fathers), mandata

Herm. sim. = Shepherd of Hermas (in Apostolic Fathers), similitudines

Herm. vis. = Shepherd of Hermas (in Apostolic Fathers), visiones

HUCA = *Hebrew Union College Annual*

Ign. = Epistles of Ignatius (in Apostolic Fathers)

Ign. Eph. = his epistle to the Ephesians

Ign. Mg. = his epistle to the Magnesians

Ign. Tr. = his epistle to the Trallians

Ign. Rom. = his epistle to the Romans

Ign. Phld. = his epistle to the Philadelphians

Ign. Sm. = his epistle to the Smyrneans

Ign. Pol. = his epistle to Polycarp

Iren. = Irenaeus, "Against Heresies"

it = itala, the pre-Vulgate Old Latin translations of the NT taken as a whole

J. Theol. Stud. = *Journal of Theological Studies*

Jahrb. d. theol. Schule Bethel = *Jahrbuch der theologischen Schule Bethel*

JBL = *Journal of Biblicial Literature*

Joh.-Ev. = Rudolf Bultmann, *Das Evangelium des Johannes* (1941), (2nd ed., 1950)

Justin Ap. = Justin Martyr, "Apology"

Justin Dial. = Justin Martyr, "Dialogue with Trypho"

Kerygma Pet. = Kerygma Petri, fragments of a second century writing

I–IV Kingdoms = I and II Samuel and I and II Kings in the nomenclature of the Septuagint

KJ = the King James translation of the Bible (1611)

l.c. = loco citato

LXX = the Septuagint translation of the Old Testament

Marb. Theol. Stud. = *Marburger Theologische Studien*

Mart. Pol. = Martyrdom of Polycarp (in Apostolic Fathers)

mg = marginal reading

n.d. = no date

op. cit. = opere citato

Origen, c. Cels. = Origen, "Contra Celsum"

par in references to the Synoptics = parallel (i.e., see the parallel "Q"-passage in Mt. or Lk.)

Past. = the Pastoral Epistles in the New Testament

Pol. (or Polyc) Phil. = the Epistle of Polycarp to the Philippians (in Apostolic Fathers) pr. = proemium (the unnumbered introductions in the Apostolic Fathers)

Princeton Theol. Rev. = *Princeton Theological Review*

Ps.-Aristeas = Pseudo-Aristeas, the so-called "Letter of Aristeas" in the Old Testament Pseudepigrapha

Ps.-Clem. hom. = Pseudo-Clementine Homilies

Q = the hypothetical second source (Quelle) common to Matthew and Luke

Realenzykl. der Klass. Altertumswiss. = *Realenzyklopädie der Klassischen Altertumswissenschaft,* Pauly-Wissowa-Kroll

RGG = *Religion in Geschichte und Gegenwart,* 2nd ed. (1927)

RSV = Revised Standard Version of the NT (exactly: The New Covenant commonly called the New Testament of our Lord and Savior Jesus Christ, Revised Standard Version, 1946)

see above, see below = these references always refer to something which precedes or follows *within the same section* (§)

Sitzungsb. d. Heidelb. Akad. d. Wiss., Phil.-hist. Kl. = *Sitzungsbericht der Heidelberger Akademie der Wissenschaften, philosophisch-historische Klasse*

Sitzungsb. d. Preuss. Akad. d. Wiss., Phil.-hist. Kl. = *Sitzungsbericht der Preussischen Akademie der Wissenschaften, Philosophisch-historische Klasse*

Str.-B. = Strack-Billerbeck, *Kommentar zum NT aus Talmud und Midrasch*

Symb. Bibl. Upsal. = Symbolae Biblicae Upsalienses

Theol. Bl. = *Theologische Blätter*

ThR, NF = *Theologische Rundschau,* Neue Folge (New Series)

ThStKr. = *Theologische Studien und Kritiken*

ThWB. = *Theologisches Wörterbuch zum Neuen Testament,* G. Kittel, editor

tr. in bibliographies = translated

tr. after a Biblical reference = translator, signifying that the translator of this book felt it necessary to translate the Greek text quoted by Bultmann in the latter's sense where this was not identical with a common English translation

Trajan ep. = Epistles of the Emperor Trajan (to and from Trajan)

ZNW = *Zeitschrift für die neutestamentliche Wissenschaft*

ZsystTh = *Zeitschrift für systematische Theologie*

ZThK = *Zeitschrift für Theologie und Kirche*

Bibliographies

[As in the original, the bibliographies are given not for the work as a whole but for the sections (§§) and chapters to which they pertain. Wherever possible, two bibliographies are given, one wholly in English, the other covering non-English languages. Each English bibliography contains, first, English works cited by Bultmann along with English translations of works cited by him from the original languages, and, second, pertinent works in English added by the translator at the author's request. The second bibliography (non-English) may be assumed to be Bultmann's (with some additions made by him since the publication of the German edition) except that it has not been felt necessary to give the original titles of works translated into English and already included in the English bibliography.]

For Chapter I as a whole. *English:* Wilhelm Bousset: *Jesus,* tr. by Janet P. Trevelyan, 1906; Rudolf Bultmann: *Jesus and the Word,* tr. by Louise P. Smith and Erminie Huntress, 1934; F. C. Burkitt: *Jesus Christ,* 1932; Maurice Goguel: *The Life of Jesus,* tr. by Olive Wyon, 1933; A. C. Headlam: *Jesus Christ in History and Faith,* 1925; T. W. Manson: *The Teaching of Jesus,* 1935; Rudolf Otto: *The Kingdom of God and the Son of Man,* tr. by Floyd Filson and B. L. Woolf (1938 and 1943 from 2nd German ed., on which see R. Bultmann in *ThR* NF 9, 1937); Albert Schweitzer: *The Quest of the Historical Jesus* (1910 and 1931; 2nd English ed. 1911, often reprinted, most recently 1948, of the first German ed.: *Von Reimarus zu Wrede*); Henry J. Cadbury: *Jesus, What Manner of Man?,* 1947; Martin Dibelius: *Jesus,* tr. by Charles B. Hedrick and Frederick C. Grant, 1949.

Catholic: Karl Adam: *The Son of God,* tr. by Philip Hereford, 1934; August Reatz: *Jesus Christ,* tr. by G. Brinkworth, 1933.

Non-English: Ad. Jülicher: *Die Religion Jesu und die Anfänge des Chistentums bis zum Nicaenum* (Die Kultur der Gegenwart I, 4, 2nd ed., 1922); Paul Wernle: *Jesus,* 2nd ed., 1916; Wilhelm Heitmüller: *Jesus,* 1913; Ad. Schlatter: *Die Geschichte des Christus,* 2nd ed., 1923; Karl Bornhäuser: *Das Wirken des Christus durch Taten und Worte,* 2nd ed., 1924; Karl L. Schmidt: "Jesus Christus," (*RGG,* 2nd ed., III, 110–151); Walt. Grundmann: *Jesus der Galiläer und das Judentum,* 1940; Rudolf Meyer: *Der Prophet aus Galiläa,* 1940.

BIBLIOGRAPHIES

§1. *English:* E. C. Hoskyns and F. N. Davey: *The Riddle of the New Testament,* 1938.

Non-English: Joh. Weiss: *Die Predigt Jesu vom Reiche Gottes,* 2nd ed., 1900; H. D. Wendland: *Die Eschatologie des Reiches Gottes bei Jesus,* 1931. For the presuppositions in the field of comparative religion: Wilh. Bousset: *Die Religion des Judentums in der späthellenistischen Zeit,* 3rd ed., 1926; also the literature cited for Chapter I.

§2: *English:* See the literature for §1. Also: B. D. T. Smith: *The Parables in the Synoptic Gospels,* 1937; C. G. Montefiore: "The Originality of Jesus," *Hibbert Journal,* XXVIII (Oct. 1929), 98–111; the same: *Rabbinic Literature and Gospel Teachings,* 1930; A. Lukyn Williams: *Talmudic Judaism and Christianity,* 1933; E. F. Scott: "The Originality of Jesus' Ethical Teaching," *JBL,* XLVIII (1929), 109–115; A. N. Wilder: *Eschatology and Ethics in the Teaching of Jesus,* 1939; Henry J. Cadbury: *The Peril of Modernizing Jesus,* 1937; G. F. Moore: *Judaism in the First Centuries of the Christian Era,* I. II., 1927.

Non-English: Joh. Weiss (as in §1): E. Grimm: *Die Ethik Jesu,* 2nd ed., 1917; E. Klostermann: *Jesu Stellung zum AT,* 1904; Fr. K. Karner: *Der Vergeltungsgedanke in der Ethik Jesu,* 1927; H. Windisch: *Der Sinn der Bergpredigt,* 1929; E. Lohmeyer: *Kultus und Evangelium,* 1942; on Jewish ethics, besides Bousset (§1) and Moore, above: Reinh. Sander: *Furcht und Liebe im palästinischen Judentum,* 1935; Erik Sjöberg: *Gott und die Sünder im palästinischen Judentum,* 1939.

§3: See the literature for Chapter I. Also: Joh. Leipoldt: *Das Gotteserlebnis im Lichte der vergleichenden Religionsgeschichte,* 1927; Rich. Ad. Hoffmann: *Das Gottesbild Jesu,* 1935; Walt. Grundmann: *Die Gotteskindschaft in der Geschichte Jesu und ihre religionsgeschichtlichen Voraussetzungen,* 1938.

§4: *English:* Edwin A. Abbott: *The Son of Man,* 1910; Vincent Taylor: *Jesus and his Sacrifice,* 1933; R. H. Lightfoot: *History and Interpretation in the Gospels,* 1934; Rud. Otto: *The Kingdom of God and the Son of Man,* tr. by Floyd Filson and B. L. Woolf [1938 and 1943, 2nd German ed., on which cf. R. Bultmann *ThR* NF 9 (1937), 1–35]; Gustav Dalman: *The Words of Jesus Considered in the Light of Post-Biblical Jewish Writings and the Aramaic Language,* tr. D. M. Kay, 1902; see also: *Jesus-Jeschua: Studies in the Gospels,* tr. by Paul Levertoff, 1929; C. H. Kraeling: *Anthropos and Son of Man,* 1927.

Non-English: Wm. Wrede: *Das Messiasgeheimnis in den Evangelien,* 1901; H. J. Holtzmann, *Das messianische Bewusstsein Jesu,* 1907; Ad. Schlatter: *Der Zweifel an der Messianität Jesu,* 1907; A. Frövig: *Das Selbstbewusstsein Jesu als Lehrer und Wundertäter,* 1918; the same: *Das Sendungsbewusstsein Jesu und der Geist,* 1924; the same: *Der Kyriosglaube des NT und der Geist,* 1928; R. Bultmann: *ZNW* 19 (1919–20), 165–74; the same: *Gesch. d. synopt. Trad.,* 2nd ed., 1931, 263–281, also 147–150; Hans Jürg. Ebeling: *Das Messiasgeheimnis und die Botschaft des Marcus-Evangelisten,* 1939 (Beiheft 19 of *ZNW*); specifically on the Son of Man question see H. Lietzmann: *Der Menschensohn,* 1896 (whose thesis, however, Lietzmann later retracted); Arn. Meyer: *Jesu Muttersprache*, 1896, 91–100, 140–149; Paul Fiebig: *Der Menschensohn*, 1901; Jul. Wellhausen: *Einleitung in die drei ersten Evangelien*, 2nd ed., 1911, 123–130; Wilh. Bousset: *Kyrios Christos*, 2nd ed., 1931, 5–13; Joach. Jeremias: *Erlösung und Erlöser im Urchristentum*, 1929.

For Chapter II as a whole. *English:* Carl Weizsäcker: *The Apostolic Age of the Christian Church*, tr. from 2nd German ed. by James Miller, 1894–99; Paul Wernle: *The Beginnings of Christianity*, tr. by G. A. Bienemann, 1903–4; F. J. Foakes Jackson and Kirsopp Lake: *The Beginnings of Christianity*, I–IV, 1920–1933; Joh. Weiss: *The History of Primitive Christianity*, ed. by F. C. Grant, 1937; C. H. Dodd: *The Apostolic Preaching and its Developments*, 1936.

Non-English: Ernst V. Dobschütz: *Probleme des apostolischen Zeitalters*, 1904; Rud. Knopf: *Das nachapostolische Zeitalter*, 1905; Ad. Jülicher: see Chapter I; Wilh. Bousset: *Kyrios Christos*, 2nd ed., 1921; Hans Achelis: *Das Christentum in den ersten drei Jahrhunderten*, 2nd ed., 1925; Rol. Schütz: *Apostel und Jünger*, 1921; Wilh. Michaelis: *Täufer, Jesus, Urgemeinde*, 1928; Ed. Meyer: *Ursprung und Anfänge des Christentums* III, 1923; Karl Kundsin: *Das Urchristentum im Lichte der Evangelien-forschung*, 1929; Ernst Lohmeyer: *Galiläa und Jerusalem*, 1936; W. G. Kümmel: *Kirchenbegriff und Geschichtsbewusstsein in der Urgemeinde und bei Jesus*, 1943.

§5: See the literature for Chapter II. Also C. H. Dodd: "The Gospels as History: A Reconsideration," *Bull. of the John Rylands Library*, Vol. 22, No. 1, 1938; the same: *History and the Gospels*, 1938.

Non-English: Joh. Weiss: *Jesus im Glauben des Urchristentums*, 1910.

§6: *English:* See the literature given in §1, 3, p. 10. Also: George Johnston: *The Church in the New Testament*, 1943.

§7: See the literature for Chapter II, especially W. Bousset: *Kyrios Christos*; and for §5. Also: W. Staerk: *Soter* I, 1933; Paul Volz: *Die Eschatologie der jüdischen Gemeinde*, 1934.

§8: *English:* See the literature for Chapter II. Also: Floyd V. Filson: "The Separation of Christianity from Judaism," *Anglican Theol. Rev.*, 21 (1939), 171–185; B. H. Streeter: *The Primitive Church*, Chap. III, 1929; A. C. McGiffert: *History of Christianity in the Apostolic Age*, Chap. V, VI, 1897; A. B. Macdonald: *Christian Worship in the Primitive Church*, 1934. Ernst Troeltsch: *The Social Teaching of the Christian Churches*, tr. by Olive Wyon, 1931.

Non-English: Lyder Brun and Anton Fridrichsen: *Paulus und die Urgemeinde*, 1921; Walter Bauer: *Der Wortgottesdienst der ältesten Christen*, 1930; Jos. Mar. Nielen: *Gebet und Gottesdienst im NT*, 1937; Ernst Lohmeyer: *Kultus und Evangelium*, 1942; Oscar Cullmann: *Urchristentum und Gottesdienst*, 1944.

For Chapter III as a whole. See the literature for Chapter II. Also: *English:* B. H. Streeter: *The Rise of Christianity* (The Cambridge Ancient History XI), 1936.

Non-English: Walter Bauer: *Rechtgläubigkeit und Ketzerei im ältesten*

Christentum, 1934; the relevant sections in histories of the primitive church are, of course, also pertinent here.

§9: Ad. v. Harnack: *The Mission and Expansion of Christianity in the First Three Centuries*, tr. by James Moffatt, 2nd ed., 1908; M. Dibelius: *From Tradition to Gospel*, tr. by B. L. Woolf, 1934. Also: *Gospel Criticism and Christology*, 1935.

Non-English: K. Axenfeld: "Die jüdische Propaganda als Vorläuferin und Wegbereiterin der urchristlichen Mission," in *Missionswissenschaftliche Studien* (Festschrift für G. Warneck), 1904, 1–102; Albr. Oepke: *Die Missionspredigt des Apostels Paulus*, 1920; Ed. Norden: *Agnostos Theos*, 1913; Mart. Dibelius: *Paulus auf dem Areopag* (Sitzungsber. d. Heidelb. Akad. d. Wiss., Phil,-hist. Kl. 1938–39, 2. Abh.), 1939; Wilh. Schmid: "Die Rede des Apostels Paulus vor den Philosophen und Areopagiten," *Philologus*, 95 (1942), 79–102; Max Pohlenz: "Paulus und die Stoa," *ZNW*, 42 (1949), 69–104. Here the various investigations of Alfr. Seeberg should be named; they show the stock of traditional formulations which gradually crystallize out of missionary preaching and from which ultimately the creed (in various forms) develops. Only Seeberg makes the mistake of placing a more or less definitely formulated "catechism" at the beginning of the development. Read from the standpoint of tradition-history (Bultmann's paraphrase of and improvement upon Dibelius' term "form-history") these investigations, which also reveal the connection of Christian preaching with Jewish tradition, have a high value: *Der Katechismus der Urchristenheit*, 1903; *Das Evangelium Christi*, 1905; *Die beiden Wege und das Aposteldekret*, 1906; *Die Didache des Judentums und der Urchristenheit*, 1908; *Christi Person und Werk nach der Lehre seiner Jünger*, 1910; on sub-section 5: Jul. Schniewind: *Euangelion*, Lieferung 1 und 2, 1927–31; Einar Molland: *Das Paulinische Euangelion*, 1934; Ad. Schlatter: *Der Glaube im NT*, 4th ed., 1927; R. Gyllenberg: *Pistis* (in Swedish), 1922.

§10: *English:* Ernst v. Dobschütz: *Christian Life in the Primitive Church*, tr. by Geo. Bremner, 1904; the same: *The Apostolic Age*, tr. by F. L. Pogson, 1910.

Non-English: N. A. Dahl: *Das Volk Gottes*, 1941; Ed. Grafe: *Das Urchristentum und das AT*, 1907; O. Michel: *Paulus und seine Bibel*, 1929; H. Jacoby: *Neutestamentliche Ethik*, 1899; Mart. Dibelius: Excursus on Herm. sim II 5 in the supplement volume of Lietzmann's *Handbuch zum NT*, IV, 555f.

§11: See the literature for §8 and the works listed in §8, 2. Also: Rud. Knopf: *Das nachapostolische Zeitalter*, 1905, 346–369; Hans Wenschkewitz: *Die Spiritualisierung der Kultusbegriffe. Tempel, Priester und Opfer im NT*, 1932.

§12: *English:* See the literature for Chapter II. Also: Martin Dibelius: *Gospel Criticism and Christology*, 1935; Joh. Weiss: *Christ, the Beginnings of Dogma*, tr. by V. D. Davis, 1911.

Non-English: W. Bousset: *Kyrios Christos*; M. Dibelius: "Christologie des Urchristentums," in *RGG* I, 1592–1607. On 1. see W. Bauer, J. M.

Nielen, O. Cullmann as listed in §8. Also: R. Knopf: *Das nachapostolische Zeitalter*, 1905, 222–252; Andr. Duhm: *Gottesdienst im ältesten Christentum*, 1928. On 2. see §7, 5 and W. Graf Baudissin: *Kyrios*, II, 257–301; Ed. v. d. Goltz: *Das Gebet in der ältesten Christenheit*, 1901; A. Klawek: *Das Gebet zu Jesus*, 1921; On 3 see: G. P. Wetter: *Der Sohn Gottes*, 1916; Ludw. Bieler: ΘΕΙΟΣ ANHP I, 1935, 134–140; M. Dibelius: Excursus on Col. 1:17 in Lietzmann's *Handbuch zum NT*, 12, 2nd ed., 1927, 9–12.

§13: *English:* J. C. Lambert: "The Passover and the Lord's Supper," *J. Theol. Studies*, IV, 1903, 184–193; H. E. D. Blakiston: "The Lucan Account of the Institution of the Lord's Supper," *J. Theol. Studies*, IV, 1903, 548–555; Jacob Mann: "The Last Supper as a Paschal Meal," *HUCA*, I, 1924, 177; C. C. Richardson: "Early Patristic Evidence for the Synoptic Chronology of the Passion," *Anglican. Theol. Rev.*, 22, 1942, 299–308; G. H. Box: "The Jewish Antecedents of the Eucharist," *J. Theol. Stud.* 3, 1902, 357–367 and 10, p. 106; F. C. Burkitt: "St. Luke 22:15,6: What is the General Meaning?" *J. Theol. Stud.*, 9, 1908, 569–571; the same: "The Lord's Supper and the Paschal Meal," *J. Theol. Stud.*, 17, 1916, 291–297; R. H. Kennett: *The Last Supper, its Significance in the Upper Room*, 1921; W. O. E. Oesterley: *The Jewish Background of the Christian Liturgy*, 1925; G. H. C. Macgregor: *Eucharistic Origins*, 1928; F. Gavin: *The Jewish Antecedents of the Christian Sacraments*, 1928, 1933; T. W. H. Marfield: *The Words of Institution*, 1933; V. Taylor: *Jesus and His Sacrifice*, 1937, 1943; F. L. Cirlot: *The Early Eucharist*, 1939; L. S. Thornton: *The Common Life in the Body of Christ*, 1941; G. Dix: *The Shape of the Liturgy*, 1944; K. Barth: *The Teaching of the Church Regarding Baptism*, tr. SCM Press, 1948.

Non-English: On 1: R. Knopf: *Das nachapostolische Zeitalter*, 271–290; W. Heitmüller: *Im Namen Jesu*, 1903; the same: *Taufe und Abendmahl im Urchristentum*, 1911; Joh. Leipoldt: *Die urchristliche Taufe im Lichte der Religionsgeschichte*, 1928; Rich. Reitzenstein: *Die Vorgeschichte der christlichen Taufe*, 1929; Jos. Thomas: *Le mouvement baptiste en Palestine et Syrie*, 1935; Eth. Stauffer: "Taufe im Urchristentum," in *RGG*, 2nd ed., V, 1002–1010. On 2: Lietzmann, Cullmann, Lohmeyer as given in §8, 3. Also: R. Knopf: *op. cit.*, 253–271; W. Heitmüller: see above at §13, 1; Maur. Goguel: *L'Eucharistie des origines à Justin Martyr*, 1910.

§14: *English:* H. B. Swete: *The Holy Spirit in the New Testament*, 1910; E. F. Scott: *The Spirit in the New Testament*, 1923; W. R. Shoemaker: "The Use of Ruach in the OT and of Pneuma in the New Testament," *JBL*, XXIII (1904); Vincent Taylor: *The Holy Spirit* (Headingley Lectures), 1937; H. Wheeler Robinson: *The Christian Experience of the Holy Spirit*, 1928.

Non-English: Paul Volz: *Der Geist Gottes und die verwandten Erscheinungen im AT und im anschliessenden Judentum*, 1910; Herm. Gunkel: *Die Wirkungen des Heil. Geistes nach der populären Anschauung der apostolischen Zeit und der Lehre des Apostels Paulus*, 3rd ed., 1909; Heinr. Weinel: *Die Wirkungen des Geistes und der Geister im nachapos-*

tolischen Zeitalter bis auf Irenäus, 1899; Friedr. Büchsel: *Der Geist Gottes im NT*, 1926; Mart. Dibelius: Excursus on Herm. mand V 2, 7 in the supplement volume to the *Handbuch zum NT*, IV, 517–519.

§15: *English:* Carl H. Kraeling: *Anthropos and Son of Man*, 1927; F. C. Burkitt: *Church and Gnosis* (written against Bultmann among others, though he is never named. Nevertheless it contains information on Gnosticism not elsewhere available in English), 1932.

Non-English: Wilh. Bousset: *Hauptprobleme der Gnosis*, 1907; Paul Wendland: *Die hellenistisch-römische Kultur in ihren Beziehungen zu Judentum und Christentum* (*Handbuch zum NT* I, 2, 2nd and 3rd ed.), 1912, 163–187; Rich. Reitzenstein: *Die hellenistischen Mysterienreligionen*, 3rd ed., 1927; Hans Jonas: *Gnosis und spätantiker Geist*, I. *Die mythologische Gnosis*, 1934; Heinr. Schlier: *Religionsgeschichtlichen Untersuchungen zu den Ignatiusbriefen*, 1929; the same: *Christus und die Kirche im Epheserbrief*, 1930; Ernst Käsemann: *Leib und Leib Christi*, 1933; the same: *Das wandernde Gottesvolk*, 1939; Hans-Werner Bartsch: *Gnostisches Gut und Gemeindetradition bei Ignatius von Antiochien*, 1940; Walter Bauer: *Rechtgläubigkeit und Ketzerei im ältesten Christentum*, 1934.

Part II as a whole. *English:* Alb. Schweitzer: *Paul and His Interpreters*, tr. by W. Montgomery, 1912; Ferd. Chr. Baur: *Paul, the Apostle of Jesus Christ*, tr. by A. Menzies, 1876; Otto Pfleiderer: *Paulinism*, tr. by Edward Peters from 2nd German ed., 1890; cf. by same author: *The Influence of the Apostle Paul on the Development of Christianity*, tr. by Fred Smith, 1885; Wm. Wrede: *Paul*, tr. by Edward Lummis, 1908; Ad. Deissmann: *Paul, a Study in Social and Religious History*, tr. by Wm. E. Wilson from 2nd German ed., 1926; Alb. Schweitzer: *The Mysticism of Paul the Apostle*, tr. by Wm. Montgomery, 1931; Wilfred L. Knox: *St. Paul and the Church of Jerusalem*, 1930; the same: *St. Paul and the Church of the Gentiles*, 1939.

Non-English: Ernest Renan: *St. Paul*, 1869; Carl Holsten: *Das Evangelium des Paulus*, I, II, 1880, 1898; Ernst Lohmeyer: *Grundlagen paulinischer Theologie*, 1929; Rud. Bultmann: "Paulus," (*RGG*, 2nd ed., IV, 1019–1045).

§16: *English:* On the problem "Paul and Jesus": Arnold Meyer: *Jesus or Paul?* 1907; C. A. A. Scott: "Jesus and Paul" (in *Essays on Some Biblical Questions of the Day*, ed. by H. B. Swete), 1909; B. W. Bacon: *Jesus and Paul*, 1920; Joh. Weiss: *Paul and Jesus*, tr. by H. J. Chaytor, 1909.

Non-English: On the conversion of Paul: W. G. Kümmel: *Römer 7 und die Bekehrung des Paulus*, 1929; Robert Steiger: *Die Dialektik der paulinischen Existenz*, 1931; Ottfried Kietzig: *Die Bekehrung des Paulus*, 1932; R. Bultmann: "Kritischer Bericht über einzelne neuere Untersuchungen zum Werdegang und zur Bekehrung des Paulus," *ThR*, NF 6 (1934), 229–246.

On the problem "Paul and Jesus": Maurice Goguel: *L'apôtre Paul et Jésus Christ*, 1904; Ad. Jülicher: *Paulus und Jesus*, 1907; Arnold Meyer:

Wer hat das Christentum gegründet, Jesus oder Paulus?, 1907; Wilh. Heitmüller: "Zum Problem Paulus und Jesus," *ZNW*, 13 (1912), 320–337; the same: "Jesus und Paulus," *ZThK*, 25 (1915), 156–179; Paul Wernle: "Jesus und Paulus," *ZThK*, 25 (1915), 1–82; R. Bultmann: "Die Bedeutung des historischen Jesus für die Theologie des Paulus," (in *Glauben und Verstehen*, 1933, 188–213); the same: "Jesus und Paulus," (in *Jesus Christus im Zeugnis der Heiligen Schrift und der Kirche*, 1936, 68–90).

On I Pet. 3:18–22 see R. Bultmann: *Coniectanea Neotestamentica* XI (1949), 1–14; on Col. 1:15–20 see E. Käsemann: *Bultmann-Festschrift*, 1949, 133–148.

Chapter IV A: *English:* Franz Delitsch: *A System of Biblical Psychology*, tr. by A. E. Wallis, 1867; John Laidlaw: *Bible Doctrine of Man*, 2nd ed., 1895; W. P. Dickson: *St. Paul's Use of the Terms Flesh and Spirit*, 1883; H. Wheeler Robinson: "Hebrew Psychology in relation to Pauline Anthropology" in *Mansfield College Essays*; the same: *The Christian Doctrine of Man*, 3rd ed., 1926.

Non-English: Herm. Lüdemann: *Die Anthropologie des Apostels Paulus*, 1872; Walter Gutbrod: *Die paulinische Anthropologie*, 1934.

§17: *English:* E. de Witt Burton: *Spirit, Soul, and Flesh*, 1918; M. Scott Fletcher: *The Psychology of the NT*, n.d.; H. Wheeler Robinson: *The Christian Doctrine of Man*, (Chapter II, "The New Testament Doctrine of Man"), 3rd ed. 1926; A. B. D. Alexander: *The Ethics of St. Paul*, (Chapter III, "The Psychology of Paul"), 1910.

Non-English: Ernst Käsemann: *Leib und Leib Christi*, 1933; P. Torge: *Seelenglaube und Unsterblichkeitshoffnung im AT*, 1909; W. Georg Kümmel: *Das Bild des Menschen im NT*, 1948.

§18: F. C. Porter: "The Pre-existence of the Soul in the Book of Wisdom and in the Rabbinical Writings," in *Old Testament and Semitic Studies in Memory of Wm. Rainey Harper*, 1908; F. C. Burkitt: "Life, Zoe, Hayyim," *ZNW*, 12, 1911, 228–230.

Chapter IV B, §21: Günther Bornkamm: "Die Offenbarung des Zornes Gottes," *ZNW*, 34 (1935), 239–252; Heinr. Schlier: "Uber die Erkenntnis Gottes bei den Heiden.," *Ev. Theol.*, 1935, 9–26.

§22: H. Lüdemann and W. Gutbrod: (for titles see the literature for Chapter IV A); E. Käsemann: (See the literature for §17); Wilh. Schauf: *Sarx*, 1924.

§24: Werner Georg Kümmel: *Römer 7 und die Bekehrung des Paulus*, 1929; Rud. Bultmann: "Römer 7 und die Anthropologie des Paulus," (in *Imago Dei, Festschrift für G. Krüger*, 53–62), 1932; Paul Althaus: *Paulus und Luther über den Menschen*, 1938.

§27: *English:* Wilfred L. Knox: *St. Paul and the Church of Jerusalem.*

Non-English: Ed. Grafe: *Die paulinische Lehre vom Gesetz*, 2nd ed., 1893; the same: *Das Urchristentum und das AT*, 1907; Otto Michel: *Paulus und seine Bibel*, 1929; Ad. Schlatter: *Der Glaube im NT*, 4th ed., 1927, 323–399; Käte Oltmanns: *Theol. Bl.* 8 (1929), 110–116; R. Bultmann: see literature for §24.

BIBLIOGRAPHIES

For Chapter V A as a whole. *English:* Th. Häring: *The Christian Faith,* tr. by John Dickie and George Ferries, 1913; Floyd V. Filson: *St. Paul's Conception of Recompense,* 1931.

Non-English: H. Cremer: *Die paulinische Rechtfertigungslehre im Zusammenhang ihrer geschichtlichen Voraussetzungen,* 2nd ed., 1910. The abundant recent literature is given in the article δικαιοσύνη in Bauer's *Wörterbuch zum NT;* see especially: E. von Dobschütz: "Uber die paulinische Rechtfertigungslehre," *ThStKr,* 85 (1912), 38–87; W. Michaelis: "Rechtfertigung aus Glauben bei Paulus," *Festgabe für Ad. Deissmann:* 1927, 116–138; Herb. Braun: *Gerichtsgedanke und Rechtfertigungslehre bei Paulus,* 1930; Wilh. Mundle: *Der Glaubensbegriff des Paulus,* 1932; R. Gyllenberg: "Die paulinische Rechtfertigungslehre und das AT," *Studia Theologica* I (1935), 35–52; Hans-Wolfgang Heidland: *Die Anrechnung des Glaubens zur Gerechtigkeit,* 1936.

§28: J. H. Ropes: "Righteousness in the OT and in St. Paul," *JBL,* XXII, 1903, 211–227; F. B. Westcott: *St. Paul and Justification,* 1913.

For Chapter V B as a whole. *English:* J. Moffatt: *Grace in the NT,* 1931; W. T. Whitley: *The Doctrine of Grace,* 1932.

Non-English: G. P. Wetter: *Charis,* 1913; J. Wobbe: *Der Charisgedanke bei Paulus,* 1932.

§32: G. Bornkamm: "Die Offenbarung des Zornes Gottes," *ZNW,* 34 (1935), 239–262.

§33: *English:* W. E. Wilson: "The Development of Paul's Doctrine of Dying and Rising again with Christ," *Expos. Times,* 42 (1930–32), 562 ff.

Non-English: A. Seeberg: *Der Tod Christi in seiner Bedeutung für die Erlösung,* 1895; Theod. Hoppe: *Die Idee der Heilsgeschichte bei Paulus,* 1926; Joh. Schneider: *Die Passionsmystik des Paulus,* 1929; Karl Mittring: *Heilswirklichkeit bei Paulus,* 1929; Emil Weber: *Eschatologie und Mystik im NT,* 1930; Gustav Wiencke: *Paulus über Jesu Tod,* 1939; on 6b, Heinr. Schumacher: *Christus in seiner Präexistenz und Kenose,* 1914; Ernst Barnikol: *Philipper 2,* 1932; the same: *Mensch und Messias,* 1932.

§34: *English:* A. B. Macdonald: *Christian Worship in the Primitive Church,* 1934.

Non-English: On 1: Otto Schmitz: *Die Bedeutung des Wortes bei Paulus,* 1927; R. Bultmann: *Glauben und Verstehen,* 1933, 153–187; Einar Molland: *Das paulinische Euangelion,* 1934; On 2: Traug. Schmidt: *Der Leib Christi,* 1919; Wilh. Koester: *Die Idee der Kirche beim Apostel Paulus,* 1928; Gerh. Gloege: *Reich Gottes und Kirche im NT,* 1929; Heinr. Schlier: *Christus und die Kirche im Epheserbrief,* 1930; Ernst Käsemann: *Leib und Leib Christi,* 1933; Alfred Wickenhauser: *Die Kirche als der mystische Leib Christi nach dem Apostel Paulus,* 1940; Franz-J. Leenhardt: *Etudes sur l'Eglise dans le NT,* 1940; Otto Michel: *Das Zeugnis des NT von der Gemeinde,* 1941; Nils A. Dahl: *Das Volk Gottes,* 1941; Ernst Percy: *Der Leib Christi,* 1942. On 3: see literature for §13; also: Ad. Deissmann: *Die neutestamentliche Formel "in Christo Jesu,"* 1892; Otto Schmitz: *Die Christusgemeinschaft des Paulus im Lichte seines Genetivgebrauchs,* 1924; Wilh. Weber: *Christusmystik,* 1924;

Erwin Wissmann: *Das Verhältnis von* Πίστις *und Christusmystik bei Paulus,* 1926; Alfr. Wickenhauser: *Die Christusmystik des heiligen Paulus,* 1928; Wilh. Mundle: *Der Glaubensbegriff des Paulus,* 1932; Werner Schmauch: *In Christus,* 1935; M. Dibelius: *Paulus und die Mystik,* 1941.
   For Chapter V C as a whole.
   Non-English: Ad. Schlatter: *Der Glaube im NT,* 4th ed., 1927; Raf. Gyllenberg: *Pistis,* 1922 (in Swedish). In addition to the works by Schmitz, Wissmann, Mundle and Wilh. Michaelis, named for §34, see Wilh. Michaelis: "Rechtfertigung aus Glauben bei Paulus," *Festgabe für Ad. Deissmann,* 1927, 116–138.
   §35: W. Morgan: *The Religion and Theology of Paul,* 1917; W. H. P. Hatch: *The Pauline Idea of Faith in its relation to Jewish and Hellenistic Religion,* 1917.
   §36: A. B. D. Alexander: *The Ethics of St. Paul* (Chapter V, "The Dynamics of the New Life"), 1910.
   Non-English: See the literature for §34, 3; also: Ernst Sommerlath: *Der Ursprung des neuen Lebens nach Paulus,* 1923.
   For Chapter V D as a whole. Joh. Weiss: *Die christliche Freiheit nach der Verkündigung des Paulus,* 1902; Otto Schmitz: *Der Freiheitsgedanke bei Epiktet und das Freiheitszeugnis des Paulus,* 1923; Mich. Müller: "Freiheit," *ZNW,* 25 (1926), 177–236; Hans Jonas: *Augustin und das paulinische Freiheitsproblem,* 1930; K. Deissner: *Autorität und Freiheit im ältesten Christentum,* 1931; W. Brandt: *Freiheit im NT,* 1932; Heinr. Schlier: the article, "ἐλεύθερος," *ThWB* II, 484–500.
   §38: *English:* Albert Schweitzer: *The Mysticism of Paul the Apostle,* tr. by Wm. Montgomery, 1931; J. E. Frame: "Paul's Idea of Deliverance," *JBL,* 49, 1930, 1–12; M. S. Enslin: *The Ethics of Paul,* 1930; H. R. Hoyle: *The Holy Spirit in St. Paul,* 1918.
   Non-English: Paul Wernle: *Der Christ und die Sünde bei Paulus,* 1897; Rud. Bultmann: "Das Problem der Ethik bei Paulus," *ZNW,* 23 (1924), 123–140; Hans Windisch: "Das Problem des paulinischen Imperativs," *ZNW,* 23 (1924), 265–281; Wilh. Mundle: "Religion und Sittlichkeit bei Paulus," *ZsystTh,* 4 (1927), 456–482; Hans v. Soden: *Sakrament und Ethik bei Paulus (Marb. Theol. Stud.* I), 1931; On 2 and 3: H. Gunkel und Fr. Büchsel: (see literature given in §14); E. Sokolowski: *Die Begriffe Geist und Leben bei Paulus,* 1903; Alfr. Juncker: *Die Ethik des Apostels Paulus,* I, II, 1904, 1919; K. Deissner: *Auferstehungshoffnung und Pneumagedanke bei Paulus,* 1912; H. Bertrams: *Das Wesen des Geistes nach der Anschauung des Apostels Paulus,* 1913; W. Reinhard: *Das Wirken des Heiligen Geistes im Menschen nach den Briefen des Apostels Paulus,* 1918; Otto Schmitz: "Der Begriff δύναμις bei Paulus," *Festgabe für Ad. Deissmann,* 1927, 139–167; Herb. Preisker: *Geist und Leben,* 1933; On 3: E. G. Gulin: *Die Freude im NT,* I, 1932.
   §39: *English:* James Moffatt: *Love in the NT,* 1925.
   Non-English: See the literature for Chapter V D. Also: on 3: Wilh. Lütgert: *Die Liebe im NT,* 1905; Herb. Preisker: "Die Liebe im Urchristentum und in der alten Kirche," *ThStKr,* 95 (1924), 272–294; the same:

[365]

BIBLIOGRAPHIES

Die urchristliche Botschaft von der Liebe Gottes, 1930; Günther Bornkamm: "Der Köstliche Weg (1. Kr 13)," *Jahrb. d. theol. Schule Bethel,* 1937, 131–150.

§40: *English:* G. Vos: "The Pauline Doctrine of the Resurrection," *Princeton Theol. Rev.* 27 (1929), 1–35, 193–226; F. C. Burkitt: "Life, Zoe, Hayyim," *ZNW,* 12 (1911), 228–230.

Non-English: See the literature for §38. Also: K. L. Schmidt: "Eschatologie und Mystik im Urchristentum," *ZNW,* 21 (1922), 277–291; Hans Emil Weber: *"Eschatologie"* und *"Mystik" in NT,* 1930; On 1: Rich. Kabisch: *Die Eschatologie des Paulus,* 1893; E. Teichmann: *Die paulinischen Vorstellungen von Auferstehung und Gericht,* 1896; On 2: Arn. Steubing: *Der paulinische Begriff "Christusleiden,"* Heidelberg dissertation, 1905; Ernst Lohmeyer: Σὺν Χριστῷ (*Festgabe für Ad. Deissmann,* 1927, 218–258); Joh. Schneider: *Die Passionsmystik des Paulus,* 1929; M. Dibelius: *Paulus und die Mystik,* 1941.

Theology of the New Testament

THEOLOGY

OF THE

NEW TESTAMENT

by

RUDOLF BULTMANN

Professor Emeritus of New Testament,
University of Marburg

VOLUME II

TRANSLATED BY
KENDRICK GROBEL

CHARLES SCRIBNER'S SONS

PRINTED IN THE UNITED STATES OF AMERICA

This translation was supported in part by funds
made available jointly by the Carnegie Foundation
and Vanderbilt University. The author and the
translator are solely responsible for the statements
made in this book.

Contents

CONTENTS

PART THREE

THE THEOLOGY
OF THE GOSPEL OF JOHN
AND THE JOHANNINE EPISTLES

CHAPTER I

Orientation

§ 41. The Historical Position of John

1. To determine the historical locus of the Gospel of John (with which the Epistles of John are closely connected*) a *comparison with the synoptics*, which for the time being must confine itself to form and characteristic themes, is of service. The distance which separates John both from the proclamation of Jesus and from that of the oldest Church is straightway apparent. Whether John was acquainted with one or more of our synoptics is debated; at any rate, it cannot be proved with certainty that he was. Nevertheless, he is familiar with the tradition which is worked into shape in them, as is clear from certain sayings of Jesus, from certain miracle stories, and especially from the account of the passion. The miracle stories, which the evangelist presumably took from a written source, indicate by their very style a more advanced stage of development than that of the synoptic tradition.† Originally, their point lay in the miracle they report, but for the evangelist they take on a symbolic or allegorical

---

* Whether the Epistles were written by the author of the Gospel himself or simply came out of his "school," can here be disregarded. In the following discussion, references to the Gospel are given simply by chapter and verse; references to the Epistles have I Jn., etc., prefixed.
Quotations from the Bible are given according to the Revised Standard Version, copyrighted 1946 and 1952, with the kind permission of the copyright owner, Division of Christian Education, National Council of the Churches of Christ in the U.S.A., unless there is an indication to the contrary. "Blt." (=Bultmann's version) means that the author himself translated the passage into German, for which an English equivalent is here offered; "tr." (=translator's version) means that the author quoted only the Greek text, which the translator of this book felt compelled to translate anew in the sense implied by the author's context. Rarely King James or a modern private translation is quoted, and always by name.
† For this assertion and all that follows I refer to my commentary "Das Evangelium des Johannes" in Meyer's *Kommentar*, 2nd ed., 1950.

meaning, and throughout the Gospel he uses them as points of departure for discourses or discussions, which, throughout his presentation, are the form of Jesus' activity. The result is a stylistically and historically completely different picture from that depicted by the synoptics. The latter offer short dialogues with disciples or opponents in which Jesus answers the honestly inquiring or his opponents with a short, striking saying (often formulated as a counter-question or a figurative saying). Instead of this, we find in John an extended discourse of Jesus or a dialogue occasioned by the miracles or by ambiguous statements or concepts like being born ἄνωθεν, 3:3f. ("again" or "from above") or ὕδωρ ζῶν, 4:10ff. ("running water" or "living water"). While the speeches of Jesus in the synoptics are mostly sayings strung on a string, in John they are coherent discussions on a definite theme. Into such discourses and dialogues are woven the few sayings which John adopted out of the synoptic tradition (2:19; 4:44; 12:25f.; 13:16, 20; 15:20). The themes taken up are not those found in the synoptics. In John, Jesus appears neither as the rabbi arguing about questions of the Law nor as the prophet proclaiming the breaking in of the Reign of God. Rather, he speaks only of his own person as the Revealer whom God has sent. He does not argue about the Sabbath and fasting or purity and divorce but speaks of his coming and his going, of what he is and what he brings the world. He strives not against self-righteousness and untruthfulness but against disbelief toward himself. And precisely where a theme of Jesus' synoptic preaching seems to lie before us—the accusation of breaking the Sabbath, ch. 5 and ch. 9—the difference is apparent. For here attention is not focused upon the question how far the Sabbath-commandment has validity for *man* (as in Mk. 2:23–3:6); rather, the authority of Jesus as Son of God is being demonstrated. The parables so characteristic of the synoptic Jesus are completely lacking; in their place appear the great symbolic discourses of the good shepherd (ch. 10) and the true vine (ch. 15) which by a symbolic figure represent Jesus as the Revealer. They belong to a cycle of words and discourses whose distinguishing characteristic is the "I am . . ." of the Revealer, and are without analogy in the synoptics. Even the passion narrative, in whose outline John is, relatively speaking, nearest to the synoptics, is completely transformed. Jesus' last meal with his disciples is no longer the Passover meal, nor does it institute the Lord's Supper; it is the

[4]

point of departure for long farewell discourses which are without parallel in the synoptics. The dialogues in the hearings before the Sanhedrin and Pilate are completely transformed, as is the account of the crucifixion, which closes with the Revealer's utterance, "It is accomplished" (tr.)—just as in the beginning of the Gospel the Baptist is no longer the preacher of repentance but the witness to Jesus as the Son of God.

While in the synoptics the vicissitudes, the problems, and the faith of the earliest Church are reflected, scarcely anything of the sort can any longer be discovered in John. The questions that were characteristic for the earliest Church—the validity of the Law, the coming or the delay of the Reign of God—have died out. The problem of the mission to the Gentiles is no longer actual, as a comparison of Mt. 8:5–13; Lk. 7:1–10 with Jn. 4:46–54 indicates: a story which once told about the faith of a Gentile now serves to answer the question about the relation between faith and miracle. Proof from prophecy plays a scanty role: only in 2:17; 12:14f., 38, 40; 13:18; 15:25; 19:24, 36f. and perhaps in 6:31 and 45 does it occur. The single problem that has retained its old importance is that of the relationship of Jesus and the Church to the Baptist and his followers (*cf.* Mk. 2:18 and parallels, Mt. 11:2–19, par., Lk. 11:1), indeed it has gained in importance (1:6–8, 15, 19–36; 3:23–30; 5:33–35; 10:40–42), and Acts 18:25 and 19:1–7 also show that this problem was occupying the Hellenistic Church. So far as the situation of the Church is reflected in the Gospel of John, its problem is the conflict with Judaism, and its theme is faith in Jesus as the Son of God. The Christian congregation is already excluded from the synagogue association (9:22; 16:1–3)—in fact, the evangelist feels the Church's estrangement from Judaism to be so great that in his account Jesus already appears as no longer a member of the Jewish people or its religion but speaks to the Jews of their Law as "your Law" as if he were a non-Jew (8:17; 10:34; *cf.* 7·19, 22). In John, "the Jews" no longer appear in their concrete differentiation as "pious" and "sinners," tax-collectors and harlots, scholars in the Law or fishermen, but simply as "the Jews," differentiated only into "the multitude" and the leaders, who are called "the rulers" or the "high-priests" or "the Pharisees," the last of whom are often conceived as a sort of official board (7:45, 47f.; 11:47, 57). Furthermore, for John "the Jews" are representatives of "the world" in general which refuses to respond to Jesus with faith.

[5]

2. The observation that in John the Pauline discussion about the Law plays no role has often led to the false deduction that John must be regarded as the culmination of the development that leads out beyond Paul, a culmination in which the debates about the Law are a thing of the past. But the *relation of John to Paul* cannot be understood on a linear scheme of development from the theology of the earliest Church; the two lie in quite different directions. Since John is somewhat remote from the earliest Church, he is likely younger than Paul; but he does not presuppose Paul as a link between himself and the earliest Church. The later development of Paulinism is shown by the deutero-Pauline literature (Col., Eph., II Thess., the pastorals, I Pet.)—it is a different world from that of John.

It is true, however, that in regard to the *current religious atmosphere* Paul and John have certain things in common. Both come within the sphere of a Hellenism that is saturated with the Gnostic stream, so that a certain agreement between them in dualistic terminology is not surprising. Both use the term "world" (κόσμος) in the dualistic depreciatory sense and also agree in understanding "world" as basically the world of men (3:16f., etc.; for Paul see § 26). The antitheses typical of John—"truth-falsehood" (8:44; I Jn. 2:21, 27), "light-darkness" (1:5, 8:12; I Jn. 1:5, etc.)—also occur, at least occasionally, in Paul (Rom. 1:25; II Cor. 4:6).* The antithesis "earthly-heavenly" is found in both (3:12; I Cor. 15:40; *cf.* Phil. 2:10). Above all, in both John and Paul christology is formed after the pattern of the Gnostic Redeemer-myth (§ 15, 4c, I, pp. 174–6): the sending of the pre-existent Son of God in the disguise of a man (Phil. 2:6–11; Jn. 1:14, etc.). The parallel Adam-Christ, it is true, is not drawn in John as it is in Paul (Rom. 5:12ff.; I Cor. 15:21f., 45f.). Yet for John, too, the sending of the Redeemer is the eschatological event; it is the turning-point of the ages (3:19; 9:39, etc.; Gal. 4:4). However, the Johannine terminology of the Redeemer's "coming" and "going" (8:14, etc.) and John's ambiguous "be exalted" (ὑψωθῆναι, 3:14, etc.) are lacking in Paul. John, for his part, avoids expressions that stem from Jewish apocalyptic and are frequent in Paul ("this age," I Cor. 1:20, etc.; "the fulness of time," Gal. 4:4; a "new creation," II Cor. 5:17; Gal. 6:15 and the like).

* II Cor. 6:14 is not cited because it is non-Pauline; see I, p. 202, note 1. For "darkness" Paul says not σκοτία but σκότος, a word which occurs in John only at 3:19 and I Jn. 1:3.

Nor is it surprising that Paul and John agree to a certain extent in the use *of common-Christian terminology*. Like Paul and the rest of the New Testament John, too, naturally speaks of "life (eternal)" as that which salvation gives, though he scarcely speaks of the Reign of God any more (3:3, 5; I, p. 76). The terms "joy" (17:13, etc.; Rom. 14:17, etc.) and "peace" (14:27, etc.; Rom. 14:17, etc.) serve to describe the gift of salvation, though they are used by John in a peculiar way: as gifts of the departing Jesus to the Congregation remaining behind in the world. Agreement in the use of "send" (ἀποστέλλω and πέμπειν) for the sending of Jesus (Gal. 4:4; Rom. 8:3, Jn. *passim*), or of "give" (διδόναι 3:16, for which the common-Christian expression is παραδιδόναι, "give up" Rom. 8:32, etc.) for God's bestowal of him, are of course no indication of any special relation between John and Paul. Neither is their agreement on Jesus' exaltation to lordship in "glory" (17:5, etc.; Phil. 2:9; 3:21, etc.). The sending of the Spirit (15:26) to the Church after Jesus' exaltation is a common-Christian view (§ 14), not specifically Pauline, and there is no parallel in Paul for the name Paraclete which the Spirit bears in John. Though Is. 53:1 is quoted in defensive argument both in Jn. 12:38 and Rom. 10:16, that, of course, does not prove John's dependence upon Paul. If in the tradition utilized by John the saying of Jesus about following him quoted in 12:26 was already formulated with the word "servant" rather than "disciple" (Lk. 14:27), that may well be due to the influence of Pauline or of deutero-Pauline usage (II Cor. 3:6; Eph. 3:7, etc.).

Since there is such contact with common-Christian terminology in both John and Paul, it is all the more significant that *the specifically Pauline terminology is missing in John*. Though Paul and John both use the term "world" and in the same sense (see II, p. 6), Paul's dominant contrast "flesh-spirit" retreats far into the background in John, occurring only at 3:6 and 6:63. In fact, "flesh" only rarely occurs (1:13f.; I Jn. 2:16—except in the passages that speak of Jesus' coming "in flesh": I Jn. 4:2; II Jn. 7). The characteristic Pauline expression "according to flesh (κατὰ σάρκα, see § 22, 3) has an analogy, if at all, only in κατὰ τὴν σάρκα, 8:15. "Desire" (ἐπιθυμία, § 23, 2) occurs only in 8:44, I Jn. 2:16; the verb "desire" (ἐπιθυμεῖν) never does. Paul's characteristic anthropological terminology derived from the Old Testament is not found in John: *soma* and *psyche* in the Pauline sense do not occur, "heart" is relatively rare (13:2; 14:1, 27;

16:6, 22 in addition to the quotation 12:40, with which *cf.* I Jn.
3:19–21), "mind" (νοῦς or νόημα) is completely missing. Also missing
are "boast" and its cognates (καυχᾶσθαι, καύχημα, καύχησις) and
"care," noun and verb (μέριμνα and μεριμνᾶν). Likewise missing are
the terms that Paul took over from the Stoic-Cynic *diatribe*:
"conscience," "virtue," "nature."

Still more important is the fact that *Paul's terminology relating
specifically to the history of salvation is not encountered in John.* He
does not know "God's righteousness" (δικαιοσύνη θεοῦ) as a designation for salvation itself; δικαιοσύνη occurs only in 16:8, 10 (where it
means Jesus' "vindication"; i.e. his victory in the suit with the
world in which he is involved) and in I Jn. 2:29; 3:7, 10 in the Old
Testament phrase "to do righteousness." Naturally, then, rightwising
(δικαιοῦσθαι, "to be justified") and the antithesis "by works of the
Law—by faith" are lacking; in fact the noun "faith" is found only
at I Jn. 5:4. For while πιστεύειν (believing) is demanded, it is
demanded not in the specifically Pauline but in the common-Christian
sense (I, pp. 88f.). Faith as the right way to salvation is not contrasted with false "zeal for God" (Rom. 10:3); in John the way to
salvation as a problem actual for the Jew is not under discussion. The
antithesis "law-grace" occurs only at 1:17, and here we evidently do
have an echoing of Pauline terminology; but even in this case the
Pauline antithesis is altered by the fact that the "grace" which is
set up against "law" is combined with "truth." Otherwise, "grace"
occurs only in 1:14, 16 and in the salutation-formula II Jn. 3; χάρισμα
(an act of grace) and χαρίζεσθαι (to be graciously treated) are
completely missing. The passion-narrative, Jn. 19, naturally mentions
"the cross" and "crucify"; but it is not as terms of the history of
salvation that these words are used. Hence, they occur neither among
the words of Jesus nor in the Johannine epistles.

The history-of-salvation perspective as a whole is lacking in John.
True, the Johannine Jesus appeals to Abraham against the Jews and
denies their descent from Abraham (8:33–58); and in conflict with the
Jews he knows Moses to be on his side (5:45f.; *cf.* 1:45). But the idea
of God's covenant with Israel or of the new covenant, God's election
of Israel and His guidance of the People play no role. Hence, it is
quite understandable that the proof from prophecy scarcely plays
any role (see above) and that the history-of-salvation term for the
Congregation, *viz.* Church (ἐκκλησία, § 6, 2; § 10, 1) does not occur

[8]

n John. The word is found only in III Jn. 6 and 9f., where it denotes
he individual congregation. Of "calling" in the history-of-salvation
sense, the "call," and "the called" (§10, 3) there is no mention. The
verb "choose" (ἐκλέγεσθαι, 6:70; 13:18; 15:16, 19) may be an echoing
of Paul's technical term, though in John it says of Jesus what otherwise is ascribed to God (I Cor. 1:27, etc.). But the nouns "choice" or
"election" (ἐκλογή) and "the chosen" (ἐκγεκτοί, § 10, 3) are missing.*
The designation of Christians as "saints" (ἅγιοι) or "sanctified ones"
ἡγιασμένοι, § 10, 3) is also missing, though Jn. 17:17 and 19 may be
echoes of it. The Hellenistic ecclesiological terminology is also lacking
—at least in the original text of the Gospel—and so is any reference
to the Kyrios-cult and the sacraments. Kyrios occurs in redactional
glosses in 4:1; 6:23; 11:2; otherwise only in ch. 20, the Easter story, as
a designation of the risen Jesus. The sacraments were subsequently
introduced into the text by editorial process (3:5; 6:51b–58).† The
evangelist avoids speaking of them, evidently having misgivings
about sacramental piety, even going so far as to omit narrating the
institution of the Lord's Supper, for which he substitutes Jesus'
farewell prayer, ch. 17.

Clearly, then, John is not of the Pauline school and is not influenced by Paul; he is, instead, a figure with his own originality and
stands in an atmosphere of theological thinking different from that of
Paul. As far as that goes, even in such a different atmosphere the
influence of Paul could take effect, as Ignatius shows—a writer who
is related to John by belonging with him to a certain world of thought,
but who was nevertheless strongly influenced by Paul. Comparison
with Ignatius well shows how much John stands by himself; and this
independence of John emerges all the more clearly as one perceives
the deep relatedness in substance that exists between John and Paul in
spite of all their differences in mode of thought and terminology.
This does not mean, of course, relatedness in such details as the fact
that John like Paul can sum up the plural "works" into its singular
"work" (6:28f.)—in which, moreover, the difference is greater than
the resemblance because in John the "work" is faith and not that
working which springs from faith, as it is in I Cor. 15:58, I Thess. 1:3.
The real relatedness lies in the fact that in both of them the

---

* "Elect lady" II Jn. 1 and "elect sister" II Jn. 13, it seems, are designations
of individual Christian congregations.
    † See below, § 47, 4.

eschatological occurrence is understood as already taking place in the present, though John was the first to carry the idea radically through. In both writers the idea of Jesus' "glory" is made historical occurrence (1:14; II Cor. 3:7ff.; I, p. 334), and for both the new life appears under the mask of death (11:25f.; 16:33; II Cor. 4:7ff.; I pp. 345–7). Both John and Paul de-mythologize Gnostic cosmological dualism in the fact that by both the world continues to be understood as God's creation and in the fact that the God-concept of both contains the paradoxical union of judgment and grace. But all this must await the detailed presentation of Johannine theology for its clarification.

3. *Who the author of the Gospel and Epistles of John was* and where they were written is unknown. As to the time of writing only this much can be said: the Gospel must have originated some interval of time after the first literary fixation of the synoptic tradition but very probably still within the first century, since its existence is testified by quotations in papyri that come from the beginning of the second century.* At any rate, the thought-atmosphere out of which it (and the Epistles) grew is that of *oriental Christianity*. The Gospel as a whole was not originally written in a Semitic language (Aramaic or Syriac) and then translated into Greek, but was undoubtedly written in Greek. But its *language* is a semitizing Greek both as to grammar and to style, though in a different way from the Greek of the synoptics, of which the same is true. Furthermore, it is at least probable that the evangelist used an originally Aramaic (or Syriac) source in certain places: namely, for the prologue and the sayings and discourses of Jesus wherever they are not derived from the synoptic tradition or from the already mentioned (II, p. 3) collection of miracle-stories which also served him as a source. Whether it be that the source of Jesus' sayings and discourses—let us call it the "Revelation-discourses" after its chief content—was translated from the Semitic or was conceived in Greek, in any case its style is that of Semitic speech; more accurately, of Semitic poetry such as is known to us from the Odes of Solomon and other Gnostic texts. A definite plan, open, of course, to variation and frequently reworked into dialogues by the evangelist, underlies such revelation-discourses.

---

* The "Unknown Gospel," the fragments of which were edited in 1935 by H. Idris Bell and T. C. Skeat and especially the fragment of John edited by C. H. Roberts in 1935 indicate that John was known in Egypt about 100 A.D.

This plan includes the motif of the self-presentation of the Revealer introduced by the characteristic formula "I am . . ."; it also includes the call of invitation and promise and a threat for him who will not believe. The discourse unfolds in the parallelism of members that is characteristic of Semitic poetry. Here it displays the peculiarity that in cases of antithetic parallelism the antithesis is often not simply the opposite of the thesis (as it is, e.g. in Sir. 3:9; Mt. 8:20; Mk. 10:42–44), but a negation of the opposite made either by repeating the thesis with a negative or by some very slight alteration of its wording (e.g. 3:18a, 36a; 4:13f.; 8:23).

The stylistic form of the Revelation-discourses expresses the *basic dualistic view* which they presuppose. Also in keeping with this dualistic view are the antithetical terms which run through these discourses: light and darkness, truth and falsehood, above and below (or heavenly and earthly), freedom and bondage. We are led into the same sphere of dualistic-Gnostic thinking by the *symbols* which characterize the Revealer in his contrast to the "world" and in his meaning for salvation or which describe the gift he brings: he is the light of the world, the good shepherd, the true vine; he dispenses the water of life, the true bread from heaven. What he is and what he gives is "true" (ἀληθινός, 1:9; 6:32; 15:1; I Jn. 2:8); in fact, he can simply be called "the truth" (14:6)—which is just the mode of expression of that dualism to which everything earthly is falsehood and seeming. All that man seeks in this world and all that he thinks he finds is, in the Revealer, "truth"—i.e. reality. In all that man seeks he is seeking "life"—in the Revealer it is present. As he is "the truth," he is also "life" (14:6; I Jn. 1:2). Of course, for Paul also and for primitive Christianity as a whole, as indeed for the Old Testament and Judaism, "life" is the redemptive good that is striven for. But it came to be the dominant designation of salvation only in those circles of the Hellenistic religions, and especially Gnosticism, in which the life of this world lost its lustre and worth to such a degree that it was regarded as a mere semblance of life which in truth is death. It is from within such an atmosphere that John writes, and in his writing the terms "truth" and "life" take the place of "Reign of God" and "righteousness of God."

Terminologically, this complex of views is also expressed by the fact that Jesus as the Revealer is called he whom the Father has "sent" or "commissioned." This mode of expression, too, (πέμπειν, "send," or

ἀποστέλλειν "commission") took on a special meaning in Gnosticism.*
It is characteristic for this dualistic view because it denotes the
irruption of the beyond into the here in the person of a Revealer—
the Ambassador. In him the world of "truth" and "life" appears within
the realm of this world; the eschatological event becomes present
reality in his word which as the Ambassador he speaks in his Father's
commission. If, then, for John, as for Paul, the eschatological
salvation-event is already taking place in the present, it nevertheless
does so with a difference suggested by their very terminology.

Paul may also say, it is true, that God "sent" His Son (Gal.
4:4; Rom. 8:3); but in Paul this term plays no such role as his
expression that God "gave up" His Son. This expression was
traditional before Paul and familiar to him (παραδιδόναι Rom.
4:25; 8:32; I Cor. 11:23); he evidently recast it in speaking of the
Son's self-surrender (διδόναι, giving, or παραδιδόναι, surrendering
ἑαυτόν, of himself; Gal. 1:4; 2:20; the expression subsequently
occurs in the school of Paul at Eph. 5:2, 25; I Tim. 2:6; Tit. 2:14).
In John this "giving" (διδόναι) occurs only at 3:16 (παραδιδόναι
occurs rather often, but means "betray") and denotes simply
the sending of the Son in common-Christian terminology. For the
idea of the (self-) surrender of the Son *as sacrifice* is not present
here, since the preposition "for" (ὑπέρ Gal. 1:4; 2:20; Eph. 5:2,
25; I Tim. 2:6; Tit. 2:14) or "for the sake of" (διά Rom. 4:25),
which is characteristic of this sacrificial terminology, is missing.

While for Paul the earthly Jesus, as the pre-existent one appearing
in the form of a servant, is empty of any divine glory (Phil. 2:6ff.;
II Cor. 8:9; Rom. 8:3), in John the incarnate Logos reveals his
"glory" in his work on earth—though admittedly in a paradoxical
fashion visible only to the eyes of the believing (1:14; 2:11). Therefore, the words which the heavenly voice speaks to Jesus (Jn. 12:28)
at the turning-point of his fate can scarcely be imagined as occurring
in Paul: "I have glorified (i.e. in the Revealer's earthly activity) and I
will glorify again (i.e. through the exaltation which will take place
on the cross)."

In short, then, the figure of Jesus in John is portrayed in the
forms offered by the Gnostic Redeemer-myth (§ 15, 1, I, p. 166)
which had already influenced the christological thinking of Hellenistic

* On which see especially: Geo. Widengren, *The Great Vohu Manah and the
Apostle of God*, 1945; and *Mesopotamian Elements in Manichaeism*, 1946. *Cf.* also
Hans Jonas, *Gnosis und spätantiker Geist* I, 1934, 120ff.

Christianity before Paul and then influenced him (§ 15, 4c). It is true that the cosmological motifs of the myth are missing in John, especially the idea that the redemption which the "Ambassador" brings is the release of the pre-existent sparks of light which are held captive in this world below by demonic powers (§ 15, 1, I, pp. 165f.). But otherwise Jesus appears as in the Gnostic myth as the pre-existent Son of God whom the Father clothed with authority and sent into the world. Here, appearing as a man, he speaks the words the Father gave him and accomplishes the works which the Father commissioned him to do. In so doing, he is not "cut off" from the Father but stands in solid and abiding unity with Him as an ambassador without fault or falsehood. He comes as the "light," the "truth," the "life" by bringing through his words and works light, truth, and life and calling "his own" to himself. In his discourses with their "I am . . ." he reveals himself as the Ambassador; but only "his own" understand him. So his coming accomplishes the separation between those who hear his voice, who become "seeing," and those who do not understand his speech, who suppose themselves seeing and remain imprisoned in their blindness. In the world out of which he calls his own to himself he is despised and hated. But he leaves the world; as he "came" so he "departs" and takes leave of his own, whom in his prayer he commits to the Father's care. But his departure also belongs to his work of redemption, for by his elevation he has prepared the way for his own to the heavenly dwelling-places into which he will fetch his own. Out of Gnostic language, finally, and not, as some maintain, out of the Greek philosophical tradition comes the pre-existent Revealer's name: Logos. How John interprets this myth, and how it can serve him to express his theological thoughts will have to become clear in the exposition of the latter.

Gnostic terminology places its stamp mainly on the words and discourses of Jesus, but it is by no means confined to the Revelation-discourse source which presumably underlies them; rather, it runs through the whole Gospel and the Epistles. If the author's background was Judaism, as rather frequently occurring rabbinical turns of speech perhaps prove, it was, at any rate, not out of an orthodox but out of a gnosticizing Judaism that he came.* Especially the

* While a pre-Christian gnosticizing Judaism could hitherto only be deduced out of later sources, the existence of such is now testified by the manuscripts recently discovered in Palestine.

literary devices with which he builds the discussions—the use of ambiguous concepts and statements to elicit misunderstandings—are indicative that he lives within the sphere of Gnostic-dualistic thinking. For those ambiguities and misunderstandings are far from being merely formal technical devices. Rather, they are the expression of his underlying dualistic view: the Revealer and the "world" cannot understand each other; they do not speak the same language (8:43); the world confuses truth with appearance, the real with the unreal and cannot but drag down into the realm of the unreal what the Revealer says of the real and thus cannot but misunderstand it.

CHAPTER II

Johannine Dualism

§ 42. World and Man

1. John's proclamation consists of the message that God so loved the world that He sent His "only-begotten" Son—not to judge it, but to save it (3:16; I Jn. 4:9, 14). Judgment would be what it deserves, for "the whole world lieth in wickedness" (I Jn. 5:19, KJ); it stands in need of being saved.

As for Paul (§ 26), so for John the *kosmos* means primarily the world of men; on it the judgment falls that it is evil and would be lost were it not for the coming of the "Son." In its radical opposition to God it is characterized as in Paul by the term "this world" (ὁ κόσμος οὗτος 8:23; 9:39; 11:9; 12:25, 31, 13:1; 16:11; 18:36; I Jn. 4:17), which comes from apocalyptic eschatology. In this term, the point is the contrast between the nature of the world and God, not a contrast between two ages (except in the quotation at 12:25). Accordingly, John speaks neither of "this age" or "the present (ἐνεστῶς) age" nor of the "future" (μέλλων) or "coming (ἐρχόμενος) age."

But what is *the essence* of the *kosmos*?

The sentence: "It (the light) was in the world, and the world came into being through it, yet the world did not recognize it (the Logos)" (1:10 tr.) corresponds to the sentence: "The light is shining in the darkness, and the darkness has not grasped it" (1:5 tr.). The essence of the *kosmos*, therefore, is *darkness* (*cf.* 8:12; 12:35, 46; I Jn. 1:5f.; 2:8f., 11)—darkness not as a shadow lying upon the world, an affliction imposed upon it (as in Is. 9:1, for example), but as its own peculiar nature in which it is at ease and at home, for: "the light has come into the world, and men loved darkness rather than light" (3:19 RSV). Just this—that the world appropriates to itself its darkness—can come to expression in the judgment that men are blind, blind without knowing it and without wanting to acknowledge it (9:39–41; *cf.* 12:40; I Jn. 2:11). Hence, it means the same thing when the world's nature is designated as *falsehood*, which indirectly takes place by Jesus' assertion that he came into the world to bear witness to the truth (18:37). It occurs again when he promises knowledge of the truth to him who is loyal in faith (8:32) or when it is said of him that through him came grace and truth (1:17), that the word he brings is truth (17:17), that he himself is the truth (14:6, *cf.* also I Jn. 2:21; 3:19). But the world's nature is directly designated as falsehood when Jesus accuses "the Jews" of not being able to hear his word because they are of the devil, i.e. sprung from falsehood, and therefore do not believe when Jesus says the truth (8:43–45; *cf.* I Jn. 2:21, 27). Whoever does not acknowledge Jesus as the Messiah is a "liar" (I Jn. 2:22). Furthermore, this compound of darkness and falsehood that is characteristic of the world, which it, itself, has appropriated as its own, is a power to which the world has fallen into bondage—an idea that is expressed by the promise of freedom to those who know the truth (8:32). *Kosmos*, then, is in essence *existence in bondage*. The "ruler of the (or this) world" is the devil (12:31; 14:40; 16:11). Because he is their father, the "Jews" are his offspring (8:44); so are the "sinners" (I Jn. 3:8, 10). For bondage to the devil is synonymous with *bondage to sin*, which is the very thing from which the knowledge of the truth emancipates men (8:32–34). To love darkness more than light means to do evil (3:19f.). To be blind means to be left stuck in one's sin (9:41)—which in turn means to be *under the sway of death*. In their sins the "Jews" will die (8:21, 24). In fact, the world is really already dead; for of him who believes in Jesus it is said that he has already gone over into life from death (5:24). Whenever Jesus' word sounds forth, the hour of the resurrection of the dead has arrived (5:25), and it is just because the world lies in death that Jesus brings the water of life and the bread of life (4:10, 6:27ff.), that he is the light of life (8:12), the resurrection, and life itself (11:25; 14:6). But the most ghastly thing of all about its bondage to death is the world's enmity to life. As the devil is by nature (ἀπ' ἀρχῆς 8:44) a murderer, so likewise are they murderers who spring from him like Cain (I Jn. 3:12) or the "Jews" (8:40). Hatred of one's brother is nothing less than such will to murder (I Jn. 3:15; *cf.* 2:9, 11). Hence, Jesus' "new commandment" is that of brotherly love (13:34f.; I Jn. 2:7ff., etc.), and as he who believes is said to have gone over from death into life, the same is said of him who loves his brother (I Jn. 3:14).

Is the devil a reality for John in the mythical sense? That is very doubtful, to say the least. But be that as it may, he represents in any case the power to whose domination the world has surrendered itself: the power of darkness and falsehood, the power of sin and death. The devil is God's antagonist; i.e. darkness and falsehood, sin and death are the enemies of light and truth, freedom and life. But the devilish power of all evil is not gnostically conceived as a cosmic power under whose domination men have come by a curse inflicted upon them. The world does not have its origin in a tragic event of primeval time (see I, pp. 165f.). Rather, *the world is the creation of God*. For everything was created by the Word (1:3) which was with God in the beginning and, indeed, was God. And that means that God revealed Himself in His creating; the same implication lies in the fact that the Word, insofar as it was "life" for that which was created, was also the "light" for men.*

2. John's concepts, light and darkness, truth and falsehood, freedom and bondage, life and death, come from Gnostic dualism, but they take on their specific Johannine meaning only in their relation to the idea of creation. For what does *light* mean? Naturally it means in John, as in religious language everywhere, that which is salutary. But how can we more exactly determine its meaning? The way is indicated by those sentences that speak of "walking" or "working" in the light (or, by day) or of the opposite, "walking" in darkness (or in the night). Only in the light is it possible to walk and work sure of one's way; in the dark a man is blind and cannot find his way (9:4; 11:9f.; 12:35; I Jn. 2:11). Light, that means, is understood in its original sense: the daylight in which man is able not only to orient himself about objects but also to understand himself in his world and find his way in it. But the "true light" (1:9; I Jn. 2:8) is not the light of literal day, which makes orientation in the external

---

* This somewhat ambiguous sentence of John (1:3–4; ὁ γέγονεν, ἐν αὐτῷ ζωὴ ἦν) means either "That which came into being—(for it) there was life in it (*sc.* the Word)" (in more tolerable English: "In the Word there was life for that which was created") or it means "That which came into being—in it (the Word) was the life" (in better English: "In that which was created the Word was the life").

But the ultimate meaning is the same in either case; see my *Kommentar*, pp. 20–22.

world possible, but the state of having one's existence illumined, an illumination in and by which a man understands himself, achieves a self-understanding which opens up his "way" to him, guides all his conduct, and gives him clarity and assurance. Since creation is a revelation of God and the "Word" is at work as the "light" in that which was created, then man is given the possibility of a genuine self-understanding in the possibility of understanding himself as God's creature. *Darkness*, then, means that a man does not seize this possibility—that he shuts himself up against the God revealed in the creation. It means that instead of understanding himself as creature he arrogates to himself a self-sovereignty that belongs to the Creator alone. To the question whence darkness comes, John gives no mythical answer. For the possibility of darkness—illusory self-understanding—is provided by the possibility of light—genuine self-understanding. Only because there is revelation of God, is there enmity toward God. Only because there is light, is there darkness. Darkness is nothing other than shutting one's self up against the light. It is the turning away from the origin of one's existence, away from that which alone offers the possibility of illumining one's existence. When the world shuts itself up against the light it thereby rebels against God, making itself independent of the Creator—i.e. attempts to do so, vainly imagines it can do so. So, being in darkness, the world is simultaneously *in falsehood*. For it is this illusion about itself, not some immoral conduct, that is the lie—an illusion, however, which is no mere error in thought, but the illusion of a false self-understanding out of which any immoral conduct that may develop proceeds to grow—a self-understanding which is revolt against God, against the "truth."

For just as "falsehood" has no merely formal meaning in John, neither does "*truth*" (ἀλήθεια), as if it meant the nakedness of that-which-is in general or reality in the purely formal sense in which that can be predicated of any object (in contrast to a mistaken notion about it). Rather, the basic meaning of "truth" in John is God's reality, which, since God is the Creator, is the only true reality. The emancipating knowledge of the truth (8:32) is not the rational knowledge of the reality of that-which-is in general; such a knowledge would at best free one from the prejudices and errors occasioned by tradition and convention. No, this knowledge of the truth is the knowledge, granted to men of faith, of God's reality; it frees one of

[18]

sin (8:32–34). True, ἀλήθεια does have the formal meaning "truth" when it is said that Jesus tells the truth (8:45), or that the Spirit guides us into all the truth (16:13). But the truth into which the Spirit guides is factually the reality of God; and Jesus does not merely *tell* the truth but also *is* the truth (14:6; § 48). So truth is not the teaching about God transmitted by Jesus but is God's very reality revealing itself—occurring!—in Jesus. For whoever has seen him has seen the Father (14:9); in him the Father is and works (14:10f.); and as he is the "truth," for that very reason he is also "the life" (14:6). If, as the incarnate Word, he is full of "grace" and "truth" (1:14), that says in a hendiadys that in him God's reality encounters men as a gracious gift. If God's word is the "truth" (17:17), that is because it is in his word that God's reality becomes manifest. And if believers are to be "consecrated" (17:17=set apart) by the truth, that will occur in this way: that the reality of God, manifesting itself in the Word, takes them, though still in the world, out of the world's sphere of power (17:14–16). If God demands such worshipers as worship him "in spirit and in truth" (4:23), here again we have a hendiadys which means that true worship of God is solely such worship as is brought about by God's power and His own revealing of Himself. But the world has become indifferent to the reality of God with an indifference expressed by the question with which Pilate shrugs it off: "What is truth?" Nevertheless, as "to be of the truth" (18:37; I Jn. 2:21; 3:19) is synonymous with "to be of God" (7:17; 8:47; I Jn. 3:10; 4:1ff.; 5:19), so "to be of the world" (8:23; 15:19; 17:14, 16; 18:36; I Jn. 2:16; 4:5) or "of the earth" (3:31) is synonymous with "to be from below" (8:23) and "to be of the devil" (8:44; I Jn. 3:8).

Now if truth is the reality of God as the only true reality, then *the lie* which denies this reality is not merely a false assertion. Rather, the "liar" withdraws from reality and falls into the unreal, *death.* For if God is the sole reality, then *life* is simply openness to God and to him who makes God manifest: "And this is eternal life, that they know thee the only true God, and Jesus Christ whom thou hast sent" (17:3 RSV—"eternal life" is equivalent to "life"; the terms are used interchangeably by John with no difference in meaning). In turning its back to the "truth," the world simultaneously turns away from "life" and thereby turns itself into a specious reality, which, being a lie, is simultaneously death. This specious reality is the Nothing which professes to be something, and which cheats of his life him who takes it for truth; it is a murderer (8:44).

In its rebellion against God, the world remains God's creation; i.e. man can produce only a specious reality which actually is a lie, a nothing. For, being a creature, he does not, like God, live out of his own resources, but ever lives only out of an uncontrollable origin which has power over him. He always comes from a Whence, and for him there is only the possibility to be from God or from the world, which means: from God or from falsehood, from God or from Nothing. If he repudiates his origin from God, then his origin is Nothing, to which he has given power over himself. In John "to be from" and "to be born from," the expressions which serve to characterize men and their conduct, have lost the cosmological sense that they have in the Gnostic myth and denote the individual's essence which asserts itself in all his speaking and doing and determines the Whither of his way. Face to face stand the opposing possibilities: "to be of (=from) God," etc., or "to be of the world," etc. (see above); or "to be born of (=from) God" (1:13; I Jn. 3:9; 4:7; 5:1, 4, 18—or "from above" 3:3, 7—or "of the Sprit" 3:6) or "to be born of the flesh" (3:6). This means a man is determined by his origin and in each present moment does not have himself in hand; he has only one alternative: to exist either from God (reality) or from the world (unreality). By man's Whence, his Whither is also determined; they who are "from below," "of the world," will die in their sins (8:21–23); "the world" and its "lust" pass away (I Jn. 2:17). The *bondage*, therefore, to which the world has surrendered itself, consists in this: that by disavowing God the creator as its origin it falls into the hands of Nothing. And *freedom* is this: that, by acknowledging the truth the world opens itself to the reality from which alone it can live.

The concepts light, truth, life, and freedom explain each other: so do the concepts darkness, falsehood, death, and bondage in the contrasting group. They all derive their meaning from the search for human existence—for "life" as "life eternal"—and denote the double possibility of human existence: to exist either from God or from man himself. They all imply that only in the knowledge of his creaturehood can man achieve true understanding of himself; this is the *light* that illumines his way. Only in such knowledge does he perceive the *truth*—the true reality which makes itself available to him in the revelation of God; and only so does he escape the delusion that he himself can establish a reality of his own by forming a world in rebellion to God. Only in such knowledge does he achieve *freedom* from specious reality, which actually is darkness, falsehood, bondage, and death. And only in such freedom does he have *life*, for in that freedom he is living out of and by his true origin. Each man is, or once was, confronted with deciding for or against God; and he is confronted anew with this decision by the revelation of God in Jesus. The cosmological dualism of Gnosticism has become in John a *dualism of decision*.

§ 43. Johannine Determinism

1. The language of this "dualism" is that of Gnosticism. In particular *the division of mankind into two groups*—those who are "of God" or "of the devil," "of the truth" or "of the world," "from above" or "from below"—makes it seem as if mankind falls into two classes each of which is from the outset determined as to its essence and its fate by its specific nature. Is not each man stamped by his origin? Does not his origin determine the direction of his way?—even his decision in regard to Jesus, in whom God-made-manifest encounters him? Is it not true that only he whom the Father "draws" comes to Jesus (6:44), only he to whom it is "given" by the Father (6:65; *cf.* 6:37, 39; 17:2, 6, 9, 12, 24)? Is it not said that only he can "hear his voice" who is "of the truth," who is "of God" (18:37; 8:47)—that only he can believe who belongs to his "sheep" (10:26)? And is it not solely "his own" whom he calls to himself (10:3f.), whom he knows and who know him (10:14, 27)? And does not the prophet's word (Is. 6:10) confirm the opinion that unbelief rests upon the hardening imposed by God (12:39f.)?

But how can that be?—for Jesus' demand for faith goes forth to all! And the assertion that they are stuck in darkness and blindness and stand under the wrath of God applies to all men. And men are asked, one and all, whether they want to *remain* in this situation (3:36; 9:41; 12:46). But—Jesus' words are not didactic propositions but an invitation and a call to decision.

Typical are the utterances which contain a promise in the main clause. By having a prefatory participle which states the condition for receiving what is promised, they are also calls to decision. (The italicized words represent participles in the Greek text.)

5:24: "Truly, truly, I say to you,
he who hears my word and *believes* him who sent me,
has eternal life; he does not come into judgment,
but has passed from death to life."

Or 6:35: "I am the bread of life.
He who comes to me shall not hunger;
and *he who believes* in me shall never thirst."

Or 8:12: "I am the light of the world.
He who follows me will not walk in darkness,
but will have the light of life."

(*Cf.* further 3:18, 33, 36; 6:47; 11:25f.; 12:44f.).

No less typical are the utterances in which the invitation
(which may be paralleled by a threat) is preceded by an if-clause
in place of a participle:

6:51: "I am the living bread . . .
if anyone eats this bread,
he will live for ever."

Or 7:16f.: "My teaching is not mine,
but his who sent me;
if any man's will is to do his will,
he shall know whether the teaching is from God. . . ."

Or 8:51: "Truly, truly, I say to you,
if any one keeps my word,
he will never see death."

(*Cf.* further 10:9; 12:26; 14:23 and the clauses containing
"unless"—ἐὰν μή τις—3:3, 5; 15:16)

All forms of this cry of invitation and decision are combined
in 12:46–48:

"I have come as light into the world,
that whoever believes in me may not remain in darkness.
If any one hears my sayings and does not keep them,
I do not judge him. . . .
He who rejects me and does not receive my sayings,
has a judge. . . ."

[22]

In 7:37 the invitation is formulated in the imperative, and the following participle, though it does not formulate the condition as a demand, nevertheless in substance has the same implication:

"If any one thirst, let him come to me,
and let him drink *who believes in me*" (tr.).

Inasmuch as the assertion that no one can come to Jesus whom the Father does not "draw" (6:44) is followed by the statement, "Every one who has heard and learned from the Father comes to me," the πᾶς by itself ("every one") indicates that everyone has the possibility of letting himself be drawn by the Father (and also the possibility of resisting). The Father's "drawing" does not precede the believer's "coming" to Jesus—in other words, does not take place before the decision of faith—but, as the surrendering of one's own certainty and self-assertion, occurs in that coming, in that decision of faith, just as Paul's "being led by the Spirit" does not mean being carried along willy-nilly by the Spirit, but is the decision of faith, the decision to surrender to God's demand and gift (§ 38, 3; I, p. 336). As in Paul (§ 37) John's predestinatory formulations mean that the decision of faith is not a choice between possibilities within this world that arise from inner-worldly impulses, and also mean that the believer in the presence of God cannot rely on his own faith. He never has his security in himself, but always in God alone. So if faith is such a surrender of one's own self-assertion, then the believer can understand his faith not as the accomplishment of his own purposeful act, but only as God's working upon him. This and nothing else is the meaning of the statements that only he comes to Jesus to whom it is "granted" (6:65) by the Father, only those whom the Father "gives him" (6:37, 39; 17:2ff.).

2. The expression "to be (or be born) of . . .," which makes it seem as if John attributed a man's conduct to his "nature" (φύσις— a Gnostic term which John significantly avoids), in reality intends to attribute all specific conduct to a man's *being*, in which his conduct is founded. Since man never exists by his own power, but can only commit himself to a power that controls him, reality or unreality, God or Nothing—and since factually "the world" exists from Nothing (§ 42, 2)—the encounter with the Revealer calls into question whether this existence-from-Nothing is existence at all. And the decision in

response to the Revealer's word, unlike decisions within this world, does not take place out of man's still unquestioned existence, as if the decider, having chosen this or that, could remain what he was. On the contrary, here he is asked just this: whether or not he wills to remain what he was—i.e. to remain in his old existence or not. This is clearly said by the sayings that speak of "remaining" in the old situation:

> 3:36: "He who believes in the Son has eternal life;
>   he who does not obey the Son shall not see life,
>   but the wrath of God *rests* (KJ: abides = remains)
>   upon him."

> 12:46: "I have come as light into the world,
>   that whoever believes in me may not *remain* in darkness."

> 9:39, 41: "For judgment I came into this world,
>   that those who do not see may see,
>   and that those who see may become blind. . . .
>   If you were blind, you would have no guilt;
>   but now that you say, 'We see,' your guilt *remains*."

It is clear: before the light's coming all were blind. "Those who see" are only such as imagine they can see. "The blind" are such as knew of their blindness or know of it now that the light encounters them. The "blind" and the "seeing," accordingly, are not two groups that were already present and demonstrable before the light's coming. Now, and not before, the separation between them takes place in that each one is asked whether he chooses to belong to the one group or the other—whether he is willing to acknowledge his blindness and be freed from it or whether he wants to deny it and persist in it.

The conduct of every man, therefore, corresponds to his origin, i.e. to what he is, his essence. But, unlike Paul, John does not attribute the fact that all men in their essence are evil, or that "the whole world lieth in wickedness" (I Jn. 5:19 KJ), to Adam's fall (§ 25, 3). Does he attribute that fact to the *devil*? Not necessarily. Admittedly, John's "of the devil" (synonymous with "of the world," "from below") applies to all men; and the statement that God sent His Son into the world to save the world (3:17) means the same thing as I Jn. 3:8: "The reason the Son of God appeared was to destroy the works of the devil." But his conception is not that men, because of a trespass committed by the devil in primeval time, are enmeshed in sin as a sinister heritage. Rather, his conception is that the devil lurks behind every particular sin; for "he was a murderer"— not "in the beginning," but "from the beginning" onward (8:44), or still more clearly in the present tense: "the devil sins from the beginning on" (I Jn. 3:8 tr.). It is in this sense, therefore, that "he who commits sin stems from the devil" (I Jn. 3:8 Blt.). That is, having the devil as one's father is a term to describe the sinner's existence. Or, said in another way, sin is not an occasional evil occurrence; rather, in sin it comes to light that man in his essence is a sinner, that he is determined by unreality, Nothing.

The *universality of sin*, i.e. the determination of men by unreality, is therefore not attributed to a mythical cause but simply shows itself to be *a fact*—a fact by virtue of the light's coming: "The light shines in the darkness, and the darkness did not grasp it. . . . It was in the world and through it the world had come into being, yet the world did not recognize it. It came into its own (*viz.* the world), and its own (=men) did not receive it " (1:5, 10f. tr.). "And this is the judgment, that the light has come into the world, and men loved darkness rather than light" (3:19). Not only because men (by and large) refuse to believe does the universality of sin show itself to be a fact but equally by the circumstance that there are those who come to faith ("but as many as received him" 1:12 KJ, 3:21). For faith, as we have seen, is the admission that one has hitherto languished in blindness, has been enmeshed in the "works" of the devil, and has now come over from death into life (9:39; I Jn. 3:8; Jn. 5:24; I Jn. 3:14).

In short: before the light's coming the whole "world" is in darkness, in death. But by the light's coming the question is put to man whether he chooses to remain in darkness, in death. By sending His Son into the world God put the world, so to say, in the balance (*in suspenso*): "If I had not come and spoken to them, they would not have sin; but now they have no excuse for their sin" (15:22). Man cannot act otherwise than as what he is, but in the Revealer's call there opens up to him the possibility of *being* otherwise than he was. He can exchange his Whence, his origin, his essence, for another; he can "be born again" (3:1ff.) and thus attain to his true being. In his decision between faith and un-faith a man's being definitively constitutes itself, and from then on his Whence becomes clear. The

"Jews," who are asserted to be "from below" (8:23) and are reviled as children of the devil, are those who by refusing to believe have anchored themselves to their sins (8:44). The children of God and the children of the devil are henceforth recognizable by whether one "does right" and "loves his brother" (I Jn. 3:10)—for brother-love is the fulfilment of the "new" commandment (13:34; I Jn. 2:7ff.), which has now become possible to those who "have passed out of death into life" (I Jn. 3:14; 2:8). By its opposition to the Revealer the "world" definitively constitutes itself as "world"; thereby the "world" and its ruler are "judged" (12:31; 16:11).

§ 44. The Perversion of the Creation into "the World"

1. The fact that God holds His judgment in the balance, so to speak, until men, in view of the sending of His Son, have either anchored themselves by un-faith to their old existence or have appropriated by faith the new possibility of existing, indicates that in spite of its rebellion against God, human life before the encounter with the Revealer has no unambiguous meaning. For even in its rebellion the world does not escape being God's creation (II, p. 20). This comes to light in the fact that *man's life is pervaded by the quest for reality* (ἀλήθεια), the quest for life. John gives expression to this quest in his sayings that deal with that which is "true" (ἀληθινόν).

When Jesus is called the "true light" (1:9; I Jn. 2:9)—the real, genuine, authentic light—it is presupposed that man does know of light (in general) and is in quest of it. For he must walk his way through the world; to do so he needs an understanding of himself in his world. He can, of course, go astray and follow a false light; but even though he factually does so and is a blind man supposing himself to have sight and a slave imagining himself free, he nevertheless shows himself consciously or unconsciously concerned with a quest for light. When Jesus calls himself the light of the world (8:12), he is presenting himself as that which the world is seeking. Human existence knows, overtly or covertly, of its dependence upon that from which it can live. It hungers and thirsts, for it has a will to live. And though this will is directly concerned with mere food and drink, the imaginative mythical notions of miraculous food (6:31) and life-giving water (4:15) indicate in themselves that its longing is ultimately for life itself. When Jesus calls himself the bread and the water of life (6:27ff.; 4:10ff.; *cf.* 7:37), he assumes such a preliminary understanding as is expressed in mythology. He is the fabled tree of life told about in myth (15:1ff.). The "I-am" pronouncements are the answer to this quest for life. For the "I" in them is a predicate nominative, not the subject (§ 48, 2), and they mean: in him that for which man seeks is here. In him it is very reality in contrast to all seeming. The "true bread from heaven" (6:32) is he; the "true vine" (15:1) is he. The same is meant when he calls himself the "good shepherd" (10:11; 10:14); here "good" (καλός), instead of the usual "true" (ἀληθινός), denotes the real shepherd in contrast to the "hireling." His "I am" offers the answer to man's quest for life, his quest for "abundance" (περισσόν, 10:10, the more-than-enough which definitively stills all longing); it presupposes man's overt or covert knowledge of being dependent upon Him who bestows life.

2. The delusion that arises from the will to exist of and by one's self *perverts truth into a lie, perverts the creation into the "world."* For in their delusion men do not let their quest for life become a question about themselves so as to become aware of their creaturehood, but instead they give themselves the answer so as to have a security of their own. They take the temporary for the ultimate, the spurious for the genuine, death for life. They give themselves the answer *in their religion,* in which, it must be conceded, they show that they have a knowledge of something beyond man and his world. But by supposing themselves made secure by their religion they pervert this knowledge. The various religions debate against each other, and each disclaims the validity of the other's worship. But neither in Jerusalem nor on Mount Gerizim is God legitimately worshiped; the "true worshipers" are they who worship Him "in Spirit and in reality." Right worship of God, that is, is an eschatological occurrence which God Himself brings about by His Spirit, and it becomes a reality by the coming of the Revealer (4:19–24).

Taking the *Jewish religion* as an example, John makes clear through it how the human will to self-security distorts knowledge of God, makes God's demand and promise into a possession and thereby shuts itself up against God. In so doing, John takes as his starting-point not the Jewish striving after "righteousness" but the will-toward-life (§ 41, 3; II, p. 11) which is active in every religion. The sin of "the Jews" is not their "boasting" on the basis of works, as in Paul (§ 23, 2; I, pp. 242f.), but their imperviousness to the Revelation

[27]

which throws into question their self-security—which in substance, of course, is the very same sin. One might almost say: the sin of "the Jews" lies not in their ethics, as in Paul, but in their dogmatics. They search the Scriptures because in them they suppose themselves to "have eternal life," and therefore reject Jesus, who otherwise could bestow life upon them (5:39f.). They pervert the meaning of Scripture; for they do not see that it is just of Jesus that it bears witness—Jesus, who as God's Revelation shatters all self-security. The very Moses they appeal to, on whom they have "set their hope," becomes their accuser (5:45). Their religion, which ought to cast them into unrest and keep them open for the encounter with God, is to them a means of rest and shuts them up against God. Actually they do not know God at all (5:37b.; 7:28; 8:19, 55; 15:21; 16:3). For knowing Him does not mean having thoughts about Him, even right ones perhaps, but acknowledging Him as Creator and being open for the encounter with Him.

Hence, all that is right becomes false in their mouths. They appeal to *their Law* in order to set aside the disturbance which Jesus is for their self-security (ch. 5). The argument of 7:19–24, which accuses "the Jews" of not keeping their Law (v. 19) and of breaking the sabbath-law in order to be true to the Law (v. 23), indicates that the Law is not an unambiguous entity capable of granting security. They ought to recognize that by the conflict of the circumcision-law with the sabbath-law Moses is directing them to inquire into the true meaning of the Law. The way "the Jews" use the Law only as a means of security for themselves is shown by 7:49f.: Nicodemus accuses the Jewish councillors of having condemned Jesus without giving him a hearing, thus violating the Law. But they have their reply ready: according to Scripture no prophet is to arise out of Galilee. Their search of Scripture stands in the service of a dogmatics which gives them self-security by furnishing them criteria for judging the Revelation, but this makes them deaf to the living word of the Revealer. Chapter 9 also shows that with them misuse of the Law for their own purposes is compatible with complete correctness toward the Law. The verses 8:17f., finally, pour ridicule on appeal to the Law; here Jesus applies the principle that a matter is to be regarded as proved by the testimony of two witnesses (Deut. 17:6; 19:15) to his own testimony and that of the Father. For reflection on this ordinance of the Law ought to indicate that it is only applicable to men, and that God's Revelation does not have to present its credentials to men. God's word cannot be subjected to the human demand for substantiating testimony; for if it could, then that statute would have to be applied—which would be absurd!

"The Jews" play off *the revelation in their history*, documented in Scripture, against Jesus. How can he raise a claim that would make him one greater than Abraham (8:25)! But Abraham did not suppose that in himself God's gift to Israel was once for all accomplished, but looked forward to the eschatological day of fulfilment (8:56). As in their appeal to Moses "the Jews" do not understand the meaning of the Law, neither do they understand in their appeal to Abraham that his meaning for them is not that of a possession but that of a promise. They consider themselves Abraham's children (8:33) and therefore free, not recognizing that freedom cannot be a possession but can only be an eschatological gift. They would have the right to appeal to their descent from Abraham if they understood its meaning to be that of a promise which points into the future and puts them under obligation to the future. Looking back into their history ought not to make them feel secure, but ought to obligate them to faithfulness toward God's dealing, which points man away from himself toward God's future, for which it is man's duty to keep himself open. Whether they understand Abraham—whether faithfulness to their past will turn out to be openness for God's future—that necessarily shows up at their encounter with Jesus. By closing themselves up against him and wanting to kill him they show that they are not Abraham's children.

Certainly, "the Jews" have *a hope of their own* and to that extent are oriented toward the future. But they have converted their hope into a theology of the Messiah, by which they have robbed themselves of freedom for the future. They know that the Messiah's place of origin will be mysterious—and protest that Jesus' home town and his parents are known (6:41f.; 7:27; *cf.* 1:46)! And even in this protest there is still correct knowledge embedded: what encounters man in the Revelation is not something human but something divine. But this knowledge is perverted! For in their theology they conceive the divine as a phenomenon whose divineness man can verify by means of his own criteria rather than as an occurrence which destroys the man who here tries to verify. Their resisting protest fails to understand that the divine cannot be contrasted with the human in *such* a manner as they in the security of their judgment suppose: "How can a mere man claim to be the Revealer?" Just this—for human thinking an absurdity—is the mystery of the Revelation, which is understood only when a man lets go of his self-security, in which he supposes he can distinguish the divine and the human as verifiable phenomena. What "the Jews" call mystery is no genuine mystery at all; for in their mythologizing theology they make the other-worldly— Jesus' mysterious origin in God—into a this-worldly thing that is subject to their approval or disapproval. There is no longer any mystery at all for him who professes to be able by criteria at his disposal to establish whether and when God's mystery stands before him; for what the recognition and acknowledgment of God's mystery presupposes is exactly that the acknowledger shall have been cast into doubt as to the validity of the prevailing standards. That is why the "world" remains blind when faced with the Revelation, and just because it "knows," it knows nothing. The true mystery is comprised in "The word became flesh" (1:14), and John either does not know or refuses to know anything of an attempt to draw this mystery down into terms of this world by a story of a mythological birth (*cf.* 1:45; 6:42; 7:27f.); "the Jews" are in error not because they are misinformed about Jesus' origin but because they apply the wrong standard to him.

Others play off another messianic dogma against Jesus: the Messiah must be a son of David born in Bethlehem, but Jesus comes from Nazareth (7:42)!—and by their wrong question they block up the door by which they might enter into faith. They know that the Messiah when he comes will remain forever (12:34)! They await the Messiah, that is, as one who will realize human air-castles, one who will make the salvation he brings into a lasting earthly condition— so the attempt was made to make Jesus king because he miraculously filled the hungry (6:15). They do not know that the salvation which the Messiah brings is the calling-into-question and the negating of the world, nor that to accept him means to surrender all air-castles. However, the Revealer will remain with his own if they faithfully remain with him (15:4f.)—but not in such a way that he will become a this-worldly figure! No, his earthly presence will come to an end, and not until he has departed from the earth will he come again to his own and along with the Father make his home with them (14:23) in a manner that will be hidden from the world (14:22).

[30]

The world in general knows the right concepts and the right quests. It speaks of "*honor*" (δόξα; also="glory"), and in its craving for honor (mutual approval) the correct knowledge comes to light that man, just by being man, is insecure and must seek for approval from outside himself. But the world perverts this proper quest by providing itself with its own answer. The world fails to realize that man's existence as a whole, being that of a creature, is in question and that the court of which it should seek approval or standing is God. But the "honor" that God gives is not sought by the world. For to seek it would mean to recognize the utter insecurity of all human existence and to relinquish one's self-created security. Instead of doing that, men in their need for standing take honor from each other, each conceding the other his "honor" in order that the other in turn may let him have standing (5:44). And thereby they are shutting themselves up against God's Revelation.

The world is acquainted with *love* of course! But it loves only its ἴδιον, what is "its own" and familiar to it (15:19). Ultimately, then, it loves only itself and hates him who exposes its own problematical character. The world is acquainted with joy and proves thereby that human existence, if it were in accord with its own character, would find fulfilment in the joy in which all seeking ceases, the joy which the Revealer bestows (15:11; 16:24; 17:13). But the world knows no true, and therefore eternal, joy, but only joy over its own (seeming) success. The world speaks of freedom and is unaware that it is in bondage; that is to say, in sin (8:32–36).

The world speaks of *sin, righteousness, and judgment*, but understands these terms in its own sense, and the judgment which the Revelation brings consists in disclosing the true meaning of these terms (16:8–11). What is sin? It is the unbelief in which the world anchors itself to itself, as becomes apparent in its attitude to Jesus. What is righteousness (or vindication)? To the world it means to turn out to be in the right, to be crowned with visible success; in reality it means to prevail over the world, as Jesus does at his departure from the world (Jesus' "vindication" is his "victory" in 16:33; *cf.* νικήσεις, "prevail" [RSV] or "overcome" [KJ], in the context of Rom. 3:4). What is judgment? The judgment (the context indicates that God's judgment is meant), in the world's opinion, takes place in that which is visible, either as a cosmic catastrophe (the apocalyptic view) or in catastrophes within world history (the expectation of the Old Testament prophets and, in part, of Judaism). In reality the judgment takes place in the decision of men toward Jesus as the Revealer of God, so that he who does not believe is already condemned (3:18; 12:48), as the "ruler of this world" is also condemned when Jesus by his death is "lifted up" (12:31).

Thus the world creates for itself a *security* of its own and operates within it as that which is *familiar and to be taken for granted*. It shrugs off the disturbance which is created for it by the appearing of Jesus with its incredulous question: 'How can this be?" (3:9), or with similar "how's" (6:42; 7:15; 8:33; 12:34). No, it does not reject everything new without discussion, but it tests it by the standard of the old that it knows and is certain of: "Search and you will see that no prophet is to rise from Galilee" (7:52). The world asks for Jesus' credentials (5:31ff.); it has its experts whose opinions it follows: "Can it be that the authorities really know that this is the Christ?" (7:26). The world has its ideals, too; instead of being extravagant one ought to aid the poor (12:5). That which is tangibly present ($\sigma \acute{\alpha} \rho \xi$, "the flesh") is regarded as the real. Jesus' saying about rebirth is unintelligible to the world because it reckons only with the possibilities of the natural, not with God's wonder-working power the Spirit (3:3-8). It judges "according to the flesh" (8:15) or, synonymously, "by appearance" (7:24).

The world also knows an institution which takes care of justice on earth: the *state*. To it the world flees in order to be rid of the disturber of its peace, Jesus. But not only does the state turn out to be too weak to accomplish its task when it shuts itself up against the Revealer's word, but, above all, the world itself perverts the meaning of the state by misusing it to fulfill its own wishes and in doing so resorts to lies and defamation (19:12).

CHAPTER III

The "Krisis" of the World

§ 45. The Sending of the Son

1. *Within this world of death life appeared* (I Jn. 1:2), into the world of darkness came the light (1:5; 3:19)—it came by *the coming of the Son of God* into the world. Jesus is he. Though he came after the Baptist in time, he nevertheless was prior to him (1:15, 30). He even claims that he was before Abraham (8:58); yes, even more: that he was before the foundation of the world (17:5, 24). It is he in whom the Christian Congregation believes as the one "who is from the beginning" (I Jn. 2:13f.). In him the "Word" which in the beginning was with God became flesh (1:1f., 14) and came into its (his) own property—i.e. into the world, which belongs to it, and hence to him, as the one through whom it came into being (1:9–11).

To what extent are such statements, which speak of Jesus in mythological form as the pre-existent Son of God who became man, to be understood in the actual mythological sense? That can only be answered in the course of more detailed interpretation. At any rate, the beginning of the first Epistle, intending to say the same thing as the prologue to the Gospel, significantly speaks of the *life* that in the beginning was with the Father, and has audibly, visibly, and tangibly appeared (in Jesus, of course—that goes without saying). It speaks of this *life* as "*that which* was in the beginning," as a thing and not as a person (I Jn. 1:1f.). At any rate, it is clear that in the person of Jesus the transcendent divine reality became audible, visible, and tangible in the realm of the earthly world. Jesus is "the Christ, the Son of God, he who is coming into the world" (11:27).

In all that he is, says, and does, he is not to be understood as a figure of this world, but his appearing in the world is to be conceived as an *embassage from without, an arrival from elsewhere*. Jesus is he "whom the Father consecrated and sent into the world" (10:36).

That the Father sent him is testified by his works (5:16); this (his sending) is what is to be believed (6:29; 11:42; 17:8) or acknowledged (17:25); for eternal life is this: to "know thee the only true God, and Jesus Christ whom thou hast sent" (17:3). So God's name accordingly is: "the Father who sent me" (six times) or simply: "(he) who sent me" (nineteen times). (Both expressions, as crystallized participial phrases, might better be translated with nouns: "my Commissioner, the Father," and "my Commissioner.") And so the congregation confesses: "And we have seen and testify that the Father has sent his Son as the Savior of the world" (I Jn. 4:14). The counterpart of his sending is his "coming" or his "having come." The sending and the coming may, of course, be combined in the same statement. Being the envoy, he did not come on his own initiative: "for I went forth from God and have come (hither). For I am not here ($\dot{\epsilon}\lambda\dot{\eta}\lambda\upsilon\theta\alpha$, perfect) of my own accord, but he sent me" (8:42, tr.; *cf.* 7:28f.; 17:8). Repeated time and again are statements that he "came into the world" (3:19; 9:39; 11:27; 12:46; 16:28; 18:37), or that he "came from the Father (or God)"—(8:42; 13:3; 16:27f., 30; 17:8), or simply that he "has come" (5:43; 7:28; 8:14; 10:10; 12:47; 15:22).* This is just the thing that his own have come to know and to acknowledge (17:8) and is what faith confesses (11:27), while "the Jews" know not whence he comes (8:14) or have a false notion about his origin (7:28f.), and the false teachers deny that Jesus Christ has come "in the flesh" (I Jn. 4:2; II Jn. 7). In more vividly mythological formulation it is also possible to say that he came down from heaven (3:13; 6:33, 38, 41f.).

His coming is the Revelation of the divine reality in the world; this aspect of his coming is emphasized by *the correspondence of his departure to his coming.* By his coming, that is, he does not become a phenomenon of the world, a figure within world-history. He is here, so to speak, only as a guest; the hour is coming when he must depart (13:1; *cf.* 1:14 "he tented among us" tr.). He came and will go again (8:14):

> "I came from the Father and have come into the world;
> Again, I am leaving the world and going to the Father."

(16:28; *cf.* 13:3; 14:12, 28; 16:5, 10, 17). The time of his sojourn on

---

* Many of the references in all three groups contain the Greek perfect tense. Its full translation would be cumbersome: "being come, I am here," but frequently the overtone "I am here" is at least as strongly sounding as the fundamental tone, "I have come" (Tr.).

arth is but short, and when he is gone he will be sought in vain
7:33; 8:21; *cf.* 13:33). As he came down from heaven—mythological
anguage again—he will ascend again thither where he previously
vas (6:62; *cf.* 3:13). He will be "elevated" (3:14; 12:32, 34; *cf.* 8:28);
ae will be "glorified" (12:23; 13:31f.; 17:1; *cf.* 7:39; 12:16), glorified
vith the "glory" that he had had in pre-existence with the Father
17:5, 24). His coming and his going belong together as a unit, the
anity of his activity as Revealer; this is indicated by the fact that
ooth his coming and his going (3:19 and 12:31) can be termed the
udgment and by the fact that both his exaltation and his sending
:an be regarded as the basis for the gift of eternal life (3:14 and 3:16).

   2. The sending of the Son is *the deed of God's love*: "In this the
ove of God was made manifest among us, that God sent his only Son
nto the world, so that we might live through him" (I Jn. 4:9). "For
God so loved the world that he gave his only Son, that whoever
oelieves in him should not perish but have eternal life" (3:16).

> That it is God's love that is manifested in the sending, is
> expressed both by the content of the sentence and by its formula-
> tion. The latter uses not only the word "gave" (ἔδωκεν), which
> suggests the common-Christian term παρ-έδωκεν ("delivered up
> to death"; see I, pp. 82f. and II, p. 12 and Rom. 4:25, I Cor.
> 11:23), but also the characterization of the Son as μονογενής
> ("only," "unique"). Only in Jn. 3:16, 18; I Jn. 4:9 (and probably
> also in Jn. 1:18, though the wording of the text is not certain
> here) does "only Son" occur in the New Testament as a
> characterization of Jesus. This designation will probably have to
> be understood on the basis of its use in the Septuagint as an
> epithet of value, meaning "beloved above all," and synonymous
> with ἀγαπητός. In Jn. 1:14, however, where it is used without any
> noun, it is probably to be regarded as stemming from Gnostic
> mythology—on which see my *Johanneskommentar*, p. 47.

The intent of this sending is therefore fulfilled in those who
believe in Jesus as the Son sent from God: they receive the love of
God—"we have come to know and to believe the love God has for us"
(I Jn. 4:16 tr; *cf.* Jn. 17:26; I Jn. 2:5; 3:17; 4:7–12), while he who loves
the world is not embraced by the love of God (I Jn. 2:15, understanding the genitive, with KJ, as subjective, not objective).

The fact that the love of God is the basis for the sending of the
Son is expressed by the way in which *the purpose of his sending or*

coming is given. He came into the world only "to bear witness to the 'truth' " (18:37), or, meaning the same thing, he came into the world as "light," in order "that whoever believes in me may not remain in 'darkness' " (12:46). Again, it means the same when Jesus says he came "that they may have life and have abundance" (10:10 tr.), or when the author says God "gave" him in order that "whoever believes in him might not perish but have eternal life" (3:16), or that God sent him into the world "so that we might live through him" (I Jn. 4:9), or that he sent him as "the expiation for our sins" (I Jn. 4:10, if this sentence is not a redactional gloss). In altogether general formulation it is also said that God sent him "that the world might be saved by him" (3:17).

Jesus, accordingly, can be called *"the savior of the world"* (4:42; I Jn. 4:14). While in this term he is accorded the specifically Hellenistic title of the salvation-bringer (see I, pp. 79f.), the meaning of his sending is more frequently expressed by the title that comes out of the Jewish and earliest Christian tradition: Messiah; whereas the Kyrios-title is completely missing.

Not until ch. 20 (and the added chapter, 21) does the *Kyrios-title* appear in John. That is, it is not used previous to the Easter accounts, for the occurrences of it in 4:1; 6:23; 11:2; are due to a glossator. Various manuscripts also insert it in II Jn. 3. Did the evangelist wish to avoid the application of the cultic title (§ 12, 2) to the earthly Jesus in order to reserve it for the risen Jesus? If so, why is it missing in the Epistles of John? Was it too strong a reminder of the "many lords" (I Cor. 8:5) of the Hellenistic religions (F. C. Grant, *The Growth of the Gospels*, 1933, p. 207)? Was it incompatible with the view that Jesus' disciples were not "slaves" (δοῦλοι) but "friends" of Jesus (15:14f.; W. Bousset, *Kyrios Christos*, 2nd ed., 1921, p. 155)? Or was the title avoided, or at least greatly repressed because John took so reserved an attitude toward the whole realm of the cultic and the sacramental, and because this title was not adapted to expressing just that which was the essential thing to John: Jesus as an eschatological figure?

Jesus is the *Messiah* (1:41; 4:25) or "the Christ" (which in both passages is explicitly pointed out to be the translation of "Messiah," see I, p. 80). Whether he is to be accorded this title, is a question that again and again comes up for discussion among "the Jews" (7:26f.,

31, 41f.; 9:22; 10:24; 12:34; *cf.* 1:20) and is answered in the negative by the false teachers (I Jn. 2:22), but the believers' confession of faith is that he is the Messiah (11:27; 20:31; I Jn. 5:1). The old royal meaning of the messiah-title is retained, for "*King of Israel*" occurs as an alternate for it (1:49) and when it is explained by the term "*Son of God*," then the latter, too, evidently has as its immediate meaning the old messianic one (§ 7, 5), even though in the intent of the evangelist something more is expressed by it in keeping with the differentiated Hellenistic understanding of the term (§ 12, 3). Likewise out of Jewish and earliest Christian tradition comes, finally, the title "*Son of Man*" (§ 5, 1; § 9, 4). Though John mostly understands it in the sense of the Gnostic myth as a designation for the pre-existent one who became man and must be exalted again (1:51; 3:13f.; 12:23, 34; 13:31 and elsewhere), he nevertheless is referring to the Jewish and earliest Christian meaning in letting Jesus' office as judge of the world be founded upon his being Son of Man (5:27, unless this sentence is a redactional gloss).

3. What is expressed by all these titles is that Jesus is the eschatological salvation-bringer, that *his coming is the eschatological event.* By his coming the predictions of Moses and the prophets are fulfilled (1:45; *cf.* 5:39, 46). To the Samaritan woman who expects enlightenment from the Messiah, Jesus answers, "I who speak to you am he" (4:25f.). The Jewish expectation that the Messiah, as the "second redeemer," will bestow bread from heaven as Moses, the "first redeemer," did of yore is fulfilled by Jesus who bestows the true bread of heaven (6:31f.). When he calls his coming "my day" which Abraham rejoiced to see (8:56), that means that his coming is "the Messiah's day" which was part of the Jewish and earliest Christian expectation (see I, pp. 75f.).

But the assertion that his coming-and-going, which constitute a unity as we have seen (see 1 in this §), is the eschatological event is primarily made in those sentences where his coming or going is termed *the judgment of the world*:

"And this is the judgment, that the light has come into the world,
    and men loved darkness rather than light" (3:19).

"For judgment I came into this world,
    that those who do not see may see,
    and that those who see may become blind" (9:39).

The historizing of eschatology already introduced by Paul is radically carried through by John in his understanding of κρίσις and κρίμα as both having the double sense "judgment" and "sunderance." The judgment takes place in just the fact that upon the encounter with Jesus the sunderance between faith and unfaith, between the sighted and the blind, is accomplished (3:19; 9:39). He who believes is not judged (i.e. not condemned), but he who does not believe remains in darkness, remains under the wrath of God, and is thereby judged (i.e. condemned):

"He who believes in him is not condemned,
  he who does not believe is condemned already" (3:18).

Right now, while Jesus' word is sounding forth, the "sunderance" which is also "judgment" is taking place:

"He who hears my word and believes him who sent me,
  has eternal life; he does not come into judgment (=condemnation),
  but has passed from death to life."

". . . the hour is coming, and now is,
  when the dead will hear the voice of the Son of God,
  and those who hear will live" (5:24f.).

In sending Jesus into the world the Father gave him authority to raise the dead and hold judgment (5:21f., 26f.). Therefore, he who believes in him already has life:

"He who believes in the Son has eternal life;
  he who does not obey the Son shall not see life,
  but the wrath of God rests (i.e. remains) upon him" (3:36;
  cf. 6:47; I Jn. 5:12).

Jesus declares:

"I am the resurrection and the life;
  he who believes in me, though he die, yet shall he live,
  and whoever lives and believes in me shall never die" (11:25f.;
  cf. 8:51).

The judgment, then, is no dramatic cosmic event, but takes place in the response of men to the word of Jesus. As it accordingly may be said that Jesus came into the world for judgment (9:39), so it can also be said that God sent him not to judge but to save (3:17). He can say that he judges no one (8:15), and again can say that he judges nevertheless (8:16; 5:30). It is not he who is the actual judge, but the word that he speaks:

"If any one hears my sayings and does not keep them,
    I do not judge him
    For I did not come to judge the world
    but to save the world.
    He who rejects me and does not receive my sayings
    has a judge;
    the word that I have spoken will be his judge" (12:47f.).

A later ecclesiastical redaction has here added "on the last day," "correcting" the text by introducing the traditional futuristic eschatology, just as it did in 6:39, 40, 44 by inserting the refrain "but (or "and") I will raise him up at the last day." This is a sentence which has an organic place in 6:54 within the passage 6:51b–58, which likewise was inserted by ecclesiastical redaction; in this passage the bread of life, which in the preceding discourse is Jesus himself, is equated with the Sacrament of the Lord's Supper and the latter is understood (in Ignatius' sense) as the "medicine of immortality." Even more jarring than these additions, if that be possible, is the insertion of 5:28f., where in direct contradiction of v. 25 the "hour" of the resurrection is transferred from the present to the future. On I Jn. 2:28; 3:2 see below (§ 50, 6).

The theme of whole sections is that Jesus' coming-and-going is the "judgment" of the world (3:1–21, 31–36; 4:43–46; 7:15–24; 8:13–20). A concrete scene, 6:60–71, depicts the "sundering" which takes place through his word: at his "hard saying" true and false disciples are put asunder, they separate themselves. Moreover, the sundering accomplished by Jesus' ministry is underscored by the author's dividing his portrayal of this ministry into two parts: chs. 2–12 portray Jesus' revealing-activity to the world, and chs. 13–17 (or 13–20) his revealing-activity to the community of believers.

The historizing of eschatology* also finds expression in the fact that the world is oblivious to what is happening. In its sight there is only a disturbance, a commotion that leads to "divisions" (7:43; 9:16; 10:19). It has no inkling that in these "divisions" a decision

* A specific example of John's de-mythologizing of eschatology in his interpretation of the mythical figure, Antichrist. In I Jn. 2:18, 4:3 the appearing of false teachers is interpreted as the coming of the Antichrist. It is even said: "now many antichrists have come!"

and a sunderance are being reflected. This obliviousness grimly demonstrates that the world is judged—condemned. While for it the hour of the passion is the hour of triumph and joy (16:20) because in it the "ruler of the world" seems to be in command (14:30), in reality this hour is just the opposite: the judgment of the world and judgment over its "ruler" (12:31; 16:11).

§ 46. The Offense of the Incarnation of the Word

1. How does God's Son come into the world? As a human being. The theme of the whole Gospel of John is the statement: "The word became flesh" (1:14). This statement is defended by I and II John against the false teachers. These are evidently Christian Gnostics who deny the identity of the Son of God with the human Jesus either by asserting that their union was only temporary or by flatly rejecting the reality of the human Jesus and docetically regarding the human form of the Son of God as only a seeming body. John's answer to them is: every spirit that does not confess that Jesus Christ came in the flesh, that does not confess Jesus (the man as the Son of God) is not "from God"; indeed, such false doctrine is nothing less than the work of Antichrist (I Jn. 4:2f.; II Jn. 7). Just because John makes use of the Gnostic Redeemer-myth (§ 41, 3) for his picture of the figure and activity of Jesus, a demarcation of his own position from that of Gnosticism is particularly incumbent upon him.

It is clear to begin with that for him *the incarnation of the Son of God is not*, as it is in Gnosticism, *a cosmic event* which sets into motion the eschatological occurrence (the unfolding of redemption) as a process of nature by which the union of the essentially opposite natures, light and darkness, is dissolved. The Gnostic Redeemer releases the pre-existent human selves, who by virtue of their light-nature are related to him, out of the matter (body and "soul") that trammels them, and then leads them to the world of light above. John eliminated both the Gnostic concept of $\phi\acute{v}\sigma\iota\varsigma$ ("nature") and the Gnostic notion of the pre-existence of human selves and their unnatural imprisonment in the material world. He does not accept the Gnostic trichotomy of man, according to which man's true *self* is imprisoned in a *body* and a *soul* (I, pp. 165, 168). Neither is the incarnation of the Son of God for John a device for transmitting "Gnosis" to men in the form of teachings about cosmogony and anthropology or for bringing them secret formulas and sacraments, on the strength of which their selves can safely make the journey to heaven (§ 48,3).

The Revealer appears not as *man-in-general,* i.e. not simply as a bearer of human *nature,* but as a *definite human being in history*: Jesus of Nazareth. His humanity is genuine humanity: "the word became flesh." Hence, John has no theory about the pre-existent one's miraculous manner of entry into the world nor about the manner of his union with the man Jesus. He knows neither the legend of the virgin birth* nor that of Jesus' birth in Bethlehem—or if he knows of them, he will have nothing to do with them. Jesus comes from Nazareth, and this fact, offensive to "the Jews," is emphasized (1:45; 7:52) rather than deprecated. "The Jews," knowing Jesus' place of origin and his parents (7:27f.; 6:42), are not in error as to the facts, but err in denying the claim of this Jesus of Nazareth to be the Revealer of God. They err not in the matter upon which they judge but in making a judgment at all κατὰ σάρκα (according to the "flesh" —according to external appearances).

Neither does the Revealer appear as a mystagogue communicating teachings, formulas, and rites as if he himself were only a means to an end who could sink into unimportance to any who had received his "Gnosis." Though Jesus says in departing from the earth, "I have manifested thy name to the men whom thou gavest me out of the world" (17:6; *cf.* v. 26), still he has imparted no information about God at all, any more than he has brought instruction about the origin of the world or the fate of the self. He does not *communicate anything,* but *calls men to himself.* Or when he promises a gift, he is, himself, that gift: he himself is the bread of life that he bestows (6:35); he himself is the light (8:12); he himself is life (11:25; 14:6).

Jesus, the Son of God who has become man, is a genuine man— which again does not mean that in his personality the divine became visible so as to fill men with enthusiasm and touch their feelings or to fascinate and overwhelm them. If that were the case, the divine would then be conceived of simply as the human exalted and intensified. But according to John, the divine is the very counter-pole to the human, with the result that it is a paradox, an offense, that the Word

---

* In some Latin witnesses to the text of Jn. 1:13 "*qui . . . natus est*" (who . . . was born) is found instead of "who . . . were born"; this is certainly a "correcting" of the original text.

became flesh. As a matter of fact, the divinity of the figure of Jesus in John is completely lacking in visibility, and the disciples' relation to him as "friends" (15:14f.) is by no means conceived of as a personal relation of human friendship. It is the farewell discourses especially that strive to teach this distinction by making clear that the disciples will not achieve the right relation to him until he has departed from them—indeed, that he is not in the full sense the Revealer until he has been lifted up and glorified (see especially 14:28; 16:7; § 50, 6).

2. In what sense, then, can it be said of the incarnate Word, "We have beheld his glory" (1:14)? Is his human figure, so to speak, a translucent picture through which his divinity gleams? On first thought it might seem so, for many passages of the evangelist represent *Jesus as the "divine man"* (θεῖος ἀνήρ) in the Hellenistic sense (I, pp. 130f.)—a man who has miraculous knowledge at his command, does miracles, and is immune to the plottings of his enemies.

It is as a "divine man" that *Jesus sees through the people he meets* (Peter, 1:42; Nathanael, 1:47f.) and knows the past of the Samaritan woman (4:17f.). But to the evangelist these stories taken from tradition are symbolic pictures which indicate that the believer feels himself searched and known by God and that his own existence is exposed by the encounter with the Revealer. When 2:24f., generalizing, says that Jesus sees through men, the author is not thinking of a supranatural ability but of the knowledge about man which arises from knowing God, and therefore knows what a stumbling-block God is to men. The same motif underlies the words, "But I know that you have not the love of God within you" (5:42)—Jesus deduces this from the unbelief of the "Jews"; he knows that face to face with the divine Revelation human resistance to God comes to light. Thus he knows that men mutter when they hear the Revealer's "hard saying" (6:60f.) and knows what oppresses believers and limits their comprehension, so long as they have not freed themselves from the notion that the Revelation ought to cause an alteration within this world (16:19).

Jesus' omniscience is confirmed by the disciples: "Now we know that you know all things" (16:30)—but not because he has demonstrated it by miraculous knowledge, but because now at his farewell he has spoken "plainly" (παρρησίᾳ) without any "figure" (παροιμία, "riddle," 16:29). But in reality it is not some progress in Jesus' conduct that is characterized in the transition from "riddles" to

[42]

"openness" but a change in the disciples' situation. For in the end Jesus has not said anything materially different from what he had always been saying, but what he had previously said now is seen in a new light; for in the light of Jesus' departure it now appears as something provisional for which only the future can bring a definitive unveiling—that is to say, a genuine understanding (16:12–28, especially vv. 25f.). The disciples' confession therefore anticipates this future and simply means that in Jesus' work as Revealer, which has now reached its end, all knowledge is contained. In keeping with this the confession continues not, "and you need to question no one," but: "And no one needs to question you." The "omniscience" of Jesus is therefore not understood to be his super-human ability, but his knowledge which is transmitted to the believer: whoever has recognized him as the Revealer by knowing that one thing knows everything, and Jesus' promise is fulfilled: "On that day you will ask me no questions" (16:23).

The mention of *Jesus' miraculous knowledge* in the story of Lazarus is the result of unconsidered adoption of tradition (11:4, 11–14). Naturally, Jesus knows of his coming betrayal by Judas before the event (6:64, 70; 13:18). Perhaps this is due to an apologetic motif (if it is allowable even to look for such in this Gospel). But in addition to this possible motif, it is probably another idea that is dominant here: the idea that in the very nature of the Revelation— because it arouses man's resistance—there lies the possibility for the apostasy even of a disciple. Faith has no guarantee, and the Church must surmount the stumbling-block created by the fact that the devil finds his tool even in her own midst. Jesus' prediction of the disciples' flight and of persecution for the Church (16:32; 15:18–16:4a.) is to be interpreted in a similar fashion: it is a foreknowledge which results from insight into the nature of the Revelation. That is also the way in which Jesus' knowledge of the fate that awaits him is to be understood. He is both the bringer of the Revelation and is himself the Revelation. Therefore he knows what is to befall him (2:19, 21); he knows "the hour" (13:1; 18:4; 19:28). For him, the perfect "Gnostic" (i.e. knower), fate is no riddle.

Several times *Jesus eludes harm* or is snatched out of his enemies' hands until his hour is come (7:30, 44; 8:20, 59; 10:39). This motif has the purpose of demonstrating the fact that the Revealer's fate is not determined by human will but is in the hands of God.

[43]

3. Jesus *performs miracles*, a fact that is sometimes mentioned in general terms (2:23; 3:2; 4:45; 7:3, 31; 10:41, 11:47; 12:37; 20:30) and sometimes is depicted in accounts of specific miracles (2:1–12; 4:46–54; 5:1–9; 6:1–25; 9:1–7; 11:1–44). The term used for these miracles is σημεῖα ("signs" and, secondarily, "miracles"), and in John this word retains its true meaning of "sign." The "signs" reveal Jesus' glory (2:11; *cf.* 9:3; 11:4), and the disbelief that refuses to be convinced by so many miracles is reproved (12:37). On the other hand, however, Jesus says in rebuke: "Unless you see signs and wonders you will not believe" (4:48). And the risen Jesus addresses to Thomas the reproving word: "Do you believe now because you have seen me? Blessed are those who see (me) not and yet believe" (20:29 tr.). It is an indication of disbelief when "the Jews" ask: "Then what sign do you do, that we may see, and believe you? What work do you perform?" (6:30; *cf.* 2:18). They ask for a miracle analogous to the manna-miracle of Moses, and have no understanding of the work Jesus is performing. The fact that their question chronologically follows the sign of the bread-miracle makes it clear that the meaning of the sign does not lie in the miraculous occurrence. In fact, this had already been said in v. 26: "You seek me, not because you saw signs, but because you ate some of the loaves and were filled" (6:26 tr.).

As "signs" the miracles of Jesus are ambiguous. Like Jesus' words, they are misunderstandable. Of course, they are remarkable occurrences, but that only makes them indicators that the activity of the Revealer is a disturbance of what is familiar to the world. They point to the fact that the Revelation is no worldly occurrence, but an other-worldly one. They are pictures, symbols. The wine-miracle, an epiphany (2:1–12) symbolizes what occurs in all Jesus' work: the revelation of his "glory"—not the glory of a miracle-worker, but that of him by whom the gift of "grace and truth" is made. The cure of the official's son (4:46–54) and the healing of the lame man at the pool (5:1–9), both miraculous, are "signs" only in the general sense that they point to the Revealer's work as of life-promoting kind. But the bread-miracle (6:1–15), the cure of the blind man (9:1–7), and the raising of Lazarus (11:1–44) have specific symbolic meaning: they represent the Revelation as food, light, and life, respectively. It can hardly be decided whether the walking on the water is appended to the multiplication of the loaves only by the force of tradition or whether it is meant to convey that the Revealer and the Revelation are not subject to the laws of natural life.

We have already seen how 6:26 and 30 indicate that the "signs," though they are miraculous occurrences, do not furnish Jesus with legitimating credentials. The remark that the faith of the many, which rests upon the miracles, is no trustworthy faith (2:23–25) indicates the same thing. John's whole presentation shows, rather, that if the miracles are not understood as signs, they are an offense! The healing of the lame man and the cure of the blind man both elicit enmity and persecution, and the raising of Lazarus brings Jesus to the cross. The miracles may be for many the first shock that leads them to pay heed to Jesus and so begin to have faith—for this purpose, miracles are, so to speak, conceded; nevertheless, for the leaders of the people, the representatives of "the world," the miracles are the offense that leads them to condemn him to death (11:47; *cf.* 12:18f.).

4. Just because the miracles are "signs" which require understanding, they also provide the possibility of *misunderstanding.* After the bread-miracle which raises the question whether he is "the prophet who is to come into the world" (6:14), the crowd wants to make him king (6:15) because it expects material benefits of him (6:26). His brothers want to take him to Jerusalem to the Feast of Tabernacles so that he may make himself conspicuous there, saying: "For no man works in secret if he seeks to be known openly. If you do these things, show yourself to the world" (7:4). They do not understand the way in which the Revelation works. They do not understand that from the world's standpoint the Revelation must always be a "hidden thing" (*cf.* "in secret" 7:4) and that it nevertheless occurs "openly"—not, however, with demonstrative obtrusiveness but with the unobtrusiveness of everyday events. What is true of the miracles is true of all that Jesus does: it is not understood. Even the disciples understand the cleansing of the temple no more than "the Jews" do. Not until after the resurrection does its meaning dawn upon them (2:17); likewise with the entry into Jerusalem (12:16). Peter does not grasp the meaning of the foot-washing (13:4ff.).

As Jesus' actions are *misunderstood,* so are *his words* so long as they are conceived in the categories of worldly thought. "The Jews" cannot but grossly misunderstand the saying about the destruction and rebuilding of the temple (2:20). As Nicodemus is able to understand re-birth only in the external natural sense (3:4), so the woman of Samaria misunderstands the saying about "living water" first to mean running water and then to mean miraculous water (4:11, 15). The disciples cannot conceive what food Jesus means as his secret nourishment (4:33), nor can "the Jews" guess what the bread from heaven is that Jesus bestows (6:34). Jesus' saying about his departure is misunderstood as an intention to go to the Dispersion (7:35f.) or even to kill himself (8:22). The disciples misunderstand the sentence addressed to Judas: "What you are going to do, do quickly" (13:27f.). And Thomas cannot cope with the statement that the disciples know the way which Jesus will take (14:4). The disciples do not understand the "little while" used by Jesus of his approaching departure and return (16:17f.). They do not see why Jesus does not wish to manifest himself to the world (14:22). The incomprehension of the crowd is symbolically illustrated by the fact that some misunderstand the heavenly voice in answer to Jesus' prayer as thunder and others understand it as the angel voice which it is, but without perceiving that it is really speaking not to Jesus but to them (12:28–38).

In all these misunderstandings the offense of the assertion, "the word became flesh" finds expression. This offense lies in the fact that the Revealer appears as a man whose claim to be the Son of God is one which he cannot, indeed, must not, prove to the world. For the Revelation is judgment upon the world and is necessarily felt as an attack upon it and an offense to it, so long as the world refuses to give up its norms. Until it does so, the world inevitably misunderstands the words and deeds of the Revealer, or they remain a riddle for it (10:6; 16:25, 29), even though Jesus has said everything openly all along (18:20). The world's inner incapacity to understand comes most crassly to expression in the demand, "If you are the Christ, tell us plainly." Jesus, of course, had been telling them for a long time, so he can only answer, "I told you, and you do not believe" (10:24f.). Evidently he is to the world a foreigner whose language it does not understand. Why not? Not because he is not a real man, but because he, a mere man, demands credence for his claim to be the Revealer: "Why do you not understand what I say? Because you cannot hear my word" (8:43 tr.). Why do "the Jews," who know him and his home town, nevertheless not know who he is nor where he comes from? Because they do not know God (7:28)! So, on the one hand, Jesus can say that he does not bear witness for himself; if he did, his testimony would not be true (5:31f.). On the other hand, he is constantly bearing witness for himself by claiming to be the Revealer, and can assert that his testimony is true when he does so (8:14). Each statement is true, according to which point of view is adopted: such a testimony as the world demands, a legitimation, he cannot and must not give. But there is a testimony which consists of his claim to be the Revealer, a claim which denies the world's competence to judge; in the world's opinion this cannot be considered true testimony (8:13). But this testimony he must bear.

The offense of the assertion, "the word became flesh," comes most clearly to light in the *direct contradiction of Jesus' claim* (see II, pp. 29f.). It can only appear as an insane blasphemy that he, a man, makes himself equal to God, and the authorities seek to kill him (5:17f.). His claim calls forth the accusation that he is demon-possessed and a "Samaritan" (8:51f.). So does his assertion that whoever keeps his word will not see death (8:51f.). And when he claims that he is older than Abraham (8:57), they want to stone him 8:59). His assertion that he and the Father are one fills them with such indignation that once more they want to stone him (10:30f.). In short, his "hard word" is intolerable to hear. And his persistence in his claim results in the apostasy of all but a few of his very disciples (6:66). What a scandal (σκάνδαλον) his cross will one day be to men, he hints in the words: "Does this (his "hard word") scandalize you? What, then, if you see the Son of Man ascending where he was at first?" (6:61f., tr.)—a saying of remarkably double meaning, for the world will, of course, perceive only the outward form of his "ascending": his crucifixion. John at the end brings this *skandalon* drastically into view when he has Pilate present the scourged and thorn-crowned Jesus to the crowd with the words, "Behold the man!" (19:5 KJ) and, "Behold your king!" (19:14 KJ). Here and in the inscription over the cross (19:19) the paradoxical stumbling-block of Jesus' claim is presented in a symbol of tremendous irony.

5. By his presentation of Jesus' work as the incarnate Son of God John has singularly developed and deepened Mark's theory of the *Messiah-secret* (§ 4, 4). Over the figure of Jesus there hangs a mystery, even though—or rather just because—he quite openly says who he is and what claim he makes. For to the world he is still in spite of all publicity the hidden Messiah, not because he conceals

anything or commands anything to be kept secret, but because the world does not see with seeing eyes (12:40). His hiddenness is the very *consequence* of his self-revelation; his revealing of himself is the very thing that makes "those who see" become "blind" (9:39).

His work as a whole, which forms a unity framed by his coming and his departure (see 2 in this §), *is both revelation and offense.* His departure or "exaltation" (i.e. upon the cross) not only belongs to the whole as its culmination but is that which makes the whole what it is: both revelation and offense. The possibility considered by Jesus in the meditation which is John's substitute for the Gethsemane scene of the synoptic tradition, "What shall I say? 'Father, save me from this hour'?" Jesus immediately rejects: "No, for this purpose I have come to this hour" (12:27). In his passion the meaning of the sending of Jesus is fulfilled. And by his conceiving and accepting it as the fulfilment of the mission enjoined upon him by the Father (14:31), it becomes the hour of exaltation, the hour of glorification. Seen from the vantage-point of this fulfilment the whole work of the man Jesus is a revelation of the divine glory. Whereas in the Gospel of Mark we can recognize the historical process by which the un-messianic life of Jesus was retrospectively made messianic, in John the inner appropriateness of that process is made clear. This is expressed by the evangelist by means of the petition of Jesus which follows the deliberation mentioned above: "Father, glorify thy name" (12:28) and by the heavenly voice which answers this prayer, "I have glorified it, and I will glorify it again" (12:28). Hence, the glorification of God's name which begins with Jesus' exaltation by crucifixion and the glorification of God's name by the ministry of the earthly Jesus (17:4) are a unity. Neither exists without the other; each exists only through the other. But the glorification of the name of God is also the glorification of Jesus himself, and Jesus' other prayer, "Father, the hour has come; glorify thy Son" (17:1), corresponds to this one ("Father, glorify thy name"). And the motive for this prayer—"that the Son may glorify thee"—makes the unity of God's glory and Jesus' glory evident. And when the motive is further developed in the words "since thou has given him power over all flesh" (17:2), the unity of his glory after the exaltation with that before it is once again made clear. Both unities are once more expressed in the words which pronounce the granting of this prayer:

> "Now is the Son of man glorified,
>   and in him God is glorified;
> if God is glorified in him,
>   God will also glorify him in himself
> and glorify him at once" (13:31f.).*

In the "now" of the "hour" when the Son of God departs from the world the past and the future are bound together, as it were. And since not until the future will the past be made into what it really is (*viz.*, the revelation of the "glory"), the disciples can only be glad that Jesus is going away (14:28; 16:7).

Faith in Jesus, then, is faith in the exalted Jesus, but not as if he were a heavenly being who had stripped off the garment of earthly-human existence as the Gnostic Redeemer was conceived to do. Rather, the exalted Jesus is at the same time the earthly man Jesus; the "glorified one" is still always he who "became flesh." In other words, Jesus' life on earth does not become an item of the historical past, but constantly remains present reality. The historical figure of Jesus, i.e. his human history, retains its significance of being the revelation of his "glory" and thereby of God's. It is the eschatological occurrence. Of course, this is not visible to the world, for the exalted Jesus does not reveal himself to it (14:22)—indeed he cannot, for it cannot receive the Spirit of truth which gives knowledge to those who believe (14:17; 16:13f.). But those who believe can now look back upon Jesus' earthly life and say, "We have beheld his glory" (1:14). What, then, is the picture of that life at which faith arrives?

§ 47. The Revelation of the Glory

1. In the hour of Jesus' departure Philip asks him: "Lord, show us the Father, and we shall be satisfied." The answer he gets is: "Have I been with you so long, and yet you do not know me, Philip? He who has seen me has seen the Father . . . Do you not believe that I am in the Father and the Father in me?" (14:8–10). In the person of the man Jesus—and only in him—is God Himself to be met, for: "no one comes to the Father, but by me" (14:6). In constantly varying expressions *this unity of Jesus the Son with God the Father* is insisted

---

* In the text of John as we now have it this passage precedes the prayer by some chapters. But the original arrangement has been disturbed. This section, 13:31f., must be the sequel to ch. 17; see my *Kommentar*, pp. 350f.

upon: "I and the Father are one" (10:30). With a formulation from the Gnostic myth it is said: he is not alone, but the Father who sent him is with him (8:16, 29; 16:32). Formulations from mysticism are pressed into service to describe this unity: the mutual knowledge of Father and Son (10:14, 38) and the mutual immanence of each in the other (10:38; 14:10f., 20; 17:21–23). Or, in mythological language once more, we read that the Father "loves" the Son (3:35; 5:20; 10:17; 15:9; 17:23f., 26) and that the Son "abides in his love" (15:10). The continuation of the answer to Philip nevertheless indicates that in none of these expressions is either mythology or mysticism really present, nor is a metaphysic in the sense of the later two-nature doctrine. This continuation is an exegesis of "I in the Father and the Father in me": "The words that I say to you I do not speak on my own authority; but the Father who dwells in me is doing his works" (14:10 tr.). In the work of Jesus, therefore, God appears, but God is not perceptible, as Philip's request implies, to the gaze of an observer. He is perceptible only to that man who has the openness to let himself be reached by the work of Jesus, the man who can "hear" his word (8:43). Yes, God in Jesus encounters even him who shuts himself up against his word—encounters him to judge him. In I Jn. the unity of Father and Son often has the peculiar result that it is impossible to decide whether the author is talking of God or of Jesus (e.g. 5:14f.).

God Himself encounters men in Jesus, a Jesus moreover who is a man in whom nothing unusual is perceptible except his bold assertion that in him God encounters men. In that fact lies the *paradoxical nature* of the *concept of Revelation*, a paradox which John was the first to see with any distinctness. It never occurs to Paul to reflect about the revelation which took place in the human figure of Jesus and his work and fate. For him the earthly Jesus is only the "emptied" one (Phil. 2:7), the "impoverished" one (II Cor. 8:9), not one who in his earthly interlude bears heavenly glory and riches. But John emphatically expresses this paradox. He accordingly presents the fact that in Jesus God encounters man in a seemingly contradictory manner: in one direction by statements that declare that Jesus has equal dignity and rights with God, or even that God has abdicated His rights to Jesus, so to speak. In the other direction, John declares that Jesus speaks and acts only in obedience to the will of the Father and does nothing on his own authority. Returning to

the former direction, we read that God gave Jesus His (God's) name
(17:11)*, gave "all things" into his hand (3:35; 13:3), gave him
"power over all flesh" (17:2), granted him "to have life in himself,"
as God Himself has life (5:26), and correspondingly gave him
"authority to execute judgment" (5:22, 27). Consequently, he wakes
the dead as the Father does and makes alive whom he will (5:21); he
works as the Father does (5:17), and is entitled to claim the same
veneration as He (5:23). But in the other direction, we find Jesus
declaring: "I have come down from heaven, not to do my own will.
but the will of him who sent me" (6:38). He acts in obedience to the
"charge" which he received from the Father (10:18; 12:49f.; 14:31;
15:10). Only in that charge does he have his existence: "My food is to
do the will of him who sent me, and to accomplish his work" (4:34).
In keeping with this saying, the last word uttered by the crucified
Jesus is: "It is accomplished" (19:30 tr.). His work is to accomplish
the task enjoined upon him by the Father (5:36; 9:4; 10:32, 37; 17:4),
which he does, not to his own glory but for the sake of the Father's
glory (7:18; 8:49f.; *cf.* 11:4). As for Jesus' own glory, the Father sees
to that (8:50, 54; *cf.* 16:14).

The negative formulations of this theme are repeated again and
again: Jesus did not come of his own accord or on his own authority
(7:28f.; 8:42; *cf.* 5:43). Of himself he can do nothing; he acts only
according to the Father's instruction (5:19f., 30; 8:28). He speaks and
teaches not of his own accord, but only speaks the words which the
Father has bidden him speak (7:17f.; 12:49; 14:10, 24; 17:8, 14). Of
course, the intent of such statements is not to diminish the authority
of Jesus and his words, but just the opposite: to establish it. Just
because he does not speak of his own accord it can be said that he
speaks the words of God (3:34), or that whoever hears him hears the
words of God unless his mind is hardened (8:47), or that whoever
hears his word has life insofar as he believes (5:24). These negative
formulations are not in the least meant as descriptions of Jesus'
humility; the high priest does not speak "of his own accord," either
(11:51), any more than long ago Balaam did (Num. 24:13). The notion
that it is Jesus' humility that is being described by them is refuted
by 5:17f.; for "the Jews" are quite right in being enraged at
Jesus' words; regarded from the human standpoint they would be

* The text of 17:11 should be read with ᾧ "which," not οὕς "those whom."
The latter is a correction, attempting to approximate this verse to v. 6.

blasphemous presumption. But it is just this standpoint, from which Jesus' character would be measured by ethical standards, which is the wrong one; and what the author is trying to make clear is not Jesus' humility but his authority: the paradoxical authority of a human being speaking the word of God. In other words, it is the idea of the Revelation that the author is setting forth.

2. But now let us inquire what *the works* are that Jesus accomplishes in his Father's commission. Or what is his one *work*? For the "works" which Jesus does at his Father's behest (5:20, 36; 9:4; 10:25, 32, 37; 14:12; 15:24) are ultimately one single work. At the beginning of his ministry we read: "My food is to do the will of him who sent me, and to accomplish his work" (4:34) and in retrospect we are told a very similar thing at the end of it: "I glorified thee on earth, having accomplished the work which thou gavest me to do" (17:4).

In the *kerygma* of the Hellenistic Church Jesus' death and resurrection are the *facts of salvation* (§ 9, 4, I, pp. 80ff.). Being a unity, they might have been called "the work" of Jesus, though this terminology does not occur. Neither does Paul speak of "the work" of Christ, even though he, too, might very appropriately have so spoken of Jesus' death and resurrection.* Though for Paul the incarnation of Christ is a part of the total salvation-occurrence, for John it is the decisive salvation-event. While for Paul the incarnation is secondary to his death in importance (§ 33, 1), one might say that the reverse is true in John: the death is subordinate to the incarnation. But on closer inspection it turns out that incarnation and death constitute a unity as the coming (incarnation) and the going (death) of the Son of God (§ 45, 1). But within that unity the center of gravity is not in the *death*, as it is in Paul. In John, Jesus' death has no preeminent importance for salvation, but is the accomplishment of the "work" which began with the incarnation (§ 46, 5): the last demonstration of the obedience (14:31) which governs the whole life of Jesus. The phrase "obedient unto death" (Phil. 2:8), quoted by Paul from a Christ-hymn (see I, pp. 131, 298), is developed by John in the whole sweep of his representation of Jesus. Thus Jesus' death takes on a double aspect in John: it is the completion of his obedience, but it is also Jesus' release from his commission, and he can return to the

---

* "The work of Christ" in Phil. 2:30 is not what the earthly Jesus accomplished but the *work* of Christian missions carried on in the service *of Christ*.

glory he previously had in pre-existence (6:62; 17:5). Therefore the crucifixion, which John, of course, narrates, is regarded from the outset as Jesus' "elevation" (ὑψωθῆναι), a peculiarly ambiguous word (3:14; 8:28; 12:32, 34), or as his "glorification" (7:39; 12:16, 23; 13:31f.; 17:1, 5). But the Pauline vocabulary, the "cross" and "the crucified" (§ 41, 2, II, p. 8), is not found in John; and in Jesus' predictive words about his death the terms "be exalted" (or elevated) and "be glorified" have supplanted the terms "be killed" and "be crucified" known to us from the synoptic predictions of the passion. Of course the way to exaltation leads through death (12:24), in which the sending of Jesus finds its meaning fulfilled (12:27; § 46, 5). But his death is not an event whose catastrophic nature could be removed only by his subsequent resurrection. On the contrary, his death itself is already his exaltation. And that means: John has subsumed the death of Jesus under his idea of the Revelation—in his death Jesus himself is acting as the Revealer and is not the passive object of a divine process of salvation. John does not use the term "suffer" (πάσχειν) of Jesus, nor speak of his "sufferings" (παθήματα). The synoptists said that Jesus "must suffer" (Mk. 8: 31, etc.). A similar unfathomable "must" (see I, pp. 46f.) occurs once in John, but its complementary infinitive is not "suffer" but "be exalted" (3:14). And 14:31 does not say "so it must be" (cf. Mt. 26:54) or the like, but simply "so I do." John's passion-narrative shows us Jesus as not really *suffering* death but *choosing* it—not as the passive victim but as the active conqueror.

The common Christian *interpretation of Jesus' death as an atonement for sins* (I, pp. 46f., 84f.) is not, therefore, what determines John's view of it. At the most, one may wonder whether in using certain expressions John was adapting himself to this common theology of the Church. When John the Baptist points out Jesus with the words: "Behold the Lamb of God who takes away the sin of the world" (1:29), "take away" is the literal translation of what Jesus does;* I Jn. 3:5 is parallel: "he appeared to take away sins." The figure of the Lamb, probably taken from Christian tradition by John, compels us to think of sacrifice. But nothing compels us to conclude that the evangelist sees this sacrifice only in Jesus' death rather than

* Αἴρειν means "remove," "carry away" in John, agreeing with the basic meaning of the verb; it does not here mean "take upon himself"—cf. I Jn. 3:5 with I Jn. 1:9.

in his whole ministry. The latter view would correspond to John's total view of Jesus. I Jn. 1:7, I admit, is a different matter: "the blood of Jesus . . . cleanses us from all sin"—certainly the common Christian conception of Jesus' death as an atoning sacrifice is present here. But the clause lies under suspicion of being redactional gloss. It competes with v. 9, just below, "If we confess our sins, he [God] is faithful and just, and will forgive our sins and cleanse us from all unrighteousness." The two sentences which refer to Jesus as "the expiation for our sins" (I Jn. 2:2; 4:10) are probably likewise redactional glosses.

Outside of I Jn. 1:7, Jesus' blood is mentioned a few other times. In the Gospel we find it in 6:53–56—i.e. within the passage (6:51b–58) inserted by an ecclesiastical editor, which reinterprets the preceding discourse or discussion (in which Jesus had revealed himself as the bread of life) as referring to the sacrament of the Lord's Supper (§ 47, 4). It occurs again in 19:34b, where the ecclesiastical editor has given the spear-wound a deeper significance by adding: "and at once there came out blood and water." This deeper meaning can only be that both sacraments, Lord's Supper (blood) and baptism (water) are founded upon Jesus' death. The case of I Jn. 5:6 is different: "This is he who came by water and blood, Jesus Christ." For here "water" and "blood" denote not the sacraments but the points of time at which his ministry began and ended: his baptism by John and his death. The purpose of the remark is to assert the reality of the Redeemer's human life against the views of the docetic Gnostics. That is why the sentence continues: "not with the water only but with the water and the blood"—i.e. let no one think that the Redeemer united with the human Jesus only at his baptism and then departed from him before his death; no, the Redeemer also suffered death. There is no allusion at this point to the death or blood of Jesus as having significance for salvation.

Whatever may be the origin of these passages, the thought of Jesus' death as an atonement for sin has no place in John, and if it should turn out that he took it over from the tradition of the Church, it would still be a foreign element in his work. It is significant that John does not narrate the founding of the Lord's Supper, in the liturgy of which (I, p. 146) the atonement idea occurs in the words "for you" (or "for many"). He substituted for it the farewell prayer of Jesus, in which the words, "And for their sake I consecrate myself" (17:19), are a clear allusion to those words of the Lord's Supper. These words do characterize Jesus' death as a sacrifice, it is true, but here, as everywhere else in John, his death is to be understood in connection with his life as the completion of his work. His life-work as a whole is sacrifice—an idea well expressed in the description of Jesus as he "whom the Father consecrated and sent into the world" (10:36).* Neither does "he gave his only Son" (3:16) specifically mean God's giving him up to death, but His sending Jesus to men. Neither is it said that his sacrifice is an atoning sacrifice for sins. Neither Jn. 17 nor the other farewell discourses deal with forgiveness of sin. In the whole Gospel, in fact, forgiveness of sin is mentioned only once—20:23—where the authority of the disciples to forgive sins is attributed to a saying of the risen Jesus. This passage alludes to ecclesiastical practice; so does I Jn., which takes ecclesiastical terminology into account more than the Gospel does. Twice forgiveness of sin is mentioned in I Jn.: it is conferred by God upon him who confesses his sins (1:9 see above, II, p. 53) and it is a characteristic of members of the Church that their sins are forgiven (2:12). In the Gospel, however, it is promised that release from sin will come through Jesus' word, or through the "truth" mediated by his word: "If you continue in my word, you are my disciples, and you will know the truth and the truth will make you free"—free from sin, as the sequel says (8:31–34). A parallel to this is the statement that whoever accepts Jesus' ministration is "clean" (13:10); for this service of his consists in his having revealed to his own the name of the Father, and given them the words that the Father had given him (17:6, 8). And 15:3 says: "You are already made clean by the word which I have spoken to you." So now at last the full meaning of 17:17 ("for their sake I consecrate myself") becomes evident, for it continues: "that they also may be consecrated in truth." This clause, however, only says how a fulfilment of the prayer, "Consecrate them in truth," is to come about (the explanation in 17:17b explicitly identifies "truth" with "thy word": "thy word is truth"). Jesus' death, therefore, is not a special work, but is conceived as of one piece with the whole life-work of Jesus, being its completion.

* However, the possibility must be left open that 10:34–36 with the apologetic scripture proof may be a later interpolation. Even so, v. 36 is a formulation quite in John's manner and thought.

3. If Jesus' death on the cross is already his exaltation and glorification, *his resurrection* cannot be an event of special significance. No resurrection is needed to destroy the triumph which death might be supposed to have gained in the crucifixion. For the cross itself was already triumph over the world and its ruler. The hour of the passion is κρίσις (of the world) and means the fall of the "ruler of this world" and his condemnation (12:31; 16:11). As a conqueror over whom the "ruler of the world" has no power, Jesus strides on to meet his passion (14:30 and see above, II, p. 53). There is not a word in John of the idea that not until the resurrection and exaltation after his death was Jesus made lord of all cosmic and demonic powers (*cf.*, for example, Phil. 2:11; Eph. 1:20f.; I Pet. 3:21f.; Pol. Phil. 2:1). For the Father did not delay the gift of life-creating power to him until the resurrection but gave it to him from the outset: "he has granted the Son also to have life in himself" (5:26). It is as he who is the resurrection and the life, or the way, the truth and the life (11:25; 14:6) that he encounters men and calls the believer into life now (5:24f.; 11:25f.), as the raising of Lazarus demonstrates (ch. 11). That is why we also fail to find in Jesus' words in John the prediction of his "rising" or "being raised" as we know it from the synoptics. The evangelist himself mentions it only in an aside (2:22): "When therefore he was raised from the dead, his disciples remembered. . . . " But as a substitute for it we find in 12:16: "but when Jesus had been glorified, then they remembered" . . . (tr.). "To rise" (ἀναστῆναι) occurs only in a redactional gloss at 20:9 and "to be raised" (ἐγερθῆναι) only in the redactional epilogue (21:4). Both terms are completely lacking in the Epistles of John.

It is not surprising that the evangelist, following the tradition, narrates some *Easter-stories*. The question is, what do they mean to him? The original close of the Gospel (20:31) just after the Easter-stories says, "Now Jesus also did many other signs." Evidently, then, the resurrection appearances just like the miracles of Jesus (§ 46, 3) are reckoned among his "signs." They symbolize the fulfilment of the prediction of 16:22: "So you have sorrow now, but I will see you again and your hearts will rejoice" (*cf.* 16:16). So far as they are actual occurrences—and the evangelist need not have doubted their reality—they resemble the miracles in that ultimately they are not indispensable; in fact, there ought to be no need for them, but they were granted as a concession to man's weakness. The Thomas-story is used to make this idea clear: his wish to see the risen Jesus in the body, even to touch him, is granted. But in the same moment he is reprimanded: "Because you have seen me have you come to faith? Blessed are those who though they do not see me yet believe" (20:29 tr.). It is hard to believe that the evangelist closes his representation of Jesus with this as his last word without a deep intention behind it. In it lies a criticism of the small faith which asks for tangible demonstrations of the Revealer. It also contains a warning against taking the Easter-stories for more than they are able to be: signs and pictures of the Easter faith—or, perhaps still better, confessions of faith in it.

The same conclusion can be drawn from the promises made in the farewell discourses. Parallel to the Easter-promise ("but I will see you again," 16:22, already mentioned above, within the whole passage 16:16–24) is another, 14:18; "I will not leave you desolate; I will come to you." This is the promise of his "coming," i.e. his parousia. But when it continues: "Yet a little while, and the world will see me no more, but you will see me; because I live, you will live also," the promise of the parousia is merging into the Easter-promise. What this means is that Jesus' resurrection and parousia are identical to John. Not only that, but parallel to these parallel promises stands a third, the promise of the Spirit (the Paraclete 14:15; 16:33), i.e. the promise of Pentecost. Hence, for John Easter, Pentecost, and the parousia are not three separate events, but one and the same. Consequently, the terminology appropriate to Easter again and again mingles with that appropriate to the parousia—reunion with him is mentioned in 14:19; 16:16, 19, 20; the fact that he lives, 14:9; his appearing to the disciples, 14:21f. But out of the traditional parousia-expectation these themes occur: his coming, 14:3, 18, 23, 28; and the phrases characteristic of eschatology, "in that day" 14:20; 16:23, 26 and "the hour is coming," 16:25. And into the midst of these the promise of the Spirit is thrust: 14:15–17, 26; 15:26; 16:7–11, 13–15. But the one event that is meant by all these is not an external occurrence, but an inner one: the victory which Jesus wins when faith arises in man by the overcoming of the offense that Jesus is to him. The victory over the "ruler of the world" which Jesus has won, is the fact that now there exists a faith which recognizes in Jesus the Revelation of God. The declaration, "I have overcome the world" (16:33), has its parallel in the believer's confession: "this is the victory that overcomes the world: our faith. Who is it that overcomes the world but he who believes that Jesus is the Son of God?" (I Jn. 5:4f.). In the short dialogue between Judas and Jesus it is explicitly stated that this is a matter of inward occurrence: "Lord, how is it that you will manifest yourself to us, and not to the world?" Jesus answers, "If a man loves me, he will keep my word, and my Father will love him, and we will come to him and make our home with him" (14:22f.). The same is said of the sending of the Spirit—"the Spirit of truth, whom the world cannot receive, because it neither sees him nor knows him; you know him, for he dwells with you, and will be in you" (14:17).

If, as John maintains, Jesus' original coming is already the κρίσις (judgment), then it is evident that for him the parousia is not an impending cosmic drama (see § 42, 1). Accordingly, John contains none of the synoptic parousia-predictions of the coming of the Son of Man in the glory of his Father, on the clouds of heaven, or the like (Mk. 8:38; 13:26f., etc.; see I, p. 29).

4. As we have seen, the "facts of salvation" in the traditional sense play no important role in John. The entire salvation-drama— incarnation, death, resurrection, Pentecost, the parousia—is concentrated into a single event: the Revelation of God's "reality" (ἀλήθεια) in the earthly activity of the man Jesus combined with the overcoming of the "offense" in it by man's accepting it in faith. It is only consistent with this concentration that *the sacraments* also play no role in John. It is true that he clearly presupposes that baptism ιs a practice of the Church when he reports in 3:22 that Jesus is winning and baptizing disciples. (The reader is assured by way of correction in 4:2 that not he himself but his disciples did the baptizing. Is this an ancient gloss?) But in the text that has come down to us in 3:5 ("unless one is born of water and the Spirit, he cannot enter the kingdom of God") the two words "water and" are clearly an interpolation made by an ecclesiastical editor, for what follows deals only with rebirth by the Spirit with no mention of baptism. Besides, it would contradict the untrammeled blowing of the Spirit (v. 8) if the Spirit were bound to the baptismal water. The foot-washing (13:4ff.) has often been taken to represent baptism, but this is an error. It depicts, rather, the service of Jesus in general which makes his disciples clean; according to 15:3, it is the word Jesus has spoken to them that has made them clean. The ecclesiastical redaction

of the account of the spear-wound (19:34a) made a gloss (34b, 35), and saw in the blood and water flowing from the wound symbols of both sacraments (II, p. 54). The knowledge-bestowing ointment (χρῖσμα) which I Jn. 2:20, 27 says the Church has received (it "abides in you, . . . and teaches you about everything, and is true . . ." v. 27) is the "Spirit of truth," of which the same statement is made (14:17: "it dwells with you and will be in you" [tr.]; 14:26 "it will teach you all things [tr.] *cf.* 16:13). Whether the author thinks of this Spirit as mediated by baptism—the term "ointment" would make it a natural assumption—is a question one may properly ask. But since the Spirit of truth in the Gospel (14:17, 26: 16:13) is the power of the word at work in the Church (§ 50, 7), the epistle's "ointment," too, is probably the word filled with power.

The Lord's Supper is introduced by the ecclesiastical redaction not only at 19:34b but also in 6:51b–58 (II, p. 54). For in the latter passage the "bread of life" of Jesus' preceding words surely does not mean the sacramental meal, but (like "water of life" and "light") means Jesus himself as the one who brings life in that he is life (11:25; 14:6). Again the notion of a "medicine of immortality" contained in 6:51b–58 does not agree with John's eschatology (§ 45, 3, II, p. 39). Finally, the offense which the "Jews" take at Jesus' offer of his own flesh as food is of a quite different sort from the Johannine *skandala* that arise from the peculiar Johannine dualism which is missing here. In John's account of Jesus' last meal there is no mention of the institution of the Lord's Supper, and for it the farewell prayer of Jesus is substituted (II, p. 54). John also substitutes the "new commandment" (13:34) for the "new covenant," of which the traditional eucharistic sayings speak (I Cor. 11:25). But the editorial appendix, ch. 21, reports in v. 13 a mysterious meal which the risen Jesus grants the disciples, and this evidently does mean the Lord's Supper.

It is therefore permissible to say that though in John there is no direct polemic against the sacraments, his attitude toward them is nevertheless critical or at least reserved.

§ 48. The Revelation as the Word

1. We have still to ask what the works are that Jesus accomplishes and that "bear witness" to him (5:36; 10:25). Are they *the "signs,"* the

miracles which Mt. 11:2 calls the "works of the Christ" (tr.)? No, at least not in the sense of being an unambiguous legitimation. For, as we have seen (§ 46, 3), they are ambiguous signs whose meaning can only be found in faith. In that respect they resemble Jesus' words. which are just as ambiguous and open to misunderstanding (§ 46, 4). In fact the miracles in John are neither more nor less than words, *verba visibilia*. Otherwise, it would be incomprehensible how Jesus' ministry could be called in retrospect a "doing of signs" (12:37; 20:30), whereas in the actual account of his ministry the "signs" are secondary in importance to the "words"—and the farewell prayer, looking back, describes Jesus' ministry as the passing on of the *words* God gave him.

That is the fact—the *works of Jesus* (or, seen collectively as a whole: his work) *are his words*. When Jesus says, "The works which the Father has given me to accomplish, these very works which I am doing, bear me witness that the Father has sent me" (5:36 tr.), the words of the preceding discussion (5:19ff.) indicate what the true works of Jesus are: "judging" and "making alive." They also indicate how these works are accomplished: by Jesus' word. Numerous formulations indicate that to John deed and word are identical.

8:28: "then you will know that I am he and that on my own authority I *do* nothing; but as the Father taught me, that I *speak*."

14:10: "The *words* that I *say* to you I do not speak on my own authority; but the Father who dwells in me *is doing* his *works*" (tr.).

15:22, 24: "If I had not come and *spoken* to them, they would not have sin . . . If I had not done among them the *works* . . . they would not have sin."

In addition *cf.* in 8:38 the interchange between "speak" and "do"; in 17:4, 8, 14 the equivalence of "work," "words" ($\acute{\rho}\acute{\eta}\mu\alpha\tau\alpha$) and "word" ($\lambda\acute{o}\gamma os$). There is a corresponding interchange between "see" and "hear" in 8:38, etc.; on which see below. 10:38 and 14:11 seem to contradict our assertion that the works are not added to the words to substantiate them but are nothing but the words themselves. Both times we read: "even though you do not believe *me*, believe the *works*" (in one case "for the sake of the works"). Does not "me" mean "my works"? But 14:11 is the continuation of 14:10, and together they indicate that the "works" of v. 11 are neither more nor less than the "words" of v. 10. When Jesus thus points away from himself to his working, that can only mean that he is rejecting an authoritarian faith which will meekly accept what is said *about* Jesus. In its place he is demanding a faith that understands Jesus' words as *personal address* aimed at the believer—i.e. as Jesus' "working" upon him. This is the sense in which Jesus refuses the demand of "the Jews" that he openly say whether or not he is the Messiah (10:24f.). The answer to that they ought to gather from his works—or workings—which bear witness for him.

The identity of work and word can be further seen in what is said of the effect of the word. "The words that I have spoken to you are spirit and life," (6:68). This is followed by Peter's confession: "You have the words of eternal life." Whoever believes the word of Jesus and Him who sent him, has eternal life, has stepped over from death into life (5:24). Whoever keeps his word will never see death (8:51). *His word therefore bestows life.* And neither more nor less than that is meant when it is said that his word leads to knowledge and hence to freedom (8:31f.). His word cleanses and consecrates (15:3; 17:17), Therein, of course, the word is *also the judge* over unbelief:

"If any one hears my words and does not keep them,
   I do not judge him . . .
He who rejects me and does not receive my words
   has a judge:
the word that I have spoken judges him" (12:47f. Blt.).

2. Now what of *the content of Jesus' word* or words? *What Jesus saw or heard with the Father* he speaks. (Or, as a consequence of identifying word and deed, John may also say that he "shows" it or "does" it.) This is in accord with the final sentence of the prologue: "No one has ever seen God; the only Son, who is in the bosom of the Father, he has made him known" (1:18; *cf.* 6:46).

Jesus testifies or speaks what he saw with his Father (3:11; 8:38) or what he saw and heard (3:32) or simply what he heard (8:26, 40; 15:15; *cf.* 5:30—the same thing is said of the Spirit in 16:13). He speaks what the Father taught him to speak (8:28, *cf.* 7:17), or commanded him to speak (12:49). He speaks the words that the Father gave him (17:8). He does what he sees the Father do, what the Father shows him (5:19f.). Expressed also in a very general way: he reveals the Father's name (17:6, 26).

It makes no difference whether the present tense is used of what the Son sees and hears (5:19f., 30), or a past tense of what he saw and heard (all the other passages), any more than there is a difference between "all that the Father *gives* me" (6:37) and "my Father who *has given* them to me" (10:29).

But the astonishing thing about it is that Jesus' words never convey anything specific or concrete that he has seen with the Father. Not once does he communicate matters or events to which he had been a witness by either eye or ear. Never is the heavenly world the theme of his words. Nor does he communicate cosmogonic or soteriological mysteries like the Gnostic Redeemer. His theme is always just this one thing: that the Father sent him, that he came as the light, the bread of life, witness for the truth, etc.; that he will go again, and that one must believe in him. So it is clear that the mythological statements have lost their mythological meaning. Jesus is not presented in literal seriousness as a pre-existent divine being who came in human form to earth to reveal unprecedented secrets. Rather, the mythological terminology is intended to express the absolute and decisive significance of his word—the mythological notion of pre-existence is made to serve the idea of the Revelation. His word does not arise from the sphere of human observation and thought, but comes from beyond. It is a word free of all human motivation, a word determined from outside himself, just as men's speech and deeds can only be determined from outside themselves when they oppose themselves to his word as enemies—determined in the latter case, of course, by the devil (8:38, 41). Therefore his word is not subject to men's scrutiny or control. It is an authoritative word which confronts the hearer with a life-and-death decision.

The same thing is meant by the solemn affirmation that Jesus does or says nothing on his own authority (see § 48, 1). Such statements have the purpose of underlining the authority of Jesus, whose words, although spoken by a man, still are not human words: "No man ever spoke like this man" (7:46). To a certain extent, the word of the Old Testament prophets is analogous in that they also do not speak by their own authority but are inspired by God. But the analogy also uncovers the difference: Jesus' words are not *from time to time* inspired, but he speaks and acts *constantly* from within his one-ness with God (§ 48, 1). Unlike the prophets' words, Jesus' words do not thrust the concrete historical situation of the People into the light of

God's demand with its promise or threat; they do not open men's eyes to what some present moment demands. Rather, the encounter with Jesus' words and person casts man into decision in his bare, undifferentiated situation of being human. None of the prophets was of absolute importance; one followed upon another. No new revealer follows Jesus; in him the Revelation of God is once for all given to the world, and this Revelation is inexhaustible. For whatever new knowledge may yet be given the Church by the Spirit, it will all be only a reminder of what Jesus said (14:26)—or, as Jesus says, "he will select from what is mine and declare it to you" (16:14 tr.; § 50, 7).

Thus comes to light the deeper meaning of that peculiar fluctuation of expression between "speak" and "do" and between "word" and "work." Jesus' words communicate no definable content at all except that they are words of life, words of God. That is, they are words of life, words of God, not because of their content, but because of *whose* words they are. They are something special and decisive not in and by their timeless content, but in and by the act of being uttered—and that is why they are just as much "works" as "words": Whatever Jesus does is a speaking, whatever he says is a doing. His actions speak, his words act.

For that very reason practically all the words of Jesus in John are *assertions about himself* and no definite complex of ideas can be stated as their content and claimed to be the "teaching" of Jesus. Hence the radical difference between Jesus' preaching in John and that in the synoptics; John took over only a minimal quantity of the traditional words of Jesus (§ 41, 1). His words are assertions about himself. But that does not mean christological instruction, or teaching about the metaphysical quality of his person. On the contrary, to understand them in that way would be to misunderstand them; for it would be a failure to understand that his "words" are "deeds." Anyone so understanding him would have to let himself be referred to Jesus' deeds, as were "the Jews" who required of him a clear statement whether he were the Messiah or not (10:24f.; see II, p. 16).

His words are utterances about himself; *for his word is identical with himself* (II, p. 19). What is said of his word is also said of himself: his words are "life," they are "truth" (6:63; 17:17); but so is he himself—"I am the way, and the truth, and the life" (14:6). Whoever hears his word and believes Him who sent him has Life (5:24), but that is what he himself is—"I am the resurrection and the life;

he who believes in me, though he die, yet shall he live" (11:25). His words (12:48; 17:8), his "testimony" (3:11, 32f.), must be "accepted" (λαμβάνειν)—so must he (1:12; 5:43; *cf.* 13:20). To reject him (ἀθετεῖν) is identical with not accepting his words (12:48). That his own "abide" in him and he in them means the same thing as that his words "abide" in them (15:4–7). He is the judge (5:22, 27)—so is his word (12:48). No wonder, then, that the evangelist can confer upon him for his pre-existent period the mythological title: *Word* (Logos)!

Certain though it is that *Logos* (Jn. 1:1ff.) is meant not as a common noun but as a proper noun, it is also certain that the everyday meaning ("Word") behind the name "Logos" is present in the evangelist's mind. For he is hardly likely to have begun his Gospel with the sentence, "In the beginning was the Logos," without thinking of "In the beginning" at Gen. 1:1 and of the recurrent phrase "God said" in the creation story of Gen. 1. And the same conclusion is to be drawn from I Jn. 1:1, where instead of the personal Word the common noun "word," ("of life") is used as a synonym ("That which was from the beginning, which we have heard . . . concerning the word of life"); here its everyday meaning is clear. The title "Logos" is not derived from the Old Testament, for in it—as also in Judaism—we hear of the "word of God" but never find the unmodified expression, "the Word." But "word of God"—like the rabbinic equivalent דִּי מֵימְרָא—does not mean a concrete figure (neither a person nor a cosmic power or "hypostasis"), but the manifestation of God's power in a specific instance. Nor is the title "Logos" derived from the Greek philosophical tradition in general or from Stoicism in particular and transmitted to the evangelist by Philo of Alexandria, for the philosophical idea of *logos* as the rational orderliness of the divine cosmos is quite foreign to John. The figure of the "Logos" is derived, rather, from a tradition of cosmological mythology which also exercised an influence upon Judaism, especially upon Philo. In the literature of the Old Testament and of Judaism there is a figure "Wisdom," which is a parallel to John's "Word." Both figures, "Word" and "Wisdom," appear side by side in Philo. In Gnosticism, which also influenced Philo, the figure "Logos" has not merely cosmological but also soteriological functions. It is within this sphere that the origin of the Johannine Logos lies.

His words are utterances about himself. Accordingly, all the

Revelation that he brings is concentrated in the great "*I-am*" *statements*.

"The bread of life—it is I.
    He who comes to me shall not hunger,
        and he who believes in me shall never thirst" (6:35 *cf*. 6:51a
        Blt.).
"The light of the world—it is I.
    He who follows me shall not walk in darkness
        but shall have the light of life" (8:12 Blt. tr.).
"The door is I" (10:9 Blt.). "The good shepherd is I" (10:11,
    14 Blt.).
"The resurrection and the life are I" (11:25 Blt.).
"The way, the truth, and the life are I" (14:6 Blt.).
"The true vine is I" (15:1, 5).

In fact, Jesus can pronounce this "It is I" absolutely, without any real subject: "unless you believe that it is I, you will die in your sins" (8:24 Blt.) and: "when you have lifted up the Son of man, then you will know that it is I" (8:28 Blt.). What is to be supplied as the real subject in place of "it"? Obviously nothing definite or specific, but something of this sort: "all that I say is I"—or perhaps better: "he upon whom life and death, being and non-being depend"—"he for whom all the world is waiting as the bringer of salvation." For let it be observed that in these "I"-statements the "I" is a predicate nominative and not the subject.* The meaning is always: "in *me* the thing mentioned (bread of life, light, etc.) is present; it is I" (II, pp. 26 f.).

All these figures of speech—that of the bread and the light, the door and the way, the shepherd and the vine—mean what John, without using a figure, calls life and truth. That is, they all mean that which man must have and longs to have in order to be able truly to exist. With his "It is I" Jesus therefore presents himself as the one for whom the world is waiting, the one who satisfies all longing. This is symbolically represented in the scene at the well in Samaria. The woman of Samaria says, "I know that Messiah is coming . . . when he comes he will show us all things." To which

---

* In Greek there is no change in the person of the verb between "I *am* he" and "it *is* I"—both are ἐγώ εἰμι (contrast, for instance, in both KJ and RSV Jn. 4:26 with Mk. 6:50—both translate ἐγώ εἰμι). The context must determine which is meant. See Bultmann's *Kommentar* p. 167, note 2, on these and two other meanings of the Greek formula "I am." (Tr.).

Jesus replies: "I who speak to you am he" (4:25f.). He similarly answers the healed blind man's question who the Son of Man is: "You have both seen him and it is he who is speaking to you" (9:37 tr.). The world's longing takes form in the concept of the *salvation-bringer* in his various forms, with his various titles. So the titles of the salvation-bringer from both the Jewish and the Hellenistic tradition (§ 45, 2) are conferred in John upon Jesus. Jesus is he in whom the old hope is fulfilled; his coming is the eschatological event (§ 45, 3). But all the traditional titles are insufficient, as is suggested by the title which occurs in Peter's confession: "and we have come to believe and to know that you are the Holy One of God" (6:69 tr.). Only one other time does this title occur in the New Testament: in the demon's confession at Mk. 1:24; it has no tradition (at least no recognizable one), for though Jesus is called "the holy one" at I Jn. 2:20 and Rev. 3:7, in these passages it is not a title but means simply "he who is holy." The title designates Jesus as the absolutely transcendent one whose place is at the side of God and who stands over against the world as the representative of God. At the same time, however, the reader is probably expected to hear in it the etymological overtone: holy—hallow (ἅγιος—ἁγιάζειν) and to remember that Jesus is he "whom the father hallowed and sent into the world" (10:36) and he who hallows himself for his own (17:19; II, p. 55).

3. Thus it turns out in the end that Jesus as the Revealer of God *reveals nothing but that he is the Revealer*. And that amounts to saying that it is he for whom the world is waiting, he who brings in his own person that for which all the longing of man yearns: life and truth as the reality out of which man can exist, light as the complete transparence of existence in which questions and riddles are at an end. But how is he that and how does he bring it? In no other way than that he says that he is it and says that he brings it— he, a man with his human word, which, without legitimation, demands faith. John, that is, in his Gospel presents only the fact (*das Dass*) of the Revelation without describing its content (*ihr Was*).

In the Gnostic myth, whose language John uses as his means of expression, it suffices that the Revelation consists of nothing more than the bare fact of it (its *Dass*)—i.e. the proposition that the Revealer has come and gone, has descended and been re-exalted. For even though Gnosticism speaks at length in cosmogonic and soteriological speculations about the content of the Revelation, nevertheless the decisive thing for it is the bare fact of Revelation. The reason for this is that for it the Redeemer is a cosmic figure and that redemption is ultimately a cosmic process by which the light-particles imprisoned in the material world are released and guided to the world of light above (II, pp. 40 f.). Cosmic connection between the Redeemer and the redeemed—that is to say, the identity of their nature (φύσις)—is the presupposition for redemption. By virtue of this identity his fate is theirs, and to know this—i.e. to know one's own nature (φύσις) and its unity with the Redeemer's nature—is the content of the Revelation and is the Gnosis ("knowledge") in which the Revelation is appropriated. But since John eliminates from the myth its cosmological presuppositions, since he does not speak of the "nature" common to the Redeemer and the redeemed or of the fate of human "selves," he appears to retain in his book only the empty fact of the Revelation. He does not give content to the Revelation by filling it with rational or speculative insights, nor by reproducing the message preached by the synoptic Jesus. Consequently, it was natural enough for investigators to declare John a mystic. For the negation of all definable Revelation-content has a counterpart in mysticism: the soul's experience, the content of which goes beyond any possibility of expression. But John is no mystic. The mystic formulas adopted by him he wishes to be understood in the sense of his Revelation-idea (§ 47, 1). Any interest in disciplining the soul or cultivating experiences of the soul ("mystical experiences") is lacking. The negative predications of God characteristic of mysticism are missing. And the negation of the world in John does not have the same meaning that it has in mysticism. That is, it does not have the ontological meaning of describing God's mode of being by the *via negationis*. John's negation of the world does mean the condemnation of man, because John sees the "world" as a historical force—*viz.*, as the world constituted of men in rebellion against God (§§ 42, 44). Therefore, his negating of the world means the rejecting and condemning of man's presumptuous independence and of the norms and evaluations emanating therefrom.

But if the Revelation is to be presented neither as the communication of a definite teaching nor as the kindling of a mystical experience of the soul, then all that can be presented is the bare fact of it. This fact, however, does not remain empty. For the Revelation is represented as the shattering and negating of all human self-assertion and all human norms and evaluations. And, precisely by virtue of being such negation, the Revelation is the affirmation and fulfilment of human longing for life, for true reality. That the Revelation is this positive thing can only be seen by such a faith as overcomes the "offense" and subjects itself to that negation, acknowledging its own blindness in order to receive sight (9:39). Then it becomes clear that the man called to have faith can ask for no credentials, no legitimation, no "testimony" ($\mu\alpha\rho\tau\upsilon\rho\iota\alpha$) to the validity of the word of the Revelation (II, p. 45).

Jesus cannot legitimate himself, cannot present "testimony" in the sense in which such is demanded by the world. The "Scriptures" do indeed bear witness to Jesus (5:39) but their meaning has been perverted by "the Jews" (II, p. 28). God, too, bears him witness (5:31f.), but this witness is not accepted by the world because it does not know God (5:37; 7:28; 8:19, 55; 16:3). And how does God bear him witness? Through Jesus' own "works" (5:36f.)! But these works, as we have seen, are identical with his word (II, pp. 60 ff.)—identical, that is, with his claim to be the Revealer. The testimony, therefore, is identical with that which is to be substantiated! Hence, contradictory statements can stand in the Gospel, one of which says that Jesus does not bear witness to himself (5:31ff.) and the other that he does (8:14, 18). He bears witness to himself with his "It is I." But only by faith is this testimony understood as testimony: "He who accepts his testimony has affixed his seal that God is true" (3:33 tr.). "He who believes in the Son of God has the testimony in himself. He who does not believe God has made him a liar . . ." (I Jn. 5:10). The paradox is that the word of Jesus does not find its substantiation by a backward movement from the attesting word to the thing attested—as it might if the thing itself were confirmable irrespective of the word—but finds it only in a faith-prompted acceptance of the word. This is also what is meant by the following saying: "if any man's will is to do his will, (i.e. God's) he shall know whether the (*sc.* my) teaching is from God or whether I am speaking on my own authority" (7:17). For "doing the will of God" here is not meant morally, as if the sentence were urging men to begin with ethics and promising that from it an understanding for dogmatics would of itself arise. No, the will of God demands nothing more nor less than faith (6:29). Only in faith is the attested matter seen, only in faith is the witness recognized as legitimate. In other words, the object of faith makes itself accessible to nothing but faith. But whoever, having such faith, "has the testimony in himself," thereby has Life itself: "And this is the confirmation: the fact that God gave us eternal life" (I Jn. 5:11 tr.).

Now it also becomes clear that the Revealer is nothing but a definite historical man, Jesus of Nazareth. Why this specific man? That is a question that must not, may not, be answered—for to do so would destroy the offense which belongs ineradicably to the Revelation. This Jesus had to meet men in a definite form, of course, but John confines himself to letting only that about Jesus become visible which was an "offense." If he presupposes that a traditional picture of Jesus and his proclamation lives on in the congregations for which he is writing, he, at any rate, wishes that picture to be understood in the light of his Revelation-idea. That would mean that he sees the meaning of the synoptic message of Jesus to be that ultimately it is the shattering and negating of the "world's" understanding of itself. In any case, he does not consider the task of the Church's proclamation to be the transmitting of the historical tradition about Jesus. The testimony of the Church is the testimony of the Spirit that was given it. The Spirit, as the "other Counselor," is Jesus' substitute (14:16). And when the Spirit "reminds" believers of all that Jesus said (14:26), this reminding is not an evocation of the past by historical reproduction. Rather, it is that which makes present the eschatological occurrence which with him burst into the world (16:8–11). When it is said that the Spirit "will guide you into the whole truth" (16:13 Blt.), that means that the Spirit teaches the believer by the light of this occurrence to understand each particular present hour (§ 50, 7).

Beyond the mere statement that the Revelation in Jesus took place, is it only by describing it as the "offense," the judgment over the "world," the negation of human self-assertion that anything can be said about that Revelation? There is one way left to try. Since it is to *faith* that it makes itself available as Revelation, the meaning of the Revelation can be further clarified by showing what happens when *faith* takes place.

CHAPTER IV

Faith

§ 49. Faith as the Hearing of the Word

1. The Gospel of John was written "that you may believe that Jesus is the Christ, the Son of God, and that believing you may have life in his name" (20:31). John the Baptist was sent from God to bear witness to Jesus "that all might believe through him." God sent his "only Son"—in order "that whoever believes in him may not perish but have eternal life" (3:16 tr.). To those "who believe in his name" the Incarnate One gave the "power to become children of God" (1:12). "He who believes in the Son has eternal life" (3:36). This demand that one *believe* (or *have faith*) runs through the whole Gospel and the first Epistle (6:29; 12:36; I Jn. 3:23); so does the promise made to him who believes (6:35, 40, 47; 7:37, 38a, 11:25f.; 12:44–46; 14:12; I Jn. 5:1, 10, 13).

Certain figurative expressions mean the same thing. To "come" to Jesus means neither more nor less than to believe in him (5:40; 6:37, 44f., 65), and both are found in synonymous parallelism (6:35; 7:37). Whoever "follows" him as the "light of the world" receives the same promise as he who "believes" in him (8:12). The same is true of him who "enters" through him, "the Door" (10:9) or who "drinks" of the "water" that he bestows (4:13f.; *cf.* 6:35; 7:37). Other expressions also mean believe in him: "accept" or "receive" him (λαμβάνειν, 1:12; 5:43), and "love" him (8:12; 14:15, 21ff.; 16:27).

In his terminology John takes the general Christian usage as his starting-point. In it πιστεύειν (believe) means the acceptance of the Christian message (see I, pp. 89f.; John uses the *verb* throughout, with the sole exception of I Jn. 5:4, which contains the noun πίστις). Hence the object of belief can be specified by a ὅτι-clause ("to believe that. . . ." 6:69; 10:38; 11:27, 42; 17:8; 20:31; I Jn. 5:1, 5, etc.). In place of the foregoing, the abbreviated expression "believe in . . ." (πιστεύειν εἰς) may appear (thus *passim* in Jn. and 1 Jn.; alternating with "believe that πιστεύειν ὅτι . . ." in 11:25–27). Equivalent to the last expression is "believe in his name" (1:12; 2:23; 3:18, I Jn. 5:13; *cf.* the alternation in Jn. 3:18). *Πιστεύειν* by itself has the same sense and can alternate with "believe that . . ." (11:40, 42; 16:30f.) as well as with "believe in . . ." (3:18; 4:39, 41). But it is a specifically Johannine characteristic that in addition to all these expressions πιστεύειν can also be used with the plain dative (in which case it is correctly translated "believe him" not "believe in him": 5:38, 46; 8:45f., etc.; in alternation with "believe in" 8:30f.; πιστεύειν τῷ ὀνόματι ["believe his name"] takes the place of "believe in his name" I Jn. 3:23).

Since Jesus and his word are identical (§ 48, 1), his words can also be named as the object of faith (5:47; *cf.* 2:22)—likewise the "works," which are identical with the words (10:38). Just as he himself is said to be "received" or "accepted" (see above), so are his "words" (12:48; 17:8) or his "testimony" (3:11, 32f.; *cf.* I Jn. 5:9). That explains why "believe him" (simple dative) and "believe in him" are identical for John. It is not as if one first had to believe him, trust him, *in order* that one might believe *in* him, but that one ought to believe him, and in so trusting him is in fact believing *in* him; one can do neither without doing both. Thus it becomes clear that in the proclaimed word the Proclaimer himself is present, acting. This unity is what John is expressing in this usage: "to reject him" and "not to receive his words" are identical (12:48); disbelief (primarily of his words, of course) means "disobeying" the Son (3:36).

A counterpart to the identity of Jesus' word and person is the fact that faith proceeds from *hearing* (5:24), or even directly *is* hearing—provided it is genuine hearing: not mere perception, but a hearkening-and-learning (6:45), or a hearing-and-keeping (12:47). So not all hearing is of the same kind:

> "The hour is coming, and now is,
>   when the dead will hear the voice of the Son of God,
>   and those who hear will live" (5:25).

"The Jews' " incapacity to "hear" Jesus word (8:43, 47) is synonymous with their incapacity to believe him (8:45f.). Whoever is "of the truth" hears his voice (18:37). Or the same thing is said through a figure: the sheep heed the voice of their shepherd (10:3, 16, 27).

The identity of Jesus' person with his word—or of his "work" with his word—makes it possible for John to speak of "*seeing*" just as he does of "hearing." The two verbs are united in 5:37 and I Jn. 1:1, 3 (*cf.* Jn. 3:32), and in 8:38 one alternates for the other. Just as "hear" and "believe" can be united, so "see" and "believe" can be joined or made parallel to each other (6:40; 12:44f.).

The various Greek verbs for "see" are used by John without distinction: ὁρᾶν (ἰδεῖν, ὄψεσθαι), βλέπειν, θεᾶσθαι and θεωρεῖν. What is seen may be persons, things, or occurrences which are generally perceptible in the visible world of earth (1:38, 47; 9:8, etc.). But beyond that it may be supranatural things or occurrences which can only exceptionally be perceived by certain people (1:32ff.; 20:12, 14, etc.). While in both these cases seeing is a sense-perception, in other cases it denotes the inner perception of matters having no sensory perceptibility; this is the specifically Johannine usage: the "sight" which recognizes the Son of God in the Incarnate One. Paradoxically, this inner sight may coincide with a sensory perceiving of Jesus (1:14; 6:40; 12:45; 14:9 and elsewhere), but the two may also be kept separate as in I Jn. 4:14: "And we have seen and testify that the Father has sent his Son as the savior of the world" (inner sight only). There is no point in dealing here with general figurative usages of "see" (4:19; 7:52, etc.) or with its use in traditional formulas (3:3;, 36; 8:51, etc.).

The parallelism—or rather, identity—of believing, hearing, and seeing indicates by itself that sight to John is not mystical contemplation. Sight, or seeing, is to him faith's perception: faith recognizes in the historical Jesus the "truth" and "life" which only he transmits and which therefore are not perceptible to direct contemplation. This is explicitly pointed out in Jesus' reply to Philip's request: "Lord, show us the Father, and we shall be satisfied." His reply is: "Have I been with you so long, and you have not yet come to know me, Philip? He who has once seen me thenceforth sees the Father" (14:8f. tr.; *cf.* 12:45). Hence "the word became flesh" is also followed by a "seeing": "and we beheld his glory" (1:14). This "beheld" does not mean that "we" were "eye-witnesses" in the sense that is meant in historical inquiry; for in that sense the unbelieving Jews were also eye-witnesses and yet saw nothing of the "glory."

But this "we" includes not merely the believing contemporaries of Jesus (the original disciples), but also the believers of all times. For it was not just once upon a time that the Revealer was incarnate—he remains so forever. Never can faith turn away from him, as if the "glory"—or the "truth" and "life"—could ever become directly visible, or as if the Revelation consisted of a certain thought-content, and the incarnation of the "Word" were only a device, henceforth superfluous, for transmitting that content. Therefore, the role of the believing contemporaries of Jesus is not that they give a certifying guarantee to the faith of following generations by their eye-witness testimony, but that they pass on to them the "offense" of "the Word become flesh."

2. Sight, then, is *the knowing* that is peculiar to faith. Hence "see" and "know" can be combined or be used as alternatives (14:7, 9, 17; I Jn. 3:6; also compare 5:37 with 8:55, or 6:46 with 17:25). *Faith is genuine* only insofar as it is a *knowing* faith. This is expressed by Jesus' promise of knowledge of the truth to believers if they loyally "abide" in his "word" (8:31f.). Genuine faith must not be confused with a seeming faith that is aroused by Jesus' "signs" (2:23f.; 7:31; 10:42; 11:45; 12:11) or may also be evoked by his discourse (8:30). Such faith may be a first tentative step toward him, but it has yet to prove itself as genuine faith. As "hearing" the word must be supplemented by "keeping" it, so genuine faith can be called "keeping" the word (8:51; 14:23; 15:20; 17:6) or as "abiding in the word" (8:31 tr.). Expressions synonymous with both of these are: abiding in the Revealer himself (15:4–7; I Jn. 2:6, 27f.; 3:6, 24; *cf.* abiding in God, I Jn. 4:13, 15f.; abiding in the light I Jn. 2:10; in love Jn. 15:9f., I Jn. 4:16) and the abiding of his words in the believers (15:7; I Jn. 2:24).

The formulation of 8:31f.: "If you continue in my word . . ., you will know the truth," might easily suggest that *knowledge*, instead of being a property already possessed by *any genuine faith*, is some advance beyond faith. But it would be a misconception to take it so. It is immediately apparent that faith and knowledge do not differ as to their substance. That the Father sent Jesus is equally what is believed (11:42; 17:8, 21) and what is known (17:3). That Jesus came from the Father is believed (16:27–30), just as it is known that his teaching derives from the Father (7:17). As "truth" is what knowledge knows (8:32), so faith believes in him who is "truth" (14:6). That

Jesus is the Christ, is believed (11:27; 20:31) but also known (6:69). The unity of the disciples will bring the world both to the belief (17:21) and to the knowledge (17:23) that the Father sent Jesus. A parallel statement is made about believers:

> ". . . they truly recognized that I came from thee
> and believed that thou didst send me" (17:8 tr.).

Since the content of the subordinate clauses is identical, it is clear that "recognizing" and "believing" are not two different acts. Only in cases where "believe" means a first turning toward Jesus, not yet developed into full faith, can "know" be distinguished from "believe" as a distinct act. This distinction is made in 8:30–32 where "the Jews who had come to believe him" are told: "if you abide in my word . . ., you shall know . . ." (tr.). The same distinction is certainly present in 10:38: "Even though you do not believe me, believe the works (the working of my words), that you may begin to know and ever be aware that the Father is in me and I in the Father" (tr.; see II, p. 60). Perhaps this is also meant in 6:69: "we have come to believe and to know that thou art the Holy One of God" (tr.). But believing in the full sense and knowing are not two different acts or stages—this is quite clear from the fact that the order can be reversed as in 17:8 and also in 16:30 and I Jn. 4:16: "And we have come to know and to believe the love which God has for us" (tr.).

Faith and knowledge, we conclude, cannot be distinguished as two stages. In the Christian Church there are not two classes of people, as there were among the Gnostics, who distinguished between "*pistics*" (men of faith) and "*gnostics*" (men of knowledge). Faith is not the acceptance of a dogma upon which there follows a disclosure of items of esoteric knowledge or a mystic vision. No, faith is everything. Knowledge cannot cut loose from faith and soar on out beyond it; faith, however, also contains knowledge—faith itself knows. Since for John all knowing can only be a knowing-in-faith, faith comes to itself, so to say, in knowing. Knowing is a structural aspect of believing.

Accordingly, Jesus' relation to God is never called "believing" but always "knowing" (10:15; 17:25). But all human knowing of God must always be a believing knowledge. This "must" will not cease until earthly existence is over and "believing" is succeeded by a direct "seeing" that is no longer directed toward the "glory" veiled in "flesh" but has "glory" itself for its object (17:24).

§ 50. Faith as Eschatological Existence

1. For John, as for Paul, faith is the way to salvation, the only way. However, "by faith alone" is so taken for granted by John that he does not explicitly emphasize it. The Pauline antithesis "faith—works of the Law" is not found in John; therefore the term "grace" plays no role of importance either (II, p. 8). For John *the central topic for discussion is not what it is for Paul: what is the way to salvation?* For John *the central topic is salvation itself.* He does not address himself to man's longing for "righteousness" nor attack the Jewish error that a man can earn righteousness by his own works. Instead, he addresses himself to man's longing for life and attacks a false understanding of life. The world longs for life, thinks it knows it, finds it, or even has it (5:39). The world is told it is in death (*cf.* 5:25). The world thinks it sees and is told it is blind (9:39). It supposes it knows God, but the "true God" (17:3; I Jn. 5:20) is unknown to it (5:37; 7:28). The true light, the true bread of life, the true tree of life, all are unknown to it (1:9; I Jn. 2:8; Jn. 6:32; 15:1; § 42). But the world is not simply in error; it is a liar. It does not believe Jesus—precisely because he tells the truth. The world does not want to come to the light (3:19).

The demand for faith, therefore, is the demand that the world surrender the understanding it has had of itself hitherto—that it let the whole structure of its security which it has erected in presumptuous independence (§ 42; § 44) of the Creator fall to ruins. The inner unity of this demand with Paul's concept of faith (§ 35) is clear in spite of its orientation against other antitheses than his. Faith is turning away from the world, the act of desecularization, the surrender of all seeming security and every pretense, the willingness to live by the strength of the invisible and uncontrollable. It means accepting completely different standards as to what is to be called death and what life. It means accepting the life that Jesus gives and is (5:19ff.; 11:25f.)—a life that to the world's point of view cannot even be proved to exist.

Faith, then, is *the overcoming of the "offense"*—the offense that life meets man only in the word addressed to him by a mere man— Jesus of Nazareth. It is the offense raised by a man who claims, without being able to make it credible to the world, that God is encountering the world in him. It is the offense of "the word became

[75]

flesh" (§ 45; § 48). As victory over this offense, faith is victory over the world (I Jn. 5:4).

But faith is *not a dualistic world-view*. It does not arise by a man's wavering in his security and getting bewildered at the world and so turning away from it to waft himself up into a world beyond by speculative thought or devout silence. Faith is not an act that can be consummated by man on his own initiative, as if Jesus were only the "impulse" toward it. Rather, it is exactly Jesus toward whom faith is directed: he who is the way, the truth and the life, and without whom no one comes to the Father (14:6; § 46, 1). Faith is not flight from the world nor asceticism, but *desecularization* in the sense of a smashing of all human standards and evaluations.* It is in this sense that the believer is no longer "of the world" (15:19; 17:14, 16); i.e. since the world is no longer his determining origin (§ 43, 2), he no longer belongs to it. That is why the world does not "recognize" the believers just as it did not recognize him (I Jn. 3:1); in fact, it hates them as it hated him (15:18–20; I Jn. 3:13). As Jesus' way led him to death, so the way of those who are his, will lead them to persecution and death (12:24–26; 16:1–4). But their not being "of the world" must not be confused with a retreat out of the world. Jesus prays the Father: "I do not pray that thou shouldst take them out of the world, but that thou shouldst keep them from evil" (17:15). As God sent him into the world, so he sends his own into the world (17:18), not out of it.

In Gnosticism the world is a cosmic power foreign to man's nature ($\phi\acute{\upsilon}\sigma\iota\varsigma$, which belongs to the world of light), which encompasses man with fateful compulsion. Not so for John. For him the world is a historical power constituted by man who has rebelled against God (§§ 42–44). The membership of a person to the world of darkness or to the world of light is determined not by his fate nor by his "nature" but by his decision. The Gnostic dualism of fate has become a dualism of decision (II, p. 21). And faith is neither more nor less than the *decision*, achieved in the overcoming of the offense, *against the world* for God.

2. This decision does not proceed from motives of this world, but

---

* It would not violate Johannine meaning to add: faith is "conversion" or "repentance." But $\mu\epsilon\tau\acute{\alpha}\nu o\iota\alpha$ and the cognate verb, already avoided by Paul (I, p. 287), are entirely lacking in John—evidently because of the possibility of moralistic misunderstanding.

is a decision against the world; it becomes a possibility only through the fact that God appears to man as He who is revealed in Jesus. Since this is so, the decision seems to be determined, but it is not (§ 43, 1). Admittedly, it is wrought by God, but not as if the working of God took place before faith or, so to speak, behind it; rather, God's working takes place exactly in it. For when the Revelation encounters faith, the reply which faith makes to the Revelation's question feels itself to have been wrought by the question itself. In making its decision, faith understands itself as a gift. The disciples did not choose Jesus; he chose them (15:16).

That is where *faith's assurance* rests. The ear of faith hears this promise: "him who comes to me I will not cast out" (6:37) and this: "no one shall snatch them (my sheep) out of my hand" (10:28). Faith knows that it is "protected from evil" in the world, even as the petition of the departing Revealer had prayed the Father for them (17:9–19). In the shepherd-discourse faith's assurance is depicted by the figure of the mutual recognition of the Revealer and the believers: "I know my own and my own know me . . ." (10:14–18, 27–30). Indeed John can even venture to say in the mythological language of Gnosticism: "Every one born of God does not sin; for God's seed abides in him, and he cannot sin because he is born of God" (I Jn. 3:9 tr.)—a sentence that can be rightly understood only in its dialectic relation to another: "every one who does right is born of him" (I Jn. 2:29). That is, every one who does right (but no one else) is born of him. Of this, the former verse is the converse: Every one who is born of God (as is shown by his deeds) does not sin (see below).

Faith's assurance is both subjective and objective. As subjective assurance it is described in the shepherd-discourse: the sheep know the shepherd's voice and with sure instinct refuse to follow a stranger's call (10:3–5, 8). This assurance belongs to faith because faith is simple hearing and obeying. If it began to ask reasons for its right to exist or a guarantee for its own validity, it would have lost its assurance. As faith that hears, it is to itself the proof of its own assurance; by accepting the testimony, it confirms God's truth (3:33; I Jn. 5:10; II, p. 69). But as a faith that hears, it finds its assurance not in itself, but in that in which it believes. "My own know me" has its counterpart in "I know my own"—an expression of the objective side of faith's assurance, which must not be confused with any sort of guarantee. Faith's overcoming of the world (I Jn. 5:4) means just this: the assurance of faith is solely that of hearing. This assurance cannot be reduced to an experience within this world, and for that very reason it cannot be shaken.

3. As an overcoming of the offense and as a decision against the world faith is desecularization, *transition into eschatological existence.* In the midst of the world the believer is lifted out of secular existence —though he is still "in the world," he is no longer "of the world" (17:11, 14, 16). He has already gone through the Judgment and gone over into Life (3:18; 5:24f.). He already has Death *behind* him (8:51; 11:25f.); he already *has* Life (3:36; 6:47; I Jn. 5:12; § 45, 3). To him "the darkness is passing away and the true light is already shining" (1 Jn. 2:8). As Jesus was a foreigner in the world because of his foreign "glory," so the believers who belong to him are also foreigners, and he can say as he departs, "I have glorified myself in them" (17:10 tr.) and "the glory which thou hast given me I have given to them" (17:22).

In what does the "glory" consist which has become the property of believers? The first answer must be: in the *knowledge* which in faith is given to the believer. The statement that Jesus gives his "glory" to his own is synonymous with the other, that he gives them "eternal life" (17:2)—and what is it? "This is eternal life: to *know* thee the only true God, and Jesus Christ whom thou hast sent" (17:3). This double knowledge (of God and of Christ) is really one single knowledge—for God is known only through the Revealer, and the latter is known only when God is recognized in him. Now this double-single knowledge is identical with the "truth" (8:32) which is promised the believer; identical, that is, with the knowledge which grasps the idea that God is the unique Reality and sees through the world's "reality" as sham (§ 42:2). But this knowing is a believing knowledge, not one that stands off in aloof contemplation. Rather, it is such a knowledge that its possessor lets himself be determined by what he knows. It is an existing in what he knows; hence, his relation to what he thus knows can be expressed as a "being in" or a "remaining in" the Revealer of God (15:3f.; 17:21).

Freedom is promised to the possessor of this faith-knowledge. From what? From the world, from sham "reality," from both its seductiveness and its open enmity (§ 42, 2). As Jesus overcame the world (16:33), so faith is victory over the world (I Jn. 5:4). As the "ruler of this world" is defeated and powerless to harm Jesus (12:31;

14:30), neither can he harm the believers, for they "have overcome the evil one" (I Jn. 2:13f.). For that reason, freedom from the world is also *freedom from sin* (8:31–36). He who is born of God can no longer sin (I Jn. 3:9; II, p. 77). He no longer sins, and "the evil one" cannot take hold of him (I Jn. 5:18). Believers, having permitted Jesus' service to them (depicted in the foot-washing), are "clean" (13:10); they have become clean by means of the word which Jesus spoke to them (15:3). He "hallowed" himself in order that they might be "hallowed in truth" (17:19 tr.; II, p. 55), and he prays the Father: "Hallow them in the truth; thy word is truth" (17:17).

The fact that both this prayer and another, "that thou shouldst keep them from evil" (17:15), exist in addition to the declarative statements quoted in the paragraph above is significant. They indicate that freedom from sin is not endowment with a new nature (φύσις) to which sinlessness belongs as a natural quality. Sinlessness, rather, is inherent to faith. But faith itself is not a once-for-all rationally acquired and henceforth possessed conviction, but is the overcoming of the world which must be done over and over again. Declarative statements such as "faith is the victory over the world" and "the believer can no longer sin," have in their context the meaning of imperative sentences. They set before the eyes of those addressed what the faith is, for which, as believers, they have decided—and imply the exhortation: "make it so in you!" "He cannot sin" could, in Gnosticism, describe the empirical condition of its believers. Not so for John. To him it says *what it means* to believe.

Although Paul clearly saw the problem of *indicative and imperative and their relation to each other* (§ 38, 1) and to Christian conduct, he did not treat it in connection with the sinning of believers which factually takes place again and again. He did not so treat it because of his expectation of the rapidly approaching end of the world. With John it is different, for to him eschatology as a time-perspective has dropped out because he has so radically transposed eschatological occurrence into the present. He sees the peculiar *paradoxical tension* that exists between the declaration that the believer does not sin (I Jn. 3:9; 5:18) and the confession: "If we say we have no sin, we deceive ourselves, and the truth is not in us" (I Jn. 1:8). The whole passage (I Jn. 1:5–10) is intended to show that the believer's "walking in the light" and his confession of his sin constitute a paradoxical unity. John's statement, "he cannot sin" does not lead to false security but does the very opposite: it makes radical the consciousness of being a sinner. The believer, knowing his constant need of forgiveness, also knows that he can always be confident of receiving it, if he lets his relationship to God be determined by Jesus Christ. This confidence is expressed in a mythologically formulated statement: "If any one does sin, we have a *paracletos* (intercessor, advocate) with the Father" (I Jn. 2:1; Jn. 16:26 shows that this verse is not to be interpreted mythologically—see below, II, p. 88).

The discourse on the tree of life (the "vine" of 15:1ff.)* depicts *the dialectical relationship between indicative and imperative.* It is doing so when it makes "fruit-bearing" the condition for "abiding" in Jesus, but then (in v. 4) makes the latter the condition for the former. It is also doing so when it represents "cleanness" (v. 2) as bestowed ever anew for each bearing of fruit and yet says, "You are already clean" (v. 3 tr.). And the reason given for this statement, "on account of the word which I have spoken to you" indicates that this cleanness is well described by what Luther called a *"Reinheit extra nos"* (a purity outside ourselves). It is our confession of sin that makes this purity ours, for it is he who confesses his sin who can be confident of being forgiven (I Jn. 1:9; *cf.* I Jn. 2:12; 3:5). Since true faith is a "keeping" of the word (II, p. 73), it is also a keeping of Jesus' "commandments." And keeping his commandments is the condition upon which one may "abide in love" (15:10), which is identical with "abiding in his word" (8:31). "Keeping his commandments" and "keeping his word" constitute an inseparable unity. Consequently, either of two statements can take the other's place: "If a man loves me, he will keep my word" (14:23) and "If you love me, you will keep my commandments" (14:15). Similarly, faith and love can be thrown together as the content of one and the same commandment:

"And this is his commandment,
  that we should *believe* the name of his Son Jesus Christ
  and *love* one another, just as he has commanded us" (I Jn. 3:23).

Hence, "keeping his commandments" is the means of deciding whether we "know" him (I Jn. 2:3–6). The imperative "Keep my commandments," then, reminds the believer what he already is, thanks to the prevenient love of God, encountered in the Revealer (15:9; I Jn. 4:10).

* In Greek and German a grapevine is a tree. (Tr.)

4. The content of keeping "his commandments" can first be set down generally. Since the believers remain in the world (17:11), a place full of temptation, this injunction has the initial negative meaning of not "loving" the world (I Jn. 2:15). That is, concretely, to keep one's self free of "worldly desire" (ἐπιθυμία, I Jn. 2:16 tr.). Whoever hopes "to see him as he is," "dedicates himself as he is dedicate" (I Jn. 3:3 tr.)—in accord with the almost identical prayer of the departing Jesus (17:17; II, p. 79). Positively, what this commandment demands can be described as doing "what pleases him" (I Jn. 3:22) or as "walking in the light" (I Jn. 1:6f.).

But "walking in the light" gets a more precise definition in I Jn. 2:9–11; it is to love one's brother. And brotherly love, or "loving one another," is the actual content of Jesus' "commandments," which can also be called collectively his "commandment" (15:12; I Jn. 3:23; 4:21). In this commandment the inner unity of indicative and imperative becomes apparent. Out of the love we have received arises the *obligation to love*: "A new commandment I give you: to love each other as (καθώς) I loved you, in order that you, too, should love each other" (13:34 Blt. tr.)—in which καθώς means both "as" and "because" (i.e. it states both the manner and the cause of this love). "Beloved, if God so loved us, we also ought to love one another" (I Jn. 4:11). "We love, because he first loved us" (I Jn. 4:19). A further indication that a close relationship exists between a believer's receiving the loving service of Jesus and the passing on of that service in mutual love is furnished by the order of the two interpretations the gospel gives of the foot-washing. The first one (13:4–11) sets forth the service which Jesus performs. The second (13:12–20) entitles this service an "example" for the disciples. That faith and love are a unity is shown by the discourse on the tree of life (the true vine, 15:1–17). In it the imperative "abide in my love" (v. 9) which, according to vv. 1–9, is an exhortation to be loyal in faith, is followed by the indicative formulation: "If you keep my commandments, you will be abiding in my love" (15:10 tr.). Furthermore, this unity of faith and love is the chief theme of I Jn.—along with its polemic against false teachings.

The unity of "keeping the word" and "keeping the commandments" signifies that in genuine faith the foundation for all one's future conduct is provided, and also that it is impossible for such conduct to derive its motivation from the world. In faith it is decided in advance, as it were, that all one's conduct is to be conduct in love.

That is why it is in love that faith makes good its freedom from the world—and in this triumph of faith over the world lies the reason why God's "commandments" are not "burdensome" (I Jn. 5:3). It is in this same sense (*viz.*, in relation to its freedom from the world) that the love-commandment is called a "new commandment." For this newness is not its relative historical novelty, for that, of course, would quickly cease to be new. And anyhow from the world's point of view, to which the epistle shifts for a moment, it is not new but old: "I am writing you no new commandment, but an old commandment which you had from the beginning" (I Jn. 2:7). It is "new" because it is the commandment that comes to realization in the new— the eschatological—existence: "Yet I am writing you a new commandment—(a statement) which is true in him and in you—for the darkness is passing away and the true light is already shining" (I Jn. 2:8). Whoever hates his brother is in darkness (I Jn. 2:9, 11), he is a murderer like that fratricide Cain (I Jn. 3:12, 15). Whoever mercilessly shuts the door on a brother in need does not have God's love abiding in him (I Jn. 3:17). Whoever claims to love God while he hates his brother is a liar (I Jn. 4:20). In the act of fulfilling the love-commandment believers will be aware of their eschatological existence: "We know that we have passed over from death into life by the fact that we love our brothers" (I Jn. 3:14 tr.). Consequently, its fulfilment is the criterion by which the world is to know that these are the disciples of Jesus (13:35).

> The Christian commandment to love one's neighbor is, of course, neither limited nor annulled by the Johannine commandment to "love one another." Rather, the Johannine demand for brotherly love is the legacy bequeathed by the departing Revealer to the intimate circle of "his own" who have been the recipients of his love: this commandment is to be the rule within the disciples' circle. But this is no closed group. On the contrary, it is the eschatological Congregation whose vocation it is to "bear witness" (15:27). Therefore, the world constantly has the possibility of being drawn into this circle of mutual love. Furthermore, the statements of I John about brother-love seem not at all to be restricted to one's *Christian* brother (e.g. I Jn. 3:17).

5. Two characteristics of eschatological existence are "*peace*" (εἰρήνη) and "*joy*" (χαρά), terms familiar from tradition as descriptions

of eschatological salvation (*cf.* Rom. 14:17, etc.). Εἰρήνη is "well-being" in the full sense of the Semitic word שׁלוֹם (shalom), which includes as one component of its meaning our more restricted term "peace." It is this "well-being" which Jesus gives his own as his farewell gift. "Peace I leave with you," he says; but when he adds "my peace I give to you; not as the world gives, do I give to you" (14:27), that indicates that this "peace" is an eschatological possibility lying beyond all possibilities that are of this world. It is not something that can be realized in the external conditions of life or in some state of mind. On the contrary, since it can be seized as a reality by faith alone, it can no more become a state or condition than can "freedom." In the world believers have not peace, but "trouble" (θλῖψις); it is only "in him" that they have "peace" (16:33). Here again, as in the case of purity (II, p. 80), the *"extra nos"* character of faith's gifts is apparent.

The same is true of *"joy."* It, too, is conferred upon his own as "his" joy (15:11; 17:13), which makes it different from every joy of this world—it differs also in the fact that what this joy rejoices in is neither said nor can be said. The modifying participle πεπληρωμένη (full, fulfilled, realized, perfect, brought to pass, 16:24; 17:13) also stamps this as eschatological joy. But this joy, although a gift of the Revealer, is never a definitively realized state, but always lies ahead of the believer as something to be realized. This paradox is expressed by the juxtaposition in 15:11: "that my joy may be in you and your joy be brought to pass" (tr.). Joy, being eschatological, can never become a static condition. But it can very well become real in occurring—a kinetic reality, so to speak. It does so in the act of faith which overcomes the "sorrow" (λύπη) that assails the believer in the world (16:20–22). "Joy" also occurs when brother encourages brother; it takes place in both the encourager and the one encouraged: "And we are writing this in order that our joy may come to pass" (I Jn. 1:4 tr.*; *cf.* II Jn. 12). Against the assault of the "world" with its cares and troubles, eschatological joy must be struggled for, but it thereby becomes invincible: "and your joy no one takes from you"

---

* The unexpected and difficult reading ἡμῶν (our), rather than the expected ὑμῶν (your, plural), is probably the right one after all. "Our" joy, then, is the joy of the "you" and the "us" of v. 3 taken together as a larger "us." But even if "your" is the original reading, it is still true in the resulting sentence that joy comes to pass as an event.

(16:22 tr.). Though it has no describable object in which it rejoices, it nevertheless has an existential significance: "On that day (the day of "joy") you will ask me no questions" (16:23). In "joy" all questioning is over, all riddles solved. Once the "offense" is overcome, the Revealer's word seems no longer to be spoken "in riddles" (ἐν παροιμίαις) but in "frankness" (παρρησίᾳ) (16:25 Blt. tr.). In faith the believer has found the understanding of his own existence, because he no longer understands it from the world's standpoint but from God's—and thereby it has lost for him its enigmatic quality. The promise is fulfilled: "While you have the light, believe in the light, that you may become sons of light" (12:36). The "son of light" is in the daylight, the medium in which he understands himself in his world and knows his way (II, p. 17).

6. Another way John uses to describe eschatological existence is to say that the believers *are in the Revealer* or *he in them* in such a way that they are bound together into a unity among themselves and with him. This latter aspect of the unity is simultaneously unity with the Father, in whom the Son is and who is in the Son. So we find it said as both exhortation and promise: "Abide in me, and I (shall abide) in you" (15:4; *cf.* v. 4b, 5) or as sheer promise: "In that day you will know that I am in my Father, and you in me, and I in you" (14:20). In the farewell prayer it is said:

> "The glory which thou hast given me I have given them,
> that they may be one even as we are one,
> I in them and thou in me,
> that they may be perfected into unity" (17:22f. tr.).

The same thing is meant in those passages which formulate the relation between Jesus and his own as a mutual "knowing" (10:2f., 14f., 27). Whereas this manner of speaking comes out of the tradition of mystical language, other sayings that have the same purport use a formulation colored by apocalyptic language: the promise that the Revealer will return and be seen again (14:18f., 28; 16:16f.), particularly 14:23: "If a man loves me, he will keep my word, and my Father will love him, and we will come to him and make our home with him."

It is just as certain that the latter group of sayings is not talking about a realistic parousia of Jesus (II, pp. 57f.) as it is that the former group is not speaking of a mystical relationship (II, p. 50) between

Jesus and his own. All these sayings are describing the believer's eschatological existence withdrawn from the world. But only in faith is this existence a reality—*not in any direct relationship to Jesus or to God*. God is available only through Jesus, which is to say: only through the Incarnate One—and this in turn means: God is never available except when man overcomes that offense (II, p. 48). Neither is there any direct way or direct relationship to the Exalted One—until He Himself fetches the believers to Himself (14:3), whereupon they may behold His glory without a veil between (17:24). So long as they are "in the world" direct sight is withheld. For John the direct personal relationship of the disciples to the historical Jesus was not yet faith-relationship to him as the Son, but only became so "afterward" (13:7): namely, "on that day" (14:20; 16:23, 26), the Day when he was recognized as the Exalted One. In a similar way the faith-relationship of the believer to the Exalted One is no direct one. As Jesus had once said to "the Jews" (7:33f.), so in parting he also says to the disciples: "Yet a little while I am with you. You will seek me; and as I said to the Jews, so now I say to you, 'Where I am going you cannot come' " (13:33). His departure, which dissolves their hitherto direct relationship and interposes a separation between him and them, is necessary, for it is only from across this separation that he can be recognized as he who for them he is. Therefore they ought to be glad that he is going away from them (14:28). His departure is good for them, for if he did not go away he could not send them the Helper, the Spirit (16:7). But this return in the Spirit is the only way in which he will return. John has abandoned the old conception of Jesus' parousia held by the earliest Church. The "world" will see nothing of his coming again (14:21f.; II, p. 57).*

The farewell discourses depict the situation of believers in the world as that of forsakenness—and represent this as the very situation in which the Revelation takes on its real meaning (II, p. 42). Within the world is the very place where believers have the possibility of being detached from the world. This is the possibility that is to become reality by faith's success in penetrating through "trouble,"

---

* I Jn. 2:28; 3:2 mention a future "appearing" of Jesus (φανερωθῆναι) and his "coming" (παρουσία), and 4:17 uses the term "day of judgment." These may be cases of addition by an ecclesiastical editor (like Jn. 5:28f., etc.). If they are not, the only way to interpret them is to follow the guidance of the farewell discourses and regard the coming that is promised in Jn. 14:3 as the "coming" and the "day of judgment" that the epistle means.

"sorrow," and "perturbation" (the noun implied by ταράσσειν, 14:1) to "peace" and "joy." Believers are not removed out of the world but within it have their task (17:15, 18; II, p. 76). Within this world faith does not yet become direct vision. Faith is a desecularization not because its culmination is some world-canceling ecstatic experience. No, faith is itself desecularization—detachment within the world from the world. Or, better: faith as the act of believing constantly brings about this desecularization. It is true faith only when it has this constancy; i.e. when it "abides," when it is faithful (II, p. 73).

The kind of *faithfulness* that is demanded by "abide in me!" (15:4) again indicates that the believer does not stand in direct personal relation to the Revealer. The peculiar thing is not merely that this "abiding" in him is identical with "abiding in his word" (8:31), but particularly that the fidelity between Jesus and the believers is not like that between human friends. The latter are, in principle, equal partners, each both giving and taking, each living both from the other and for the other. But here Jesus alone is the giving one from whom the other lives, as the figure of the vine indicates. And though Jesus does call the believers his "friends" (15:15f.), he immediately forestalls a natural misunderstanding by adding, "You did not choose me, but I chose you" (15:16). So the believer's relation to him always remains that of faith.

Inasmuch as a relationship to God is mediated to the believer by the Revealer, the relationship is that of *prayer*. Both the certainty of the believer that he is united with God and also the separating interval between God and the believer find expression in it. Prayer, too, shows that the believer is still "in the world," but is nevertheless an expression of his eschatological existence which is no more "of the world." For he who prays can be certain that he will be heard: "If you abide in me, and my words abide in you, ask whatever you will, and it shall be done for you" (15:7). In characteristic variations this promise is repeated. In one place it is prayer addressed to the Father "in Jesus' name" that the Father will grant (15:16; 16:24, 26) or that He will grant "in Jesus' name" (16:23). In another place it is Jesus himself who will grant prayer uttered "in Jesus' name" (14:13f.). In all their variations these statements mean just one thing: such prayer is possible only to him for whom a relationship to God has been opened up by Jesus and through him ever remains open. And as he who prays such a prayer makes confession of Jesus in the phrase "in

Jesus' name," so God also makes confession of Jesus, as it were—acknowledges him as his own—by granting the petition "in Jesus' name." So it amounts to the same thing whether God or Jesus is asked, whether prayer is granted by God or by Jesus. But in order to preclude the mythological notion that the exalted Jesus is conceived as an intercessor standing between God and man, an explicit denial is made, "I do not say to you that I shall pray the Father for you; for the Father himself loves you, because you have loved me . . ." (16:26f.). I Jn. 2:1 is to be interpreted consistently with this. There prayer is also the subject, though a specialized kind: prayer for forgiveness of sin—"if anyone does sin, we have an advocate with the Father, Jesus Christ the righteous" (II, p. 80). "Advocate" (or ("intercessor") is a mythological concept, but here the term means neither more nor less than what the author otherwise means by prayer "in Jesus' name."

Because such prayer flows out of his eschatological existence, the believer can be sure that it will be heard. For he who in faith has gained the upper hand over the world is also master of the world in his praying; i.e. his praying is no longer determined by wishes and fears as to his worldly future. Recall that the granting of prayer is promised to him who "abides in" Jesus and in whom Jesus' words abide (15:7), and also that prayer is explicitly called an "asking according to his (God's) will" (I Jn. 5:14). The author indicates that the answering of prayer does not consist in the fulfilment of whatever worldly wishes one may express in it. That is the inference to be drawn from the following words, "And if we know that, whatever we ask, he hears us, we know that we (therein) have the requests that we made of him" (I Jn. 5:15, tr.)—i.e. no matter what may happen, that which does happen is God's answer to the prayer. Or rather: prayer itself is already its own answer. But this is true only when in praying a believer, eschatologically existing, is making certain of his eschatological existence by asking God "in Jesus' name" to make it a reality.

This attitude in prayer is called "*confidence*" (I Jn. 5:14). This "confidence" is ours "if our hearts do not condemn us" (I Jn. 3:21)—i.e. if we are not obliged to condemn ourselves as sinners. But for the believer there goes hand in hand with this self-condemnation the knowledge that "God is greater than our hearts and he knows everything" (I Jn. 3:20)—the knowledge, that is, that we can be certain of God's forgiveness. And it is just this knowledge which confirms to

[87]

us that we are "of the truth" (v. 19).* This attitude of "confidence" therefore is a paradoxical one in that it denotes that freedom toward God which springs from self-condemnation before Him; yet this very self-condemnation, if it leads us to "confess our sins" (I Jn. 1:9), is really itself already an evidence of "confidence." This is also the "confidence" that the believer has when Jesus comes (I Jn. 2:28), or that he has "on the day of judgment" (I Jn. 4:17), if these expressions are native to the epistle and not formulations due to an ecclesiastical editor (II, p. 85, footnote).

7. A final criterion of eschatological existence is the *possession of the Spirit*: "We know that he abides in us by this: the Spirit which he has given us" (I Jn. 3:34, tr.). "We know that we abide in him and he in us by this: the fact that he has given us of his Spirit" (I Jn. 4:13 tr.). In the farewell discourses the Spirit is called the Paraclete whom Jesus promises his own (14:16f., 26; 15:26; 16:7–11, 12–15). That the Spirit and the Paraclete are one is made explicit where the latter is identified as "the Spirit of Truth" (14:17; 15:26; 16:13) or the "Holy Spirit" (14:26).† In I Jn. the Spirit is also called the "unction" ($\chi\rho\hat{\iota}\sigma\mu\alpha$, I Jn. 2:20, 27 KJ) possessed by believers.‡ In this evaluation of the Spirit, John takes up the common Christian conception of the Spirit as the eschatological gift (§ 14, 1), which Paul also shared (§ 38, 2). But for John, the Spirit is neither the power that causes miracles and striking mental phenomena, nor the power and norm of Christian conduct (thus Paul; § 38, 3). It is *the power within the Church which brings forth both knowledge and the proclamation of the Word.*

Appropriate to the designation "Spirit of Truth," the Spirit's activity consists in "teaching all things" (14:26), and "guiding into

* Both the text and the interpretation of I Jn. 3:19, 20 are uncertain. I take ἐν τούτῳ (v. 19) as referring ahead to the second ὅτι-clause and assume that an οἴδαμεν has dropped out of the text in v. 20 before ὅτι μείζων ἐστὶν ὁ θεός. (The two verses would then read: "We shall know that we are of the truth and reassure our hearts before him by this: that when our hearts condemn us [we know] that God is greater than our hearts and knows everything." (Tr.)

† The designation "Paraclete" for the Spirit comes out of a tradition—presumably Gnostic—that has not yet been identified with certainty. The meaning of the term here is "helper," not "advocate" as it is at I Jn. 2:1.

‡ In using this designation "unction" John apparently has adopted a term of some Gnostic mystery-cult, against which he turns the barb of his remarks in their own language. Possibly the cult applied the term "chrisma" to baptism; in I John, however, it apparently means the Spirit as the power working behind and in the proclamation of the word (II, p. 59).

all the truth" (16:13). And the consequence, for those who have the Spirit, is that they all "know the truth" (I Jn. 2:20f.) and "have no need that any should teach" them (I Jn. 2:27). However, the knowledge bestowed by the Spirit is not a quantum of information or doctrine supplemental to what Jesus said or surpassing it (II, pp. 62f.). The Spirit will only "remind" believers what Jesus said (14:26). He will not speak "on his own authority" but will only say what he has "heard"; he will take of what is mine" (16:13f.). He will "bear witness" for Jesus (15:26). It is nothing new that the Spirit will teach, but whatever Jesus taught or did will appear in new light under the Spirit's teaching, and thus for the first time become clear in its true meaning (II, pp. 69f.). Jesus' promise, "What I am doing you do not know now, but later you shall know" (13:7), will be fulfilled. In departing Jesus says, "I have yet many things to say to you, but you cannot bear them now" (16:12). This does not refer to any quantitative incompleteness in Jesus' "teaching," but to the non-terminated character of it which is part of its very essence and meaning. For what teaching could still be lacking if it is true, as Jesus says, "all that I have heard from my Father I have made known to you" (15:15)? Or this: "I have manifested thy 'Name' (=Self) to men . . ." (17:6) and also this: "I have made known to them thy Name (=Self)" (17:26)? Furthermore, this last sentence goes on: ". . . and I *shall* make it known" (tr.). This interplay of tenses indicates that the Revelation brought by Jesus is neither a sum of doctrines nor a terminated occurrence but that it is what it is only by constantly occurring anew. And causing this to happen is exactly what constitutes the activity of the Spirit. As a matter of fact, Jesus brought no "doctrine" capable of being summarized in propositions; his word, we have seen, is he himself (§ 48, 2). But what he is, what his coming and his going mean, what it means to be encountered by him—namely: the "sifting" ($\kappa\rho\iota\sigma\iota\varsigma$) of the world which is the judgment of it—all this one must know with ever greater clarity, and must achieve this knowledge anew in ever Now. The Spirit's "testimony" which "calls to mind" Jesus' words consists in the fact that Jesus' word is constantly being understood anew while it remains the same—indeed, it remains the same because of the very fact that it is constantly new. This is the way in which the Spirit "glorifies" Jesus (16:14).

When in relation to Jesus the Spirit is called the "other Paraclete"

(14:16), he appears to be Jesus' substitute, so to speak, after Jesus' departure. Actually, it is Jesus himself who in the Spirit comes to his own, as is indicated by the correspondence between the promise of the Spirit (14:16f.; 16:12–15) and the promise of Jesus' return (14:18–21; 16:16–24; II, p. 57). Thus it is said of the Spirit, just as it is of Jesus, not only that he will be and abide *with* the believers (14:16f.) but that he will be and abide *in* them (14:17; I Jn. 2:27). As the world did not know Jesus (8:19; 17:26), neither has it any means of knowing the Spirit (14:17), and hence the world does not know the believers either (I Jn. 3:1). And as it was said of Jesus that his word is "heard" only by him who is "of God" or "of the truth" (8:47; 18:37), so the same is said of the Church's word (I Jn. 4:6).

Going back to 15:26 with its declaration that the Paraclete "will bear witness to me," we find its continuation to be: "and you also bear witness" (tr.). That means that the knowledge bestowed by the Spirit is to have its activity in the *proclamation*, in *preaching*. It is in and through it that the Revelation time and again becomes event. That occurs particularly in the "convincing" (16:7–11) which the Spirit does: "he will convince the world of sin and of righteousness and of judgment"—i.e. in its proclaiming the Church is to show the world what "sin" is (namely, sheer disbelief, imperviousness to the Revelation), what "righteousness" is (namely, Jesus' victory in his "suit" with the world), and what "judgment" is (namely, the very situation in which the unbelieving world stands condemned (II, p. 31). That is, the eschatological occurrence which took place in Jesus' coming and going is to continue to take place in preaching. This continuing eschatological occurrence is the Spirit's activity in preaching.

As this occurrence takes place in the Spirit's "convincing," it likewise takes place in the brotherly love which also manifests itself in the fellowship of believers (13:35). For brotherly love, too, is an eschatological phenomenon (II, p. 82). The task, then, which the believers have received, and through which the Church's life in the world makes sense, is this: that it exist as a non-worldly eschatological entity within the world, having been "sent," as Jesus was (17:18), into the world from without. Delimited from the world as the Congregation of the "hallowed" (ἡγιασμένοι, 17:17, 19), a constant offense to the world and hence persecuted by it (15:18–16:4), nevertheless united with the Father and the Son, the Church constantly offers the world the possibility of believing (17:20–23). Since it is

Jesus himself who speaks in the Church's word, wherever it sounds forth it again and again becomes true that ". . . the hour is coming, and now is, when the dead will hear the voice of the Son of God and those who hear will live" (5:25). John indicates that the Church's word must sound forth ever the same yet in ever new form. How it may do so, the Gospel of John itself illustrates by the way in which it both adopts and sovereignly transforms the tradition.

8. All the foregoing (1–7) has more or less implied what needs to be said about the Johannine view of the *Church.* That it has not been treated as a topic by itself up to this point is due to the fact that John himself never takes the concept "Church" for a theme as Paul does. The Church is only indirectly dealt with, and the word ἐκκλησία does not occur at all (except in III Jn. 6 and 9f., where it does not mean "Church" but "a church"). No specifically ecclesiological interest can be detected. There is no interest in cult or organization.* But that does not entitle one to conclude that interest in the Church is completely absent. On the contrary, there is a lively interest in it, as I John in particular and also in their own way II and III John confirm. But John does not speak of the Church in the terminology that comes from the traditional account of the plan of salvation which is common to the Old Testament, Judaism, and the earliest Church. For this tradition, the Church (or Congregation in Jewish tradition)—an eschatological entity—is the People of God at the time of the End, in whom the history of salvation has reached it, completion (§ 10). The terminology typical of this whole cycle of ideas is missing in John (§ 41, 2; II, p. 8). The Johannine terminology pertaining to the Church comes, instead, from the area of Gnostic thought. In it, the "pneumatics" (spiritual men), in whom dwell the pre-existent sparks of light (§ 15, 1 and II, pp. 13f.), constitute a potential unity which becomes reality through the fact that the Redeemer gathers together the scattered sparks of light and unites them with himself. This idea had already influenced the development of the Church-concept in Paul and elsewhere in Hellenistic Christianity (§ 15, 4e). It is at work in John, too. But it is significant that the term "body of Christ" (§ 34, 2), so important in Paul and the deutero-Pauline literature, never occurs in John's writings—and, in fact, that he has no designation in the singular

* In fact, from III Jn. one can deduce a Johannine opposition to the ecclesiastical organization which was then developing.

number for "Church" at all. Those who are bound together in the fellowship of the Church are termed Jesus' "disciples" (e.g. 13:35; 15:8), and his "friends" (15:13ff.), and are also termed, by a specifically Gnostic designation, his "own" (ἴδιοι 13:1, *cf.* 10:3f.). This peculiarity of calling it only by terms in the plural defines the Church as a Church of gathered individuals who become his disciples by their decision of faith (especially 6:60–71).

In a certain sense the Church is conceived in John as the "invisible Church," insofar as they who are "of the truth" belong to it, even though they have not yet heard his voice but are yet to hear it (18:37; *cf.* 10:3). They prove to be "his own" when the call goes out to them and they follow him (10:1–6). That is why a unity of his own in "one flock" is still a thing of the future (10:16; 17:20f.); to work toward it is a duty for those who already are believers (17:18). His own, scattered throughout the world, must be gathered together and led to unity with him (17:21f.). This process, however, has been set going by the coming of the Revealer (as in Gnosticism), and thus the invisible Church is gradually being realized in the visible Church of the disciples.

Negatively, this Church is already recognizable as a unity by the fact that it is delimited from the world, in fact exposed to its hatred (§ 50, 7 and especially 14:17, 19, 27; 15:18–16:11; 17:14, 16; I Jn. 3:1, 13; 4:4f.; 5:4). Positively, it is recognizable by the fact that it is the Church of those whose existence is eschatological, those whose freedom from the world and sin is founded upon their relation to Jesus as the Revealer (§ 50, 1–3 and 4). The unity in which they are bound together is primarily the unity of each individual with him, the "shepherd" (ch. 10), the "tree of life" (ch. 15). It is the unity of faith (§ 50, 6). But as their freedom from the world and from sin includes the imperative, "Keep yourself free!" (§ 50, 3), the fellowship of the believers with him is also their fellowship with each other which is governed by the commandment of love (§ 50, 4). It is not through a discipline of abstention from the world, an ascetic conduct of life, or a sacramental cult that this Church seeks to achieve its eschatological character, for it is the Church of the Word—the Word from which it lives, the Word which is also its commission to the world. Its life is impelled by the living Spirit within it: it is the power which brings forth both knowledge and the proclamation of the Word (§ 50, 7).

PART FOUR

THE DEVELOPMENT TOWARD
THE ANCIENT CHURCH

CHAPTER V

The Rise of Church Order and its Earliest Development

§ 51. Eschatological Congregation and Church Order

1. No human society can have permanence in history without regulations. Hence, it is self-explanatory that regulations gradually developed in the primitive Christian congregations—both for the constitution of the local congregations and for their relation to each other and to the totality of the Church. As the congregations grew and Christianity spread, these regulations were formed, unified, and solidified until the organization of the ancient catholic Church stood created, or, rather, had grown into being.

But is the Ecclesia in the New Testament sense a historical entity —a thing of history at all? Is it not, rather, the eschatological Congregation of those who are divorced from the world (§§ 6; 10, 4; 34)? Then would it not be a falling away from its own nature, if the Ecclesia should nevertheless come to constitute itself as an entity within the world, having, as such an entity, a history in which it works out its regulations? And what if these regulations become regulations of law enforced by compulsion; what if their execution becomes the concern of an office? Will they not then directly contradict the nature of the Ecclesia? For its regulations—if it be permissible to speak of such at all—are created from case to case by the free sway of the Spirit. In the Ecclesia can the leaders' authority have any other foundation than the gracious gift of the Spirit?

These synonymous questions are *the theme of the still unconcluded discussion once held between Rudolf Sohm and Adolf Harnack.* According to Sohm, any such thing as ecclesiastical law stands in contradiction to the nature of Ecclesia; with such a thing a notion (first visible in I Clem.) invades the Church that the authority of Spirit-endowed persons is the authority of office. But that is the sinful fall of the Church; by it she denies her own nature. Harnack endeavors to prove that, on the contrary, from the very beginning there were in primitive Christianity regulations which had the character of law and necessarily developed into full legal regulations, and that such regulations by no means need to contradict the nature of Ecclesia.

2. In order to judge the right and wrong of these mutually contradictory views we must make clear to ourselves *the difference between the Ecclesia as an historical phenomenon and the Ecclesia as the eschatological Congregation guided by the Spirit's sway*, which it understands itself to be. Harnack focuses upon the Ecclesia as historical phenomenon; Sohm understands it from the point of view of its own understanding of itself. As an historical phenomenon, the Ecclesia is subject to the laws to which all historical phenomena are subject, and its history is an object for historical, sociological, psychological consideration. Undoubtedly, as an historical religious society the Ecclesia is constituted by its members who join it by their own free decision (so long, at least, as there is still no such thing as a "folk-church," into which one is born). But the Ecclesia itself understands itself quite differently. That is, it understands itself as the eschatological Congregation of the "called," the "chosen," the "saints" (§ 10, 3), and the believer attributes his membership in it not to his own decision but to the call of God and to the sacrament of baptism, which (in Pauline formulation) incorporates him into the Body of Christ (§ 34, 2 and 3). Undoubtedly, insofar as the eschatological Congregation, which, *as such*, is invisible, is visibly embodied in an historical society, it cannot escape the force of historical laws. Nevertheless, one must certainly inquire whether and to what extent the Ecclesia's self-understanding is itself a factor that has determined its form and history. While Sohm professes to construe the form and earliest history of the Church purely on the basis of its understanding of itself, Harnack loses sight of that self-understanding and understands its form and history from historical and sociological motifs alone.

In point of fact *the Ecclesia's self-understanding was a decisively important factor*. That is most clearly recognizable by the fact that the union of the local congregations into the total Ecclesia, in which union the Christian religion is distinct from the Hellenistic mystery-congregations, was really caused not by the empirical facts and necessities of interchange, mutual help, or an urge toward power—

though such factors may, of course, have been incidentally at work—but rather by just that self-undestanding of the Ecclesia, according to which the total Church takes precedence over the local congregations (§ 10, 1, I, pp. 93ff.), no matter whether the Church-concept is oriented more toward the idea of the People of God or more toward that of the Body of Christ. For that reason the "autonomy" of the local congregations is no contradiction of the idea of the total Church; it cannot be, because in each local congregation the total Church presents itself.

But also *the incipient regulation of the local congregations* is determined by the congregation's understanding of itself as an eschatological community ruled by the Spirit. It is so determined, first, by the fact that out of this self-understanding *the exclusivity of the Christian congregations* results, giving them their special character over against the mystery-congregations (§ 10, 3), and by the fact that this exclusivity at the same time means that *delimitation from the "world"* (§ 10, 4) in which there originates a disciplining of life which will eventually lead to the development of the penance-discipline. It is so determined, secondly, by the fact that the characteristic way in which the church offices arose and took on form was founded upon the congregation's self-understanding. *The chief persons of authority are those endowed with gifts of the Spirit*, beside whom those who act for the external order and welfare of the congregation's life play at first a subordinate role. The character of those having Spirit-gifts is determined by the fact that the eschatological congregation knows itself called into existence by the proclaimed word (§ 8, 4; 34, 1 and 2), and therefore gathers about the word, listening and also speaking (I Cor. 14). The Spirit-endowed, then, are primarily *proclaimers of the word*, and that fact stamps the character of the incipient churchly office from the outset. Even when the sacrament, which stands by the side of the word, receives a greater weight in the self-understanding of the congregation and its leaders take on a priestly character, they nevertheless remain proclaimers of the word also, and the congregation continues to be the listening congregation gathered about the word.

3. In this sense Sohm's conception of the Church as a society constituted not by a code of law but by the sway of the Spirit must be considered valid. He is right, further, in maintaining that the congregation, so understanding itself, needs no law; in fact *that legal regulation contradicts the Church's nature—in case, that is, such law*

ceases to be regulative and becomes constitutive. Sohm's error, however, lies in his failure to recognize that a regulative legal provision not only does not stand in opposition to the Spirit's sway, but may actually be the creation of the Spirit. Quite rightly Karl Holl pointed out in refutation of Sohm that *the word of the Spirit-endowed, being an authoritative word, creates regulation and tradition.* What Paul writes to his congregations as one who claims to "have the Spirit of God" (I Cor. 7:40; *cf.* 14:37 and also 2:10ff.) creates tradition. And the author of the Apocalypse attributes canonical authority to his prophetic book (Rev. 22:18f.). The New Testament would never have been written, or passed on, or canonized as authoritative, if the charismatic word and regulative tradition were contrary to each other.

Sohm one-sidedly pictures the members of the Christian congregations as religious individualists and enthusiasts and one-sidedly conceives *the working of the Spirit* as taking place in inspirations of the moment. What Paul combats as a danger or what he at least restricts (I Cor. 12 and 14), Sohm regards, so to say, as the normal thing. No matter how much momentary inspiration may be characteristic of the word of the Spirit-endowed—*the word which they proclaim* does not derive its content from a revelation personally vouchsafed to them in inward illumination, but instead they proclaim "the word of faith" (Rom. 10:8), the "gospel" at whose center stands Christ and the occurrence of salvation in him: "the word of the cross," "the reconciliation." Richly varied as the form of that word may be—as the New Testament abundantly testifies—it is a definite word mediated by tradition; there never was a "gospel" without "tradition" (παράδοσις—see I Cor. 15:1f.).

The Spirit works, however, not only in the proclaimers of the word, but *also in the congregations.* And here again the Spirit's work manifests itself not only in momentary inspirations, remarkable psychic phenomena, and the capacity to do things that surpass the normal (§ 14, 1), but also in the order-creating activities of individual members, in their various services to the group, which Paul teaches his readers to regard as being spiritual gifts, too (I Cor. 12:5ff., 28; Rom. 12:7f.; see I, pp. 154, 336). The Spirit also works in the congregations in such a way that definite decisions are made and put into action. The Spirit founds in the beginning something like a "*congregational democracy,*" which is very well able to exist side by side with an "aristocracy" consisting of the Spirit-endowed. Of course, one cannot say that there was a democratic constitution as an institutional legal ordinance which guaranteed each individual his rights and assigned him his duties, so it would be better to call it a "pneumatocracy" or, less felicitously, a "Christocracy" (Eduard Schweizer). Nevertheless, such terms are not very clear, for neither pneumatocracy nor Christocracy is a genuine opposite to democracy (nor to aristocracy or monarchy, either). For the real question is just this: in what form will the rule of the Spirit, or of Christ, realize itself in history? At any rate, it is incontestable that the later order (in which congregational officials have superseded the Spirit-endowed, a monarchical episcopate has developed, and the distinction between priests and laymen has arisen) was preceded by an order that must be called democratic. For notwithstanding the authority of the Spirit-endowed—for this is not an authority of office—the congregation takes action as a totality. It not only has itself the charismatic right to "test" the charismatics (=the Spirit-endowed; see I Thess. 5:21; I Cor. 12:10, 14:29; Did. 11:7–12; Herm. mand. XI) but also sends out missionaries (Acts 13:2) or delegates (I Cor. 16:3; II Cor. 8:19, Acts 15:2, probably also Ign. Philad. 10:1; Sm. 11:2; Pol. 7:2). It holds sessions, sometimes court-sessions (I Cor. 4:3, 5:3f.) in which majority decisions may be reached (II Cor. 2:6). In Acts 6:2, 5, 15:22, 30 we evidently have a reflection of a practice by which recommendations or proposals offered by the leaders of the congregation are voted into force by the whole congregation. In I Clem. 54:2 the recalcitrant one is exhorted to do "that which is ordered by the congregation." Even when in the course of time installation of congregational officials arises, the congregation is evidently also active in the process, for in all probability it is from the congregation that the prophet-voices arise which point out the persons to be installed (I Tim. 1:18, 4:14; *cf.* Acts 20:28). At any rate, I Clem. 44:3 explicitly says that presbyters were appointed in the congregations by the successors of the apostles "with the approval of the whole congregation." And Did. 15:1 in harmony with this commands: "therefore appoint for yourselves bishops and deacons."

Hence, it is not justified to place the inception and development of church order and church office in such opposition to the sway of the Spirit as Sohm does. Intelligent conduct which arises from a recognition of what the situation demands does not exclude the possibility that the Spirit is working in such conduct. It is no less true that the services performed through the Spirit in and for the congregation do not contradict the nature of the Spirit simply because of being connected with an office. Such a conclusion would be necessary only if the Spirit's sway were regarded as restricted to the phenomena of an individualistic Spirit-possession. Early Christianity was spared from such a narrow view of the Spirit by the influence of Pauline and Johannine theology and, secondarily, by that of the synogogal tradition—or that of the Old Testament and Judaism.

The development about to be described, therefore, is viewed from the point of view of this critical question: were the incipient regulations appropriate to the nature of the Ecclesia as an eschatological congregation constituted by the word of proclamation?—or, to what extent were they appropriate, and how appropriate did they continue to be? This question includes the further question: did this budding ecclesiastical law have regulative character or constitutive, and did it retain its original character? But the rise of ecclesiastical law itself is regarded from the point of view of two questions: 1. From what time, and how, is the observance of regulations guaranteed by penalties? For as soon as that occurs, the regulations take on the character of legal regulations. 2. What are the sources of authority that establish regulations and watch over their observance? Are they the congregations—either each congregation, or the totality of all the congregations—or are they individuals either empowered by the congregation or authorized by some other kinds of power? If the authority behind the regulations is represented by individuals, then the ecclesiastical office arises.

§ 52. The Ecclesiastical Offices

1. Neither in the earliest Palestinian Congregation nor in earliest Hellenistic Christianity was there originally any thought of instituting church regulations or offices—which is just what one would expect in view of their eschatological consciousness of standing at the end of time. The consequence even of this single fact was that the earliest Church in Palestine at first remained within the regulations of the Jewish Congregation and had no intention to constitute itself a new religious community (§ 8, 1). Although baptism and the Lord's Supper already delimited the Palestinian Congregation from Judaism and later delimited the Hellenistic Church from heathen cults, still

neither in the Palestinian Church nor originally in the Hellenistic Church was there a priestly class. As late as I Pet. (*cf.* 2:5, 9) the Congregation is "a holy priesthood," "a royal priesthood"; i.e. all Christians have priestly quality. But to the extent that both branches of the Church had need of some sort of order and guidance, such was given by persons of authority who were still far from being officials. In the Palestinian Congregation these were Peter, John, and James, the Lord's brother (§ 8, 4); in the Hellenistic congregations they were, quite naturally, the "apostles" who had founded these congregations. Since the apostles are not resident in a particular congregation, we find in addition to them other proclaimers of the word: "prophets" and "teachers." Neither are these men officials. Rather, they are persons called individually by the Spirit, no matter whether they were settled in one congregation or whether like the apostles they wandered from place to place.

But presently there appears *in the early Congregation of Palestine the office of the "elders"* (§ 8, 4). There was little need to feel a conflict between this office and the persons of authority, because one of the latter, James, was in all likelihood also chairman of the board of elders. A council of "elders," as a matter of fact, is an institution in which respect for personal authority is united with the authority of office; such a council was an excellent means of enhancing the authority of leading persons. The formation of a board of elders, furthermore, could scarcely seem to the Christian Congregation to be anything out of the ordinary, because therein it was only following the pattern of the synagogue congregations.* The earliest Church at first took the form of a synagogue within Judaism, as is well known.

As for *the Christian congregations in the Hellenistic world*, which had developed out of synagogue-congregations or had attached themselves to such, much the same thing holds true. Here, too, "elders" led the congregations. This is clear from the fact that in the very sources where the adoption of synagogal tradition is evident (not in the Didache, however), *presbyteroi* (elders) appear as congregational leaders; it is so in Acts, James, I Clem., Hermas, and II Clem. (17:3–5). For the early period at least we may assume that the title denoted both office and age; it clearly does in I Pet. 5:1–5. In the

---

* See Schürer, *A History of the Jewish People in the Time of Jesus Christ*, II, part I, pp. 149ff.; Strack-B.IV 145; Joachim Jeremias, *Jerusalem zur Zeit Jesu*, II B (1937), 88ff.

partially or totally Gentile congregations the leaders bear the title *episkopos*, which is known to us in pagan Greek usage as the title of certain municipal officials and also of officers of associations and cultic societies.* Christian *episkopoi* appear for the first time at Phil. 1:1, and there *diakonoi* are named with them—a title which is likewise known to us as one used for municipal officials and for officers of associations.† It can be inferred from the Christian use of these terms that the activities which at first were voluntarily assumed by individuals on the basis of their personal authority gradually became the functions of formal officials. In place of the early informal designations "those who labor among you" ($\kappa o\pi\iota\hat{\omega}\nu\tau\epsilon\varsigma$, I Thess. 5:12), "fellow workers" ($\sigma\nu\nu\epsilon\rho\gamma o\hat{\nu}\nu\tau\epsilon\varsigma$, I Cor. 16:16 and elsewhere), your "leaders" (or "chairmen" Heb. 13:7) there now appear the more formal ones, "elders" or "episkopoi" (and *diakonoi*, "assistants"); yet, in addition to these, more general designations continue to be used, such as $\dot{\eta}\gamma o\acute{\nu}\mu\epsilon\nu o\iota$ or $\pi\rho o\eta\gamma o\acute{\nu}\mu\epsilon\nu o\iota$ ("leaders," I Clem. 1:3, 21:6; Herm. vis. III 9:7). The difference between presbyters and *episkopoi* is probably just a difference of terminology. Both titles alike evidently mean the leaders of the congregation—though it must be left open what powers and duties, and how many of them, were apportioned to the leaders in the one case and the other. It is probably a result of intercommunication between the congregations that here and there both titles were used side by side for the same persons, as in I Clem. and Hermas (*cf.* also Acts 20:17 with 20:28, where "guardians" translates *episkopoi* in RSV). This is particularly clear in the pastoral epistles. To their author the familiar title is evidently presbyter, elder. (I Tim. 4:14, 5:17, 19; especially Tit. 1:5). But when he specifies the qualifications for this office he takes over an already formulated tradition in which the qualifications for the office of *episkopos* were enumerated—and retains the latter title without changing it (I Tim. 3:2, Titus. 1:7). Probably a distinction in meaning between these two titles develops only when the monarchical episcopate arises. Then the *episkopos* is the chairman of the board of elders, a situation for which Ignatius is the earliest witness.‡

---

* See M. Dibelius on Phil. 1:1 in Lietzmann's *Handbuch*; H. W. Beyer in *ThWB* II, 908ff.

† See Dibelius in the preceding note, *op cit.*, same page.

‡ See M. Dibelius on Herm. sim. IX 27:3 in the supplement volume of Lietzmann's *Handbuch*; also W. Bauer on Ign. Mg. 2:2 in the same volume.

Within the framework of a theology of the New Testament it is not necessary to trace this development in detail, even so far as the paucity of sources grants us insight into it. In various regions it took place in varying ways and with varying speed. But the important thing is to clarify the character of this incipient office.

2. First, we must clarify *the distinction between the congregational officials and the "charismatics,"* who also play a leading role in the young congregations. This distinction has become common since the discovery of the Didache (1883) and Harnack's evaluation of it. It means that the congregational offices possess administrative and jurisdictional functions for each particular congregation, but that the elders and *episkopoi* are not proclaimers of the word—at least not by virtue of their office. Rather, it is the *apostles, prophets, teachers,* whom I Cor. 12:28 places at the head of the list of the "charismatics," who are *the proclaimers of the word.** These are in no sense officials of a specific congregation, but have their calling, or rather their "call," for the whole Church. Theirs is not an official activity, as we clearly see in the case of the apostles: they were called by the Lord and are not in charge of an office which must be filled again after their death. But the same is true of the prophets and teachers. They are called by the gift of the Spirit, and at first, at least, any member of the congregation may become the recipient of the gift ($\chi\acute{a}\rho\iota\sigma\mu\alpha$) of the Spirit. Neither is their commission restricted to that congregation to which they belong. As the Didache and Hermas show, they like the apostles may also travel as wandering preachers from congregation to congregation, especially after the apostles, along with the rest of the first generation, have died out.

In order to indicate this distinction there are those who term the "office" of the apostles, prophets, teachers, a "charismatic office" in contrast to the institutional office of the elders or episkopoi. But it would be better to avoid the term "office" for the proclaimers of the word. At any rate, one should not talk of a "double organization" (one for the specific congregation and one for the Church as a whole), for the work of the apostles, prophets, and teachers cannot be termed an organization. But it is correct to say that the activity of the elders and episkopoi is restricted to their specific congregation, while by

---

* Apostles and prophets, Acts 18:20, Did. 11; prophets and teachers, Acts 13:1, Did. 13:1f.; apostles and teachers, Herm. sim. IX 15:4, 16:5, 25:2; while in Herm. vis. III 5:1 apostles, bishops, teachers, and deacons are combined.

the person and the work of the apostles, prophets, and teachers the Ecclesia is represented as the *one* Church. But this oneness is at first not an organizational but a charismatic unity wrought by the Spirit.

In the fact that the activity of proclaiming the word, which we have seen really constitutes the Church (§ 8, 4; § 34, 1 and 2), is not at first tied to an office, we have solid evidence that *the Church at first knows no office or law by which it is constituted as the Church.* What there is of office and law—the institution of congregational officers (presbyters and episkopoi)—does not constitute the Church, but regulates the practical side of congregational life. Now, according to Paul's view the tasks and activities within the compass of congregational life (the "varieties of service," the "helps" and "administrations" I Cor. 12:5, 28 tr.) are also gifts of the Spirit. To that extent it may be justified to term the offices of "presbyter" and "episkopos" charismatic, but in so doing one must be aware that although this corresponds to Paul's specific understanding of the matter, it nevertheless does not agree with the oldest usage of Hellenistic Christianity (§ 14, 1, I, p. 154). This general Hellenistic usage agrees with the usual philologically established usage, according to which being empowered and commissioned by a *charisma* (supernatural gift) is in sharp contrast with natural endowment and legal commission. The charismatic (or "pneumatic") man, then, is the inspired man endowed with miraculous power.

Charisma (considered always as the miraculous gift bestowed by the Spirit) was capable of being regarded in three different ways: 1. as the power which manifests itself as the momentary, or violent, or extraordinary event (such as glossolalia or ecstasy) which occurs in specific miraculous phenomena; here a man's *charisma* is the particular miraculous deed accomplished through him. 2. As the power with which certain individuals ($\pi\nu\epsilon\nu\mu\alpha\tau\iota\kappa o\iota$) are endowed. 3. As the manifestation of that which is miraculous in respect of its significance ($o\grave{\iota}\kappa o\delta o\mu\acute{\eta}$, edification). With the coalescing of the second and third viewpoints there arises the ecclesiastical conception of the *charisma* of office.

3. The *course of development* now is a double one. On the one hand, the charismatics, so far as they are proclaimers of the word, more and more become officials; that is, their *charisma*, which was originally given to the person, is now understood as an office-*charisma* conveyed by ordination (I Tim. 4:14, II Tim. 1:6). On the

ɔther hand, the proclaiming of the word is transferred as a right or duty of office to the officials (elders or episkopoi) of the congregation ʻpastoral letters, Did., Herm.).

At the head of the charismatics stands the apostle. At first he was the proclaimer of the word called by the Lord or the Spirit (Rom. 10:14ff.; Mt. 28:18ff.; Lk. 24:46ff.; Acts 1:8, 13:2 and elsewhere), the missionary to the Jewish and to the Gentile world. He can be called ʻ"herald" (κῆρυξ), as his preaching can be called *kerygma* (herald-service, proclamation); see Rom. 10:8ff.; I Cor. 1:23, 9:27; I Tim. 2:7; II Tim. 1:11 and elsewhere). His designation as "sent man," ʻ"messenger" (שָׁלִיחַ, ἀπόστολος), was probably taken over from the Jewish institution of שְׁלִיחִים (messengers) of the Sanhedrin. But whereas the office of the Jewish שָׁלִיחַ expires with the performance of his errand, the Christian apostle remains what he became by his call. As the unmodified use of the word "apostle" indicates, his commission cannot expire. The apostle proclaims the risen Lord. Indeed, in the apostle, as the representative of Christ, the Lord himself encounters men. Not only Paul so formulates it (II Cor. 5:20), it is also expressed in the saying of Jesus at Mt. 10:40; Lk. 10:16; Jn. 13:20. Thus the concept of the apostle as the proclaimer sent out by the risen Lord is primarily determined by the *idea* of *authorization*; his word is the word legitimated by the Lord. In addition to this, *the idea of tradition* gradually achieves preponderance, an idea which, of course, was not absent at the beginning (I Cor. 15:3, 14f.). The "testimony" (μαρτύριον), which at first meant primarily an appeal as if by oath (I Thess. 2:12: "we *charged* you"), takes on more and more the meaning of "attestation," i.e. attestation of the facts experienced by the apostles as eye-witnesses, especially to the resurrection of Christ (Acts 1:22, 2:32, 3:15, etc.). The resultant narrowing down of the title "apostle," which originally was accorded to all missionaries, to include only the twelve (Paul is the only exception to this restriction) is clear evidence that the apostles were regarded as the guarantors of the Church's tradition. According to Eph. 2:20 the Church is built upon the foundation of the apostles and prophets; and the latter belong with the former as recipients of revelation (3:5). Christ established both, along with the evangelists, pastors, and teachers, as the authorized bearers of the tradition (4:11; *cf.* Herm. sim. IX 25:2). The apostles, of course, begin the list; their names, according to Rev. 21:14, are inscribed on the twelve foundation stones of the New Jerusalem's walls (see, further, § 55, 5). Especially significant is the legend of the election of a substitute for Judas Iscariot to the college of the twelve (Acts 1:21–26). Also indicative, probably, is the distinction made between apostle and evangelist (Eph. 4:11; *cf.* II Tim. 4:5; Acts 21:8); the latter title fell to missionaries as soon as the title "apostle" was reserved for the twelve. (It was not able to establish and maintain itself as a common title because the congregational officials gradually took over the function of proclaiming the word.) Since the apostles are regarded primarily as guarantors and mediators of the tradition, the Church's "deposit-in-trust" ($\pi\alpha\rho\alpha\theta\acute{\eta}\kappa\eta$ I Tim. 6:20; II Tim. 1:12, 14 tr.), they come to be regarded in the same light as were the congregational officials, upon whom, next after the apostles, the responsibility for preserving the tradition rests. Hence, the notion can now arise that the apostles must have successors (pastoral epistles, Acts 14:23; I Clem. 44:2; see immediately below). The conception of apostleship as an office could find support in sayings which grant the apostle the right to support by the congregations (I Cor. 9:17–18; II Cor. 11:7–12; Lk. 10:7; for "teachers," Gal. 6:6) or also in the fact that the claim to be called an apostle was conditioned by the fulfilment of certain qualifications (I Cor. 9:1f.; II Cor. 3:2f.; 12:12).

Now comes a further development. The *apostolate* comes more and more to be seen from the standpoint of the organization of the whole Church and to be conceived as an office which, unlike that of the bishops and elders, pertains to the whole Church. This finds expression in the fact that the organizing of the individual congregations is attributed to the apostles. And this is not incorrect insofar as the apostles, as Paul's letters show, not only founded the congregations but thereupon claimed the right—though not a legal one—to guide them with advice and exhortation by letters and visits. In so doing they not only concerned themselves with right understanding of the faith and combatted heresy, but also worked for proper order (*cf.* I Cor. 4:15; 9:1f.; II Cor. 3:1–3; 10:13–16; Gal. 4:17–20; and compare the restraint that Paul exercises toward the congregation at Rome). But it is something new when *the appointment of elders and episkopoi is traced back to the apostles*. This is already done in Acts 14:23, and again in the pastoral epistles.

It is done indirectly in Tit. 1:5 by the order of the pretended apostle to the recipient that he appoint elders in every city. What "Titus," who is to act in the apostle's place, is considered to be, may probably be inferred from II Tim. 4:5: an evangelist. That is, he is practically an apostle himself except that after the reservation of the title "apostle" to the twelve and Paul (see II, p. 105), he can no longer receive that title. However that may be, the author of the pastorals does not venture to ascribe direct apostolic appointment to the elders and "bishops" who in his time are functioning as congregational officials, but injects Timothy and Titus, pupils of the apostle, as an intermediate link. It amounts to the same thing whether the author says the charisma of office was conferred upon "Timothy" by the laying on of the apostle's hands (II Tim. 1:6) or whether he says that it was mediated by the laying on of the hands of the presbytery (I Tim. 4:14), which was itself guided by "prophecy" (I Tim. 1:18, 4:14). Evidently the latter corresponded to the practice of the author's own time.

This view is fully developed in I Clem. Jesus Christ, commissioned by God, on his part commissioned the apostles (42:1f.). They then spread the proclamation through lands and cities and everywhere appointed bishops and deacons (42:4; 44:2) and authorized them to arrange for their own successors (44:2)—for which Scripture proof from the Old Testament is then provided (43). Here, then, the congregational office as obligatory for all congregations is traced back to the apostles; the latter, that is, appear as the organizers of the whole Church.

The decisive step has then been taken: henceforth the office is regarded as *constitutive of the Church.* The whole Church rests upon the office-bearers, whose office is held to go back in uninterrupted succession to the apostles (=the twelve). The tradition of the proclamation, and the succession which guarantees its continuity, are no longer left, as they originally were, to the sway of the Spirit (I, pp. 60f.) but are institutionally safe-guarded. The Spirit is henceforth bound to the office and is transmitted by a sacramental act, ordination by the laying on of hands (Acts 6:6; 13:3; I Tim. 4:14; II Tim. 1:6 perhaps also I Tim. 5:22). For a while the freely acting Spirit is still at work in this process. We see this in the fact that prophet-voices from the congregation precede the act of the laying on of hands (Acts 13:2; I Tim. 1:18; 4:14). We also see it in the further fact— which may amount to the same thing—that the predecessor does not simply name his successor, but that the congregation gives it approval (I Clem. 44:3).

In the case of ordination it is probable that synagogal tradition was influential. But more important is the insight that this develop ment is understandable from the fact that *the proclamation of the word became the affair of the congregational officials.* For this, Did 15:1f. is clear evidence. There it is explicitly said that the bishop and deacons perform the service of the prophets and teachers and are to be honored as these are. Such a situation had to come because the original apostolate gradually died out, also because the wandering prophets (and teachers) gradually became suspect (Did. 11, Herm mand. XI), and, above all, because the danger of "heresy" became acute. This is already evident in "Paul's" speech to the elders of Ephesus, in which they are exhorted above all to protect the con gregation from perverse teachers (Acts 20:28–30). The same is evident in the pastorals. The qualities demanded in them for elder or "bishops" pertain not only to their administrative tasks (such as "sensible," "hospitable," "no lover of money," etc., I Tim. 3:2ff. Tit. 1:6ff.) but also to their activity as teachers ("an apt teacher," I Tim. 3:2; II Tim. 2:24; Tit. 1:9: "he must hold firm to the sure word as taught, so that he may be able to give instruction in sound doctrine and also to confute those who contradict it"; *cf.* II Tim. 2:24–26). Keeping watch over right doctrine and doing battle against false doctrine are particularly urged as duties upon Timothy and Titus (I Tim. 1:3; 4:6f., 11ff.; 6:3, 20; II Tim. 2:14ff.; 3:1ff.; 4:1ff.; Tit 1:10ff.; 2:1ff., 15; 3:8ff.). Indeed, the charisma of office seems to manifest itself most particularly in their teaching activity, since after the exhortation "attend to the public reading of scripture, to preach ing, to teaching" is added: "Do not neglect the gift you have" (I Tim. 4:13f.). In Hermas, though the duties connected with organization and charity are in the foreground, nevertheless the congregational officials are named in vis. III 5:1 in such close connection with the apostles and teachers that one must conclude that like the latter they, too, are proclaimers of the word, especially since for Hermas the apostles belong to a bygone time. Similarly, according to II Clem. 17:3–5 the elders are those who "put minds right" and "proclaim concerning salvation."

4. But in the formation of the congregational office still a further element comes in: namely, that the *bishops* become *the leaders of the*

cramental cultus. This is all the more important the more the
*s*crament comes to be regarded, along with the word or even instead
f the word, as the factor which is constitutive for the Church.

Of this, there is still nothing to be seen in the New Testament.
We may assume that the direction of the congregational worship
service and hence also the administering of the sacraments,
except where everything was left to the sway of the Spirit in the
charismatics, was in the hands of those who had a personal
authority—"those who labor among you and are over you"
(I Thess. 5:12, I Cor. 16:16, Rom. 12:8, etc.)—so far as there
was any ordering direction in worship and the administration of
the sacrament. For I Cor. 11:17ff., 12, and 14 show that at least
at Corinth in Paul's time there was no such direction. Paul
directs that "all things be done decently and in order" (I Cor.
14:40; *cf.* I Clem. 40:2). But if his admonition was to be carried
out, it was soon necessary to designate persons to be responsible
for it, just as in the mysteries of Andonia it was the business
of the ῥαβδοῦχοι (staff-bearers) to see to it "that all things be
done decently and in good order by those who are present"
(Inscriptiones Graecae V 1, 1390 § 10). In the Christian congregations it was just this which became the concern of the *episkopoi.*
The Didache evidently testifies to this when directly after the
ordinance for the Lord's Day it says, "Therefore" (οὖν) choose
for yourselves bishops and deacons. . . ." (15:1). Since it is said that
these perform for the congregation the service of prophets and
teachers, then evidently prophets and teachers—charismatics,
that is—had at first been the leading persons in the celebrations
of worship; so the prophets were explicitly permitted to say as
many prayers of thanksgiving in addition to the liturgical
prayers as they wished (10:6). Since I Clem. 44:7 terms the elders
(or "bishops") "those who offer gifts," they are evidently the
leaders of the celebration of the Eucharist. With some degree of
probability it can be deduced that according to Hermas likewise
the leadership of the sacramental cultus fell to the lot of the
"bishops." At any rate, in Ignatius it is clear that the "bishop"
(here already the monarchical bishop) is the administrator of the
sacrament of the Lord's Supper (Eph. 5:1f., Mg. 7:1, Tr. 2:2,
7:2, Philad. 4f., 7:2). In Justin (Apol. I 65:3, 67), finally, the
congregational leader (προεστώς) clearly stands forth as the
leader of the congregational worship and of the cultic celebration.

This fact takes on special importance as soon as the cultus is no

longer conceived as the self-presentation or the appearing of th
eschatological Congregation, which in worship is filled with th
powers of the Spirit as the firstfruit of coming salvation (Rom. 8:23
cf. Heb. 6:4f.), but, having as its focus not the word but the sacramen
of the Lord's Supper, is conceived as an institution of salvation whicl
mediates the "medicine of immortality" (Ign. Eph. 20:2; see § 13, 3
I, pp. 150ff.). Then eschatological consciousness is over-shadowec
or supplanted by sacramentalism, and *the bishop* who leads wor
ship and administers the sacrament *becomes the priest*, whos
office gives him a quality which separates him from the rest of th
congregation, making them laymen. This is all the more the cas
when the sacrament is conceived as a sacrifice. Such a conception is
prefigured in the language in which the Didache and Ignatius describ
worship, is further prepared for in I Clem., and then actually exists
in Justin Martyr; for to him the Eucharist is a sacrifice (§ 13, 2, I
pp. 149f.).

Something decisive has occurred here. The order which regulates
the cultus is now regarded as that which guarantees its efficacy.
Thereby the persons who carry out the cultus achieve priestly
character, and the distinction between priests and laymen, unknown
to the New Testament and, indeed, contradictory to it, develops. The
position that the leader of the cultus cannot be deposed (I Clem.) is
not in itself a symptom for the rise of a divine ecclesiastical law, but
its resting upon the priestly ordinances of the Old Testament is
(I Clem. 43).

In view of the special character of the Christian Congregation,
this has a far-reaching consequence. It brings it about that *the regula-*
tions of the Church all together become ordinances of divine law and
make the Church into an institution of salvation. For in all cults,
even pagan ones (the mystery-cults, for example), cultic ordinances
are, of course, conceived as those of holy law. But in the Christian
Church that has other special consequences. The Church as an
eschatological entity is lifted out of the profane regulations of the
world, and hence, for the members of the Church, religion is not an
isolated territory of their secular life which in other respects is geared
into the regulations of the world. Rather, their life is completely
determined by the fact that they belong to the Church. The Church's
claim is a total claim, and it leaves no secular areas of life that could
be subject to the claim of worldly law. While for Paul it was a

misconception of the Church's eschatological character for a Christian to seek his rights from a worldly court, now what is true of the cultic ordinance is transferred to all the ordinances of life. They all participate in the sacral character of the cultic ordinance.

Of course, so long as primitive Christianity lives in the expectation of the imminent end of the world, it has no interest in regulating the orders of profane life, but takes these as they are (I Cor. 7:14–24), and leaves the control of them to the state (Rom. 13:1–7). But in the course of time the more development there is toward the formation of Christian regulations for living, the more the territory of divine law will expand outward from its center in the cultic ordinance. This tendency takes on concrete form by the fact that the Old Testament is taken over by the Church; hence, its legal regulations—since the ordinances of divine law cannot change—are regarded as authoritative. Naturally, these can only become pertinent for specific questions, such as that of matrimonial law. This development lies beyond the period of primitive Christianity and need not here be further pursued. It suffices to have pointed out the origin of the development.

We need further to consider only (1) that the execution of a regulation of life by legal ordinance requires the establishment of penalties (it will be shown in § 61 that the establishment of such penalties is already beginning in early Christianity) and (2) that ecclesiastical legal ordinances, because they require the power of compulsion, can really receive validity only by delegation of power from the state. But when the Church now conceives itself as the original source of legal authority, it necessarily comes into competition with the state and in the end has to develop the theory that it is the Church which delegates the state to exercise the power of compulsion.

§ 53. The Transformation of the Church's Understanding of Itself

This development, the outcome of which lies beyond the boundary of the New Testament, though it is presaged within it, is ultimately *a transformation in the Church's understanding of itself.* Originally the Church conceives itself as the eschatological people of God, the Congregation of the saints, those who are called out of the world and divorced from it. The Church senses this transcendent character of itself by the gifts of the Spirit which are at work in it. But the Spirit is the earnest-money or the pledge of the coming glory, the eschato logical fulfilment (I, p. 155). Hence, the Church lives in hope of th fulfilment and documents its transcendent character in its exclusiv ness and by the conduct of its members as "strangers" in the worl (§ 10, 3 and 4).

While the consciousness of being a non-worldly society belongin to the other world and filled with its powers does not actually ge lost, it nevertheless suffers a peculiar transformation. In consequenc of the delay of the expected parousia *the transcendent character of th Church* gradually comes to be seen not so much in its reference t the future as *in its present possession of institutions* which are alread mediating transcendent powers in the present: a sacramental cultu and finally a priestly office.

Of course, *that reference to the future* does not get lost, but it, too becomes peculiarly modified. The future salvation toward whic hope is directed comes to be seen less in the completion of the histor of salvation and the transformation of the world at the dawn of th new age (as in Rom. 9–11 and 8:19–22) than in the future life of th individual beyond death. Certainly the traditional picture of the end drama continues to be passed on, and at certain times and situation may take on living power as in Rev. and I Pet. Still, the most im portant thing in the picture of the future is the expectation of th resurrection of the dead and the last judgment (I, pp. 74–77); i.e interest is concentrated upon that which is decisive for the individual It is just this interest which at an early time finds solid formulatio in the statement about Christ as judge of the quick and the dead (I, p. 78)—the only item in the second article of the Apostle's Cree which deals with the eschatological future. And, correspondingly, the third article of the Creed speaks of a hope only for the resurrection of the flesh and life eternal.

Correspondingly, *the meaning of the sacraments* comes to be seen in the fact that they mediate the powers of the future life to the individual. The effect of baptism is the overcoming of death and the acquisition of eternal life (I, pp. 140–142; see further Herm. vis. III 3:5: "Your life was and will be saved by water"). The Lord's Supper becomes the "medicine of immortality" (I, pp. 147f.).

In Hellenistic Christianity this development is implicit from the outset, as the practice of vicarious baptism indicates for the con ception of baptism (I Cor. 15:29). The reason it is implicit is that in ddition to the conception of the Church as the People of God, the rue Israel (I, p. 97), there came the interpretation of the Church as he sacramental unity of the "body of Christ" (I, pp. 178f.). Paul, t is true, knew how to unify the idea of the body of Christ with the lea of the Israel of God, since for him the body of Christ is precisely he eschatological Congregation (I, pp. 311f.) and the realm of Christ I, p. 312). For him the eschatological future realizes itself in the way he baptized leads his life (I, pp. 312f.) and in the fellowship of life nto which baptism unites believers (I Cor. 12:12–27; for the Lord's upper, see I Cor. 10:17). Nor was his understanding of baptism urrendered in the school that followed him (Col. 3:1–17; Eph. 4:1–5, 1; Tit. 2:11–14). But the more the Christian's new way of life comes o be understood not as the demonstration of the new (eschatological) xistence but as the condition for achieving future salvation (the atter especially in Hebrews; see 2:1–4; 10:19–31; 12:25–29 and see § 58, 59), the more this reference to the future loses the meaning it ad had in Paul; the dialectic relation between indicative and mperative (I, p. 332) is surrendered. Then the effect of baptism is imited to forgiveness of the sins committed in one's pre-Christian period, and the problem of sins committed after baptism arises §§ 58 and 59).

In John the idea of the eschatological People of God plays no ole, and the term "Ecclesia" is missing (II, pp. 8, 91). And though or him the individual's salvation, his "life," is in the foreground, still he retained the idea of the unity of believers (§ 50, 8)—and did so even though he gave up founding it upon the sacrament (§ 47, 4). Along with the history-of-salvation perspective John also lacks the traditional Jewish-Christian eschatology (§ 45),* but not the believer's relation to the future. Like Paul, John understands the believer's existence as eschatological existence (§ 50, especially II, pp. 79 f.). However, the Gospel and Epistles of John did not at first influence the development of theology.

But when this Pauline-Johannine dialectic is missing and the knowledge is lost that the future so qualifies the present that believers already exist eschatologically now, understanding for the paradoxical quality of the Christian situation (I, pp. 95f.) gradually disappears,

* Ecclesiastical revision, however, endeavored to inject the traditional eschatology into the Gospel and the Epistles of John by means of certain glosses; see II, p. 39 and 85 footnote).

[113]

and the Church has changed from a fellowship of salvation to ar institution of salvation, even when, and particularly when, it holds fast to the traditional eschatological conceptions. Its transcendence is understood no longer as pure reference to the future, but primarily as a sacramental quality. The Spirit is no longer the power that now and again breaks out in the "gifts"—the words and deeds and conduct of the believers—but is a power immanent in the institutions, particularly in the sacramental cult; it is the office-bearers' equipment for office. The officers have taken on the quality of priests, while it is only through their mediation that the Spirit is indirectly at work in the laymen.

2. But there is still another way in which this reference to the future is modified: the eschatological tension relaxes. The expectation of eschatological fulfilment is not simply given up, but the fulfilment of the hope is pushed forward into *a time that lies in the indeterminate distance.*

II Pet. 3:1–10 shows by its polemic against doubt of the coming of the promised parousia that there were even groups in which the glow of the expectation had gone out or was threatening to do so. The same doubt is combatted in I Clem. 23:3–5 and II Clem. 11 and 12. The exhortations to wait patiently likewise show that hope was in danger of exhausting itself: Jas. 5:7–11, Heb. 10:36, II Clem. 12:1, Herm. vis. III 8:9. The same thing is indicated by the exhortations to be awake and watching in such later synoptic passages as Mt. 13:33–37, Lk. 12:35–38, Mt. 24:43–51 and, outside the synoptics, Rev. 3:3, 16:15, Did. 16, and the exhortations of Hermas not to let the remaining interval before the impending end go by without repenting—for example, sim. X 4:4.

Admittedly, this was not a smooth and everywhere identical development. In times of peril and persecution the consciousness that the end is breaking in can vividly and passionately flare up, as in Rev. and I Pet. Again and again voices arise, crying: "The end of all things is at hand" (I Pet. 4:7), "Near is the day" (Barn. 21:3; *cf.* 4:3, 9), "the last times" (Ign. Eph. 11:1; *cf.* also Heb. 1:1; 9:26, Herm. sim. IX 12:3 and the eucharistic prayers of Did. 9f.). But at the same time the pastoral epistles and Acts show that to a large extent Christians are preparing for a rather long duration of this world and that the Christian faith, losing its eschatological tension, is becoming a Christian-bourgeois piety.

As a matter of course the preaching of the coming judgment belongs to the Christian proclamation for the author of Acts (17:30f.), to whom the "last days" of Joel 3 have become present reality in the pouring out of the Spirit (2:16f.). While Christ tarries in heaven Christians await "times of refreshing" (3:19), "times of restitution of all things" (3:21 KJ). Though it is first said that the predictions of the Old Testament apply to this "restitution," nevertheless the goal of the prediction is then regarded to be the historical coming of Jesus (v. 22). How different it is in I Pet. 1:1–12: Here the goal of prediction is "the sufferings of Christ and the subsequent glory" (the glorification of the risen Lord), and the intention of the reference to prophecy is not as in Acts 3:26 to make a moral appeal but to fortify the hope of the eschatological fulfilment. While Acts 3:20f. without any tone of impatient expectation says, "that times of refreshing may come. . . . and he (God) may send the Christ, Jesus, whom heaven must receive until the time of restitution," according to I Pet. 1:5 believers "are guarded through faith for a salvation ready to be revealed in the last time" and they rejoice in having "now for a little while to suffer various trials" (v. 6). Indeed, it is already characteristic that at the beginning of Acts impatient hope is corrected when the risen Jesus not only answers the question, "Will you at this time restore the kingdom of Israel?" by saying that the time for this is hidden from men, but also announces that the Christian mission must first be carried "to the end of the earth" (1:6–8).

By the pastorals, also, it is taken for granted that the life of believers is a life in hope (I Tim. 1:1, Tit. 1:2, 2:13, 3:7). They await "the appearing of the glory of our great God and Savior Jesus Christ" (Tit. 2:13, I Tim. 6:14, II Tim. 4:1), they hope for "life eternal" (I Tim. 1:16, 4:8, 6:12, 19), for "salvation" (I Tim. 2:15, 4:16, II Tim. 2:10), and fear the judgment (I Tim. 5:24, II Tim. 4:1; *cf.* I Tim. 6:9). But the historical coming of Jesus can also be called the "appearing" (ἐπιφάνεια) of Christ; already he has destroyed death through the Gospel and brought life and incorruption to light (II Tim. 1:10); already the promised "life" is present reality in the fact that the proclamation is present (Tit. 1:2f.); already God has "saved" us (II Tim. 1:9), having done so by means of baptism (Tit. 3:5). This, it is true, is thinking in the line of Paul's thought, to which the eschatological event takes place in the proclamation (§ 34, 1), but Paul's understanding of the eschatological character of the present has greatly paled (see below, § 58, 3m) and there is no longer a trace either of the tension between the present and the future or of longing for the fulfilment. Righteousness is no longer the eschatologically present essence of salvation but is now—side by side with εὐσέβεια ("religion, piety")—moral uprightness (I Tim. 6:11, II Tim. 2:22, 3:16). Similarly the "last days," in which false messiahs and false prophets according to apocalyptic prediction will appear (Mk. 13:21f. par.) are interpreted to be the present time with the false teachers that are appearing in it (I Tim. 4:1, II Tim. 3:1), much as in I Jn. 2:18. That the world is calculated to last for a considerable time yet is indicated by the prayer for the civil authorities—particularly its purpose-clause: "that we may lead a quiet and peaceable life in all piety and respectability" (I Tim. 2:2; the same conclusion is implicit in the traditional prayer for the civil government preserved in I Clem. 61). The grace of God, described as σωτήριος (full of salvation), is also called παιδεύουσα (educative)—educating the Christian: namely, to morally impeccable conduct (Tit. 2:12). The parenesis of the pastoral epistles agrees, offering as its norm a picture of Christian-bourgeois piety (§ 60).

3. So it is not surprising that the Christian Church conceives of itself *as a new religion* existing side by side with the Jewish and the heathen religion (the latter regarded as a unity). This found terminological expression peculiar to the book of Acts in the term "the Way." Saul goes as a persecutor to Damascus where he will perhaps find people "belonging to the Way," (9:2), and later he describes himself as one who "persecuted this Way to death" (22:4). The Jews in Ephesus "speak evil of the Way" (19:9), and a disturbance arises concerning "the Way" (19:23). The procurator Felix is informed about "the Way" (24:22). Everywhere this term ὁδός can be translated "direction, tendency," as in the eyes of the Jews this Christian "direction" is a "sect" (αἵρησις, 24:14). In point of fact, however, the Christian religion is meant, irrespective of whether Christian teaching or the Christian fellowship is uppermost in the author's thought. In the same sense Christians will later be spoken of as the "third kind" (I, pp. 107f.).

The author of Luke and Acts is guided in his presentation by *a conception of Christianity as an entity of world history.* In contrast to the other evangelists he endeavors as an historian to describe the life of Jesus in his Gospel. In the proemium he assures the reader that he has acted as a conscientious investigator in having taken pains with the sources (Lk. 1:1–4). And in the narrative itself he strives not only to give a better connected account than Mark, but also to bring the narrated events into chronological relation with world history. He is already doing this at 1:5 by dating Zacharias in the time of Herod, then especially by dating Jesus' birth (2:1–3) and again by dating the appearing of John the Baptist with a six-fold synchronism (3:1f.). It is also significant that in 21:20–24 he transforms the apocalyptic prediction of the "abomination of desolation" and its subsequent catastrophes (Mk. 13:14–20) into a prediction of the siege and destruction of Jerusalem by the Romans. In Acts correspondingly he offers a history of the earliest Church, the beginnings of Christian missions, and Paul's missionary journeys down to his imprisonment in Rome. The very fact that he writes an account of the origin and earliest history of the Christian Church—in which the eschatological Congregation, of course, would have no interest—shows how far removed he is from its own way of thinking. The fact that he wrote Acts as a sequel to his Gospel completes the confirmation that he has surrendered the original kerygmatic sense of the Jesus-tradition (§ 54, 3) and has historized it. Whereas for the eschatological faith not only of the earliest Church but also of Paul the history of the world had reached its end, because in Christ the history of salvation had found its fulfilment and hence its end, according to the viewpoint of Acts the history of salvation now continues. While for Paul, Christ, being the "end of the Law" (Rom. 10:4), is also the end of history, in the thought of Acts he becomes the beginning of a new history of salvation, the history of Christianity. Later on he will be regarded by universalistic thinking as the middle-point and turning-point of history.

The author of Acts further classifies Christianity as a religion within world history by letting Paul in the Areopagus-discourse appeal to heathen piety by the reference to an inscription on an Athenian altar and to the Stoic belief in God (17:23, 28). This amounts to acclaiming "heathen history and culture and the heathen religious world as Christianity's pre-history."* And the conception of the relation of Christianity to Judaism found in Acts corresponds to this: Paul's teaching on the Law is no longer understood, and Jewish history has simply become the pre-history of Christianity.

* See Vielhauer, "Zum Paulinismus der Apostelgeschichte," *Evangelische Theologie*, 1950–51, pp. 1–15.

It is further significant, finally, that at the climaxes of his narrative the author of Acts, following the pattern of ancient historians, puts into the mouth of Peter and especially of Paul speeches which express the situation-transcending significance of the event (10:34–43; 11:5–17; 15:7–11; 17:22–31; 20:18–35; 22:1–21).

CHAPTER VI

The Development of Doctrine

§ 54. Paradosis and Historical Tradition

1. According to Jude 3 Christian teaching is "the faith once for all delivered (παραδοθείση) to the saints"; according to II Pet. 2:21 it is "the holy commandment delivered (παραδοθείση) to them." And according to Pol. Phil. 7:2 "the word delivered (παραδοθείς) from the beginning."* The Christian Church, called by the word and ever and again reconstituted by the word, does indeed need *tradition* (I, pp. 59f.). Παραδιδόναι, "to pass on by tradition or as tradition," its noun παράδοσις "tradition" and παραλαμβάνειν, "to receive by or as tradition," are from the beginning technical terms for the tradition-process (I Thess. 2:13; 4:1; Gal. 1:9; I Cor. 11:2, 23; 15:1, 3; Phil. 4:9; and, after Paul, Col. 2:6; II Thess. 2:15; 3:6; Jude 3; II Pet. 2:21; I Clem. 7:2; Did. 4:13; Barn. 19:11), and παραθήκη is the term in the pastorals for the *deposit* of teaching offered by the tradition (I Tim. 6:20; II Tim. 1:12, 14; *cf.* 2:2), a juristic term perhaps intentionally chosen to avoid the term παράδοσις, which through Gnosticism had become suspect (v. Campenhausen). Usually the content of the "tradition" (or "deposit") is right teaching in contrast to false teaching; but it can also mean that which is ethically required (Did. 4:13; Barn. 19:11; I Clem. 7:2; and in II Pet. 2:21 probably both the ethical demand and the tradition of teaching are meant as one). The apostles' proclamation founded the tradition, and in the apostle concept the idea of tradition becomes the dominant factor (II, p. 105).

While every religion requires transmission, transmission or *tradition* in Christianity not only plays a special role but also takes on a peculiar character. In pagan religions transmission is confined

* Unfortunately, English lacks a verb on the same root as the noun tradition to show the intimate connection of the Greek verb παραδιδόναι with its noun παράδοσις (Tr.).

primarily to cultic acts and the liturgical formulas which accompany them; there may in addition be an etiological myth which tells of the origin of the cult. In a more developed stage cosmogonic myths may also enter in or replace the old formulas, as in the religion of Egypt or in so-called Orphism or in Gnosticism. Then one may properly speak of doctrine and theology, and these, too, may be transmitted as tradition. However, they are subject to great variability, as is indicated, for instance, in the manifold allegorizations of old myths in the Gnostic systems or in those of the Osiris myth (Plutarch: *De Iside et Osiride*).

The *Israelitic-Jewish religion* naturally also requires transmission of its cultic acts and liturgy. In addition, the transmission of laws regulating life plays a greater role in it than in most pagan religions, even where these have developed beyond the primitive stage (as was especially the case in the Greek world, where ethics became independent of the official religion). In Judaism the Old Testament tradition is supplemented by that of the scribes (sopherim) who were responsible for the interpretation of the old tradition in regard to its application in the present. Here, too, the terminology of "taking over" (παραλαμβάνειν, קִבֵּל) and "passing on" (παραδιδόναι, מָסַר) prevails. The decisive difference between the religion of the Old Testament and of Judaism and the pagan religions in respect to tradition is this: in the former the cultic-legal tradition is supplemented by an historical one. And this historical tradition has not merely the etiological function of explaining the origin and form of cult and rite but tells the history of the people, since here God is primarily the God of history who reveals Himself in the history of the people. In this respect, too, it is fundamentally different from the Greek world, in which the writing of history developed as secular history without connection with the official religion, although (as in Herodotus) the viewing of history was not necessarily devoid of religious reflection.

2. But what was the nature of tradition in earliest Christianity, and what meaning did it have? I Cor. 11:23–25 shows for the case of the Lord's Supper that *in Hellenistic Christianity* there was a *"tradition" of cultic formulas*: "for I received . . . what I also delivered to you, etc." (I, pp. 145f.). For the case of baptism, at the beginning there was only the naming of Christ over the one being baptized (I, pp. 137f.). There is no need here to deal with the further develop-

ment of the baptismal liturgy, which lies beyond the time of the New Testament (I, pp. 133f.); we need only to point out the origin of certain formulas which in part were later united and supplemented in the Apostles' Creed (i.e. the Symbolum Romanum).

A Christian *tradition* corresponding to the cult-myth is offered by Paul in I Cor. 15:3f. ("For I delivered to you . . . what I also received . . ."). It sums up in one short sentence the salvation-event which took place in Christ, his death and resurrection. The precipitate of *paradosis* is further found in statements about Christ as he "who is ready to judge the living and the dead" (I Pet. 4:5, etc.; see I, p. 78) and about his rising or his being raised from the dead (Rom. 10:9; II Tim. 2:8, etc.; see I, p. 80) and about his exaltation (I, p. 82). Sentences like Rom. 1:3f.; 4:24–26; I Cor. 8:6(?); I Tim. 3:16; 6:13; II Tim. 2:8; 4:1; I Pet. 1:20f.; 3:18f., 22; 4:5; Ign. Eph. 18:2; Tr. 9; Sm. 1:1f.; Pol. Phil. 2:1f., and others, are obviously citing or alluding to confessional formulas or hymns that had already become traditional. In addition to such christological formulas it is likely that others early took form which expressed monotheistic faith and later found solid shape in the first article of the Apostles' Creed (I, pp. 68–70).

Now when historical data like "descended from David" (Rom. 1:3) and "under Pontius Pilate" (I Tim. 6:13) occur in the christological formulas, that brings to light a characteristic difference between Christian confessional formulas and *paradosis* and those of the heathen: *the occurrence of salvation*, of which the Christian formulas speak, is peculiarly *bound up with history, world history*. It took place not in some mythical time, neither is it a timeless occurrence in some transcendent sphere, but it took place here on earth, and not long ago, either. The saving event of the crucifixion took place "under Pontius Pilate," the resurrection is testified by a series of people, "most of whom are still alive," and the list of their names is an appendix to the *paradosis* (I Cor. 15:5–8). That is, to the *paradosis* belongs history, an account about historical events. Hence, the conception of the author of Luke-Acts (II, pp. 116f.) in fitting the story of Jesus and the earliest period of the Church into the context of world history is understandable enough, even though in the process the eschatological character of this history gets lost.

The problem of the relationship between *history of salvation* and *world history*, or between *revelation* and *history*, is posed by the paradosis in which both are united—posed anew as compared with the Old Testament and Judaism. For historical tradition could no longer have the meaning which it had had in the Old Testament and Judaism. The revelation of God in Jesus was not an event in the history of the People, to which one could look back as to Moses' history, the exodus from Egypt, the seizure of Canaan, or the history of the judges and the kings. The "new covenant" (I, p. 98), unlike the old, is not the founding event of a people's history, but, however much it arises from a historical event, the death of Jesus, it is nonetheless an eschatological event, and the "People of God" with which this covenant is made is an entity not of world history but of eschatology (I, p. 98). Participation in the Lord's Supper makes the participant a member not of a national commonwealth but of the eschatological Congregation which sojourns in this world as in a foreign land (I, p. 100). For Christ is the end of history, and because he is thereby the fulfilment of the history of salvation it was possible for the Christian Church to take over the Old Testament with its historical account, but only by understanding Old Testament history as history of salvation in a new sense and by comprehending the Church's continuity with the history of Israel as the continuity of the divine plan of salvation which governs that history and has now reached its fulfilment (I, p. 97). So the story of Jesus and the call of the eschatological Congregation appeared as the fulfilment of the Old Testament's predictions, especially in Matthew's presentation. Such a view, however, was not inescapable. In contrast to Matthew, Mark did not write the story of Jesus with constant reference to prediction, and in John the history-of-salvation perspective is completely absent (II, p. 8).

Furthermore, it could happen that the history-of-salvation sense of Old Testament history got completely lost. It did when the figures of Israel's history were adduced, following synagogal tradition, as examples for pious or moral conduct or for patient suffering, as in I Clem. and also Jas. 5:10f., Heb. 11:17ff. Then, of course, the suffering Jesus could also be adduced as a model to follow, as in I Pet. 2:21, Heb. 12:2. The extent to which such a procedure forsakes the history-of-salvation point of view is shown by I Clem., which in addition to Biblical examples can also cite "examples of the heathen" (55:1f.).

At any rate, Old Testament history could not be continued as an historical account of the life of Jesus and the history of the Church unless their eschatological meaning were to be sacrificed, as was done in Luke-Acts (II, pp. 116f.).

3. But how much, and in what way, did faith have need of an account of historical events? Passages like II Cor. 5:18f.; 8:9; Phil. 2:6–11 indicate that it was possible *to formulate statements of the paradosis without mentioning historical facts.* So does Paul's attitude to the Palestinian Jesus-tradition, which he all but ignores (I, pp. 188f.), for it could lead to fixing one's attention upon the "Christ according to the flesh" whom Paul wants no longer to know (II Cor. 5:16; I, p. 294). In a way John indicates this, too, by his free treatment of the tradition and by the independent way in which he formed his Gospel (II, pp. 3f.). Altogether it is strange how little reference is made in apostolic and post-apostolic literature to Jesus' life—apart from the Gospels and Acts (see especially 2:22f.; 10:37–39) only at I Tim. 6:13 and Heb. 2:18; 4:15; 5:7; 12:2.

On the other hand, it is clear that passages like II Cor. 5:18f.; 8:9; Phil. 2:6–11 make sense only because they speak *at the same time of an historical person, Jesus.* And it is precisely the humanity of Jesus which is strongly emphasized in Phil. 2:7f.: ". . . becoming a man like other men and being recognized as truly human" (Weymouth; *cf.* Rom. 8:3; Gal. 4:4). The humanity of Christ—the fact, that is, that the saving event took place in the sphere of "flesh"—is essential: "He was manifested in the flesh" (I Tim. 3:16; *cf.* also Col. 1:22, Heb. 2:14; 5:7; 10:20; I Pet. 3:18; 4:1). For John, too, it is essential that Jesus was a man: "The Word became flesh" (1:14); he comes from Nazareth and his parents are known (II, pp. 41f.). To deny his humanity is a false teaching (II, pp. 40f.). Ignatius, also, like I John, combats the docetism of Gnostic heretics (Ign. Eph. 7, 18:2; Tr. 9–10; Sm. 1–3; 4:2; 5:2; 7:1).

But was it not enough merely to declare and insist upon the fact of Jesus' humanity? Was information about the manner of his historical life also necessary? Certainly Luke thought so and proceeded to give his Gospel a corresponding form (II, p. 116). In Paul, however, there is no trace of such an interest. When he refers to the obedience of Christ (Phil. 2:8; Rom. 5:19) or to his exemplary love (II Cor. 8:9; Rom. 15:3) he is thinking of the self-abasement and sacrifice of the pre-existent Christ and not of the concrete conduct of the historical Jesus. It is also something other than simple appeal to the historical Jesus when "*words of the Lord*" are appealed to, as is occasionally done by Paul (I, pp. 188f.). Outside of the Gospels, it is true, a saying of Jesus is directly cited only once in the New Testament (Acts 20:35), but there can be no doubt that sayings of Jesus were pretty generally passed on in the congregations, and certain quotations in the so-called Apostolic Fathers confirm that this was so. The logia-collection worked into Matthew and Luke was evidently soon superseded by the synoptic Gospels. It may still have remained in use here and there for a while, and we have no way of knowing whether, or to what extent, words of the Lord such as are quoted in Did. 1:3–6; I Clem. 13:2; II Clem. 2:4; Barn. 4:14; Pol. Phil. 2:3, and elsewhere, and others to which Ignatius occasionally alludes, come from oral tradition or from a written collection of sayings—it is at least doubtful whether they come from any one of our four Gospels. That such collections existed is also testified by papyrus finds.

But it is clear that the passing on of words of the Lord was motivated not by historical-biographical interest but by the practical concern to regulate the way of life of believers and to keep their hope alive. The one whom they heard speaking in the words was not the historical Jesus, but the Church's heavenly Lord. But then, we must ask, how is Matthew to be understood, who presents the words of the Lord in the framework of a history of Jesus? And above all how is Mark to be understood, who in his account also made use of words of the Lord but gave more room to the account of Jesus' deeds and his fate? It is in these two evangelists that it becomes clear to what an extent the historical tradition belongs to the kerygma or could be combined with it—and that it could be combined under various points of view.

That neither Matthew nor Mark wrote his Gospel out of historical interest, as Luke did, is clear; but they also differ from each other. Matthews presents Jesus as the one in whom the history of salvation has found its fulfilment. Running all through his Gospel is the demonstration that in the life and work of Jesus the predictions of the Old Testament are fulfilled: "This (or, all this) occurred in order that that which was spoken (by the Lord through the prophet) might be fulfilled" (1:22, etc.). But in addition he represents Jesus as the authoritative interpreter of the Law, or rather as the bringer of the new Torah, the messianic Torah, with his claim: "You have heard that it was said . . . but I say to you" (5:21–48). Insofar, then, as Matthew offers an account of the history of Jesus, he thereby makes visible the fact that eschatological salvation became history; the Jesus whom he depicts is to be understood not as a figure of world history but as its conclusion. Hence, in comparison with his source, Mark, he repeatedly enhances the divinity of the figure of Jesus (*cf.* especially 19:17 in contrast with Mk. 10:18). And then in depicting Jesus as the teacher of the Congregation he makes clear that this is the eschatological Congregation. Once more, his historical account expresses that fact (that eschatological salvation became history) by making the reader conscious that the present is eschatological in character; he does this by showing that the present stands under the dominion of the eschatological King, as his conclusion (28:18–20) clearly expresses: "All authority in heaven and on earth has been given to me," etc.

Mark in his own way also brings to view that fact that eschatological salvation became history. Fulfilment of prediction is of minor importance in his Gospel and occurs in pure form only at 4:12, though 7:6f.; 9:12; 11:9f.; 12:10f.* are related. Chief emphasis falls upon the miracles and miraculous events like the baptism and the transfiguration. In these the true nature of the Son of God, though in general hidden, appears—but only to the readers of the Gospel, for that nature was to remain hidden from his contemporaries (I, p. 32). While Matthew kept within the conceptual horizon of the Old Testament and Judaism, Mark expresses the kerygmatic character of the historical account in the manner of Hellenistic thinking: Jesus' life is not an episode of world history but the miraculous manifestation of divine dealing in the cloak of earthly occurrence. By including the debates of Jesus along with the miracles Jesus is presented less than in Matthew as teacher of the Church and more as the Son of God, who unmasks the anti-godliness of Jewish tradition. By giving baptism and the Lord's Supper their origin in Jesus' own baptism by John and in his last meal, Mark is likewise giving the history of Jesus the character of occurring revelation. By the account of the transfiguration, finally, he shows that only from the standpoint of faith in the risen Lord (9:9) can the "history" of Jesus be recognized as being in its inner nature epiphany of the Son of God.

4. Matthew and Mark, as we have just seen, made the historical account serviceable to the kerygmatic character of the "Gospel." But there was something intrinsically problematical in that procedure.

---

* Mk. 1:2f. is probably an ancient gloss.

The problem lay in the fact that both Mark and Matthew, following his lead, gave their writings the form of an historical presentation, a "life of Jesus," in which the single bits of the old tradition are united into a chronological-geographical continuity—and some of even the old bits of tradition themselves exhibit novelistic details which bear witness to a biographical interest on the part of the congregations which passed them on. This problem arises from the fact that the Christian Church, knowing itself to be the eschatological Congregation of men called out of the world and belonging to the coming aeon, was nevertheless not called by a revelation from the beyond—whether a revelation given in the pictures of ecstatic visionaries, or a revelation brought by some unconfirmable myth—but by an historical figure, Jesus, in whom it heard the word of God calling it. As it is the Church's duty to manifest its non-worldly character in its existence within the world, so it is also its duty not completely to sublimate into myth him who called it into existence—however much it may express his significance in the language of traditional mythology. The tradition about Jesus, therefore, has this special character: that it speaks simultaneously of the eschatological occurrence and of an historical occurrence. The question is whether this paradoxical character was maintained.

While in the presentation of Luke-Acts this paradox was resolved in favor of a theology of history which knows only a history of salvation unrolling as world history (II, pp. 186f.), it was also resolved in another direction by sacrificing from the kerygma its reference to the historical occurrence. This happened in Gnosticism. In it the occurrence of salvation is understood with a consistent one-sidedness as transcendental, and, in consequence of divorcing it from history, the occurrence of salvation becomes mythical. Unlike heathen Gnosticism, Christian Gnosticism naturally could not give up all connection with the historical person Jesus and thus transplant the occurrence of salvation into a mythical past. But it did surrender the historical reality of the Redeemer when it denied the identity of the Son of God with the historical Jesus by teaching either that the Son of God only temporarily—from the baptism of Jesus, say—united with the human Jesus and then left him before the passion, or that the Redeemer's human form was only seemingly a body (docetism).

This solution of the paradoxical problem inevitably seemed heretical to the majority of the congregations (I, p. 169; II, p. 40f.).

But the very writings that most emphatically assert against Gnosticism that "the Word became flesh" and see the incarnation of anti-Christ in those "who do not confess that Jesus Christ came in flesh"—John, I and II John, and Ignatius, too—demonstrate the relative appropriateness and the intent of Gnostic teaching; in opposition to a historizing of the eschatological occurrence, it expresses a legitimate interest of faith.

The meaning of that paradox was grasped most clearly of all by John and is most clearly set forth in his Gospel. In the very fact that he dealt so freely with the tradition of Jesus' life (II, pp. 3f.), he most sharply made clear the meaning it has for the kerygma by reducing the revelation of God in the man Jesus to the mere fact that He so revealed Himself (§ 48, 3, esp. II, pp. 67 and 69) and by uncovering in the most extreme fashion the paradox of "the Word became flesh" (§ 46, especially II, pp. 40f.)—the paradox that God's word went forth in a definite historical person and remains a present reality. He presents this person not as a reliably testified person of the past but as he is constantly present in the word which proclaims him in the power of the Spirit (II, p. 90). For John, therefore, the tradition is not historical transmission, which establishes the continuity of historical occurrence, but is the Church's preaching, in which Jesus is present in the Spirit (§ 50, 7). The succession which the kerygmatic tradition requires is here not yet conceived as an institutional one (as in Acts, the pastorals, and I Clem., § 52, 3) but as a free, Spirit-wrought succession. While Paul—inconsistently with his basic insight—still tries to guarantee the resurrection of Jesus by the enumeration of witnesses, as if it were an historically visible fact (I Cor. 15:5–8; see I, p. 295), John concludes his Easter-stories with the sentence: "Blessed are they who have not seen and yet believe" (20:29; see II, pp. 56f.).

§ 55. The Problem of Right Teaching and the Rise of the New Testament Canon

1. Christianity did not become a mystery-religion because in it salvation rests primarily not upon a sacramental cult which professes to mediate divine powers through material elements (I, p. 135), but upon the proclamation of the word, in which the grace of God by being proclaimed encounters the hearer and demands of him personal

faith. The proclamation, telling of God's deed in Christ, is at the same time personal address to the hearer; and at the same time as it brings knowledge of what God has done in Christ it also brings the hearer a new knowledge of himself. It is the "knowledge of the truth" which frees the hearer from "ignorance" and "error" (I, p. 67), and in which knowledge and acknowledgment are bound together into a unity. In the same way Paul understands the "knowledge" which he spreads abroad by his preaching (II Cor. 2:14; 4:6)—this knowledge means: "to gain Christ and be found in him" (Phil. 3:8f.).

This "knowledge" (whether ἐπίγνωσις or γνῶσις) scarcely differs in substance from "faith," except that it emphasizes *the element of knowing which is contained in the very structure of* "*faith.*" This appears most clearly in John by the way in which he understands the relationship between "believing" and "knowing" (§ 49, 2). For the believer must, of course, understand what is proclaimed to him about God and Christ and also how his own situation is thereby qualified. The theological expositions in Galatians and Romans have no other purpose than to unfold the knowledge which is the concomitant gift of faith. Paul clearly saw that this knowledge is not merely capable of development, but also stands in need of development. Faith must prove itself to be living faith by reaching in each case a right judgment as to what is required of the man of faith, for whatever does not come from faith is sin (Rom. 14:23). Paul wishes for his readers that their power of judgment may grow and gain in certainty (Rom. 12:2; Phil. 1:9f.; Philm. 6; see I, pp. 326f.). Similarly Col. 1:9f. wishes: "that you may be filled with the knowledge of his will in all spiritual wisdom and understanding, to lead a life worthy of the Lord . . ." (*cf.* 3:10). Also similar are the prayer II Pet. 1:3 and the exhortations that correspond to it (1:5 and 3:18), and Barnabas wishes: "May God . . . give you wisdom, insight, knowledge, understanding of his just demands" (21:5); γνῶσις (knowledge) for him means not merely theoretical but also practical knowledge (5:4; 18:1; 19:1; *cf.* 16:9: "wisdom in regard to his just demands"). As Paul rejoices that such "knowledge" is alive and at work in the congregation (I Cor. 1:5; II Cor. 8:7; Rom. 15:14), so I Clem. praises the "complete and dependable knowledge" of that Corinthian congregation (1:2), and Did. 11:2 orders that wandering teachers are to be received if their activity is conducive to "increasing uprightness and knowledge of the Lord."

2. Such "knowledge" or "wisdom" is the knowledge of God's will; i.e. the power of judgment that lies within the Christian's ethical willing and which it is every believer's duty to cultivate and activate. To be distinguished from it is *a special "knowledge" or "wisdom"*; its content is the divine plan of salvation and the saving occurrence which is described in the kerygmatic formulations of the paradosis. Already to Paul the divine plan of salvation and its realization in Christ seemed a "mystery" (I Cor. 2:6f.; 15:51; Rom. 11:25); it seemed even more so to writers later than Paul (for Colossians and Ephesians, see no. 3, below; also II Thess. 2:7 [Rom. 16:25], I Tim. 3:9, 16; Rev. 10:7; Ign. Eph. 19:1; Mg. 9:1; Tr. 2:3). The formulations of the paradosis needed interpretation. Their concepts and statements were not only subject to various interpretations but they also led inevitably to further thinking, to questions: what theological and christological, cosmological and anthropological consequences necessarily result? Which ones are legitimate deductions? This is the origin of Christian theology. In the course of time Christians also had to come to terms with heathen thinking, its mythology and philosophy; there had to come a theology which finally in the apologetes became a sort of Christian philosophy.

This "knowledge," too, has its origin in faith, though it is not for all believers to develop such knowledge independently. That is a special gift not given to all (I Cor. 12:8). But whoever has it is to communicate it to others and these are to listen to him; indeed, he who has it may wish that all might achieve it (Eph. 1:17). This knowledge as well as that described under 1, above, also has a practical purpose, since in its light the situation of the Christian becomes clear, and in it he learns to understand himself. Thus the theological expositions of Galatians and Romans teach one to understand the emancipation of Christian existence from the Law and the cosmic powers; so do those of Colossians. Paul's discussion with his gnosticizing opponents in Corinth shows how one's understanding of "freedom" and "authorization" (ἐξουσία) leads to a particular way of living. The critical question for the development of theology is how far it sticks to being an unfolding of the knowledge contained in faith. That is equivalent to saying how far it is the explication of the kerygma and of Christian existence as it is determined by the kerygma. It has cut itself loose from its origin and become mere speculation or rational construction when it no longer rightly sees the connection between the knowledge of God and His dealing and the knowledge of the Christian's situation determined by it.

Motivation for the development of a Christian theology was furnished not only by the necessity of interpreting the kerygma but also by the Old Testament, which had been taken over by the Church and also required interpretation. II Pet. 1:20f. shows the embarrassment they were in; the readers are warned that the prophecy of Scripture is not to be interpreted in the light of one's private understanding but only in accordance with its pneumatic origin. We have already dealt in § 11 with the multiple possibilities and attempts at interpretation. Here we need only briefly consider what meaning the interpretation of the Old Testament had for the development of a Christian theology. The situation was not merely that the Church had to overcome the difficulties offered by the Old Testament, but also that the Old Testament could serve as a source of Christian "knowledge" when its mysteries were interpreted by means of allegory. For the author of Ephesians one such mystery is the saying in Gen. 2:24 which he interprets as applying to the union of Christ with the Ecclesia (5:31f.). The author of Hebrews (§ 11, 2c) is manifestly proud of what he is able to offer his readers in the way of knowledge. By his solemnly rhetorical introduction to his interpretation of the Old Testament cult and to his theory of the high-priesthood of Christ he is explicitly reminding the reader that his knowledge rises above the level of a Christianity that is primitive (5:11; 6:12). Though in Barnabas "knowledge" and "wisdom" play no role as technical terms, its author (§ 11, 2b) specifically calls his interpretation of the Old Testament "knowledge" (6:9; 9:8; 13:7; *cf.* "to know" 7:1; 14:7; 16:2; "to make known" 1:7; 5:3; "to make wise" 5:3). He praises the Lord "who placed in us wisdom and understanding of his secrets" (6:10), and he writes his book in order that the readers may go on beyond their "faith" to a "perfect knowledge" in order that faith and the Christian virtues may be enriched by the addition of "wisdom, prudence, understanding, and knowledge" (2:2f.). The allegorical method by means of which Hebrews and Barnabas and later Justin Martyr (§ 11, 2f.) get knowledge is also occasionally used by I Clem. (§ 11, 2d), though as a rule he uses the Old Testament as a book of ethical examples. He, too, calls his art of interpretation a γνῶσις (40:1: "we have looked into the depths of divine knowledge").

It soon became apparent that even authoritative Christian writings needed exposition. Understandably, such a need was first felt in regard to the Pauline letters, in which according to II Pet. 3:16 there is much that is hard to understand, giving rise to false interpretation by false teachers. Polycarp also confesses that neither he nor others are able completely to grasp the wisdom of the "blessed and renowned" Paul, but that his letters are able to bestow edification upon him who ponders over them. And can the treatment of the theme "faith and works" in Jas. 2:14–26 be understood in any other way than that it is a debate against misunderstood ideas of Paul? In the mind of the Church the interpretation of Paul is not an exegesis concerned with merely understanding his wording but is motivated by the practical interest of ascertaining the meaning of Paul's utterances for the present situation, or of preventing the misuse of them. Hence, interpretation of Paul can be undertaken by letting Paul speak anew—i.e. by writing a new letter in his name. Thus in a certain sense II Thessalonians is a commentary on I Thessalonians. For the expectation of the imminent end of all things expressed in the earlier letter—whether against a too enthusiastic eschatological mood or (more likely) against doubts that had arisen in view of the delay of the parousia—is restricted in the later letter: before the End comes all sorts of things must first take place (II Thess. 2:1–12).

We must mention, finally, the exposition of other texts of mysterious content or of apocalyptic pictures and terms. God's plan of salvation is a "mystery" (Col. 1:26f., Eph. 1:9, etc.); so are the apocalyptic seer's visions "mysteries," and he interprets them (Rev. 1:20, 17:5, 7) or he may only hint at their meaning (Rev. 13:18): "This calls for wisdom: let him who has understanding reckon the number of the beast." The name for the "understanding" of the mysterious "booklet" of which Hermas learns from the "old lady" who appears to him is γνῶσις; and the cognate verb (γινώσκειν) constantly recurs in Hermas—the term means the process of understanding the visions and allegories (vis. III 1:2, 4:3; sim. V 3:1; IX 5:3, etc.).

3. This Christian γνῶσις (knowledge or understanding) which arises out of the elements discussed above leads before long to the problem of right teaching. *Paul* himself already knew two "wisdoms": the paradoxical wisdom of the cross and a wisdom available only to the "mature" (τέλειοι) and penetrating into the depths of divinity

(I Cor. 2:6ff.; see I, pp. 181 and 327). The latter is certainly not the product of rational thought, for Paul attributes it to revelation by the Spirit (2:10), and in the end it also flows into a recognition of God's gift and of the situation of the believer (2:12; see I, p. 327). Still it is clear that in this wisdom fantasy and speculative thought are at work as well as motifs of the apocalyptic and mythological tradition. For a part of this wisdom is the mythological theorem of the deception of the "rulers" by the disguise of the pre-existent Christ (2:8; see I, pp. 175f.). Probably the notion of the fall and liberation of the creation, to which Paul allusively refers in Rom. 8:20ff., also goes back to such mythological tradition, and certainly secrets like the eschatological "mystery" of I Cor. 15:51ff. do; whereas the history-of-salvation mystery in Rom. 11:25ff. is derived from speculative fantasy.

Though Paul himself is already under the influence of *Gnostic thinking* (§ 15, 4), his correspondence with the congregation at Corinth permits us to see in young Christianity there were circles which had fallen under the power of such influence to such an extent that the Christian message was emptied of its true content or perverted. Such are the members of the congregation who boast of their "wisdom" and "knowledge" (I Cor. 1:18ff.; 8:1ff.); so are the apostles who have worked their way in from the outside—false apostles, to Paul (II Cor. 2:13)—for whom Paul claims to be a match in "knowledge" (II Cor. 11:6). The struggle between this gnosticizing wing and the ultimately victorious orthodoxy has not died out even after Paul's time. Its tenacity indicates that in circles of considerable extent there was a craving for a knowledge that would go beyond faith. That the "false teachers" opposed by I John were characterized by a claim to possess knowledge is indicated by the author's effort to make clear what "to know God" in reality means (2:3ff.; 3:6; 4:6ff.). Similarly, in his battle against Gnostic teachers Ignatius asks, "Why have we not all become wise, having received the knowledge of God— that is, Jesus Christ?" (Eph. 17:2). And he praises Christ who has "made wise" his readers—made them solid, that is, in the orthodox faith (Sm. 1:1). The false teachers in Thyatira, against whom Rev. 2:18–29 polemizes, evidently boasted of their knowledge of the "deep things of Satan" (or, in case this is a polemic distortion of their claim, what they really claimed was knowledge of the deep things of God). Col., the pastorals, Jude, and II Pet. also polemize against a gnosticizing Christianity.

One way of meeting this danger was *to reject such striving after knowledge altogether*. That is the attitude we meet in the pastorals. Here "false teaching" is not combatted with counter-arguments but all debate with it is declined: it is simply "falsely called knowledge." "Timothy" is advised to "charge certain persons not to teach any different doctrine nor to occupy themselves with myths and endless genealogies which promote speculation rather than the divine stewardship (*v. l.* training) that is in faith" (I Tim. 1:3f.; *cf.* 4:7; 6:20). Or he is exhorted: "Have nothing to do with stupid, senseless controversies; you know that they breed quarrels" (II Tim. 2:23; *cf.* 2:16; Tit. 3:9). He is to stick to "the words of the faith and of the good doctrine," the "sound words" of the Lord, the "sound doctrine" (I Tim. 4:6; 6:3; Tit. 1:9, etc.). Neither does Acts 20:29f. enter into discussion with the false teachers, but is content to call them "men speaking perverse things." Jude and its imitator, II Pet., deal still more summarily with the false teachers: here there not only is no suggestion of a refutation by argument, but they are directly accused of moral turpitude and immoral conduct. I Jn. also, unlike Paul, does not enter upon a theological discussion with the false teachers, but simply thrusts before these "antichrists" the statement of the true humanity of the Son of God. One may concede that he does offer a refutation to the extent that he makes clear the existential meaning of faith by uncovering the unity of indicative and imperative, the unity of faith and love (II, pp. 80–82), whereas Ignatius gets stuck in dogmatic polemics and stays there.

The method represented by the pastorals could be successful in limited circles at the most; for the urge for knowledge could not be rooted out—and, after all, was it not in itself legitimate? At any rate, such an urge is expressed in *Colossians* and *Ephesians* in their further development of Pauline motifs—in Col. in a struggle against false teachers, in Eph. in a non-polemic explication of Christian knowledge.

Colossians warns the reader against the "φιλοσοφία (literally "philosophy," but, of course, not Greek philosophy is meant but Gnostic speculation) and empty deception whose norm is human tradition and the elemental spirits of the universe, and not Christ," 2:8 tr.). Though the author does not carry out a true discussion in debate form and though it is almost entirely by indirection that he allows the opposing view to be recognized, he nevertheless sets up against it his own view of the theme under discussion—the relation of Christ to the angelic or cosmic powers—and is convinced that in Christ "are hid all the treasures of wisdom and knowledge" (2:3). Here "wisdom and spiritual understanding" (1:9 tr.) is by no means restricted to the judgment of the ethical will (see above, II, p. 129) but certainly includes a theoretical "wisdom" by which the "mystery" (the divine plan of salvation is often so termed: 1:26f., 2:2; 4:3) is unfolded by describing the cosmic status of Christ and by describing the reconciliation of the cosmos brought about by the work of salvation, a cosmos torn by recalcitrant powers and reconciled in the fact that the latter are overcome (1:15–20; 2:9–15). At the same time, the transcendent nature of the Ecclesia is characterized as that of the "body of Christ." The fact that the author in 1:15–20 made use of a pre-Christian hymn that had already received a Christian editing before him* proves to what an extent Christian craving for knowledge had already mingled with cosmological speculation.

The interest of the author of *Ephesians* is not polemic. But for him, too, God's plan of salvation is the "mystery" which was imparted by revelation to the Paul whose mask the author adopts (3:3; *cf.* 1:9; 6:19). By that which he writes the readers are to recognize what "insight into the mystery of Christ" he possesses (3:4) and how he is able "to preach . . . the unsearchable riches of Christ, and to make all men see what is the plan of the mystery" (3:8f.). He abundantly shares his knowledge with the reader, and while the author of Col. wishes his readers "wisdom and spiritual understanding to lead a life worthy of the Lord" (Col. 1:9f.), the author of Eph. wishes in the parallel passage "that God . . . may give you a spirit of wisdom and of revelation in the knowledge of him . . . that you may know what is the hope to which he has called you, etc." (1:17–19). Later he wishes that his readers may be able to comprehend "what is the breadth and the length and height and depth and to know the love of Christ which surpasses knowledge" (3:18f.). Like Col. (which he is probably using) he also describes the work and dignity of Christ in the cosmological terminology of Gnosticism (1:10, 20–22; 2:14–16). His theme, however, is not the reconciliation of the cosmos but the unity of the Church and Christ's relation to it (2:11–22; 4:1–16; *cf.* 5:29–32). For this he has at his disposal a special wisdom in scriptural interpretation by

* See E. Käsemann, *Eine christliche Taufliturgie*, in *Festschrift für Rudolf Bultmann*, 1949, pp. 133–148.

which he reads out of Ps. 68:19 Christ's descent to earth and his victorious ascent (4:8–10) and interprets the "great mystery" of Gen. 2:24 as applying to Christ and the Church (5:31f.).

4. The diversity of theological interests and ideas is at first great. A norm or an authoritative court of appeal for doctrine is still lacking, and the proponents of directions of thought which were later rejected as heretical consider themselves completely Christian—such as Christian Gnosticism (§ 15, 3). In the beginning, *faith* is the term which distinguishes the Christian Congregation from Jews and the heathen, not *orthodoxy* (right doctrine). The latter along with its correlate, *heresy*, arises out of the differences which develop within the Christian congregations. In the nature of the case this takes place very early; even Paul already curses the Judaizers who offer a "different gospel" in wanting to impose the yoke of the Law upon converted Gentiles (Gal. 1:6–9). He likewise polemizes against those in Corinth who deny the resurrection (I Cor. 15) and against the gnosticizing preachers who proclaim "another Jesus" (II Cor. 11:4). We have just shown (in 3, above) that battles with Gnosticism continued to be fought.

It is understandable that in such battles $\pi\iota\sigma\tau\iota\varsigma$ takes on the meaning of right belief (I, p. 90) and also that $\pi\iota\sigma\tau\iota\varsigma$, retaining its primary meaning "the faith with which one believes," can come to mean the right kind of faith. It must be meant in one or the other of these senses when we hear of men who "have made shipwreck of their faith" or "have missed the mark as regards the faith" (I Tim. 1:19; 6:21), who "have failed the test in regard to faith" (II Tim. 3:8 tr.), or when in a (pretended) look into the future it is said of the false teachers: "some will depart from the faith" (I Tim. 4:1). At any rate, right doctrine is meant when the proper servant of Christ is described as "nourished on the words of the faith and of the good doctrine which you have followed" (I Tim. 4:6—here "faith" and "good doctrine" constitute a hendiadys). And the right kind of faith is meant when it is said of the false teachers: "They are upsetting the faith of some" (II Tim. 2:18). In Tit. 1:13 and 2:2 occurs the expression "to be sound (literally, "healthy") in faith," which evidently means to be orthodox, and from this expression the pastorals found a solid technical term for right doctrine: "sound (or "healthy") teaching" (I Tim. 1:10; II Tim. 4:3; Tit. 1:9; 2:1; *cf.* "sound $\lambda\acute{o}\gamma o\varsigma$," Tit. 2:9, which RSV renders "sound speech," but it may also mean doctrinally sound preaching; *cf.* also "sound words," I Tim. 6:3; II Tim. 1:13). The word *pistis* also contains the meaning "right doctrine" in Eph. 4:5, even though in the explanation "one Lord, one faith, one baptism . . ." faith evidently means primarily that confession of faith at baptism which Rom. 10:9 mentions. Nevertheless the word "one" in "one faith" indicates that in the author's mind hovers a contrast with other confessions (as does a contrast with other lords in the case of "one Lord"), and hence the idea of the *right* confession is also present. It means the same thing as is meant by the "faith of equal standing" (or "faith of the same sort," tr.) which the "Peter" of II Pet. 1:1 and his readers have received in common. Certainly right doctrine is meant by "the faith which was once for all delivered to the saints," Jude 3 (*cf.* Jude 20: "your most holy faith"; on the implications of "delivered" see § 54, 1).

In Rom. 10:9 "*to confess*" (ὁμολογεῖν) means: to make the baptismal confession, with no thought as yet of a *right* confession in contrast to a heretical one. Hebrews uses the word "confession" (3:1; 4:14; 10:23) in this same sense, though here the reader is urged to hold fast his confession in contrast to neglecting it or being anxious in regard to it. Mt. 10:32 ("confessing Jesus") already has this meaning and so do Jn. 9:22; 12:42 and Herm. sim. IX 28, 4 and 7 (where ὁμολόγησις also occurs). But "the good confession" of I Tim. 6:12 means the right confession in contrast to heresy, and the verb "confess" is often used with the same implication (I Jn. 2:23; 4:2: "that Jesus has come in the flesh"; 4:3; 4:15: "that Jesus is the Son of God"; II Jn. 7; Ign. Sm. 5:2: "that he was clothed in flesh"; Pol. Phil. 7:1).

Thus a *terminology* develops for indicating *orthodoxy*. Words with the prefix "ortho-" do not yet appear, for the ὀρθοποδεῖν of Gal. 2:14 ("walk straightly in regard to the truth of the gospel") is a purely figurative expression; likewise ὀρθοτομεῖν in II Tim. 2:15 ("rightly handling the word of truth"). In the apostolic and post-apostolic period the actual words "orthodox," "orthodoxy," and the verb "be orthodox" (ὀρθόδοξος, ὀρθοδοξία, ὀρθοδοξεῖν) do not yet occur; they belong to philosophic usage. And "dogma" (δόγμα) also occurs only in the general sense of "regulation," "ordinance," "directive" (Ign. Mg. 13:1; Did. 11:3; Barn. 1:6; 9:7; 10:1, 9f.).

To designate *false teaching*, *heresy*, formations with the prefix "hetero-" were immediately available: ἑτεροδιδασκαλεῖν ("to teach otherwise"—I Tim. 1:3; 6:3; Ign. Pol. 3:1; *cf.* Gal. 1:6; II Cor. 11:4), ἑτεροδοξεῖν ("to have other opinions"—Ign. Sm. 6:2), ἑτεροδοξία ("other doctrine"—Ign. Mg. 8:1). So were formations with the prefix "pseudo": pseudoprophet (I Jn. 4:1), ψευδοδιδάσκαλος, "false teacher," (II Pet. 2:1), ψευδοδιδασκαλία, "false teaching," (Pol. Phil. 7:2), ψευδολόγος "false word" (I Tim. 4:2). Ἁίρεσις (*hairesis*, the Greek parent of our word "heresy") means in the beginning a school or party (Acts 5:19 "of the Sadducees"; 15:5 "of the Pharisees"; *cf.* 26:5) and in this sense can be applied by non-Christians to the Christian faith (Acts 24:5, 14; 28:22; RSV renders "sect"), then it also means a faction (Gal. 5:20; I Cor. 11:19). Even in II Pet. 2:1 the αἱρέσεις are not heresies but the factions evoked by the false teachers. The αἱρετικὸς ἄνθρωπος of Tit. 3:10, however, in the context can only be the heretic, and in Ignatius (Eph. 6:2; Tr. 6:1) αἵρεσις at least approaches the meaning "heresy"—the meaning which became the common one in the ancient Church—though perhaps all Ignatius means is "faction."

W. Bauer has shown that that doctrine which in the end won out in the ancient Church as the "right" or "orthodox" doctrine stands at the end of a development or, rather, is the result of a conflict among various shades of doctrine, and that heresy was not, as the ecclesiastical tradition holds, an apostasy, a degeneration, but was already present at the beginning—or, rather, that by the triumph of a certain teaching as the "right doctrine" divergent teachings were condemned as heresy. Bauer also showed it to be probable that in this conflict the Roman congregation played a decisive role. Later, but independently of Bauer, M. Werner* defended a similar thesis, regarding heresy as a symptom of the great crisis of the post-apostolic period, which, according to him, consisted of the fact that in consequence of the delay of the parousia a chaos of teachings arose. Since Christians wanted to hold fast to the tradition but now had to reinterpret it, a multitude of attempts at reorientation was called forth. "By the continuing delay of the parousia the inner eschatological logic, the dominating connectedness of meaning in the doctrine of Christ and salvation received from the apostles and Paul, is broken, and the several items and concepts of faith thereby lose their unambiguity" (pp. 131f.). All the attempts at reorientation were originally "heresies"—also the Christianity of the "great

* *Die Entstehung des christlichen Dogmas*, 1941, pp. 126–138. For Bauer, see *Rechtgläubigkeit und Ketzerei im ältesten Christentum*, 1934.

Church" which finally gained the day; the "great Church" is only the most successful heresy. In this thesis the influence of the non-occurrence of the parousia is obviously greatly overestimated. Granted that this non-occurrence was one reason for the formation of heresies, nevertheless it was only one among others. Indeed, we probably ought to call this non-occurrence a *conditio sine qua non* rather than a positive cause. For the differentiation of the various shades of teaching did not first arise in the post-apostolic period but was already present in the time of Paul, who in Galatia, Corinth and elsewhere had to contend with "false teachers." The motifs of later heresies are already partially present in the Hellenistic Christianity of the apostolic period when the Christian message had penetrated the world of Hellenism from its mother-soil in Palestine and the influences of the mystery religions, particularly of Gnosticism, set to work. Christian Gnosticism is not the result of disappointed expectation of the parousia; rather vice versa, as the Corinthian letters already show, the rejection of realistic eschatology is a consequence of the Gnostic thinking which even then was penetrating into the Christian congregations.

5. In view of the differences in doctrine and of the conflict between them the question necessarily arose *concerning the authority which might determine "right" doctrine*. To whom could one appeal in a given case for the correctness of one's opinion? To the *Lord* himself? Appeal to a revelation directly accorded by the Lord or by the Spirit could only make the problem all the more delicate and the embarrassment all the greater. In this situation only such words of the Lord could claim authority as were regarded as vouched for as words of the historical or of the risen Jesus—but that means the factual authorities could only be the people who were bearers of reliable tradition, primarily *the apostles*. When Serapion (*ca.* 200 A.D.) says, "The apostles we accept as the Lord," he is only expressing what had long been taken for granted. The element of tradition had long ago become the decisive thing in the apostle-concept (§ 52, 3). According to Acts 2:42 what the Jerusalem Church held to was "the teaching of the apostles." Jude 17 refers the reader to the words of "the apostles of our Lord Jesus Christ" against the heretics; likewise II Pet. 3:2, where "the commandment of the Lord and Savior through your apostles" takes its place by the side of the canonical authority of the Old Testament prophets. How the authority of the Lord is

concentrated in the person of the apostles is shown by the ranging of the apostles with the Lord in I Clem. 42:1f.; Ign. Mg. 7:1; 13:1; Pol. Phil. 6:3.

It must be recognized, of course, that the apostles could become an indubitable authority only when with the disappearance of the first generation they themselves already belonged to the past, and the conflicts of the apostolic period in which Paul had been involved had died away. Another presupposition for such apostolic authority is the restriction of the title "apostle" to the twelve (§ 52, 3), for, of course, it was not possible to appeal with success to one of those missionaries who had earlier also borne the title apostle. When one appealed to individual apostles such as Peter or Paul (*cf.*, for example, Ign. Rm. 4:3), it was not as individualized and significant personalities that they were appealed to, but as undoubted authorities whose personal differences were of no concern. Apostolic authority is basically that of the college of the twelve, with which only that of Paul is considered equal. It is significant that the Church's first manual of ethics and congregational order was given the title "Teaching of the Twelve Apostles."

But how did this apostolic authority concretely present itself after the twelve and Paul were no longer alive? It was not adequate simply to appeal to the oral tradition by which the words of the apostles had come down to any particular present. At first, it is true, one could still name disciples of apostles and so-called "elders" who had still (actually or allegedly) associated with the apostles or at least with their pupils (Papias, Clement of Alexandria). But that this was an uncertain matter comes to light in the conflict with Gnosticism, for it, too, appeals to oral tradition, "the apostolic tradition which we, too, have received by succession" (Ptolemy to Flora, 10:5). It was Gnosticism particularly which made oral tradition suspect.

But there was a way out of this if one could point to certain persons as authorized bearers of the tradition, and one could. These persons were the congregational officials, *the bishops*, whose appointment, according to common conviction, went back to the apostles (II, pp. 106f.). They represent the legitimate "succession" (διαδοχή)*.

---

* This term first appears in Hegesippus (Eusebius, *Historia Ecclesiastica*, IV 22:3) and Irenaeus I 27, 1. Nevertheless, the cognate verb (διαδέχεσθαι) in this sense is already found in I Clem. 44, 2.

The address of "Paul" to the elders of Ephesus (Acts 20:18ff.) and also the pastorals and Ignatius show what significance the congregational office takes on as bearer and guarantor of the apostolic tradition in the struggle over right doctrine; it was not until the consolidation of the monarchical episcopate that this significance was fully established.

But apostolic authority also lives on in *the written tradition*, the weight of which could only become the greater when oral tradition came into discredit through the Gnostics. Around the middle of the second century words of the Lord in a written tradition already count as Scripture (II Clem. 2:4); the public reading of Gospels in worship is testified by Justin (Apol. I 67). In the book of Revelation it is presupposed that this book is to be read to the congregation (1:3). In the case of Paul's letters it had long been taken for granted that they were to be read in the worship service (I Thess. 5:27; Col. 4:16); at an early time they were exchanged by the congregations to which they had been addressed, and relatively early there must have been collections of Pauline letters. I Clem. 47 refers the readers to Paul and his first letter to the Corinthians. For Ignatius, as for Polycarp, Paul is an authority taken for granted. Jas. 2:14–26 and II Pet. 3:15f. testify that his letters were much read. It is due to the important role of apostolic literature that Paul, though not one of the twelve, nevertheless counts as an apostle—indeed in the end as *the* apostle. In his genuine letters the Church possessed truly apostolic writings, and how much it needed such is indicated by the deutero-Pauline literature which circulated under his name: II Thess., Col., and Eph. as well as the pastorals. So do other writings to which the names of other apostles were attached. Some of these were published under such pseudonyms: the letters of Peter and Jude, and James also, as written by a brother of the Lord, could be reckoned to the same class. Other writings of this sort were attributed to an apostle as an afterthought; such were the originally anonymous Epistles of John and the Epistle to the Hebrews and also the book of Revelation, whose author was some man named John. Then, of course, the Gospels that were in church use also had to be attributed to apostles (Matthew, John) or to disciples of apostles (Mark, Luke) and so did Acts as the sequel of one of them. The tendency at work here is testified, finally, by the fact that a work could be written with the title "Teaching of the Twelve Apostles."

The problem now, however, was the selection of those writings out of the swelling literary production which could count as apostolic. The historical process had to lead to *the formation of a new canon* which took its place beside the Old Testament canon. Within the framework of a theology of the New Testament the detailed stages of this process cannot be described.

Though they cannot be dealt with here, the chief questions are the following: How did it happen that four Gospels were taken into the canon and that the attempts to reduce their number from four to one, either by accepting only one (Luke by Marcion, Matthew by the Ebionites) or by the preparation of a Gospel harmony (Tatian), did not succeed? How did the delimitation of the "apostle" portion come about and why did contested writings like Heb. and Rev. achieve canonical standing while others like I Clem., Barn., and Herm. were excluded? In such decisions how important was the fact that congregations were simply accustomed to certain writings, and how important were criteria of content (such as was the case in the exclusion of the Gospel of Peter, concerning which Bishop Serapion convinced himself that it had to be rejected as Gnostic)?

The essential fact is that in determining what is to be regarded as authoritative apostolic tradition for the Church, the office of bishop and the weight of written tradition worked together. In the end the authority of the bishop-office decided the matter: for the Greek Church, the thirty-ninth paschal letter of Athanasius (367 A.D.) conclusively set the extent of the New Testament at twenty-seven writings, and in the West this decision achieved recognition through Pope Innocent I (405 A.D.).

Unity of doctrine was assured by the canon and not by some normative system of dogmatics. But that means this unity is *only a relative one.* For in point of fact, the canon reflects a multiplicity of conceptions of Christian faith or of its content. Hence, its inner unity becomes a question. At any rate, such inner unity as is there does not appear with the unanimity of dogmatically formulated propositions. Beside the synoptics, which even among themselves exhibit differences, stands John, and beside the Gospels as a whole stands Paul! On one side of Paul stands Hebrews, on the other James! These variations were not necessarily felt as opposites, and they were at first so felt only in border cases as in the question whether Heb.

and Rev. ought to belong to the canon. But in the course of history these differences inevitably worked out as opposites, and when it finally came about that the various Christian confessions and sects all appeal for authority to the canon, that is possible only because in each of them one of the various motifs contained in the canonical writings has become the dominant one. Hence, the judgment is valid: "The New Testament canon, as such, is not the foundation of the Church's unity. On the contrary the canon, as such—i.e. as a fact as it is available to the historian—is the foundation of the multiplicity of confessions" (Käsemann).*

§ 56. Motifs and Types

Before we set forth what themes engage the desire for knowledge it is advisable to cast a glance at the various motifs which determine theological thinking and at the various types in which they take form.

1. *A special influence emanates from the Pauline letters.* Upon the editing of the Gospels, however, the theology of Paul had no influence. The Paulinism which is occasionally supposed to be found in Mark is limited to ideas which are the common property of Hellenistic Christianity. But Luke also contains no specifically Pauline ideas. Matthew need not even be considered, and John is likewise independent of Paul—at the most it contains an echo of Pauline terminology in the antithesis Law—grace (§ 41, 2). Some echoes of the Pauline doctrine of rightwising are found in Acts (13:38f.; 15:8–10). Nevertheless, it did not occur to the author of Acts to utilize the Pauline letters for his presentation. Of the Apostolic Fathers, I Clement, Ignatius, and Polycarp show the influence of Paul.

It is due to the influence of Paul's letters, at least for the most part, that the letter form plays a dominant role in ancient Christian literature. Letters are written not only after the example of Paul (especially Ignatius) but also under his name, so that one may speak of a Pauline school, to which II Thess., Col., and Eph. and, more remotely, the pastorals belong (see II, p. 140). I Pet. too, though it was not placed under the name of Paul, also belongs here, whereas the remaining "catholic" letters are not influenced by Pauline theology but only demonstrate that the letter form had become

---

* In America one would add (or substitute): (and) of denominational types of theology (Tr.).

customary. It is especially characteristic that the tract which came to be known as I Jn. cleverly imitates letter style in its introduction and in what was presumably its original close (5:13).* The discourse entitled Epistle to the Hebrews is provided with an ending which belatedly gives the writing the appearance of being a letter (13:18–25). Later falsifications further testify to the continuing influence of Paul's letters; among such works are: III Corinthians (preserved in Armenian and Latin), the letter to Laodicea (found in some Latin Biblical MSS), the correspondence between Paul and Seneca, and the Epistula Apostolorum (preserved in Coptic and Ethiopic; discussions in letter form between Jesus and his disciples after the resurrection).

2. The *tradition of the Hellenistic synagogue*, already at work in Paul himself, exerts greater influence in the pastorals. An important document of the Christianity which arose out of the Hellenistic synagogue is I Clem.; another is the Shepherd of Hermas, which comes out of the Roman congregation. In the latter, Jewish tradition is utilized to such an extent that it has been surmised—not without probability—that its substructure is a Jewish document which has received Christian editing. The same is true of James, in which that which is specifically Christian is surprisingly thin. At any rate, a Jewish catechism, the doctrine of the Two Ways, is worked into the Did. (1–6, 16:3–8) and also into Barn. (18–20). In all these writings it is especially the homiletic and parenetic tradition of the synagogue which continues to operate; in addition to this, in Heb. and in Barn. 1–17 it is also the tradition of the Hellenistic-Jewish Scripture-theology, *viz.*, its allegoristic exegesis (§ 11, 2b and c). In a somewhat different way Matthew shows the after-effect of Jewish scribalism in his proofs of prediction and in his conception of Jesus as the bringer of the messianic Torah (II, p. 124).

In particular the *apocalyptic literature of Judaism* exercised great influence. It is not only detectable in the whole epistolary literature of the New Testament and not only led to the weaving in of apocalyptic tradition in Mk. 13 and Did. 16, but it also led to the writing of a Christian apocalypse, that of John, in which, moreover, older Jewish tradition was utilized. Hermas also professes to be an apocalypse, but in it the apocalyptic form is essentially only the framework for hortatory remarks. This influence is further shown by the fact

---

* *Cf.* R. Bultmann, *Die kirchliche Redaktion des ersten Johannesbriefes. In Memoriam Ernst Lohmeyer*, 1951, 189–201.

that Jewish apocalypses were taken over by Christianity and handed on down with editorial alterations of greater or less degree. The Apocalypse of Peter is a case by itself; here, in addition to the influence of Jewish tradition, another tradition is at work: that of an oriental eschatology which had penetrated into Gentile Hellenism bringing along its special notions of the world beyond and especially of the underworld.

3. In part by way of the synagogue, in part directly, comes the influence of *Hellenistic popular philosophy* in the diatribe with its natural theology and ethical parenesis, as we already saw it affecting Paul (I, pp. 71f.). This influence manifests itself especially in "Paul's" Areopagus discourse (Acts 17:22–29) and in the parenesis of the pastorals, but also in Jas., especially in 3:1–12 and on a large scale in I Clem. Later on, this influence comes to full development in the apologetes and in the so-called Epistle to Diognetus.

4. To conclude the list, the tradition of *Gnostic mythology and terminology* which had already affected even Paul and John continued to have effect. It did so not merely in the fact that the terminology of Gnostic dualism and of dualistic parenesis often occurs (I, pp. 173f.) nor merely in the fact that single motifs of Gnostic mythology occur as in Rev. and Herm. but primarily in the fact that central motifs of christology, ecclesiology, and eschatology were worked out in Gnostic terminology—as we find them in Col., Eph., and the letters of Ignatius. Also, in the production of apocryphal gospels and acts of apostles Gnostic influence was at work. At first the boundary between this literature and literature which was rejected as heretical by the school of thought that had come to dominate was fluid, and it took some time until apocryphal gospels and acts in which Gnostic fantasy was let loose were excluded.

§ 57. Theology and Cosmology

PRELIMINARY REMARK

It is characteristic that theological thinking in the post-apostolic period also was not guided by a striving after a dogmatic system but was determined by concrete occasions. Consequently, many themes which became important to a later time do not enter the field of reflection, and many ideas taken over from tradition as undiscussed presuppositions are not explicitly developed. Hence, it is not appropriate to offer here a summary of the theological thoughts of the New Testament organized according to traditional *loci* in the form of a dogmatic. The themes intertwine. Since practically all of them are to be heard in the central theme of christology, and since the christological ideas are developed not as free speculation but in the interest of soteriology, the right course seems to be to make this section primarily a presentation of christology and soteriology. But since in the background of all these ideas stands the idea of God, it is advisable to preface the section with a presentation of *theology* in its narrower sense. And since theology like christology was not speculatively developed but God was spoken of only in His relation to the world, the first theme will have to be that of theology and cosmology. In developing it, the intertwining of the themes will become apparent in the fact that theology and cosmology cannot be presented without considering certain christological ideas.

Although in this section and in the rest of the book the literature of the so-called Apostolic Fathers is cited more copiously than usual, our interest in so doing is not to depict the historical development, as such, but rather through a consideration of it to clarify the motifs governing the New Testament way of thinking and to uncover the problems that lie within that thinking. The more inclusive one's view of the total development, the more light falls upon the New Testament itself.

1. It is true that in opposition to Gentile polytheism it is again and again emphasized that only one is *God* (I, pp. 67f.); but the need to prove to sceptical doubters or atheists that this God *exists* is not yet present. On the whole, it is the tradition of the Old Testament and Judaism that prevails when God is mentioned: God is the Creator and Lord of the world; He is the Judge before whose judgment-seat everyone will someday have to stand (I, pp. 73 and 75–77), but He is also the Father of Jesus Christ. As such a God He is praised in songs that come out of Christian worship or are patterned after such songs (Rev. 4:8, 11; 5:13; 15:3f.; Herm. vis. I 3:4; *cf*. I Clem. 33:2f.). Eschatological hymns which praise God's act of salvation in anticipation lie behind Lk. 1:46–55, 67–79 and perhaps also Rev. 11:15, 17f. Beyond this, thoughts taken from the natural theology of Stoicism are put to service, as they already had been in Paul, to describe the origin of the world out of God and His governance of the universe (I, pp. 70f.). Both motifs, the Hebrew and the Stoic, appear side by

side in I Clem. 33:3, for instance, as they do in the Areopagus discourse (Acts 17:24–29). As a matter of fact, natural theology is never treated by and for itself, as if in the interest of a theodicy, for instance; its ideas are only incidentally put to use. Thus the reference to the divine διοίκησις (governance) of the universe, I Clem. 20, is made in the service of an exhortation to peace and harmony, and in I Clem. 24 the reference to God's providence which makes itself known in the regular cycles of nature is forced to serve as proof for faith in the resurrection.

No necessity for a *theodicy* is felt; for to the problem of suffering a double answer is always possible. In keeping with the tradition of the Old Testament and Judaism it can be regarded as punishment for sin and hence as an instrument of God's discipline (Heb. 12:4–11; Herm. sim. VI 3–5, VII) or of His testing (Jas. 1:2f.; I Pet. 1:6f.; II Clem. 19:3f.). Or all evil can be attributed to Satan and the demons or to demonic powers of the cosmos, and here, too, the idea of testing—the eschatological πειρασμός (both "testing" and "temptation")—may be combined with it (e.g. Rev. 2:10, 3:10). Sufferings, especially those of persecution (Rev. and I Pet.) are the trials of the last days, in which faith must stand the test; they last only a little while, and so they can actually serve to strengthen hope (I Pet. 1:6f., 4:12–19, 5:10, Did. 16:5). In addition, one may find the specifically Christian thought that suffering brings one into fellowship with Christ (I Pet. 2:20f., 4:13). The depth of Paul's thinking on the subject (I, pp. 349ff.), one must admit, is never again reached; in the main, the idea gets no further than the notion of the suffering Christ as an example to be followed (I Pet. 2:21, 3:18, 4:1; Heb. 12:1f.; Ign. Eph. 10:2f.; Pol. Phil. 8:1f.).

No theoretical interest in God's general relation to the world, aside from the history-of-salvation relation, exists as yet, and the Stoic conception of the *logos*, which was later taken up by the apologetes, is not yet put to service to explain the relation of the transcendent God to the world—not by John, either, for the Logos (Word) of his prologue comes not from the philosophical but from the mythological tradition and is not used to serve the cosmological interest (II, p. 64). The same is true of the angels, who according to the tradition of the Old Testament and Judaism constitute, as it were, the courtiers of God (Heb. 1:4ff; 12:22; II Thess. 1:7; I Tim. 5:21; Rev. 5:11; 7:11; I Clem. 34:5; Herm. vis. II 2:7, sim. V 6:4, 7).

Through them God once upon a time caused the Law to be proclaimed (Acts 7:53; Heb. 2:2); they helpfully bring God's people protection and guidance (Acts 5:19; 8:26: 12:7; 27:23); in particular they mediate revelation (Rev. 1:1; 22:6, 16; Herm. mand. XI 9 and *passim.* Hermas is acquainted not only with an angel of repentance (vis. V 7, etc.) and one of righteousness (mand. VI 2:1ff.), but also with one in charge of the beasts (vis. IV 2:4) and of course Michael, too, as the angel who rules the People of God (sim. VIII 3:3). God also lets sentences of punishment be carried out by angels (Acts 12:23; Herm. sim. VI 3:2, VII 1f., 6) and in Revelation it is angels who set going each act of the eschatological drama (Rev. 5–20). They are only servants of God and must not be worshiped in any manner (Rev. 19:10; 22:8f.). There are, of course, other angels that do not serve God but are evil (Barn. 9:4; 18:1, Herm. mand. VI 2:1ff.). But we also hear of angels that have still another quite different meaning: the angelic beings of the cosmos whose origin lies not in the genuine Old Testament-Jewish tradition but in that of Gnosticism. These are the "angels, principalities, authorities, and powers" which are already found in Paul (I, p. 173); and they also include the "rulers of this age" (I Cor. 2:6, 8) and the "thrones" (Col. 1:16) and "dominions" (Col. 1:16; Eph. 1:21). Such beings, like other Gnostic motifs, had already been adopted by the Jewish apocalypses, the eschatology of which was shaped by cosmological speculation, as we have seen (I, pp. 172f.).

All such things, whether adopted from Jewish apocalyptic or from Gnostic tradition, even though they may not entirely have lost what cosmological meaning they once had, were nevertheless made *to serve the history-of-salvation understanding of the relation between God and the world.* If thought about them had been consistent, they would have called into question the idea of creation—as radical Gnosticism recognized. For the notion of the aeons and of Satan as well as that of the cosmic rulers originated in the mythology of a dualistic understanding of the universe. Nor can it be denied that the belief in creation was somewhat obscured by the acceptance of such dualistic notions; but—except in radical Gnosticism—it was not called into question.

Neither did the *figure of the devil*, which has its origin in the mythological dualism of Iranian religion, become, either in Judaism or in Christianity, the representative of a cosmic principle opposed to the divine world of light, but became, instead, an inferior opponent of God whose tempting and destructive power is, indeed, a constantly threatening danger. For Paul, Satan was essentially the tempter (I, p. 258). But just as even Paul could occasionally attribute to him the spoiling of his plans (I Thess. 2:18), so in the time after Paul the devil is held to be the instigator of all evil. He "prowls around like a roaring lion, seeking someone to devour" (I Pet. 5:8). He is the one "who has the power of death" (Heb. 2:14). He is Christ's antagonist who deceives the whole world (Rev. 12:9); he lurks behind the mysterious Antichrist (II Thess. 2:9) and behind "the beast" and the lying prophet of Rev. 13:2, 4. Above all, he is the instigator of sin. As once he seduced Judas (Lk. 22:3; Jn. 13:27; see II, p. 17), so now he is still the seducer (Acts 5:3; I Tim. 5:15; Ign. Eph. 10:3, 8:1; Herm. mand. IV 3:4, 6, V 1:3, etc.). The thing to be done is to resist him in faith (I Pet. 5:9; Eph. 4:14, 6:11; Jas. 4:7) and to beware of falling into his snare (I Tim. 3:6f.; *cf.* 6:9). A human tempter may be reviled as a "son of the devil" (Acts 13:10). Behind persecutions he is lurking, tempting people to apostasy (I Pet. 5:8f.; Rev. 2:10; Ign. Rom. 5:3). Naturally, it is also he who leads the teachers of error astray (II Tim. 2:26; Pol. Phil. 7:1). The heathen temple (of Zeus? of Augustus and Roma?) in Pergamun is his throne (Rev. 2:13), and even the Jewish synagogue may be called the "synagogue of Satan" (Rev. 2:9). It is characteristic that for Ignatius separation from one's bishop is service of the devil (Sm. 9:1), and that the cultic unity of the congregation breaks the devil's might (Eph. 13:1). Because whoever falls into his power thereby pulls down judgment upon himself, the devil's "snare" can also be called his "judgment" or "condemnation" (RSV I Tim. 3:6), and "Paul" can deliver the heretics up to Satan (I Tim. 1:20). Nevertheless, his end is certain (Rev. 20:2, 10).

Even in Rev., where the notions of apocalyptic mythology play their largest role, God still remains the "Almighty" (παντοκράτωρ— nine times in Rev., elsewhere in the New Testament only once [II Cor. 6:18]). Close to the beginning we read: " 'I am the Alpha and the Omega', says the Lord God, who is and who was and who is to come, the Almighty"—(1:8). Satan and his demonic helpers can there-fore play only that role which God has appointed them in the eschatological drama. By a heavenly act like the opening of the book of fate (6:1ff.), the blowing of the seven trumpets (8:7ff.), the emptying of the seven bowls (16:1ff.), by the call, "Come!" (6:1), by the command of an angel (7:2; 10:1ff.; 14:15, 18; 19:17) the demonic powers are given the signal, so to speak, to begin their raging; and their lack of independent action is repeatedly marked by saying "and power was given them (or him)" (6:8, 9:3; 13:5, 7; *cf.* 9:11) or simply "it was given . . ." (6:4; 7:2; 9:5; 13:7, 14f.).

2. At the same time, there were circles in which *angelic beings of the cosmos* played a different role. The New Testament and the Apostolic Fathers, it is quite true, are free from that radical Gnosticism which even in Ptolemy's moderate form (I, pp. 112f.) refuses to ascribe the creation of the world to God and ascribes it to a subordinate or even inimical Demiurge instead (I, pp. 109f.). But when I Jn. 1:5 insists that God is pure light without any darkness, that is probably a polemic against a gnosticizing Christianity which has given up the idea of creation in favor of the idea of emanation. For according to the latter idea, if the lower world of darkness developed by a series of steps out of the world of light, then the darkness must ultimately have its origin in God. It is unlikely that the heretics against whom he is writing actually said that, themselves, but the author sees that that is the logical consequence of their thinking (I, p. 170).

The dualistic view of the world could also be combined with the belief in *creation* in such a way that a fall of the creation was assumed. This is directly said by the Jewish apocalypses (IV Ezr. 3:4ff.; 7:11f.; II Bar. 23:4; 48:24f.) and is allusively suggested by Paul also (Rom. 8:20ff.; I, p. 174). However, Adam's fall, especially its cosmic significance, at first plays no role in ancient Christian literature; only in I Tim. 2:14 is there a hint of it. But when Col. 1:20 nevertheless characterizes the work of Christ as "reconciling all things to himself" and Eph. 1:10 calls it "uniting all things in him," that presupposes that prior to Christ the world had fallen into disorder and contention. Here Biblical tradition has been forsaken and Gnostic mythology is at work. Col. shows that as in Paul and John Gnostic motifs on the one hand have been taken up and that on the other hand Gnostic teachings are being combatted.

Colossians is directed against a heresy which evidently combines speculations of a syncretistic, i.e. Gnostically influenced, Judaism with the Christian faith. In it the dignity and work of Christ are impaired by the veneration of cosmic powers, which are called "elemental spirits of the universe" (2:8, as in Gal. 4:3, 9), "angels" (2:18) and "principalities and powers" (2:10, 15). The author offers no extended description of this "elements"–doctrine. But when he describes the cosmic status of Christ (1:15–20)—quoting a traditional hymn (II, p. 134 footnote)—in whom all cosmic powers have their origin and continue to exist, and when he contrasts Christ with the elemental spirits, calling him the one in whom "dwells the whole fullness of deity bodily" (2:9), we can infer that the heretics must have ascribed to the cosmic powers some sort of participation in the divinity which —in the author's view—dwells in Christ alone, or must have transferred to them a portion of the lordship which is Christ's alone. They appear to have worshiped the angelic powers (2:18); at least they served them by subservience to their δόγματα—i.e. certain ritualistic or ascetic regulations (2:16, 20f.). For that reason, the author, equating such regulations (perhaps rightly) with demands of the Old Testament Law, reminds the reader that Christ has set aside the Law (" the bond which stood against us with its legal demands", 2:14), triumphed over the angelic powers, and stripped them of their power (2:9–15).

Now, it is not as if the author of Col. contested the existence of these cosmic powers. For him, they belong to the totality of the cosmos, whose structure he conceives to be "Christ's body," of which Christ himself is the "head." It is just this which that hymn in 1:15–20 says, and so does the statement of 2:9 that the fullness of divinity dwells in Christ as its body. When the author explains the "body of Christ" as "the Church" (1:18), he conceives the latter to be a cosmic entity that reaches out beyond the empirical Church. To this cosmic "Church," then, those angelic powers also belong. Christ, by being the head of this "Church," is also "the head of every principality and power" (2:10 tr.). It is clear that here a mythological cosmology has been taken over—already taken over in the Christian redaction of that hymn* and then taken over by the author himself—in order to describe the stature and the work of Christ in comprehensive fashion; and the effort to combine the cosmological terminology with traditional Christian terminology is apparent. Christ's work of cosmic reconciliation is at the same time the reconciliation, founded

---

* Detectable in its introduction, vss. 12–14, and in the insertion of "the church" in v. 18 and of the words "by the blood of his cross" in v. 20.

in the cross of Christ, by which the former enemies of God (the heathen world sunk in its sins) were reconciled with God (1:21f.). And when the heretic is described as one "not holding fast to the Head, from whom the whole body, nourished and knit together through its joints and ligaments, grows with a growth that is from God" (2:19), a mythical terminology in which the universe is conceived as an organism is being used to describe the believer's relation to Christ. But factually the exhortation to "hold fast to the Head," which is implicit in this description, means neither more nor less than what our author soon after says in Pauline terminology: "If then you have been raised with Christ, seek the things that are above, where Christ is, seated at the right hand of God. Set your minds on things that are above, not on things that are on earth" (3:1f.).

Matters are not basically different in *Ephesians*. Here, too, the cosmological terminology has been taken over with only this difference, that here the cosmology has been more consistently reinterpreted into a history-of-salvation meaning. In the process a strange mixture of cosmological and history-of-salvation terminology often results (e.g. 2:11–22). The author does not have to fight heretics, and only occasionally does he warn against false doctrines (4:14). With no sense of impropriety he takes over Gnostic concepts to describe the work of salvation. Having first described it as "redemption" through Christ's blood, which he explicitly defines as "the forgiveness of our trespasses," he then brings in the idea of the reconciliation of the cosmos (1:10). But when he applies this idea, he interprets it as the unification of Jews and Gentiles in one "body" (2:11–22). But this "body" does not consist of cosmic powers, but is identical with the "Church" (1:22f.). Yet he uses Gnostic terminology more copiously than Colossians does, especially the myth of the Redeemer's* descent to earth and his reascension (4:8–10), which the author derives by peculiar exegesis from Ps. 68:19, also the myth that the ascending Redeemer* tore down the wall of separation that divided the lower from the upper world (2:15)—for him, however, this has become only a metaphor. The author also utilizes the picture found in Col. 2:19

---

* The author wrote "Christ's" and "Christ," but inasmuch as the "myth" alluded to comes over from pre-Christian Gnosticism (see I, pp. 167, 175), the translator has taken the liberty of substituting "Redeemer"—whom the author of Ephesians, of course, equates with Christ (Tr.).

of the connectedness of the universe as that of a body growing as a unified organism, indicating as the goal of its growth: "upbuilding in love" (4:15f.). In doing so he confuses the figure by mixing the picture of the growing body with the picture of a structure being built (still more acutely in 2:21f.).

The cosmic powers figure in Eph. not as beings belonging to the total structure of the universe who by Christ have been drawn into the reconciliation of all things, but only as enemy powers. They have now been made subject to Christ who sits in glory at God's right hand (1:20–22); that is, Christ here (as in Col. 2:15) is conceived of as their conqueror. But they are still considered threatening powers, and the author classified them with the devil (6:11f.). Men of faith are indeed freed from their rule, to which they once were subject (2:2–6), but they still have a battle to fight against them (6:10–13). Basically, everything mythological or cosmological about the idea has been here given up; for in point of fact the rule of the powers consisted of the sins and lusts of the flesh (2:1, 3). Rescue from their rule was brought about by the mercy and grace of God and by faith (2:4, 8), a rescue which manifests itself in good works (2:10). The battle against these powers is fought by the faith which holds fast to God's word and by prayer, for that is what the armor described in 6:14–18 amounts to.

The Jewish apocalypses already betray a *feeling about the world* which Paul later shares—a feeling which is no longer determined purely by the tradition of the Old Testament faith in God and creation. It is the feeling of people who feel themselves prisoners in a world pervaded with sinister powers—or if not prisoners, at least strangers in an enemy's land. Upon the soil of such a feeling it is quite understandable that the dualism and mythology of Gnosticism could take root and become influential, and that redemption through Christ could be, and was, interpreted as emancipation from these cosmic powers. Though for the "heretics" Gnostic ideas became dominant, the deutero-Pauline literature shows how the intellectual power of Paul asserted itself there and prevented any such thing. For he himself had paralyzed the dualistic mythology by his ability to make it the expression of his understanding of human existence as an historical existence (§ 26, especially 3). It is an aftermath of this element in Paul which is at work in Col. and especially in Eph., though in neither is the depth of Paul's thoughts reached.

[152]

It was also an idea of Paul's that the work of Christ was a *victory over the cosmic powers* (I Cor. 2:6–8; 15:24–26), and even before Paul the idea had already been expressed in the Christ-hymn quoted by him at Phil. 2:10f. But the characteristic idea of Paul is the conception that although the cosmic drama—begun with the resurrection of Christ—is being played in the present, it is by no means already finished. Christ's battle against the powers fills the time between his resurrection and his parousia; not until the latter will the last enemy, death, be destroyed (I Cor. 15:20–27; *cf.* I, p. 347). This corresponds to the hope of Jewish and the earliest Christian eschatology, in which the close of the cosmic drama and the triumph of God and His Messiah still lie ahead. But in keeping with Gnostic thinking is the conception that Christ's resurrection, or—here more important—his ascent, is already the glorious victory over the cosmic powers. The formulation of Phil. 2:10f. leaves it unclear whether the homage of the powers is considered already present reality or as still a thing of the future. But Col. 2:15 clearly speaks of Christ's triumph as already achieved. This conception became traditional and left its expression in a series of liturgical formulas or hymns. The hymn which underlies I Pet. 3:18–22 presumably closed with the following sentence, which we reconstruct out of v. 19 and v. 22:

Πορευθεὶς (δὲ) εἰς οὐρανὸν ἐκάθισεν ἐν δεξιᾷ θεοῦ ὑποταγέντων αὐτῷ ἀγγέλων καὶ ἐξουσιῶν καὶ δυνάμεων.
("And going into heaven he sat down at God's right hand,
With angels, authorities and powers in subjection to him." tr.)

Pol. Phil. 2:1 quotes a liturgical text which speaks of believing in

"Him who raised our Lord Jesus Christ from the dead
And gave him glory and a throne at His right hand,
To whom are subject all things in heaven and earth."

Christ's glorious ascent to heaven is also described in the hymnic fragment quoted at I Tim. 3:16, for that is what "seen by angels" and "taken up in glory" allude to. "Seen by angels" has a parallel in Ignatius: "in the sight of those in heaven and on earth and under the earth" (Ign. Tr. 9:1), even though the object of that sight named here is his crucifixion and death, for they are meant as cosmic occurrences, as which they constitute a unity with his resurrection— or, rather, his exaltation. The point of view which lies behind all these formulations comes most extensively to view in Ign. Eph. 19:

"And hidden from the ruler of this world remained the virginity of Mary and her child-birth, likewise also the Lord's death—three loudly-crying mysteries that took place in the silence of God. How, then, did it become manifest to the Aeons? A star flashed forth in heaven outshining all the stars, and its light was indescribable, and its newness caused astonishment. (Not the star of Mt. 2:2 is meant, but the luminous ascent of Christ.) . . . Thenceforth all magic was destroyed and every fetter disappeared; malignity's ignorance was canceled, the old regime was annihilated, for God had revealed himself in human form (in Jesus' birth, which is the beginning of the cosmic drama) in order to bring about new, eternal life. That began which, for God, was already completed. Thenceforth all things (=the universe) were agitated, because this would lead to the destruction of death" (Blt., tr.). Here, as the closing sentence shows, the idea of victory already won is combined with that of the conquest of death yet to come, as elsewhere the idea of victory won is combined with the traditional proposition of Christ the Judge who is to come (I Pet. 4:5; Pol. Phil. 2:1; I, p. 78).

Jude 8–11 also shows how the cosmic beings occupy the thinking of believers. Here the heretics are accused of defiling the flesh, rejecting "lordship" (κυριότητα), and reviling the "glorious ones" (δόξας), whereas the archangel Michael did not presume to revile even the devil. This allusive description cannot be interpreted with certainty; nevertheless, it is clear that κυριότης and δόξαι denote angelic powers. Perhaps we have here a case opposite to that of the heretics of Col., who out of respect for the angelic powers regard all manner of ritualistic and ascetic regulations as binding, while the heretics of Jude in the consciousness of their freedom adopt the opposite attitude and are libertines. The author, who, of course, does not need to have belonged to the angel-worshipers combatted in Colossians, at least respects those powers.

CHAPTER VII

The Core of Development

§ 58. Christology and Soteriology

To the extent that christological ideas are inseparable from cosmological ones, it was necessary to discuss some of them in the preceding section. A further interwining of themes now becomes apparent in the fact that soteriology, which forms a unity with christology, cannot be set forth without an anticipatory treatment of the problem of ethics, because the understanding of salvation is intimately connected with one's conception of the foundation of Christian living.

1. In all congregations *Jesus Christ* was worshiped *as the bringer of salvation*. It is he who is confessed at baptism, he who is worshiped in the cult as the present Kyrios (I, pp. 124f.), he who is awaited as the coming Judge and Savior (I, pp. 78f.). How important the service of worship is, is shown by the exhortations to attend the gatherings for worship (Heb. 10:25; Did. 16:2; Barn. 4:10; II Clem. 17:3; Ign. Pol. 4:2), particularly to participate in the Lord's Supper (Ign. Eph. 13) and to pray together (Ign. Tr. 12:2). The cultus has power: "Be zealous, therefore, to gather more frequently together for God's Eucharist and to give praise. For when you frequently gather together, Satan's powers are annihilated and his destructive power is destroyed by your unity of faith" (Ign. Eph. 13:1). In worship songs are sung to the praise of God and Christ. Paul already presupposes that "psalms" are sung in worship (I Cor. 14:26) and Col. 3:16 urges the singing of Spirit-given psalms, hymns, and songs; *cf.* Eph. 5:19, which is similar. Ignatius not only figuratively says that concord and the Congregation's harmony of love are a song of praise to Christ (Ign. Eph. 4:1), but also presupposes that in worship songs of praise and supplication were sung (Rom. 2:2; 4:2). In addition to (or combined with) hymns in praise of God, there were Christ-hymns. One example is the hymn which Paul quotes in Phil. 2:6–11, others are

the many hymnic fragments or sentences of liturgy which here and there are woven into the epistles and other writings.

The motifs seen in Phil. 2:6–11 are found, singly or together, in many places: the incarnation of the pre-existent one, the cross, and the exaltation. Incarnation and exaltation are sung in I Tim. 3:16. The exalted Christ and Christ the Judge to come are sung in Pol. Phil. 2:1 (see II, p. 153). If I Pet. 1:20, 3:18, 22 may be combined as fragments of a confession of faith, then it contains all three of those motifs plus a statement of the purpose of Christ's passion: it was "for sins . . . that he might bring us to God" (3:18; see also II, p. 153). I Pet. 2:21–24 perhaps also comes from a hymn; here the theme is the vicarious suffering of Christ. Christ's cosmic significance and his work of redemption is the theme of Col. 1:13–20 (from a baptismal hymn?), while Ign. Tr. 9:1f. deals with Christ's incarnation and with his resurrection which will be followed by the resurrection of the faithful. Rev. 5:9, 12 is a song of praise to "the Lamb that was slain" and by his blood obtained salvation. The salvation brought by Christ is described in I Clem. 36:1f.—evidently sentences out of a liturgy:

"Through him we fix our gaze on the heights of heaven,
  Through him we see the reflection of His (God's) faultless and
    lofty countenance,
  Through him the eyes of our hearts were opened,
  Through him our foolish and darkened understanding blossoms
    toward the light,
  Through him the Master willed that we should taste the
    immortal knowledge."

The *titles* which are given to Christ are manifold. He is the Son of God (I, pp. 128f.), the Lord (I, pp. 124f.), the Savior (I, p. 79; II, p. 158), the Judge (I, p. 78); but the old title Son of Man is no more to be found (I, pp. 79f.). In place of it other designations occasionally appear such as Pioneer (of life or of salvation; see Acts 3:15; 5:31; Heb. 2:10; 12:2; II Clem. 20:5) and High Priest (Heb. 2:17; 3:1, etc.; I Clem. 36:1; Ign. Philad. 9:1; Pol. Phil. 12:2), but also Teacher (I Clem. 13:1; Ign. Eph. 15:1; Mg. 9:1f.).

As for *Christ's person*, the reflections about his relation to God which later occupied the ancient Church are still far off. God is his Father whom he obeys (Ign. Sm. 8:1; *cf.* Mg. 7:1); the designation of

Christ as God occurs almost solely in Ignatius (see I, p. 129). Just as remote in this period are reflections about the relation between the divine and the human nature in Christ. The belief that the pre-existent one became man and was re-exalted to glory at God's right hand was sufficient. Only the miracle of his birth from a virgin here and there occupies the imagination of a writer (Mt. 1:18–25; Lk. 1:34f.; Ign. Eph. 18:2; 19:1; Sm. 1:1). Measured by later ways of putting the question the generally dominant christology would have to be called a Spirit-christology rather than adoptionistic. Only in Hermas do the motifs of an adoptionistic and of a Spirit-christology combine (sim. V), and there the combination is decidedly unclear.

The *work of salvation* as a whole consists of Christ's incarnation, his passion and death, his resurrection and exaltation, but sometimes one item, sometimes another, may be mentioned or emphasized. By and large, however, the chief emphasis lies upon his passion and death. Christ's death is the sacrifice made for us (I, p. 85). It is in this sense that his blood poured out for us is mentioned (I, p. 85), or the cross (Col. 1:20; 2:14; Eph. 2:16; Barn. 9:8; 12:1; Ign. Eph. 9:1; Tr. 11:2, etc.), or his suffering ($\pi\acute{\alpha}\sigma\chi\epsilon\iota\nu$: Mk. 8:31; Lk. 24:46; Acts 3:18; 17:3; Heb. 2:18; 9:26; I Pet. 2:19, 21; Barn. *passim*, II Clem. 1:2; Ig. Sm. 2:7; 7:1, etc.) or his sufferings ($\pi\alpha\theta\acute{\eta}\mu\alpha\tau\alpha$: Col. 1:24; I Pet. 1:11; 4:13; 5:1; Heb. 2:9f.; I Clem. 2:1) or his passion ($\pi\acute{\alpha}\theta os$, very often in Ignatius). He is "the Lamb that was slain" (Rev. 5:6ff., etc.; *cf.* Acts 8:32; I Pet. 1:19; 2:22ff.; I Clem. 16:7; Barn. 5:2; 8:2). The salvation wrought by Christ's sacrifice is generally termed forgiveness of sin, release ($\dot{\alpha}\pi o\lambda\acute{\upsilon}\tau\rho\omega\sigma\iota s$, "redemption"), rightwising ("justification"), sanctification, or purification, when it is being described in its effect upon believers (I, p. 85). In addition, it is termed victory over the cosmic powers, especially over death (see II, pp. 153f.). The benefit of the work of salvation is appropriated by baptism, the effect of which is termed as a rule forgiveness of sin (I, p. 136). Baptism is probably always in mind when forgiveness of sin is mentioned, even though it may not be explicitly named (e.g. Lk. 24:47; Acts 2:38; Herm. vis. III, 3:5).

2. But the *concept of salvation* is unambiguous only insofar as it in any case means life and rescue from death.

II Tim. 1:10 formulates it thus: Christ is he "who abolished death and brought life and immortality to light...." It is in this sense that Christ is the Savior ("rescuer"—II Tim. 1:10; Tit. 1:4, 2:13, 3:6; Acts 5:31, 13:23; II Pet. 1:1, 11, 2:20, 3:2–18; Ign. Eph. 1:1; Mg. intr., Philad. 9:2; Sm. 7:1; Pol. Phil. intr.; II Clem. 20:5; see I, p. 79) or the pioneer of salvation (Heb. 2:10) or of life (Acts 3:15; *cf.* 5:31), the "source of eternal salvation" (Heb. 5:9). In him salvation is given (II Tim. 2:10, 3:15; *cf.* Acts 4:12). He rescues from death because he himself conquered death (Heb. 2:14f.; Rev. 1:18; Barn. 5:6f.; *cf.* I Pet. 1:3, 21). The Christian message, accordingly, is called the "gospel of salvation" (Eph. 1:13), the "word of salvation" (Acts 13:26; *cf.* Heb. 2:3); its content is the "way of salvation" (Acts 16:17). "Salvation" and "life" are identical, and both may be combined in a hendiadys (Ign. Eph. 18:1; II Clem. 19:1).

But here *the views of salvation differentiate themselves* according to what is regarded to constitute the power of death and hence what kind of salvation or life corresponds to it; and further—related to this—according to whether the rescue is considered to be solely future or already present; and, finally, according to how the mediation and appropriation of salvation is conceived.

Whatever else it means, death is probably always also thought of as the literal end of natural life. Paul, however, had understood this "natural" life not as a mere phenomenon of nature, but as the human person's activity within his own history (I, pp. 209f.). Neither had he understood death as a mere event of nature, but simultaneously understood it as the already present nothingness of a life estranged from God (I, pp. 246ff.). Consequently, he had also understood the life conferred by Christ as a present reality given to a Christian in the gift of righteousness (I, p. 279), not, of course, as simply a state of being but as that freedom from sin which contains within itself the ethical imperative, and which maintains itself in hope, in the conquest of suffering and fate, and in emancipation from the world and its powers (§ 40). For Paul, that is, "life" is paradoxically a present reality. In substance the same is true of John (§ 42 and § 50, 3). To what extent has this Pauline and Johannine understanding of "life" (and "death") been retained?

Statements predominate in which *salvation is conceived as a thing of the future*. It is for "salvation" that Christ will someday appear for the benefit of those who await him (Heb. 9:28), who, by the power of God through faith are preserved "for a salvation ready to be revealed in the last time" (I Pet. 1:5; *cf.* 1:9; 2:2). Whoever calls upon the name of the Lord will (quoting Joel) be saved (Acts 2:21; *cf.* 15:11, 16:30f.).

It will be by repentance and the fear of God that one will be saved (Herm. mand. IV 3:7; VII 1, IX 6; *cf.* sim. I 11, IX 12:3; II Clem. 8:2, 13:1). Women will be saved by the bearing of children (I Tim. 2:15). The future tense of "save" or "be saved" is also used elsewhere: I Tim. 4:16; II Tim. 4:18; Did. 16:5; Barn. 1:3; Ign. Pol. 1:2; very frequently in II Clem. e.g. 4:2, 14:1.

Life is likewise often spoken of *as a life that is yet to come*—for instance when the "crown of life" is promised (Rev. 2:10; Jas. 1:12), or in the expression "hope of life (eternal)" (Tit. 1:2; Barn. 1:4, 6; Herm. sim. IX 26:2; *cf.* 14:3) or "the life which lies ahead" (Ign. Eph. 17:1), or when "salvation" and life" are combined (Ign. Eph. 18:1).

In general "life eternal" is understood (otherwise than in John) as the life to come (I Tim. 1:16, 6:12; Tit. 1:2, 3:7; Acts 13:46, 48; Jude 21; Herm. vis. II 3:2). The verbal expression "live forever" has the same meaning (Barn. 8:5, 9:2, 11:10f.). But "life" alone (Herm. vis. I 1:9) or "to live," by itself, (Heb. 12:9; Barn. 6:17; Herm. vis. III 8:5; mand. IV 2:3f., XII 6:3) also means the same thing. The future meaning of the following expressions is clear: "to obtain life" (Herm. mand. III 5; sim. VI 5:7; *cf.* "to obtain glory, honor," etc., I Clem. 54:3; Herm. mand. IV 4:2; sim. V 3:3) and "to inherit eternal life" (Herm. vis. III 8:4; *cf.* "heirs of eternal life," Tit. 3:7). To "inherit salvation" (Heb. 1:14, tr.) or "inherit the blessing" (I Pet. 1:4, tr.) also refers to future life. Just as this "inheritance" can be called "imperishable" (ἄφθαρτος, I Pet. 1:4), so in place of being called "life (eternal)" it may be called "incorruption" (ἀφθαρσία; Eph. 6:24; Ign. Philad. 9:2; II Clem. 20:5), or "incorruption" and "life eternal" may be combined with each other (Ign. Pol. 2:3; II Clem. 14:5; *cf.* "life in immortality," I Clem. 35:2).

But in other passages "*salvation*" or "*life*" is meant as *present life*. Just as believers may be called "those who are being saved" (σῳζόμενοι, Acts 2:47; I Clem. 58:2) or even "those who have been saved" (σεσωσμένοι, Eph. 2:5; Pol. Phil. 1:3), they may also be called "the living" (II Clem. 3:1). God's deed rescued them. It is God who "delivered us from the dominion of darkness and transferred us to the reign of his beloved Son" (Col. 1:13, tr.). How that deliverance is to be understood is shown by the remainder of the sentence: "in whom we have redemption, the forgiveness of sins" (1:14). In so writing, the author probably has baptism in mind—in keeping with the likelihood that the hymn which he adapts in vss. 15–20 comes out of a baptismal liturgy. From the fact that he prefaces the hymn with the statement: "giving thanks to the father, who has qualified you (*v. l.* us) to share in the inheritance of the saints in light" (v. 12), we see that he so relates present and future salvation as to regard the state of present salvation as an anticipation of that future salvation which is guaranteed by baptism. So, in spite of 1:14, true "life" is, itself, still future; as 3:3 puts it, it is "hid with Christ in God" and, further, "When Christ who is our life appears, then you will also appear with him in glory" (3:4). Consequently, the author can say that the Gospel proclaims "the hope laid up for you in heaven" (1:5; *cf.* 1:23, 27).

What we have here observed in Col. is typical. In similarly paradoxical manner Eph. speaks of the present reality of salvation: "but God . . . even when we were dead through our trespasses, made us alive together with Christ . . . and raised us up with him and made us sit in the heavenly places in Jesus Christ" (2:5f.). This author, too, is thinking of *baptism* (*cf.* 5:26), and present salvation is anticipatory of the future; for the content of the "illumination" brought by the Gospel is knowing "what is the hope to which he has called you . . ." (1:18; *cf.* 4:4). That the deliverance was accomplished by baptism is said in many places (Tit. 3:5; I Pet. 3:21; Barn. 11:11; Herm. vis. III 3:5; mand. IV 3:1; sim. IX 16:2ff.). It is just because baptism has taken place that it can be said of the deliverance ("salvation") that it has already occurred (*cf.* in addition to the last list of passages: II Clem. 1:4; 2:7; 3:3; 9:2, 5; Herm. sim. VIII 6:1; IX 26:8).

Just as the acquisition of salvation can be attributed to baptism, so it can also be attributed to being "*called*," without any substantial difference in meaning, for by his "calling" the Christian is called into the Church, and he is received into the Church by baptism. (In Hermas κλῆσις—"calling"—is actually a direct designation of baptism; mand. IV 3:6; *cf.* 3:4; sim. VIII 11:1; sim. IX 14:5). The "saved" or the "living" therefore may also be called "the called" (Heb. 9:15; Herm. sim. IX 14:5) or "the called, sanctified ones" (κλητοὶ ἡγιασμένοι, I Clem., intr.). God, or Christ, called them "into his marvelous light" (I Pet.

2:9), "from darkness into light" (I Clem. 59:2; *cf.* II Clem. 1:2, 8). They were called "to the peace of Christ . . . in one body" (Col. 3:5; *cf.* Eph. 1:11 in the text of ADG it, 4:4), to "eternal life" (I Tim. 6:12), to "the obtaining of glory" (II Thess. 2:14; *cf.* I Pet. 3:9, 5:16). Κληθῆναι ("to be called") often occurs without any complement (Eph. 4:1; II Tim. 1:9; I Pet. 1:15; II Pet. 1:3; II Clem. 2:4, 7, 5:1, etc.); so does κλῆσις ("calling": Eph. 1:18, 4:1, 4; II Thess. 1:11; II Tim. 1:9; Heb. 3:1; II Pet. 1:10; I Clem. 46:6; Herm. mand. IV 3:6; sim. VIII 11:1). The relation of the believer to the future is perhaps more strongly expressed by his "calling" than it is by the term "deliverance"; at least it is in II Thess. 1:11, or in expressions like "the hope of your calling" (Eph. 1:18) and "the calling of his promise" (Barn. 16:9); *cf.* also the "heavenly call" of Heb. 3:1.

3. The decisive question now is how *the relation between salvation's present reality and its futurity is conceived.* Has the dialectic understanding of this relation, such as we found it in Paul and John been retained? Is it still understood that it is the situation of the Christian to be in that peculiar "betweenness"—between "no longer" and "not yet" (see I, p. 322)? In very general terms it may be said that through the call into the Church, through the present forgiveness of sin mediated by baptism, the possibility of future salvation is bestowed; and likewise that the present stands under the ethical imperative, the fulfilment of which is the condition for achieving future salvation. But the real question is: is future life regarded as already a present reality in the very fulfilling of the imperative? To ask it differently: which is true—that the forgiveness mediated by baptism is conceived as absolution from the debts contracted up to the time of baptism and from the punishment they deserve? or that it is conceived as emancipation from the power of sin?

a. The problems involved in the situation may perhaps be made clearest by examining an extreme case. Such is the *Shepherd of Hermas.* Here we read (vis. III 3:5): "your life was saved and shall be saved through water"—the baptism which has saved you will bring about your future salvation. But this is dependent upon a pure conduct of life. The "heavenly letter" which Hermas receives, assures him: "But what saves you is the fact that you have not fallen away from the living God, and your sincerity, and your great continence. These things have saved you on condition that you persevere in them, and they save all who do likewise and walk in innocence and sincerity" (vis. II 3:2 tr.). Baptism brings about salvation only insofar as it frees one from his previously committed sins (mand. IV 3:1–3; 4:4) and thereby makes possible a new beginning for his life; but henceforth he must lead his life on his own responsibility in obedience to the commandments of God which Hermas constantly urges upon his readers. In the end, then, not baptism but his own good conduct saves the believer. For good conduct, "life" is promised (e.g. mand. III 5, IV 2:4, XII 6:3). No wonder that the problem of sins committed after baptism then arises. The revelation which Hermas professes to have received is just this: that after the benefit of the first repentance (at baptism) has been trifled away, now one last time before the impending end the possibility of repentance has been given by God (vis. II 2:4–8, mand. IV, 3, sim. IX 26:6). The Christian stands, indeed, between the past and the future, but this "between" is only a chronological one; it is a between-time, an interval which must be utilized for repentance. The whole book is a call to repentance, and the author is at pains to show that "repentance" is an "insight," the effect of which is to cause the sinner to recognize and repent his sins and to walk henceforth according to the commandments of God (mand. IV 2:2–4, etc.). It is characteristic of Hermas that for him "Faith" is one of the virtues (mand. VIII 8f., XII 3:1, sim. X 4:2), in fact, the chief virtue to which Continence, Simplicity, Knowledge, Innocence, Reverence, and Love are "daughters." But this *pistis* is nevertheless nothing other than faith in the one God (mand. I).

b. The exhortations of *James* also are pervaded with reference to the coming retribution and the judgment. He takes it for granted that the Christian is subject to the Law, the authority of which he emphasizes with the adjectives "perfect" and "royal" (1:25; 2:8), and that the Law, as a whole, must be observed (2:13f.). Why he also calls it "Law of freedom" (1:25; 2:12) is a riddle.* At any rate, the Pauline idea of freedom is just as remote from the author's mind as is Paul's concept of faith. Works of good conduct are required, and of the "doer of the Law" it is said: "he shall be blessed in his doing" (1:25).

This attitude finds its strongest expression in the polemic against a point of view which claims that salvation is awarded

---

* "Law of freedom" is probably a Jewish term; it seems that it occurs three times in the "Dead Sea Manual of Discipline" (M. Burrows, *Dead Sea Scrolls* II 2, 1951). *Cf.* E. Stauffer in *Th. L. Z.* 77 (1952), 577ff.

to a faith that is without works (2:14–26). The fact that the author polemizes against the proposition that Abraham was justified by faith alone makes it likely that that point of view is supposed to be Paul's or that of some group claiming Paul as its authority. If so, Paul's concept of faith is thereby utterly misunderstood. For Paul would certainly have agreed with the proposition that a faith without works is dead (2:17, 26) but never in the world with the thesis that faith works along with works (2:22). James can so speak only because he understands by faith merely the theoretical conviction of the existence of the one God, a belief which even the demons have (2:19).

Every shred of understanding for the Christian's situation as that of "between-ness" is lacking here. The moralism of the synagogue-tradition has made its entry, and it is possible that James not merely stands in the general context of this tradition but that its author took over a Jewish document and only lightly retouched it (see II, p. 143).

c. To this type belongs also *the Didache*, in the first part of which a Jewish catechism for proselytes is woven in (see II, p. 143), and which contained ethical commandments and prohibitions according to the scheme of the "Two Ways," and which the author enriched by interpolating words of the Lord. Naive belief in retribution dominates the exhortations, and the conclusion of the book, which refers to the coming judgment and exhorts the reader to "be watchful" (16:1) and promises salvation to those who "endure in their faith" (16:5), probably also comes out of the Jewish catechism.

d. *Barnabas*, too, took over that Jewish catechism (18–21). Its author also stands within the tradition of the Hellenistic synagogue with his allegoristic method of interpreting the Old Testament (§ 11, 2b). Nevertheless, his understanding of Christian existence, no matter how inconsistently he carries it out, goes beyond that of Herm., Jas., and the Did., and approaches that of the deutero-Pauline writings; this is all the more noteworthy in that the author is not under the influence of Pauline theology. It is true, he knows the forensic concept of "righteousness" (13:7, following Gen. 15:6; otherwise, he uses "righteousness" in the ethical sense: 1:4, 6; 5:4; 20:2—likewise "righteous": 10:11; 19:6), but Christians are not, for him, already rightwised (4:10; *cf.* 15:7). Salvation is a future thing (6:17–19; 15:5–9); believers are already at the last time (4:3, 9; 21:3) and have to prepare themselves by conscientious fulfilment of "the new law of our Lord Jesus Christ" (2:6), or of the "ordinances" (2:1; 10:11, etc.) or "commandments" (4:11; 16:9, etc.) "of the Lord" —for the judgment according to one's works lies ahead (4:12; *cf.* 15:5; 21:1, 3), the judgment which Christ as the coming Judge will hold (5:7; 7:2). The call to repentance, however, is missing; "repentance" occurs only once (16:9), but there it evidently means baptismal repentance.

Nevertheless, the present existence of Christians is already a new one. They are the "new People" (5:7; 7:5), the "People of the inheritance" (14:4), the "holy People" (14:6) to whom God's covenant pertains (13, 14)—in contrast to the Jewish people, which never had a true covenant with God (§ 11, 2b). The Christians' situation has become a new one by the fact that Christ, the Son of God, came and revealed himself in the flesh (5:6, 10f.; 6:7, 9, 14; 12:10), suffered for us on the cross and died (5:1f., 12f.; 7:2f. 12:1ff.), and thus by his blood (5:1) achieved for us the forgiveness of sins (5:1f; 7:3, 5) and by his resurrection destroyed death and gave us life (5:6; 7:3; 12:5). By these means he "renewed" us so that we now have the souls of children; he "created us anew" (6:11, 14; 16:8). His work is appropriated by us in baptism (11:8, 11; *cf.* 8:3; 16:9), which establishes a new life by the gift of the Spirit (1:2f.). Hence, the Christian can be called "a spiritual temple being built for the Lord" (16:10), and yet can be exhorted: "Let us be spiritual, let us be a perfect temple for God" (4:11, tr.). Otherwise, however, the Spirit plays no essential role, and the contrast between flesh and spirit occurs only at 7:3, where Christ's flesh is called "the vessel of the Spirit" (*cf.* 11:9). *Pneuma* denotes mainly the prophetic spirit of the Old Testament, except where the author is speaking non-technically of the "spirit" or "spirits" of his readers (*cf.* 11:11 where "in the spirit" parallels "in the heart"—a parallelism missed by Lake's translation). The new existence of Christians as "God's temple" is described in 16:9: "His word of faith, his call of promise, the wisdom of the ordinances, the commandments of the teaching, he himself prophesying in us, he himself dwelling in us, he leads us who were enslaved to death— opening the door of the temple (that is, the mouth) and giving us repentance—into the incorruptible temple."

Corresponding to the fact that in this description the "word of faith" stands first, "faith" is again central where it is said of the Christians "we are made alive" (N.B.: not "rightwised") by faith in the promise and by the word" (6:17). The "word" which is to be believed (9:3; 11:11) contains, of course, the message of Christ's work, which is the object of "believing" (7:2). But Christian existence can also be described as "believing God" (16:7) and occasionally also by just the noun "faith" (4:9) or just the verb "believe" (3:6 and 13:7 quoting Gen. 17:4f. and 15:6). Nevertheless, the concept of "faith" is not emphasized, nor is it sharply outlined; it is not placed in contrast to "works." The term "grace" correspondingly scarcely plays a role; it is used of Old Testament prophecy (5:6) and of baptismal grace (1:2); the content of the cross (9:8) and of preaching (14:9 quoting Is. 61:1f.) is "grace" (also used in a formula of greeting at the close, 21:9). In the obviously traditional triad "faith, love, hope" (1:4, 6; *cf.* 11:8), which are descriptive of Christian existence, the terms are not sharply distinguished from each other; according to 1:4 "faith" and "love" dwell in the Church "in the hope of his life," and according to 1:6 "the hope of life" is the beginning and end of faith. The new covenant is to be sealed in the heart "in the hope which belongs to faith in him" (4:8). Faith, for Barnabas, evidently is essentially hoping trust (*cf.* 12:7), a meaning that is also apparent in the fact that to believe in Jesus and to hope in him are interchangeable expressions (*cf.* 6:3 with 6:9; 11:11; 12:2f.; 16:8); in reference to God the verbs can also interchange: 19:7 uses "hope in God" in place of "believe in God." If faith's helpers are "fear" and "patience" (2:2), that points to a meaning of "faith" that lies in the same direction

But more important and more characteristic is the connection between "faith" and "knowledge." The author writes to his readers "in order that along with your faith you may have your knowledge complete (or perfect)" (1:5). The content of this "knowledge" is "the way of righteousness" (5:4), which primarily means the knowledge, given by the Old Testament, of that which is past, present, and future (1:7; 5:3), along with which, of course, knowledge of the "ordinances" is also given (21:5; *cf.* 6:9; 19:1). This knowledge is the new knowledge given by God, who is called He "who placed in us wisdom and understanding of his secrets" (6:10; *cf.* 5:3; 7:1). It is conferred upon him who has faith and virtue (2:3). Because "knowledge" and "teaching" constitute a unity, God can also be called He "who placed the implanted gift of his teaching in us" (9:9).

All in all, the understanding of Christian faith is less legalistic in

Barn. than in Herm., Jas., and the Did. The paradox of Christian existence between "no longer" and "not yet," and hence the determination of the present by the future, is not clearly set forth, it is true, yet occasionally it is involuntarily expressed. The exhortation "let us become spiritual" (4:11) is directed to such as have already received the Spirit and are "the temple of God." And it is as men "made alive by the word" (6:17) that they will receive the life to come.

e. Related to Barnabas is *Hebrews*. For its author, too, the life of the believer stands essentially under the demand of God. Responsibility has become greater for Christians than it was for Israel (2:2f.; 10:26–31; 12:25). God is an unbribable judge (4:12f.), and it is a fearful thing to fall into His hands (10:31). But the relation of the present to the future goes beyond the relation between human conduct and divine retribution, because the present is in a certain sense already a time of salvation. The believers' present situation is characterized by the fact that they are "those who have once been enlightened and have become partakers of the Holy Spirit, and have tasted the goodness of the word of God and the powers of the age to come" (6:4f.). And yet—does all this solemn description really mean anything more than that they have been baptized? Otherwise the essential description given of the present is that it is the time of the New Covenant (8:6–13; 10:15–18) which came into being by the sacrifice of himself which Christ as High Priest made, so that the entrance to the sanctuary stands open (10:19f.) and believers, freed from the fear of death (2:14f.), now have access to God and "confidence" and "hope" (3:6; 4:16; 6:11, 18; 7:19, 25). They can confidently approach the "throne of grace" (4:16—in prayer is probably meant, after all; *cf.* 7:25; 10:22). Nevertheless, the Christian is conscious of his accountability to the heavenly Judge, and the resultant paradox is misunderstood if one regards the new thing in the present reality of salvation to be that it contains the possibility, after the release (by baptism) from one's past sins, of achieving salvation by the Christian's new kind of conduct.

The problem of sins committed after baptism did not, in itself, oppress the author. To be sure, "deliberate" sins are unforgivable (10:26–31), and for grave sins, especially that of apostasy, there is no possibility of repentance (6:4–6; 12:16f.). The intercession of Christ for the believers (7:25; *cf.* 2:17) apparently means no more than that they can receive forgiveness for occasional sins. Unlike Hermas, the author does not call his readers to repentance; evidently the baptized have repented once for all (6:1, 6). He does call them to "endurance" (ὑπομονή, 10:36; 12:1), to hold fast to their "confidence" and "hope" (3:6, 14; 6:11; 10:23, 35); the really sinful sin is precisely that of apostasy. In harmony with this conception is Hebrew's concept of faith (I, p. 91). "Faith" first means, of course, acceptance of the missionary message (6:1; 11:6), then also trust (10:22), but above all it means faithfulness, fidelity (6:12; 10:22, 11 *passim*, 13:7; it is synonymous with ὑπομονή, "endurance," *cf.* 10:35–39) and hope (11 *passim*).

The "faith" by which the "righteous one" will live (10:38) is his "endurance"; the faith by which Abel was approved as "righteous" (11:4) can hardly be defined in any other way than simply belief in God. The contrast between "faith" and "works" plays no role in Heb.; neither does "rightwising by faith" or Paul's "righteousness from God." (*Dikaiosyne* in Heb. means "uprightness" in 1:9, 11:33, 12:11; or "the right," 5:13; or the "justice" of a ruler, 7:2; only once does it mean the substance of salvation: the "righteousness" which Noah achieved by virtue of his obedience, 11:7). The believer's trust, it is true, is toward the grace of God, and in 12:15 "grace" evidently means saving grace—probably also in 13:9 and 10:29. But the contrast between "grace" and "works" is missing; and in 4:16, where "grace" and "mercy" are co-ordinated, that is the grace of God which the one praying hopes to find "in time of need"—i.e. help in each particular time of need. What is important to the author is, rather, that Christians are "purified" and "sanctified"—i.e. by baptism. Christ's blood "purifies our conscience from dead works in order that we may serve the living God" (9:14 Blt.; *cf.* 1:3, 10:22; for "sanctify," which according to 9:13f. is synonymous with "purify," see 2:11, 10:10, 14, 29, 13:12). No reconciliation between these indicatives and the imperative "strive . . . for sanctification" (12:14 tr.; *cf.* 12:10) is attempted, nor between the two uses of τελειοῦν. This word means in 9:9 (*cf.* 9:14) and 10:1, 14 just what καθαρίζειν and ἁγιάζειν mean: "dedicate" or "sanctify"; but in 11:40 and 12:23 (*cf.* 12:2) it means "bring to completion or perfection" (the verb has this meaning even where applied to Christ: 2:10, 5:9, 7:28). The explanation for this double usage is that the dedication proleptically places the dedicated into heavenly existence, i.e. separates him from the world's sphere, desecularizes him. But the inner connection between the desecularization which takes place in the dedication and the desecularization which is to be brought about by one's own effort (13:13f.) is not made evident by the author. The imperative is here not truly founded upon the indicative. The purification of the conscience in 9:14 (*cf.* 10:2, 22) is simply the forgiveness of former sins conferred in baptism, and the "good conscience" of the baptized consists in their desiring to "act honorably in all things" (13:18). Of dying and rising with Christ there is no mention. The cross of Christ is referred to as an example for the Christian to follow (12:2f., 13:13). The author does know of "distributions of the Holy Spirit" (i.e. gifts distributed by the Holy Spirit), 2:4, and knows that in baptism the Spirit is given (6:4), and says (10:29) that he who has fallen away from the faith has insulted the "Spirit of grace." But the Spirit which is the power of Christian living (Paul's view) is not what he is talking about. Instead he is trying to teach the believer to understand the woes that come upon him as the discipline of God (12:4–11).

Because the dialectic relationship between imperative and indicative has been lost from sight, salvation is really only future, and the present simply stands under God's demand; insofar as the present is a "between," it is only a between-time, an interval that will last for a little while longer, in which by his "endurance" the believer must hold out (10:36, etc.). It is significant that the problem of legalism does not concern the author; all that interests him about the Torah is the sacrificial-ceremonial law which he interprets allegorically (§ 11, 2c).

f. The opening section of *II Peter* creates a first impression that its author has an understanding of Christian faith that goes beyond the field of legalistic moralism; for it is also true that the influence of the synagogue tradition is scarcely detectable in II Pet. In 1:3–11 the ethical imperative is given its foundation in the indicative—out of the "faith" by which the divine gift was accepted a whole chain of attitudes or modes of acting is derived: "virtue—knowledge—self-control—steadfastness—godliness—brotherly affection—love." But the unfolding of these modes of acting is made the responsibility of the believer's own σπουδή (effort, diligence)—the Spirit is mentioned only in 1:21, where it means that which inspires prophecy—and this "effort" has for its goal the confirmation of one's "call" and "election" (1:10). In point of fact, for this author God's gift is limited to His calling the believer to future salvation (1:3f.), or one might also say limited to baptism, which cleanses one from his former sins (1:9). When the author is defining the purpose of the promises given in God's call ("in order that you may share a divine nature, escaping the worldly corruption that lies in desire," 1:4, tr.), it is not clear whether his intention is to describe the present state of the Christian or to describe future salvation. Even if the former is his intention the present reality of salvation is still not conceived as a paradoxical one but as a quality of one's nature (a quality acquired through baptism). At any rate, in spite of all the author's high words about the already received gift of God (1:3f.), for him salvation lies basically in the future. For his purpose in writing is clearly to combat doubt about the coming of Christ (1:16; 3:4, 12) and to impress upon his readers the seriousness of the coming judgment and their consequent responsibility to lead a pure life (3:14, 17f.).

The situation is much the same in *Jude*, except that his exhortation looks forward not like II Pet. to "the day of judgment and destruction of ungodly men" (II Pet. 3:7) but to "the mercy of our Lord Jesus Christ" which will bestow upon us "eternal life" (Jude 20f.). That such expectation is founded upon pure living is the indirect implication not only of his description of the heretic's blasphemous way of life which the judgment will condemn, but also of the closing doxology with its confidence that God will keep the readers faultless and unblemished (24).

g. There is a clear-cut peculiar kind of Christian legalism in *II Clement*. The document bearing this title is an exhortatory and penitential sermon which looks forward to the coming judgment and the salvation promised to the pious. Judgment will be according to one's works (6:9; 11:6; 16:3; 17:4) and the whole life of a Christian must be an athlete's "contest" and for victory in it a crown beckons (7:1ff.). But the author's exhortation is motivated by reference to the Christian's present as it is conditioned by the work of Christ. Though "salvation" is mostly conceived as future (e.g. 19:3, "that we may be saved at the end"), believers are nevertheless already saved (3:3; 9:2). Christ who came as the "savior" and the "pioneer of incorruption" (20:5) saved them (1:4, 7; 2:7; 9:5); he called them (1:2, 8, etc.); he suffered for their sake (1:2). Believers are his "body" (14:2), that is, "the Church," which, as spiritual Church, was pre-existent and with the appearing in the flesh of the spirit-Christ has now likewise appeared in the flesh (14:1ff.). Those received by baptism into the "Church" must now keep pure their baptism or "seal" (6:9; 7:6; 8:6). They must give thanks for the gift of salvation and requite it (ἀντιμισθία, 1:3, 5; 9:7; 15:2) with a confession which consists in deeds (3:1ff.; 4:1ff.) and repentance (9:8). To keep baptism or "the seal" pure also means "to keep the flesh pure" (8:4, 6; 9:3; 14:3); i.e. to renounce the world and its desires (5:4; 6:4; 16:2, etc.) and to lead one's life in good works, in "uprightness," as one who is "upright," "holy," "reverent" (6:9; 11:7; 12:1; 15:3; 19:2f., etc.). Though love (ἀγάπη, 4:3; 9:6; 12:1; 13:4; 15:2; 16:4) is also regarded as a "virtue" (10:1), yet for II Clem. the characteristic virtue is ἐγκράτεια (self-control, abstinence, continence—4:3; 15:1), which even goes to the extent of sexual asceticism (12:5).

It is possible to find in II Clem. a founding of the imperative upon the indicative, but the Pauline paradox of it is lacking, and consequently so is the paradoxical realization of the future in the present. Here, too, then, the "betweenness" of Christian existence is that which determines only its chronology and not its character.

How far removed the author is from Paul may also be seen from the fact that though he occasionally speaks of temptation, to which he himself, being "altogether sinful" (πανθαμαρτωλός, 18:2), is also subject, he does not speak of the power of sin nor of its cancellation. "The flesh" for him is not an evil power, but is the sphere of the earthly (5:5, 8:2, 9:1ff., 14:3ff.), and as he urges men to "keep the *flesh* pure," he also teaches the resurrection of the "flesh" (9:1ff.). Similarly, *pneuma* is not the eschatological gift and power but indicates anything that is of heavenly nature (9:5, 14:1ff.). "Righteousness" is not the very substance of eschatological salvation (the cognate verb, δικαιοῦσθαι, "rightwise," never occurs), but is the uprightness that must be practised ("do righteousness", 11:7, 19:3) and the δίκαιοι (in Paul: "the righteous") here are really the good (11:1, 17:7, 20:3). The combination of δίκαιος with ὅσιος ("pious") is significant of their related meanings (5:6, 6:9, 15:3), and the occurrence of the terms εὐσεβής, εὐσέβεια, θεοσέβεια ("pious," "piety," "piety toward God"—the latter almost="religion"; *cf.* RSV I Tim. 2:10—II Clem. 19:1, 4, 20:4) is also characteristic. Significant by comparison with Paul is the author's moral consolation in regard to suffering: if piety were already to receive its reward now, we would be practising trade and not religion (20:4); and he accompanies his exhortation to renounce the world with the consoling assurance: "the sojourn of this flesh in this world is slight and short of duration" (5:5; *cf.* 6:6, 7:1). Religious enthusiasm and charismatic phenomena are also completely lacking.

The Christianity of II Clem., then, is no less a legalistic one than is that of Herm., Jas., Did., Barn., and Hebrews, differing from theirs only in the fact that its legalism (as in II Pet. and Jude) is less shaped by the synagogue tradition and is more strongly influenced by certain Hellenistic tendencies of asceticism and flight from the world.

h. The *Letter of Polycarp*, consisting essentially of ethical exhortations ("concerning uprightness", 3:1), is the document of a Christianity estranged from the world and conditioned by hope in the future (8:1). Christians still live in the present age and look for the age to come (5:2). They hope for the resurrection of the dead (2:2; 5:2) and look ahead to the coming judgment which Christ will hold (2:1; 6:2; 11:2). Doubt of the resurrection and the judgment is combatted as heresy (7:1). In this present time the Christian's relatedness to the future must be carried out in the form of renunciation of the world: ἀπέχεσθαι ("to refrain from . . ." 2:2; 5:3; 6:1, 3; 11:1f.) and ἀπολείπειν ("to put aside", 2:1; 7:2) are the key words that pervade the exhortations; worldly desires are to be rooted out (5:3; *cf.* 7:1 and "continence" in 4:2). Thus the future conditions the present only negatively; of the idea that the future also positively conditions the present because the future is paradoxically present, there is no trace. The statements about Christ—that he came in the flesh (7:1) and suffered and died for us and our sins (1:2; 8:1; 9:2), that he arose and is exalted to be the ruler and judge (1:2; 2:1f.; 9:2)—amount only to this: that by them Christian hope in the coming resurrection is well founded (2:2; 8:1). There is no mention of the Spirit as the eschatological gift and the power of the new life, nor of the charismatic gifts. Christ, characteristically, is termed our "pledge" (of righteousness) who died for our sins (8:1). Similarly there is also no mention of *Sarx* as the power of sin. An echo of Gal. 5:17 is heard in the formulation, "every lust wars against the Spirit (spirit?)," in which it is doubtful whether the Holy Spirit is meant or merely man's better self (as in the quotation from Mk. 14:38 at 7:2). At any rate, Holy Spirit (πνεῦμα ἅγιον) does not occur. Nor is the present reality of future life through the sacraments touched upon; the sacraments are not mentioned.

[171]

Although the author knows some Pauline letters, Paul's doctrine of justification is echoed in 1:3 only: "knowing that by grace you are saved, not by works but by the will of God through Jesus Christ" (dependent upon Eph. 2:5, 8f. ?). The author does not speak of "being rightwised" (nor of "salvation" or of "being saved") and uses δικαιοσύνη (with the possible exception of 8:1) only in the sense of ethical "uprightness" (2:3, 3:1, 3, 4:1, 9:1f.); except in 1:3 "grace" occurs only in the closing wish (which is known to us only in Latin translation). *Pistis* in the Pauline sense plays no role; the word (usually absolute) is most frequently used: to denote Christianity 1:2 (the verb "believe" in the same way, 5:2), often in combinations: with "hope" and "love" 3:2f.; with "love" and "purity" 4:2; with "uprightness" 9:2; with "patience" 13:2; its object is often given by an εἰς ("in"): "in the Lord" 1:2 (?) ,13:2; "in him who raised the Lord" 2:1, 12:2; by an objective genitive: 4:3. Christian teaching may be called "the word concerning truth" 3:2, "the word handed down to us from the beginning" 7:2, "the word of righteousness" 9:1.

The statements about Christ's suffering and dying for our sins of course imply the thought of forgiveness brought by Christ; but the problem of post-baptismal sins does not engage the author. He knows that we all "owe the debt of sin" and hence must hope for future forgiveness at the judgment (6:1f.). That the sinner must repent is said in connection with a particular case (11:4); otherwise, "repentance" and "repent" are not mentioned. But forgiveness will be granted in the judgment only to those who serve Christ "with fear and reverence" (6:3). Exhortations to serve God or Christ in fear (2:1, 4:2, 6:3), to fulfill the "commandment of uprightness" (3:3), to obey the "word of uprightness' (9:1), to do the will of Christ or God and to walk in his "commandments" (or "worthily of his commandment" 2:2, 4:1, 5:1) run all through the letter. This manner of "walking" is concretely described in virtue-catalogues and especially in vice-catalogues (4:3, 5:2f., 6:1f.). Wives and widows are exhorted on the Haustafel pattern (4:2f.), as are the deacons, the youths and the maidens (5:2f.), and then the elders (6:1). Once he uses a word of the Lord for his parenesis (2:3—see Mt. 7:1f., Lk. 6:37f., or perhaps I Clem. 13:2). That the "commandment of uprightness" culminates (or is summed up) in "love" is. said in 3:3: "for he who has love is far from all sin" (a quotation?). Furthermore, "love" in combination with "faith" and "hope" characterizes Christian existence (see foregoing paragraph).

Throughout this book, then, the life of the Christian is understood as a preparation for coming salvation made by fulfilling the "commandments," by a way of life which renounces the world. The present is not understood as already full of the future's power and Paul's founding of the imperative (upon the indicative) has been forgotten. An echo of it can be found, if one likes, in 2:1, where the reminder, "by grace ye were saved" (1:3) is followed by the exhortation: "therefore . . . serve God." Anyway, a clear echo does occur in 8:1f., where after reference has been made to Christ's suffering for our sins we read: "Let us then be imitators of his endurance" (*cf.* 10:1). But that the believer is set free to the freedom of obedience, is a lesson the author did not let Paul teach him; in fact the term "freedom" (ἐλευθερία) is completely missing.

i. The threatening judgment which *the Revelation of John* proclaims in chapters 6–18 (–20) is the judgment over the world at enmity with God. It threatens the Church, too, one must admit: that is why it is admonished, especially in the letters to the seven churches in chapters 2, 3 (especially 3:2f.; later also 16:15), to be watchful and true to the faith. But it is primarily to comfort and strengthen it that the Church is made to contemplate the coming judgment. This very fact indicates that in a certain sense the author knows of a future power at work in the present—that sense, however, goes no further than this: that the hope in which the Church lives is certain of fulfilment. This certainty finds expression in the hymns and triumph-songs sung in heaven in praise of God's eternal reign and of His and "the Lamb's" eschatological victory (*cf.* especially 11:15, 17f.; 12:10f.; 19:1f., 6–8) and, at the end of the book, in the fact that future salvation is beheld in the picture of the New Jerusalem which is already present in heaven and is only awaiting the hour, so to speak, to let itself down upon the earth (21:1–22:5). Such a hope, one readily sees, harmonizes with thoughts of Paul (Rom. 8:24f., 31–39), for whom "faith" is simultaneously "hope" (§ 35, 3); and in the hope which faith is, the Church already has in its possession, as it were, a present treasure, which, for all its poverty, makes it rich (2:9), while the seemingly wealthy one is in reality poor (3:17). But for Paul future life is nonetheless present reality in a different way, inasmuch as Paul understands suffering as the weakness in which the power of the Lord comes to perfection (I, pp. 349–51). It may be that such an understanding can be surmised behind the words of

Rev., but it is never put into words—for this reason, if for no other, that as suffering the author has one-sidedly in view the sufferings of persecution (2:3, 9f.; 6:9; 7:14; 12:12, 17; 13:7). For him the consolation consists in the fact that the "crown of life"—heavenly reward—is certain for him who is faithful (*passim*—e.g. 2:10; 7:13–17; 14:3; 22:14) and, beyond that, that the Church will be preserved in the midst of the terrors of the end (3:10; 7:1–8; 14:1–5). In addition, the idea occurs that suffering is a salutary discipline (3:19).

The certainty of this hope is founded upon the death of Christ, "the Lamb that was slain" (5:6, 9; 13:8), whose blood redeems and cleanses (5:9; 7:14). What sort of relationship exists between Christ and his own is a question that cannot be clearly answered, because the author does not reflect about it; at any rate, the verb "believe" is not used to denote that relationship. *Pistis* occurs a few times (2:13; 13:10; 14:12; combined with "love" 2:19), but with the meaning "faithfulness," just as πιστός means the faithful, dependable one (2:10, 13; 17:14). Christ himself is the "faithful (or "reliable") witness" (1:5; 3:14) and the words of the book are "reliable and true" (21:5; 22:6 tr.). *Pistis* is usually combined with "endurance" (2:19; 13:10; 14:12), and the praise of "endurance," or exhortation to show endurance, pervades the whole book. Worthy of the highest praise is he who has carried "endurance" to the point of martyrdom (2:13; 6:9–11; 7:9–17). Christ's word is the "word of endurance" which is to be held fast (3:10; *cf.* 3:3, 8), and it means the same thing when the author urges the "keeping" of the words of his book (1:3; 22:7, 9); likewise the exhortation to "hold fast what you have" (2:25; 3:11). "Holding fast the name" (2:13) has its negative parallel in "not denying the name" (3:8) or "the faith" (2:13). One must also "keep my works" (2:36) or "keep the commandments of God" (12:17; 14:12), or, in figurative language, "keep one's garments" (16:5). Besides "endurance," "works" are demanded (2:2, 19). According to his works each man will be recompensed (2:23; 20:12f.; 22:12); and the works of those who die "in the Lord" will follow them (14:13). By the words of the heavenly Lord, "I know your works," the churches receive comfort or warning as the case may be (2:2; 2:13, variant reading, 2:19; 3:1, 8, 15); they are urged to do "works" (2:5, 26, etc.) or are praised for their works (2:2, 13, 19) or rebuked for them (2:19, 22; 3:1f., 15); and condemnation, correspondingly, will fall upon unbelievers for their works (9:20f.; 16:11; 18:6). By the "works" that are required of Christians pure conduct is meant—not only according to ethical commandments (3:4?; 21:8, 27; 22:15) but also according to ritualistic commandments (2:14, 20); but one of the "works" demanded is undoubtedly faithfulness to the faith. But as there is a call for faithfulness there is also a call for repentance (2:15, 16; 3:3, 19; *cf.* 2:21f.; 9:20 f.; 16:9, 11).

The Christianity of Revelation has to be termed a weakly Christianized Judaism. The significance of Christ is practically limited to this: that he gives the passionate eschatological hope a certainty which the Jewish apocalyptists lack. To him as Lord over life and death (1:17f.; 2:8), as the heavenly comforter and ruler, is transferred what Judaism says of God. What gives the impression that the present is already illumined by the light of the future is the certainty of eschatological hope and the conviction that the end is near at hand (22:10 "the time is near"; 22:12: "behold, I am coming soon"). But the peculiar "between-ness" of Christian existence has not been grasped. In fact, not even in the chronological sense does the present possess the character of an interval, because the author does not reflect about the past which in Christ has been brought to its end and out of which believers have been transplanted into a new beginning. Hence the present is understood in a way not basically different from the understanding of it in the Jewish apocalypses: namely, as a time of temporariness, of waiting. The clear symptom of this understanding is the fact that *pistis* is essentially conceived as "endurance," as in Judaism.

k. Wherever the Pauline tradition continues effective, particularly in *Colossians* and *Ephesians*, there prevails a situation decidedly different from that in Revelation and in all the other writings considered up to this point. In these two writings the basic (i.e. non-chronological meaning of the "between"-situation is grasped, for the determination of the present by the future is grasped. The chronological sense of the Christian's "between-ness" plays a slighter role here simply because the nearness of the parousia is not discussed. Of course, that does not mean that the reference to the future which belongs to Christian existence has disappeared. "Hope" is not seldom mentioned; it is directed toward the prospective "revealing" of Christ (Col. 3:4), before whom believers will someday stand as saints (Col. 1:22f.). Hope also looks forward to the life which with Christ will then be revealed (Col. 3:3f.), to the salvation prepared in heaven

(Col. 1:5; Eph. 1:18), to the rewarding of all good deeds (Eph. 6:8). "This aeon" will be followed by the age "which is to come" (Eph. 1:21; *cf.* 2:2). Nevertheless, more emphasis falls upon salvation as a present state than upon an anticipation of future salvation (II, p. 160). Present conduct, it is true, may also be regarded as the condition for receiving future salvation—perfectly legitimately when such conduct is synonymous with "abiding in the faith" (Col. 1:23 tr.), less legitimately, from the standpoint of faith in God's grace, when the ethical exhortation is supported by a reference to reward (Col. 3:24).

But the thing characteristic of both Col. and Eph. is that the present is conceived as a time of salvation brought about by God's deed in Christ—a time of salvation, that is, in view of the fact that the cosmic powers have been disarmed (Col. 1:20; 2:15; see II, p. 153). By appropriating this occurrence through baptism (Col. 2:12; *cf.* 2:20; 3:3; Eph. 4:5), believers are emancipated from domination by the powers, from the "dominion of darkness," and transferred to the Reign of Christ (Col. 1:13). This "redemption" of theirs is the "forgiveness of sins" (Col. 1:14; *cf.* 2:14; Eph. 1:7; 5:26)—but not as if their life were now placed under an imperative, the fulfilment of which would be the condition for obtaining salvation, but rather thus: that with forgiveness the might of sin is broken and in their obedient conduct Life has become a present reality. Believers have died with Christ, been buried and raised with him, made alive (Col. 2:12f., 20; 3:3). Upon this indicative the imperative is founded (Col. 3:5ff., 12ff.; Eph. 4:1ff., 17ff., 25; 5:8ff.; *cf.* Col. 1:21f.; Eph. 2:5f.). The idea is peculiarly formulated in Eph. 2:10: we, saved by God's grace, are "his workmanship, created in Christ Jesus for good works, which God prepared beforehand, that we should walk in them." The formulation of Col. 3:2f. is especially clear: "Set your minds on things that are above, not on things that are on earth. For you have died, and your life is hid with Christ in God." The paradox: present, and yet future—or, future, and yet present—is here recognized. That paradox is preserved also in the fact that in spite of—or, rather, just because of—the Christian's having died with Christ the author still exhorts: "Put to death therefore what is earthly in you" (Col. 3:5; *cf.* Eph. 4:22), and that in spite of their emancipation from the evil powers believers are charged with the duty of fighting against them (Eph. 6:10ff.). The quality of being constantly menaced, which Christian living has, is clearly seen. There is, it is true, no mention of the "flesh" which strives against the "Spirit" (Gal. 5:17) nor of tempt-ations (neither πειράζειν, "to tempt," nor πειρασμός, "temptation," occurs). The "flesh" with its "desires" (or "lusts") is regarded as done away with in baptism (Col. 2:13; Eph. 2:3), yet, in spite of that, exhortation to do battle against the desires and the vices does not drop out, but, having received a foundation in the indicative, remains. The conception that evil is one coherent power, and that the life of the believer consequently is a constant battle, finds expression in mythological language in the exhortations of Eph. 6:10–20: the devil and the demonic powers must be resisted and fought as with soldier's weapons. (The whole sphere of beings and things at enmity with God is occasionally also called "world," κόσμος, in the Pauline and Johannine sense: Col. 2:8, 20; Eph. 2:2; 2:12?). The Spirit given in baptism is the guarantee (ἀρραβών) of future salvation (Eph. 1:13f.); but it is also the power that is bestowed in the present in the process by which one constantly becomes new (Eph. 3:16; 4:23), and this Spirit must not be "grieved" (Eph. 4:30) by bad living.

"In Christ"—Paul's own phrase to denote Christian existence —occurs here in various ways. In a set formula (Col. 1:2; Eph. 1:1), it means "Christian." As in Paul, it may mean the fellowship with Christ established by baptism (Col. 2:12; Eph. 2:6, 10, 13, 3:6). The same is probably also meant in Col. 1:28, 2:9f., Eph. 1:10, 2:15, 21f.; in all these cases the Gnostic conception of the cosmic Anthropos which underlies the phrase (*cf.* especially Eph. 4:13) comes into view. Several times "in Christ" has a repre-sentational meaning: "in—i.e. *with*—Christ" salvation is given, Col. 2:3, Eph. 1:3, 6; 2:7; 4:32; but it may also be that the ἐν is meant to be instrumental, as it probably is in Eph. 1:20, 2:15 (i.e. "*by* Christ"). "Chosen *in Christ*" seems to have a special meaning: through the fact that Christ was chosen before all time by God, believers in him are also chosen—Eph. 1:4, 9; 3:11. Nevertheless, the phrase in liturgical language had evidently already crystallized into a set formula (*cf.* Eph. 3:21) so that frequently its exact sense can scarcely be determined.

Salvation has become available through preaching, the "word of truth," the "Gospel" (Col. 1:5; Eph. 1:13), which has revealed the hidden secret (or mystery) of God (Col. 1:25ff.; 4:3; Eph. 3:1ff.; 6:19); consequently, this "word" of preaching must be kept alive in the Church (Col. 3:16). In that word, or in the knowledge which results

[177]

from it, salvation is present reality. To denote this knowledge a whole series of terms is used: γνῶσις (knowledge) and ἐπίγνωσις (full knowledge), σοφία (wisdom), σύνεσις (understanding), φρόνησις (comprehension, insight).

In distinction from Paul, "believe" and "faith" play a relatively unimportant role. "Believe" never occurs in Col., and in Eph. only at 1:13, 19, where the πιστεύσαντες or πιστεύοντες are simply "the Christians" (I, p. 90). The use of *pistis* varies. Sometimes it means the Christian religion, "Christianity" (Col. 1:23; Eph. 1:15, 3:12) or the degree to which one exhibits Christianity, especially in combination with "love" (Col. 1:4; Eph. 1:15). *Pistis* may then be followed by a phrase of specification, though only rarely: just once by εἰς (which in Paul occurs after "believe" but never after "faith")—"in Christ" (Col. 2:5)—by ἐν (=εἰς) Col. 1:4: "in Christ Jesus"; Eph. 1:15: "in the Lord Christ Jesus" (in Paul perhaps at Gal. 3:26; in the pastorals at I Tim. 3:13; II Tim. 3:15); once by an objective genitive, Col. 2:12: "faith in (lit. "of") the working of God"; but never by the objective genitive so frequently found in Paul, "faith *of* Jesus (Christ)," meaning "faith *in*."

Often *pistis* probably places more emphasis upon "faith" as a subjective attitude (Col. 2:7; Eph. 3:17, 6:16–23); in other places it has the objective meaning, so that *pistis* means belief, the "confession" or "creed" of the Christian, as in the characteristic juxtaposition "one Lord, one belief, one baptism" (Eph. 4:5, tr.—from liturgical tradition?) and perhaps in Eph. 4:13. Only once does *pistis* occur in combination with "grace" in the Pauline antithesis to "works" (Eph. 2:8f.; *cf.* 2:5); however God's "grace" bestowed in Christ or the Gospel is mentioned a few times (Col. 1:6; Eph. 1:6f., 2:7; *cf.* 4:7). But it is characteristic that in such phrases they do not use Paul's typical verb "rightwised" (by "grace" or "faith") but "saved" (σεσωσμένοι)—indeed the verb δικαιόω (to rightwise) is missing in both writings. In Col. "righteousness" (δικαιοσύνη) is also missing; it does occur in Eph. (4:24, 5:9) but not in the forensic sense denoting the essence of (eschatological) salvation, but as an ethical term, i.e. "uprightness" (similarly τὸ δίκαιον Col. 4:1; Eph. 6:1, "justly," "right"), appearing at Eph. 4:24 in combination with ὁσιότης ("piety"), a word, not found in Paul, which corresponds more or less with the εὐσέβεια (godliness, piety, religion) of the pastorals.

The thought that what distinguishes Christian existence is specifically knowledge, and that knowledge consequently must be constantly growing, is especially characteristic of Col. and Eph. God's deed of grace, which takes effect in preaching, is a causing to know ("make known" Col. 1:27; Eph. 1:9; 6:19), just as by revelation the apostles were "caused to know" the "secret" or "mystery" of the plan of salvation (Eph. 3:3f., 5) which constitutes the subject and content of preaching (Col. 1:25–27; 4:3; Eph. 1:9; 3:9; 6:19). The content of the "secret" is nothing other than God's plan of salvation (Col. 1:26; Eph. 1:9f.; 3:9f.) or, as it may also be phrased, simply: "Christ, in whom are hid all the treasures of wisdom and knowledge" (Col. 2:3; *cf.* 1:27). The content of the knowledge mediated by preaching is then at the same time Christ's love which surpasses all knowledge (Eph. 3:19); but God's will which demands worthy living (Col. 1:9f., 28; 4:5; Eph. 5:17) is also what that knowledge knows.

The authors may also say—summing up, as it were—that salvation is present in the Ecclesia as the "body of Christ," into which believers have been taken up by baptism (Col. 1:18, 24; 2:19; 3:15; Eph. 1:21f.; 2:6; 5:23, 30). Not that that is a guarantee, for the Church must prove that it really is the body of Christ by holding fast to Christ the Head of the body (Col. 2:19) in the unity of love (Col. 3:14f.; Eph. 4:2f.)—also in suffering for the Church (Col. 1:24), in mutual instruction and admonition (Col. 3:16), and in the thanksgiving and the songs of the assembled congregation (Col. 1:12; 2:7; 4:2; especially 3:16; Eph. 3:21; 5:19f.). Interest in the Church is more prominent in Eph. than in Col. not only because the union of Jews and Gentiles (as Christians) into one temple of God is a special theme of Eph. (2:11–22), but also because it is an important thought for its author that the Church is founded upon "the holy apostles and prophets" (2:20; 3:5) and is directed by them along with the evangelists, pastors, and teachers (4:11). The ancient catholic Church's idea of authority is beginning to come alive; nevertheless, the Church's leaders still have no priestly character; their office is that of preaching the word. Neither is there any mention yet of a special Church discipline. The members are to train one another (Col. 3: 13–16; Eph. 4:2f., 32; 5:19–21). Though the life of believers is released from worldliness ("desecularized") because it is the life of men who have died with Christ, who have renounced and are to renounce their former way of life (Col. 1:21; 3:5ff.; Eph. 2:1ff.), who are no longer oriented toward the "things that are on earth" but toward those "that are above" (Col. 3:2; see above), and because it is a life lived within the Church, nevertheless it is not a life that flees the world. The ascetic and ritualistic regulations of the heretics are opposed (Col. 2:16, 21; see II, p. 150). It is a pious life, borne up by brotherly love, in the forms of bourgeois existence; the pattern for it is provided (as in the pastorals) by the Haustafeln (Col. 3:18–4:1; Eph. 5:22–6:9).

It cannot be denied that in Col. and Eph. there is a certain doctrinarianism and moralization in their understanding of salvation. The nature and origin of sin are not grasped with such depth as in Paul and John. Sin is regarded as a sinister power, it is true; but its essence is seen only in a life of vice—pagan living is described in catalogues of vice (Col. 3:5, 8; Eph. 2:1ff.; 4:18f.). Consequently, *pistis* also is not understood with such radicality as in Paul and John. Their language also is to a large extent conventional; it is nourished by the Pauline tradition and—especially in Eph.—by liturgical tradition. Nevertheless, fundamental motifs of Paul's theology remain alive in them, particularly in their understanding of the believer's paradoxical situation "between the ages," in their understanding of the present's reference to the future, and in their basing the imperative upon the indicative.

1. Related to Col. and Eph. is *I Peter*; in it, however, the Christian's relation to the future is more prominent. Hope for coming salvation is predominant (1:3ff., 13; 3:9; 4:13; 5:4), yet not so as to exclude thinking of the judgment (4:6, 17ff.). In fact, even the expectation that the End is near is still (or once more) alive (4:7). Consequently, divorce from the world is also more prominent. (But the Pauline and Johannine use of the term κόσμος is lacking; and the term αἰὼν οὗτος—"this world" and also "this age"—is not found.) Christians are often described as "holy"; this is not a mere technical designation but an expression of the fact that they no longer belong to the present world. The Christian Church is a "spiritual house," a "holy priesthood," a "holy nation" (2:5, 9f.), designations that include responsibility for holy conduct (1:15). Toward the world Christians must know themselves to be "aliens" and "exiles" (2:11; *cf.* 1:1, 17). The present has the character of the temporary (1:17), though this idea is used mainly as consolation in the sufferings of the present (1:6; 5:10). But the "between-ness" in which believers now stand is not mere chronology. For inasmuch as they are already

"holy," one may say that salvation has a present reality. They are made holy (sanctified) by the Spirit conferred in baptism, which bestows upon them the efficacy of Christ's blood (1:2; *cf.* 1:18–21). Baptism, which receives its power from the resurrection of Christ (3:21; 1:3), rescues them and gives them a new relation to God (3:21).* So they are born again (or begotten anew 1:23). But 1:3 significantly adds that it was to a "living hope" that God caused them to be reborn (or begot them). Hence the present reality of salvation manifests itself in the fact that they are hopers: their "faith," as such, is "hope."

But the present reality of salvation is also clearly shown in that new conduct in which one's renunciation of the world is to be carried out (1:13ff.; 2:1ff.; 4:1ff., 7ff.). The sacrament of baptism did not simply bestow upon the believer a new nature, the possession of which guarantees future salvation; rather, all the way through we find the indicative furnishing the basis for the imperative in genuinely Pauline fashion (1:13ff., especially v. 15; 1:23; 2:11, 24; 3:9); once the Pauline motif of "freedom" also occurs (2:16). On the other hand, an exhortation is occasionally supported by a reference to the approaching End (4:7; 5:6). The idea of the Spirit given at baptism is not, as it is in Paul, made to bear fruit in parenesis; and "flesh" as the power of sin is mentioned allusively at the most (2:11: "abstain from the passions of the flesh"); and sin is recognized only in a life of vice (2:1; 4:2f., 15), in the passions (1:14; 2:11; 4:2f.), which, significantly are called "human passions" (4:2). So it is not surprising that *pistis* except where it means confident hope (1:9, 21), has the general meaning: "the Christian faith"—with here and there the nuance of "loyal faith" (1:5, 7; 5:9; the verb πιστεύω with the same nuance: 1:8; 1:21 in text of ℵ C 33)—and the "believing" (πιστεύοντες) or the "faithful" (πιστοί) are simply the "Christians" (1:21; 2:7; *cf.* 5:12). The antithesis of "faith" to "works" is lacking; it is said, rather, that God judges each man according to his "work" (1:17), and believers are to distinguish themselves by their "good works" (2:12). Mention of God's "grace" does occur. It is spoken of as the grace given by God through Christ (1:10; 3:7; 5:12) or the grace to be expected in the future revealing of Jesus Christ (1:13) or as the varied grace of God which manifests itself in charismatic gifts (4:10;

---

* The words συνειδήσεως ἀγαθῆς ἐπερώτημα εἰς θεόν probably mean: the prayer which issues from a consciousness of the purity acquired through baptism.

cf. 5:10) or in strength to endure undeserved suffering (2:19). But "grace" no longer has the specifically Pauline meaning. Neither is "rightwising" mentioned; δικαιοσύνη is here not "righteousness" but "uprightness" (2:24; 3:14) and δίκαιος means the "upright," "innocent" one (3:12; 4:18).

The Pauline idea of suffering and dying with Christ is modified in a strange manner. To interpret suffering in persecution as a sharing in the sufferings of Christ (4:13) is not in itself un-Pauline. But the genuinely Pauline thought is echoed only at 4:2: *viz.*, that fellowship with Christ's suffering takes place in the decision of faith and hence is a goal ever to be won or, better, is a process constantly taking place in the life of the believer (I, pp. 349f.). Elsewhere the author understands that thought thus: that a connection with Christ is brought about by the suffering of Christians because following Christ brings with it the suffering of persecution. Hence the crucified Christ is not the "power and wisdom of God" (I Cor. 1:24) but the pattern for the believer's suffering (2:21ff.: 3:18)—though, of course, he leaves intact the (traditional) statement that Christ's death was a death for our sins (1:18f.; 2:21, 24; 3:18). The thought that taking up the cross is radical divorce from the world and the giving up of all boasting (Gal. 6:14; Phil. 3:3ff.; I Cor. 1:18ff., etc.) has been lost. In fact, suffering is regarded at all only as innocent suffering resulting from human malice or from the enmity of the heathen to the Christians (3:13ff.; 4:12ff.)—similarly πειρασμός is never used as "temptation" but always means "trial," the trial of sufferings.

Eschatological consciousness with its aloofness from the world is more prominent in I Pet. than in Col. and Eph. (and the pastorals), a fact that is certainly conditioned by the situation of threatened and in part actual persecution of the Christians by the heathen. This gives the parenesis its peculiar character. Both the admonitions to obey the public authorities (2:14–17) and the Haustafeln (2:18–3:7) exhort the reader not only to a decent and clean bourgeois life but to a specifically Christian attitude: by his good conduct the believer is to bring honor to the faith and be prepared to endure. The admonition to patient endurance runs through the whole writing (1:6f.; 2:20f.; 3:16f.) and with it the exhortation to love (both ἀγάπη and φιλαδελφία, 1:22, 2:17; 3:8; 4:8). In addition, the admonition to "humility" is characteristic (3:8; 5:5f.). Not only in these admonitions to brotherly love but also in special admonitions the thought is expressed that the Church's nature as a "holy priesthood" realizes itself in a Church life ruled by brotherly love: each is to serve the whole with his special gift (4:10f.). The "elders" receive a special exhortation in this direction (5:1–4), and so do the "younger men" (5:5).

m. In a different way, more or less in the same direction as in Col. and Eph., the Pauline tradition works on in the *pastoral epistles*. Here the expectation of the future parousia has lost still more of its tension, and the Christian faith is becoming a piety which, though it by no means surrenders its aloofness from the world, nevertheless is making a place for itself within the framework of bourgeois living. It is characteristic that though there are echoes of some Pauline ideas, other important concepts of Paul's theology have either disappeared or have lost their old meaning. Thus "to save" (and "be saved") has taken the place of "rightwise" (and "be rightwised"); and "salvation" has replaced "righteousness" (II, p. 115).

Only in Tit. 3:7, echoing Paul, does "rightwised by his grace" occur. Otherwise δικαιοῦν does not occur except in the quotation I Tim. 3:16, where its passive is used of Christ and means not "rightwised" but "vindicated." Δικαιοσύνη means "uprightness" —to it one is trained by Scripture (II Tim. 3:16), for it one must strive (I Tim. 6:11; II Tim. 2:22), as reward for it a wreath (crown) stands in prospect at the end (II Tim. 4:8). The δίκαιος, correspondingly, is the "upright" man (I Tim. 1:9; Tit. 1:8).

"To believe" very rarely occurs, and, when it does, not in Paul's sense, as the combination of πιστεύειν with ἐπί and the dative suffices to indicate (I Tim. 1:16, a construction found in Paul only within the repeated quotation at Rom. 9:33; 10:11). Paul's πιστεύειν εἰς ("believe in" followed by accusative) and πιστεύειν ὅτι ("believe that . . .") do not occur. Πιστεύειν in the pastorals means "trust, depend upon" (I Tim. 1:16; II Tim. 1:12; probably also Tit. 3:8 with θεῷ as object). Πίστις occurs frequently and sometimes has the complement "in Christ Jesus" (I Tim. 3:13; II Tim. 1:13; 3:15), but in general it has the worn-down meaning of "Christianity," "Christian religion"; as the context may demand, it can mean the subjective faith with which one believes or faith as the object which one believes, "belief" (*cf.* I Tim. 1:5; 2:15; 3:9; 5:8; 6:12; II Tim. 1:5; 4:7; Tit. 1:1), in fact it can actually mean "right doctrine," orthodoxy.

Characteristic expressions are the set formula ἐν πίστει= "Christian" (I Tim. 1:2, 4; Tit. 3:15; *cf.* "in a common faith" Tit. 1:4). Another formula is "faith and love" (I Tim. 1:14; II Tim. 1:13) as a designation for the state of being a Christian. *Pistis* is, above all, proper faith in contrast to a wrong kind, both in the subjective sense of the right quality or degree of faith and in the objective sense of right doctrine (see II, p. 135). As the right quality or degree of faith, *pistis* loses its character of that which is the basis of Christian existence and becomes a virtue. The very fact that it can be given the adjective "unfeigned" (ἀνυπόκριτος, I Tim. 1:5; II Tim. 1:5), which Paul gives only to "love" (Rom. 12:9; II Cor. 6:6; *cf.* I Pet. 1:22), is indicative. This "unfeigned faith" may indeed appear as the root of "love" (I Tim. 1:5) but coupled with a "pure heart" and a "good conscience." Especially characteristic are combinations with other virtues: with "love" I Tim. 1:14; II Tim. 1:13, also Tit. 2:2 which also adds "steadfastness" (ὑπομονή), and I Tim. 4:12, where "faith" and "love" are combined with "conduct" and "purity." In I Tim. 6:11 "faith" even appears as one member in a whole catalogue of virtues: "uprightness, godliness, faith, love, steadfastness, gentleness." II Tim. 2:22 and 3:10 are similar.

The characteristic designation of the Christian attitude is εὐσέβεια, "the attitude pleasing to God," "piety."

The substantive occurs ten times, the verb (εὐσεβεῖν) at I Tim. 5:4, and the adverb (εὐσεβῶς) at II Tim. 3:12 and Tit. 2:12. The adjective is missing but is replaced by ὅσιος "holy" or "pious" (I Tim. 2:8; Tit. 1:8). Like *pistis*, "piety" can mean simply "Christianity"—I Tim. 3:16, 6:3; II Tim. 3:5.

Piety makes itself known in respectable conduct (I Tim. 2:2; 5:4; 6:11; II Tim. 3:12; Tit. 2:12) such as is described in the Haustafeln (I Tim. 2:8–15; 6:1f.; Tit. 2:2–10). So it is the opposite of a former heathen life of vice (Tit. 3:3). It is the renunciation of "irreligion" and "worldly passions" (Tit. 2:12; I Tim. 6:9; II Tim. 2:22; 3:6; 4:3), yet it bears no traits of a flight from the world but is characterized by a "sensibleness" (σωφροσύνη) which avoids licentiousness and excess (I Tim. 3:3, 8; Tit. 1:7; 2:3) and is frugal (I Tim. 6:6–10) but still does not practice asceticism (I Tim. 4:4f., 8; 5:23; on the subject of marriage, see § 60, 5).

Such "piety" holds promise both for the present life and for the life to come (I Tim. 4:8). For believers are waiting for the "appearing" of Christ (I Tim. 6:14f.; II Tim. 4:1; 4:8?; Tit. 2:13), they have the hope of eternal life (Tit. 3:7; 1:2; II Tim. 1:1), the recompense which "on that Day" the Lord as Judge will provide for faithfulness to the faith (II Tim. 4:8; *cf.* 4:1). Nevertheless, the present no longer stands in the eschatological tension that Paul knew; instead the Church has settled down to the prospect that the world will last a while yet (II, p. 116). When it is time to do so, God will bring to pass the appearing of Christ ("at the proper time," I Tim. 6:15). It is never said that this event lies near ahead, but neither can one detect any such thing as disappointment at the delay of the parousia. It is significant that the eschatological term ἐπιφάνεια ("appearing") can also be used in this literature to denote the historical appearing of Christ (i.e. Jesus) upon earth (II Tim. 1:10; *cf.* Tit. 2:11; 3:4). Reference to the future recedes behind the consciousness of present salvation. The pastorals know, in fact, that the present is under grace, which once was hidden but now with the "appearing" of Christ has been revealed (II Tim. 1:9f.; Tit. 1:2f.; 2:11). They also know the importance of the Gospel as the proclaimed word by which salvation was and continues to be revealed (II Tim. 1:10; Tit. 1:3; *cf.* I Tim. 3:16) and know what importance preaching has for the Church (I Tim. 5:17; II Tim. 2:15; 4:2; Tit. 1:9; *cf.* also I Tim. 2:7; II Tim. 1:11; 2:9; 4:17). They also know that not our works but grace saved us (II Tim. 1:9; Tit. 3:7). It becomes ours through baptism, and baptism gives us a new possibility of life as it does in Hermas and Hebrews, but not as a new chance by the forgiveness of our former sins ("forgiveness of sins" is lacking in the pastorals as in Paul!) but as the "working of regeneration and renewal in the Holy Spirit" (Tit. 3:5).

The paradox of Christian existence— a new existence within this old world (Tit. 2:12)—is here grasped: in other words the qualitative (and not merely chronological) sense of the Christian's "betweenness" is grasped. The present has not come under a new bondage to the Law, although as in Herm., Barn. and Heb. it is subject to new conditions, but is under the sway of the Gospel in which grace has come to be a present reality (II Tim. 1:9f.; Tit. 1:3). God gave the Spirit which is characterized by power, love, and self-control (II Tim. 1:7); it also aids the Christian in fulfilling his duty (II Tim. 1:14). The period of religious ecstasy, however, is past; particular charismatic gifts are not mentioned except that of office (the preaching-teaching office—I Tim. 4:14; II Tim. 1:6, probably also II Tim. 2:1, translating χάρις not as "grace" but as "gift"). The life of the believers, accordingly, is beginning to be subjected to an ecclesiastical discipline not only in the fact that the congregational officers rebuke and correct teachers of error (II Tim. 2:25; Tit. 1:9, 13) and, if need be, excommunicate them (I Tim. 1:20; Tit. 3:10f.), but also in the fact that they supervise the ethical life of the members and keep them in control (I Tim. 5:3–16, 19f.; II Tim. 4:2; Tit. 2:15). Thus, somewhat as in Col. and Eph. the present reality of salvation is incorporated, so to speak, in the Church, which is "the pillar and bulwark of the truth" (I Tim. 3:15). Nevertheless, the concept Ecclesia is not emphasized as it is in Eph. (the word Church occurs in the pastorals only in I Tim. 3—vss. 5, 15, and 16), and there is no mention of the "body of Christ."

The Christianity of the pastorals is a somewhat faded Paulinism— nevertheless, the Pauline tradition works on in it. The way in which grace is spoken of does not sound very Pauline, it is true; nevertheless, it is understood in Paul's sense as a power that transforms our present living when Tit. 2:11f. describes it as that which "trains" us to "godly living." For here the imperative is understood to be founded upon the indicative, even though the Pauline paradox is not expressed. Grant all the following: (1) that the believer's divorce from the world is not grasped with such radicality as it was by Paul, because the depth of Paul's understanding of sin (and hence also of faith) is no longer grasped; (2) that κόσμος (I Tim. 1:15; 3:16; 6:7) no longer means "world" in Paul's sense except in the adjective "worldly" (Tit. 2:12); (3) that the struggle between "flesh" and "Spirit" is not mentioned ("flesh" never occurs at all except in the quotation I Tim. 3:16); (4) that dying with Christ to live with him is not found, and that Paul's resulting description of Christian life as a living "in Christ" occurs at the most in II Tim. 3:12, if it does there.* Nevertheless, for all its plodding one-sidedness, it is a legitimate extension of Paul's thinking to understand grace as a power that molds everyday bourgeois living; and when this everyday living is placed under the light of grace something also remains of Paul's "as if . . . not" (I Cor. 7:29ff.; I, p. 351f.).

* "In Christ" otherwise is an adjectival complement to "faith" (see above, II, p. 183) or to both "faith" and "love" (I Tim. 1:14; II Tim. 1:13), or, as in Col. and Eph. (see II, p. 177), it has representational meaning (II Tim. 1:1, 9, 2:1, 10).

n. Closely related to the pastorals is the *First Letter of Clement.* It, too, is under the influence of the Pauline tradition, though much more under that of the Hellenistic synagogue, so that of genuine Paulinism there is little or almost nothing left. It is quite a problem to say what it really is that makes I Clem. a Christian document. Is it anything more than the consciousness of being certain of God's grace, thanks to the occurrence of salvation in Christ? That is to say, is it anything more than a "Church"–consciousness (see I, p. 37f.), such as the Jewish congregation also had, but a consciousness now made alive, strong, and certain?

As in the pastorals, though looking to the eschatological future has not been given up, the eschatological tension has disappeared. Hope, it is true, is not infrequently mentioned; in fact "hope" can denote the Christian attitude as a whole (51:1: "the common ground of our hope," tr., 57:2). But the hope in God (59:3) which Christians have in common with the pious men of the Old Testament (11:1; *cf.* the quotation from Ps. 31:10 in 22:8 and from Prov. 1:33 in 57:7) is for the most part simply trust in God; in this sense πιστεύειν ("to trust") and "to hope" may be combined, as the nouns *pistis* ("trust") and "hope" also may (12:7; 58:2). The statement made of God, "he is near" (21:3; 27:3), does not refer to the proximity of the End but means God's omnipresence, and the congregational prayer (59–61) comes to a close without any eschatological look toward the future. But, of course, the author can also speak of the coming Reign of God (42:3; 50:3); the Lord (God? Christ?) will suddenly come (23:5, after Is. 14:1; Mal. 3:1); the judgment is to come (28:1f.) and it will requite men according to their works (34:3 quoting Is. 40:10, etc.). There is no delineation of the events of the End at all and the glory of the salvation to come is only mentioned in allusions (34:7f.; 35:3f.). Only in the truth of the belief in resurrection is any living interest shown. The doubts about it are refuted (23–26), and it is significant that the chief role in this argumentation is played not by the raising of Jesus but by proofs taken from nature (alternation of day and night, of seed-time and harvest, the Phoenix), seconded by words of Scripture and a reminder of God's truthfulness—while the raising of Jesus is only cited as the "first-fruits" of the "coming resurrection" (24:1) without being meant in the sense of I Cor. 15:20.

For the Christian Church salvation is in a certain manner present reality: it is, in just the fact that it is conscious of being the Christian

Church. The technical term "Church of God" occurs, it is true, only in the conventional salutation; otherwise *ecclesia* means only a particular congregation (44:3, 47:6). But the author calls Christians by the old titles of the eschatological Congregation. They are "called" and "sanctified" (salutation), they are "the holy portion" (30:1); God made them the "portion of his choice" for Himself (29:1) and sanctified them through Christ (59:3); hence they are the "chosen (of God)" (1:1; 2:4; 6:1; 46:4; 49:5; 58:2; 59:2) or the "chosen by God through Jesus Christ" (50:7), "the called by his will in Jesus Christ" (32:4; *cf.* 59:2; 65:2; also 46:6: "one calling in Christ"). They are the "flock" of Christ (16:1; 44:3; 54:2; 57:2).

As these expressions show, it was through Christ, our "means of salvation" (36:1), that salvation was brought about. He is the foundation of the Christian's relationship to God, because through him God chose (50:7) and called (59:2; 65:2) us and bestowed upon us right knowledge of Himself (36:1f.). He is the gate of righteousness into life (48:2–4). One's gaze is to be fixed upon his sufferings (2:1), his blood (7:4). (The cross is not explicitly named, but his blood is: 7:4; 12:7; 21:6; 49:6. His sufferings, furthermore, are described not according to the synoptic tradition but according to Is. 53, ch. 16). All such expressions are already highly formalized into set phrases; the author can only say in general that Christ's blood was given "for us" (21:6; 49:6; *cf.* 16:7 modeled on Is. 53:6)—as he also says of heathen heroes for their peoples (55:1)—that it brought us "redemption" (12:7) and gave the whole world the "grace of repentance" (7:4; *cf.* 8:1).

Though the possibility of repentance has always existed (7:5ff.; 8:1ff.), it has once more become actual to the present by the death of Christ. There is no explicit reference to baptism whatever; the only presupposition mentioned for forgiveness is repentance. And repentance, one must recognize here, is connected with the fulfilment of the commandments. In fact, it can be said that the "commandments" of Christ (37:1) as the "yoke of his grace" (16:7) represent the soteriological meaning of the present. Thus the ethical demands, or the virtues that correspond to them, are called the "paths of blessing" (31:1), and among the "blessed and wonderful gifts of God" appears "continence in holiness" along with terms which denote the possession of salvation: "life in incorruption, splendor in righteousness, truth in boldness, faith in confidence" (35:1). To that extent it might be said

[188]

that for the author indicative and imperative constitute a unity. Such a unity is also expressed in the sentence: "Being, therefore, a holy portion, let us do all that belongs to sanctification" (30:1 tr.). But this unity is not the paradoxical unity of the future and the present. Rather, it is the same unity as in Judaism, for with the consciousness of being God's chosen, holy People it also combines knowledge of its responsibility and its obligation to holy conduct. Hence the significance of Christ consists, on the one hand, in his having given the Church by his death the consciousness of being the Congregation of the elect, the People of God (59:4, 64) and, on the other hand, of his therefore being the teacher and law-giver of the Church.

Christ is the teacher who taught "gentleness and long-suffering" (13:1). There is constant mention of his "command-ment" (ἐντολή), his "injunctions" (παραγγέλματα), "orders" (προστάγματα), and "just demands" (δικαιώματα) (2:8; 13:3; 27:2; 37:1; 49:1). But his "injunctions" are identical with the old commandments of God, "the glorious and venerable rule (κανών) of our tradition" (7:2). As one may speak of Christ's "orders," one may therefore also speak of God's "orders" (3:4; 40:5; 50:5; 58:2), "just demands" (58:2), and "statutes" (νόμιμα, 1:3; 3:4; 40:4). The only difference is in the name appended: Christ's or God's. In substance it remains the same whether one fixes his regard on Christ (2:1; 7:4; 36:2) or on God (19:2; *cf.* 34:5). *Pistis* (or πιστεύειν, which usually is used absolutely) may have Christ for its object (22:1: "in—ἐν—Christ"; never εἰς, never χριστοῦ as objective genitive) but more frequently God is the object (3:4; 27:3; 34:4, and, of course, everywhere where the faith of pious men of the Old Testament is mentioned). The meaning proper to Christian "faith" cannot assert itself under such circumstances.

The problem of legalism, therefore, does not exist for the author, although he took over from Paul the thought that we are rightwised ("justified") not by our works but by faith (32:4). He can both quote Gen. 15:6 like Paul (10:6) and also say that "Abraham performed (ποιήσας) uprightness and truth through trust" (31:2, tr.). Δικαιοσύνη and δίκαιος (the latter co-ordinated with ὅσιος—almost = "proper"—, with "innocent," or with "pious," 14:1; 46:4; 48:4; 62:1) are ethical terms for the author (*cf.* δικαιοπραγία, "just dealing", 32:3), even though he defines the "gate of uprightness standing open into life"

as the "gate in Christ" (48:2–4—see especially the expansion in 48:4).
It is self-evident, therefore, that in this document *pistis* cannot have
the Pauline (or Johannine) meaning. Except where it means trust in
God (see especially 26:1; 35:5—πιστῶς) and is related to "hope" (see
above, II, p. 187), *pistis* is only one of the many virtues (1:2; 35:2;
62:1) and is specifically paired with "hospitality" (10:7; 12:1). It
can also mean simply the Christian attitude as a whole (5:6; 6:2; 27:3)
and so be equivalent to εὐσέβεια, "piety" (*cf.* 1:2 with 22:1; 11:1
with 10:7; 12:1—εὐσέβεια also at 15:1; 61:2; 62:1) or to "holiness of
soul" (29:1; *cf.* 48:4; 60:4; he is fond of ὅσιος, "holy": 2:3; 6:1; etc.).
So, in a faded sense, *pistis* can mean "Christianity" (22:1; *cf.* similar
use of the verb "believe": 12:7; 42:4).

Neither "sin" nor "flesh" is mentioned as a power to which man
has fallen victim. Of the Holy Spirit, or the "Spirit of grace" it is
said that it has been given to the Church. The apostles also worked
by its power (42:3; 47:3), and the author writes his own letter "through
the Holy Spirit" (63:2). But nowhere do we hear of the struggle
between flesh and Spirit, nor is the Spirit appraised as the "first-
fruit" or "guarantee" of the final consummation of salvation. For
the most part, *pneuma* is the Spirit which inspires the words of the
Old Testament (8:1; 13:1, etc.). Ecstatic possession by the Spirit has
disappeared; the Spirit that was given to the Church is conceived
as working in the virtues (2:2). God's "grace" is the saving grace
which brought the new possibility of repentance (7:4; 8:1) or grace in
an altogether general sense (30:3) in which the pious men of the Old
Testament also shared it (50:3; 55:3). In the plural it means God's
favors in general (23:1). The Pauline antithesis between "grace" and
"works" is not present, nor is that between "faith" and "works."
Only in the conventional closing greeting does "the grace of our
Lord Jesus Christ" appear. Once χάρισμα (gift) occurs (38:1) meaning,
as in I Pet. 4:10, the gift given to an individual which is to be used
to the advantage of the fellowship. "Knowledge," which is often
mentioned, is not a special gift and has no specific content (unless
perhaps in 48:5, but the meaning here is obscure) but is Christian
knowledge in general (1:2; 36:2; 41:4; 48:5; *cf.* also the verb "know":
7:4; 59:3; ἐπίγνωσις 59:2; ἐπιγινώσκειν 32:1) or, specifically, the understanding of the Old Testament (40:1)—by which, however, he does
not mean the art of allegory as Barnabas does.

Inasmuch as the Church was called by Christ and looks forward to the coming Reign of God, the Church stands in an intermediate time; and since there is present enjoyment of the "blessed and wonderful gifts of God" (35:1), it might be said that this "between-ness" determines not merely the chronology but also the character of Christian existence. But it disintegrates into a mere temporariness, more or less as in the book of Revelation, because, despite what the author says of Christ, he does not bring to expression how it is that in Christ anything really decisive took place, founding a new relation to God. Ultimately, the only relation to God that the author knows is the old one, for the characteristics of Christian existence are also attributed to the pious men of the Old Testament: "piety," "faith," "hope," and "repentance." As God's "injunctions" are the same for Christians as for the Old Israel, so the virtues of Christians are none other than those of the pious men of the Old Testament, who, indeed, are to be regarded as patterns for Christians to follow. Ultimately, all that Christ has done is to strengthen and make certain the Church's consciousness of being the Church, so that from the author's point of view Christ has his appropriate title when he is called "protector and helper of our weakness" (36:1).

o. *Ignatius* represents a completely different type from all the writings so far considered. Like the last few types described he also is under the influence of Paul's theology. But this takes on a special form with him because his antecedents lie not in the tradition of the synagogue but in the thought-world from which John also came (§ 41, 3), a fact which accounts for many points of contact between him and John.* Salvation is called by Ignatius, as by John, usually "life," and also "truth."

> "Life" without a modifier Mg. 9:1; "true life" (τὸ ἀληθινὸν ζῆν) Eph. 11:1, Tr. 9:2 (in apposition to "Christ" Sm. 4:1); "true life" (ζωὴ ἀληθινή) Eph. 7:2; "our inseparable life (ζῆν, likewise in apposition to "Christ") Eph. 3:2; "our life through all (time?)," epithet of Christ, Mg. 1:2; "life eternal," Eph. 18:1; Pol. 2:3; equivalent to these expressions are the terms (lacking in John) "immortality" (Eph. 20:2) and "incorruption," Eph. 17:1; Mg. 6:2; Philad. 9:2; Pol. 2:3. The opposite term is "death" (*passim*) which, in turn, for its opposite may have "truth" (Sm. 5:1; Pol.

---

* It has often been asserted (most recently by Christian Maurer, *Ignatius von Antiochien und das Johannesevangelium*, 1949) that Ignatius is dependent upon John. But such is not likely the case.

7:3). In parallel meaning we find "light of truth," Philad. 2:1, and "pure light," Rom. 6:2; the Church can be termed "enlightened" (φωτισμένη) Rom. intr.

"Life" is a thing of the future ("the life which lies before you," Eph. 17:1) and Christ can be called our "hope" (Eph. 21:2; Mg. 11, etc.) as well as our "life." And the Gospel is called "the Gospel of the common hope" (Philad. 5:2), as the Christian faith can be called simply: "hope" (Mg. 9:1). That which is hoped for is the "rightwising" that is to come (Philad. 8:2), or especially the resurrection (Tr. 9:2; Eph. 11:2; Tr. intr., Rom. 4:3; Sm. 5:3; Pol. 7:1), or the gaining of "pure light." A special technical term for the object of hope is "attaining to God" (θεοῦ τυγχάνειν or ἐπιτυγχάνειν); this usually refers to what Ignatius expects as the fruit of his martyrdom (Eph. 12:2; Mg. 14, etc.), but it is also the hope of all Christians (Eph. 10:1; Mg. 1:2; Sm. 9:2; Pol. 2:3).

But the traditional picture of early Christian eschatology has to all intents and purposes disappeared. We read once, it is true: "These are the last times" (Eph. 11:1). Nevertheless, calling salvation "immortality," "incorruption," and "attaining to God" indicates that the hope here implied is a hope for the salvation of the individual. The two aeons are not mentioned. Even though Satan is called "prince of this αἰών" (Eph. 17:1; 19:1; Mg. 1:2, etc.) this is no exception, for the time-aspect of the concept is subordinate here, while the contrast between this world and the other world is emphasized, as the parallelism of "this aeon" to "the world" in Rom. 6:1 indicates. Of the old apocalyptic pictures, at least that of the judgment and the "wrath to come" is retained (Eph. 11:1; Sm. 6:1); the idea of coming reward and punishment is used (Eph. 16:2; Mg. 5:1; Sm. 9:2). But of the future coming of Christ there is at the most a single allusion (Pol. 3:2). The "coming of the Savior" (Philad. 9:2) is not the eschatological coming but the entrance into history of Jesus, who "in the end was made manifest" (Mg. 6:1); through him "grace" came (Sm. 6:2) and became a present reality (Eph. 11:1; Mg. 8:1). The cosmic catastrophe, which apocalyptic eschatology expected to occur in the future, has already taken place in the birth, death, and resurrection of Jesus (Eph. 19; *cf.* Mg. 11, Tr. 9; Philad. 8:2; Sm. 1; see II, pp. 153f.). So salvation is present now. Since Christ is our life (Eph. 3:2; Sm. 4:1), then to be in Christ already means to be in life. Believers are "members" of Christ (Eph. 4:2; Tr. 11:2) or "branches of the cross" (Tr. 11:2); as those who are united in the Ecclesia they are the body of Christ, of which he himself is the head (Sm. 1:2; Tr. 11:2). Whereas they are in life, the heretics are already in death; they are "clothed with death" (νεκροφόροι, Sm. 5:2; cf. Philad. 6:1). "To live after the manner of men" (Rom. 8:1; 6:2) would in reality be to die, while to die the death of a martyr means to live (Rom. 4:3, 6; cf. Mg. 5:2). Indeed, not until one belongs to Christ does one even *exist* (Mg. 10:1). The existence of the heretics is only a "semblance" (δοκεῖν, Sm. 2, Tr. 10) of existing.

But with this individualistic piety there is combined an ecclesiastical piety: salvation is available to the individual in the Church. That is why the unity of the Church and the unity of each congregation under the guidance of its one bishop is one of the chief concerns of Ignatius (Eph. 4:2; Mg. 6:2; Sm. 8:2, etc.). In the united congregation the power of prayer is mighty (Eph. 5:2) and Satan's power is overcome (Eph. 13:1). Baptism plays a curiously unimportant role in Ignatius (Eph. 18:2; Sm. 8:2; Pol. 6:2); the Eucharist plays a far greater one as the "medicine of immortality" (Eph. 20:2). To partake of it the congregation ought to gather more frequently (Eph. 13:1. Philad. 4). In the Eucharist the eschatological occurrence takes place as present event (Eph. 13:1f.), and it brings about "union" (ἕνωσις) with the flesh and blood of Christ (Philad. 4; Sm. 7:1).

Still, it would be wrong to conceive the Christianity of Ignatius as being mere sacramentalism in the sense that receiving the sacrament guarantees salvation. The peculiar thing is that Ignatius considers the believer's whole life to be stamped by sacramental union with Christ, receiving thereby a sacramental character, so to speak. For this thought Ignatius uses Paul's formula "in Christ" not only to designate the coming fulfilment as one that takes place in Christ (Eph. 11:1; Rom. 4:3, etc.), but also to describe the conditioning of present living by fellowship with him (Eph. 1:1; 8:2; 10:3, etc., see below). But union with Christ is determined by his paradoxical nature— Christ who was the pre-existent Son of God (Mg. 6:1; 7:2; 8:2), became man, suffered, died, and rose again. He was "God humanly manifested" (Eph. 19:3), a paradox that is emphasized again and again (especially Eph. 7:2) and is passionately defended against the denials of the heretics. Everything depends upon the reality, the actuality of the humanity and the suffering of Christ and upon the reality of his resurrection (Tr. 9f., Sm. 2f., 7:2). The resurrection itself is physical, of the flesh: the risen Christ ate and drank with his disciples "as a person in the flesh, though spiritually he was united with the Father" (Sm. 3:3, tr.; *cf.* 12:2). Just for the sake of this paradox Christ is also called "God" (Eph. intr., 1:1; 15:3, etc.), though, of course, God is his Father, and he is the Son (Eph. 2:1; 4:2, etc.) subordinate to his Father (Sm. 8:1; Mg. 13:2), but joined with Him in unity (Mg. 7:1; Sm. 3:3, etc.). He is the will ($\gamma\nu\omega\mu\acute{\eta}$, Eph. 3:2) of God, his "word proceeding from silence" (Mg. 8:2; *cf.* Rom. 8:2; Philad. 9:1 for similar metaphors).

Christ, both God and man at once—everything hangs upon this paradox, because through it man, too, can attain to a paradoxical existence: the correlate to "God became man" is "man becomes God." Ignatius avoids, it is true, the actual word $\theta\epsilon\omega\theta\hat{\eta}\nu\alpha\iota$ ("be deified"). But other expressions do service for it: ($\dot{\epsilon}\pi\iota)\tau\upsilon\gamma\chi\acute{\alpha}\nu\epsilon\iota\nu\ \theta\epsilon o\hat{\upsilon}$ ("attain to God" but also: to get, or obtain, God; see above, II, p. 192), $\theta\epsilon o\hat{\upsilon}\ \mu\epsilon\tau\acute{\epsilon}\chi\epsilon\iota\nu$ ("to have, partake of, or enjoy God"), $\theta\epsilon o\hat{\upsilon}\ \gamma\acute{\epsilon}\mu\epsilon\iota\nu$ ("be full of, or filled with, God," Mg. 14), "to be (or become) God's" (Mg. 10:1; Rom. 6:2; 7:1). The formula "in Christ" (see above) is interchangeable with "in God" (Eph. 1:1; Mg. 3:1; Pol. 6:1); and the phrase "Christ in us" (Mg. 12; Rom. 6:3) has its parallel in "God in us" (Eph. 15:3). Christians are both $\theta\epsilon o\phi\acute{o}\rho o\iota$ ("wearers of God") and $\chi\rho\iota\sigma\tau\acute{o}\phi o\rho o\iota$ ("wearers of Christ"); they are $\theta\epsilon o\delta\rho\acute{o}\mu o\iota$ (literally "God-runners," prob.="soarers to God," Philad. 2:2; Pol. 7:2).

The Christian's new mode of being can be indicated, as in Paul, with the term *pneuma*. Christians are contrasted to non-Christians as the "spiritual" to the "carnal" ($\sigma\alpha\rho\kappa\iota\kappa o\acute{\iota}$ Eph. 8:2; the opposite to "spiritual" can also be "human", Eph. 5:1; *cf.* "in human fashion," Tr. 2:1; Rom. 8:1). The chains which Ignatius wears as a "captive in Christ" (Tr. 1:1, etc.) are "spiritual pearls" (Eph. 11:2). But Ignatius differs from Paul in the fact that for Ignatius "the flesh" is merely the sphere of the earthly, the visible (Mg. 3:2), the evident ($\phi\alpha\iota\nu\acute{o}\mu\epsilon\nu o\nu$, Rom. 3:3; Pol. 2:2), the sphere of transitoriness and death, and not also the power of sin; for in place of "flesh" he can say "matter" ($\H{\upsilon}\lambda\eta$, Rom. 6:2; *cf.* 7:2). Of course, the sphere of the earthly can become a sinister power to a man if he lets himself be led astray to think or act "according to the flesh" (Mg. 6:2; Rom. 8:3; Philad. 7:1). But the term "flesh" serves Ignatius primarily to describe the paradoxical nature of human existence as being both "spiritual" and "of the flesh" at once. By the fact that Christ is "both flesh and Spirit" (Eph. 7:2), or that his resurrection is "both of flesh and of Spirit" (Sm. 7:2), "flesh" has been rendered capable of union with "Spirit." Ignatius wishes for the congregations a "union with the flesh and spirit of Jesus Christ" (Mg. 1:2; *cf*. Mg. 13:2); he wishes for the Ephesians that they may "abide in Jesus Christ both physically (σαρκικῶς) and spiritually" (Eph. 10:3); he wishes for the Magnesians that in all they do they may have success "in the flesh and in the spirit" (Mg. 13:1; *cf*. further: Tr. intr., 12:1; Sm. 1:1; 13:2; Pol. 1:2; 2:2; 5:1). This paradox is expressed with particular clarity when Ignatius says: "They who are carnal cannot do spiritual things, neither can they who are spiritual do carnal things" and shortly thereafter assures them, "But even what things you do according to the flesh are spiritual, for it is in Jesus Christ that you do them all" (Eph. 8:2).

Since "flesh" is the sphere of death, the union of "flesh" and "spirit" made possible by Christ can also be understood as the uniting of death and life. For Christ, Ignatius says, is "true life in death" (Eph. 7:2); that is why in his passion he calls us to himself as his members (Tr. 11:2).

"The distinction of the Gospel" over the Old Testament dispensation is "the coming, the passion, and the resurrection" of Christ (Philad. 9:2; *cf*. Eph. 20:1; Sm. 7:2). By his "passion" he gave the baptismal water its power (Eph. 18:2); his "cross" is the elevator (μηχανή) which lifts believers to God (Eph. 9:1). Christ's passion, death, and resurrection are understood as events which continually condition Christian existence, not as an occurrence of the past the benefit of which is appropriated in baptism as the cancellation of one's former sins. The phrases which express this traditional view occur very rarely in Ignatius. The phrase "for us" (referring to the suffering and dying of Christ) appears only in Rom. 6:1 and Sm. 1:2; "for our sins" only at Sm. 7:1. (Otherwise, neither "sin" nor "sinner" occurs; the verb "sin" appears only in the characteristic sentence: "No man who professes faith sins," Eph. 14:2.) By this omission Ignatius is also spared from limiting the effect of the salvation-occurrence to the cancellation of sins committed in one's pre-Christian period.

The Christian's fellowship with the suffering and dying of Christ is described with a variety of expressions, such as "to suffer with him" (Sm. 4:2), "to die through him in his passion" (Mg. 5:2, etc.). Christians are "branches of the cross"

(Tr. 11:2); they are "nailed to the cross" (Sm. 1:1). Ignatius says of himself: "My selfish love (ἔρως) is crucified" (Rom. 7:2). In addition compare, for example, Eph. intr., 1:1; Tr. 4:2; Rom. 4:3, and for its paradox, the closing salutation: "in the name of Jesus Christ and in his flesh and blood (which is) both a passion and a resurrection having the nature of both flesh and spirit" (Sm. 12:2 tr.).

Beyond doubt Ignatius thinks that the Christian's sharing of death and life with Christ is brought about by the sacraments (see above II, p. 193). But this sharing with Christ gives the whole of life a sacramental character, though in a different way than in Paul. For the latter, "being crucified with Christ" (Rom. 6:6; Gal. 5:24; 6:14) constantly takes place in the battle against sin and in renunciation of the world. Not so Ignatius. For him it takes place in literal suffering and in the willingness to die as the imitation of Christ (Sm. 5:1; Mg. 5:2). From this view comes Ignatius' craving for martyrdom (especially in Rom.); for not until he is martyred will that be truly actualized which was potentially or approximately given in the sacrament and in the conduct of his life. Not until his martyrdom will Ignatius be truly an "imitator of the passion of my God" (Rom. 6:3), even though all Christians may be called, or ought to be able to be called, "imitators of God" (Eph. 1:1; 10:3; Tr. 1:2; Philad. 7:2). While every Christian is a "disciple of Jesus Christ" (Mg. 9:1; 10:1; Rom 3:1; Pol. 2:1), nevertheless it is the martyr who is the true disciple (Eph. 1:2; 3:1; Tr. 5:2; Rom. 4:2; 5:1, 3; Pol. 7:1).

Furthermore, the ethical life of believers is conditioned by this sacramental fellowship, although Ignatius does not call it dying and rising with Christ. One must not merely be called a "Christian," but must also "live according to Christianity" (κατὰ Χριστιανισμόν, Mg. 4; 10:1; *cf.* Rom. 3:2f.; Pol. 7:3).

Christian living is rarely described concretely. Usually Ignatius simply refers to the "commandment(s) of Christ" (Eph. 9:2; Rom. intr.; Philad. 1:2), for Christ is for him also the "teacher" (Eph. 15:1; Mg. 9:1); or he refers to the "ordinances" (δόγματα) of the Lord and the apostles" (Mg. 13:1). He evidently presupposes something like a catechism of Christian living. Specifically, he admonishes his readers to love for the brethren and unity (Mg. 6:2; Tr. 8:2; Philad. 8 and elsewhere), to prayer for non-Christians and to patient endurance of scorn and injustice

(Eph. 10), to worthy conduct which will not offend the heathen (Tr. 8:2). It is characteristic of him that his warnings against heresy outweigh his ethical parenesis. "To be firm in the faith" (Eph. 10:2) is the thing that counts.

Again and again "faith" and "love" are named as marks of Christianity (Eph. 1:1; 9:1; 14:1f.; 20:1; Mg. 1:2, etc.); "faith" is the "flesh," "love" the "blood" of Christ (Tr. 8:1). In this combination "faith" generally means, probably, the acceptance of right doctrine or the holding fast to it. But in Ignatius faith as orthodoxy is not to be separated from faith as an attitude of life, the will to share in suffering with Christ; thus Ignatius can speak of "believing in his death" (Tr. 2:1) or believing "in the blood of Christ" (Sm. 6:1).

The source of "faith" or "believing" lies, as we have seen, in the mystery of Christ's death and resurrection (Mg. 9:1). The opposite of "faith" is an un-faith (ἀπιστία, Eph. 8:2; Mg. 5:2) for which the cross is a "scandal" (Eph. 18:1). The "disbelievers" (ἄπιστοι) are heretics who deny the reality of Christ's passion (Tr. 10:1; Sm.2) and by their "false teaching" corrupt "the faith for the sake of which Jesus Christ was crucified" (Eph. 16:2). This is the "teaching of the prince of this world" (Eph. 17:1), while the true teaching is the "doctrine of incorruption" (Mg. 6:2).

Beyond doubt right faith for Ignatius is not merely assent to dogmatic propositions but is an existential attitude.* But nowhere in his letters does "faith" have that meaning which Paul expresses by contrasting "faith" and "works." Only the (Pauline) motif of rejecting "boasting" and "being puffed up" occasionally occurs (Eph. 18:1; Mg. 12; Tr. 4:1; 7:1; Sm. 6:1; Pol. 4:3; 5:2), but the opposite is not "faith" but "non-boasting" (ἀκαυχησία, Pol. 5:2) and "humility" (Tr. 4:2) or "being modest" (Mg. 12) and "restraining one's self" (Tr. 4:1). Ignatius also catches up Paul's expression "I am not thereby rightwised" from I Cor. 4:4 (tr.), applying it to his own progress toward martyrdom (Rom. 5:1). He hopes to be "rightwised" by the death and resurrection of Christ and by faith (Philad. 8:2). But these are rare echoes of Pauline language. "Righteousness" as designation for the essence of salvation never occurs at all; its adjective (δίκαιος) in Ignatius refers to moral uprightness (Mg. 12 quoting Prov. 18:17; used also in a play on words Eph. 1:1—see

* I.e. an attitude which involves the whole being and the whole doing of the believer (Tr.).

Bauer *ad loc.* in Lietzmann's *Handbuch*). As "flesh" does not mean the power of sin (see above II, p. 194), neither does Spirit mean the power behind ethical conduct, but means the other-worldly sphere (see above, II, p. 194), or is used in conventional phrases. However, Ignatius does speak of God's "grace" as a power at work in the Church (Sm. 9:2, Rom. intr., Mg. 8:2)—a power, furthermore, which is specially incorporated in the congregational officers (Mg. 2; Pol. 1:2). χάρισμα ("gift") he uses in the same sense (Sm. intr.; Pol. 2:2). Otherwise "grace" is God's, or Christ's, gracious will (e.g. Rom. 1:2; Philad. 8:1; 11:1; Sm. 11:1) or, in an objective sense, is the salvation wrought by God (Eph. 11:1; Mg. 8:1; Sm. 6:2). But "grace," like "faith," never stands in antithesis to "works."

Ignatius has here been treated at considerable length. That was necessary partly because from him a light is cast backward upon the theology of Paul, partly because Ignatius, in contradistinction to all other writers of early Christianity after Paul and John, is a figure having originality. But it was primarily necessary because through him the problems clearly emerge which confronted a genuine appropriation of the Christian kerygma which had received its first theological explication at the hands of Paul. Almost everywhere else Christian faith sank back into legalism, even though Col., Eph., and I Pet. as well as the pastorals hold fast to some motifs of Paul's theology and make them effective. But Ignatius learned from Paul to understand Christian faith as a truly existential matter. He did not reach emancipation from Hellenistic dualism, it is true—on the contrary, it is within such dualism that he understands the antithesis of "flesh" and "Spirit." Since he knows "flesh" not as the power of sin but only as the sphere of transitoriness and death, he did not grasp the meaning of Paul's doctrine of justification ("rightwising" by faith) nor of his concept of "faith." Neither does he understand Paul's concept of Christian "freedom," for to his mind "freedom" is to be achieved only after death (martyrdom)—Rom. 4:3. Nor did he understand Paul's concept of the Christian's relation to the suffering and dying of Christ, but understood it to be an imitating of Christ. But Ignatius did comprehend the paradoxical character of Christian existence: an existing between "already" and "not yet." In fact, because he did not take over the apocalyptic doctrine of the two aeons, for him that "between-ness" shrinks to the time between the believer's baptism and death (or, rather, resurrection) and consequently well-nigh loses its chronological sense and to a considerable extent becomes that which determines the character of Christian existence. Legalism is no problem for Ignatius. The reason for that is not (as it generally is with other writers) that he thinks legalistically and hence does not find it problematical that fulfilling the "(new) law" is the condition for achieving future salvation. Rather, the reason for it is that it would never occur to him that salvation might be won by one's own merit. That which is new in the Christian situation lies, for him, not in the granting of a new chance but in the transformation of one's existence. For him the effect of the salvation-occurrence is not limited to the cancellation of past sins but is a power experienced in the present. Though the traditional eschatology plays no role in Ignatius' thought, he nevertheless understood Christ as the eschatological event. Hence he knows the dialectic of Christian existence: the paradox that it unites indicative and imperative. Christians who are "disciples" or "imitators" of God or Christ (Mg. 10:1; Eph. 1:1; Tr. 1:2) must nevertheless still become such (Mg. 9:1; Eph. 10:3; Philad. 7:2). By the indicative they may be described as "belonging to God" (ὄντες θεοῦ, Eph. 8:1), or as "in all ways adorned by the commandments of Jesus Christ" (Eph. 9:2), but they can likewise be admonished by the imperative as people who have yet to become "sanctified in all things" (Eph. 2:2). The paradox of Gal. 5:25 reappears in this form: "Since you are perfect, then also strive after perfect (deeds)" (τέλειοι ὄντες τέλεια καὶ φρονεῖτε, Sm. 11:3 tr., to which he immediately adds, "For if you desire to do well, God is ready to help you." *Cf.* Eph. 15:3; Mg. 12).

4. In the preceding survey we have examined a certain body of literature. We did so under a guiding question: how is the present conceived to be related to future salvation, and in what way is the Christian situation understood to be that peculiar situation of "between-ness"? The answers yield a series of differences, an abundance of nuances. In some writings there is no understanding of that "between-ness" at all. In them the present is not conceived as a period basically new as compared with the past, but is a temporary and preparatory period quite as in Judaism. Of this sort are Jas., Did., Rev., and I Clem. In most other cases, however, the present is distinguished from the past as something made new by the coming of Jesus, or by his death and resurrection. Nevertheless, here the "between-ness" of the present is conceived as that which determines

only the chronology of the Christian situation and not its character; it is the period of a new chance for man's effort in behalf of his future salvation—ultimately, therefore, here, too, only a temporary and preparatory period. Only where the Pauline tradition continues to work controllingly does the basic (non-chronological) sense of that "between-ness" come forth—radically in Ignatius, with some power also in Col., Eph., and I Pet. and more weakly in the pastorals and even in Barn., though he is not under the influence of Paul. The basic sense has completely paled down in Herm. and Heb., in both of which, as in I Clem., Jas. and Did., the synagogue-tradition has become dominant. But even where the synagogue-tradition is weak or missing, as in II Pet., Jude, and Pol., the same is true.

The more prominent the chronological meaning of the believer's "between-ness" becomes—even to the point of becoming its sole meaning—the more salvation's present reality comes to be seen solely in the fact that one's former sins are canceled by the work of salvation (Jesus' death and resurrection) appropriated in baptism, and that thereby the possibility of a new beginning is conferred upon the present. This possibility, however, is understood to mean that now by obedience to God's demands a man can successfully exert himself to fulfil the condition for attaining future salvation: do the good works on the basis of which he will be acquitted in the judgment by God (or Christ), who will judge according to works. This legalism is not relinquished but is at the most only modified when the Spirit's assistance in this human effort is mentioned, or when the consciousness is alive that Christians are the new People of God (especially Barn. and Heb.), called, and in an anticipatory sense "saved" (II, p. 159), and hence also have hope. Neither is it any relinquishing of legalism when a possibility exists of obtaining God's forgiveness by repentance for sins committed after baptism. That the question concerning such a possibility can arise (Herm. but also Heb.) is a clear symptom of legalistic thinking. It is significant how rarely faith in the radical sense, as we find it in Paul and John, is understood as a new relation to God. As a rule *pistis* is understood as trust in God, as confident hope, or as patient faithfulness. Even in Col. and Eph. and in the pastorals Paul's antithesis of "faith" to "works" is only faintly echoed; otherwise it is entirely lacking (for which in Ignatius there is a special reason; see II, p. 199) or is simply reproduced in conventional phrases (I and II Clem.). Man is thrown back upon his own strength and nothing remains of the insight, "if anyone is in Christ, he is a new creation" (II Cor. 5:17). The consequence of this is probably clearest in I Clem. For him the difference between Christians and the pious men of the Old Testament disappears.

5. What does this mean for *christology*? The Christ who is worshiped in the cultus as the present Kyrios (II, p. 155) is truly thought of as Lord of the present only when the present is understood as made absolutely new by him—i.e. when Christ's appearing is understood in Paul's sense (Gal. 4:4, etc.) and John's (Jn. 5:25, etc.) as the eschatological event which terminated the old world and when, correspondingly, Christian existence is understood as divorced-from-the-world, eschatological existence. The decisive question is whether this end which has been imposed upon the world is understood only chronologically as the end of the course of time or whether it is also and essentially understood as the end of the worldliness of man, who, having become, as a believer, a new creature, has stepped over from death into life. This qualitative meaning of the eschatological occurrence had been completely cut loose from the chronological meaning by John (§ 45, 3), while in Paul the two are still combined. The radicality of John is well-nigh achieved by Ignatius, while Paul's understanding is to some degree preserved in Col. and Eph. and even in the pastorals. Hence in them, too, the salvation-character of the present is seen in the fact that in the present the word of the proclamation is sounding forth (II, pp. 177, 185)—i.e. that here, as in Paul (I, p. 302), Christ is present in the proclaimed word. Everywhere else Christ's eschatological significance (except where it entirely disappears, as in Jas. and Herm.) is seen only in the fact that he will (soon) put the world's temporal course to end when he returns to hold judgment and bring salvation. As the coming Judge he is, consistently, for the present time the teacher and law-giver, not the founder of a new relation to God. Paul's expression "in Christ," which denotes the believer's present existence, is still found in this sense in Col. and Eph. but is also already becoming a conventional phrase meaning "Christian" (II, p. 177). As such a formula it is used in the pastorals (II, pp. 186f.) and in I Pet. (3:16; 5:10, 14), rather often in I Clem., and once in Pol. (1:1). Once in Rev. the phrase "in the Lord" (14:13) occurs. "In Christ" does not occur in Heb., Barn., Jas., Did., II Pet., II Clem., or Herm. Only in Ignatius does it have once more its old strength (II, p. 193).

[201]

Participation in the suffering and death of Christ meant, in Paul, the shaping of Christian living by that divorce from the world which is to be constantly accomplished in the battle against sin (Rom. 6:6; Gal. 5:24; 6:14). It still has this meaning in Col. 2:12, 20; 3:3, perhaps in II Tim. 2:11f., and certainly in I Peter 4:1f. But already in I Pet. there is combined with it the idea of the *imitatio Christi* (II, pp. 182f.), which later is so important in Ignatius (II, p. 195). In this idea of imitation Christ is not regarded as the eschatological emancipator but as an example (so also in I Clem. 16:17; Pol. 8:2). While for Paul sharing the suffering and death of Christ is at the same time a present sharing of his life (II Cor. 4:8ff., etc.), in the notion of imitation the life is the future life which is to be conferred at the resurrection.

The presence of Christ here and now—where it is anything more than his presence as teacher, law-giver, and example—according to Col., Eph., and the pastorals is experienced in the proclaimed word; but otherwise it is experienced in the cult, particularly by receiving the sacraments of baptism and the eucharist. Since the sacraments have their foundation in the death and resurrection of Christ, in a certain sense they give present reality to the salvation-occurrence by mediating its benefit: the forgiveness of sins and the gift of eternal life (Ignatius).

Except in Ignatius *the incarnation* of the pre-existent Son has no significance of its own but is only the necessary pre-supposition for his passion and death or also for his activity as teacher and founder of the Church by his commissioning of the apostles. In Ignatius, as a consequence of his conception of "flesh" and "spirit," the incarnation has a special meaning; by it that which is of the earth and the flesh is enabled to participate in that which is otherworldly and spiritual (II, pp. 193f.). The incarnation regarded as an act of obedience and love, which is the dominant view in Paul and John (Phil. 2:8; Rom. 15:3; II Cor. 8:1; Gal. 2:20; Jn. 3:16, 4:34, 12:49f.; I Jn. 4:9), has disappeared except for a remnant (Sm. 8:1; Mg. 7:1).

The more Christian faith degenerates into legalism, the more Christ's significance is reduced to that of being at work in the Church's sacrament. The less Christ is felt to be present in the proclaimed word, the more the Church becomes a sacramental institution of salvation (II, p. 114). Christology, as soon as it ceases to be naive and becomes a matter of reflection, will have to find its task in furnishing a foundation for the sacramental significance of Christ.

CHAPTER VIII

The Problem of Christian Living

§ 59. The Understanding of the Imperative

1. The problem of Christian living, among other problems, was present to the Church from the beginning (§ 10, 4; § 11, 3c)—not only and not primarily as a problem of the practical side of living, but mainly as a problem of the Christian's understanding of himself. The problem was set by the paradoxical situation of the Church: as the eschatological entity which it is it belongs not to the old but to the future world and yet must lead its life within the old world between "no longer" and "not yet." As a new life no longer belonging to the old aeon it can be described in the indicative; but as long as it must be led in the old world, it stands under the imperative. As new life it stands under God's grace; as life within the old world it stands under His law, under ethical demand (§ 11, 3c). The problem therefore resolves itself into this question: how is the relation between the present and the future, between the indicative and the imperative, understood? Paul had solved the problem by his understanding of Christian freedom (§ 38) and had conceived the relation between the present and the future as a dialectic one (§ 40)—and John likewise (§ 50). The question was whether or not this understanding would be retained—whether Christian freedom would be understood as the freedom to obey, obedience itself then being understood as the gift of grace or of the Spirit, or whether obedience would be conceived as an accomplishment and hence as the condition to be fulfilled in order to obtain salvation (I, pp. 119f.), and then whether the imperative would receive again the character of a law in the sense that had been demolished in Paul's doctrine of justification: the character of a way to salvation.

In most essentials the answer to these questions has already been given in the discussions of soteriology (§ 58) because on account of the peculiar nature of the Christian understanding of salvation the themes of soteriology and ethics cannot be separated. They cannot be separated because the question of the relation between present and future salvation is most intimately bound up with the question of the relation between indicative and imperative. In our discussion it developed that the Pauline tradition is still alive only in Col., Eph., I Pet., and, more weakly, in the pastorals, and that everywhere else a sinking back into legalism takes place except in Ignatius, who, while he has learned decisive things from Paul, nevertheless re-interprets him under the influence of sacramental thinking. The fact is that on the average the insight of Paul and John that the occurrence of salvation means eschatological occurrence was not grasped; instead it was reduced to an event—the death and resurrection of Jesus—the effect of which, when appropriated in baptism, is to cancel the sins of the past. The man who is purified from his former guilt has henceforth the chance of a new beginning but is now left to rely on his own strength to become worthy of the coming salvation by his obedience. The knowledge that the gift of grace (Paul) or of God's love (John) makes a man radically new is lost. Gone is the knowledge that a man without God's grace is a victim to the power of sin and death, that he has lost his freedom and is living in disobedience to God even if his conduct be correct, because God's law is to him a means of asserting himself before God. Vanished is the knowledge that his release from the powers that controlled him is a release to genuine obedience, but that he is never cast loose from the giving and forgiving grace of God nor left to rely upon his own strength.

2. Hence *the failure to see any longer man's radical fallen-ness to* the power of sin, falsehood, darkness is an understandable develop-ment. The conversion of the heathen was regarded—both from the Gentile-Christian and the Jewish-Christian view-point—as the acquiring of a new and correct knowledge of God, as the transfer from the "darkness" of "ignorance" and "error" into the light of the knowledge of the one God (§ 9, 2; *cf.* especially II Clem. 1:6f.), and at the same time as a turning away from a life sunk in vices (§ 9, 3), which, as such, is a life under the power of death. Rescue from this death occurs by the forgiveness of sins which is made available by Christ's death and is appropriated in baptism (I, pp. 84f., 136f.). The last statement also applies, of course, to the Jews who turn to the Christian faith.

[204]

The "*slavery*" into which man prior to faith has fallen is no longer understood as slavery to sin (and the Law) as it is in Paul and John (Gal. 4:24; 5:1; Rom. 6:16–20, 8:15; Jn. 8:32–36), but to "death" and "corruption" (Heb. 2:15; II Pet. 2:19)— a view that is likewise found in Paul, it is true (Rom. 8:21). The only exception is Tit. 3:3 ("slaves to various passions and pleasures"). "*Freedom*" in I Pet. 2:16 perhaps means freedom from the Law and from sin; in Ign. Rom. 4:3; Pol. 4:3 it means freedom from death. Otherwise, the term "freedom" as a mark of Christian existence no longer occurs at all unless one is inclined to find it in the heretics' slogan at II Pet. 2:19. On the "law of freedom (or "liberty")" Jas. 1:25, 2:12, see II, p. 162 footnote.

In no case is conversion understood as the radical transformation of the old man. There are indeed echoes of Paul's thought of the destruction of the "old man" (Rom. 6:6; 7:6; I Cor. 5:7f.) and also of the "newness" ($\kappa\alpha\iota\nu\acute{o}\tau\eta\varsigma$) of Christian life (Rom. 6:4). But the paradox of the statements: "If anyone is in Christ, he is a new creation" (II Cor. 5:17; *cf.* Gal. 6:15) and: "our inner (man) is being renewed every day" (II Cor. 4:16; *cf.* Rom. 12:2) is scarcely understood any longer. Only rarely is there a train of thought in which there is any grasp of man's renewal in the sense of Paul's understanding of indicative and imperative. The clearest case of this sort is Col. 3:1ff.: "If then you have been raised with Christ, seek the things that are above . . . for you have died . . . put to death therefore your members that are on the earth . . . having put off the old man . . . and having put on the new man which is being renewed; . . . put on then . . ." (*cf.* 2:12f.). In Tit. 3:3–7 the paradox is also still preserved in that the imperative is founded upon the "renewal" brought about by the "Holy Spirit." In Eph. 2:1–10 the quoted sentences from Colossians are echoed, but their paradox is now only weakly expressed: "you who were dead through your trespasses and sins . . . he made alive together with Christ . . . created in Christ Jesus for good works." Likewise in the admonition of Eph. 4:22–24: "Put off your old man . . . and be renewed in the spirit of your minds and put on the new man created after the likeness of God. . . ." The catch-word "renewal" is echoed in Heb. 6:6; but here the meaning of renewal as including the imperative is given up when it is said that after baptism it is impossible to "restore again ($\pi\acute{\alpha}\lambda\iota\nu$ $\dot{\alpha}\nu\alpha\kappa\alpha\iota\nu\acute{\iota}\zeta\epsilon\iota\nu$) to repentance" the (grave) sinners. And the threat of divine retribution, which he says is so much more terrible for Christians than for Jews (2:2f.; 10:28f.; 12:25), indicates that the author did not understand the Christian's radically different standing before God. If either of them understood it, it was rather the author of Barnabas: "Because we received the remission of sins and hoped in the Name, we have become new, created again from the beginning" (Barn. 16:8). Or again (6:11): "Since, then, he made us new by the remission of sins, he made us another type, that we should have the soul of children, as though he were creating us afresh." But because the author knows nothing of present righteousness (4:10), neither did he understand the renewal radically. This judgment is not altered by his term "the new law of our Lord Jesus Christ" (2:6), for this consists of "ordinances" and "commandments," as we have seen (II, p. 164). Even when Christians are called the "new People" (5:7; 7:5), this "new" denotes only the chronological not the qualitative newness of the eschatological Congregation. Hermas, too, speaks of the renewal which (by baptism) the Christian has experienced (vis. III 8:9: "the renewal of your spirits") or which he now receives by the Lord's revelation and call to repentance (vis. III 12:3; sim. VIII 6:2; IX 14:3; *cf.* VI 2:4). But precisely by speaking of the renewal now made possible for one last time he shows that he does not understand renewal in Paul's sense. If for him Christ is the "new door" (sim. IX 12:1–3), he is so only in the chronological sense.

A particularly revealing passage is Herm. mand. XII 3:4–5:4: Hermas has learned from the "Shepherd" what the commandments of God are and confesses in fright: "But I do not know whether these commandments can be kept because they are exceedingly difficult." But he has to be told in answer that he is mistaken—rather, the commandments are easy, and merely to regard them as difficult is already a sin. If a man only desires to do so from his heart, he can keep them; since man received from the Creator lordship over the world, why shouldn't he also have the strength to keep the commandments? If he only does not fear the devil, the devil will flee before him!

An understanding for "the old has passed away, behold, the new has come" (II Cor. 5:17)—i.e. for the total otherness of the Christian situation—is really found only in Ignatius. He really understood the salvation-occurrence as eschatological and consequently grasped the paradox of Christian existence. He understood the release of man from

his old nature not as release from the power of flesh and sin, it is
true, but as release from transitoriness and death (II, p. 195). That
is understandable from a recognition of Ignatius' different presuppositions: the Hellenistic-Gnostic dualism, out of which he comes,
and his sacramentalism. Elsewhere than in Ignatius understanding
for what Paul and John called sin gets lost in moralistic-legalistic
thinking—essentially under the influence of the synagogal tradition.

The manner in which *sin* is generally spoken of indicates that the
radical fallen-ness of man outside of Christ is no longer seen. Almost
nowhere is sin any longer regarded as a unified power, or, seen from
man's side, as a unified attitude toward living; only in Colossians and
Ephesians is sin still seen as a power that threatens even the Christian (II, pp. 176f.). Of course, we often hear of "sins" (ἁμαρτίαι and
ἁμαρτήματα) and "transgressions"; and such confessions as the following occur: "my sins are many and manifold" (Herm. mand IV 2:3),
or "I myself am altogether sinful (πανθαμαρτωλός) and have not yet
escaped temptation" (II Clem. 18:2), or "we all owe the debt of sin"
(Pol. Phil. 6:1). But practically never is sin mentioned as a power
that dominates man; at the most sin is regarded as a unity in Heb.
9:26; 12:1, 4 and Pol. Phil. 6:1. When the men prior to Christ are
regarded as sinners whom he came to save, the authors are thinking
of the heathen life of vice (I Tim. 1:9; *cf.* Col. 1:21; 3:7f.; Eph. 2:3;
Tit. 3:3; I Pet. 1:14, 18; 4:3); they were "dead in trespasses" (Col.
2:13; Eph. 2:1, 5; *cf.* Herm. sim. IX 16:3ff.), their "works" were
"dead" (Heb. 6:1; 9:14; said of sinful Christians, Herm. sim. IX 21:2;
cf. Rev. 3:1).

If we leave Ignatius out of account (II, p. 195), *the flesh* also is
scarcely spoken of in the Pauline sense any longer, either. In Col.
2:11, 13 "flesh," if not the power of sin, is at least the sphere of sin:
in baptism took place "the putting off of the body of flesh," and
God made alive those who were dead "in trespasses and in (?) the
uncircumcision of the flesh" (*cf.* Jude 23). A number of times the
"desires of the flesh" are mentioned (Eph. 2:3; I Pet. 2:11; II Pet.
2:18; Did. 1:4; Barn. 10:9). But otherwise *sarx* now means as in
Ignatius only the sphere of the earthly, that which is of the body.

Thus *sarx* is used neutrally, e.g. in II Clem. 8:2; Herm. vis.
III 9:3, mand. III 1 and elsewhere. It is several times said that
Christ revealed himself and suffered in the flesh (Barn. 5:6, 10ff.,
6: 7, 9, etc.; II Clem. 9:5; Herm. sim. V 6:5ff.) or that man must

not defile his flesh but keep it pure (II Clem., see II, p. 170; Herm. mand. IV 1:9; sim. V 7:1f.; *cf.* "pure in the flesh" I Clem. 38:2). Paul's "according to the flesh" no longer occurs at all as the characteristic of sinful conduct; to denote a natural relation-ship (I, pp. 236f.) the phrase still occurs but only in Col. 3:22, Eph. 6:5 (the earthly—κατὰ σάρκα—masters, i.e. masters of slaves) and I Clem. 32:2 (Jesus, Abraham's descendant "accord-ing to the flesh"). II Clem. like Ignatius, teaches the resurrection of the flesh (9:1ff.).

Hence, *the contrast between "flesh" and "Spirit"* in Paul's sense no longer plays any role but only denotes the contrast between the earthly and the divine (the other-worldly). This is true not only in Ignatius but also elsewhere—e.g. I Tim. 3:16; Barn. 7:3; II Clem. 9:5; 14:3ff.; Herm. sim. V 6:5ff., etc.; Col. 2:5 is somewhat different. More frequently found is the contrast "world—God," which may be expressed in full (Jas. 4:4; Ign. Mg. 5:2; Rom. 2:2) or only implied by speaking of "this world" (Eph. 2:2; Did. 10:6; Barn. 10:11; II Clem. 5:1–5 "this world of the flesh"; 8:2; 19:3; Ign. Mg. 5:2; Herm. vis. IV 3:2–4, sim. V 5:2), or by simply using "the world" in a derogatory sense (Jas. 1:27; 4:4; II Pet. 1:4; 2:20; Ign. Rom. 3:2f.; 7:1; Pol. Phil. 5:3). In such cases "world" for the most part does not mean a power inimical to God (which it clearly does mean in Jas. 4:4) but the sphere of the earthly, and the usage is less indicative of man's being fallen or threatened than of the negativity of ethical demand—as when "worldly passions" are mentioned (Tit. 2:12; II Clem. 17:3; *cf.* Pol. Phil. 5:3: "the lusts that are in the world") or simply "worldly things" (κοσμικά, II Clem. 5:6).

The contrast between *the present and the future aeon* lives on in some writings. It may be explicitly formulated (Eph. 1:21; II Clem. 6:3; Herm. sim. III–IV) or only one or the other may be named: "this" or "the present" aeon (I Tim. 6:17; II Tim. 4:10; Ign. Rom. 6:1; Pol. Phil. 5:2; 9:2, frequently in Hermas—"ruler of this world" several times in Ignatius), or only "the coming aeon" (Heb. 6:5: "the age to come," ὁ μέλλων; Herm. vis. IV 3:5: "the coming, ἐρχόμενος, aeon"; Barn. 10:11: "the holy, ἅγιος, aeon"; II Clem. 19:4: "the age without sorrow," ἀλύπητος). This usage, too, is characteristic for negative ethics, as one may see especially clearly in Hermas who

* The antecedents of the pronouns in I Clem. 32:1, 2 are far from clear. Perhaps 32:2 refers to Jacob, not Abraham (Tr.).

warns against the "lusts" (and "deceptions") of this aeon (mand. XI 8, XII 6:5; sim. VI 2:3; 3:3, etc.) or against its "vanities" (mand. IX 4, sim. V 3:6), its "wickednesses" (sim. VI 1:4) and its "occupations" (mand. X 1:4). One's belonging to the coming aeon appears essentially as the obligation to free one's self from the old world by obedience to the "new law of the Lord" (Barn. 2:6), to its "commandments" and "ordinances" and by renunciation of "fleshly" or "worldly" desires. The indicative upon which this imperative is founded is limited to the fact that former sins are forgiven: henceforth the baptized man is on his own responsibility and must fulfil the condition for achieving future salvation by his own good works. The consciousness of being freed from the power of sin and of being borne up by the strength of the Spirit is in the process of getting lost.

Freedom from sin is understood in the moral sense: as sinlessness. Therefore, where the contrast between the past and the present is taken seriously, the problem of post-baptismal sins—at least the grave ones—necessarily arises along with the question whether there is a possibility of renewed repentance (Heb., Herm.). Though it is true that in parenesis the contrast between "once" and "now" plays a great role (I, pp. 105f.). But where the contrast is only that between one's present baptismal purity and one's former sins, and is not a description of a once hidden salvation now revealed, a motivation for the imperative is furnished by means of an indicative, but their paradoxical relation to each other is not expressed. Sinlessness has thereby become a task to be accomplished; and to the extent that sinlessness shows itself to be unfulfillable or unfulfilled, refuge is sought in repentance and divine forgiveness. For by and large this is assumed without reflection to be an existing possibility—an assumption which is also an aftermath of the synagogal tradition. While Herm. calls men to repentance because that possibility is now once again opened to them but for the last time, II Clem. is a penitential sermon with the presupposition that repentance is possible at any time. The cry, "Repent!" pervades the letters to the seven churches in Revelation, and the repentance of Christians is dealt with in II Tim. 2:25; I Clem. 57:1; 62:2; Did. 10:6; II Pet. 3:9; Ign. Philad. 3:2; 8:1; Sm. 4:1; 5:3;, 9:1. In I Clem. 7–8 we hear of "repentance" as a possibility existing for Christians as it once did for the pious men of the Old Testament. Even though it is occasionally said that an opportunity for repentance is given us only so long as we tarry on earth (II Clem. 8:1–3; 16:1; Ign. Sm. 9:1), it is clear that repentance is now still constantly possible, a situation for which II Pet. 3:9 explicitly gives the long-suffering of God as the reason. Like repentance, forgiveness, too, always stands open (Jas. 5:15; Pol. Phil. 6:2).

Repentance is, of course, the condition for forgiveness (expressly stated in Ign. Philad. 8:1). Occasionally forgiveness is conditional to the requirement that man fulfil the commandments of God in love (I Clem. 50:5), for "love covers a multitude of sins" (I Pet. 4:8; Jas. 5:20; I Clem. 49:5; 50:5; II Clem. 16:4). The same thing is also accomplished by "doing good" (Pol. Phil. 10:2; Barn. 19:10; Did. 4:6); indeed, according to II Clem. 16:4 almsgiving is as good as repentance and better than prayer and fasting. Herm. sim. V 1 goes even further: here ritual fasting is rejected, and the teaching is presented that the genuine way to "fast" is to fulfil the commandments. In sim. V 3:7, contrariwise, fasting is approved but is put to charitable service: the food saved by fasting is to be turned to the benefit of widows, orphans, and the destitute. Such passages indicate that there were Christian circles in which fasting was deemed meritorious; in Pol. Phil. 7:2 it appears in combination with prayer, and in Did. 8:1 the Christian fast on Wednesday and Friday is contrasted with the Jewish fast on Monday and Thursday. A somewhat different case is the fast which is a preparation for the receiving of revelation (Herm. vis. II 2:1, III 1:2, 10:6f.) or for baptism (Did. 7:4). Suffering, too, if it leads to repentance, has a sin-canceling effect, so Hermas says (vis. III 7:6, sim. VI 3–5, VII); I Pet. 4:1 is hardly interpretable in this sense, but perhaps Jas. 5:14–16 is.

In the congregational prayer at I Clem. 60:1 forgiveness is implored under appeal to divine mercy. As in I Jn. 1:9, the confessing of sin is often mentioned (Jas. 5:16; I Clem. 51:3; 52:1; Barn. 19:12; Did. 4:14; 14:1; II Clem. 8:3; Herm. vis. I 1:3; III 1:5f.; sim. IX 23:4). Probably such confession is generally presupposed.

3. Corresponding to the fact that sin is no longer taken with radical seriousness, neither is *the grace of God* any longer radically understood. The "grace" of God is, indeed, often mentioned, but the antithesis of "works" to "grace" is only rarely echoed (Eph. 2:5, 8f.; II Tim. 1:9; Tit. 3:5, 7).

Quite often divine "grace" in a very general sense is mentioned (II Thess. 1:12, 2:16; I Tim. 1:14; Acts 11:23; 14:26;

15:40; I Clem. 30:2f.; 50:3; II Clem. 13:4; Ign. Sm. 12:1; Pol. 2:1; Herm. mand. X 3:1). In such cases "grace" · is scarcely distinguishable from "mercy" (ἔλεος, I, pp. 282f.). "Grace" and "peace" are often combined, both in greetings (I Tim. 1:2; II Tim. 1:2; Tit. 1:4 *v.l.*; II Jn. 3; Ign. Sm. 12:2) and elsewhere (Heb. 4:16); the place of "grace" can be taken by "mercy" (Eph. 2:4; Tit. 3:5). "Grace" may also be seen in God's granting of repentance (I Clem. 7:4, where, unlike Acts 5:31; 11:18, the author evidently is not thinking of baptismal repentance alone).

In general "grace" denotes the saving grace manifested in Christ (e.g. Tit. 2:11). The Christian message can be called the "Gospel" or "the word" of "grace" (Acts 20:24, 32). To become a Christian can be termed a hearing and understanding of God's grace (Col. 1:6). To be a Christian is to have come under the "yoke of grace" (I Clem. 16:17) or be under "present grace" (Ign. Eph. 11:1; *cf.* I Pet. 5:12). Heretics "have divergent notions (ἑτεροδοξοῦντες) concerning the grace of Jesus Christ" (Ign. Sm. 6:2); the sin of apostasy is called insulting "the Spirit of grace" (Heb. 10:29). "Grace" appears to be conceived as a power which aids one to a proper Christian attitude, in such expressions as say that the Church has received the "Spirit of grace" or "the grace of the spiritual gift" (I Clem. 46:6; Barn. 1:2) or that it is full of the "grace of God" (Ign. Rom. intr.). *Cf.* also I Clem. 23:1; 46:6; Barn. 1:3; on grace as a power see also I Clem. 55:3.

It is evident now that *pistis* (and its verb *pisteuein*) also cannot here mean, as in Paul, the obedience which faith is, but—except where it means hopeful trust or fidelity—is becoming a historical term, so to speak, a term for becoming or being a Christian or also for Christianity in the sense of the content of its belief (II, pp. 135f.). When the antithesis between "works" and "faith" gets lost, it is not surprising that the demand for good works (and warning against evil ones) is everywhere heard—in the pastoral epistles as in I and II Clem. and Barn. For the judgment and its retribution will turn out according to one's works (I Pet. 1:17; Rev. 2:23; I Clem. 34:3; Barn. 4:12; II Clem. 6:9, etc.). Jas. 2:24 explicitly assures the reader that man will be "justified" by works and not by faith alone (*cf.* I Clem. 31:2). Therefore, Hermas begs the "Shepherd" to instruct him "that I may know what works I must do in order to have life" (mand. IV 2:3, tr.; *cf.* VIII 8) and he constantly receives instruction about "wicked works" and "upright" ones, about the "works of God" and those "of the devil," etc. Certainly, exhortation to good work and reference to the judgment also occur in Paul (I Cor. 15:58; II Cor. 5:10; see I, pp. 320f., 332f., 337f.). But now that takes on another meaning because the imperative no longer has its foundation in the indicative as it did in Paul; because "grace" is no longer conceived in Paul's radical sense (I, pp. 289f.); and because the Spirit is no longer understood as uniting in itself both power and norm (I, pp. 336f.). Symptomatic of this change in meaning is the fact that "repentance" and "forgiveness of sins" which Paul almost never mentions (I, pp. 287, 317) now become prevalent.

As the term "faith" loses its Pauline (and Johannine) meaning, so does the term *"righteousness."* "Righteousness of God" in Paul's sense is no longer found at all (on Jas. 1:20; II Pet. 1:1, see I, p. 285). Also the unmodified noun "righteousness" and the unmodified verb "be rightwised" are only rarely used in the forensic-eschatological sense, and even then it is not always clear whether the reference is to the rightwising of the believer which has already occurred (certainly so in Tit. 3:7; perhaps in I Clem. 35:2) or to the rightwising which is to come (Barn. 4:10, where it is said in so many words that we are not yet "made righteous"; 15:7; Pol. Phil. 8:1; Ign. Philad. 8:2; II Clem. 11:1; probably also I Clem. 30:3; 32:4). In the majority of cases *dikaiosyne* and *dikaios* denote moral uprightness (§ 58, 3 *passim*). When Polycarp writes "concerning *dikaiosyne*" (Pol. Phil. 3:1) that means that he is giving an ethical parenesis.

Dikaiosyne as uprightness or moral conduct—see, for instance: Eph. 4:24; 5:9; I Tim. 1:9; 6:11; II Tim. 2:22; 3:16; Acts 13:10; Jas. 5:6, 16; I Pet. 3:12; II Pet. 2:7f.; Rev. 22:11; Barn. 1:6; 19:6; Pol. Phil. 9:2; mostly so in I Clement, consistently so in Didache and II Clement, almost always so in Hermas. The following expressions are typical: "do, ποιεῖν, uprightness," already found in I Jn. 2:29; 3:7, 10, then in Rev. 22:11; I Clem. 31:2; II Clem. 4:2; 11:7; "practice, ἐργάζεσθαι, uprightness" Acts 10:35; Heb. 11:33; I Clem. 33:8 ("work a work of uprightness"), often in Hermas (e.g., mand. VIII 2: "practice great uprightness"): "do, πράσσειν, uprightness" II Clem. 19:3. (*cf.* δικαιοπραγία, "exercise-of-uprightness," I Clem. 32:3); "to will upright things" Herm. vis. I 1:8; "way of uprightness" II Pet. 2:21; Barn. 1:4, 5:4; II Clem. 5:7; "reward of uprightness," Did. 5:2; Barn. 20:2; II Clem. 20:4. *Dikaiosyne* as the summation of all "virtues" (ἀρεταί), Herm. mand. 1:2, sim. VI 1:4; combined with "virtue" (ἀρετή), Herm. mand. XII 3:1, sim. VIII 10:3. The "angel of uprightness" and the "angel of wickedness" stand opposed to each other in Herm. mand. VI 2:1ff. *Dikaiosyne* as a virtue is often mentioned with one or more other virtues; e.g. with "love," II Clem. 12:1, with *pistis* (probably "fidelity") Pol. Phil. 9:2, with "hope" and *"pistis"* Barn. 1:6, with "purity" Herm. sim. IX 16:7, with "truth" I Clem. 31:2; Herm. sim. IX 25:2, or in a catalogue of virtues I Clem. 62:2; Herm. mand. VI 2:3, VIII 10, XII 3:1; with "humble" Did. 3:9; Barn. 19:6, with "worthy," σεμνός, Herm. sim. VIII 3:8. Particularly characteristic is the combining of "uprightness," "upright" or "uprightly" with ὅσιος ("devout," "pious") or its derivatives: I Clem. 14:1; 48:4, II Clem. 5:6; 6:9; 15:3, or with the equivalent adverb εὐσεβῶς, "piously," Tit. 2:12; I Clem. 62:1.

This terminology reveals that an ideal of moralistic piety is beginning to replace and to a considerable extent already has replaced the eschatological consciousness and endowment with spiritual gifts. As in Judaism it is the ideal that the servants of God shall live in piety and the fear of God as the condition for participating in future salvation. As *dikaiosyne* in the sense of right conduct takes on the meaning of "piety," so the number of expressions which denote "piety" increases.

The terms εὐσέβεια ("piety, religion" and the corresponding adjective and verb) and θεοσέβεια (once) do not occur in the New Testament until the pastorals and II Pet., then they become frequent in I and II Clem. Ὅσιος, "devout," and ὁσιότης, "devoutness" occur in the New Testament only in Eph. 4:24 and the pastorals, but are common in I and II Clement. Σεμνότης, "reverence" already emerges in the New Testament at I Tim. 2:2, occurs rather often in I Clem., and then is a great favorite with Hermas, for whom Reverence, personified, is one of the seven virgins (=virtues) who are building the tower of the Church (vis. III 8).

The use of "*fear (of God)*" and "to fear (God)" is especially revealing. Paul, too, sometimes speaks of the "fear of God" (Rom. 3:18 quoting LXX Ps. 35:2) or "of the Lord" (II Cor. 5:11), but the expression does not become a technical term for the Christian attitude until it appears in Acts 9:31, in the interpolation II Cor. 7:1, and, as "fear of Christ," in Eph. 5:21. The unqualified word "fear" is used with the same meaning in I Pet. 1:17; 3:2, 16 (combined with πραΰτης, "gentleness"), Jude 23. Later "fear of God" (or "of the Lord") and "fear," unqualified, frequently occur in I Clem., Barn., Pol., and especially in Herm., who treats at length the two kinds of fear—of the Lord and of the devil (mand. VII). In the New Testament the verbal form, "to fear God (or "the Lord"), aside from the technical designation of proselytes or semi-proselytes as "God-fearers," is still only seldom used as a characterization of the Christian attitude (Col. 3:22; I Pet. 2:17; Rev. 11:18; "to fear thy name" Rev. 19:5; *cf.* 14:7; 15:4), then it becomes more frequent in I and II Clem. and Herm. The related designation of the pious as "slaves of God" or "of Christ" likewise becomes more and more frequent.

Within the New Testament the term "slave of God" (or "of Christ" or "of the Lord") occurs in the word-play of I Cor. 7:22 but not yet in the technical sense. In the technical sense (approximately equivalent to "Christian") it occurs in Col. 4:12; Eph. 6:6; II Tim. 2:24; I Pet. 2:16; Rev. 1:1; 7:3; 19:2, 5; 22:3. To be distinguished from this is the use of the term as a title for distinguished persons like Moses (Rev. 15:2), the prophets (Rev. 10:7; 11:18), and the apostles (current in Paul and then present in Tit. 1:1; Acts 4:29; Jude 1; II Pet. 1:1). "To serve (or to be a slave of) δουλεύειν, God" occurs only at Mt. 6:24=Lk. 16:13. "To serve Christ" or "the Lord" is a term not unknown to Paul, but one which he uses comparatively seldom and then only when it is specially motivated by the context (Rom. 7:6 [25]; *cf.* 6:6; Gal. 4:8f.; I Thess. 1:9). As characterization of the Christian attitude: Col. 3:24; Acts 20:19. In Hermas "slave" (or "servant") "of God" is a current term for "Christian"; it also occurs in the congregational prayer I Clem. 60:2; also in II Clem. 20:1. Likewise, "serving God" or "the Lord" is common in Hermas; it is also found in I Clem. 26:1; 45:7; II Clem. 11:1; 17:7; 18:1; Pol. Phil. 2:1; 6:3. In Hermas the term is so worn down that he can also say "serve faith" (mand. IX 12), "serve good things" (neuter, mand. VIII 8), "serve the virtues" (vis. III 8:8), "serve the good desire" mand. XII 2:5, 3:1). But nowhere except in I Pet. 2:6 is the paradox grasped as in Paul (I Cor. 4:19; Gal. 5:13) that this slave-existence is at the same time an existence as a free man. That is, nowhere else is it radically understood what it means to be a "slave of God" or of "Christ"; nowhere else is the moralistic sense of "servitude" overcome.

4. Both in terminology and in substance it is *the influence of the synagogue* that is here at work pushing aside the theology of Paul (and of John). Not only in Heb. and Barn., in Rev., Jas., and the Did., in I Clem. and Herm. is the tradition of the synagogue dominant —partly in the form of written sources—but it is also detectable in the deutero-Pauline literature: Col., Eph., the pastorals, and I Pet. The Church is on the way to straying into a religious moralism. Besides the writings of Paul and John the forces which work against this are two. On the one hand there is the tradition of Jesus' preaching contained in the synoptics; its radical demand for obedience and its message of grace could hamper the development of moralism, but it could also come to be of service to such a development. On the other hand there is the Kyrios-cult and sacramentalism. *The effect of Jesus' preaching* remained at first remarkably weak. Is it detectable at all in any other way than that the love-commandment generally appears as the highest of the ethical demands? At any rate, it is striking that sayings of Jesus are extraordinarily seldom quoted.

Paul rarely quotes words of Jesus (I, pp. 188f.); elsewhere in the New Testament a saying of Jesus is quoted only at Acts 20:35 and perhaps at I Tim. 5:18 in case the "scripture" here quoted is intended to be Lk. 10:7. In Jas. there are perhaps some allusions to words of Jesus (e.g. 5:12), but no quotations. After the New Testament the only quotation of considerable extent is Did. 1:3–6; quotations of smaller extent: Did. 8:2 (the Lord's prayer), 9:5; 15:3f.? (in addition perhaps a few allusions: 11:7; 13:1; 16:1f.?); I Clem. 13:2; 46:8; Pol. Phil. 2:3; 7:2; in II Clem. rather numerous (2:4 as "scripture"; 3:2; 4:2, 5; 5:2–4; 6:1f.; 8:5; 9:11; 12:2 quite apocryphal, 13:4; 14:1?). In Ignatius there are at the most a few allusions (Eph. 14:2; Pol. 2:2; Sm. 1:1?). Barnabas places Old Testament sayings or sayings that he himself has formed upon the lips of Jesus (7:5, 11), but quotes none of the words of Jesus known to us in the tradition; allusions to such: 5:9; 7:9?; 21:2?. Hermas once expressly adduces a saying of Jesus (sim. IX 31:2) and several times is perhaps alluding to a saying of Jesus (mand. IV 1:6; sim. IX 20:3?; 29:1–3). Nevertheless, words of Jesus, as papyrus finds prove, must have circulated abundantly in the congregations. Those which are quoted by the so-called Apostolic Fathers are all incorporated in ethical parenesis.

At any rate, only *the Kyrios-cult with its sacramentalism* directly constitutes a real counterbalance to moralism. That is clearest in Ignatius, for whom the effect of baptism does not lie exclusively in the cancellation of former sins: in union with the Eucharist it gives the entire Christian life a sacramental character (II, pp. 193 f.). Nevertheless, Ignatius is the only one after Paul and John who grasped the fact that Christian existence is transcendent in character and is determined by the Spirit, even though he understands divorce from the world not primarily as freedom from the power of sin but as freedom from transitoriness. It is also significant that he is almost the only one for whom the Eucharist plays a role, whereas even in Colossians and Ephesians, in which sacramentalism and the pneumatic character of the Ecclesia do also come into play, only baptism is mentioned. In the context of regulations for the congregation the Did. naturally gives directions not only for baptism but also for the Eucharist (9–10, 14:1) and in the eucharistic prayer of thanksgiving we read: "but to us thou hast given the gift of spiritual food and drink and of life eternal through thy Servant (or Child)" (10:3). Otherwise, the Eucharist is only seldom mentioned (Acts 2:42; 20:7; Jude 12). Of course, the celebration of it is everywhere presupposed, and it is likely included among the "sacrifices" and "services" of I Clem. 40:2. As Justin Martyr and the well-known letter of Pliny show, it is an identification mark of the Christian congregations. But there is nothing to indicate that it was significant for the self-understanding of Christian existence. In spite of that, however, it must have been one factor among others that gave the Church the consciousness of being a fellowship borne up by forces that are not of this world.

For the Church is also conscious of having been called by divine grace and of having been given the Spirit (see above, II, p. 200.) Though it is difficult to say how "grace" and the "Spirit" determine Christian existence when they are not understood in Paul's sense, the conviction is still there that they manifest themselves in Christian conduct (II Tim.:7; I Clem. 2:2; Barn. 1:2ff.; Ign. Sm. intr.). And though no unity is achieved between such statements and the imperatives in which the winning of salvation is made dependent upon one's own effort, such statements nevertheless testify to a consciousness of being borne up. This consciousness finds manifold expression; for instance: Col. 1:12–14, 24; 2:10–15; Eph. 1:6–14; 2:1–9; Tit. 2:11–14; I Pet. 1:3–12; 2:7–10; II Pet. 1:3f., in the triumph-songs of Revelation (II, p. 173), I Clem. 36:1f. (II, p. 188), Barn. 16:9 (II, p. 164), II Pet. 1:6f. It is alive in the consciousness of belonging to the Ecclesia (Col., Eph., the pastorals, I and II Clem.) or to the new People of God (I Pet., Heb., Barn.).

Neither is the knowledge lost that the activity of grace and the Spirit manifests itself in the capacity (and the obligation which it involves) given to the individual to exert himself on behalf of the congregation, as the following passages show: Eph. 4:7; I Pet. 4:10f.; I Clem. 38:1f.; 48:5f.; Did. 1:5. Do miraculous phenomena such as healings (I, p. 154) still occur? If they do, they play no role in the literature, at any rate (Heb. 2:4 is speaking of the past). In quite general terms Ignatius mentions spiritual gifts ($\chi\alpha\rho\acute{\iota}\sigma\mu\alpha\tau\alpha$) that were given to the congregation or its bishop (Sm. intr., Pol. 2:2); in so speaking, he is thinking, immediately at least, of the manifestation of Christian and dutiful conduct. It may be that he also includes experiences of pneumatic inspiration in the service of worship such as the one he reports of himself (Philad. 7:1f.; *cf.* Rom. 7:2) and certainly also includes the singing of "psalms, hymns, and spiritual songs" of which Col. 3:16 and Eph. 5:19 speak (Ign. Eph. 4:2; Rom. 2:2). The old activity of Christian prophets (I, pp. 41 and 154) lives on (Eph. 2:20; 3:5; 4:11; I Tim. 1:18; 4:14; Rev. 2:20; 22:6, 9; Did. 11–13; 15:1f., Herm. mand. XI) but it begins to be suspect, as the Did. and Herm. and also Rev. 2:20 indicate, and one must take care to distinguish the genuine from the false prophets. Books of revelation also continue to be written, as Rev. and Herm. show, but reflection on the part of the author (especially in Herm.) outweighs the prophetic inspiration.

According to Did. 15:1 the place of the prophets (and teachers) is being taken by the congregational officials, and the direction of development is that the "gift" is becoming the official equipment of these officers (§ 52, 3). But the consciousness of belonging to a fellowship filled with pneumatic forces lives on even when these forces are administered by an ecclesiastical institution—in fact, in just such a situation it may become especially strong and certain. And this consciousness creates a compensation for the consciousness of being under the demand of the imperative and left to one's own efforts for salvation. An organic unity of both motifs—though not in Paul's sense—will be achieved only when the sacrament of penance develops, a sacrament by which the effect of baptism can be again and again renewed. And it sounds almost like a reference to that which is to come when I Clem. 7:4 calls the "grace" given the world by Christ's death the "grace" (or "gift") "of repentance"; for under this term the author understands not baptismal repentance alone. But until the time when "repentance" will be regulated by the sacrament of penance, the Church will be afflicted by the inner contradiction which exists between having its conduct placed under the "new law" with its "ordinances" and "commandments, on the one hand, and the claim or the assurance, on the other hand, that in baptism it has received the Spirit which makes life new.

§ 60. The Content of the Ethical Demand

1. What is the content of the "new law"? What do the "commandments," the "ordinances," and the "commands" ($\pi\rho o\sigma\tau\acute{a}\gamma\mu\alpha\tau\alpha$) demand? What must one do to obey?

The consciousness of belonging to the Ecclesia, which by its very nature does not belong to the world, the consciousness of the Church's separateness and its delimitation from the world remained alive generally (§ 10, 3 and § 53, 1). Consistent with this is *the basic character of the ethical demand*. Its immediate character is *negative*: they who (by baptism) are purified and sanctified are called to purify and sanctify themselves (§ 10, 4) to renounce "worldly" or "fleshly" desires and refrain from all evil (see especially I, pp. 104f. and what is said at II, p. 208 concerning "world," $\kappa\acute{o}\sigma\mu o\varsigma$).

In *catalogues of vices* lists are made, as they already were by Paul, of the desires and sins that one must avoid (I, p. 72). Frequently, as already in Gal. 5:19–23, they are paralleled with a contrasting *catalogue of virtues* (Col. 3:5–14; Eph. 4:31f.; I Tim. 6:4–11; Jas. 3:15–18; *cf.* also I Clem. 35:5; II Clem. 4:3; Herm. sim. IX 15: opposed to the twelve virtue-virgins stand twelve women clad in black, the vices); but the catalogues of virtues may also stand by themselves (Eph. 4:2f.; II Pet. 1:5–7, Herm. vis. III 8). Side by side with these catalogues or mingled with them there are also *lists resembling catechisms* of commandments and prohibitions according to the scheme of the "two ways," the ways of life and death or of light and darkness. This scheme, like the catalogues, was taken over from the Hellenistic synagogue. In Did. 1–6 and Barn. 18–20 a catechism for proselytes arranged according to this scheme has been worked in.

Into it words of Jesus have been inserted in Did. 1:3–6. Similarly
sayings of Jesus also appear elsewhere in parenesis (II, p. 215). As a
matter of course Old Testament sayings of an exhortatory or threatening character are also adopted (I Pet. 3:10–12; Jas. 4:6; Heb. 3:7–11;
10:37f.; 12:12; I Clem. 8:4; 14–15; Barn. 2:10; 3:3–5; 4:11, etc.). The
vices listed include typical sins such as sensual greed and sexual
passion, envy and covetousness, wrath, hatred, evil words and lying,
etc. The listing is not determined by any systematic order nor are
the several vices or virtues derived from a principle, an ethical ideal.
The listing is loose, guided by associations of content or form.

In addition to pareneses offered in the form of catalogue or
catechism there is also *the developed parenesis*. The warning against
vices and the admonition to exercise the virtues in I Clem. is developed
with homiletical breadth according to such catch-words as "jealousy"
(3–6), "humility" (13–16), "harmony" (20–22). In the process,
examples from the Old Testament are abundantly given, but also
some from the present and even from heathen saga and history (e.g.
3–6, 11–16, 20–22, 55). Developed parenesis also occurs in James, the
author of which dwells rather long upon single themes (2:1–13:
partiality; 3:1–12: sins of the tongue; 3:13–18: conceit over wisdom;
4:1–5: contention and desire for the world; 4:13–17: admonitions to
business men; 5:1–6; warnings to the rich). Especially in the *Mandata*
Hermas describes virtues and vices with their blessing or terrifying
consequences, often in dialogue-form. He contrasts against each other,
for example: "simplicity" and "evil-speaking" (mand. II), "truth"
and "falsehood" (mand. III), "purity" and "adultery" (mand. IV),
"long-suffering" and "quickness to wrath" (mand. V), "grief" and
"joyfulness" (mand. X); or he describes the two kinds of "fear"—of
God and of the devil (mand. VI) and likewise the two kinds of
"temperance" (mand. VIII), and of "desire" (mand. XII), and of
"luxury" (sim. VI).

2. Seen as a whole all the separate commandments stand under *the
demand for sanctification*: the renunciation of "the world," of one's
former (heathen) way of life, and of the fleshly desires. Now the
decisive question is whether this demand for sanctification is understood and unfolded solely, or at least in essence, in the negative sense,
resulting in asceticism and hence in the ideal of the individualistic
holiness of the *homo religiosus*—or whether, as in Paul (§ 38, 3), it
simultaneously has a positive sense as the demand which points the

individual into fellowship with others, in which he is to do the good in selflessness. As long as "the world" is understood as the sphere of sin which by men's own fault has become a power over them (§ 26, 2 and § 44), the demand for renunciation of the world will be a genuine ethical demand, and the unity of the negative and the positive sense of sanctification will be preserved. It is probably necessary to acknowledge that from the beginning both tendencies—the purely negative and the also positive—are present and competing with each other, for even in Paul a dualistic-ascetic motif is already at work, as we have seen (I, p. 202). Historically regarded, it is a question of how the influences of the synagogal tradition and of popular-philo-sophical (Stoic) ethics, on the one hand, and of Hellenistic-Gnostic dualism, on the other hand, work with each other or against each other. In the course of time two different types of Christian piety develop, depending upon whether the one or the other of these two tendencies preponderates; for the most part, however, the boundary between them cannot be sharply drawn.

That unity stands forth, preserved, where the catalogue of vices is paralleled by a corresponding catalogue of virtues (see above, II, p. 218), but also wherever the admonition to abstain from the "passions of the flesh" has the demand for "good works" combined with it, as I Pet. 2:11f. formulates it (*cf.* Tit. 3:8). It is generally so in the pareneses of Col. and Eph., of the pastorals, Heb., Jas., I Clem., and Pol. to the Philippians. The preponderance of the positive sense of sanctification also expresses itself in the fact that the positive sense is developed by means of a host of single terms and instructions, while only a few terms are on supply to denote the negative sense. Those used for the negative sense, in addition to the general ones like "faithfulness" (πίστις), "uprightness," "piety" (εὐσέβεια), "rever-ence" (σεμνότης), are: ἐγκράτεια "self-control" in general, often specifically "continence"), ὑπομονή ("patience," "endurance"), ἀκακία ("innocence"), ἁπλότης ("simplicity," "generosity"), ἁγνεία ("purity") —though in individual cases where they are used one can be in doubt whether they mean more the Christian's negative relation to the world or whether they have a reference to living in fellowship with others.

Particularly indicative of the double-sidedness of the ethical demand is the virtue of "self-control" (ἐγκράτεια) only rarely used in the New Testament but later more frequently named, which primarily denotes the negative side of sanctification. But it scarcely stands out as the one dominant demand; rather it is cited, as it already is in Gal. 5:23, as one virtue among others in catalogues of virtues (Tit. 1:8; II Pet. 1:6; I Clem. 30:3; 35:2; 38:2; 62:2; 64; II Clem. 4:3; Barn. 2:2; Pol. Phil. 4:2; 5:2). Nevertheless, a pre-eminent importance is ascribed to it when according to Acts 24:25 the moving theme of Paul's address before Felix and Drusilla is "righteousness and self-control." Likewise, when II Clem. 15:1 designates the author's intention in writing by saying that he has given the readers weighty advice "concerning self-control," which also is in harmony with his admonition to "keep the flesh pure" (II, p. 170). Or again when Hermas (mand. I 2, VI 1:1) regards the first commandment after that of "faith" and "fear (of God)" to be "self-control" or when in the dance of the Virtues "Self-control" is the daughter of "Faith" and the foremother of all the ensuing Virtues (vis. III 8:4ff.; *cf.* sim. IX 15:2). Even by Hermas, however, "self-control" is conceived not as asceticism but rather as abstinence "from all evil," and its opposite is "doing good" (mand. VIII); though it must be granted that ascetic features are not lacking in Hermas (vis. II 2:3, sim. IX 11; see below).

The positive sense of abstinence from the world comes out in one way in the fact that practically everywhere "good works" are demanded, but above all it comes out in the fact that among all the commandments the love-commandment occupies the highest place. The demands for living in fellowship all stand ultimately under the commandment of love. It appears in almost all pareneses and only in the writings which are most dependent upon Jewish tradition (such as Rev., Heb., Jas., and Herm.) is it more rarely found, while it occurs frequently within the circle of Pauline influence. "Love" (noun or verb) often appears in catalogues of virtues, frequently receiving in them a special accent by being placed at the beginning of the list (as in Gal. 5:22 and II Clem. 4:3) or at the end. Thus the list in Col. 3:12–14 closes with the sentence: "And above all these (put on) love, which is the uniting-band of perfection" (tr.). "Love" is at the end of the series at II Pet. 1:5–7, and in Herm. vis. III 8:5, 7 it is the last-named of the Virtues (*cf.* sim. IX 15:2; 18:4). I Clem. 49 is a panegyric on love (under the influence of I Cor. 13), the bond which unites us with God, and 50:1 draws this conclusion: "See . . . how great and marvelous love is! Nor is there any describing of its perfection" (tr.). "Love" is often used with "faith" as if to denote the essence of Christianity (I Tim. 1:14; 2:15; 4:12; II Tim. 1:13; 2:22; Barn. 1:4; 11:8; II Clem. 15:2; Herm. sim. IX 17:4). This is especially frequent in Ignatius who asserts in Sm. 6:1: "For the whole of the matter is faith and love, than which nothing is more highly esteemed" (tr.) (*cf.* Eph. 14:1f.; Philad. 9:2). Occasionally "hope" is associated with them, resulting in the triad of I Cor. 13:13; it is so in Pol. Phil. 3:2f., at the end of which we read: "for he who has love is far from all sin" (*cf.* Barn. 1:4–6; Heb. 10:22–24). Other combinations also occur (with "sanctification" I Tim. 2:5; with "purity" I Tim. 4:12; Pol. Phil. 4:2; with "fear" I Clem. 51:1; with "righteousness" II Clem. 12:1). That love brings about forgiveness of sins is often said (II, p. 210). Barnabas addresses his readers as "children of love" (9:7; 21:9), and in Ignatius "love" is the bond which binds the congregation together into the unity of a choir (Eph. 4:1f.; Rom. 2:2) and also the bond which unites the writer with his readers (Eph. 1:1; Tr. 12:3). Demonstration of love is what all the single virtues ultimately are: "mildness," "long-suffering," "meekness," "humility," "harmony," "compassion," "brotherly love," "hospitality"; also: "helping each other" (ἀντέχεσθαι ἀλλήλων) and "forgiving one another" and conducting one's self as one who is ἀνυπόκριτος ("un-hypocritical," "genuine"), "peaceful," "reasonable," "docile," "merciful," etc. All such virtues are singled out *not as traits of character but as modes of conduct in fellowship with others.* They are not derived from an ideal picture of humanity or personality, even when here and there Greek virtues are taken over such as σωφροσύνη ("prudence" and "moderation"), αἰδώς ("modesty"), ἐπιείκεια ("reasonableness") or the term κόσμιος ("that which is comely or becoming") and κοσμεῖσθαι ("to be adorned"; see below). There is no thought of character-education, just as there is none of education in general.

Now one must, of course, concede that such virtues for the most part have a *negative character* in that they ultimately demand one thing: selflessness, the waiver of one's own advantage and one's own right—and that they have *purely formal character* in that they do not set up concrete goals of action, do not sketch a program for molding society. But in both respects they are the appropriate explication of the love-commandment because by its own nature it will not tolerate formulated positive determinations (§ 2, 4) if it is not to relapse into law. It is completely described both in the "Golden

Rule" (Mt. 7:12) as well as in Paul's sentence "Love does no wrong to a neighbor" (Rom. 13:10). For in both cases action arising from love is guided not by looking toward some "work" (ἔργον) that is to be accomplished but by asking what needs and troubles of my neighbor or of society encounter me in any particular here and now. Christian freedom must also prove itself in just this situation: the Christian must be able to judge without a legal statute what God's will demands of him at any given moment. Whether the liberty and the duty to do this "distinguishing" (δοκιμάζειν, Rom. 12:2; Phil. Phil. 1:10; § 39, 1) for one's self will continue to be held fast, is just the question. The explicit admonition to distinguish "what is pleasing to the Lord" is found after Paul only in Eph. 5:10; it may be permissible to discover it in Barn. 21:6 also: "And be taught of God, seeking out what the Lord requires of you." But it may probably be regarded as implicitly contained in the purely negative and formal exhortations—at least to a large extent.

3. However remote any notion of an ideal picture of human personality may have been as a point of reference for orienting conduct, other ideal pictures did force their way in: *the ideal of perfectionism and the ideal of holiness as a personal quality.*

The more the ethical demands made of the Christian come to be regarded as the "commandments," the "commands" and "ordinances," which must be fulfilled as the condition for obtaining life or salvation—and the more conduct is governed by the notion of merit and by consideration of the judgment according to one's works —the more there develops a striving after perfection. Then the waiver of self demanded by the commandment of love is no longer motivated by interest in one's neighbor and interest in fellowship with others but by interest in one's own salvation. This can come to the surface anywhere, but it appears in particularly crass form in Hermas (e.g. mand. II, 4–6, sim. I, V 3:7f.). The influence of Hellenistic dualism, especially of the Gnostic kind (I, pp. 107, 173–175) operated in the same direction as the notion of merit. The demand for holiness changes its meaning just as the demand for love does, and there arises the notion of holiness as a quality to be won by renunciation of the world.

One consequence of perfectionism and the striving after holiness is that the demand for *asceticism* becomes a temptation. That this demand had been raised at an early time is indicated by the very passages which polemize against it or at least admonish the ascetic to modesty about his asceticism. I Tim. 4:3 is directed against the heretics "who forbid marriage" and demand "abstinence from foods" (*cf.* 2:15; 5:23; Tit. 1:14f.; perhaps also Col. 3:16–23, where it is not clear whether it is truly ascetic tendencies that are being combatted or merely ritualistic ones). But such a writing as II Clem. with its demand "to keep the flesh pure" (8:4; 14:3) and its ideal of celibacy or virginity (12:5) indicates where this path is leading. Perhaps by the "virgin (men)" who "have not defiled themselves with women" Rev. 14:4 means ascetics. In any case Herm. sim. IX 11 proves that the practice of "subintroduction" (I, p. 103 n.) which comes to view at Corinth as early as Paul's time (I Cor. 7:25, 36f.) continues to exist. Indications that Hermas himself is not far from such tendencies are not only his designation of himself as "Hermas the abstinent" (or "continent"), vis. I 2:4; *cf.* II 3:2, and his admonition: "Keep this flesh of yours pure and undefiled" (sim. V 7), but also the role which "abstinence" and "purity" and also "desire" in specific reference to sexual life play in his book, and likewise his interest in the question of marriage (the "wife" of Hermas shall become his "sister," vis. II 2:3; and in mand. IV 1 and 4 marriage is advised against).

The demand for asceticism as a demand applying to all Christians did not establish itself, but as a commandment which individuals take upon themselves, it was not contested. And the admonitions that the ascetic is not to be haughty (I Clem. 38:2; 48:6; Ign. Pol. 5:2) indicate by themselves that the way is being prepared for the differentiation of two levels of morality. But it is not merely this striving after ascetic holiness which leads to the differentiation of a perfect holiness from a lower level of morality: perfectionism operates in the same direction. For it necessarily quickly became evident that the demand for "abstinence" in the sense of consistent refraining from all worldly needs, pleasures, and occupations was not universally practicable—as the pastorals and Hermas illustrate. Therefore, it cannot surprise us that the concept of "perfection" ($\tau\epsilon\lambda\epsilon\iota\acute{o}\tau\eta s$, $\tau\acute{\epsilon}\lambda\epsilon\iota o\nu$) takes on a new meaning. In Mt. 5:48 $\tau\acute{\epsilon}\lambda\epsilon\iota o s$ (Lk. 6:36 has a different word) seems still to be used in the sense of Hebrew שָׁלֵם or תָּמִים (whole and complete, whole-hearted, without breach or inner dividedness). In Mt. 19:21 (not found in Mk. 10:21) it means, on the contrary, "perfect" in the sense of perfectionism; likewise in Did.

1:4; 6:2, in the latter of which two levels of morality are clearly distinguished. Though Paul had used τέλειος not with the Semitic but with a Greek meaning, he meant by it not "perfection" but "adulthood" (I Cor. 14:20; Phil. 3:15); the same meaning appears in Heb. 6:1. But Ignatius urges for perfection (Eph. 1:1; 15:2; Sm. 11:2f.); in him the negative admonition to divorce from the world quite overweighs the positive admonition to love, and for him the ideal of the *homo religiosus* is embodied in the figure of the martyr. Hermas, too, takes the pre-eminent rank of the martyr for granted (vis. III 1:9–2:1; 5:2; sim. IX 28:1ff.); and in other ways, too, he differentiates two levels of morality, for he not only distinguishes the upright from those who need repentance (vis. III 5:3f.) but also recognizes a meritorious conduct which goes beyond the measure of the required (sim. V 2:4ff.; 3:3ff.).

4. Side by side with these tendencies, which find their fulfilment in the notion of holiness and in the differentiation of a double morality in the ancient Church, there runs another hortatory tendency of which the Haustafeln and the pastoral epistles as a whole are typical. In it the conception comes to light that the Christian conduct of life derives its Christian character not from the fulfilling of special moral demands and from an idea of perfection or holiness upon which they depend, but from *following such simple ethical demands as can be familiar to anyone.* Here Paul's admonition is followed: "whatever is true, whatever is respectable, whatever is right, whatever is innocent, whatever is well-regarded, whatever is reputable—anything that is a virtue, anything that deserves praise—think about it" (Phil. 4:8 tr.). The specifically Christian element in this can only lie in the fact that just as all the commandments of the Torah are fulfilled in the demand for love (according to Rom. 13:8–10; Gal. 5:14) so every "virtue" is understood as a requirement of love and is to be fulfilled by the power of love. Though a distinction from Greek ethics is present in the fact that "virtue" is not considered from the viewpoint of shaping character but rather under that of brotherly fellowship (in Pauline language: of "edification," οἰκοδομή), it is also clear that these demands in themselves require nothing which a heathen's judgment would not also acknowledge to be good. If the Christian Church is to bring honor to God or to the Christian faith by its ethical conduct (a view already present in I Thess. 4:12; I Cor. 10:32 and then in Col. 4:5; I Tim. 3:7; 6:1; Tit. 2:5; 8:10; I Pet. 2:12,

15; 3:1, 16; I Clem. 1:1; 47:7; Ign. Tr. 8:2), then agreement between the moral standards of Christians and those of the heathen is presupposed.

Futhermore, Christian exhortation ingenuously takes over from *the ethics of popular philosophy* and from the store of ideas of *bourgeois morality* certain concepts and patterns of arrangement.

The schemata of moral teaching, particularly Haustafeln (schedules of household duties), such as Hellenistic Judaism had already taken over from the hortatory practice of Hellenism, are now impressed into Christian service. Such lists of duties are found in I Tim. 3:2ff.; Tit. 1:5ff.; Pol. Phil. 5:2, where the qualifications for "bishops" and "deacons" are enumerated. Especially favored are the "Haustafeln": Col. 3:18–4:1; Eph. 5:22–6:9; I Tim. 2:8–15, 6:1f.; Tit. 2:2–10; I Pet. 2:13–3:7; Did. 4:9–11; I Clem. 21:6–9; Pol. Phil. 4:2–6:2; Barn. 19:5–7 (woven into the parenesis); the praise of the Corinthian congregation, I Clem. 1:3, also follows this pattern.

The terms *"virtue," "what is proper"* (τὸ καθῆκον), and *"conscience"* (I, p. 71), all of which had already appeared in Paul, continue to occur. Especially significant is the increasingly frequent mention of "good conscience" (συνείδησις ἀγαθή, καθαρά, and the like): I Tim. 1:5, 19; 3:9; II Tim. 1:3; I Pet. 3:16, 21; Heb. 13:18; Acts 23:1; 24:16; I Clem. 1:3; 41:1; 45:7; II Clem. 16:4; Ign. Tr. 7:2; Pol. Phil. 5:3; corresponding mention of "bad (πονηρά and the like) conscience": I Tim. 4:2; Tit. 1:15; Heb. 10:2, 22; Barn. 19:12; Did. 4:14; Herm. mand. III 4.

A general characterization of Christian conduct is furnished by the terms δικαιοσύνη and εὐσέβεια—terms which on Hellenistic honorific inscriptions customarily described reverent, virtuous conduct and now also count as Christian virtues (II, p. 213). Also σεμνότης and σεμνός are taken over as designations of dignity and respectability (II, p. 213). Likewise σωφροσύνη ("prudence") is taken up among the Christian virtues: I Tim. 2:9, 15; Acts 26:25; I Clem. 62:2, 64, Ign. Eph. 10:3 (σώφρων, "prudent, sensible" I Tim. 3:2; Tit. 1:8; 2:2, 5; I Clem. 1:2; 63:3; "prudently, soberly," Tit. 2:12; σωφρονεῖν, "to be prudent, sober, sensible" in Paul at Rom. 12:3, then in Tit. 2:6; I Pet. 4:7; I Clem. 1:3; Pol. Phil. 4:3; *cf.* II Tim. 1:7; Tit. 2:4). Ἀιδώς ("modesty") is still rare (I Tim. 2:9; Heb. 12:28, *v.l.*) and so is χρηστότης ("mildness, kindness") as a Christian virtue (Col. 3:12; Eph. 4:32; I Clem. 14:3); less rare is ἐπιείκεια ("reasonableness,

considerateness"; also ἐπιεικής, "reasonable")—already used by
Paul, Phil. 4:5, it also occurs in I Tim. 3:3; Tit. 3:2; I Pet. 2:18;
Jas. 3:17; I Clem. 1:2; 21:7; 30:8; 56:1; 58:2; 69:2; Ign. Eph. 10:3;
Philad. 1:1f. A word which occurs in honorific inscriptions as a
virtue, especially as a womanly virtue, κόσμιος ("decent, proper,
moral") was also taken over into Christian usage: in I Tim. 2:9
as a virtue of women: in 3:2 named after σώφρων ("prudent") as
a qualification for the "bishop" (*cf.* also κοσμεῖσθαι—which in
these places ought perhaps to be translated not "be adorned,"
but "be kept in order"—I Clem. 2:8; 33:7; Ign. Eph. 9:2).

5. *The extent of the departments of living* toward which moral
reflection and parenesis are directed is still a decidedly limited one.
This is only natural because the Christian faith is in the main still
restricted to people in humble circumstances or at least to the lower
middle class. Their interests, it is true, already include, in addition
to those of their own immediate circle of living, those of property
and business. There are even slave-holders among them. But to
undertake great enterprises, in particular to take a responsible part
in politics, is still far from their mind, nor have they any such
ambition. They also lack any regard for the problems and tasks of
social life.

In *the high esteem for marriage* and in the views about *the disciplining of married life* the tradition of the Old Testament and
Judaism, or the influence of the Hellenistic synagogue, is undoubtedly
at work; also at work in addition to this is the influence of Stoic
morality, for which purity of marriage and the rejection of fornication
and adultery belong to the demands that are taken for granted (see
especially Musonius and Epictetus).

Among the chief vices combatted in the catalogues of vices
and elsewhere are "fornication," "adultery," "uncleanness" and
the like. The rejection of adultery plays an especially prominent
role in Hermas (mand. IV). In the Haustafeln husbands are
admonished to love their wives, wives to obey their husbands,
children to obey their parents, parents to be kind to their
children (Col. 3:18–21; Eph. 5:22–25; 6:1–4; I Tim. 4:11; Tit.
2:4f.; I Pet. 3:1–7; *cf.* I Clem. 1:3; Ign. Pol. 5:1). Women are
admonished to be modest and chaste and are warned against
personal vanity (I Tim. 2:9; Tit. 2:4f.; I Pet. 3:3f.; I Clem. 1:3;
21:7; Pol. Phil. 4:2). Their duty to bear children is emphasized
in I Tim. 2:15; 5:14, probably in opposition to Gnostic-ascetic

tendencies (I Tim. 2:15; 5:14), the influence of which is detectable in the exaggerated demand for chastity in II Clem. and Herm., but on the whole these tendencies were rejected. They remain only in the advice against remarrying (as in I Cor. 7:11, 39f.; perhaps I Tim. 5:9, and Herm. mand. IV 4)—either after divorce or after the death of the first mate—and also in the fact that remarriage is evidently forbidden to the "bishop" or the "deacon" (I Tim. 3:2, 12; Tit. 1:6). The duty of training children to piety is often emphasized (I Tim. 3:4, 12; Tit. 1:6; especially I Clem. 21:8; Pol. Phil. 4:2; Did. 4:9; Barn. 19:5) and on occasion reference is made to the good tradition of a family (II Tim. 1:3–5, 16; 3:14f.). Even though the responsibility for the family, of which Hermas so often emphatically speaks (vis. II 2 and 3, sim. VII and elsewhere), is only a symbol for responsibility for the Christian Church, such symbolism nevertheless presupposes that duty to one's actual family is vitally felt.

Even living together in the more comprehensive community has, as it were, the character of living in a family. As parents and children are admonished to fulfil their duties toward each other, so old and young within the congregation are admonished (I Pet. 5:1–5, where the "elders" are both the "older ones" and the "presbyters," the leaders of the congregation; further: I Clem. 21:6; *cf.* 1:3; Pol. Phil. 5:3; 6:1; II Clem. 19:1). The leaders of the congregation are correspondingly directed to behave rightly toward old and young and to admonish them to perform their duties (I Tim. 5:1f.; Tit. 2:3–8). Special mention is made of duties toward widows, but also of the right conduct that is expected of them (I Tim. 5:3f.; Ign. Pol. 4:1; Pol. Phil. 4:3; Herm. mand. VIII 10, sim. IX 27:2). Providing for widows and orphans is often mentioned as a duty (Jas. 1:27; Barn. 20:2; Ign. Sm. 6:2; Pol. Phil. 6:1; Herm. vis. II 4:3, mand. VIII 10, sim. I 8, V 3:7; IX, 27:2). At an early time there was already an officially recognized status of "widow" which was marked off by special rights and duties (I Tim. 5:9ff.), and it appears to have been possible for virgins, too, to be taken into this class (Ign. Sm. 13:1). In gnosticizing circles women played a role as prophetesses or teachers as in the early period (Acts 18:26: Priscilla; Acts 21:9: Philip's four daughters as "prophesying virgins"). In the trend within the Church which had become dominant this role was denied them (I Tim. 2:1f., the interpolation I Cor. 14:34f.; Rev. 2:20). Applying to all members of the congregation and particularly to its officials we find exhortations to love, kindliness, and

humility and also to agreeableness and truthfulness, and warnings
against anger and envy, gossiping and lying, uncleanness and
drunkenness. That the virtues demanded are "bourgeois" ones is not
surprising; nevertheless, it is striking that while there is admonition
to "good works," there is only rarely an exhortation to diligent toil
(in Paul I Thess. 4:11f.; then also II Thess. 3:6–12; Did. 12:3f.), and
that such exhortation represents this toil as having charity or penance
for sins as its purpose (Eph. 4:28, Barn. 19:10). Negative exhortation
preponderates: one must not walk ἀτάκτως ("lazily"; "in idleness,"
II Thess. 3:6, 11), not "be a busybody" (περιεργάζεσθαι, II Thess.
3:11; I Tim. 5:13), not be a "meddler in others' affairs" (I Pet. 4:15,
tr.: ἀλλοτριοεπίσκοπος);* in short, it is the admonition to ἡσυχία
("quietness") or ἡσυχιάζειν ("to live quietly")—see I Thess. 4:11;
II Thess. 3:12; I Tim. 2:2, 11f.; I Pet. 3:4; Did. 3:8; Barn. 19:4; Herm.
mand. V 2:3–6, VI 2:3, VIII 10, XI 8. The ambition of the Congregation is none other than that which is given as the purpose of praying
for the officials of the state: "that we may lead a still and quiet life
in all piety and respectability" (I Tim. 2:2 tr.).

Christian conduct toward non-Christians is sketched in the
advice given at Tit. 3:1f.: "Admonish them to submit to
authorities and officials, to obey, to be prepared to do any good
work, to defame no one, to keep from quarreling, to be reasonable, and in every respect to behave agreeably toward all men"
(Blt., tr.). On the attitude toward the state, see below. The
admonition to be kind to non-Christians and the warning not to
repay evil with evil is urged in I Pet. 3:15f. (probably already in
3:9 also) and Ign. Eph. 10:2f. A special admonition to such
conduct is laid upon Christian wives toward their heathen
husbands (I Pet. 3:1f.); a corresponding admonition is addressed
to Christian slaves (I Pet. 2:18f.). Christians in general are to
bring honor to God and to their faith by the way they live
(II, p. 225). The Church's prayers include intercession for all
men (I Tim. 2:1; I Clem. 60:4; Ign. Eph. 10:1; Pol. Phil. 12:3).

How far the Christian Church was from thinking of remolding the
world, of adopting an economic or political program, is indicated by
its attitude toward property, slavery and the state. As for the
matter of *property*, the picture of the original Church's "love-communism" sketched in Acts 2:45; 4:32–35 stands isolated in the

* The meaning of the compound can only be conjectured (Tr.).

tradition and is representative only insofar as it is a pattern for the love which is prepared to bring about that "equality" of which Paul speaks in II Cor. 8:13f.: the surplus of one man is to supply the need of another. The custom of setting aside money for the needy on Sunday (I Cor. 16:2) became the fixed practice of taking up a collection in the Sunday worship-service, which is placed at the disposal of the congregation's leader for charity (Justin Martyr, apol. I 67:6). "Love-communism" of this sort always remained a voluntary matter; just as Paul neither knew a "command" to this effect (II Cor. 8:8) nor wished that giving should be done "reluctantly or under compulsion" (II Cor. 9:7), neither did the succeeding period. Therefore, it is no surprise to discover that in that succeeding period economic equality does not exist in the congregations but rich and poor are found side by side. But we can well understand that a distrust of wealth arises (Jas. 2:1–7) and that admonitions to the rich and warnings against acquisitiveness and greed increase in number (I Tim. 6:6–10, 17–19; Jas. 5:1–6; Heb. 13:5; Herm. vis. III 6:5–7, sim. I, VIII 9:1, etc.). Especially Hermas exhorts his readers to charity, which benefits the rich man himself, because the poor man's prayer of thanksgiving ascends in his favor (vis. III 9:2–6, mand. II 4–6, VIII 10, especially sim. II). Hand in hand with the warning against wealth goes that against business and worldly "pursuits" and "occupations" (II Tim. 2:4; Jas. 4:13–16; Herm. vis. I 3:1, III 6:5, mand. III 5, X 1:4f., sim. IV 5, VI 3:5, VIII 8:1f., IX 20:1f.).

In the matter of *slavery* Paul's standpoint is maintained (I Cor. 7:21f.; *cf.* Philemon); i.e. so far as it is a matter of this world's social order, the slavery question does not exist for the Christian Church. The fact that slavery exists is accepted as a part of the given world order which it is not the task of Christians to alter. Hence it also causes no offense that there are Christian masters who own slaves. But the Christian faith's independence from and superiority to the world's order demonstrate themselves in the fact that within the Church the difference between master and slave has no validity because both, as Christians, are brothers. Nevertheless, the slaves must not deduce from that fact a right to be disrespectful to their Christian masters (I Tim. 6:1f.; Ign. Pol. 4:3) nor raise a claim to be bought free at the expense of the congregation (Ign. Pol. 4:3). For the masters, whether Christian or heathen, are their masters only κατὰ σάρκα, "according to the flesh"—on the world's plane—(Col. 3:22;

Eph. 6:5); their true master is Christ, and in fear of him they are to serve their earthly masters faithfully as if it were a service rendered to their true Lord (Col. 3:22–25; Eph. 6:5–8 *cf.* I Tim. 6:1f.; Tit. 2:9f.; Did. 4:11; Barn. 19:7). They are patiently to endure whatever unjust treatment they may experience and remember the innocent suffering of Christ (I Pet. 2:18–25). But the masters are also correspondingly admonished to grant their slaves whatever is right and fair (Col. 4:1), not to deal threateningly with them (Eph. 6:9; Did. 4:10; Barn. 19:7), and not to be haughty toward them (Ign. Pol. 4:3).

As for *the Christian relation to the state*, here, too, it holds true that the Christian is to submit to it as a given order, for it was instituted by God (as in Rom. 13:1–7, so also in I Clem. 61:1). The Christian owes it obedience (Tit. 3:1; I Clem. 60:4) even when, and precisely when, he is under its suspicion as a Christian (I Pet. 2:13–17; 4:16). At an early time the Christian Church took over from the synagogue the custom of praying for the civil authorities (I Tim. 2:1f.; I Clem. 61:1f.; Pol. Phil. 12:3). The author of Acts takes pains to emphasize the loyalty of Christians to the state and to prove the assertion that they were enemies of the state to be a Jewish slander (18:12ff.; 21:27ff.; 23:29; 25:18f.; 26:31). The hatred toward Rome which breaks out in Rev. rests not upon a rejection of the existing civil order on principle but upon indignation over its demand of emperor-worship, at which Christian obedience naturally draws the line. For that reason one must not regard the attitude of Revelation as contradictory to the general Christian acknowledgment of the civil order. This order is simply not questioned, but it belongs, of course, to the transitory orders of this world. Consequently, no obligation is felt to take over responsibility for it or for the just administration of it—a situation for which one of the causes, of course, is the fact that the Christians still belonged primarily to those social classes for which such responsibility was out of the question.

§ 61. Church Discipline

1. Concern for *the purity of the Church* has its foundation not merely in the individual's interest in salvation but is also a concern of the Church as a whole, for it as a whole is supposed to be and professes to be the Congregation of the saints. It lies in its own interest, therefore, to develop a discipline which by admonition or

punishment trains the individual members and in the extreme case eliminates unworthy members. But the purity of the Church is endangered not only by unethical conduct of its members but also by false teaching. This, too, ranks as sin (see especially Ignatius), and it accords with Jewish tradition that a causal connection like that between heathenism and a life of vice (I, p. 72) is seen between false teaching and the vices, as the polemic found in the pastorals and Jude and II Pet. indicates.

Responsibility for the purity of the Church resides at first—and in a certain sense we may say continually—*in all members of the congregation*. As Paul had admonished the Thessalonians: "Exhort one another and build one another up" (I Thess. 5:11, tr.) and specifically: "set right the idle" (5:14, tr.) and as he had assumed in the Roman Christians the ability to "set yourselves right" (νουθετεῖν ἑαυτούς, Rom. 15:14, tr.), so similar admonitions continue to be given: "to set yourselves (or ἀλλήλους, "each other") right" (Col. 3:16; I Clem. 56:2; II Clem. 17:2); "to exhort" (παρακαλεῖν, Heb. 3:13; 10:25; Barn. 19:10; Herm. mand. VIII 10, XII 3:2); "to reprove" (ἐλέγχειν, Did. 15:3; cf. 2:7; 4:3; Barn. 19:4; also Eph. 5:11, but this probably refers not to erring Christians but to pagans; to whom Jude 22 refers is not clear). Fathers and mothers, specifically, have the duty of disciplining their children or their family (παιδεύειν, see Eph. 6:4; I Clem. 21:8; Pol. Phil. 4:2; Herm. vis. II 3:1f.; νουθετεῖν, "correct, set right" Herm. vis. I 3:1f.); older persons have the same duty toward younger persons (I Clem. 21:6).

But this task pertains particularly to certain responsible persons, especially to *the leaders of the congregations* whose duty it is to "admonish," as the pastorals again and again urge (I Tim. 4:13; 5:1; 6:3; II Tim. 4:2; Tit. 1:9; 2:6, 15; also Ign. Pol. 1:2), and this is given as their purpose in writing by the author of Hebrews (13:19, 22) and repeatedly by Ignatius (Eph. 3:2; Mg. 14:1; Tr. 6:1, etc.). Upon the leader of the congregation falls the duty of παιδεύειν ("correcting, disciplining," II Tim. 2:25; Herm. vis. III 9:10; cf. sim XI 31:5f.), or of νουθετεῖν ("setting right,"—the same term as in I Thess. 5:12— presupposed to be the leader's duty in Col. 1:28; Acts 20:31; II Clem. 17:3; 19:2 and exercised as his duty in I Clem. 7:1) or of ἐλέγχειν ("reproving, rebuking," I Tim. 5:20; II Tim. 4:2; Tit. 1:9, 13; 2:15).

2. In particularly bad cases *the sinner* (or the teacher of error, as the case may be) *must be excluded from the congregation*—whether it

be because his sin is so great as to make association with the sinner utterly impossible or because the attempts at admonishing and correcting him have been in vain. From Rev. 2:14f., 20f. it is to be gathered that heretics must be excluded; from Rev. 22:15, that all gross sinners must. Paul himself had already demanded that the evil-doer who was "living with his father's wife" be "delivered to Satan" (I Cor. 5:1–5)—which must mean be excommunicated. The author of the pastorals similarly says that he has delivered two heretics to Satan (I Tim. 1:20), while the "Paul" of II Thess. 3:6, 14f., though he does forbid the readers to associate with the sinner, nevertheless evidently means this only in a limited and temporary way, for he says: "Do not regard him as an enemy, but set him right as a brother" (tr.). The advice given in Pol. Phil. 11:4 is similar. II Tim. 2:25f., too, admonishes the leader of the congregation to correct the heretics in kindness in order that they may come to repentance and knowledge and escape the devil's snares. But in case kindly correction fails, exclusion must follow, according to Tit. 3:10. That is probably also the meaning of Jude 22f., but they are verses having a very uncertain text-transmission. In Did. 14:2 temporary suspension of association with people who are quarreling is demanded until they are reconciled with each other; in 15:3 association with a member who has wronged another is likewise forbidden until he has repented. Jas. 5:19f. also admonishes Christians to lead back the brother who has wandered away from the truth (*cf.* II Clem. 15:1). The same attitude toward a sinner is recommended by Herm. mand. IV 1:9, but Ignatius advises that one should not even speak with heretics either in private or in public (Sm. 7:2; *cf.* Eph. 7:1).

Definite rules soon had to be created both for the *restitution* of a temporarily excluded member and for the *conclusive exclusion of* a notorious and incorrigible sinner (or heretic), but in the sources at our disposal there is little to be learned about such rules. We probably can assume that at first it was the assembled congregation that made the decision on conclusive exclusion, as Paul had demanded of the Corinthians (I Cor. 5:4f.). The presupposition for the restitution of a repentant sinner was certainly from the outset a confession of repentance made before the congregation. So we read in Did. 4:14: "In the congregation you shall confess your transgressions and not proceed to your prayer with a bad conscience," even though here those who are to be received back after temporary exclusion are not thought of as especially grave sinners. (The same direction is found in Barn. 19:12, but in this case "in the congregation" is lacking.) The confession of sin demanded of the rebels at Corinth in I Clem. 51f. is surely meant to be one to be made before the whole congregation. The same thing is to be deduced from Ign. Philad. 3:2, where we hear of those who "having repented come to the unity of the Church," and from 8:1, where repentance is described as a "repenting to the unity of God and (to) the bishop's council." Since the restitution was undoubtedly confirmed by admitting the penitent to the congregation's service of worship and specifically to the Lord's Supper, it is to be assumed that that is just where the confession of repentance was made. This may also be gathered, probably, from the fact that according to Did. 14:1 the whole congregation is to confess its "transgressions" before participating in the Eucharist (in some such way as in the prayer of I Clem. 60:1f.); this must apply, then, all the more to the graver sinners. They may be meant by the call which precedes the celebration of the Eucharist: "If anyone be holy, let him come (to the Eucharist); if he be not, let him repent" (Did. 10:6). In Herm. vis. III 1:5ff. Ecclesia raises Hermas, who has confessed his sins, from his knees. Is this scene composed on the pattern of a liturgical usage in which the sinner after confessing his sins before the congregation was raised up and comforted by the leader of the congregation? And is the angel of repentance in Hermas patterned after the congregational officer effecting the acceptance of the penitent? When Hermas is ordered to communicate the instructions he has received from the lady Ecclesia (vis. II 4:3) to Clement and to the "elders who preside over the congregation," the purpose surely is that they may act according to them. Aside from this we learn nothing further of any officially granted absolution (see vis. II 2:4f.) from this early period.

3. But it was inevitable that the question of *distinguishing between light and grave sins* should soon arise. In I Jn. 5:14–21, a supplement made by some ecclesiastical revision, verse 16 distinguishes between sins that are "not mortal" ($\mu\grave{\eta}\ \pi\rho\grave{o}s\ \theta\acute{a}\nu\alpha\tau o\nu$) and those that are "mortal" ($\pi\rho\grave{o}s\ \theta\acute{a}\nu\alpha\tau o\nu$), and for the latter even intercession is declined. What sort of sins that means, is not said. The ideal of a sinless Church naturally could not be maintained: it was necessary to be content with an average uprightness on the part of the members of the Church. In distinction from "deliberate" sins

(Heb. 10:26) one could put up with "unintentional" sins (I Clem. 2:3) as inevitable, and one could trust that the congregation's general confession of sin and prayer for forgiveness would bring about forgiveness. Only notorious heresy and gross moral trespasses inevitably remained an offense, particularly apostasy and denial of the faith in times of oppression. The excommunication of "heretics" certainly did not always take place by an explicit ban such as I Tim. 1:20 presupposes and Rev. 2:14f., 20 demands. The "heretics" probably often removed themselves from the "orthodox" congregations on their own volition (*cf.* I Jn. 2:19), claiming orthodoxy for themselves and accusing the others of heresy. III John and Ignatius give us some idea of how such splits inevitably arose.

There were grave sins which caused temporary exclusion but which could be forgiven after confession and repentance. Evidently of this sort at first were adultery and fornication, as their position in the catalogues of vices and also the admonitions referring to them indicate. That they were regarded in many circles as unforgivable may be taken to be indicated by Heb. 12:16f.; 13:4, and by the later practice of the Church down to the edict of Callixtus (217/18 A.D.). Murder, which like the two vices just mentioned was later reckoned among the mortal sins, is at first scarcely mentioned; it is named only in traditional lists of commandments and vices (Did. 2:2; 3:2; 5:1f.; Barn. 19:5; 20:1f.). The sin of apostasy does play a role, however. To a large extent it evidently was regarded as unforgivable (Heb. 6:4–8; 10:26–29) and later was considered a mortal sin for which until the Decian persecution no forgiveness was granted. Hermas still regards apostasy and denial of the faith as forgivable, even though it is the gravest of sins (*cf.* sim. VIII 6:4, IX 18:3; 19:1), but he considers it unforgivable only in the case of impenitence (vis. III 7:2; *cf.* vis. III 5–7 as a whole, sim. VIII 6:4–6). Hermas does know of sinners so hardened that repentance is denied them (sim. IX 6:2; 19:1). Nevertheless, in general and in keeping with the purpose of his book of repentance, he proclaims the possibility of repentance for all sinners (*cf.* especially sim. VIII 11:1–3) and while he does distinguish various classes of sinners (*cf.* especially vis. III, sim. VIII and IX) he still does not know any basic distinction between light sins and mortal sins. This distinction, suggested in I Jn. 5:16 and Heb. 10:26, is likewise unknown in the other writings of the apostolic and post-apostolic period. I Clem.'s call to repentance knows no limitation (chapters 7 and 8), neither does that of II Clem. Even Ignatius assumes the possibility of repentance for the heretics (Philad. 3:2; 8:1; Sm. 5:1; 9:1), though he considers it difficult (Sm. 5:3).

The direction that further development would have to take is clear. To distinguish between light and grave sins imperils from the outset the radical understanding of sin, as it had been conceived by Jesus, Paul, and John. But that understanding is completely surrendered when this distinction is combined with a distinction between two kinds of repentance. Though the latter distinction is not made in so many words, factually it is nevertheless made in the fact that for the grave sins an official ecclesiastical repentance (penance) comes to be required. For this is quite another thing from the repentance to which all Christians are again and again called (II, p. 209), quite another thing from the penitent disposition in which the congregation prays for forgiveness of its sins (I Clem. 60:1; Did. 14:1). Inasmuch as with the penetration of legalism into the Church the genuine understanding of grace like that of sin was lost (§ 59, 3), the sinner who was excluded from the fellowship of the Church now had to be regarded as one no longer standing under the forgiving grace of God. What he had been given in baptism, he had lost. If the Church then in view of his penance granted him forgiveness and took him back into its fellowship, this act, so far as its meaning is concerned. necessarily became a repetition of his baptism. Since baptism was a sacrament, the churchly institution of penance also necessarily became a sacrament. When this development should have taken place, the Church's character as institution of salvation (II, pp. 110. 202) would be complete.

*Epilogue**

1. The Task and the Problems of New Testament Theology (the Relation between Theology and Proclamation)

The science called New Testament theology has the task of setting forth the theology of the New Testament; i.e. of setting forth *the theological thoughts of the New Testament writings,* both those that are explicitly developed (such as Paul's teaching on the Law, for example) and those that are implicitly at work in narrative or exhortation, in polemic or consolation. The question may be raised whether it is more appropriate to treat the theological thoughts of the New Testament writings as a systematically ordered *unity*—a New Testament system of dogmatics, so to say—or to treat them in their *variety,* each writing or group of writings by itself, in which case the individual writings can then be understood as members of an historical continuity.

The second procedure is the one chosen in the treatment here offered. By this choice the opinion is expressed that there can be no normative Christian dogmatics, in other words, that it is not possible to accomplish the theological task once for all—the task which consists of unfolding that understanding of God, and hence of the world and man, which arises from faith, for this task permits only ever-repeated solutions, or attempts at solution, each in its particular historical situation. Theology's continuity through the centuries consists not in holding fast to once formulated propositions but in the constant vitality with which faith, fed by its origin, understandingly masters its constantly new historical situation. It is of decisive importance that *the theological thoughts be conceived and explicated as thoughts of faith,* that is: *as thoughts in which faith's understanding of God, the world, and man is unfolding itself*—not as products of free speculation or of a scientific mastering of the problems involved in "God," "the world," and "man" carried out by the objectifying kind of thinking.

Theological propositions—even those of the New Testament—can

* The Epilogue reproduces with slight alterations and additions my contribution to the volume honoring Maurice Goguel, *Aux sources de la tradition Chrétienne,* published by Delachaux et Niestlé in 1950 (Neuchâtel and Paris).

[237]

never be the *object* of faith; they can only be the *explication* of the understanding which is inherent in faith itself. Being such explication, they are determined by the believer's situation and hence are necessarily incomplete. This *incompleteness*, however, is not a lack to be remedied by future generations, each generation supplying what is still lacking, so that by an ever-continued summation a complete dogmatics would finally result. Rather, the incompleteness has its cause in the inexhaustibility of believing comprehension, which must ever actualize itself anew; this incompleteness consequently signifies a task and a promise. Furthermore, my understanding of myself in my world of work and destiny by the light of a love conferred upon me or of a responsibility entrusted to me is necessarily always incomplete. It is self-evident, for example, that the New Testament's thought about the state and society are incomplete because the possibilities and the problems of forms of the state and society which history has introduced in the meantime could not be present to the minds of the New Testament authors. It is likewise clear that the world of modern science and technology imposes upon believing comprehension new tasks which could not yet occur to minds of the New Testament period. Therefore the theological thoughts of the New Testament can be normative only insofar as they lead the believer to develop out of his faith an understanding of God, the world, and man in his own concrete situation.

But from the fact that theological statements are by nature the explication of believing comprehension it also follows that *these statements may be only relatively appropriate, some more so, others less so.* The possibility exists that in some of them the believing comprehension may not be clearly developed, that it may be hindered—bound perhaps by a pre-faith understanding of God, the world, and man and by a corresponding terminology—and consequently may speak of God's dealing and of the relation between God and man in juristic terms, for instance. Or it may speak of God's relation to the world in mythological or cosmological terms which are inappropriate to faith's understanding of God's transcendence. Or the consequence may be that it expresses God's transcendence in the terminology of mysticism or of idealistic thinking. From this possibility arises the task—even in the case of the New Testament writings—of *content-criticism* (Sachkritik) such as Luther, for example, exercised toward the Epistle of James and the Revelation of John.

But the most important thing is that basic insight that the theological thoughts of the New Testament are the unfolding of faith itself growing out of that new understanding of God, the world, and man which is conferred in and by faith—or, as it can also be phrased: *out of one's new self-understanding.* For by the believer's new understanding of himself we, of course, do not mean "understanding" as in a scientific anthropology which objectifies man into a phenomenon of the world, but we do mean an existential understanding of myself which is at one with and inseparable from my understanding of God and the world. For I am I, of course, not as an isolable and objectifiable world-phenomenon but I am I in my particular existence inseparably bound up with God and the world.

If the scientific presentation of the theological thoughts of the New Testament has the task of pointing them out as the unfolding of believing self-understanding, it then presents *not the object of faith but faith itself* in its own self-interpretation. But here arises the real problem of the presentation! For can one concentrate upon faith without seeing at the same time that toward which it is directed, its object and content?

For in the New Testament, faith is not understood as a self-understanding arising spontaneously out of human existence but as an understanding made possible by God, opened up by His dealing with men. Faith is not choosing to understand one's self in one of several possible ways that are universally available to man but is man's response to God's word which encounters him in the proclamation of Jesus Christ. It is *faith in the kerygma,* which tells of God's dealing in the man Jesus of Nazareth.

When, therefore, the science of New Testament theology seeks to present faith as the origin of the theological statements, it obviously must present the kerygma and the self-understanding opened up by it in which faith unfolds itself. And that is just where the problem lurks! For both the kerygma and faith's self-understanding always appear in the texts, so far as they are expressed in words and sentences, already interpreted in some particular way—i.e. in theological thoughts. Although there are single statements in the New Testament which can be designated as specifically kerygmatic, even they are always formulated in a particular theological terminology—take, for instance, that simplest sentence, "Jesus, Lord" (II Cor. 4:5), for it presupposes a particular understanding of the term "Lord."

[239]

Therefore, it is *not possible simply and sharply to distinguish kerygmatic statements in the New Testament from theological ones,* nor to derive from the New Testament a self-understanding not formulated in theological statements. Nevertheless, he who sets forth a New Testament theology must have this distinction constantly in mind and must interpret the theological thoughts as the unfolding of the self-understanding awakened by the kerygma if he is to avoid conceiving them as an objectifying kind of thought cut loose from the act of living, no matter whether such thought be attributed to the intellect or to "revelation." For when revelation is conceived as an arrangement for the impartation of teachings, these teachings have the character of the objectifying thought of science, a kind of thought which dims their existential reference to living into a mere object of thought—but then they are pseudo-scientific teachings. Such a procedure leads to the misunderstanding that theology, conceived as the "right teaching," is the object and content of faith, when actually it is only the kerygma that may be regarded as the "right teaching" which is the object and content of faith. Though the propositions of philosophy, so far as they contain truth, are in themselves "right teaching," the propositions of theology are not themselves "right teaching" but, so far as they contain truth, teach what the "right teaching" is—a teaching which is not found by investigation but is given in the kerygma. But the kerygma is just what theology can never seize in definitive form; it can always take hold of it only as something conceptually stated, and that means as something already theologically interpreted.

This state of affairs reveals itself in its problematical character all the more when the theologian holds fast to the insight that faith can be nothing else but the response to the kerygma, and that the kerygma is nothing else than God's word addressing man as a questioning and promising word, a condemning and forgiving word. As such a word it does not offer itself to critical thought but speaks into one's concrete existence. That the kerygma never appears without already having been given some theological interpretation rests upon the fact that it can never be spoken except in a human language and formed by human thought. This very fact confirms its kerygmatic character; for it makes clear that the statements of the kerygma are not universal truths but are personal address in a concrete situation. Hence they can appear only in a form molded by an individual's understanding of his own existence or by his interpretation of that understanding. And correspondingly they are understandable only to him who is able to recognize the kerygma as a word addressed to him in his situation—to recognize it immediately only as a question asked him, a demand made of him.

Differently expressed: the kerygma is understandable as kerygma only when the self-understanding awakened by it is recognized to be a possibility of human self-understanding and thereby becomes the call to decision. For the theological investigator obviously cannot presuppose his own faith as an epistemological instrument and make use of it as a presupposition for methodical work. What he can and should do is keep himself ready, open, free. Or, better, keep himself questioning—or knowing the questionability of—all human self-understanding, in the knowledge that existential* understanding of one's self (in distinction from existentialistic† interpretation of Man's being) is real only in the act of existing and not in the isolated reflection of thought.

2. The History of New Testament Theology as a Science

A survey of the history of New Testament theology as a science may clarify the problem.‡ Its origin lies in the "Collegia biblica" ("Biblical collections") of the *old-Lutheran orthodoxy*, those collections of scriptural quotations which as "dicta probantia" were intended to furnish the scriptural proof for the statements of dogmatics. In them, passages of the Old and the New Testament are indiscriminately arranged according to the *loci* of dogmatics as, for instance, in **Sebastian Schmidt's** *Collegium biblicum, in quo dicta Veteris et Novi Testamenti juxta seriem locorum communium theologicorum explicantur* (1671; 2nd ed., 1689). They take for granted the assumption that both the statements of dogmatics and the teaching of Scripture are, as "right teaching," the object and content of faith. That is, kerygma

* German text: *existentiell*. See the following note (Tr.).

† German text: *existential*. The terminology of existentialism thus far devised in English is highly unsatisfactory. This might be a useful way of distinguishing between these perplexing twin words (Tr.).

‡ Amos N. Wilder also develops the problems of New Testament theology by means of a survey of its history in the volume edited by Harold R. Willoughby, *The Study of the Bible Today and Tomorrow* (University of Chicago Press, 1947), pp. 419–436.

and theology are naively identified with each other. In *pietism* it is just the same, except that here, where the title "Biblical Theology" is first encountered,* scriptural doctrine was treated independently of dogmatics.† The theologians of the *Enlightenment* continue in the same direction, and for them scriptural doctrine set free from dogmatics is the critical norm by which dogmatic theology is to be measured. Even the titles of some of these works are eloquent: in the years 1771–75 **G. T. Zachariae** published his *Biblische Theologie oder Untersuchung des biblischen Grundes der vornehmsten theologischen Lehren* (*Biblical Theology, or Investigation of the Biblical Foundation of the Most Eminent Theological Doctrines*). In 1787 appeared **Johann Philipp Gabler's** *Oratio de iusto discrimine theologiae biblicae et dogmaticae regundisque utriusque finibus* (*A Discourse on the Proper Distinction between Biblical and Dogmatic Theology and the Boundaries to be Drawn for Each*). When **Lorenz Bauer** gave separate treatment to *Theologie des Alten Testaments* (*Theology of the Old Testament*) 1796–1803 and *Theologie des Neuen Testaments* (*Theology of the New Testament*) 1800–02, this very separation indicates a parting from dogmatics and an intention to present the theology of Scripture as an historical phenomenon. Likewise, **Martin Leberecht de Wette's** *Biblische Dogmatik des Alten Testaments und Neuen Testaments, oder kritische Darstellung der Religionslehre des Hebraismus, des Judentums und des Urchristentums* (*Biblical Dogmatics of the Old and New Testament, or Critical Presentation of Hebrew, Jewish, and Early Christian Teaching on Religion"*) 1813. More and more it is taken for granted that Christianity is the rational religion—proved to be so by the right interpretation of Scripture. For it is maintained that interpretation has to demonstrate that everything in Scripture which contradicts the principles of reason and experience is accommodation to "erroneous folk-concepts."

It is fully clear that here as in old-Lutheran orthodoxy New Testament theology is regarded as the right doctrine, except that here this doctrine is not founded upon the authority of Scripture but is worked out by rational thought and is only rediscovered in Scripture

---

* As the title of C. Haymann's book, *Biblische Theologie*, 1708.

† Example: A. F. Büsching, *Epitome theologiae e solis sacris literis concinnata* (*Epitome of theology compiled from the Sacred Writings alone*), 1756; *Gedanken von der Beschaffenheit und dem Vorzug der biblisch-dogmatischen Theologie vor der scholastischen* (*Thoughts upon the nature of biblical-dogmatic theology and its superiority to the scholastic*), 1758.

—regardless of how much Christian tradition may be at work in that which it was thought possible to establish as the content of rational thought. Like orthodoxy, the Enlightenment is also unaware of theology's reference to the kerygma, only now one can no longer say that kerygma and doctrine are identified with each other, because Biblical doctrine is regarded as an historical ("symbolical") embodiment of rational truths and hence cannot be the authority for faith. In reality the Enlightenment walked to its consistent end the path which orthodoxy had begun. The two agree in not seeing the difference between theology and kerygma and in confusing approval of theological statements with faith in the kerygma. For both viewpoints these theological statements have the character of general, timeless truths. The difference is only that for orthodoxy the theological statements are utterances of Scripture conceived as authority, while for the Enlightenment they are truths founded upon reason and discovered by rational thought. That is, whereas for the Enlightenment the kerygmatic character of "right teaching" has altogether disappeared, it is retained by orthodoxy to the extent that for it the theological statements of Scripture are authority and are regarded as the object and content of faith—though it thereby misunderstands both kerygma and faith.

With the Enlightenment there took place not only a parting from the authority of Scripture but also another change. If right interpretation of Scripture is to demonstrate the Christianity to which it bears witness to be the rational religion, then this interpretation must peel off everything local and temporal, everything individual and particular, in order to win that which is timelessly general. But quite understandably attention is more and more directed at just those things; for general truth is known beforehand, and a historical presentation can only be made, of course, from individual phenomena determined by their time in history. Thus, those presentations of New Testament theology arise which are (1) interested in the individual differences of the New Testament authors, differences which they characterize as so many "concepts of doctrine," and which (2) place the various formations of New Testament thought into a context of historical relations. Finally—and in this respect the tradition of the Enlightenment works on in the nineteenth and twentieth centuries—New Testament theology comes to be understood as a phenomenon of the history of religions, and it is then no longer proper, so it seems, for the science which presents it, being an historical science, to be interested in the question of truth.

This development might have been prevented if the work of **Ferdinand Christian Baur** had been destined to exercise a decisive influence.* Unlike the Enlightenment, Baur did not distinguish between eternal rational truths of timeless character and their imperfect, time-bound formulation which an enlightened reason overcomes, but sees (following Hegel) that truth always and everywhere can be grasped only in a particular historical form and that it unfolds itself as *the* truth only in the totality of the historical course of development. The subject in which and to which this development takes place is the human mind, and history is "the eternally clear mirror in which the mind regards itself, contemplates its own image, in order to be what it is in itself and also for itself, for its own consciousness, and to recognize itself as the moving power of that which has historically come to be."†

Since, therefore, historical reflection is the way to grasp the truth, then historical investigation of the history of Christianity—primarily of its origin and hence of the New Testament—is the way to grasp the truth of Christian faith, a truth which for Baur is unquestionably no other than the truth of the human mind in general. Hence New Testament theology must understand the interpreting of the New Testament to be the unfolding of Christian consciousness, which is itself understood as a decisive stage in the process by which the human mind comes to itself.

With this view Baur hit upon the real meaning of New Testament theology in the respect that it is the explication (in thought) of believing self-understanding. Though orthodoxy had solidly retained the insight that by the New Testament a word that man is to believe is said to him, orthodoxy nevertheless replaced the kerygma with theological doctrine and made the latter the object of faith; Baur overcomes this danger. But by reducing faith's self-understanding to a consciousness which arises in historical development out of man himself so that in him the mind comes to consciousness of itself, he eliminates the kerygma. Yet he does this not as rationalism does—its thinking knows no authority—but in such a way that history itself

---

* After Baur's death (1860) his lectures on New Testament theology were published by his son (1864).

† F. C. Baur, *Lehrbuch der christlichen Dogmengeschichte*, 1847, p. 59.

becomes authority and takes the place of the kerygma through the fact that he regards backward-directed reflection upon history as the way by which the mind of man comes to itself.

The fruitful way in which Baur put the question was already lost by his followers. They retained the conception of history as a process of development and likewise the concrete view of history which Baur had drawn up according to Hegel's scheme of thesis, antithesis, and synthesis: out of the struggle of the Torah-free Gospel of Paul (thesis) with the Torah-bound Jewish Christianity (antithesis) there finally emerged in a series of compromises the ancient Catholic Church (synthesis). But after Baur the question of the meaning of history and of historical reflection got lost. The work of investigation proceeded in the direction that had been taken by the Enlightenment— except that belief in the eternal verities of reason, or the consciousness of having definitively recognized them, got lost, and the Christian faith was no longer regarded as the "rational" religion. That meant, then, that investigation fell victim to a historism which conceived early Christianity and with it the New Testament as a phenomenon within the closed continuum of world history linked together by cause and effect.

The logical consequence would have been a complete relativism. This consequence was avoided by idealistically interpreting history's course of development as one having meaning: even without binding one's self to Hegel's philosophy of history one could perceive the power of the mind at work in history and could believe in a progress in which the eternal verities and norms are more and more clearly grasped. Under the influence of romanticism one could also conceive personality as a history-forming power. Thus this period found in the teachings of the New Testament the expression of the Christian *Weltanschauung*—which it described as "religious-ethical"—and saw the significance of Jesus in the fact that he was the proclaimer of religious-ethical truths and that he effectively and uniquely embodied them in his own person. Representative examples of this conception are **H. J. Holtzmann's** *Lehrbuch der Neutestamentlichen Theologie* (1896–7, 2nd ed., 1911), a model of critical conscientiousness, and **Paul Wernle's** sprightly and impressive book *Die Anfänge unserer Religion* (1901, 2nd ed., 1904).

A decisive turn, the importance of which could not at first be foreseen, took place in the *history-of-religions school*. **William Wrede's** essay *Über Aufgabe und Methode der sogenannten neutestamentlichen*

Theologie (*Concerning the Task and Method of So-called New Testament Theology*, 1897), may be regarded as the statement of its program. Wrede combatted the method of "concepts of doctrine" because he contended that an intellectualistic understanding of Christianity underlies it; after all, Christian faith is religion and not a system of thoughts! The scientific task, he therefore maintained, is to present as New Testament theology the living religion of earliest Christianity. Obviously, a right insight was here at work in that theological teachings were understood as an expression of faith and not as the object of faith—now understood, however, not as the unfolding of believing self-comprehension but as subsequent reflective thinking about the objects of faith. The connection between the act of living and the act of thinking was here torn apart, as Adolf Schlatter used to say.

The cause of this shortcoming lies in the fact that a clear concept of faith and religion was missing. There was only an awareness that religion is not a theoretical attitude, but that it is a feeling, that it is piety; and there was an awareness that it can take form in various types. It can appear as a trust in God. And since it is taken for granted that God is the holy will which determines and demands the good, trust in God includes the consciousness of ethical obligation, and from such trust flows a positive relation to the world as the place in which the ethical will must prove itself in the execution of concrete tasks. But religion can also be "redemption-religion." In it the thought of the demanding will in the concept of God recedes behind the thought of transcendence. A negative relation to the world is the result, and this piety which flees from the world can intensify itself to the point of mysticism. However, the idea of redemption can also be taken up into that religion of trust in God and of a feeling of duty as the idea of redemption from sin. Accordingly, **Heinrich Weinel** in his *Biblische Theologie des Neuen Testaments* (1911; 4th ed., 1928) against a background of orientation in the general history of religions presents Jesus' "religion" as an "ethical religion of redemption" in contrast to that "mythical religion of redemption" ("esthetic religion" in the first edition), motifs of which, he concedes, then united themselves in various ways with that of Jesus in the "religion" of earliest Christianity. **Julius Kaftan** also conceives the religion of the New Testament as an ethical religion of redemption (forgiveness of sins) in his concise and spirited treatment: *Neutestamentliche Theologie im Abriss dargestellt* (1927). In **Wilhelm Bousset's** brilliant *Kyrios*

Christos (1913; 2nd ed., 1921) the religion of earliest Christianity appears, on the contrary, as essentially a cult-piety which sent forth as its flower: mysticism. One-sidedly but powerfully the basic idea is here carried through; and because many things are here seen in a new way, the problems which are active in New Testament theology emerge into a new light.

In the history-of-religions school, religion had been recognized as an independent force, the essence of which does not lie in acknowledging general timeless truths, whether they be mediated by a supranatural "revelation" or discovered by rational thought. Religion is rather—for the intention of the history-of-religions school can evidently be so interpreted—an existential attitude. And though the legitimate meaning of the theological statements was not grasped by its adherents, they were nevertheless evidently on the right path.

An indication that they were on the right path is the fact that in the exegetical labor of this school those terms which are characteristic of religion as an independent attitude directed toward the transcendent God and distinct from every worldly attitude were grasped anew. Decisive for the discovery of the importance of eschatology to the New Testament was **Johannes Weiss'** *Jesu Predigt vom Reiche Gottes* (1892; 2nd ed., 1902). Another important insight was that *pneuma* in the New Testament does not mean "mind, spirit" as understood by the Greeks and by idealism but does mean the miraculous working of the transcendent God, as was first shown by **Heinrich Gunkel** in his book, *Die Wirkungen des Heiligen Geistes nach der populären Anschauung der apostolischen Zeit und nach der Lehre des Apostels Paulus* (1898; 3rd ed., 1909). Various works of **Wilhelm Heitmüller** pointed out the meaning and importance of the sacraments to earliest Christianity,* and in connection with them a new insight into the meaning of Ecclesia was won and also into the peculiar nature and significance of the idea "church" in earliest Christianity.†

It was only natural that in addition to the research of the historical school and of the history-of-religions school the work of conservative

---

* *Im Namen Jesu.* An investigation of the New Testament from the linguistic and history-of-religion standpoint, in particular concerning Christian baptism, 1903. See also his articles "Abendmahl" and "Taufe" in *RGG* I and V (1909 and 1913).

† *Cf.* Olof Linton, *Das Problem der Urkirche in der neueren Forschung*, 1932. Since then various essays by Maurice Goguel in the *Revue d'Histoire et de Philosophie religieuses*, 1933, 1938, and Nils Alstrup Dahl, *Das Volk Gottes: Eine Untersuchung zum Kirchenbewusstsein des Urchristentums*, 1941.

scholars under the influence of the orthodox tradition continued, and likewise that in their discussions with those of other trends they were also considerably influenced by the questions and the results of those others. In the tradition of the "concept-of-doctrine" method stand the very carefully written *Lehrbuch der Biblischen Theologie des Neuen Testaments* by **Bernard Weiss** (1868), 7th ed., 1903—English translation: *Theology of the New Testament*, 1892, from the third German edition) and the concise *Grundriss der neutestamentlichen Theologie* by **Theodor Zahn** (1928). More deeply influenced by modern statements of the questions involved, yet conservative in its results, is the *Theologie des Neuen Testaments* by **Paul Feine** (1910; 8th ed., 1950). It is significant that both B. Weiss and P. Feine later added to their presentations of New Testament theology a book on the "religion" of the New Testament.* It can scarcely be claimed that in these works new insights into the problem of the relation of theology to the kerygma were opened up. Nor can that claim be made for the *Theologie des Neuen Testaments* by **Friedrich Büchsel** (1935; 2nd ed., 1937), even though it bears the sub-title, "Geschichte des Wortes Gottes im Neuen Testament" ("History of the Word of God in the New Testament"), for the theological teachings are not differentiated from the kerygma which the word is, but are, themselves, taken to be God's word. Neither is **Ethelbert Stauffer's** very original *Theologie des Neuen Testaments* (1941; 4th ed., 1948) determined by that problem. Stauffer does indeed break away from the "concept-of-doctrine" method and from the notion of schematic development. After a short survey of the "course of development of primitive-Christian theology" he sets forth the thought-world of the New Testament as a unity under the title, "The New Testament's Christocentric Theology of History" and thus transforms theology into a religious philosophy of history.

A place by itself in this whole development is occupied by **Adolf Schlatter**. His book *Der Glaube im Neuen Testament* (1885; 4th ed., 1927) can in itself be termed a New Testament theology *in nuce*. It was followed by his *Theologie des Neuen Testaments* (1909–10).† He

---

*B. Weiss, *Die Religion des Neuen Testaments*, 1903, 2nd ed., 1908 (English translation: *The Religion of the New Testament*, 1905). P. Feine, *Die Religion des Neuen Testaments*, 1921.

† In 1921 the two volumes of this work appeared under new titles: *Die Geschichte des Christus* and *Die Theologie der Apostel*.

set forth his conception of the task in a small volume, *Die Theologie des Neuen Testaments und die Dogmatik* (1909). He marks off the boundaries of his own position against three frontiers: against the "statistical" inventories of New Testament thoughts found in orthodoxy, against the rationalistic "concept-of-doctrine" method, and against the history-of-religions school. He accuses them all, rightly, of separating the act of thinking and the act of living. But he does not see the unity of these two acts as Baur did in the fact that theological thoughts are the explication of man's understanding of himself as mind (reason). For Schlatter understands man from the standpoint of his will and sees the origin of his thoughts to lie in his willing and his acting. "They (i.e. the "men of the New Testament") frustrate the attempt to separate the act of thinking from the act of living, and that is why they do not even create the appearance of laying before us timeless items of knowledge independent of historical conditions. Rather, their labor of thought stands in conscious and independent combination with their willing and acting; this labor has its foundation and its material in their experiences and serves them as a means for carrying out their profession. Their thoughts are components of their deeds and hence of their history. Therefore, the task of New Testament theology is not yet exhausted by setting up a catalogue of the thoughts of Jesus and his disciples. By doing this an historical caricature easily arises: a sum of abstract, timeless 'doctrines,' which are conceived as the content of a consciousness cut off from willing and acting. But Jesus and his disciples did not carry their thoughts within them in this form. In order to observe rightly we must make clear to ourselves the context which engenders their thoughts and into which their thoughts immediately return as the basis for what they proceed to do."* From this it also follows that the presentation must distinguish the individual "metaphors of teaching" (Lehrtropen), in order to make clear that primitive-Christian history "has its basis in those events which constitute the personal life-situation of the individual."†

Such sentences might be understood in the sense of historical relativism, but, of course they are not so meant. What Schlatter terms the "experiences" of the "men of the New Testament" which are the foundation and the material for the formation of their

* *Neutestamentliche Theologie*, I, pp. 10f.
† *Das Neue Testament und die Dogmatik*, p. 40.

thoughts, or what he terms "personal life-situation" has its origin in the encounter with the person of the historical Jesus. Primitive-Christian history begins with the "inward life of Jesus himself,"* that is, with the fact that Jesus knows himself to be the "Christ" and works as such. Now, inasmuch as encountering Jesus and acknowledging him as "Christ" is faith, the theological thoughts consequently are the unfolding of faith, each thought called forth by a concrete historical task. And we may probably add, keeping within Schlatter's intent, they are the unfolding of the new self-understanding which is conferred with and by faith; for we may probably assume that Schlatter took it for granted that faith includes an understanding in which a man understands God, the world, and himself anew.

In spite of all this, it seems to me that Schlatter did not clearly see the problem of the relation between theology and the kerygma. What he does not see is that it is in the kerygma that the historical Jesus first appears as the "Christ." Consequently, in his thought the place of the kerygma is taken by the historical Jesus—under the assumption that Jesus can be made visible as the "Christ" by historical investigation, whereas in reality at the most a messianic consciousness might be made visible in this way. That is probably the reason why in all questions of historical criticism, particularly in regard to the literary-critical investigation of the Gospels, Schlatter is subject to peculiar inhibitions, and why he wants to interpret the formation of theological thought in the New Testament one-sidedly out of the Old Testament-Jewish tradition in which Jesus himself stands, failing to recognize the importance of Hellenistic syncretism. The kerygma of the Church then factually becomes a passing on of historical tradition; that is, the passing on of the picture of the historical Jesus (that picture as Schlatter happens to see it), in which Jesus is thought to be already perceptible as the "Christ." The peculiar problem how Jesus the proclaimer comes to be "Christ" the proclaimed is thereby covered over and by just this covering the peculiar essence of the kerygma is also obscured.

The presentation of New Testament theology offered in this book stands, on the one hand, within the tradition of the historical-critical and the history-of-religion schools and seeks, on the other hand, to avoid their mistake which consists of the tearing apart of the act of

* *Ibid.*, p. 60.

thinking from the act of living and hence of a failure to recognize the intent of theological utterances.

Since the New Testament is a document of history, specifically of the history of religion, the interpretation of it requires the labor of historical investigation. The method of this kind of inquiry has been worked out from the time of the Enlightenment onward and has been made fruitful for the investigation of primitive Christianity and the interpretation of the New Testament. Now such labor may be guided by either one of two interests, that of reconstruction or that of interpretation—that is, reconstruction of past history or interpretation of the New Testament writings. Neither exists, of course, without the other, and they stand constantly in a reciprocal relation to each other. But the question is: which of the two stands in the service of the other? Either the writings of the New Testament can be interrogated as the "sources" which the historian interprets in order to reconstruct a picture of primitive Christianity as a phenomenon of the historical past, or the reconstruction stands in the service of the interpretation of the New Testament writings under the presupposition that they have something to say to the present. The latter interest is the one for which historical labor is put to service in the presentation here offered.

But that is just the reason why it was so urgent to interpret the theological thoughts of the New Testament in their connection with the "act of living"—i.e. as explication of believing self-understanding. For they can claim to have meaning for the present not as theoretical teachings, timeless general truths, but only as the expression of an understanding of human existence which for the man of to-day also is a possibility for his understanding of himself—a possibility which is opened to him by the New Testament itself, in that it not only shows him that such self-understanding is the reply to the kerygma as the word of God addressing him, but also imparts to him the kerygma itself.

To make clear this believing self-understanding in its reference to the kerygma is the task of a presentation of New Testament theology. This clarification takes place directly in the analysis of the theology of Paul and John. It takes place indirectly in the critical presentation of the development toward the ancient Church, because in this development both the problems of believing self-understanding and the problems of the kerygmatic formulations conditioned by such self-understanding become visible.

[251]

Bibliographies

For §§ 41–50 as a whole. In addition to the commentaries* on John and the relevant sections in the theologies of the New Testament, see the following for the history of investigation. *English:* B. W. Bacon: *The Fourth Gospel in Research and Debate*, 2nd ed., 1918; W. F. Howard: *The Fourth Gospel in Recent Criticism and Interpretation*, 1931.

Non-English: P. H. Menoud: *L'évangile de Jean d'après les recherches récentes*, 2nd ed., 1947; J. Behm: "Der gegenwärtige Stand der Erforschung des Johannesevangeliums" in *Theologische Literaturzeitung* 73, 1948, pp. 21–30.

For the characterization of the Fourth Gospel as a whole. *English:* J. E. Carpenter: *The Johannine Writings*, 1927; R. H. Strachan: *The Fourth Gospel: Its Significance and Environment* (the third edition is undated; the second edition was of 1943); W. F. Howard: *Christianity According to St. John*, 1943; William Temple: *Readings in St. John's Gospel*, 1945.

Non-English: Alfredo Omodeo: *La mistica Giovannea*, 1930; William Wrede: *Charakter und Tendenz des Johannesevangeliums*, 2nd ed., 1933.

§ 41, for section 1. *English:* F. W. Worsley, *The Fourth Gospel and the Synoptists*, 1909; P. Gardner-Smith: *St. John and the Synoptic Gospels*, 1938; Erwin R. Goodenough: "John a Primitive Gospel," *JBL* LXIV, 1945, pp. 145–182.

Non-English: Hans Windisch: *Johannes und die Synoptiker*, 1926; also, "Die Absolutheit des Johannesevangeliums," *Zsyst Th.* 5, 1928, pp. 3–54; T. Sigge: *Das Johannesevangelium und die Synoptiker*, 1935.

§ 41, for section 3. *English:* C. F. Burney: *The Aramaic Origin of the Fourth Gospel*, 1922; J. de Zwaan: "John Wrote in Aramaic," *JBL* LVII, 1938, pp. 155–171; Hugo Odeberg; *The Fourth Gospel*, 1929; E. C. Colwell: *The Greek of the Fourth Gospel*, 1931.

Non-English: A. Schlatter: *Sprache und Heimat des vierten Evangelisten*, 1902; R. Bultmann: "Die Bedeutung der neuerschlossenen mandäischen und manichäischen Quellen für das Verständnis des Johannesevangeliums," *ZNW* 24, 1925, pp. 100–146; F. Büchsel: *Johannes und der hellenistische Synkretismus*, 1928; Lothar Schmidt: *Johannesevangelium und Religionsgeschichte*, 1933; Ernst Percy: *Untersuchungen über den Ursprung der Johanneischen Theologie*, 1939 (concerning which see R. Bultmann: review in *Orientalistische Literaturzeitung*, 1940, pp. 150–175); Eduard Schweizer: *EGO EIMI*, 1939; K. Kundsin: *Charakter und Ursprung der johanneischen Reden*, 1939.

* Though this book will be read mainly by readers who do not easily read German, it may not be superfluous to call special attention to Bultmann's own commentary on John, *Das Evangelium des Johannes*, 1941–47 (2nd ed., 1950) in which many assertions in this section of the book are treated in detail (Tr.).

[253]

§§ 42–44. Besides the literature cited above for the characterization of John as a whole, see: *English:* B. F. Westcott: *The Revelation of the Father*, 1884; G. B. Stevens: *The Johannine Theology*, 1894.

Non-English: Erich von Schrenk: *Die johanneische Anschauung vom Leben*, 1898; F. Büchsel: *Der Begriff der Wahrheit in dem Evangelium und in den Briefen des Johannes*, 1911; J. B. Frey: *Le Concepte de "Vie" dans l'Évangile de Saint Jean* (Biblica I), 1920, pp. 37ff.; Hans Pribnow: *Die johanneische Anschauung vom "Leben,"* 1934. See also the articles in *ThWB* on ἀλήθεια, ζάω, θάνατος, φῶς, ψεῦδος; F. Mussner: *Die Anschauung vom Leben im 4. Evg.*, *1950*.

§§ 45–48. *English:* R. H. Charles: *A Critical History of the Doctrine of a Future Life* (Jowett Lectures, 1898–99), 1899, pp. 362–376; E. von Dobschütz: *The Eschatology of the Gospels*, 1910, pp. 187–202; H. A. Guy: *The New Testament Doctrine of the Last Things*, 1948, pp. 159–172.

Non-English: R. Bultmann: '*Die Eschatologie des Johannes-Evangeliums*' (*Glauben und Verstehen I*), 1933, pp. 134–152; Doris Faulhaber: *Das Johannes-evangelium und die Kirche*, 1935; B. Aebert: *Die Eschatologie des Johannes*, 1937; Alf Corell: *Consummatum est. Eskatologi och Kyrka i Johannes-evangeliet*, 1950; Jacques Dupont: *Essais sur la Christologie de S. Jean*, 1951.

§ 45. *English:* G. B. Stevens: *The Johannine Theology*, 1894, pp. 74–126; H. R. Mackintosh: *The Doctrine of the Person of Jesus Christ*, 1912, pp. 94–121; A. E. J. Rawlinson: *The New Testament Doctrine of the Christ* (Bampton Lectures), 1926, pp. 199–228; R. H. Strachan: *The Historic Jesus in the New Testament*, 1931, pp. 128–222.

Non-English: W. Lütgert: *Die Johanneische Christologie*, 2nd ed., 1916; W. Bousset: *Kyrios Christos*, 2nd ed., 1921, pp. 154–183; Ernst Gaugler: *Das Christus-zeugnis des Johannesevangeliums* (*Jesus Christus im Zeugnis der Heiligen Schrift und der Kirche*, second supplement to *Evangelische Theologie*), 1936, pp. 34–67.

§ 46. To the literature for § 45, add for section 2: G. P. Wetter: *Der Sohn Gottes*, 1916; for section 4: Oscar Cullmann: *Theologische Zeitung* 4, 1948, pp. 360–72.

§ 47 as a whole. Hugo H. Huber: *Der Begriff der Offenbarung im Johannesevangelium*, 1934. For section 4: J. M. Creed: "Sacraments in the Fourth Gospel," in *The Modern Churchman* 16, 1926, pp. 363–372; C. T. Craig: "Sacramental Interest in the Fourth Gospel," *JBL* LVIII, 1939, pp. 31–41; Oscar Cullmann: *Urchristentum und Gottesdienst*, 2nd ed., 1950; H. Clavier: "Le Problème du rite et du mythe dans le 4. Evg.," *R.H.Ph.Rel.*, 1951, 275–292.

§§ 49–50. *English:* W. H. P. Hatch: *The Idea of Faith in Christian Literature from the Death of Paul to the Close of the Second Century*, 1926; J. O. Buswell: "The Ethics of 'Believe' in the Fourth Gospel," in *Bibliotheca Sacra* 80, 1923, pp. 28–37.

Non-English: Adolf Schlatter: *Der Glaube im Neuen Testament*, 4th ed., 1927; Rafael Gyllenberg: *Pistis* (in Swedish), 1922; J. Huby: "De la connaissance de foi chez S. Jean," in *Recherches de Science religieuse* 21, 1931, pp. 385–421; the article πίστις in *ThWB*.

§ 50 as a whole. D. Faulhaber (see under § 45). For section 4: J. Moffatt: *Love in the New Testament*, 1929; C. R. Bowen: "Love in the Fourth Gospel," in *Journal of Religion* 13, 1933, pp. 31–41; W. Lütgert: *Die Liebe im Neuen Testament*, 1905; Herbert Preisker: *Das Ethos des Urchristentums*, 2nd ed., 1949. For section 7: see the literature for § 14 and also M. Goguel: *La notion johannique de l'Esprit*, 1902; J. G. Simpson: "The Holy Spirit in the Fourth Gospel," in *Expositor* 9, Ser. IV, 1925, pp. 292–299; H. Windisch: "Jesus und der Geist im Johannesevangelium," in *Amicitiae Corolla for R. Harris*, 1933, pp. 303–318; Anton Fridrichsen: "Die Kirche im 4. Evangelium," in *Schwedische Theologische Quartalschrift* 16, 1940, pp. 227–242.

§§ 51–53 as a whole. See the literature for §§ 8 and 10. Concerning the literature down to 1932, see: Olof Linton: *Das Problem der Urkirche in der neueren Forschung*, 1932. Out of the earlier literature, see especially Harnack: *Die Mission und Ausbreitung des Christentums in den ersten drei Jahrhunderten*, 4th ed., 1924 (for the title of an English translation of an earlier edition of the same work, see the literature for § 9); Alfred Loisy: *L'Évangile de l'Église*, 5th ed., 1929; B. H. Streeter: *The Primitive Church studied with special Reference to the Origin of the Christian Ministry*, 1929; F. J. Foakes-Jackson: *The History of the Christian Church from the Earliest Times to A.D. 461*, 1933, Chapter X; Ernst Troeltsch: *The Social Teaching of the Christian Churches* (German, 1912; translated by Olive Wyon, 1931, reprint 1949); Rudolf Knopf: *Das nachapostolische Zeitalter*, 1905, pp. 147–222. Out of the abundant literature since 1932, see Karl Müller and H. von Campenhausen: *Kirchengeschichte* I, 1, 3rd ed., 1941, pp. 116–126; Otto Michel: *Das Zeugnis des Neuen Testaments von der Gemeinde*, 1941; Eduard Schweizer: *Das Leben des Herrn in der Gemeinde und ihren Diensten*, 1946; especially Maurice Goguel: *L'Église primitive*, 1947. See also the special literature for the following paragraphs:

§ 51. *English:* Walter Lowrie: *The Church and Its Organization: An Interpretation of Rudolph Sohm's Kirchenrecht*, 1904; A von Harnack: *The Constitution and Law of the Church in the First Two Centuries* (translated by F. L. Pogson, edited by H. D. A. Major), 1910; Thomas M. Lindsay: *The Church and Ministry in the Early Centuries* (Cunningham Lectures), 1902, 2nd ed., 1903, pp. 1–36.

Non-English: Rudolph Sohm: *Kirchenrecht* I, 1892; the same: *Wesen und Ursprung des Katholizismus* (*Abhandlungen der sächsischen Gesellschaft der Wissenschaften, Philosophisch-historische Klasse* 27, 10), 1909, 2nd ed., 1912; A. von Harnack: *Entstehung und Entwicklung der Kirchenverfassung und des Kirchenrechts in den ersten drei Jahrhunderten* (for English translation, see preceding paragraph), 1910; Erich Foerster: *Rudolf Sohms Kritik des Kirchenrechtes*, 1942; Karl Holl: "Der Kirchenbegriff des Paulus im Verhältnis zu dem der Urgemeinde," in *Sitzungsbericht der preussischen Akademie der Wissenschaften*, Berlin, 1921 (reprinted in Holl's *Gesammelte*

Schriften II, 1928); Wilhelm Mundle: "Das Kirchenbewusstsein der ältesten Christenheit," *ZNW* 22, 1923, pp. 20–42; H. von Campenhausen: "Recht und Gehorsam in der ältesten Kirche," *Theol. Bl.* 20, 1941, pp. 279–295; the same: *Kirchliches Amt nnd geistliche Vollmacht in den ersten drei Jahrhunderten*, 1953.

§ 52. See the general literature for §§ 51–53; also the following: *English:* B. H. Streeter: "The Rise of Christianity," in *The Cambridge Ancient History*, Vol. XI, especially pp. 286–293; T. M. Lindsay: (see § 51), pp. 69–217; A. C. Headlam and F. Gerke: "The Origin of the Christian Ministry," in *The Ministry and the Sacraments*, 1937, pp. 326–367.

Non-English: K. L. Schmidt: "Le Ministère et les Ministères dans l'Église du Nouveau Testament," in *Revue d' Histoire et de Philosophie Religieuses*, 1937, pp. 313–336; Ph.-H. Menoud: *L'Église et les Ministères selon le Nouveau Testament*, 1949. For section 2: F. V. Filson: "The Christian Teacher in the First Century," *JBL* LX, 1941, pp. 317–328. For section 3: A. Fridrichsen: *The Apostle and His Message*, 1947; Johannes Munck: "Paul, the Apostles and the Twelve," in *Studia Theologica* III, 1950, pp. 96–110. *Non-English:* H. von Campenhausen: "Der Christliche Apostelbegriff," in *Studia Theologica* I, 1948, pp. 96–130; the same: "Lehrerreihen und Bischofsreihen," in *In Memoriam Ernst Lohmeyer*, 1951, pp. 240–249; J. Brosch: *Charismen und Ämter in der Urkirche*, 1951; H. Greeven: "Propheten, Lehrer, Vorsteher bei Paulus," *ZNW* 44, 1952, 1–43.

§ 53. *English:* T. M. Lindsay (see § 51), pp. 169–210; E. F. Scott: *The Nature of the Early Church*, 1941; G. Johnston: *The Doctrine of the Church in the New Testament*, 1943; F. C. Grant: *An Introduction to New Testament Thought*, 1950, pp. 268–299; Oscar Cullmann: *Christ and Time* (translated by F. V. Filson), 1950.

Non-English: M. Goguel: "Eschatologie et apocalyptique dans le Christianisme primitif," in *Revue d'Histoire et de Philosophie Religieuses*, 1932, pp. 381–434, 490–524; A. Fridrichsen: "Église et Sacrement dans le Nouveau Testament," in *Revue d'Histoire et de Philosophie Religieuses*, 1937, pp. 337–356; H. D. Wendland: *Geschichtsanschauung und Geschichtsbewusstsein in Neuen Testament*, 1938; O. Bauernfeind: "Die Geschichtsauffassung des Urchristentums," *Zsyst Th.* 15, 1938, pp. 347–378; Martin Werner: *Die Entstehung des christlichen Dogmas*, 1941; Ph. Vielhauer, "Zum Paulinismus der Apostelgeschichte," *Ev. Theol.*, 1950–51, pp. 1–15; M. Dibelius: *Aufsätze zur Apostelgeschichte*, 1951 (especially pp. 108ff.); G. Bornkamm: "Die Verzögerung der Parusie," in *In Memoriam Ernst Lohmeyer*, 1951, pp. 116–126; R. Bultmann: "Der Mensch zwischen den Zeiten," in *Man in God's Design*, 1952, pp. 39–59.

§§ 54–58 as a whole. *English:* B. H. Streeter: *The Rise of Christianity* (see above, bibliography for § 52), 1936; C. H. Dodd: *The Apostolic Preaching and Its Development*, 1936, 6th ed., 1950; C. T. Craig: *The Beginning of Christianity*, 1943; F. V. Filson: *One Lord, One Faith*, 1943; A. M. Hunter: *The Unity of the New Testament*, 1943; E. F. Scott: *The Varieties of New Testament Religion*, 1943.

[256]

BIBLIOGRAPHIES

Non-English: A. Loisy: *La naissance du Christianisme*, 1933; J. Lebreton and J. Zeiller: *L'Église primitive*, 1938; R. Asting: *Die Verkündigung des Wortes im Urchristentum*, 1939; J. Gewiess: *Die urapostolische Heilsverkündigung nach der Apostelgeschichte*, 1939; M. Goguel: *L'Église primitive*, 1947; the same: *Les premiers temps de l'Église*, 1949; Hannelore Schulte: *Der Begriff der Offenbarung im Neuen Testament*, 1949.

§ 54, for section 1. *English:* G. F. Moore: *Judaism* I, 1927, pp. 251–262. *Non-English:* G. van der Leeuw: *Phänomenologie der Religion*, 1933, § 64, 4; W. G. Kümmel: "Jesus und der jüdische Traditionsgedanke," *ZNW* 21, 1922, pp. 1–34; 22, 1923, pp. 257–279; 24, 1925, pp. 193–202; O. Cullmann: *Die ersten christlichen Glaubensbekenntnisse*, 1943; J. de Ghellinck: "Les origines du symbole des apôtres," in *Nouvelle revue de theologie*, 1945, pp. 178ff. For section 3: M. Dibelius: *From Tradition to Gospel*, 1934; R. Bultmann: *Die Geschichte der synoptischen Tradition*, 2nd ed., 1931; Joachim Jeremias: *Unbekannte Jesusworte*, 1951.

§ 55. A. von Harnack: *History of Dogma* (translated from the third German edition by Neil Buchanan), 1895, Vol. I, Chapter III. *Non-English:* Walter Bauer: *Rechtgläubigkeit und Ketzerei im ältesten Christentum*, 1934; M. Werner: (see lit. for § 53); G. van der Leeuw: (see lit. for § 54). For section 5: *English:* P. R. Williams: *Authority in the Apostolic Age*, 1950, especially pp. 42–74. *Non-English:* A. von Harnack: *Die Briefsammlung des Apostels Paulus und die anderen vorkanonischen Briefsammlungen*, 1926; H. Strathmann: "Die Krisis des Kanons in der Kirche," in *Theol. Bl.* 20, 1941, pp. 295–310; O. Cullmann: "Die Pluralität der Evangelien als theologisches Problem im Altertum," in *Theologische Zeitung* I, 1945, pp. 23–42; H. von Campenhausen: (see lit. for § 52); W. G. Kümmel: "Notwendigkeit und Grenze des neutestamentlichen Kanons," *ZThK* 47, 1950, pp. 277–312; E. Käsemann: "Begründet der neutestamentliche Kanon die Einheit der Kirche?", *Ev. Theol.* 11, 1951–52, pp. 13–21. In addition, see the histories of the canon, especially those within the various introductions to the New Testament.

§ 56. For section 2. *English:* Sir Robert Falconer: *The Pastoral Epistles*, 1937; B. S. Easton: *The Pastoral Epistles*, 1947.

Non-English: O. Michel: "Grundfragen der Pastoralbriefe," in the *Wurm-Festschrift*, 1949; F. Spitta: *Studien zum Hirten des Hermas* (*Zur Geschichte und Literatur des Urchristentums* II), 1896; Arnold Meyer: *Das Rätsel des Jakobusbriefes*, 1930; H. Weinel: "Die spätere christliche Apokalyptic," in *Eucharisterion* II, *Festschrift für H. Gunkel*, 1923, pp. 141–173; A. Dietrich: *Nekyia*, 1893; M. Dibelius: "Paulus auf dem Areopag" in *Aufsätze zur Apostelgeschichte*, 1951, pp. 29–70; see also Dibelius' commentaries on James (Meyer's *Kommentar*) and on the pastoral epistles (Lietzmann's *Handbuch*).

For section 4. *English:* William Manson: *The Epistle to the Hebrews*, 1951; E. F. Scott: *The Epistles of Paul to the Colossians, to Philemon, and to the Ephesians*, 1930 and later reprints; C. R. Richardson: *The Christianity of Ignatius of Antioch*, 1935.

BIBLIOGRAPHIES

Non-English: H. Schlier: *Religionsgeschichtliche Untersuchungen zu den Ignatiusbriefen*, 1929; the same: *Christus und die Kirche im Epheserbrief*, 1930; E. Käsemann: *Leib und Leib Christi*, 1933; the same: *Das Wandernde Gottesvolk: Eine Untersuchung zum Hebräerbrief*, 1939; K. L. Schmidt: *Kanonische und apokryphe Evanglien und Apostelgeschichten*, 1944.

§ 57. *English:* F. C. Grant: *An Introduction to New Testament Thought*, 1950, pp. 99–143.

Non-English: H. Schlier and E. Käsemann (see lit. for § 56); G. Bornkamm: "Die Häresie des Kolosser-Briefes," in *Theologische Literaturzeitung* 73, 1948, pp. 11–20; R. Bultmann: "Bekenntnis- und Liedfragmente im ersten Petrusbrief," in *Coniectanea Neotestamentica* XI, 1947, pp. 1–14; H. Bietenhard: *Die himmlische Welt im Urchristentum und Spätjudentum*, 1951; G. Lindeskog: *Studien zum neutestamentlichen Schöpfungsgedanken I*, 1952.

§ 58. See the literature for § 57; also: V. Taylor: *Forgiveness and Reconciliation*, 1908; F. C. Grant: *An Introduction to New Testament Thought*, 1950, pp. 187–276; W. Bousset: *Kyrios Christos*, 2nd ed., 1921; H. Windisch: *Taufe und Sünde im ältesten Christentum*, 1908; O. Cullmann: *Christ and Time*, 1946.

For section 3: E. F. Scott (see § 56, section 4).

Non-English: Ernst Percy: *Die Probleme der Kolosser- und Epheserbriefe*, 1946; H. Schlier and V. Warnack: *Die Kirche im Epheserbrief*, 1949; J. Klevinghaus: *Die theologische Stellung der Apostolischen Väter zur alttestamentlichen Offenbarung*, 1948; W. Wrede: *Untersuchungen zum ersten Klemensbriefe*, 1891; A. von Harnack: *Der erste Klemensbrief*, S. A. Berlin, 1909, pp. 38–63. Literature on Barnabas in H. Windisch, Supplement Volume III to Lietzmann's *Handbuch*, 1920; also P. Meinhold: "Geschichte und Exegese im Barnabasbrief," *Zeitschrift für Kirchengeschichte*, 1940, pp. 255–303. On the abundant literature for Ignatius see W. Bauer in Supplement Volume II to Lietzmann's *Handbuch*, 1920; also Th. Preiss: "La Mystique de l'Imitation et de l'Unité chez Ignace d'Antioche," *Revue d'Histoire et de Philosophie Religieuses* 18, 1938, pp. 197–241; K. H. Schelkle: *Die Passion Jesu in der Vekündigung des N.T.*, 1949.

§§ 59–61 as a whole. *English:* E. von Dobschütz: *Christian Life in the Primitive Church* (translated by George Bremner, edited by W. D. Morrison), 1904. A. von Harnack (see lit. for § 9); F. C. Grant: *An Introduction to New Testament Thought*, 1950, pp. 300–324; C. H. Dodd: *Gospel and Law*, 1951; Vincent Taylor: *Forgiveness and Reconciliation*, 1946.

Non-English: R. Knopf: *Das nachapostolische Zeitalter*, 1905, pp. 417–444; R. Asting: *Die Heiligkeit im Urchristentum*, 1930; M. Goguel: *L'Église primitive*, 1947, pp. 508–540; H. Preisker: *Das Ethos des Urchristentums*, 1949.

§ 59. See the literature for § 58.

§ 60. Ernst Troeltsch (see under §§ 51–53); Igino Giordani: *The Social*

Message of the Early Church Fathers (translated by A. I. Zizzamia with *imprimatur*), 1944; M. S. Enslin: *The Ethics of Paul*, 1930.

Non-English: See the general literature for §§ 59–61, to which add pp. 105–137 in Knopf and pp. 541–600 in Goguel. In addition: K. Müller and H. von Campenhausen: *Kirchengeschichte* I 1, 3rd ed., 1941, § 6, 9 and § 23; H. von Campenhausen: *Die Idee des Martyriums in der alten Kirche*, 1936; the same: *Die Askese im Urchristentum*, 1949; H. Windisch: *Imperium und Evangelium*, 1931: H. Schlier: "Die Beurteilung des Staates im Neuen Testament," *Zwischen den Zeiten* 10, 1932, pp. 312–330; K. Pieper: *Urkirche und Staat*, 1935; E. Stauffer: *Gott und Kaiser im Neuen Testament*, 1935; the same: *Christus und die Cäsaren*, 1948; G. Kittel: "Das Urteil des Neuen Testaments über den Staat," *Zsyst Th.* 14, 1937, pp. 651–680; K. L. Schmidt: "Das Gegenüber von Kirche und Staat in der Gemeinde des Neuen Testaments," *Theol. Bl.* 16, 1937, pp. 1–16; F. J. Leenhardt: *Le Chrétien, doit-il servir l'état?* 1939; O. Eck: *Urgemeinde und Imperium*, 1940; W. Bieder: *Ekklesia und Polis im Neuen Testament und in der alten Kirche*, 1941; M. Dibelius: *Rom und die Christen im ersten Jahrhundert*, S. B. Heidelberg, 1941–2, No. 2; W. Schweitzer: *Die Herrschaft Christi und der Staat im Neuen Testament*, 1949.

§ 61. *English:* O. D. Watkins: *A History of Penance*, 1920.

Non-English: H. Windisch: *Taufe und Sünde im ältesten Christentum*, 1909; S. Hoh: *Die kirchliche Busse im zweiten Jahrhundert*, 1932; B. Poschmann: *Paenitentia secunda: Die kirchliche Busse im ältesten Christentum*, 1940; P. Bonnard: "La discipline ecclésiastique selon le Nouveau Testament," in *Centenaire de la Faculté de theologie de l'église évangélique libre du Canton de Vaud*, 1947, pp. 115–135.

Bibliographical Note to the Epilogue.

The author, writing originally for persons of German tongue, was probably perfectly correct in ignoring non-German treatments of New Testament theology. It has been a singularly German branch of theology, but there have been several writers in English (as also in French and Dutch) who, stimulated by the German works, have seen the advantages of writing similar books in their own language. Their debt to German work is always great, but several of them are much more than mere imitations. A suggestive list, not meant to be exhaustive, of non-German works follows: J. J. v. Oosterzee: *De Theologie des Nieuwen Verbonds*, 1867 (English translation by M. J. Evans, 1870); E. Reuss: *Histoire de la Théologie Chrétienne du Siècle Apostolique*, 1852 and later; W. Alexander: *A System of Biblical Theology*, 1888; R. F. Weidner: *Biblical Theology of the New Testament*, 1891; W. F. Adeney: *The Theology of the New Testament*, 1894; G. B. Stevens: *The Theology of the New Testament*, 1899 and often reprinted, most recently 1947; E. H. van Leeuwen: *Prolegomena van bijbelsche godgeleerdheid*, 1890; the same: *Bijbelsche godgeleerdheit*, 1892:

BIBLIOGRAPHIES

G. G. Chavannes: *La religion dans la Bible II, le Nouveau Testament*, 1889; G. Fulliquet: *La pensée religieuse dans le Nouveau Testament*, 1893; W. Mackintosh: *The Natural History of the Christian Religion*, 1894; Orello Cone: *The Gospel and Its Earliest Interpretations, a study of the teaching of Jesus and its doctrinal transformation in the New Testament*, 1893; J. Bovon: *Théologie du Nouveau Testament*, 1893–4; D. F. Estes: *An Outline of New Testament Theology*, 1900; E. P. Gould: *The Biblical Theology of the New Testament*, 1900; H. C. Sheldon: *New Testament Theology*, 1911; A. Nairne: *The Faith of the New Testament* (Hulsean Lectures, 1919–20), 2nd ed., 1927; E. W. Parsons: *The Religion of the New Testament*, 1939; W. T. Conner: *The Faith of the New Testament*, 1940; E. F. Scott: *The Varieties of New Testament Religion*, 1947; F. C. Grant: *An Introduction to New Testament Thought*, 1950. If works on the theology of Paul or John or on separate theological concepts of the New Testament were added, the list would be much longer. (It should also be noted that several voluminous New Testament theologies written in the latter half of the nineteenth century were translated from German to English, among them theologies by C. F. Schmid, W. Beyschlag, B. Weiss, and also B. Weiss' *Religion of the New Testament*.)

Greek Index*

Ἀγάπη, I, 343f.; II, 81f., 162, 165, 168, 178, 184, 221f.
ἀγάπη of God or of Christ, I, 291f.; II, 35
ἄγγελοι (ἀρχαί, δυνάμεις, ἐξουσίαι), I, 173, 230, 257; II, 146, 149
ἁγιάζω (ἅγιος, ἁγιασμός), I, 39, 136, 276, 338f.; II, 79, 167, 189
ἄγνοια, I, 66f.; II, 128, 204
ἀθανασία, II, 193
αἰδώς, II, 226
αἰών (οὗτος—μέλλων), I, 5, 172, 256; II, 208
ἀλήθεια, I, 67, 180; II, 16, 18–21, 27, 191
ἁμαρτία, I, 239ff.; II, 172, 190, 207
ἀνάμνησις, I, 149
ἄνθρωπος (ὁ ἔσω), I, 203, 212
ἀπέχεσθαι, I, 104f.; II, 171, 221, 224
ἀποκαλύπτειν, I, 274f.
ἀπολύτρωσις, I, 85, 176
ἀπόστολος, II, 103–6
ἀρετή, I, 71, 261; II, 225
ἄρχων (ἄρχοντες), I, 173, 257f.
ἄφεσις (τ. ἁμαρτίων), I, 39, 136f., 287; II, 176, 185
ἀφθαρσία, I, 77; II, 159, 188, 191
βασιλεία (τ. θεοῦ), I, 4ff., 77, 189
Γινώσκειν (γνῶσις), I, 326f.; II, 73f., 128–34, 165, 190
γρηγορεῖν, I, 76, 174f.
Δικαιοσύνη, I, 189, §§ 28–30; II, 75, 162f., 167, 170, 172, 182, 189, 197, 212f., 225
δικαιώματα, II, 164, 188f., 206, 223
δοκιμάζειν, I, 214f.; II, 223

δουλεία (δουλεύειν, δοῦλος), I, 243f., 331f., 343; II, 205, 214
Ἐγκράτεια, II, 170, 188, 220ff.
ἐγώ εἰμι, II, 21f., 26, 63f.
εἶναι ἐκ, II, 19f., 23f.
εἰρήνη, II, 82f.
ἐκκλησία, I, 10, 38f., 94, 178f., 308ff.; II, 8f., 150, 179f., 187f., 193
ἔλεος, I, 282
ἐλευθερία, I, 180f., §§ 38–40; II, 20, 79, 198, 205
ἐλπίς, I, 319f., 347; II, 159, 165, 167, 175, 181, 187, 191
ἐντολή, II, 81f., 164, 173, 196, 206, 223
ἐξουσία, I, 180, 341
ἐπικαλεῖσθαι, I, 126ff.
ἐπίγνωσις, I, 67, 180
ἐπιείκεια, II, 226
ἐπιθυμεῖν (ἐπιθυμία), I, 104, 224f., 227, 246; II, 177
ἐπίσκοπος, II, 102–6
ἐπιστρέφειν, I, 74, 317
ἐπιφάνεια, II, 185
ἔργα, I, 279f.; II, 163, 165, 174f., 181, 190, 198, 200, 211
εὐαγγέλιον, I, 87f.; II, 177
εὐαγγελιστής, II, 106
εὐσέβεια (εὐσεβής), II, 170, 184, 190, 213, 226
Ζηλοῦν, I, 225f., 227
ζωή, I, 77, 210, 345ff.; II, 11, 61, 63, 159, 191
Ἡμέρα (ὀργῆς), etc.), I, 75f.
Θέλειν, Θέλημα, I, 223ff.
Ἱλαστήριον, I, 46, 85
Καθῆκον, I, 71; II, 226

* Because of the purpose of this translation the Greek of the original has regularly been transliterated or translated; accordingly, the words in this index may occur in the text either in Greek or Roman type or in translation, but they should still be an aid in locating pertinent discussion.

New Testament Passages Discussed

(A selection of the more important)

Subject Index

ABRAHAM, I, 6, 36, 50, 95–7, 111f., 120, 194, 234, 237, 242, 253f., 265, 267, 280–2, 310, 315, 320, 323; II, 29, 163

Abstain, I, 104f.; II, 221, 224

Acknowledgment, of God, I, 213, 215, 229, 319; of Jesus as Lord, I, 315

Adam, I, 204, 227, 230, 246, 250ff., 258, 265, 289, 347; II, 149; first, I, 300; last, I, 178, 300, 302

Adamitic man, I, 173f., 178, 249, 251ff., 277, 300, 347

Adoption to sonship, I, 278, 297, 335

Advent of Christ, I, 29, 35, 43

Aeon(s), I, 173, 177; Adam-, I, 303; Christ-, I, 303; two, I, 5; new or old, I, 5, 172f., 256n., 278, 299f., 307f., 349; II, 208f.

Agape, I, 144, 150, 183, 262, 268, 291f., 345; II, 81f., 162, 165, 168, 178, 184, 221f.

Allegory, I, 111–18, 340; II, 143, 163

Altar, I, 149f.

Angels, I, 25, 110, 128f., 158, 170, 174, 176, 230, 255, 257f., 268; II, 149ff., 152, 154

Animism, I, 155, 157, 207

Anthropology, I, 71, 168, 174, 189, 191–268; II, 40

Antioch, I, 56, 61, 63f., 96, 188

Anxiety, I, 104, 226, 235, 240, 243, 247, 320

Apocalypticism, I, 4–6, 27, 35, 38, 47, 49f., 53, 74, 76, 79f., 173, 307, 346; II, 143

Apostasy, I, 170, 241, 250

Apostles, apostleship, I, 60, 62, 68, 77, 81, 114, 121, 125f., 133, 161, 163, 170f., 217, 222, 271, 308, 314, 318, 325, 340, 343, 350, 352; II, 105ff., 138, 140

Apostles' Creed, see *Symbolum Romanum*

Apostolic Council, I, 56, 61, 95, 108, 188

Areopagus address, I, 68, 71–3, 68, 77, 92

Ascension, I, 45, 123, 127, 176

Asceticism, I, 11, 102f., 107, 110, 152, 160, 166, 170, 182, 199, 202; II, 220f., 223

Atonement I, 46, 85, 285ff., 302; II, 53f.

Attis, I, 140, 148, 167, 299

Authority, I, 61, 137, 171, 180–2, 219f., 223, 289, 294, 309; of O.T., I, 16, 118; II, 138–42

Authorization (*exousia*), I, 181, 342–344

BAPTISM, I, 39f., 57, 74, 101, 107, 114, 116, 120–2, 126, 133–44, 153, 157–63, 167–9, 180, 293, 298f., 311–14, 333, 335, 337–9, 348; II, 160, 166, 236; of Jesus, I, 26, 131; of Jewish proselytes, I, 39f.; of John, I, 39f., 59, 138; vicarious, I, 141, 169, 312

Barnabas, I, 56, 61, 64, 95, 98, 101, 108f., 155, 188; Epistle of, I, 110f., 114; II, 143, 163–5

Barth, Karl, I, 274, 295

Baur, F. C., II, 244

Belief in God, I, 67f., 73, 89f., 120, 300, 317; II, 145

Between-ness, II, 162, 163, 168, 175, 180, 185, 191, 198, 199f.

Bishop, I, 116, 135, 149, 153, 310; II, 102, 108ff., 139, 141

Blood, I, 198, 233, 244, 249, 288, 295; of Christ, I, 46, 73, 84f., 103, 111f., 142f., 146–50; II, 54; of "God", I, 129